PSYCHIATRY - THEORY, APPLICATIONS, AND TREATMENTS

SUICIDAL BEHAVIOR IN ALCOHOL AND DRUG ABUSE AND DEPENDENCE

PSYCHIATRY - THEORY, APPLICATIONS, AND TREATMENTS

Attention Deficit Hyperactivity Disorder (ADHD)
Stuart M. Gordon and Aileen E. Mitchell (Editors)
2009. ISBN: 978-1-60741-581-7

Attention Deficit Hyperactivity Disorder (ADHD)
Stuart M. Gordon and Aileen E. Mitchell (Editors)
2009. ISBN: 978-1-60876-699-4 (E-book)

Victimhood, Vengefulness, and the Culture of Forgiveness
Ivan Urlić, Miriam Berger, and Avi Berman
2010. ISBN: 978-1-60876-191-3

Psychiatric Research Trends: Dreams and Geriatric Psychiatry
Daniella M. Montez (Editor)
2010. ISBN: 978-1-60741-760-6

Psychiatric Research Trends: Dreams and Geriatric Psychiatry
Daniella M. Montez (Editor)
2010. ISBN: 978-1-61668-719-9 (E-book)

Optimization of Research and Clinical Applications for Combat-related Posttraumatic Stress Disorder (PTSD): Progress Through Modern Translational Methodologies
Seth D. Norrholm, Tanja Jovanovic, Barbara O. Rothbaum, Michael Davis, Wendy Hasenkamp, Chris Crowe, Erica Duncan, Linda Leimbach, Kelly Skelton and Bekh Bradley
2010. ISBN: 978-1-61668-027-5

Optimization of Research and Clinical Applications for Combat-related Posttraumatic Stress Disorder (PTSD): Progress Through Modern Translational Methodologies
Seth D. Norrholm, Tanja Jovanovic, Barbara O. Rothbaum, Michael Davis, Wendy Hasenkamp, Chris Crowe, Erica Duncan, Linda Leimbach, Kelly Skelton and Bekh Bradley
2010. ISBN: 978-1-61668-358-0 (E-book)

War and Suicide
Leo Sher and Alexander Vilens (Editors)
2010. ISBN: 978-1-60741-978-5

War and Suicide
Leo Sher and Alexander Vilens (Editors)
2010. ISBN: 978-1-61668-274-3 (E-book)

Post-Traumatic Stress Disorder (PTSD): Causes, Symptoms and Treatment
Sylvia J. Egan (Editor)
2010. ISBN: 978-1-61668-526-3

Post-Traumatic Stress Disorder (PTSD): Causes, Symptoms and Treatment
Sylvia J. Egan (Editor)
2010. ISBN: 978-1-61668-716-8 (E-book)

Dyslexia and Depression: The Hidden Sorrow
Neil Alexander-Passe
2010. ISBN: 978-1-60876-118-0

Dyslexia and Depression: The Hidden Sorrow
Neil Alexander-Passe
2010. ISBN: 978-1-61668-933-9 (E-book)

Stress of Family Members in Caring for a Relative with Schizophrenia
Wai-Tong Chien
2010. ISBN: 978-1-60876-145-6

Military Psychiatry: New Developments
Dennis G. Stanton and Lawrence R. Castaneda (Editors)
2010. ISBN: 978-1-60876-149-4

"Paranoia of the Millionaire": Harry K. Thaw's 1907 Insanity Defense
Emil R. Pinta
2010. ISBN: 978-1-60876-988-9

Psychoanalytic Psychotherapy: A Modern Kleinian Approach
Robert Waska
2010. ISBN: 978-1-60876-909-4

Suicidal Behavior in Alcohol and Drug Abuse and Dependence
Leo Sher and Alexander Vilens (Editors)
2010. ISBN: 978-1-60876-919-3

Neurobiology of Post-Traumatic Stress Disorder
Leo Sher and Alexander Vilens (Editors)
2010. ISBN: 978-1-61668-851-6

Neurobiology of Post-Traumatic Stress Disorder
Leo Sher and Alexander Vilens (Editors)
2010. ISBN: 978-1-61668-816-5 (E-book)

Young, Violent, and Dangerous to Know
Michael Fitzgerald
2010. ISBN: 978-1-60876-952-0

Delusional Misidentification
Garry Young
2010. ISBN: 978-1-60876-956-8

Paranoia in the "Normal" Population
Antonio Preti and Matteo Cella
2010. ISBN: 978-1-60876-984-1

Malingering Versus Posttraumatic Stress Disorder
Kenneth R. Morel
2010. ISBN: 978-1-61668-144-9

Malingering Versus Posttraumatic Stress Disorder
Kenneth R. Morel
2010. ISBN: 978-1-61668-454-9 (E-book)

Cognitive Impairment in Children with ADHD
Alasdair Vance, Catherine Mollica and Paul Maruff
2010. ISBN: 978-1-61668-197-5

Cognitive Impairment in Children with ADHD
Alasdair Vance, Catherine Mollica and Paul Maruff
2010. ISBN: 978-1-61668-476-1 (E-book)

Immigration and Mental Health: Stress, Psychiatric Disorders and Suicidal Behavior Among Immigrants and Refugees
Leo Sher and Alexander Vilens (Editors)
2010. ISBN: 978-1-61668-503-4

PSYCHIATRY - THEORY, APPLICATIONS, AND TREATMENTS

SUICIDAL BEHAVIOR IN ALCOHOL AND DRUG ABUSE AND DEPENDENCE

LEO SHER
AND
ALEXANDER VILENS
EDITORS

Nova Science Publishers, Inc.
New York

For permission to use material from this book please contact us:
Telephone 631-231-7269; Fax 631-231-8175
Web Site: http://www.novapublishers.com

LIBRARY OF CONGRESS CATALOGING-IN-PUBLICATION DATA

Suicidal behavior in alcohol and drug abuse and dependence / editors, Leo
Sher, Alexander Vilens.
p. ; cm.
Includes bibliographical references and index.
ISBN 978-1-60876-919-3 (hardcover)
1. Dual diagnosis. 2. Suicidal behavior. I. Sher, Leo. II. Vilens,
Alexander.
[DNLM: 1. Diagnosis, Dual (Psychiatry) 2. Comorbidity. 3.
Self-Injurious Behavior--epidemiology. 4. Substance-Related
Disorders--epidemiology. 5. Substance-Related Disorders--therapy. 6.
Suicide. WM 270 S948 2009]
RC564.68.S85 2009
616.85'8445--dc22

2009052743

Published by Nova Science Publishers, Inc. ✢ New York

CONTENTS

PREFACE

Suicidal behavior is a major medical and social problem. Multiple lines of evidence suggest that alcohol and drug abuse is associated with suicidal ideation, attempts and suicides. Next to depression, alcoholism and drug abuse are the psychiatric conditions most strongly associated with suicide attempts and completed suicides. Alcohol and drugs are involved in about 50 percent of all suicide attempts. About 25 percent of completed suicides occur among individuals with alcoholism or drug abuse. Acute substance use makes suicide more likely. Nearly all alcoholic suicides occur among active drinkers, and alcohol consumption often immediately precedes the suicide. Individuals who drink a significant amount of alcohol before a suicide attempt make more serious suicide attempts.

This book is dedicated to the relationship between substance use disorders and suicidal behavior. Clinical, epidemiological, neurobiological, and treatment aspects of the relation between substance use disorders and suicidal behavior are discussed in this book.

The contributors to this book are the leading international experts in psychiatry, psychology, and suicidology. We would like to acknowledge and thank all the contributors. Our task as the editors was greatly facilitated by their swift and positive response to our initial inquiry, and thereafter by producing their manuscripts diligently.

We welcome comments from readers. Please, submit your comments via the website at www.internetandpsychiatry.com

Leo Sher
Alexander Vilens
September 2009

PART I. EPIDEMIOLOGY AND PATHOPHYSIOLOGY OF ALCOHOL AND DRUG ABUSE AND DEPENDENCE

In: Suicidal Behavior in Alcohol and Drug Abuse... ISBN: 978-1-60876-919-3
Editors: L. Sher, A. Vilens, pp. 3-11

Chapter 1

EPIDEMIOLOGY OF ALCOHOL, TOBACCO AND SUBSTANCE USE

***Levent Tokucoglu*[1] *and A. Ender Altintoprak*[2]**
[1]Alman Hospital, Diyarbakir, Turkey
[2]Ege University School of Medicine, Izmir, Turkey

ABSTRACT

Tobacco, alcohol and illicit substance use continue to result in substantial morbidity and mortality rate and significant socio-economical costs despite considerable efforts to minimize use of licit substances and prevent use of illicit substances [1,2]. Substance use is associated with a wide range of risk behavior including symptom of both dependence and abuse. Consequences of alcohol and illicit/illegal substance abuse include, medical illnesses -like cirrhosis, job loss and criminal behavior related to acquisition and sale of these drugs [1]. Substance use contributes substantially to the global burden of disease. Tobacco is the fourth important risk factor causing burden of disease as expressed in the number of healthy life years (disability adjusted life years, DALYs). Alcohol is the fifth commonest disease burden and illicit/illegal drugs are in the top 20 causes of disease [3]. Illicit drug use refers to the non-medical use of variety of drugs including cannabis, amphetamine type stimulants, cocaine and opioids [3]. People use psychoactive drugs because of expecting to benefit from their use, whether by pleasure or by the avoidance of pain, including social uses. But using these substances also carries with its potentially harmful effects [4].

INTRODUCTION

Epidemiology has been defined in many ways and hereby we can describe it as the study of the incidence, prevalence and distribution of a disease in a population. Epidemiology answers the questions of who, what, where, when and how much for a particular disease [5].

Epidemiology provides a foundation for much research on drug use and its disorders by demonstrating on whom, through what agents and where drugs exert their effects [6].

Some basic terms used here should be described concisely due to understanding literature and some studies.

Prevalence denotes the percentage of persons who have a particular disorder at a given time within a specific population and incidence refers to the rate of occurrence or percentage of new cases (e.g., in a 6-month or in a-one year period) within a population [5].

For any psychoactive substance there is a range of use from what causes little or no problems to dependent use. Alcohol and other substance use can be classified into five categories: Hazardous drinking or substance use; harmful drinking or substance use; alcohol or substance abuse; alcohol or substance dependence and withdrawal syndrome [3].

ALCOHOL

Alcohol has been consumed by humans since pre-historic ages and it is part of almost every society. Although moderate alcohol consumption has some minimal specific beneficial effects on health, current alcohol use pattern impose a huge health and economical burden on society [7]. Approximately 90% of people consume alcohol at some stage and 30% develop alcohol related disorders [8].Excess alcohol consumption is the fifth largest cause of preventable disability globally [9]. Problems associated with alcohol abuse are recognized by the World Health Organisation (WHO) as a major health issue which is responsible for the 1,4 % of the total global burden of disease [10].

The level of consumption of alcohol has declined in the past 20 years in developed countries, but is increasing in developing countries, especially in the Western Pacific Region [11]. According to WHO, alcohol addiction incidence for developed and developing countries varies from %1 to 5% [12].

Data from the 2001-2002 NESARC in the US, prevalence of lifetime and 12-month alcohol abuse was 17,8% and 4,7%; prevalence of lifetime and 12-month alcohol dependence was 12,5% and 3,8% [13].

High-risk drinking is defined in gender specific terms as drinking 20 grams or more of pure alcohol per day for females and 40 grams or more for males [14]. Men who drink more than 4 standard drinks in a day or drink 14 and more per week and women who drink more than 3 in a day or 7 and more per week, are at increased risk for alcohol-related problems [17].

Currently many young people's health and well-being are seriously under threat by the use of alcohol. There is an increasing pattern towards a more hedonistic attitude to drink, conscious use of alcohol for its pleasurable effect [11]. A comparative study which has been conducted in 6 European countries found that in all countries except Italy, the young people have showed a higher frequency of intoxication than the elders [16].

In general, adults in developing countries are more likely to abstain from drinking than adults in the developed countries [17]. In much of the world, drinking by adult women has been relatively uncommon, but in some places, this is changing [17]. In terms of total years of life lost due to premature mortality and disability, alcohol's net effect is negative everywhere [18]. The burden of social problems caused by drinking is mostly unmeasured, but qualitative evidence suggests that it is also huge in many parts of the developing world [17]. For the 2002, WHO' s global burden of disease study estimated the impact of alcohol consumption cause a net harm of 4,4 of the global burden of disease [17]. Drinking is a gender issue everywhere, in that men do more (in some places, most or all of them) of the drinking, but women disproportionately suffer the consequences [17]. Epidemiological surveys show that alcohol abuse and dependence are more common among males and the younger [19]. It might be due to different cultural-social norms and roles, body size and differences in metabolism [20]. In the US, lifetime prevalence of alcohol dependence is observed in some 10% men and 3-5% women [8]. Patterns of drinking are changing globally with more females and young individuals drinking excessively and up to 10% of females continuing to drink during pregnancy [21].

In the US, nearly 8 million people aged 18 or older fulfill criteria for alcohol addiction for DSM-IV criteria [22]. Although trends in the United States and in other developing countries indicate, either flat or declining alcohol use, rates are rising in many developing countries and in Central and Eastern Europe [23].

In US, the 2007 National Survey on Drug Use and Health (NSDUH) has found that slightly half of Americans aged 12 or older (51%) reported being current drinkers of alcohol; 6,9% of the population was heavy drinker and current alcohol use among young people which aged between 12 and 17 was 15,9 in the 2007 survey [24].

In Europe alcohol abuse and addiction is responsible for 3,2% of the total causes of mortality and 4% of the total of life years in incapacity [23]. In the UK alcohol use responsible for 10% of all DALYs in 2002; male 15%, female 4% [7].

Alcohol use per capita has been considerably higher in Europe, North America and Australasia than other regions. Alcohol consumption is likely to remain stable over the 10-20 years in the most regions of the world, except Southeast Asia and Western Pacific [3].

TOBACCO

Tobacco use is the most significant public health problem globally and is the preventable cause of mortality. More than 1,1 billion people smoke worldwide and about 82% of smokers live in low-income and middle-income countries [25]. Currently 50% of men and 9% of women in developing countries smoke as compared with 35% of men and 22% of women in developed countries [4]. Per capita consumption of cigarettes in Asia and the Far East is higher than in other parts of the world, with the Americas and Eastern Europe. Per capita consumption of cigarettes is 2255, 1849, 1832, 1791 for US, Poland, Peru, Jordan and China respectively [26]. In the US, about 21% adults are current smokers [27]. Tobacco is the fourth leading risk factor of avoidable premature death, disability and burden of disease. Beside this, tobacco use is the single reversible risk factor for illness and death. Tobacco contributed 4,1% to the burden of disease in 2000 [4]. For the US, mortality due to tobacco use is greater than that attributable to HIV, illicit drug and alcohol use, motor vehicle accidents and murders combined [28]. The reason of 80%-90% of all lung cancer deaths is tobacco use [28]. The WHO estimates that about 5 million people die annually from tobacco-related disease and it will increase up to 10 million by 2030 [29].

There is strong evidence of co-morbidity between nicotine and alcohol problems. According to data from the National Epidemiological Survey of Alcohol and Related Conditions (NESARC), 12 month co-morbidity of alcohol use disorders among those with nicotine dependence is 22.8%, and 12 month co-morbidity of nicotine dependence among those with alcohol use disorders is 34.5% [30].

Current mental health disorders are also a risk factor for tobacco use. One third of people with major depression and a quarter of those with an anxiety disorder are tobacco addicted people [3].

Low levels of parental supervision and single parent families have been associated with both tobacco use and alcohol initiation [1].

Illicit Drug Use

People use psychoactive drugs expecting to benefit from their use, whether by pleasure or by the avoidance of pain, including social uses, but using these agents also carries the potential for harmful effects [4].

Illicit drugs are those banned by international drug control treaties. They include cannabis products (e. g., marijuana, hashish and bhang); stimulant drugs (e.g., cocaine and metamphetamine, ecstasy or MDMA) illicit opioid (e.g., heroin, opium) and diverted pharmaceutical opioid (e.g., buprenorphine, methadone, morphine) [31].

There is substantial and increasing demand for substance globally. Demand for and consumption of drugs is dynamic and parallel so supply of substances respond to and drive demands for substances [3]. It is hard to quantify number of how many people use illicit drugs due to its illegal feature and usually they tend to conceal the amount and pattern of their substance use. Globally there are an estimated 205 million people who make use of one or another type of illicit substance [32]. The most common is cannabis, followed by amphetamines, cocaine and the opioid [4]. Illicit substance use is more prevalent among males than females, much more so than cigarette smoking and alcohol consumption. Substance use is also more prevalent among young people than in older age groups. United Nations Office on Drugs and Crime (UNODC) data shows that 2.5% of the total global population and 3.5% of people aged 15 and above had used cannabis at least once in one year between 1998 and 2001 [4].

The 2002 NSDUH data demonstrated that nearly 46% (estimated 108 million people) have tried an illicit drug at least once in their lives ("lifetime"). 40% of them have used marijuana and 30%of have used other illicit drugs [33].

According the UNODC data, in between 2000-2001, annual prevalence estimates of global illicit substance use for all illicit substances was 3,4% of global population and, was 2,7%, 0,7%, 0,2%, 0,3% for cannabis, amphetamine-type stimulants (ATS) (amphetamine and ecstasy), cocaine and opioid respectively [32].

Cannabis is the most widely used illicit drug worldwide [34,35]. Cannabis use seems to be increasing in several countries in Latin America, Africa and Asia, whereas it is to be declining in North America, Pacific Region and Western Europe, especially among young people. Despite the increasing trend, cannabis use are still significantly lower in South

America than in North America [35]. A recent study showed that cannabis use was far higher in US and New Zealand than in any other country [2].

Stimulants are the second most commonly used illicit drugs after cannabis. In recent years, production and consumption of ATS, especially use of crystal meth, have increased substantially around the Pacific Rim [36].

Inhalants are volatile substances. According to the 2007 NSDUH, in US, about 22,5 million people aged 12 or older used inhalants at least once during their lifetime [24].

The least commonly used drugs are opioid in the worldwide. According the UNODC, in 2007, between 15-21 million people used opiates at least once in the worldwide [35].

Globally, drug use is not distributed equally. In general, the US had among the highest level of drug use. Much lower levels were observed in lower income countries in Africa and the Middle East and lower levels of use were reported in the Asia locales covered [2].

Illicit substance use is more prevalent in men and young people than women and older age people [31]. Cigarette smoking, alcohol consumption and illicit substance use are more prevalent among men than women [4]. Differences increase with age and degree of involvement [37].

There was greater drug involvement among the younger than adults in all countries. The period of risk for initiation was mostly during the period from mid to late teenage [2].

The main harmful effects of substance use are chronic health effects (e.g., alcoholic liver cirrhosis; transmission of infections such as HIV); acute/short term effects (e.g., opioid or alcohol overdose); adverse acute and chronic social consequences of the substance use [4].

Use of one substance often does not occur by itself. Alcohol users are more likely to smoke tobacco and most of substance users are multi-substance user, most of them using non-injectable drugs as well, particularly nicotine, alcohol, benzodiazepines, cannabis, prescribed and proprietary drugs [3]. Concurrent illicit drug use with alcohol was reported by 5,6% among past month alcohol users in 2006 and 2007. Most frequently used illicit drug with alcohol was marijuana by 4,8% [38].

The prevalence of alcohol and all the independent type of mood and anxiety disorders are associated with alcohol and drug dependence [39] and nearly half of all individuals with a current drug use disorder have at least one personality disorder [40]. More than 9% of adults who are currently substance users have diagnosable mood disorders and more than 5 million adult US citizens have a serious mental disorder and co-occurring substance use disorders [5].

About 40%-60% of people seen in mental health setting have a co-occurring substance use diagnosis and 60%-80 of people seen in a substance abuse facility have a co-occurring mental illness diagnosis [41].

According to ECA study, in US substance use disorders were remarkable in adults with anti-social personality, bipolar disorders and schizophrenia and less so in depression or anxiety disorder [42] and prevalence rates of substance use disorder are higher in inpatient wards and emergency services [43].

There are so many social and environmental factors that have been related to substance use and abuse. Different factors like culture, gender and ethnicity influence the psychiatric disorders as well as alcohol and substance use disorders. Socio-economic and living conditions, physical environment, access to education, health care systems can affect peoples' choice of alcohol and/or other substances and related problems [3].

As previously stated, men more likely to use all types of substances than women and young adults use more than older people. These two associations are consistent across drug types and countries [2].

Higher income is related to the lifetime use of all types of licit and illicit substances. Never married and previously married people have higher odds of lifetime use of tobacco, cannabis and cocaine than currently married people. Education is positively related to lifetime alcohol use but negatively related to tobacco use. Education is not related to lifetime illicit substance use [2].

Adolescence is a critical period. Adolescents are more likely to have a history of family alcohol use, to have pre-existing mental health problems, to have low levels of self-regulation, to come from broken families and/or to have parents who monitor their activities poorly, to be exposed to deviant peer models, to be victims of sexual or physical abuse, and to hold beliefs that encourage excessive alcohol use [44].

In pregnant women, the use of most substances -except tobacco- usually decreases during pregnancy. Alcohol use associated with fetal alcohol syndrome [37] and tobacco smoking in pregnancy is associated with lower birth weight babies [3]. In developed countries between one in five and one in three pregnant women reported smoking during their pregnancy period [45]. In the US, National Pregnancy and Health Survey between 1992-1993, of the 4 million women who gave birth during survey period, 820.000 women smoked cigarettes, 757.000 women drank alcohol, 119.000 women used marijuana and 45.000 women reported use of cocaine during their pregnancies that year [46].

CONCLUSION

Although alcohol and tobacco sale and usage are not illegal in a lot of countries in the world and might be these reasons they keep to continue as the most significant public health problem and they are easily and with a low-cost preventable cause of mortality globally. Although alcohol consumption trends are to be declining or flattening in many underdeveloped/undeveloped countries, rates are to be rising. Currently, cannabis is the most common illicit substance that has been used followed by ATS, cocaine and opioid. Addiction and related problems seem to be more common among men and younger people than women and elders. On the other hand, drinking pattern of women has been changing globally. Various factors like culture, gender, ethnicity, race, socio-economical and living conditions and income levels might influence alcohol and/or substance use pattern. The period between mid to late teenage is the most risky era to start using them.

Finally, at national and global level serious policies, organizations and initiatives for prevention and treatment approaches and available health facilities are needed in order to protect people against the negative impact of alcohol, tobacco and illicit drugs.

REFERENCES

[1] Galea S, Nandi A, Vlahov D. The Social Epidemiology of Substance Use. *Epidemiol Rev* 2004; 26:36-52.

[2] Degenhardt L, Chiu W-T, Sampson N, Kessler RC, Anthony JC, et al. Toward a Global View of Alcohol, Tobacco, Cannabis, and Cocaine Use: Findings from the World Helath Organization. World Mental Health Surveys. PLoS Med 2008; 5(7): e141.

[3] Latt N, Conigrave K, Saunders JB, Marshall EJ, Nutt D. *Oxford Specialist Handbooks Addicition Medicine.* Oxford Uni. Press, 2009, NY.

[4] World Health Organization: *Neuroscience of Psychoactive Substance Use and Dependence.* 2004 , Geneva, Switzerland.

[5] The Center for Substance Abuse Treatment (CSAT). The Epidemiology of Co-Occuring Substance Use and Mental Disorders. *COCE Overview Paper 8.* Rockville MD. SAMSHA and Center for Mental Health Services, 2007. (To Access: http://coce.samhsa.gov/cod_resources/PDF/OP8Epidemiology10-03-07.pdf)

[6] Compton WM, Thomas YF, Konvey KP, Colliver JD. Developments in the Epidemiology of Drug Use and Drug Use Disorder. *Am J Psychiatry* 2005;162:1494-1502.

[7] Balakrishnan R, Allender S, Scarborough P, Webster P, Rayner M. The burden of alcohol related ill health in the UK. *J Public Health,* 2009, (Epub ahead of print)

[8] Sher L. Alcohol and Suicide: Neurobiological Alcohol and Clinical Aspects. *Sci World J* 2006; 6:700-6.

[9] Ezzati M, Lopez AD, Rodgers A. Selected major risk factors and global and regional burden of disease *Lancet* 2002;360: 1347-1360.

[10] World Health Organization: *The World Health Report.* 2003.Geneva, Switzerland.

[11] World Health Organization:*Global Status Report on Alcohol.* 1999. Geneva, Switzerland.

[12] World Health Organization: *Global Status Report on Alcohol.* 2004. Geneva, Switzerland.

[13] Hasin DS, Stinson FS, Ogburn E, Grant BF. Prevalence, Correlates, Disability, and Comorbidity of DSM-IV Alcohol Abuse and Dependence in the US. *Arch Gen Psychiatry* 2007; 64(7):830-842.

[14] Rehm J, Chisholm D, Room R and Lopez AD. Alcohol. In: Disease Control Priorities Related to Mental, Neurological, Developmental and Substance Abuse Disorders. World Health Organization, 2006, Geneva, Switzerland.(ToAccess:http://worldebookfair.org/Members.3/World_Health_Collection/publications/2006/924156332X_eng.pdf)

[15] Helping Patients Who Drink Two Much. *A Clician's Guide.*

[16] (To Access: http://pubs.niaaa.nih.gov/publications/Practitioner/CliniciansGuide2005/guide.pdf.)

[17] Leifman H, Österberg H, Ramsted M. Alcohol in Postwar Europe, ECAS II: *A discussion of indicators and alcohol-related harm.* 2002. Stockholm, Almquist and Wiksell International.

[18] World Health Organization: *Alcohol in developing societies : a public health approach.* Summary.2002. Geneva, Switzerland.

[19] World Health Organization: Evidence-based strategies and interventions to reduce alcohol-related harm. *World Health Organization.* Sixtieth World Health Assembly. 2007.

[20] Grant BF, Dawson DA, Stinson FS et al. The 12-month prevalence and trends in DSM-IV alcohol abuse and dependence: United States 1991-1992 and 2001- 2002. *Drug Alcohol Depend* 2004; 74 (3): 223-234.

[21] Altintoprak E, Akgür SA, Yuncu Z et al. Alcohol Use-Related Problems in Women. *Turk Psikiyatri Derg.* 2008; 19:197-208.

[22] Center for Disease Control and Prevention. *Alcohol Consumption Among Women Who Are Pregnant or Who Might Become Pregnant US,* 2002. MMWR 2004; 53:1178-81. (To Access: http://www.cdc.gov/mmwr/preview/mmwrhtml/mm5350a4.htm)

[23] 22. American Psychiatry Association (APA): *Diagnostic and Statistical Manuel of Mental Disorders.* 4 th edition. 1994. Washington DC.

[24] World Health Organization: Alcohol in the European Region Consumption, Harm and Policies. 2001. *World Health Organization Regional Office for Europe,* Geneva, Switzerland.

[25] Substance Abuse and Menthal Health Service Administration (SAMSHA); *Office of Applied Studies Results from the 2007 NSDUH: National Findings. 2008.* Rockville, MD.

[26] Jha P, Chaloupka FJ, Moore J et al. Tobacco Addiction. In *Disease Control Priorities Related to Mental, Neurological, Developmental and Substance Abuse Disorders.* WHO, 2006, Geneva, Switzerland. (To access: http://files.dcp2.org/pdf/ expressbooks/noncomm.pdf)

[27] Mackay J, Eriksen M. *The tobacco atlas.* 2002. World Health Organization, Geneva, Switzerland.

[28] Center for Disease Control and Prevention. Cigarette smoking among adults- US, 2006. *Morbid. Mortal. Wkly.* 2007.Rep. 56 (44): 1157-61.

[29] US Dep. Health Hum. Serv. The Health Consequences of Smoking: *A Report of the Surgeon General.* 2004. Atlanta, GA.

[30] World Health Organization: *Annual report from WHO's tobacco free initiative.* 1999. Geneva, Switzerland.

[31] Grant, B. F., Hasin, D. S., Chou, S. P. et al. Nicotine dependence and psychiatric disorders in the United States. Arch Gen Psychiatry. 2004; 61: 1107–1115.

[32] Hall W, Doran C, Degenhardt L and Shepard D. Illicit Opiate Abuse. In *Disease Control Priorities Related to Mental, Neurological, Developmental and Substance Abuse Disorders.* WHO, 2006, Geneva, Switzerland.

[33] United Nations Office on Drugs and Crime (UNODC) : *Global illicit drug trends* 2003. New York, NY, SAMSHA, Office of Applied Studies: *Results from the 2002 NSDUH:* National Findings. 2003.

[34] Vandrey R, Haney M. Pharmacotherapy for cannabis dependence: How close are we? *CNS Drugs* 2009; 23:543-553.

[35] United Nations Office on Drugs and Crime (UNODC): *World Drug Report 2009.* (To Access: http://www.unodc.org/document/wdr/WDR_2009/WDR2009_eng_web.pdf)

[36] United Nations Office on Drugs and Crime (UNODC): *World Drug Report 2005.* Vol 1 Vienna, Austria. (To Access: www.unodc.org)

[37] Winnick C, Norman RL. Epidemiology. In: *Substance Abuse. A Comprehensive Textbook* 4. edition. Editors: Lowinson JH, Rusz P, Millman RB, Langrod JG. 2005 Lippincott Williams & Wilkins, US.

[38] SAMSHA, Office of Applied Studies: The NSDUH Report: *Concurrent Illicit Drug and Alcohol Use*. 2009. Rockville MD.

[39] Grant BF, Stinson FS, Dawson DA, et. al. Prevalence and co-occurence of substance use disorders and independent mood and anxiety disorders: Results from the National Epidemiological Survey on Alcohol and Related Conditions. *Arch Gen Psychiatry.* 2004; 61 (8): 807-816.

[40] Grant BF, Stinson FS, Dawson DA, et. al. Co-occurence of 12-month alcohol and drug use disorders and personality disorders in the US: Results from the National Epidemiological Survey on Alcohol and Related Conditions. *Arch Gen Psychiatry* 2004; 61 (4): 361-368.

[41] Mueser, KT., Drake, RE., Turner, WC., & McGovern, MP. Comorbid Substance Use Disorders and Psychiatric Disorders. In: *Rethinking Substance Abuse: What the Science Shows, And What We Should Do About It.* W.R. Miller & K.M. Carroll (Eds.). 2006. New York: Guilford Press, pp. 115-133.

[42] Regier DA, Farmer MA, Rae DS, et. al. Comorbidity of Mental Disorders with Alcohol and Other Drugs Abuse. *Results from The Epidemiologic Catchment Area* (ECA) Study. JAMA. 1990; 264 (19): 2511-2518.

[43] Ridgely MS, John S. Drug and alcohol services. In : *Textbook of Community Psychiatry* (Eds. Szmukler G, Thornicroft G). 2001 Oxford: Oxford Uni. Press.pp. 347-367.

[44] Brown SA, McGue M, Maggs J, et al. A Developmental Perspective on Alcohol and Youths 16 to 20 Years of Age. *Pediatrics* 2008;121(Supp4):S290-310.

[45] Lumley J, Oliver SS, Chaberlain C et al. (2004) Interventions for promoting smoking cessation during pregnancy. *Cochrane Database Syst Rev*. 2004 Oct 18;(4):CD001055.

[46] Through Substance Abuse Among Women in the USA. *National Pregnancy and Health Survey,* 1992. NIDA Notes, Jan/Feb. 1997. (To access: http://www.drugabuse.gov/NIDA_Notes)

In: Suicidal Behavior in Alcohol and Drug Abuse... ISBN: 978-1-60876-919-3
Editors: L. Sher, A. Vilens, pp. 13-26

Chapter 2

SEROTONIN DYSFUNCTION IN ALCOHOLISM

Eva Friedel and Andreas Heinz
Charité University Medicine, Berlin, Germany

ABSTRACT

The serotonergic system originates in the brains raphé nuclei, from where serotonergic neurons project to subcortical and cortical brain areas [1] (Figure 1). Dysfunction of central serotonergic neurotransmission has been associated with negative mood states such as anxiety and depression [2-4] as well as with suicidality and impulsivity [5, 6]. Dysfunction of serotonergic neurotransmission has also been implicated in the development and maintenance of alcohol dependent behavior [7] [8] [9]. In this chapter, we will first review studies that associate serotonin dysfunction with psychpathological correlates such as impulsivity or negative mood states, we will than review studies, that associate serotonergic dysfunction with the development of alcohol dependence and finally focus on studies, which assessed serotonin dysfunction in alcohol dependent subjects and we will try to identify a specific psychopathological correlate of serotonin dysfunction in manifest alcoholism.

INTRODUCTION

Serotonergic pathways arise from the brainstem raphé nuclei and innervate a multitude of brain areas, which may explain the variety of psychiatric disorders in which dysfunction of serotonergic neurotransmission have been implicated [1, 10] [11, 12]. Once serotonin is released into the synaptic cleft, its reuptake is regulated by the availability and function of serotonin transporters. A functional polymorphism in the regulatory region of the serotonin transporter (5-HTT) gene has been associated with a two-fold difference in serotonin reuptake rates and the risk to develop negative mood states [13, 14] but see [15]. Besides negative mood states such as anxiety and depression [5, 16-19], serotonergic dysfunction may also contribute to the pathogenesis and maintenance of excessive alcohol consumption and to impulsive behavior [6, 7]. Animal experiments and human studies suggest that the acute response to alcohol is modulated both by the structure of the 5-HTT gene and by stress factors, which affect the serotonin turnover rate and the *in vivo* availability of serotonin transporters [9, 20-23]. These observations may be relevant for the development of excessive alcohol intake and alcohol dependence, as a low level of response to acute alcohol intake is more common in the relatively alcohol-naive offspring of alcoholics and is predictive of subsequent alcohol abuse and dependence [9, 24, 25]. In this review, we will trace these lines of evidence and examine whether studies in humans and non-human primates offer a coherent view of the behavioral correlates of serotonergic dysfunction with respect to alcohol dependence.

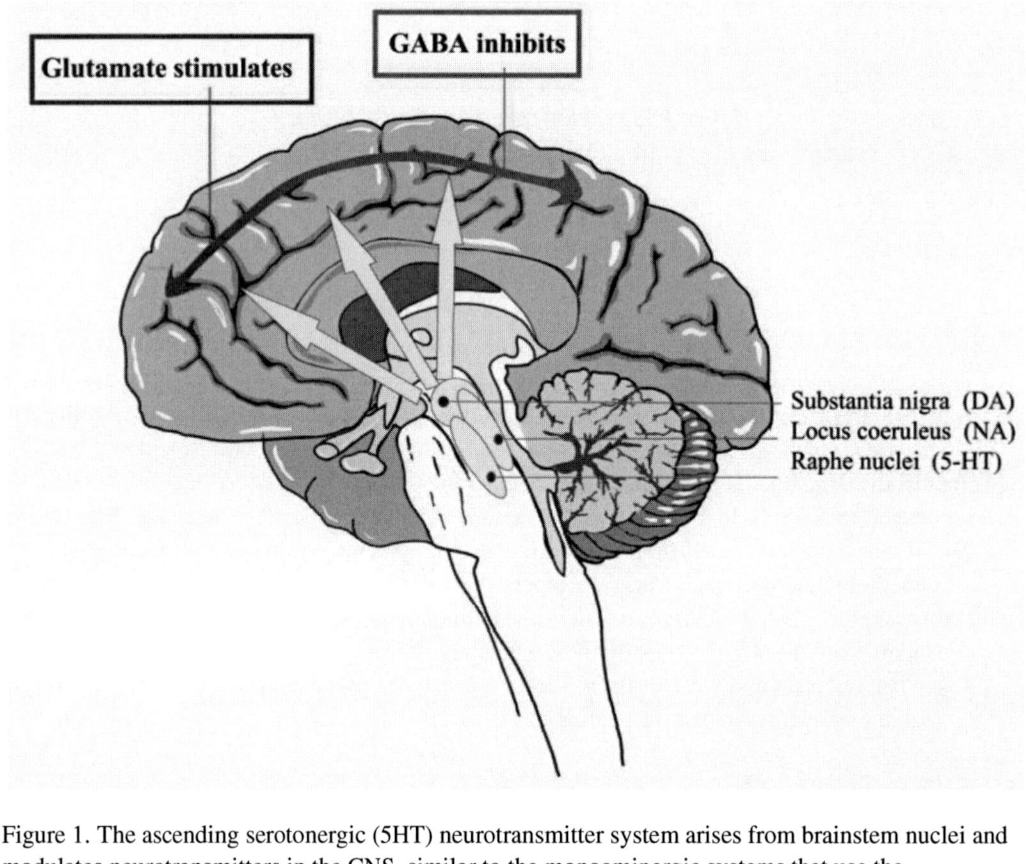

Figure 1. The ascending serotonergic (5HT) neurotransmitter system arises from brainstem nuclei and modulates neurotransmitters in the CNS, similar to the monoaminergic systems that use the neurotransmitter dopamine (DA) and noradrenaline (NA).

Studies in Non Human Primates and Humans on the Psychopathological Correlates of Central Serotonin Dysfunction

It has been suggested that aggressive and impulsive behavior is a primary or secondary correlate of dysfunctional central serotonergic neurotransmission [6]. This hypothesis was based on the work of Gray [26], who hypothesized, that serotonin activates the septo-hippocampal behavior inhibition system, and that this activation is unpleasant, experienced as negative reinforcement (punishment) and induces passive avoidance. A dysfunctional serotonergic system may thus impair the function of this behavior inhibition system, and impulsivity would be a clinical manifestation of the resulting behavior control disorder. This view was evaluated in a series of studies, in which a low serotonin turnover rate measured as the concentration of the serotonin metabolite 5-hydroxyindoleaminoacid [5HIAA] in the cerebrospinal fluid (CSF) had been associated with impulsive and aggressive behavior in both humans and non human primates [27] [6]. However, other studies suggested, that impulsive aggression is not a specific correlate of central serotonergic dysfunction, but rather a secondary consequence of serotonin associated mood state changes. For example, Knutson et al. [28] observed that acute blockade of central serotonin transporters with a selective serotonin reuptake inhibitor, which presumably increases serotonin levels in the synapse, was associated with a primary decrease in negative mood states, and that this decrease in negative mood states explained a (secondary) decrease in aggressiveness in a competitive game in healthy volunteers. Knutson suggested that negative mood states are a primary correlate of serotonin dysfunction; this hypothesis was supported by the observation that Methylendioxymethamphetamin (MDMA, "Ecstasy") acutely increases serotonin release and is associated with a dramatic reduction of negative mood states [29]. Furthermore human studies suggested that medicational selective serotonin reuptake inhibitors (SSRIs) are associated with an improvement of negative mood states due to a time-dependent increase rather than a decrease in synaptic serotonin concentrations [16, 30-32]. Likewise, human studies which measured the serotonin metabolite5-HIAA in the CSF observed that clinical remission of depressive symptoms (as an example of negative mood states) was associated with an increase in primary low CSF 5-HIAA concentrations [18, 19]. Serotonin depletion studies in humans pointed in the same direction and revealed that negative mood states were induced by reducing serotonin concentration in patients who suffered from negative mood states due to obsessive-compulsive disorder or major depression and who previously displayed a reduction of their depressive symptoms following a blockade of serotonin transporters with SSRI-medication [17, 33]. Moreover, a functional promoter polymorphism of the human tryptophan hydroxylase (TPH) 1 gene may contribute to low serotonin synthesis and was associated with both suicidality and alcohol dependence [34]. However recent studies suggest that central serotonin synthesis is driven by TPH 2 gene polymorphisms rather than TPH 1 variants [35]. All together, these studies suggested, that negative mood states are primary correlates of dysfunctional serotonergic neurotransmission and that impulsive aggression and impulsive suicidal acts (interpretated as aggression directed against the own person) may be a secondary correlate of such negative mood states. Particularly, it was suggested that individuals who are overwhelmed by feelings of threat and in security (as primary correlates of serotonin dysfunction) may respond with impulsive aggressive behavior [8].

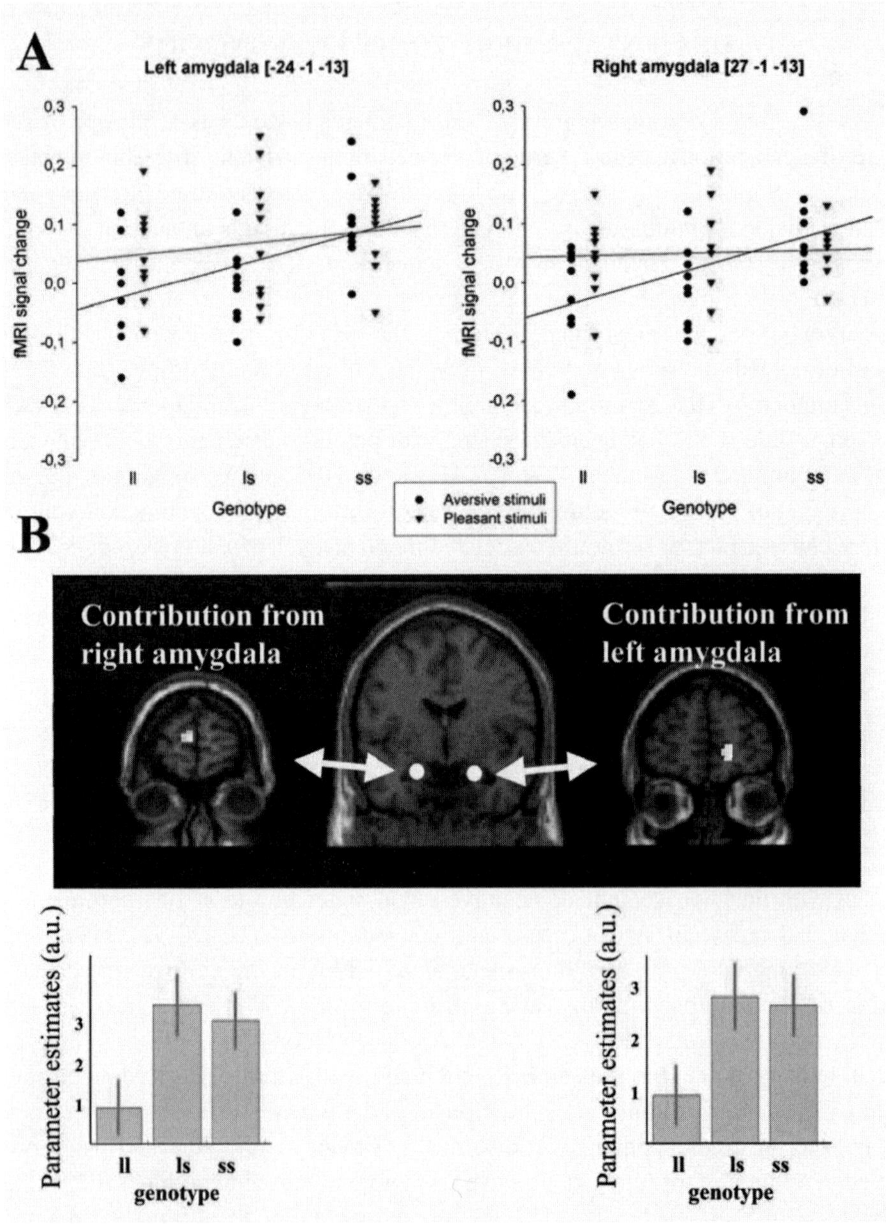

Figure 2. A. 5-HTT genotype modulates amygdala activation elicited by aversive versus neutral (circles) but not by pleasant versus neutral (triangles) pictures. B. Assessment of bilateral functional connectivity between the amygdala and medial prefrontal cortex (PFC): In healthy control subjects, 5-HTT genotypes with increased amygdala activation elicited by aversive cues also showed increased functional connectivity between the amygdalae and medial prefrontal cortex (Brodman's area: BA10), which may limit effects of limbic stimulation and facilitate cortical control (modified according to: Heinz et al. [43]) Parameter estimates of connectivity between the amygdala and medial PFC modulated by 5-HTT genotype: risk allele (s-allele) carriers display increased parameter estimates for functional connectivity.

A series of studies suggest that serotonin modulation of the amygdala and further limbic brain areas may indeed contribute to neuronal processing of threat-indicating and aversive stimuli. One line of investigation accessed the effects of serotonin transporter genotype on such amygdala responses. This inquiry was based on the study of Lesch et al. [14], who showed that carriers of one or two short alleles of a serotonin transporter polymorphism (5-HTTLPR) display about a two-fold reduction in serotonin reuptake capacity and function compared with carriers of two long alleles. Some, but not all human studies suggested that this 5-HTT genotype is directly associated with in vivo expression of serotonin transporters in the brainstem and thalamus [36-39]. Alternatively, it is possible that the serotonin transporter genotype primarily effects central serotonergic neurotransmission during neuro-development, as indicated by one study which showed that early blockade of serotonin transporters was associated with later development of increased anxiety in rodents [40, 41]. Human imaging studies showed that serotonin transporter genotype indeed was associated with amygdala responses to aversive and threat indicating stimuli [42, 43] (Figure 2) and that a genetically driven low expression of serotonin transporters is associated not only with an increased amygdala response to aversive cues but also with the strength of the functional connectivity between the amygdala and brain centers that have been implicated in emotion regulation such as the medial prefrontal cortex and anterior cingulate cortex [43, 44]. In fact, carriers of the genotype that has been associated with reduced expression of serotonin transporters displayed an increased amygdala medial prefrontal cortex connectivity, which may help to regulate increased limbic responses to threatening cues [43, 44]. This "protective" connectivity may increase resilience against aversive life events, because it allows top down cognitive control of limbic processing of aversive experiences. Indeed, one study in unmedicated patients suffering from a major depression showed that functional connectivity between the medial prefrontal cortex and the amygdala is reduced in patients suffering from major depression versus healthy control subjects: when both groups carried the loss of function 5-HTT genotype, patients versus controls showed a reduced prefrontal-amygdala connectivity which was associated with increased anxiety during exposure to unexpected compared with anticipated aversive stimuli [45].

Such findings may explain why serotonin transporter genotype has been associated with a risk to develop major depression following exposure to severe aversive life events [13].

Interestingly Caspi et al. [13] showed that carriers of the loss of function allele of the 5-HTT gene displayed a higher level of depression when exposed to severe negative life events. Human imaging studies suggest that subjects carrying this risk allele may be impaired in their cognitive control of sudden aversive or threatening stimuli [45]. Some studies appear to indicate that epigenetic processes such as CpG-methylation may affect transcription of 5-HTT mRMA [46],since women who displayed increased levels of CpG-methylation showed low levels of 5-HTT mRNA. Such epigenetic and gender specific findings deserve further exploration and may help to explain some inconsistencies in the literature with respect to the interaction of serotonin transporter genotype, severe negative life events and the development of major depression [15, 47].

Serotonin Dysfunction and the Development of Alcohol Dependence

It has been suggested that early onset of alcoholism (i.e. with a manifestation of alcohol dependence before 25 years of age) is characterized by increased aggressive behavior, impulsiveness and serotonin dysfunction [6, 8]. This hypothesis was supported by a series of animal experiments, in which non human primates showed reduced serotonin turnover and increased impulsivity and alcohol intake following early social separation stress. Further brain imaging studies revealed that in such primates, serotonin turnover (5-HIAA in CSF) is reduced and the availability of serotonin transporters in the raphé area is increased, potentially due to reduced competition between serotonin and the radioligand used to mark serotonin transporters. Reduced serotonin turnover rates and increased serotonin transporter availability was directly associated with impulsive aggression and a low response to the acute effects of alcohol intake [22]. Further behavior studies showed that these primates display low social competence and increased anxiety following separation from their mothers during the first six months of life. [22, 27].

Particularly in male rhesus monkeys following puberty, increased anxiety and perception of threatening environmental cues appears to manifest as increased impulsive aggressiveness [8]. Interestingly, in these primates, serotonin dysfunction was associated with reduced sedative effects of gabaergic drugs [21] and with reduced sedative and a toxic effect of acute alcohol intake [22]. This finding is particularly interesting, because a series of human studies suggested that a low response to acute alcohol intake is a partially heritable trade that predicts excessive alcohol intake during later life [24]. Indeed, an elevation of serotonin transporters in non human primates following early social isolation stress was associated with increased alcohol intake in a free choice paradigm [48]. As discussed above, an elevation of serotonin transporters availability can also be observed in association with the genetic constitution of the serotonin transporter gene [14, 22]. Again, carriers of a genotype with increased serotonin transporter expression displayed a low response to acute alcohol effects [9, 49] and an increased risk to develop alcohol dependence [9]. This finding was evaluated in a study in non human primates, in which a genetic constitution of the serotonin transporter that was associated with increased transporter expression also predicted increased alcohol intake [20]. In humans and non human primates, increased availability of serotonin transporters was associated with a reduced serotonin turnover rate in vivo [50, 51]. Serotonin dysfunction can contribute to low alcohol response by reducing the sedative effects of alcohol due to its effects on excitatory and inhibitory neurotransmitters (mediated in the prefrontal cortex via activation of GABA- receptors [52, 53] and by blockade of glutamatergic NMDA-receptors [53-55]), given 5-HT1a and H-HT4 [56, 57]. Altogether, these studies suggest that a high expression of serotonin transporters (may it result from early social isolation stress in association with reduced serotonin turnover rates or be associated with serotonin transporter genotype per se) contributes to a low response toward the acute effects of alcohol [9, 50]. Subjects displaying such a low response towards the acute effects of alcohol appear to lack a "warning sign" and to consume excessive amounts of alcohol, thus increasing the risk to develop alcohol dependence [9, 23].

SEROTONIN DYSFUNCTION IN MANIFEST ALCOHOLISM

A study of Mash et al. [58] showed that dysfunction of monoaminergic systems such as dopamine and serotonin neurotransmission may differ profoundly from the state of monoaminergic transmission following excessive alcohol intake. In fact, non human primates displayed a reduced turnover rate of serotonin and dopamine measured as the metabolites 5-HIAA and HVA in CSF and an increased availability of dopamine transporters before excessive alcohol consumption started. Following alcohol intake the same primate showed an alcohol-associated increase in serotonin and dopomanine turnover rates and a decrease in dopamine transporters [58]. A similar observation was made in studies accessing serotonin transporter availability: non human primates predisposed to excessive alcohol intake displayed an increase in serotonin transporter availability and a decreased serotonin turnover rate [50], while alcohol dependent patients showed a reduction of serotonin transporter availability in the brainstem (raphé) area, which was associated with the amount of lifetime alcohol intake [22]. Here, serotonin transporter availability appears to be reduced following the neurotoxic effects of alcohol intake, which may itself be modulated by serotonin transporter genotype [36] and by cortisol increases as found during acute detoxification [51].

In these imaging studies in humans, no specific effect of age of onset on serotonin dysfunction was observed. This finding contrasts to the observation that early onset alcoholism has been associated with lower cerebral spinal fluid 5-HIAA levels [6], however, it remains unclear whether comorbide and antisocial personality disorder may contribute to this finding. Since the subjects observed by Fils-Aime [6] also displayed increased anxiety, it is possible that serotonin dysfunction in association with negative mood states may contribute to impulsive aggression in alcoholics [8]. In the study of Heinz et al. [22], reduced serotonin transporter availability was associated with increased anxiety, a finding that was also observed in major depression [2]. This observation suggests that serotonin dysfunction may indeed be primarily associated with negative mood states such as anxiety. However, two further studies failed to observe a reduction in serotonin transporter availability in human alcohol dependent patients [59, 60]. These divergent results may be due to specific characteristics of the radioligand applied to quantify serotonin transporter availability: while the ligand CIT is displaced by endogenous serotonin [61], other radioligands such as DASB are not [62]. Since alterations in serotonin turnover rates had been implicated in alcoholism and were found to be inversely associated with serotonin transporter availability in both humans and non human primates [50, 51], alterations in serotonin transporters observed with radioligands like CIT may reflect altered serotonin turnover rates rather than reductions in the density of brainstem serotonin transporters per se. Nevertheless, in vitro studies also point to a reduction of midbrain serotonin transporter density in alcohol dependence [63], and this reduction may simply be the result of a neurotoxic alterations of serotonin neurons in the raphé area, the center of origin of serotonergic projections [1].

If several studies appointed to an association between mood states and alteration of serotonin transporters in manifest alcohol dependence, why are SSRIs rather ineffective in reducing the relapse risk? One prospective study that directly accessed the interaction between negative mood states and the relapse risk may help to elucidate this finding: during the first months of abstinence, high levels of anxiety are associated with reduced rather than an increased relapse risk [64]. This finding may be due to the effect that high anxiety was associated with harm avoidance, which may explain why patients with higher levels of anxiety are also more cautious and show low relapse rates. Further reduction of anxiety by SSRIs may thus not be helpful, unless major depression or anxiety disorders are manifest or suicidality should be reduced [65].

Recent studies further implicate, that the blockade of serotonin 5-HT3 receptors with ondansetrone seems to be efficient in treating alcohol dependence [66]. This observation may be due to the fact that 5-HT3 antagonists block serotonin-mediated dopamine release as well as activation of the ventral striatum elicited by alcohol-associated cues, particularly in combination with the mu-opiate antagonist naltrexone [67]. Blockade of 5-HT3 and mu-opiate receptors decreased alcohol craving [67], a finding that is in accordance with the observation that elevated mu-opiate receptors in the ventral striatum of detoxified alcoholics correlate with the severity of alcohol craving [68]. 5-HT3 antagonists may thus interfere both with alcohol-associated dopamine release in the ventral striatum and with cue-induced activation of this central region of the brain reward system.

Conclusion

Altogether, these findings show that serotonin neurotransmission may play a complex role in the development and maintenance of alcohol dependence. In subjects predisposed for excessive alcohol intake, a high availability of serotonin transporters in the brainstem (raphé) predisposes to a low response to the acute effects of alcohol. Subjects with this phenotype appear to lack a warning sign of alcohol intoxication and to carry an increased risk for excessive alcohol intake and the development of alcohol dependence [9, 49]. This association between high raphé serotonin transporter availability and a low response to alcohol appears to be independent of whether elevated serotonin transporters result from 5-HTT genotype or early social isolation stress [9, 48, 49].

Animal experiments further suggest that early social exclusion stress appears to also result in a low serotonin turnover rate, which was associated with increased threat perception and impulsive aggression, particularly in male rhesus monkeys after puberty [22, 27]. Chronic alcohol intake, on the other hand, was associated with potentially neurotoxic effects on central serotonergic neurotransmission as indicated by a serotonin neuron sprouting [69] and by a reduction in brainstem serotonin transporters, which was associated with the amount of lifetime alcohol intake and correlated with the severity of negative mood states such as anxiety and depression [50]. Interestingly, some but not all studies suggest that these alcohol-associated alterations in serotonin transporter availability are driven by 5-HTT genotype [36, 66]. The interesting interaction between social stress factors, alcohol neurotoxicity and genetic vulnerability of the serotonin system remains to be explored in further studies.

REFERENCES

[1] Baumgarten HG, Z.. Anatomy of central serotoninergic projection systems. In: *Handbook of experimental pharmacology*. Berlin, Heidelberg: Springer; 1997. p. 41 - 89.

[2] Reimold M, Batra A, Knobel A, Smolka MN, Zimmer A, Mann K, Solbach C, Reischl G, Schwarzler F, Grunder G, Machulla HJ, Bares R, Heinz A. Anxiety is associated with reduced central serotonin transporter availability in unmedicated patients with unipolar major depression: a [11C]DASB PET study. *Molecular psychiatry* 2008;13(6):606-13, 557.

[3] Asberg M, Bertilsson L, Martensson B, Scalia-Tomba GP, Thoren P, Traskman-Bendz L. CSF monoamine metabolites in melancholia. *Acta psychiatrica Scandinavica* 1984;69(3):201-19.

[4] Malison RT, Price LH, Berman R, van Dyck CH, Pelton GH, Carpenter L, Sanacora G, Owens MJ, Nemeroff CB, Rajeevan N, Baldwin RM, Seibyl JP, Innis RB, Charney DS. Reduced brain serotonin transporter availability in major depression as measured by [123I]-2 beta-carbomethoxy-3 beta-(4-iodophenyl)tropane and single photon emission computed tomography. *Biological psychiatry* 1998;44(11):1090-8.

[5] Mann JJ, Malone KM, Psych MR, Sweeney JA, Brown RP, Linnoila M, Stanley B, Stanley M. Attempted suicide characteristics and cerebrospinal fluid amine metabolites in depressed inpatients. *Neuropsychopharmacology* 1996;15(6):576-86.

[6] FilsAime ML, Eckardt, M. J., George, D. T., Brown, G. L., Mefford, I., & Linnoila, M.. Early-onset alcoholics have lower cerebrospinal fluid 5-hydroxyindoleacetic acid levels than late-onset alcoholics. *Archives of general psychiatry* 1996;53:211-216.

[7] LeMarquand D, Pihl RO, Benkelfat C. Serotonin and alcohol intake, abuse, and dependence: findings of animal studies. *Biological psychiatry* 1994;36(6):395-421.

[8] Heinz A, Mann K, Weinberger DR, Goldman D. Serotonergic dysfunction, negative mood states, and response to alcohol. *Alcoholism, clinical and experimental research* 2001;25(4):487-95.

[9] Schuckit MA, Mazzanti C, Smith TL, Ahmed U, Radel M, Iwata N, Goldman D. Selective genotyping for the role of 5-HT2A, 5-HT2C, and GABA alpha 6 receptors and the serotonin transporter in the level of response to alcohol: a pilot study. *Biological psychiatry* 1999;45(5):647-51.

[10] Cloninger CR. A systematic method for clinical description and classification of personality variants. A proposal. *Archives of general psychiatry* 1987;44(6):573-88.

[11] Meltzer H, Maes, M., & Elkis, H. The biological basis of refractory depression. In: W. Nolen JZ, S. Roose, & J. Amsterdam, editor. *Refractory depression: current strategies and future directions*. Chichester: John Wiley and Sons; 1994. p. 177 - 198.

[12] Owens MJ, Nemeroff CB. Role of serotonin in the pathophysiology of depression: focus on the serotonin transporter. *Clinical chemistry* 1994;40(2):288-95.

[13] Caspi A, Sugden K, Moffitt TE, Taylor A, Craig IW, Harrington H, McClay J, Mill J, Martin J, Braithwaite A, Poulton R. Influence of life stress on depression: moderation by a polymorphism in the 5-HTT gene. *Science* (New York, N.Y 2003;301(5631):386-9.

[14] Lesch KP, Bengel D, Heils A, Sabol SZ, Greenberg BD, Petri S, Benjamin J, Muller CR, Hamer DH, Murphy DL. Association of anxiety-related traits with a polymorphism in the serotonin transporter gene regulatory region. *Science* (New York, N.Y 1996;274(5292):1527-31.

[15] Risch N, Herrell R, Lehner T, Liang KY, Eaves L, Hoh J, Griem A, Kovacs M, Ott J, Merikangas KR. Interaction between the serotonin transporter gene (5-HTTLPR), stressful life events, and risk of depression: a meta-analysis. *Jama* 2009;301(23):2462-71.

[16] Artigas F. Pindolol, 5-hydroxytryptamine, and antidepressant augmentation. *Archives of general psychiatry* 1995;52(11):969-71.

[17] Barr LC, Goodman WK, McDougle CJ, Delgado PL, Heninger GR, Charney DS, Price LH. Tryptophan depletion in patients with obsessive-compulsive disorder who respond to serotonin reuptake inhibitors. Archives of general psychiatry 1994;51(4):309-17.

[18] Praag HM. The Harold E. Himwich Memorial Lecture. Significance of biochemical parameters in the diagnosis, treatment, and prevention of depressive disorders. Biological psychiatry 1977;12(1):101-31.

[19] Traskman-Bendz L, Asberg M, Bertilsson L, Thoren P. CSF monoamine metabolites of depressed patients during illness and after recovery. Acta psychiatrica Scandinavica 1984;69(4):333-42.

[20] Barr CS, Newman TK, Becker ML, Champoux M, Lesch KP, Suomi SJ, Goldman D, Higley JD. Serotonin transporter gene variation is associated with alcohol sensitivity in rhesus macaques exposed to early-life stress. Alcoholism, clinical and experimental research 2003;27(5):812-7.

[21] Doudet D, Hommer D, Higley JD, Andreason PJ, Moneman R, Suomi SJ, Linnoila M. Cerebral glucose metabolism, CSF 5-HIAA levels, and aggressive behavior in rhesus monkeys. The American journal of psychiatry 1995;152(12):1782-7.

[22] Heinz A, Higley JD, Gorey JG, Saunders RC, Jones DW, Hommer D, Zajicek K, Suomi SJ, Lesch KP, Weinberger DR, Linnoila M. In vivo association between alcohol intoxication, aggression, and serotonin transporter availability in nonhuman primates. The American journal of psychiatry 1998;155(8):1023-8.

[23] Hu X, Oroszi G, Chun J, Smith TL, Goldman D, Schuckit MA. An expanded evaluation of the relationship of four alleles to the level of response to alcohol and the alcoholism risk. Alcoholism, clinical and experimental research 2005;29(1):8-16.

[24] Schuckit MA, Smith TL. An 8-year follow-up of 450 sons of alcoholic and control subjects. Archives of general psychiatry 1996;53(3):202-10.

[25] Rodriguez LA, Wilson JR, Nagoshi CT. Does psychomotor sensitivity to alcohol predict subsequent alcohol use? Alcoholism, clinical and experimental research 1993;17(1):155-61.

[26] Gray J. The neuropsychology of anxiety. An inquiry into the function of the septo-hippocampal system. New York: Oxford University Press; 1982.

[27] Higley JD, Suomi SJ, Linnoila M. A nonhuman primate model of type II excessive alcohol consumption? Part 1. Low cerebrospinal fluid 5-hydroxyindoleacetic acid concentrations and diminished social competence correlate with excessive alcohol consumption. Alcoholism, clinical and experimental research 1996;20(4):629-42.

[28] Knutson B, Wolkowitz OM, Cole SW, Chan T, Moore EA, Johnson RC, Terpstra J, Turner RA, Reus VI. Selective alteration of personality and social behavior by serotonergic intervention. The American journal of psychiatry 1998;155(3):373-9.

[29] Huether G, Zhou D, Ruther E. Causes and consequences of the loss of serotonergic presynapses elicited by the consumption of 3,4-methylenedioxymethamphetamine (MDMA, "ecstasy") and its congeners. J Neural Transm 1997;104(8-9):771-94.

[30] Kreiss DS, Lucki I. Effects of acute and repeated administration of antidepressant drugs on extracellular levels of 5-hydroxytryptamine measured in vivo. The Journal of pharmacology and experimental therapeutics 1995;274(2):866-76.

[31] Limberger N, Starke K, Singer EA. Serotonin uptake blockers influence serotonin autoreceptors by increasing the biophase concentration of serotonin and not through a "molecular link". *Naunyn-Schmiedeberg's archives of pharmacology* 1990;342(4):363-70.

[32] Muck-Seler D, Jevric-Causevic A, Diksic M. Influence of fluoxetine on regional serotonin synthesis in the rat brain. *Journal of neurochemistry* 1996;67(6):2434-42.

[33] Delgado PL, Charney DS, Price LH, Aghajanian GK, Landis H, Heninger GR. Serotonin function and the mechanism of antidepressant action. Reversal of antidepressant-induced remission by rapid depletion of plasma tryptophan. *Archives of general psychiatry* 1990;47(5):411-8.

[34] Nielsen DA, Virkkunen M, Lappalainen J, Eggert M, Brown GL, Long JC, Goldman D, Linnoila M. A tryptophan hydroxylase gene marker for suicidality and alcoholism. *Archives of general psychiatry* 1998;55(7):593-602.

[35] Scheuch K, Lautenschlager M, Grohmann M, Stahlberg S, Kirchheiner J, Zill P, Heinz A, Walther DJ, Priller J. Characterization of a functional promoter polymorphism of the human tryptophan hydroxylase 2 gene in serotonergic raphe neurons. *Biological psychiatry* 2007;62(11):1288-94.

[36] Heinz A, Jones DW, Mazzanti C, Goldman D, Ragan P, Hommer D, Linnoila M, Weinberger DR. A relationship between serotonin transporter genotype and in vivo protein expression and alcohol neurotoxicity. *Biological psychiatry* 2000;47(7):643-9.

[37] Praschak-Rieder N, Kennedy J, Wilson AA, Hussey D, Boovariwala A, Willeit M, Ginovart N, Tharmalingam S, Masellis M, Houle S, Meyer JH. Novel 5-HTTLPR allele associates with higher serotonin transporter binding in putamen: a [11)C] DASB positron emission tomography study. *Biological psychiatry* 2007;62(4):327-31.

[38] Reimold M, Smolka MN, Schumann G, Zimmer A, Wrase J, Mann K, Hu XZ, Goldman D, Reischl G, Solbach C, Machulla HJ, Bares R, Heinz A. Midbrain serotonin transporter binding potential measured with [11C]DASB is affected by serotonin transporter genotype. *J Neural Transm* 2007;114(5):635-9.

[39] van Dyck CH, Malison RT, Jacobsen LK, Seibyl JP, Staley JK, Laruelle M, Baldwin RM, Innis RB, Gelernter J. Increased dopamine transporter availability associated with the 9-repeat allele of the SLC6A3 gene. *J Nucl Med* 2005;46(5):745-51.

[40] Yamada I, Iwasaki T. [Anxiety-like behavior in rats neonatally and adultly treated with 5,7-dihydroxytryptamine]. Nihon shinkei seishin yakurigaku zasshi = *Japanese journal of psychopharmacology* 2002;22(5):145-51.

[41] Andersen SL, Dumont NL, Teicher MH. Differences in behavior and monoamine laterality following neonatal clomipramine treatment. *Developmental psychobiology* 2002;41(1):50-7.

[42] Hariri AR, Mattay VS, Tessitore A, Kolachana B, Fera F, Goldman D, Egan MF, Weinberger DR. Serotonin transporter genetic variation and the response of the human amygdala. *Science* (New York, N.Y 2002;297(5580):400-3.

[43] Heinz A, Braus DF, Smolka MN, Wrase J, Puls I, Hermann D, Klein S, Grusser SM, Flor H, Schumann G, Mann K, Buchel C. Amygdala-prefrontal coupling depends on a genetic variation of the serotonin transporter. *Nature neuroscience* 2005;8(1):20-1.

[44] Pezawas L, Meyer-Lindenberg A, Drabant EM, Verchinski BA, Munoz KE, Kolachana BS, Egan MF, Mattay VS, Hariri AR, Weinberger DR. 5-HTTLPR polymorphism impacts human cingulate-amygdala interactions: a genetic susceptibility mechanism for depression. *Nature neuroscience* 2005;8(6):828-34.

[45] Friedel E, Schlagenhauf F, Sterzer P, Park SQ, Bermpohl F, Strohle A, Stoy M, Puls I, Hagele C, Wrase J, Buchel C, Heinz A. 5-HTT genotype effect on prefrontal-amygdala coupling differs between major depression and controls. *Psychopharmacology* 2009.

[46] Philibert RA, Sandhu H, Hollenbeck N, Gunter T, Adams W, Madan A. The relationship of 5HTT (SLC6A4) methylation and genotype on mRNA expression and liability to major depression and alcohol dependence in subjects from the Iowa Adoption Studies. *Am J Med Genet B Neuropsychiatr Genet* 2008;147B(5):543-9.

[47] Munafo MR, Durrant C, Lewis G, Flint J. Gene X environment interactions at the serotonin transporter locus. *Biological psychiatry* 2009;65(3):211-9.

[48] Heinz A, Jones DW, Gorey JG, Bennet A, Suomi SJ, Weinberger DR, Higley JD. Serotonin transporter availability correlates with alcohol intake in non-human primates. *Molecular psychiatry* 2003;8(2):231-4.

[49] Hinckers AS, Laucht M, Schmidt MH, Mann KF, Schumann G, Schuckit MA, Heinz A. Low level of response to alcohol as associated with serotonin transporter genotype and high alcohol intake in adolescents. *Biological psychiatry* 2006;60(3):282-7.

[50] Heinz A, Ragan P, Jones DW, Hommer D, Williams W, Knable MB, Gorey JG, Doty L, Geyer C, Lee KS, Coppola R, Weinberger DR, Linnoila M. Reduced central serotonin transporters in alcoholism. *The American journal of psychiatry* 1998;155(11):1544-9.

[51] Heinz A, Jones DW, Bissette G, Hommer D, Ragan P, Knable M, Wellek S, Linnoila M, Weinberger DR. Relationship between cortisol and serotonin metabolites and transporters in alcoholism [correction of alcolholism]. *Pharmacopsychiatry* 2002;35(4):127-34.

[52] Liljequist S, Engel J. Effects of GABAergic agonists and antagonists on various ethanol-induced behavioral changes. *Psychopharmacology* 1982;78(1):71-5.

[53] Silveri MM, Spear LP. The effects of NMDA and GABAA pharmacological manipulations on ethanol sensitivity in immature and mature animals. *Alcoholism, clinical and experimental research* 2002;26(4):449-56.

[54] Tsai G, Gastfriend DR, Coyle JT. The glutamatergic basis of human alcoholism. *The American journal of psychiatry* 1995;152(3):332-40.

[55] Krystal JH, Petrakis IL, Webb E, Cooney NL, Karper LP, Namanworth S, Stetson P, Trevisan LA, Charney DS. Dose-related ethanol-like effects of the NMDA antagonist, ketamine, in recently detoxified alcoholics. *Archives of general psychiatry* 1998;55(4):354-60.

[56] Feng J, Cai X, Zhao J, Yan Z. Serotonin receptors modulate GABA(A) receptor channels through activation of anchored protein kinase C in prefrontal cortical neurons. *J Neurosci* 2001;21(17):6502-11.

[57] Krystal J, Abi-Dargham, A., Laruelle, M., & Moghaddam, B. Pharmacological models of psychosis. In: D. Charney EN, & B. Bunney, editor. *Neurobiology of mental illness.* New York, Oxford: Oxford University Press; 1999. p. 214 - 224.

[58] Mash DC, Staley JK, Doepel FM, Young SN, Ervin FR, Palmour RM. Altered dopamine transporter densities in alcohol-preferring vervet monkeys. *Neuroreport* 1996;7(2):457-62.

[59] Brown AK, George DT, Fujita M, Liow JS, Ichise M, Hibbeln J, Ghose S, Sangare J, Hommer D, Innis RB. PET [11C]DASB imaging of serotonin transporters in patients with alcoholism. *Alcoholism, clinical and experimental research* 2007;31(1):28-32.

[60] Martinez D, Slifstein M, Gil R, Hwang DR, Huang Y, Perez A, Frankle WG, Laruelle M, Krystal J, Abi-Dargham A. Positron emission tomography imaging of the serotonin transporter and 5-HT(1A) receptor in alcohol dependence. *Biological psychiatry* 2009;65(2):175-80.

[61] Heinz A, Jones DW, Zajicek K, Gorey JG, Juckel G, Higley JD, Weinberger DR. Depletion and restoration of endogenous monoamines affects beta-CIT binding to serotonin but not dopamine transporters in non-human primates. *Journal of neural transmission* 2004(68):29-38.

[62] Hummerich R, Reischl G, Ehrlichmann W, Machulla HJ, Heinz A, Schloss P. DASB - in vitro binding characteristics on human recombinant monoamine transporters with regard to its potential as positron emission tomography (PET) tracer. *Journal of neurochemistry* 2004;90(5):1218-26.

[63] Little KY, McLaughlin DP, Zhang L, Livermore CS, Dalack GW, McFinton PR, DelProposto ZS, Hill E, Cassin BJ, Watson SJ, Cook EH. Cocaine, ethanol, and genotype effects on human midbrain serotonin transporter binding sites and mRNA levels. *The American journal of psychiatry* 1998;155(2):207-13.

[64] Heinz A, Dufeu P, Kuhn S, Dettling M, Graf K, Kurten I, Rommelspacher H, Schmidt LG. Psychopathological and behavioral correlates of dopaminergic sensitivity in alcohol-dependent patients. *Archives of general psychiatry* 1996;53(12):1123-8.

[65] Wojnar M, Brower KJ, Jakubczyk A, Zmigrodzka I, Burmeister M, Matsumoto H, Wozny E, Sliwerska E, Hegedus AM, Husar A, Slufarska A, Lipinski M, Zucker RA. [Influence of impulsivity, suicidality and serotonin genes on treatment outcomes in alcohol dependence]. *Psychiatria polska* 2006;40(5):985-94.

[66] Johnson BA. Role of the serotonergic system in the neurobiology of alcoholism: implications for treatment. *CNS drugs* 2004;18(15):1105-18.

[67] Myrick H, Anton RF, Li X, Henderson S, Randall PK, Voronin K. Effect of naltrexone and ondansetron on alcohol cue-induced activation of the ventral striatum in alcohol-dependent people. *Archives of general psychiatry* 2008;65(4):466-75.

[68] Heinz A, Reimold M, Wrase J, Hermann D, Croissant B, Mundle G, Dohmen BM, Braus DF, Schumann G, Machulla HJ, Bares R, Mann K. Correlation of stable elevations in striatal mu-opioid receptor availability in detoxified alcoholic patients with alcohol craving: a positron emission tomography study using carbon 11-labeled carfentanil. *Archives of general psychiatry* 2005;62(1):57-64.

[69] Underwood MD, Mann JJ, Arango V. Morphometry of dorsal raphe nucleus serotonergic neurons in alcoholism. *Alcoholism, clinical and experimental research* 2007;31(5):837-45.

In: Suicidal Behavior in Alcohol and Drug Abuse...
Editors: L. Sher, A. Vilens, pp. 27-38
ISBN: 978-1-60876-919-3

Chapter 3

DEPRESSED-LIKE BEHAVIOR AND ALCOHOL DRINKING ARE CO-MORBID BUT INDEPENDENT IN THE FAWN-HOODED RATS

***Amir H. Rezvani*[1] *and David H. Overstreet*[2]**
[1]Duke University Medical Center, Durham, North Carolina, USA
[2]University of North Carolina, Chapel Hill, North Carolina, USA

ABSTRACT

The Fawn-Hooded (FH/Wjd) rat is an inbred strain that exhibits symptoms analogous to those exhibited by human depressives and alcoholics. The exaggerated swim test immobility and increased basal coticosterone levels are two of the depressed-like symptoms; importantly, these symptoms are reduced following chronic antidepressant treatments. Like alcoholics, the FH rat drinks excessive amounts of alcohol voluntarily that if allowed to continue will lead to tolerance and dependence, as revealed by anxiety-like behavior upon withdrawal of the alcohol. The human literature is inconclusive on how these two comorbid conditions are related; however, data in the animals clearly points to them being independent. Genetic studies (F1 and F2 crosses, QTL) indicate no genetic overlap. Chronic treatment with antidepressants selectively reduces the depressed-like symptoms. Thus, the depressed-like behavior and excessive alcohol drinking appear to be independent traits in the FH/Wjd rat.

1. INTRODUCTION

The high comorbidity between alcoholism and depressive disorders has been well documented. Epidemiological data and clinical observations as well as some animal studies strongly support the notion of comorbidity of depression and alcoholism. However, no consensus has been reached in the scientific community regarding the mechanism(s) of this relationship. Although several groups have made attempts to determine the role of genetics in the manifestation of the comorbidity of alcoholism and depression both in humans and laboratory animals [1-6], the true nature of this association is not fully understood. This short review examines the relationship between depressed-like behaviors and alcohol-seeking behavior using a genetic animal model of comorbid depression and alcoholism.

2. Co-morbidity of Depression and Alcoholism in Humans

The co-occurrence of depression and alcoholism is very common in humans. Up to one third of alcoholics may have comorbid depressive symptoms [7]. This topic may be covered in greater detail in another chapter in this book. For the purposes of discussing the Fawn-Hooded rats as a potential model for comorbid depression and alcoholism, the present section will emphasize the issues summarized in the recent review by Davis et al. [7].

Several studies have suggested that the question is more complicated than simply a comorbid depression and alcohol abuse. Many of the patients not only exhibited depressed-like behavior, they also exhibited symptoms of anxiety disorders such as obsessive-compulsive disorder and panic disorder [7]. Furthermore, many of the patients abuse other drugs besides alcohol. Therefore, it is relatively uncommon to have patients that have just depressed symptoms and alcohol abuse. Nevertheless, a substantial number of studies have been carried out.

A key question in this field is why do the depressive disorders and alcohol abuse co-occur. Among the opinions that have been expressed are the following. 1) The depressive symptoms are secondary to the alcohol abuse, as it is well known that depressive-like symptoms are common during withdrawal from alcohol. This view has been expressed in several versions, such at "biologically driven substance-induced depression" [7] or depression related to the social, interpersonal and occupational consequences of the alcohol abuse. 2) There are common risk factors for the two conditions, such as family history and/or interpersonal relationships. There is also evidence for a mutual relationship with depressive disorders increasing the risk for alcohol abuse and alcohol abuse increasing the risk for depressive disorders. 3) The self-medication hypothesis states that the depressed individual initiates and maintains alcohol drinking to relieve the symptoms of depression. An important feature of these three opinions is that they need not be mutually exclusive. At least two of the opinions may be correct for some populations. For example, Davis et al. [7] concluded that a large study on twins [8] supported both the opinion of mutual causation (#2 above) as well as self-medication (#3 above).

Treatment of comorbid individuals is not common, but there are enough studies with antidepressants to develop some conclusions. Davis et al [7] reported that the studies on antidepressants in individuals with substance abuse were related to the baseline symptoms and the response to placebos. Individuals who responded to placebos made it more difficult to detect antidepressant-like effects. However, they can be seen and it is not clear whether having a substance abuse disorder will impair the patient's ability to respond to antidepressants. Pettinati and her colleagues have carried out a number of these trials and she has concluded that it is now possible to design appropriate trials that allow positive effects of antidepressants to be seen [9]. However, an equally important finding is that the antidepressants did not affect alcohol abuse. Thus, from a treatment perspective, the depressive disorders and alcohol abuse are independent. These findings also tend to argue against the self-medication hypothesis. If the individual is drinking to relieve the depression, then the drinking should be reduced when the depression is relieved by another means; but drinking is not reduced [9].

Thus, co-occurring depressive disorders and alcohol abuse are common conditions and there is an unresolved debate about what causes this morbidity. Each disorder being "caused" by the other and mutual interactions are the most commonly proposed hypotheses. Interestingly, no one has apparently suggested that the two conditions may be independent even though only the depressive symptoms can be reduced by antidepressant treatment. We do not know what happens to the depressive symptoms when alcoholics are given drugs for their alcoholism, such as naltrexone, because individuals with depressive symptoms have been excluded from the clinical trials.

3. Animal Model of Depression

When developing animal models of depression or when considering specially bred or treated rats as animal models, one must consider the key symptoms of depression and whether these symptoms are testable in animals. Furthermore, you must have some idea as to how many of the symptoms must be fulfilled before the animal should be regarded as a valid animal model. For example, suicidal ideation is a key symptom associated with depression, but it is unlikely that one could model such behavior in rodents. To consider this topic in more detail, a list of many of the symptoms of depression are given in Table 1, along with a statement about the extent to which the FH rat exhibits depressed-like behavior for each of the list criteria.

The key variable that differentiates the FH rats from most normal strains of rats is their exaggerated immobility in the forced swim test. In a 5-min session, normal rats are immobile for about 100-120 sec, but the FH rat is immobile for about 220-240 sec [4,10,11,12]. It is suggested that this behavior may be analogous to psychomotor retardation in human depressives, where the individual has difficulty in initiating and maintaining behavior. However, the findings that strongly argue for the swim test to be relevant are the studies showing that antidepressants will reduce the exaggerated swim test immobility. [3,12,13].

Another key symptom of FH rats is their elevated basal corticosterone levels [14]. Thus, they resemble about 50% of the human depressives, who show elevated cortisol levels [15]. Importantly, this elevated corticosterone level is normalized following a course of antidepressant treatment [16]. Thus, the FH rat resembles a subgroup of depressed patients who have elevated basal cortisol levels that decrease following the successful treatment with antidepressants.

A final aspect is the recognition that depressed individuals often exhibit somc signs of anxiety-like behavior [7]. In fact, it was pointed out earlier that the presence of anxiety-like symptoms can cloud the picture of comorbidity between depression and alcoholism. The FH rat may also show signs of anxiety-like behavior, but not in all tasks. The FH rat tends to exhibit anxiety-like behavior in social interaction tasks [17,18] but not in the elevated plus maze [19]. Thus, the FH rat may model the type of depressive-like behavior that includes an anxiety component.

It should be emphasized that there are more than one FH inbred rat strain. In addition to the strain used in our laboratory at the University of North Carolina, termed FH/Wjd to indicate its origin from W. Jean Dodds of the New York State Department of Health, there is also the inbred strain developed by Gordon Harrington at the University of Northern Iowa, which can be designated FH/Har, although they are commonly known as the Iowa Reactive Strain. (See 20) Finally, there are two lines selectively bred for differences in blood pressure at Erasmus University by Provoost and colleagues and consequently known as the FHH and FHL strains [21]. We have found the FH/Wjd and FH/Har rat strains to be very different [20] and the pattern of differences between all four strains to be complex [22]. The FH/Har strain stood out from the others in having relatively normal swimming in the forced swim test; in contrast, it exhibited anxiety-like behavior in the elevated plus maze, whereas the other three strains did not [22]. Finally, using the two-bottle choice paradigm, only the FH/Wjd strain exhibited excessive intake of alcohol [4,22,27]. Thus, only the FH/Wjd rats exhibit features of both depressed-like behavior and elevated drinking.

In conclusion, the FH/Wjd rat resembles depressed individuals in at least three ways. Some of the symptoms have yet to be tested in the FH/Wjd rat, but the degree of similarities is adequate to suggest that the FH/Wjd rat is a useful animal model of depression.

Table 1. Depressive-like Characteristics of FH/Wjd Rats

Observation in Depressed Individuals	Observation in FH/Wjd Rats
Core Symptoms	
Psychomotor Retardation	**Reduced Swim Test**
Elevated Cortisol	**Elevated corticosterone**
Anxiety of Some Types	**Anxiety in Some Tasks**
Suicidal Ideation and/or Attempt	Cannot Be Modeled
Anhedonia	Elevated Saccharin Intake
Cognitive Disturbance	No Data
Elevated REM Sleep	No Data

Bold in both columns indicates a match; i*talics in one column* and normal font in the other column indicates a mismatch.

Table 2. Drugs and pharmacological agents that are successful in reducing alcohol intake in FH/Wjd rats and selectively-bred alcohol preferring P rats

Agents	Reference
Naltrexone (opioid antagonist)	33,45
Ibogaine (African herb)	35
Noribogaine (Ibogaine metabolite)	36
St. John Wort (herbal remedy)	37
Amperozide (5-H2 antagonist)	38
MDMA (5-HT neurotoxin)	34
L-NAME (Nitric Oxide synthesis inhibitor)	39
Combination pharmacotherapy	45

4. Animal Model of Alcohol Seeking Behavior

An animal model is a non-human animal that has one or more characteristics that is similar to a human disease condition. Animal models allow to study of conditions that for ethical or practical purposes cannot be studied in humans. A valid animal model must be similar in etiology and function to the human condition. Animal models of disease can be spontaneous (i.e. naturally occurring in animals by mutations), or be induced by humans through physical, chemical, or biological means. One such model is the animal model of alcohol seeking behavior or human alcoholism. Selective breeding techniques have been utilized to generate lines of rats that drink significant amounts of alcohol compared with their counterparts, alcohol non-preferring rats. The most widely used selectively bred alcohol preferring rats are P (alcohol preferring), HAD (High alcohol drinking), AA (Alcohol accpting) and sP (Sardinian alcohol preferring rats) [23-26]. All of these lines have been generated by selective breeding. Interestingly but not surprisingly, neurochemical profiles and the patterns of drinking of these rats are different from each other. It seems that each line represents a particular aspect of human alcoholism or a sub-population of alcoholics. There is not an animal model that can represent all aspects of human alcoholism as this disease is a complex multifactorial disease.

The Fawn-Hooded (FH/Wjd) rat is a strain of alcohol-preferring rats that opposite to selectively-bred lines has not been selectively bred for excessive drinking. However, similar to other acohol preferring lines, it has a high intake for alcohol [4,22,27]. Similar to other alcohol preferring rats, the FH/Wjd rat drinks enough alcohol voluntarily in an acute session to achieve pharmacologically significant blood alcohol levels [4,27] and drinks enough alcohol voluntarily over time to become tolerant and dependent upon alcohol [27]. Also, it has been shown that the FH/Wjd rat will bar-press for alcohol at rates similar to the alcohol-preferring P rat [28,29,30]. In addition, withdrawal from alcohol following chronic alcohol self-administration in the FH/Wjd rat results in quantifiable neurochemical adaptations [31], including an up-regulation of cortical AMPA receptors, consistent with a hyper-glutamatergic state [32].

Similar to human alcoholics, FH/Wjd rats respond positively to the anti-craving of the opiate antagonist naltrexone [33,45]. Furthermore, FH/Wjd rats similar to selectively bred alcohol preferring P rats respond in similar fashion to pharmacological agents and drugs that reduce voluntary alcohol intake (Table 2). These include, the serotonin neurotoxin, MDMA [34], the herbal extracts ibogaine [35], noribogaine [36] and St. John's Wort [37], the 5-HT_{2A} antagonist amperozide [38], serotonin releaser fenfluramine, and L-NAME, an inhibitor of nitrous oxide synthesis [39]. These findings suggest the neurological regulation of alcohol intake is quite similar in the FH/Wjd and P rats. Thus, the FH/Wjd rats similar to other alcohol preferring rats satisfy most of the criteria and it is justifiable to conclude that it is a reliable animal model of alcoholism. It should be emphasized here that there can be more than one model of alcoholism, since most of the clinical literature suggests that there is more than one type of alcoholism (e.g., 40,41). The FH/Wjd rat shares some characteristics with selectively-bred alcohol preferring P rats, such as drinking enough to become tolerant and dependent, but there are also some interesting differences. The FH/Wjd exhibits depressive-like behavior while P rats do not [12,37]. Neurochemical studies of these rats indicate altered central serotonergic [42] and opioidergic activities [43] which might contribute to their excessive drinking.

5. Fawn-Hooded Rats as a Genetic Animal Model of Co-morbidity

Fawn-Hooded (FH/Wjd) rats have been around for over a quarter of century and mostly have been used for platelet disorder studies as they have both peripheral and central serotonin deficiency [46,47,48]. They trace their origins to an outbred FH strain formed by mating of Long Evans, German Brown, and Lashley Albino [20,47,49]. Later, Jean Dodds and Gordon Harrington developed two inbred strains (FH/Wjd and FH/Har) by brother-sister mating [20]. In 1990, we for the first time discovered that the FH/Wjd strain when given a choice between water and a solution of 10% alcohol, similar to selectively-bred alcohol preferring rats, drink significant amounts of alcohol [27]. Furthermore, we demonstrated that compared with Wistar and ACI/N rats, FH/Wjd rats exhibit depressive tendencies in the forced swim test [4,27,50] and elevated intake of saccharin [51]. We have shown that serotonergic compounds, when given systemically, can reduce their alcohol intake [44] and increase their mobility in the swim test [4]. Fawn-Hooded rats also exhibit elevated corticosterone levels [16] and blunted hormonal responses to serotonergic agents [14] as observed in some depressed individuals [7,52, 53].

Biochemical studying of selectively-bred alcohol preferring P rats indicates that there are major differences in brain levels of serotonin, its metabolites and serotonergic receptors in several brain loci including nucleus accumbens, frontal cortex and hippocampus [54,55]. Not surprisingly, serotonin enhancing compounds, such as fenfluramine, fluoxetine, can reduce alcohol intake in rats with serotonin deficiency [44,54]. The association between low serotonin activity in the brain and high alcohol intake also has been documented in humans [56]. The role of central serotonin in the manifestation of depression has been well established and the association of low serotonin and depression has been documented. Because of these documented associations between low serotonin activity/levels on one hand and excessive drinking and depression on the other hand and the fact that FH/Wjd rats possesses a genetic serotonin dysfunction, we in 1990 hypothesized that this strain can be a genetic animal model of comorbidity of drinking and depression [27]. Later, in several studies we demonstrated that in fact this strain meets the criteria for both disorders [27,50,58]

6. Alcohol Drinking and Depressed-like Behavior Are Independent in FH/Wjd Rats

Previous sections have clearly established that the FH/Wjd rat has characteristics consistent with its being considered a model of depression and a model of alcoholism. The question considered here is whether these two traits should be regarded as independent or as related in some way. Remember that the human literature suggested that either trait might influence the other, either as a primary disorder affecting a secondary disorder or as two equally important disorders that mutually influence each other. The fact that antidepressants reduced the depressive symptoms without affecting alcohol drinking [9] provides evidence for the independence of the two traits. The evidence we will present below also argues for the independence of the two traits in the FH/Wjd rats.

In preparation for determining the genetic correlates (QTL) of immobility and alcohol intake, a total of 612 F2 progeny from FH/Wjd and ACI/N parents were produced. Correlations were carried out between several of the key variables, including swim test immobility and alcohol intake in the two-bottle choice procedure. There was no significant correlation between alcohol intake and immobility [3,4]. Preliminary studies have revealed 15 QTL for alcohol intake and 13 QTL for immobility, without any significant overlap [57, 58]. Thus, immobility and alcohol intake appear to be genetically independent in the FH/Wjd rat.

As in depressed, alcoholic humans [9], chronic treatment with antidepressants can alleviate the depressive symptoms, but do not alter alcohol intake. Actually, the situation was more complicated. In one study FH rats that were drinking alcohol voluntarily were injected chronically with the serotonin reuptake inhibitor, sertraline. There was an initially but temporary reduction in alcohol intake, but tolerance developed. At the end of the chronic treatment a swim test was performed and it was found that the chronic treatment produced a reduction in swim test immobility [59]. In a second study, alcohol-naïve rats were chronically treated with fluoxetine for 14 days; then access to alcohol was permitted while the rats continued to receive their fluoxetine injections. There was a reduction in immobility without any change in alcohol intake [60]. Thus, the FH/Wjd rat behaves just like the comorbid patient, with the antidepressants producing selective changes in depressed-like behavior.

Therefore, both genetic and pharmacological studies indicate that alcohol drinking and swim test immobility are independent traits in the FH/Wjd rat. Pharmacological studies in humans have reached the same conclusion [9]; however, genetic studies suggest that there could be some overlap (See 7). Thus, independence of the traits is clearly seen in the FH/Wjd rat but not in the depressed alcoholic.

7. Conclusion

Clinical observations, epidemiological data and animal studies indicate the notion of comorbidity of alcoholism and depression. However, the true nature of the co-morbidity is not fully understood and it is not clear whether one of these diseases causes or predisposes to the other. Several hypotheses have been briefly discussed to explain this relationship. Fawn-Hooded (FH/Wjd) rat was used as an animal model of co-morbid depression and alcoholism to study this relationship. FH/Wjd rats exhibit depressive tendencies in the swim test and drink significant amount of alcohol volitionally. Chronic treatment with antidepressants selectively improves their depressive behavior without affecting their drinking behavior. Our quantitative genetic analysis, using F1 and F2 progeny, also suggest that high alcohol drinking and depressive like behavior are under independent genetic control. Although, our data suggest that high alcohol drinking and depressive-like behavior in FH/Wjd are independent, well-controlled clinical studies are needed to further our understanding of the association between these two diseases. The understanding of neurobiological and genetic mechanisms mediating the co-morbidity between depression and alcoholism may lead to the development of more effective treatment strategies for these disorders. Animal models of co-morbidity of alcoholism and depression, such as FH/Wjd, should be utilized to advance this goal.

8. REFERENCES

[1] Markou A, Weis, F, Gold LH, Caine SB, Schulteis G, Koob GF. Animal models of drug craving. *Psychopharmacology* 1993; 112:163-182.

[2] Nurnberger JI Jr, Foroud T, Flury L, Su J, Meyer ET, Hu H, Crowe R, Edenberg H, Goate A, Bierut L, Reich T, Schuckit MA, Reich W. Evidence for a locus on chromosome 1 that influences vulnerability to alcoholism and affective disorder. *Am J Psychiatry* 2001; 158:718-724.

[3] Overstreet DH, Rezvani AH, Djouma E, Parsian A, Lawrence AJ. Depressive-like behavior and high alcohol drinking co-occur in the FH/Wjd rat but appear to be under independent genetic control. *Neurosci Biobehav Rev* 2007; 31:103-114.

[4] Rezvani, AH, Parsian, A, Overstreet, DH. The Fawn-Hooded (FH/Wjd) rat: a genetic animal model of co-morbid depression and alcoholism. *Psychiatric Genet.* 2002; 12, 1-16.

[5] Schuckit MA, Smith TL. An evaluation of level of response to alcohol, externalization symptoms, and depressive symptoms as predictors of alcoholism. *J Stud Alcohol* 2005; 57:215-227.

[6] Vengeliene V, Siegmund S, Singer MV, Sinclair JD, Li T-K, Spanagel R. A comparative study on alcohol-preferring rat lines: effects of deprivation and stress phases on voluntary ethanol intake. *Alcohol Clin Exp Res* 2003; 27:1048-1054.

[7] Davis L, Uezato A, Newell JM, Frazier E. Major depression and comorbid substance use disorders. *Curr Opin Psychiatry* 2008; 21:14-18.

[8] Lin N, Eisen SA, Scherrer JF, Goldberg J, True WR, Lyoins MS, Tsuang MT. The influence of familial and nonfamilial factors on the associate between major depression and substance abuse/dependence in 1874 monozygotic male twin pairs. *Drug and Alcohol Depend.* 1996; 43:49-55.

[9] Pettinati HM. Antidepressant treatment of co-occurring depression and alcohol dependence. Biol. Psychiatry 2004; 56, 785-792.

[10] Overstreet DH, Friedman EF, Mathe' AM, Yadid G. The Flinders Sensitive Line rat: A selectively bred putative animal model of depression. *Neurosci Biobehav Rev* 2005; 29:739-59.

[11] Rezvani AH, Oversteet DH, Cleves MA, Parsian A. Further genetic characterization of alcohol-preferring Fawn-Hooded and -nonpreferring ACI rats and their intercrosses. *Presented at Research Society on Alcoholism Meeting*, Santa Barbara, CA, June 25-30, 2005, Abstract 550

[12] Rezvani AH, Overstreet DH, Cleves H, Parsian A. Further genetic characterization of the Fawn-Hooded (FH/Wjd) rat, an animal model of comorbid depression and alcoholism. *Psychiatric Genet.* 2007; 17:77-83.

[13] Patra B, Cleves M, Parsian AJ, Overstreet DH, Rezvani AH, Parsian A. Quantitative genetic analysis off alcohol-related phenotypes in F2 progeny derived from FH/Wjd and ACI/N strains of rat. *Presented at 29th Annual Meeting of the Research Society on Alcoholism,* June 23-29, 2006, Baltimore, MD.

[14] Aulakh CS, Wozniak KM, Hill JL, Devane CL, Tolliver TJ, Murphy DL. Differential neuroendocrine responses to the 5-HT agonist m-chlorophenylpiperazine in Fawn-Hooded rats relative to Wistar and Sprague-Dawley rats. *Neuroendocrinology* 1988; 48,401-406.

[15] Vreeburg SA, Hoogendjk NJ, Van Pelt S, Derijk RH, Van Dyck R, Smit JH, Zitman FG, Peninx BW. Major depressive disorder and hypothalamic pituitary axis activity. results from a large cohort study. *Arch. Gen. Psychiatry* 2009; 66:617-626.

[16] Aulakh CS, Hill JL Murphy DL. Attenuation of hypercortisolemia in fawn-hood rats by antidepressant drugs. *Eu.r J. Pharmacol.* 1993; 240: 85-88.

[17] Kantor S, Anheuerer ZF, Bagdy G. High social anxiety and low aggression in Fawn-Hooded rats. *Physiol. Behav.* 2000; 71:551-557

[18] Overstreet DH, Knapp DJ, Breese GR, Diamond I. A Selective ALDH-2 Inhibitor Reduces Anxiety in Rats. *Pharmacol. Biochem. Behav.* 2010 (in press).

[19] Hensler JG, Hodge CW, Overstreet DH. Reduced 5-HT_3 receptor binding and lower baseline plus maze anxiety in the alcohol-preferring inbred Fawn-Hooded rat. *Pharmacol. Biochem. Behav.* 2004: 77:281-289.

[20] Overstreet DH, Rezvani AH. Behavioral differences between two inbred strains of Fawn-Hooded rats: a model of serotonin dysfunction. *Psychopharmacology* 1996; 128, 328-330.

[21] Verseput GH, Provoost AP, Van Tol A, Koomans HA, Joles JA. Hyperlipidemia is secondary to proteinuria and is completely normalized by ACE inhibitors in hypertensive fawn-hooded rats. *Nephron* 1997; 27:346-352.

[22] Overstreet DH, Rezvani AH, Parsian A. Behavioral features of alcohol-preferring rats: Focus on inbred strains. *Alcohol Alcohol* 1999; 34, 378-385.

[23] Li TK, Lumeng L and Doolittle DP. Selective breeding for alcohol preference and associated responses. *Behav. Genet.* 1993:23, 163-170.

[24] Murphy JM, Stewart RB, Bell RL, Badia-Elder NE, Carr LG, McBride WJ, Lumeng L, Li TK. Phenotypic and genotypic characterization of the Indiana University rat lines selectively bred for high and low alcohol preference. *Behav. Genet.* 2002; 32:363-388.

[25] Colombo G, Agabio R, Lobina C, Reali R, Zocchi A, Fadda, F, Gessa GL. Sardinian alcohol preferring rats: A genetic animal model of anxiety. *Physiol Behav.* 1995; 57, 1181-1185.

[26] Sinclair JD, Le AD, Kiianmaa K. The AA and ANA rat lines, selected for differences in voluntary alcohol consumption. *Experientia* 1989; 45:798-805.

[27] Rezvani AH, Overstreet DH, Janowsky DS. Genetic serotonin deficiency and alcohol preference in the Fawn-Hooded rats. *Alcohol Alcohol* 1990; 25: 573-575.

[28] Cowen MS, Adams C, Kraehenbuehl T, Vengeliene V, Lawrence AJ. The acute anti-craving effect of acamprosate in alcohol-preferring rats is associated with modulation of the mesolimbic dopamine system. *Addict. Biol.* 2005; 10:233-242.

[29] Cowen MS, Djouma E, Lawrence. The mGlu5 antagonist MTEP reduces ethanol self-administration in multiple strains of alcohol-preferring rats and regulates olfactory glutamatergic systems. *J. Pharmacol. Exp. Ther.,* 2005; 315:190-205.

[30] Cowen MS, Rezvani AH, Jarrott B, Lawrence AJ. Ethanol consumption by Fawn-Hooded rats following abstinence: Effect of naltrexone and changes in μ-Opioid receptor density. *Alcohol. Clin. Exp. Res.* 1999; 23:1008-1014.

[31] Djouma E, Lawrence AJ. The effect of chronic ethanol consumption and withdrawal on μ-opioid, dopamine D_1 and D_2 receptor density in Fawn-Hooded rat brain. *J. Pharmacol. Exp. Ther.* 2002; 302, 551-559.

[32] Chen F, Jarrott B, Lawrence AJ. Up-regulation of cortical AMPA receptor binding in the Fawn-Hooded rat following ethanol withdrawal. *Eur. J. Pharmacol.* 1999; 384, 139-146.

[33] Rezvani AH, Overstreet DH, Janowsky DS. Drug-induced reductions in ethanol intake in alcohol preferring and Fawn-Hooded rats. *Alcohol & Alcoholism* 1991; Suppl. 1, 433-437.

[34] Rezvani AH, Garges PL, Miller D, Gordon CJ. Attenuation of alcohol consumption by MDMA in two strains of alcohol drinking rats. *Pharmacol. Biochem. Behav.* 1992; 43:103-107.

[35] Rezvani AH, Overstreet DH, Lee YW. Attenuation of alcohol intake by Ibogaine in three strains of alcohol-preferring rats. *Pharmacol. Biochem. Behav.* 1995; 52, 615-620.

[36] 36. Rezvani AH, Overstreet DH, Ying Y, Maisonneuve IM, Bandarage UK, Kuehne ME, Glick SD. Attenuation of alcohol consumption by a novel non-toxic ibogaine analog (18-Methoxycoronaridine) in alcohol preferring rats. *Pharmacol. Biochem. Behav.* 1997; 58:615-619.

[37] Rezvani AH, Overstreet DH, Yang Y, Clark Ejr. Attenuation of alcohol intake by the extract of *Hypericum Perforatum* (St. John's Wort) in two different strains of alcohol-preferring rats. *Alcohol Alcohol.* 1999; 34:699-705.

[38] Overstreet DH, McArthur RA, Rezvani AH, Post C. Selective inhibition of alcohol intake in diverse alcohol-preferring rat strains by the 5-HT2A antagonists amperozide and FG 5974. *Alcohol. Clin. Exp. Res.* 1997: 21:1448-1454.

[39] Rezvani AH, Peek AE, Grady DR, Pucilowski O. Inhibition of nitric oxide (NO) synthesis attenuated alcohol consumption in two strains of alcohol preferring rats. *Pharmacol. Biochem. Behav.* 1995; 50:265-270.

[40] Gilligan SB, Reich T, Cloninger CF. Etiologic heterogeneity in alcoholism. *Genet. Epidemiol.* 1987; 4:395-414.

[41] Parsian A, Cloninger CR. Serotonergic pathways genes and subtypes of alcoholics. Association studies. *Psychiatr. Genet.* 2001; 11:89-94.

[42] Hulihan-Giblin BA, Park YD, Aulakh CS, Goldman D. Regional analysis of 5-HT-1A and 5-HT-2 receptors in the Fawn-Hooded rat. *Neuropharmacology* 1992; 31, 1095-1100.

[43] Chen F, Lawrence AJ. 5-HT Transporter sites, 5-HT_{1A} and 5-HT_3 receptors in Fawn-Hooded rats: a quantitative autoradiography study. *Alcohol. Clin. Exp. Res.* 2000; 24:1093-1102.

[44] Rezvani AH, Grady DR. Suppression of alcohol consumption by fenfluramine in Fawn-Hooded rats with serotonin dysfunction. *Pharmacol., Biochem. Behavior.* 1994; 48, 105-110.

[45] Rezvani AH, Overstreet DH, Mason GA, Janowsky DS, Hamedi M, Clark Ejr, Yang Y. Combination pharmacotherapy: A mixture of small doses of naltrexone, fluoxetine, and a thyrotropin-releasing hormone analogue reduces alcohol intake in three strains of alcohol-preferring rats. *Alcohol Alcohol.* 2000;35:76-83.

[46] Tschopp TB, Zucker MB. Hereditary defect in platelet function in rats. *Blood, 1*972; 40:217-226.

[47] de Keizer MH, Provoost AP, Molenaar JL. Proteinuria as an early marker in the development of progressive renal failure in hypertensive fawn-hooded rats. *J. Hypertens.* 1989; 7:525-528.

[48] Raymond SL, Dodds WJ. Characterization of the fawn-hooded rat for hemostatic studies. *Thromb. Diath. Haemorrh.* 1975; 33:361-369.

[49] Harrington GM. The Har strains of rats: origins and characteristics. *Behav. Genet.* 1981; 11:445-468.

[50] Overstreet DH, Rezvani AH, Janowsky DS. Genetic animal models of depression and ethanol preference provide support for cholinergic and serotonergic involvement in depression and alcoholism. *Biol. Psychiatry* 1992; 31:919-936.

[51] Overstreet DH, Kampov-Polevoy AB, Rezvani AH, Murrelle L, Halikas JA, Janowsky DS Saccharin intake predicts ethanol intake in genetically heterogeneous rats as well as different rat strains. *Alcohol. Clin. Exp. Res.* 1993; 17:366-369.

[52] O'Keane V. Dinan TG. Prolactin and cortisol responses to d-fenfluramine in major depression: evidence for diminished responsivity of central serotonergic function. *Am. J. Psychiatry* 1991; 148:009-1015.

[53] Lesch. KP, Mayer S, Disselkamp-Tietze J, Hoh J, Wiesmann M, Osterheider M, Schulte HM. 5-HT_{1A} receptor responsivity in unipolar depression. Evaluation of ipsapirone-induced ACTH and cortisol secretion in patients and controls. *Biol. Psychiatry* 1990; 28: 620-628.

[54] McBride WJ, Murphy JM, Lumeng L, Li TK. Serotonin, dopamine and GABA involvement in alcohol drinking of selectively bred rats. *Alcohol* 1990; 7:199-205.

[55] Murphy JM, McBride WJ, Lumeng L, Li TK. Alcohol preference and regional brain monoamine contents of N/Nih heterogenous stock rats. *Alcohol Drug Res* 1987; 7:33-39.

[56] Heinz A, Mann K, Weinberger DR, Goldman, D. Serotonergic dysfunction, negative mood states, and response to alcohol. *Alcohol. Clin. Exp. Res.* 2001; 25:487-495.

[57] Parsian A, Patra B, Cleves M, Parsian AJ, Overstreet DH, Rezvani AH. QTL mapping for alcohol intake and related phenotypes in FH/Wjd X ACI/N cross. Presented at 30th Annual Meeting of Research Society on Alcoholism, Chicago, IL July 7-11, 2007.

[58] Overstreet DH, Parsian A, Rezvani AH. High immobility and excess alcohol intake may be independent traits in the Fawn-Hooded rat, an animal model of comorbid depression and alcoholism. Presented at International Behavioural and Neural Genetics Society, Dresden, Germany, June 4-8, 2009.

[59] Rezvani AH, Overstreet DH. Effects of sertraline on ethanol intake and depressive behavior in Fawn-Hooded rats. Presented at meeting of Research Society on Alcoholism, San Diego, CA, June, *Alcohol Clin Exp Res* 1992*, 394.*

[60] Overstreet DH, Rezvani AH, Parsian A. Chronic fluoxetine reduces swim test immobility but not alcohol intake in fawn-hooded rat, an animal model of comorbid

depression/alcoholism. Presented at 35th Annual Meeting of the Society for Neuroscience, Washington, D.C., November 8-12, 2005.

In: Suicidal Behavior in Alcohol and Drug Abuse... ISBN: 978-1-60876-919-3
Editors: L. Sher, A. Vilens, pp. 39-46

Chapter 4

PSYCHOPHYSIOLOGICAL ASPECTS OF ALCOHOL EPILEPTIC SYNDROME

Tatiana Elistratova and Andrey Soloviev
Northern State Medical University, Arkhangelsk, Russia

ABSTRACT

Alcohol epileptic syndrome is one of the most frequent neurologic manifestations of alcohol dependence occurring during withdrawal. The goal of the study was to investigate psychophysiological peculiarities of patients with alcohol epileptic syndrome in order to develop special diagnostic algorithms for its detection and selection of correct treatment and management approaches. The main methods of the study were screening, a clinical method, electroencephalopraphy, computerized tomography, a laboratory method. As part of the study, frequency of occurrence of separate clinical, psychophysiological and laboratory indexes was compared in patients with idiopathic, symptomatic epilepsy, alcohol epileptic syndrome.

INTRODUCTION

Among patients with alcohol withdrawal syndrome (AWS) a tendency takes place for steady growth of the number of critical, life threatening states requiring urgent intensive care [1]. Those states include alcohol epileptic syndrome (AES), which is one of the most frequent neurological disorders among patients suffering from chronic alcoholic intoxication (CAI) [2]. In 90% of cases, epileptic attacks develop in 7-48 hours after the last alcohol taking secondary to other manifestations of alcohol withdrawal syndrome and don't require any special medical treatment with antiepileptic preparations or surgical intervention in comparison with idiopathic (primary) or symptomatic (secondary) epilepsy [3].

The AWS psychophysiological mechanism is directly associated with dramatic alcohol withdrawal. It is known that on the neural level, ethanol starts up the following system brain processes: it reduces influence of GABA on chlorine canals, slows down action of glutamate on NMDA-receptors, that inhibits the excitation system and causes abnormal excitation processes, as well as increases brain concentration of adenosine, an inhibitory neurotransmitter. Abnormal regulation of GABA-mediated inhibition and activation of NMDA-receptors account for excitation effect in dramatic alcohol withdrawal [4,5,6].

However, references do not give clear criteria of AES, and the psychophysiological aspects of patients with AES are described insufficiently. Both reasons cause difficulties in ES differential diagnostics, during making expert decisions about patients' working abilities and vocational aptitude, as well as in searching for ways of adequate therapy and prevention. As a result, analysis of psychophysiological status of patients with AES acquires great practical importance for specification of AES mechanisms' development and working out of diagnostic principles of the pathology in question.

The goal of our study was to detect specific neurophysiological peculiarities of patients with AES for working out of their diagnostic algorithms.

There have been examined 251 Caucasian persons, their average age was 42.3±0.89. At the time of the study, they stayed at the Neurological Department of the Severodvinsk City Hospital, the Arkhangelsk region, Russia. In the course of the study, three groups of patients have been distinguished.

I group	patients with ES and CAI without brain localized organic damages in anamnesis (89 persons), average age 41.66±1.15 : of them, 16 persons - under 30, 67 persons – at the age 31-55, 6 persons - over 55.
II group	patients with ES without CAI (78 persons), of them 26 persons - under 30, 29 persons – at the age 31-55, 23 persons - over 55.
II-a group	patients with ES and brain localized organic damages (craniocerebral injuries, insults, tumors) in anamnesis (22 persons), the average age 54.23 ± 3.04; of them, 2 persons - under 30, 7 persons – at the age 31-55, 13 persons - over 55.
II-b group	patients with ES and without brain localized organic damages (56 persons), the average age 36.98 ± 1.86; of them, 24 persons - under 30, 22 persons – at the age 31-55, 10 persons - over 55.
III group	(comparison group) – patients with lumbar osteochondrosis, disciliculatory encephalopathy I and II stage secondary to arterial hypertension and cerebral atherosclerosis, migraine and vegetative-vascular dystonia, not suffering from ES and CAI (84 persons), the average age 43.40 ± 1.66; of them, 25 persons - under 30, 39 persons – at the age 31-55, 20 persons - over 55.

The age difference among the patients with ES was statistically significant in I and II-a groups ($p < 0.001$), in I and II-b groups ($p < 0.05$), what confirmed the fact that ES of various genesis occurred frequently in different age groups. So, attacks manifested in childhood and at a young age, were more often caused by hereditary factors, perinatal pathologies, abnormal development, at a middle and late age – by tumors, vascular diseases, brain injuries, alcoholism. AES occurred more frequently in persons at a middle age. The age difference among the patients was insignificant in the I and III groups.

The following methods were applied during the study of frequency of occurrence of different neurophysiological characteristics:

1. *Screening* – detection of sings of alcohol dependence and a high risk of its emergence with the help of the methods “Self-reporting card PAS”, AUDIT test [7].
2. *Clinical method* – neurological examination of the patients, detection of typical symptoms of the studied pathology: withdrawal signs, polyneuropathy of lower extremities [8,9], disorders in intellectual, motion activity, perception and vegetative spheres that was carried out every day during the patients' stay at the Neurological Department.
3. *ECG* recording was made on a 19-ported computer electro encephalograph “Neuron-Spectrum” with the use of the international lead system «10-20» with application of 19 active electrodes on the 1st-2nd day of a patient's admission to the Hospital, re-examination of some patients – on the 3rd-7th day.
4. For *CT* test on the 1st-3rd day of hospital admission, a computer tomograph with technology of helical scanning «High Speed Dxi General Electric» (US) was used. In the course of implementation of a layer-specific axial section test according to the international testing standards, brain sub- and supratentorial structures were analyzed. The width of scans (Tomograph step) was 1 cm, on brain base, it was 0.5 cm. If a mass brain lesion or any other local pathology was suspected, a contrast agent was administered for verification of obtained results.
5. *Laboratory method* – for study of blood serum biochemical indices - alanine aminotransferases (ALT), aspartate aminotransferases (AST), gamma-glutamyl transpeptidases (GGTP), alkaline phosphatases (APh), creatine phosphokinase (CPh) - a biochemical autoanalyzer «Vitalab Flexor E» was used. The study was conducted on the 2nd day of hospital admission. If enzymes' indexes were high, the study was repeated in 3-5 days.

In the neurological status of the patients from the I group, focal symptoms were not revealed, however in 68.5% of cases, polyneuropathy of lower extremities has been detected. In 100% of cases, EEG of the patients from the I group had the following features: low-amplitude type, absence of zonal differences and alpha-rhythm modulations, dysrhythmia, light diffuse changes in the form of slow waves, multiple artifacts of recording; epileptic and local slow wave activity was not detected on the EEG. 82.0% of the patients form the I group (of them, 10.1% were under 30, 67.4% - under 55, 22.5% - over 55) had diffuse hypotrophic hydrocephaly on brain CT. In 94.3% of the patients from the I group, high activity of blood serum ALT, AST, GGTP was registered. GGTP was most active, its activity was tens times higher and in 3-5% of cases - a hundred times higher. The level of ALT activity rated second, it exceeded the maximum allowable level 10-30 times, AST activity in 7-10% of cases was only 2-3 times higher. Almost in 90% of cases on the 5th-6th day of hospitalization, GGTP and ALT indexes were 2-3 times lower with further reduction in a week period of time to normal or slightly higher than normal indexes. The characteristic feature was that the normal level of blood serum bilirubin was accompanied by extremely high GGTP and ALT indexes what allowed to distinguish between hepatitis of different aetiology and alcoholic hepatitis.

In the neurological status of all the patients from the II-a group, focal symptoms of pyramidal insufficiency type were detected in 72.7% of cases; hemiparesis of I - IV degree - in 27.3% of cases. In this group, polyneuropathy of lower extremities was detected in 36% of the patients, on EEG in 77.1% of the patients, low-wave activity in brain injured hemispheres was determined, in 9.1% of cases - low electrobiological activity of the brain, in 3.6 % -

dysfunction of medial-stem brain structures. On CT in 100% of cases, cystic-gliostic brain changes were detected. 77.3% of the patients had higher indexes of blood serum transferases, the GGTP level was maximally high, ALT – to a lesser degree, AST - 2-4 times higher.

During collection of anamnestic data of the patients from the II-b group, it was detected that 73.2% of them had epiphenomena, 7.1% - CI in anamnesis, 3.6% - brain tumor after surgery in anamnesis, 19.4% - hereditary tainted epilepsy. During the clinical examination of 17.9% of the patients, focal symptoms were determined. Polyneuropathy of lower extremities was detected in 17.9% of the patients. On EEG of 44.6% of the patients, epileptic activity was detected in the form of commissures, discharges «peak – sharp wave», «sharp wave – slow wave»; in 25.0% - dysfunction of medial-stem structures, in 19.4% of the patients - high paroxysmal brain readiness in the form of hypersynchronous sharp alpha-rhythm, discharges of bilateral synchronous sharp alpha-rhythm polyphase alpha-kin waves with an amplitude twice as high as the background, in 10.7% - low-amplitude type and slight diffuse changes were recorded. On repeated EEG, epileptic activity was lower in 20% of cases owing to medical treatment.

On CT of the brain, 25% of the patients had indexes within the norm, 10.7% of the patients had cystic-gliostic brain changes of posttraumatic nature, 64.3% of the patients had mixed hypotrophical hydrocephaly. 3-4 times higher activity of blood serum transferases (GGTP, ALT, AST) was registered in 10.7% of the patients.

In the III group, epileptic phenomena were detected in 23.8% of the patients, anamnestic record in epilepsy among 7.1% of the patients, craniocerebral injuries in anamnesis of 4.8% of the patients. During the clinical examination, focal neurological symptoms were detected in 4.8% of the patients, and nontoxic polyneuropathy of lower extremities - in 11.9% of them. On EEG of the patients from the III group in 23.8% of cases, there was revealed a dysfunction of medial-stem structures in the form of single discharges of bilateral synchronous polyphase alpha-kin waves with the amplitude up-to-background, flatness of zonal differences; in 17.9% heightened paroxysmal brain readiness (frontier EEG type) was detected; in 4.8% of cases focal slow wave activity was registered; in 23.8% there was no pathology detected. On CT of the brain in 31.0% of cases, there were no changes registered, in 64.3% - there were signs of mixed hypotrophic hydrocephaly, in 4.7% - cystic-gliostic brain changes were registered. Higher activity of hepatic enzymes was detected in 10.7% of the patients, mostly ALT and AST indexes were higher, GGTP activity was within the norm in 30% of cases.

A comparison of indexes detected in each group is shown in Table 1 and Diagrams 1,2.

A strong direct correlation relationship between the patients' age and polyneuropathy presence was established ($R = 0.45$, $P < 0.001$), and a relationship between age and low electrobiological activity on EEG ($R=0.21$, $P<0.001$), mixed hypotrophic hydrocephaly ($R=0.29$, $P<0.001$), cystic-gliostic brain changes ($R=0.27$, $P<0.001$), high levels of blood serum transferases ($R=0.27$, $P< 0.001$) as well as an inverse relationship of age and absence of traumatological anamnesis ($R=-0.27$, $P<0.001$), focal symptoms ($R=-0.28$, $P<0.001$) and epileptic activity on EEG ($R=-0.34$, $P<0.001$). There was a statistically reliable connection between the CAI sings and the absence of epiphenomena ($R=0.5$,$P<0.001$), epileptic heredity ($R=0.22$, $P<0.001$), traumatological anamnesis and the presence of focal neurological symptoms ($R=0.9$, $P<0.001$), and a correlation relationship between alcoholic withdrawal and epileptic activity on EEG ($R=-0.3$, $P<0.001$) and transferases blood serum indexes within the norm (R=-0.8, P<0.001) has been detected. Statistically more often, EAS was detected among middle-aged men (P<0.001).

At the same time, epileptic activity on EEG typical for the patients with idiopathic ES had an inverse correlation relationship with age (R=-0.34, P<0.01), with the presence of alcohol anamnesis and withdrawal syndrome (R=-0.3, P<0.001), polyneuropathy (R=-0.24, P<0.001), the presence of low electrobiological activity on EEG (R=-0.32, P<0.001), cystic-gliostic brain changes on CT (R=-0.13, P<0.05) and high blood serum transferases' levels (R=-0.24, P<0.01). Statistically more often, it occurred in patients with hereditary tainted epilepsy (R=0.13, P<0.01), as well as the level of GGTP content in blood was insignificantly higher (R=0.14, P<0.05), probably, due to toxic influence of anti-epileptic medicines.

Table 1. The frequency of anamnestic and neurophysiological indexes detected by screening, use of clinical and laboratory methods in the groups of the studied patients (%)

Indexes	I group	II group		III group
		IIa	IIb	
epiphenomena	0	50	73.5	23.8
hereditary tainted epilepsy	0	81.8	19.4	7.1
CI, brain tumor after surgery in anamnesis	0	100	7.1	4.8
polyneuropathy of lower extremities	68.5	36.4	17.9	11.9
focal and meningeal symptoms	0	100	17.9	4.8
AWS	100	100	0	0
increased GGTP indexes more than 10 times	78.5	70.0	0	0
increased GGTP indexes 2-10 times	15.8	7.3	10.7	5.6
increased AST indexes more than 10 times	65.3	68.3	0	3.4
increased AST indexes 2-10 times	29.0	9.0	5.3	9.0
increased ALT indexes more than 10 times	5.3	4.0	0	0
increased ALT indexes 2-10 times	89.7	73.3	2.3	0

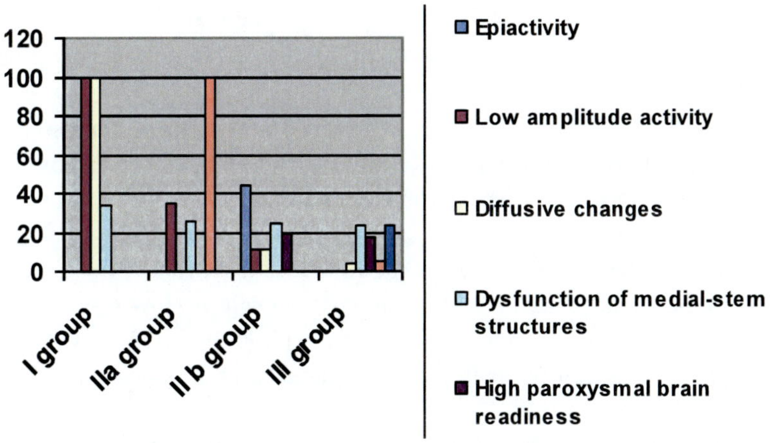

Diagram 1. The frequency of neurophysiological indexes detected by use of electroencephalographic method in the studied group and the comparison groups (%).

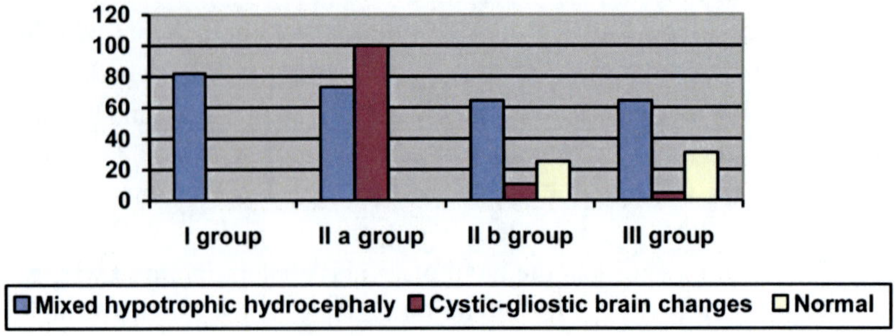

Diagram 2. The frequency of psychophysiological indexes detected by use of computerized tomography method in the studied group and the comparison groups (%).

CONCLUSION

On the basis of the study conducted, it has been concluded that the patients suffering from AES had the following significant anamnestic and neurophysiological characteristics:

- alcohol anamnesis, primary generalization of paroxysms, attacks of wakefulness,
- absence of epiphenomena, personality disorders of epileptoid type, hereditary tainted epilepsy, craniocerebral injuries and insults in anamnesis; focal and general brain symptoms during clinical examinations,
- absence of epileptic and focal activity on EEG,
- presence of low electrobiological activity, diffuse changes of the brain, superposition of muscular tremor on EEG,
- presence of mixed hypotrophic hydrocephaly on the brain CT,
- blood serum transferases' increased activity and further rapid recovery within 2-3 weeks,
- alcoholic polyneuropathy of lower extremities – a frequent concomitant pathology characterized by axonal damages of nerve fibers, and therefore by absence of delayed nerve impulse conduction on electroneurogram.

In symptomatic epilepsy, alcohol plays the role of a provocative, not a causative factor. Fixed changes in a clinical picture (focal symptoms) as well as slow wave activity on EEG, and cystic-gliostic changes on CT indicate that even without harmful influence of alcohol on the brain, epileptic attacks can occur in alcoholic patients, so it is needed to select adequate anti-convulsion medicines.

In cases of detection of epileptic activity on EEG, epileptic attacks can not be caused by alcohol. In those cases, alcohol was only an initiating agent.

Epileptic phenomena occur more often in patients with idiopathic epilepsy, who suffer neither from ES nor from CAI ($P < 0.001$).

EEG changes typical of patients with AES practically do not occur in patients with idiopathic or symptomatic epilepsy, as well as in persons who do not suffer from CAI or epileptic attacks ($P<0.001$).

A common feature for the patients with nonalcoholic ES was typical changes on EEG in the form of epileptic or slow-wave activity ($P< 0.001$).

Beside epileptic activity in the groups of the patients with nonalcoholic ES and without alcoholic ES and CAI, there were often observed changes on EEG like conditional-epileptic activity and dysfunction of medial-stem structures, that is not typical for the patients with AES [10].

Mixed hypotrophic hydrocephaly is a general sign indicating brain diffuse lesion, however in cases of CAI absence, it occurs in health only in elderly patients. Brain lesions caused by CAI result in CT – pattern of hypotrophic hydrocephaly in patients at the middle and even young age. For reference – in the age groups of the patients who suffer from idiopathic epilepsy, CT is more often within the standard ($P<0.01$). In symptomatic epilepsy, pathological focus in brain tissue is a precondition.

A correct classification of attacks and accurate detection of ES types will provide rational and individual basis for therapy, allow to improve prognosis and quality of life of patients suffering from different epileptic attacks.

Diagnostics of AES should include a total of anamnestic, clinical, laboratory and instrumental data. So, sings of «alcohol anamnesis», screening tests positive to alcohol dependence, absence of hereditary tainted epilepsy in anamnesis, epiphenomena and epileptic personality features do not mean that attacks can be only of alcohol origin. Focal or total brain and meningeal symptoms within the clinical pattern are typical for symptomatic epilepsy, and alcohol is often an initiating agent, but not a causative factor. Absence of those symptoms presupposes a possibility of intoxication or idiopathic attacks. Polyneuropathy of lower extremities as another significant sign of CAI is typical of patients with alcoholic epileptic attacks, but its occurrence together with a high level of blood serum transferases can not give a decisive answer about the reason of the epileptic attack. Immunological investigations will help to exclude another genesis of polyneuropathy of lower extremities (hereditary, autoimmunological, paraneoplastic, toxic). High activity of ALT, AST, GGTP is a biomarker of CAI [11]. It is obligatory to study brain electrobiological activity during differential diagnosis between alcoholic and idiopathic attack genesis. Detection of epileptic activity means that the attack cannot be of alcoholic genesis. CT brain testing of patients who have had primary epileptic attacks is also necessary as a final link in the diagnostic process. CT importance is in early detection of tumors, localized hematomas, cysts, which can not be detected clinically, but participate in formation of epileptic foci and development of symptomatic epilepsy.

PRACTICAL GUIDELINES

It is reasonable to use diagnostic algorithms for detection of polyneuropathy and the alcohol epileptic syndrome during differential diagnostics of epileptic attacks.

Anticonvulsants are not indicated for patients with AES because they do not develop seizures if they do not use alcohol.

REFERENCES

[1] Ogurtsov P.P., Girov I.V. Urgent Alcohol Pathology (Guidance for Doctors of Diversified hospitals). Spb.: «*Nevsky Dialect*», 2002. – 118p.

[2] Baranov V.N., Gerasimova M.M.,Chekesova I.M., Belyakova O.U. Characteristics of Neurological Manifestations of Chronic Alcoholism//*Nigegorodsky Medical Journal*. - 2002. - № 3. – p.45 - 50.

[3] Stulman D.R., Levin O.S. Neurology. *Manual for General Practitioner*//M.: MEDpress-inform, 2002.

[4] Brown T., Holms G. Epilepsy. *Clinical Guidance*. M.: «BINOM Publishing House», 2006.- 288p.

[5] Jha S., Nag D. Some observations on clinical, cognitive and neurophysiological changes in subjects consuming indigenous alcohol //*Indian J. Physiol. Pharmacol*. – 1994. – Vol. 38. - №4. – P. 277 - 280.

[6] Wallace R.H., Scheffer I.E., Barnett S. Neuronal sodium – cannel alpha 1 – subunit mutations in generalized epilepsy with febrile seizures plus // *Am J. Hum Genet*. – 2001. - № 68. – 859 – 865.

[7] Ogurtsov P.P., Nugny V.P. Express-Diagnostics (Screening) of Chronic Alcohol Intoxication in Somatic Patients. Guideline №99/ 174 Public Health Ministry RF // *Clinical Pharmacology and Therapy*. – 2001. №1. - p.22 – 26.

[8] Ammendola A., Gemini D., Iannacore S. Gender and peripheral neuropathy in chronic alcoholism: a clinical electroneurographic study // *Alcohol and Alcoholism*. – 2001. - Vol. 35. - № 4. – P. 388 – 391.

[9] Kenneth W.V. Alcoholic polyneuropathy. Pathogenesis, clinical manifestations, diagnostic criteria and therapeutic concepts. *Fortschr. Neurol. Psychiatr*. 2003. – Vol. 68. - № 5. – P. 273 – 288.

[10] Fenton G.W. *Electroencephalography*. – Wiley, Chichester, 1994. – 466 p.

[11] Piatnitskaya I.N., Naidenova N.G., Goryushkin I.I. Activity Changes of Transferase of Blood Serum as Supplementary Criteria for Diagnostics and Indicator of Pathogenetic Treatment Methods//*Manual for Doctors*, M.: Sputnik Company+, 2003.-31p.

PART II. COMORBIDITY OF ALCOHOL AND DRUG ABUSE AND DEPENDENCE WITH OTHER PSYCHIATRIC DISORDERS

In: Suicidal Behavior in Alcohol and Drug Abuse... ISBN: 978-1-60876-919-3
Editors: L. Sher, A. Vilens, pp. 49-82

Chapter 5

COMORBIDITY OF ANXIETY DISORDERS WITH ALCOHOL AND DRUG ABUSE AND DEPENDENCE: A COMPREHENSIVE REVIEW

Omer Saatcioglu
Bakirkoy Research and Training Hospital for Psychiatry, Neurology and Neurosurgery, Istanbul, Turkey

ABSTRACT

The comorbidity of anxiety disorders and drug abuse is growing because of the prevalence and negative impact of comorbidity on course, treatment outcomes and prognoses of both disorders. Most of the studies investigating the comorbidity of anxiety disorders with alcohol and/or drug abuse disorders have focused on alcohol abuse. The number of studies of the relationship between drug abuse and anxiety disorders is relatively limited because of the varying impact of misused drugs on the Central Nervous System (CNS) and compliance issues for the populations being investigated. While discussion of the casual and chronological relationships between anxiety disorders and alcohol and/or drug abuse is ongoing, there are indisputable figures indicating that these two conditions may potentially coexist. The comorbidity of substance abuse and anxiety disorders is common and has important treatment implications. A combination of pharmacotherapeutic and psychotherapeutic strategies should be used in individuals with comorbidity for treatment, but much work remains to be done.

INTRODUCTION

A common perception dating back to ancient times that alcohol alleviates stress has survived to this day. Hippocrates was quoted in 1886 as saying that "wine takes away anxiety and fear". The German neurologist, Westphal, was also known to have claimed in 1871 that agoraphobic patients could easily traverse feared places after having consumed beer or wine.

Westphal recommended a reliable companion, a walking stick and alcohol for anxious and phobic patients [1]. Isaac Marks reported in his book "Fears, Phobias and Rituals", published in 1987, that early twentieth century workers, who were employed in building zeppelins and who had to climb to significant heights, were aware of the anxiolytic effect of alcohol and consumed alcoholic beverages to relieve their anxiety [2]. So it was commonly believed that the anxiolytic effect of alcohol encouraged drinking behavior and contributed to people's pathological drinking behavior. Today, on the other hand, discussions about whether alcohol decreases stress indicate that, in fact, the answer is much more complex and depends on several factors including individual physiological variability, the amount of alcohol consumed, previous experiences with alcohol, the definitions of anxiety and stress, and expectations associated with alcohol [3,4].

Most of the studies investigating the comorbidity of anxiety disorders with alcohol and/or drug abuse disorders have focused on alcohol abuse. The number of studies of the relationship between drug abuse and anxiety disorders is relatively limited because of the varying impact of misused drugs on the Central Nervous System (CNS) and compliance issues for the populations being investigated. Horton and Bales were the first to demonstrate that tension resulted in alcohol consumption. However, it was Conger who established a theoretical model for the relationship between alcohol and anxiety. In his "Tension Reduction Hypothesis (TRH)" published in 1956, Conger pointed to the encouraging effect of alcohol and linked alcohol use with its effect of reducing the fear associated with avoidant behavior [5]. TRH, a well-established hypothesis based mainly on clinical observations of light to moderate drinkers, gained wide acceptance after it was published, and numerous comprehensive studies have been conducted over the years. In light of these discussions, Schuckit devised an alternative hypothesis several years later, namely, if small amounts of alcohol help ease mild anxiety then alcoholics may use large quantities of alcohol to resolve their severe anxiety [6]. Although there are several theoretical arguments both in support and against the TRH, since its publication it has been one of the few theories recognized by all disciplines, particularly psychoanalysts and behaviorists. While psychoanalysts believed the superego was resolved by consuming alcohol, behaviorists pointed out the negative impact of alcohol, with its anxiety-reducing attributes, on pathological behavior. When the validity of the model was tested in humans and in animal models, the model was supported by most of the animal experiments, while the human studies failed to support the model. Studies during the 1960s and 1970s demonstrated that alcohol had a biphasic effect on anxiety, that is, the anxiety-reducing effect achieved with low doses was not experienced with high doses [7].

Although it is commonly believed by the scientific community and by a significant portion of society that alcohol reduces anxiety, studies undertaken over the years to support this belief have reported conflicting results. Some of these studies demonstrated that alcohol decreased anxiety, while others either reported the opposite or indicated that alcohol had no effect on anxiety. These differences in results are because of the methods utilized. Variables such as alcohol consumption, the anxiety measurement method, environmental conditions and the sample make the results difficult to interpret and complicate any generalization of them [3,4,6,7]. Whether anxiety disorders lead to alcohol abuse or whether alcohol abuse results in anxiety symptoms and anxiety disorders are questions still being discussed today.

Schuckit et al. discussed the acute phase of the withdrawal syndrome, during which anxiety, insomnia, vigor, irritability and restlessness may develop. Findings associated with alcohol withdrawal, including anxiety, emotional instability, increased autonomic activity, sleep disorders, irritability and restlessness may persist for weeks and even months, even though these symptoms decrease significantly in severity compared with what occurs during the first few days of alcohol withdrawal. This hypothesis supported the findings from several publications, and Schuckit et al. argued that many of the psychological and physiological symptoms observed during the first few months of alcohol withdrawal were part of the subacute phase of the alcohol withdrawal syndrome [8]. Studies investigating the severity and signs of anxiety during the alcohol withdrawal period have demonstrated that anxiety symptoms that had an early onset during this period decreased in severity over time but did not completely disappear [9,10,11].

In an interesting study on this subject by George et al., 11 patients with known alcohol addiction and a history of panic attacks were given a list including 29 physical and cognitive signs. Except for vigor, the patients failed to differentiate between whether the described signs were associated with panic attacks or alcohol withdrawal [12].

Hofmann et al. suggested that anxiety disorders are associated with an increased likelihood of substance use disorders. The highest association was between posttraumatic stress disorder (PTSD) and substance use disorder. Their results showed that the presence of any anxiety disorder reduced the association between externalizing problems and substance use disorders, possibly because the fear of bodily symptoms prevents individuals with externalized problems from engaging in drug-seeking behaviors [13].

Alcohol use disorder (AUD) was registered before anxiety disorders with a greater frequency than any other disorder, because 56.9% of individuals with AUD were registered with AUD before being registered with anxiety disorders. In addition, the risk of developing anxiety disorders when registered with AUD was considerably greater than the risk of developing AUD when registered with an anxiety disorder. This, however, may reflect the fact that people with anxiety disorders are less likely to be treated and registered unless comorbid disorders are present [14].

According to earlier studies on comorbidity in addiction, phobic patients use alcohol in order to control their anxiety feelings. These studies reported that approximately one-third of agoraphobic patients with alcohol addiction started using alcohol to alleviate their anxiety, and that the majority of these patients (91%) used alcohol to control their phobic fears, while 77% reported using alcohol for its anxiolytic effect [15,16]. In contrast with these findings, Samarasinghe et al. showed that neurotic patients do not abuse alcohol regularly in order to benefit from its anxiolytic effect [17].

HYPOTHESES DESCRIBING THE PRESENCE OF DISORDERS ACCOMPANYING ALCOHOL ADDICTION

Substance-related Artifact Hypothesis

After having studied numerous findings and hypotheses, Schuckit discussed all the studies that considered the relationships between alcohol addiction/abuse and anxiety disorders. According to Schuckit, most of these studies investigated anxiety disorders in alcohol addicts who were hospitalized for treatment of alcohol addiction and who were in the first few weeks of the alcohol withdrawal period. Therefore, Schuckit argued that anxiety and mood disorders that occurred with relatively high frequencies in these studies had a clinical presentation involving the subacute phase of the alcohol withdrawal period, rather than being a separate entity or a primary condition. Schuckit also argued that another key explanation for the relatively high incidence of anxiety and mood disorders in hospitalized patients with alcohol addiction was that these patients' need for help and treatment was higher than that of alcohol addicts who did not have similar symptoms and disorders [18]. In field studies, psychiatric conditions accompanying alcohol addiction were less frequent compared with findings from clinical trials carried out with hospitalized alcohol addicts [19,20,21]. A number of studies have supported this perspective, which has been called the "substance-related artifact hypothesis" [22,23,24].

Self-medication Hypothesis

This hypothesis states that increased frequencies of accompanying conditions in alcohol abusers are associated with the fact that individuals with pre- and coexisting psychiatric disorders abuse alcohol to cope with these disorders, their addiction developing over time. Patients start using alcohol to change their moods, to alleviate their unbearable anxiety and to cope with some cognitive disorders. The self-medication hypothesis is based on, and supported by, observations from individual, dynamic-oriented psychotherapies and psychoanalyses, rather than controlled trials [22]. Khantzian's argument that opiates could be used to control anger and aggression and that opiate addicts abused these substances in order to benefit from their effects may support this hypothesis [25].

Genetic Predisposition Hypothesis

Studies investigating relationships between alcohol and anxiety also attempted to reveal familial connections. The presence of a strong familial connection has been demonstrated for the relationship between panic disorder and alcohol addiction [23,26].

GABAergic System Hypothesis

Alcohol putatively exerts anxiolytic activity on the GABAergic system. It has been emphasized that the coexistence of anxiety in alcohol addicts may be associated with disorders of this system [27].

Despite their similarities, the relationship between alcohol problems and anxiety disorders is believed to vary in individual anxiety disorders. According to Kushner et al., alcohol problems in agoraphobia and social phobia are because of the patients' attempts at self-medication to manage anxiety symptoms while, conversely, panic disorder and generalized anxiety disorder may develop as a result of pathological alcohol abuse [7]. Simple phobias increase the risk of alcoholism [28,29,30]. Two experimental studies demonstrated that simple phobic anxiety was not alleviated by alcohol consumption [31,32]. Although the frequencies of concurrent alcohol and/or substance abuse and anxiety disorders vary with subtypes of these conditions, studies indicate that the presence of one condition increases the risk of the other condition approximately threefold. *Three hypotheses* were suggested to describe this high risk of comorbidity and the chronological link between the two diagnoses.

1. Anxiety disorder leads to alcohol and/or substance use disorders.
2. Alcohol abuse disorder leads to the development of anxiety disorder.
3. A third factor (e.g., familial and/or genetic) leads to the simultaneous development of anxiety disorder and AUD [33,34,35].

While discussion of the casual and chronological relationships between anxiety disorders and alcohol and/or substance abuse is ongoing, there are indisputable figures indicating that these two conditions may potentially coexist. In reviews of the comorbidities between anxiety disorders and AUDs and their incidences, Kushner et al. reported the following findings. In individuals with AUDs, the incidence of agoraphobia was 2.4–42.2%, the incidence of simple phobia was 6.2–17%, the incidence of panic disorder was 2.4–10.8%, the incidence of generalized anxiety was 8.3–52.6% and the incidence of obsessive compulsive disorder (OCD) was 2.7–12%. In individuals with anxiety disorders, on the other hand, the incidence of AUDs was 7–27% for those with agoraphobia and 7.2–8% for those with panic disorder. The incidences of agoraphobia, simple phobia and panic disorder in the general population are 5.9%, 11.4% and 1.4%, respectively [7]. Interestingly, generalized anxiety disorder and panic disorder had high incidences in the group with AUD, while AUD was infrequent in patients with generalized anxiety disorder and panic disorder. In another study, the prevalence of anxiety disorders in the previous 12 months among 90 cannabis users was as follows: social phobia (29%), generalized anxiety disorder (17%), panic disorder with or without agoraphobia (16%), OCD (12%), agoraphobia without panic disorder (9%) and PTSD (5%) [36].

PANIC DISORDER

Panic disorder is a common disease with a chronic course, resulting in significant problems in social and occupational functionality. The key feature of this disorder is recurrent and unexpected "panic attacks" that occur in the form of sudden periods of fear, characterized by physical signs including labored breathing, palpitation and dizziness. During a panic attack, physical signs associated with sympathetic and parasympathetic stimulation occur within a few minutes, resulting in perceptions of severe fear, particularly a fear of death [37].

The anxiety the individual experiences puts the individual in a state of anxious anticipation, wondering when the next panic attack will occur. This is referred to as "anticipatory anxiety". Additionally, concerns regarding physical health associated with these attacks and agoraphobic avoidance behavior secondary to panic attacks are among the key features of the disorder. Agoraphobia, which develops in the majority of these patients, is the primary cause of disability [38,39].

Epidemiology

The prevalence of lifetime panic disorder, reported from comprehensive studies, ranges between 1% and 4%, and the prevalence of panic disorder with agoraphobia has been reported as 1.3% [40]. In some countries, studies of panic disorder are limited to small regions of their respective countries [41].

In the Epidemiologic Catchment Area (ECA) study, the prevalence of lifetime panic disorder was described as 1.5%, and comorbid alcohol and/or substance abuse disorders were identified in 36% of these individuals [20]. The risk of comorbid alcohol and/or substance abuse disorders in individuals diagnosed with panic disorder has been reported to be 2.4 times that of the general population [42]. Alcohol addiction may develop in some patients with panic disorder who attempt to alleviate their anxiety with alcohol. This may be considered a complication of panic disorder. Most of the studies that have investigated the concurrence of panic disorders and alcohol and/or substance abuse have targeted alcohol addicts rather than substance addicts.

The prevalence of panic disorder has been reported to be higher among alcohol addicts compared with the general population [15,43,44,45]. In samples that include alcohol addicts, the prevalence of panic disorder ranges between 5% and 42% [7]. Several factors account for the significant variability in these figures. For example, symptoms of panic attacks that are observed during intoxication with, or withdrawal from, the abused psychoactive substance may have a wide range. Thus, discrepancies in the time of diagnosis may result in significant differences when estimating the prevalence rates.

Prevalence rates in populations consisting of alcohol addicts were generally reported to be higher than in populations of substance addicts [46]. However, conflicting results have been reported from studies conducted in different countries. In studies of opiate addicts undergoing methadone treatment, panic disorder rates have been reported to be 6.9–13% [47,48]. Cox et al. noted that 33.8% of 144 patients presenting with alcohol and/or substance abuse disorders used several unprescribed substances to alleviate the distress they experienced. It is believed that cocaine addicts report fewer panic symptoms [49]. In a comprehensive study of a population of cocaine addicts, the frequency of panic disorder was 1.7% [50]. Brooner et al. reported the overall prevalence of lifetime panic disorder in a population of heroin addicts as 2%, being 2.1% in women and 1.8% in men [51].

Chen et al. did not identify any case of panic disorder in heroin-addicted males who underwent hospitalized treatment during 1999. These same authors reported a 0.7% prevalence of panic disorder in one of two prisons, while no case of panic disorder was noted in the other prison [52]. Matthew et al. reported that the prevalence of panic disorder was 2.1% and 1.8% in male and female heroin addicts, respectively [53].

Etiology

One of the most discussed and supported hypotheses to explain the comorbidity of panic disorder and alcohol and/or substance abuse disorders is the "self-medication hypothesis". Moreover, most of the abused substances (cocaine, marijuana, and other stimulants) may actually result in panic attacks and panic disorder during periods of acute intoxication and withdrawal [54,55]. The actions of cocaine, amphetamines and phencyclidine on the noradrenergic system may explain why they lead to panic symptoms. According to data from a few studies, cocaine may result in panic attacks in individuals with no previous history of panic disorder [55,56]. Panic attacks have also been reported following intranasal phencyclidine. Panic attacks may also develop during the withdrawal period of sedative/hypnotic agents and alcohol [57]. Moran reported six cases presenting with panic disorder and agoraphobia; in all these cases, the symptoms developed following marijuana use [54].

Treatment

Several agents, including the Selective Serotonine Reuptake Inhibitors (SSRIs), Monoamine oxidase inhibitors (MAOIs), Tricyclic antidepressants (TCAs) and benzodiazepine, are established treatments for panic disorder [58]. Particular caution should be exercised when treating panic disorder with antidepressants, such as TCAs and SSRIs. These agents may cause initial activation, leading to a reduction in panic symptoms. Worsening of the symptoms, in turn, increases the risk of a substance abuse relapse. It is recommended that initial doses of TCAs and SSRIs be kept low to prevent activation. Another problem with TCAs and SSRIs in the treatment of panic disorder is the time of the onset of their activity. A period of 2 to 6 weeks is required for these agents to exert their maximum activation, and this long period increases the risk of relapse for patients suffering from substance abuse [59].

Extreme caution should be taken while treating substance-abuse patients with an MAOI. Because the interaction of MAOIs with thiamine may result in a hypertensive crisis, a series of dietary restrictions should be ordered [60].

The efficacy of TCAs and SSRIs has been demonstrated in many studies of cases in which panic disorder and alcohol and/or substance abuse do not coexist [59,61]. However, the administration of these agents in cases of comorbidity has not been investigated systematically and comprehensively. Interestingly, some scientists have acknowledged that SSRIs are effective in reducing alcohol abuse, particularly in some subgroups [62,63]. Although, based on these data, SSRIs seem to be a reasonable choice for comorbid panic disorder and alcohol and/or substance use disorders, further studies are needed to determine the profile of an alcohol abuser that will provide the best response to this treatment approach.

Although benzodiazepines are highly effective in managing panic symptoms and symptoms of other anxiety disorders, the treatment of substance abuser populations with these agents may be objectionable because of the potential for misuse. According to clinical experience, as a rule, benzodiazepines should not be used by individuals with a current substance abuse disorder, and they should be carefully prescribed for patients with a history of substance abuse, who should be monitored. A review by Posternak and Mueller in 2001 discussed the advantages and disadvantages of benzodiazepine treatment in patients with comorbid substance addiction and anxiety disorder. This article emphasized that the restriction of benzodiazepines for treating substance addiction is in fact questionable, in light of data from several studies indicating that benzodiazepines may be an appropriate choice of treatment [64]. In a study comparing the efficacy of carbamazepine (anticonvulsant) and lorazepam during alcohol withdrawal, these two agents were determined to be equally efficient. However, the alcohol usage by the group on carbamazepine treatment was less than that of the group treated with lorazepam during the follow-up period after withdrawal management, which has been associated with the occurrence of a short-term withdrawal syndrome lasting five days following lorazepam treatment. Therefore, benzodiazepines may be considered as add-on pharmacotherapeutic agents for treating comorbid panic disorder and alcohol or substance abuse if activation problems are present or while waiting for the onset of the action of antidepressants. Benzodiazepine should be administered in low doses, and the patients should be closely monitored for any sign of relapse [65].

In a study investigating the coexistence of cocaine addiction and panic disorder [56], marked alleviation of symptoms has been noted following treatment with carbamazepine or clonazepam. Neuronal sensitization, which may lead to limbic stimulation, is known to develop with recurrent cocaine abuse [66]. According to one hypothesis, this explains the panic attack mechanism caused by cocaine. A similar mechanism may be involved in the comorbidity of panic disorder and psychostimulant abuse. Patients in this subgroup might be expected to respond quite well to anticonvulsants such as carbamazepine and valproate. However, this hypothesis should also be supported by further studies.

As in many anxiety disorders, panic disorder also responds well to nonpharmacological treatments. Behavioral approaches, such as exposure and systematic desensitization, have been found to be very effective. Relaxation and supportive therapies may also be helpful in some cases [67,68,69,70].

Social Phobia

Social anxiety disorder is an intense anxiety experienced when the person feels he/she is the focus of others. Since social anxiety disorder and social phobia are terms that are used synonymously, both terms are used in this article interchangeably. People with social anxiety cannot initiate communication, avoid eye contact, talk less than others, remain silent for a long periods of time, are late to respond, do not get as involved as others in dialogues and, when they are required to engage in dialogues because of their work, they make significant efforts to look effective and relaxed. They are self-oriented and preoccupied with how others perceive them. This self-orientation takes the form of an ongoing inner dialogue. Social anxiety may also occur as anxiety regarding physical appearance. According to the DSM-IV classification system, if the perceived anxiety has a significant impact on daily life and persists for at least six months in individuals aged 18 or less, the diagnosis of this condition is "social anxiety disorder" [37]. Cognitive perceptions in social phobia may be summarized in terms of thoughts such as "I will be disgraced", "I will be laughed at", "people will think how stupid I am", "people will understand how clumsy I am" and "no one will ever want to be friends with me". Typical physical signs include flush, palpitation, perspiration, tremor, agitation, abdominal discomfort, dry mouth, labored breathing, lightheadedness, dizziness and tinnitus.

Epidemiology

Social phobia has a high rate of comorbidity with other psychiatric disorders. Two major studies reported the prevalence of social phobia alone as being from 19% to 29%. These studies have revealed that social phobia occurs mostly with affective disorder, anxiety disorder and alcohol and/or substance abuse/addiction. In comorbid cases, the onset of social phobia occurs much earlier than the accompanying psychiatric disorder; in other words, social phobia establishes the ground for comorbidity and occurs at least one year before the accompanying psychiatric disorders in 77% of patients. Other psychiatric conditions accompany social phobia in 70–80% of these patients [71,72]. The presence of accompanying conditions aggravates the symptoms of social phobia and increases the risk of negative outcomes, including suicide.

Studies on social phobia and alcohol and/or substance abuse/addiction comorbidity date back to the 1980s. According to Sher, alcohol diminishes an individual's affective, psychophysiological and behavioral responses in the face of threatening stimulants [27]. Quintkin et al. reported that the first 10 patients with phobic anxiety attempted to self-treat their anxiety symptoms with alcohol and/or substance abuse [73]. Mullaney and Trippet found that there were agoraphobic or social phobic symptoms in two-thirds of 102 alcoholic patients [74]. In another study, the incidence of social phobia was found to be from 9.8% to 11.4% in alcohol-dependent patients [75].

While the prevalence of social phobia in individuals with alcohol problems varies between 2.4% and 57%, most studies report this prevalence as 10–20%. The prevalence rate of alcohol abuse among individuals with social phobia was 14–40%. Clinical studies, however, do not reflect the general population since serious cases would be more likely to seek professional support and present to psychiatric clinics. The prevalence of alcohol abuse/addiction and social phobia in the general population is 9–14% and 13–16%, respectively. The largest community study conducted in the USA (National Comorbidity Survey, NCS) found the frequency of lifetime alcohol addiction in patients with social phobia to be 24%, while the frequency of social phobia among individuals with alcohol addiction was reported as 19% in males and 30% in females [76]. Epidemiologic studies have reported a two- to threefold increased risk of developing alcohol abuse or addiction in individuals with social phobia, compared with those who do not have the condition. Problems associated with alcohol were reported by 2–5% of individuals with social phobia and by less than 1% of those without social phobia. In addition, 4.2% of social phobic individuals and 0.4% of subjects in the control group described that they had serious problems controlling alcohol use during hard times [77].

Social Anxiety Disorder and Substance Abuse Disorders

There are limited studies on the relationship between social anxiety disorder and substance abuse disorders other than alcohol, and this relationship has not been adequately investigated. Regier et al. reported that social phobia and simple phobia, which have an early onset in adolescents, may lead to susceptibility to substance abuse disorders [78]. Examining the relationship between shyness and substance abuse in high school students, Page reported higher rates of marijuana, cocaine, amphetamine or hallucinogenic agent use among shy students compared with others, but they did not report a correlation between alcohol use and shyness. Very shy girls consumed less alcohol than the average for shy people. These findings indicate that shyness is a more important risk factor for males and that shy young people may potentially use substances other then alcohol to alleviate the distress caused by their shyness [79]. Myrick and Brady found social phobia in 13.9% of a group of patients addicted to cocaine. In 100% of the cases, social phobia developed before the subjects started their substance abuse [46]. Milby et al. reported the frequency of social phobia as 5.9% in a group of patients on maintenance treatment with methadone [47]. In other studies, the relative frequencies of social anxiety disorder in inhalant users and opioid dependents were 36.1% [80] and 18.6% [81], respectively.

Etiology

Studies have shown that most social phobic patients use alcohol to decrease their participation anxiety [82]. Several hypotheses that have been suggested to describe the relationship between alcohol and/or substance abuse disorders and social phobia may be summarized as follows: 1) Individuals with social phobia use alcohol and/or substances because they reduce social anxiety through their psychopharmacological activity; 2) Individuals with social phobia use alcohol and/or substances because they believe that these drugs reduce anxiety; 3) Individuals with social phobia have a genetic disposition to both anxiety disorder and addiction; 4) Neurochemical alternations, which consequently result in susceptibility to alcohol and/or substance abuse, occur in individuals with social phobia; 5) Alcohol and/or substance withdrawal leads to the development of social anxiety; 6) Addiction develops as a secondary response to several problems accompanying anxiety disorders, including depression, problems at home or work and personality disorders [83,84].

Phobias (simple, social and agoraphobia) usually start before problems occur with alcohol. Typically, the onset of social phobia occurs during childhood and adolescence; in other words, it has an earlier onset than comorbid alcoholism. Schneir et al. reported an earlier onset of phobia in 82% of patients, and their data were supported by results demonstrating that in 85% of cases, social phobia has an earlier onset than comorbid alcohol abuse [72]. Similarly, Stockwell et al. reported that social phobia and agoraphobia started about two years before alcohol problems in patients being treated for alcoholism [85]. In a chronological study, Bibb and Chambless found that in 56% of patients with agoraphobia and in 31% of problem drinking started earlier, whereas in 13% of the cases, both conditions developed simultaneously [15]. Significant differences between the sexes in terms of the times of onset of alcoholism and the comorbid conditions were observed in the NCS. Males usually reported that alcohol abuse and addiction started before the comorbid conditions, whereas females indicated that alcohol abuse and addiction started in the same year either simultaneously with or after the comorbid disorders. For instance, alcohol addiction developed secondarily to social phobia in 13% of the males compared with 24% of the females. Additionally, the risk of developing alcohol abuse increased twofold in women with social phobia [76].

Social phobia that develops in most or all social settings is called generalized social phobia, while social phobia that occurs in specific situations, such as public speaking, is called nongeneralized social phobia. In 1995, Mannuzza et al. found higher rates of comorbid alcohol abuse in subjects with generalized social phobia (6% vs. 25%). There is evidence suggesting that avoidant personality disorder has a closer link with the potential for developing alcoholism than nongeneralized social phobia [86]. Morgenstern et al. determined that lifetime avoidant personality disorder occurred in 18% of alcohol addicts [87]. Stravynski et al. also found a higher frequency of avoidant personality disorder among alcoholic subjects compared with those with social phobia [88]. It should, however, be noted that these data may have different interpretations, considering the hypothesis that social phobia and avoidant personality disorder are in fact the same disorder from a clinical perspective.

Whether social phobia represents a risk for heavy drinking, alcohol abuse or addiction has been investigated prospectively. Crum and Pratt categorized cases of social phobia into two groups, those who met all the DSM-III diagnostic criteria and those who had unreasonable social fears but did not meet the diagnostic criteria for avoidant behaviors (subclinical social phobia). In this study, subjects with subclinical social phobia had a twofold increased risk of developing heavy drinking behavior, alcohol abuse or addiction compared with subjects without social phobia. Contrary to previous data, no marked relation was identified between the occurrence of social phobia and alcohol problems. This low incidence may be associated with the fact that avoidant behavior reduces social anxiety or that more individuals with social phobia diagnosed by DSM-III present to psychiatry clinics and receive earlier treatment for problematic drinking behaviors. On the other hand, the subclinical syndrome is mostly unnoticed, and these individuals do not present to psychiatry clinics unless comorbid conditions develop [89].

Does alcohol consumption actually reduce social anxiety? Although alcohol use is common among individuals with social anxiety, some studies have shown that alcohol consumption does not alleviate anxiety symptoms [90]. In a study by Himle et al., the subjects were asked to make two improvisatory speeches. Half of the subjects received placebo beverages before both speeches while the remaining subjects received a placebo beverage before the first speech and a drink containing a small dose of alcohol before the second speech. The patients' anxiety levels were rated before, after and during the speeches, and their heart rates were monitored. It was concluded that there were no differences between the groups receiving alcohol and placebo in terms of their anxiety levels and mean heart rates [91]. Consistent with Naftolowitz's study, this study concluded that alcohol was not effective in reducing social anxiety. Allen reported that alcohol's anxiety-reducing effect was not a reasonable rationale for describing how alcohol problems start, and that anxiety was a cause rather than the result of heavy drinking [92].

These data raise the question whether alcohol is consumed because it actually reduces anxiety or because it is expected to reduce anxiety. In a social setting that triggers anxiety, it is possible that any failure of alcohol to reduce anxiety may lead to increased amounts of drinking rather than being dissuasive, the perception being that the consumed dose was inadequate. Although most social phobic alcoholics indicate that the phobias started before alcohol abuse, a significant proportion of them report that their phobic anxiety peaked when their alcohol problems began. In their study of alcoholic individuals, Stockwell et al. also observed increased anxiety and dysphoria with prolonged drinking, although reduced levels of anxiety were noted after alcohol consumption in the short term. According to these authors, individuals increase their anxiety when they intend to alleviate it, and the vicious circle of anxiety and alcohol abuse develops [93].

Schuckit et al. investigated the lifetime risk of social phobia in relatives of alcohol addicts and found a prevalence of 2–3%, concluding that there was little evidence to support a common genotype for anxiety and alcohol disorders [11]. Munjack and Moss reported a history of alcoholism in first-degree relatives of agoraphobic patients [94].

Cudrin has pointed out that the relation of social phobia and agoraphobia to alcoholism may provide guidance when planning treatment. Cudrin described how many alcohol therapists and planners tried to eliminate the resistance patients showed to the idea of participating in Alcoholics Anonymous meetings, and that their patients with social phobia and agoraphobia avoided such meetings. He emphasized the prevalence of these problems, indicating that such meetings will have a key role in an effective treatment plan [95].

In their study demonstrating increased nicotine addiction in individuals with social phobia, Wittchen et al. suggested that smoking may compensate for a lack of confidence in social settings [96]. Social anxiety disorder usually starts during the early period of life (during the first decade) and is prevalent during childhood and adolescence. Thus, it can be stated that social phobia usually starts well before the age at which individuals start habitual smoking. Sonntag et al. investigated whether social anxiety affects the development of regular smoking habits and nicotine addiction. When the development of regular smoking habits and nicotine addiction in individuals with social fears or social phobia was investigated during a follow-up study after four years, an increased rate of nicotine addiction was observed in subjects with at least one social phobia who were not diagnosed with social phobia [97]. Consistent with previous studies, this study demonstrated that a DSM-IV nicotine addiction diagnosis was more likely for subjects with social phobia than for those who did not have social fears or social phobia [98,99,100]. As additional evidence to that obtained in previous studies, nicotine addiction was shown to be related with social fears and subthreshold signs of social phobia. During the four-year follow-up, the number of nicotine addicts among the participants who were not smokers or addicts increased, while the increase in the number of nicotine addicts among subjects with social phobia was not statistically significant. The finding that developing nicotine addiction over time was linked with social fears rather than social phobia may be associated with the fact that individuals with social phobia avoid social settings and engage less in social groups. On the other hand, individuals with social fears who do not have social phobia endure social settings even though they feel uncomfortable and are faced with their peers' insistence that they smoke. Therefore, individuals with social phobias have the greatest risk of smoking in order to adapt to social settings. Social fears may thus have a significant impact on the development of smoking habits in adolescents and young adults.

Treatment

Since social phobia may interrupt an individual's active treatment, early recognition of the condition has a positive effect on its prognosis. A prolonged abstinence period is not necessary for differential diagnosis in comorbid situations since experiences of anxiety while engaging in social settings are not the result of intoxication or the symptoms of withdrawal from any substance. Social fears observed during marijuana or stimulant intoxication are not considered adequate to meet social phobia criteria.

The treatment of patients with comorbid social phobia and alcohol and/or substance abuse disorders should be planned so that it considers both conditions. Because 12-step programs, such as Narcotics Anonymous (NA) or Alcoholics Anonymous (AA), are favored in most treatment units, individuals with social phobia may experience significant difficulties when participating in group therapy activities [101]. Sometimes, these patients may even be misjudged by the healthcare providers as being resistant to, and not complying with, treatment. A treatment plan that also includes individual therapy will be much more effective. Thevos et al. compared cognitive behavioral therapy (CBT) with the 12-step therapy plan in alcoholic patients with or without social phobia. Female alcoholics with social phobia who received cognitive behavioral therapy benefited more from their treatment [102]. Randall and colleagues randomly assigned patients to alcoholism treatment alone, or to alcoholism treatment plus CBT, for social anxiety disorder [103]. The findings indicated that the anxiety outcomes were similar, but that alcoholism treatment alone was superior in terms of drinking outcomes. The treatment sessions were longer for the integrated treatment. In addition, cognitive approaches that include desensitization, flooding, exposure and social skill building were found to be effective in social phobic individuals without comorbid substance abuse [103,104,105,106].

Only a few studies have investigated drug treatments for comorbid social phobia and substance abuse. In social phobic patients, however, pharmacotherapy has been investigated to a greater extent [107]. Of the studied drugs, the effectiveness of the MAOIs, the SSRIs and the benzodiazepines has been established. Paroxetine, an SSRI, has received US FDA approval for the treatment of social phobia. A placebo-controlled study demonstrated that gabapentin was also effective for the treatment of uncomplicated social phobia [108]. Other agents, including venlafaxine, bupropion, ondansetron and buspirone, may also be effective but have not been investigated adequately. In a small, placebo-controlled study in individuals with social phobia and alcohol addiction, paroxetine reduced both alcohol use and social anxiety [109]. SSRIs, gabapentin or venlafaxine will be the most appropriate first-choice treatments for comorbid social phobia and substance abuse. SSRIs may provide beneficial effects by reducing alcohol use. Caution should be exercised if benzodiazepines are used, but it should be borne in mind that these agents may be effective in alleviating symptoms until treatment with SSRIs has been initiated.

Obsessive Compulsive Disorder

Obsessive compulsive disorder (OCD) is a condition characterized by recurrent obsessions and/or compulsions with usually a chronic and sometimes periodic course that significantly affects an individual's daily life. Obsession has been described as an individual's persistent and compelling preoccupation against his/her will, which is perceived by the individual as absurd and irrational (egodystonic), anxiety-inducing, recurrent thoughts, impulses and imagery. The individual perceives his/her obsessions as a creation of his/her own mind. Compulsions are repetitive ritual behavioral or mental actions that the person feels he/she is obliged to perform in response to obsessions or according to certain rules. Those ritual acts that aim to decrease anxiety and prevent certain feared events or situations from occurring are perceived by the individual as exaggerated and irrational [37]. Although observed obsessive compulsive symptoms are often egodystonic, they are accompanied by loss avoidance and risk reduction, insight (perception of symptoms as absurd and irrational), resistance (attempting to suppress and resist the symptoms), and an absence of satisfaction (lack of pleasure despite decreased anxiety or distress).

Epidemiology

OCD may accompany several other psychiatric disorders, the most commonly reported of which are major depression, phobic disorders, schizophrenia, body dysmorphic disorder and hypochondriasis. The number of studies investigating comorbidity of OCD with alcohol and/or substance abuse disorders is limited, and this subject has not been researched adequately [110]. Rasmussen and Tsuang studied the clinical characteristics and familial history of OCD patients and identified lifetime alcohol addiction in the children of 12% of these patients [111]. In their study with 50 patients diagnosed with alcohol abuse/addiction, Eisen and Rasmussen determined that 6% met the OCD criteria according to DSM-III-R. This prevalence is three times the prevalence reported for the general population [112].

Kushner et al. reviewed a large sample of patients they were treating who had alcohol problems, and they identified OCD with a frequency of 3–12% [113]. Based on the data from the ECA study, the risk that a person using cocaine and marijuana would develop OCD was 5.6 times that for individuals who were not using any substances [114]. The same study reported an odds ratio of 2.1 for the risk of OCD in individuals using marijuana only, while the odds ratio was 3.2 for those using marijuana, cocaine and any third substance. Milby et al. reported an OCD frequency of 2.9% from their study with opiate addicts who were on maintenance treatment with methadone [47]. In another study, an OCD ratio of 3.6% was found in inhalant users [81].

Etiology

Diagnosing OCD in comorbid substance abuse is easy compared with other anxiety disorders. Symptoms that develop during any substance abuse or withdrawal are less similar to those of OCD, and the typical symptoms of OCD are highly discriminative. Knowledge from symptoms similar to OCD in substance abusers has been obtained from a limited number of case reports. One of these case reports involved patients constantly seeking cocaine hidden in an imaginary place and exerting an excessive effort to find it [115], while the other two reports described temporary obsessive–compulsive symptoms related to opiate and hallucinogen intoxication [116,117]. How abused substances induce these symptoms is not currently known.

Treatment

Although many serotonergic agents have been approved by the US FDA for the treatment of OCD, there are no case reports or controlled studies regarding their use in OCD with alcohol and/or substance abuse/addiction comorbidity. Both clomipramine and the SSRIs are effective in the treatment of OCD [58]. However, the administration of clomipramine to individuals using alcohol and/or other substances may be objectionable for a number of reasons. As with other TCAs, clomipramine may lower the level of seizure during an epileptic attack, which may pose a danger, particularly during alcohol and benzodiazepine withdrawal. Toxic interactions may occur between CNS stimulants and CNS depressants during treatment with clomipramine. Therefore, SSRIs should be considered as a first-choice option if OCD and alcohol and/or substance abuse coexist. The potential for toxic interaction or adverse effects is less when SSRIs are administered [118].

When alcohol and/or substance abuse and OCD coexist, combination treatment using psychotherapy and pharmacotherapy is of key importance. In such cases, thought stopping, exposure and response-prevention approaches to cognitive behavioral therapies are quite safe and effective. Psychotherapy and pharmacotherapy might be expected to demonstrate a synergistic effect [119,120].

Posttraumatic Stress Disorder (PTSD)

Reactions to life-threatening events typically involve terror, fear and anxiety. While these emotions result from a natural survival instinct, they also create a memory of the trauma so that the individual can avoid the trauma and cope in similar situations that might be encountered in the future. Most people who have experienced at least one trauma during their lifetime can cope and survive. However, following trauma, some experience a period of distress characterized by the symptoms of PTSD [121]. The person reacts to the experience with emotions of excessive fear, helplessness and terror. Individual symptoms include experiencing the events repeatedly in different forms, avoiding stimulants that occurred with the trauma, a reduction in overall reaction level and increased excitability.

Epidemiology

Individual reactions to trauma differ significantly, which explains why PTSD occurs not as an isolated entity but often accompanied by other disorders. Individuals diagnosed with PTSD are usually diagnosed with accompanying conditions including dissociative disorder, somatization disorder, anxiety disorder and borderline personality disorder [122]. In studies with veteran soldiers and civilians diagnosed with PTSD, the most common comorbid conditions among males diagnosed with this disorder were alcohol abuse/addiction, depression, other anxiety disorders, behavioral disorder and substance abuse/addiction. In females with PTSD, on the other hand, the most common accompanying conditions were depression and other anxiety disorders, followed by alcohol and/or substance abuse/addiction. Postwar studies were the first to describe PTSD and alcohol and/or substance use disorders comorbidity as disorders with high prevalence, as 75% of veteran soldiers with PTSD had concurrent alcohol and/or substance abuse/addiction. In studies with civilians, the reported prevalence of coexisting alcohol and/or substance abuse disorders among individuals diagnosed with PTSD varies between 25.6% and 43.0%. This ratio in the non-PTSD population ranged from 8.1% to 24.7%. The prevalence of PTSD among those using alcohol and/or substance in the general population was found to be 8.3%. Among hospitalized alcohol and/or substance users, however, the prevalence of PTSD was much higher (42.5%); this ratio may even reach as high as 62%, particularly in hospitalized pregnant alcohol and/or substance users. A PTSD prevalence of 29.2% has been observed in studies of alcohol and/or substance addiction in adolescents [123].

The most comprehensive data has been provided by the NCS. We learn from the "PTSD in the NCS" study by Kessler et al. that at least 59% of men and 44% of women with PTSD had three or more psychiatric conditions accompanying PTSD. In a study with Vietnam veterans, 66% of patients who met PTSD criteria had another anxiety or affective disorder, with 59% having alcohol and/or substance abuse disorders at the time of the study [124]. Another study with Vietnam veterans identified at least one psychiatric disorder in 98.9% of patients with PTSD. The most common comorbidity was alcohol and/or substance abuse disorders (73%), followed by antisocial personality disorder (31%) and major depression (28%) [125]. A study with 277 women who had been subjected to violence identified major depression in 60% and alcohol and/or substance abuse disorders in 25% of the subjects with PTSD, as well as very high rates of borderline antisocial and paranoid personality disorders [126].

Cottler et al., in their study using epidemiological data, showed that cocaine/opiate users had the highest risk of developing PTSD. The frequency of PTSD noted for this group was ten times that observed for the control group [127]. As shown by several studies, lifetime PTSD is observed in 30–60% of the population being treated for alcohol and/or substance abuse disorders [128].

High rates of PTSD comorbidity with alcohol and/or substance abuse disorders have been reported for individuals applying for psychiatric treatments during the past decade. Alcohol and/or substance abuse disorders have been observed in 60–80% of patients diagnosed with PTSD, while PTSD has been observed in 40–60% of individuals with alcohol and/or substance abuse disorders [129]. PTSD was observed with a rate of 46% in a study with 489 male veterans who were being treated for alcohol and/or substance abuse disorders [130]. Another study with 33 female patients treated for addiction reported a frequency of 40% [131].

Data regarding the comorbidity of PTSD and alcohol and/or substance abuse disorders are mostly from studies with Vietnam veterans. By contrast, Kilpatrick showed that female victims of crime who had developed PTSD were 3.2 times more susceptible to developing alcohol disorders compared with those who did not develop PTSD; the same subgroup was also 3.4 times more susceptible to developing substance abuse disorder. Victims of crime who had developed PTSD were 6.3 more likely to participate in alcohol and/or substance abuse programs [132]. Clinical trials have also reported very high PTSD prevalence among patients who have been followed up for alcohol/substance abuse disorder [133,134,135,136]. PTSD was found in 30.1% of a population addicted to inhalants [81]. A study of 132 patients with alcohol and substance addiction reported PTSD in 33% of the subjects [137].

PTSD Prevalence for Different Substances

The reported comorbidity rates of PTSD and alcohol and/or substance abuse disorders were always high, regardless of the type of trauma or the substance used. The relationship between trauma and PTSD and the use of cocaine and opiates was more marked than that involving marijuana and alcohol, which the general public believe to be milder substances [132].

In their research using data obtained from the St. Louis ECA study, Cottler et al. found that alcohol and/or substance users were exposed more frequently to traumatic events than were the subjects in the control group. Of the multiple substance or cocaine/opiate users, 43% had experienced a traumatic event that may have led to PTSD. This rate was reported as 23% for hallucinogen users, 18% for marijuana users, 16% for alcohol users and 13% for the control group. All groups except the alcohol group had experienced significantly more traumatic events compared with the control group. Among the subjects exposed to traumatic events, cocaine/opiate users were diagnosed more frequently with PTSD, with a 19% diagnosis rate. Thus, exposure to more traumatic events was found to be associated with higher rates of PTSD diagnosis. Among subjects who had experienced traumatic events, the lowest PTSD rate was noted for those using marijuana (2%); the PTSD rate in marijuana users was even lower than that in the control group. The PTSD rate was higher for alcohol and/or substance users compared with the controls regardless of the frequency of traumatic event exposure. The prevalence of lifetime PTSD was 0.3%, while it was 8.3% for cocaine/opiate users. Cocaine/opiate users were 10 times more likely to be diagnosed with PTSD compared with the controls, while pill/hallucinogen users were four times more likely to be diagnosed with PTSD compared with the subjects in the control group [127].

When alcohol and substance addicts with an accompanying PTSD diagnosis were compared, no differences were noted with respect to comorbid disorders. However, the symptoms of avoidant behaviors were more frequently observed in PTSD patients than in alcohol addicts. The same study revealed a significant relationship between the date of trauma and the date on which substance-addicted PTSD patients had started consuming high amounts of substances [137].

Etiology

There is a strong link between PTSD and alcohol and/or substance abuse disorders. For example, the existence of one of these disorders increases the likelihood that one of the other disorders will be developed. The possibility of the co-occurrence of these disorders in different trauma types when different substances are used is always high. Studies have shown that the possibility of those using alcohol/substances being exposed to a trauma is higher than for those who do not use alcohol/substances. Even evidence of alcohol/substance use in the family history increases the possibility of a person being exposed to traumatic events. In contrast, a history of trauma increases the likelihood of alcohol and/or substance use. Berk was the first to suggest the "Substance Abuse Disorder Traumatogenicity Theory" hypothesis, according to which trauma may increase the risk of alcohol and/or substance use [138]. According to Berk, using alcohol and/or substance reflects an attempt by the individual to treat the pain suffered [139].

Models for the Development of a Comorbid State

The high comorbidity rate of PTSD and alcohol and/or substance abuse disorders indicates that a functional link may exist between these two disorders. Four major developmental models have been proposed to explain this high comorbidity rate. In the first model, alcohol and substance abuse develops before PTSD. Some alcohol and/or substance users place themselves in danger in order to sustain their habit, and as a result, they are exposed to many physical and psychological traumas. For example, in a study conducted on a group with PTSD and comorbid cocaine use disorder, it was found that for patients who had been using cocaine previously, PTSD that developed secondary to comorbid cocaine use occurred following a traumatic event when they were either trying to access cocaine or using cocaine. It is known that chronic alcohol and/or substance use may cause overstimulation and anxiety, as well as the sensitization of some neurobiological stress systems. Alcohol and/or substance use creates a high vulnerability to PTSD development when trauma has been experienced [123].

In the second model of the development of a comorbid state, PTSD occurs before alcohol and/or substance use. In this model, alcohol and/or substance use is a type of self-treatment. According to the information obtained from patients, cerebrospinal fluid (CSF) depressants, as with opiates and benzodiazepines, provide a sharp improvement in PTSD symptoms. In line with this, the initiation and severity of alcohol and/or substance use increase in parallel with the initiation and development of the PTSD symptoms. Additionally, it is understood from some of the clinical data that selection of the substances to be used (CSF depressant or stimulant) depends on the group of PTSD symptoms from which the patient suffers the most. For example, in PTSD patients with alcohol addiction, the stimulation symptoms are much more serious that in PTSD patients with cocaine addiction [128].

In the second model, alcohol and/or substance withdrawal, in particular withdrawal involving CSF depressants, may cause a vicious cycle involving relapse and then reuse of substances. Withdrawal syndromes associated with most of the CSF depressants are confused with overstimulation syndromes from PTSD. At the beginning, alcohol and/or substances serve as a cure for the PTSD symptoms. PTSD patients report that CSF depressants cause an immediate relief in their symptoms. Apart from this, the objectively measured startle response is decreased by the effects of alcohol. The physiological stimulation caused by alcohol and/or substance withdrawal may create an additive effect on stimulation symptoms that accompany PTSD. The resulting state of overstimulation may function as a conditional reminder of traumatic events and cause an increase in reexperiencing symptoms. Exacerbation of the PTSD symptoms may cause a relapse in alcohol and/or substance use after the individual's efforts at self-treatment. Thus, PTSD patients who had difficulty coping with their current stimulation symptoms will have even more difficulty tolerating the additional stimulation induced by withdrawal. Alternatively, alcohol and substance use may be regarded as a mechanism for coping with the traumatic event itself. This model applies particularly to patients who experienced trauma in adulthood and subsequently developed PTSD. The tranquilizing effects of alcohol and/or substance use serve initially as a motivation for the patient to use substances once more when the PTSD symptoms reappear [123].

A third model might explain the high comorbidity rate between alcohol and/or substance use and PTSD. Those using alcohol and/or substances are more likely to develop PTSD after a trauma as a result of a deficiency in their coping mechanisms and/or changes in brain neurochemistry. Neurochemical changes increase the likelihood of developing PTSD and delay its progress [128].

According to the fourth model, vulnerability to PTSD and alcohol and/or substance abuse disorders has a common genetic and psychosocial basis. However, there are no clinical studies in the literature to justify this hypothesis [140].

Most studies support the second model. This model's suggestion that alcohol and/or substance use develops after PTSD was evaluated using three- and five-year observation intervals in a longitudinal study conducted by Chilcoat and Breslau in 1998. According to the investigators, a preexisting alcohol and/or substance addiction does not increase an individual's risk of experiencing a trauma or developing PTSD. Besides, it was determined that exposure to a trauma increases the risk of developing alcohol and/or substance use disorders only if it results in PTSD. A traumatic experience in itself does not increase the risk of developing alcohol/substance use disorder [141]. In another study conducted on patients diagnosed with cocaine addiction and PTSD, it was demonstrated that in cases where PTSD developed before cocaine addiction, the possibility of a comorbid major depression accompanied by benzodiazepine and opiate use is higher than in cases in which cocaine use begins earlier than the PTSD [123].

For neurobiological and psychosocial reasons, alcohol and/or substance abuse disorders are a risk factor for PTSD. Individuals lead a more risky life under the effects of alcohol and/or substances, and the biochemical characteristics of the withdrawal periods, which are similar to those of PTSD, form the neurobiological basis of PTSD. Furthermore, the comorbidity rates obtained in epidemiological studies that were conducted to investigate the relation between the two disorders confirm these findings [123].

Pathophysiology

Many neurobiological systems are involved in ensuring the development of acute and chronic adaptation by the organism against stress and substance use. The hypothalamic–pituitary–adrenal (HPA) axis, the noradrenergic, dopaminergic, GABA, benzodiazepine and serotonergic systems and the thyroid axis represent only the most important of these systems. In individuals with comorbid PTSD and alcohol and/or substance abuse, the interaction between these systems is extremely complicated. The HPA axis and the noradrenergic system are the most extensively studied systems [123].

The HPA Axis in Cases in which PTSD and Addiction Coexist

Acute stress in humans and animals initiates a series of neurohormonal events. Norepinephrine turnover occurs in the terminal extension of the locus ceruleus, and the hypothalamic Corticotropin Releasing Hormone (CRH) is released and discharged into the pituitary portal system. CRH stimulates ACTH release from the pituitary, which results in cortisol (for humans) or corticosterone (for mice) secretion from the adrenals. Research conducted on humans and animals has demonstrated that these series of reactions form the basis for the pathophysiology of both PTSD and alcohol and/or substance abuse disorders [123,142].

Alcohol and/or substance addicts report stress and negative mood as the most common causes of relapse and ongoing alcohol and/or substance use. In some recent studies that have examined cocaine addicts using the personal stress imaging method, it was noted that both the craving for cocaine and the cortisol level in the saliva increased. In animal studies, mice were first taught how to use heroin and cocaine, and they were then deprived of these substances for a long period; the animals' use of heroin and cocaine relapsed upon application of stress. Similarly, in animals using other substances, a broad range of stressors increases the tendency of the animals to consume substances. Further, in studies conducted on the pathophysiology of this phenomenon, corticosteroids played a mediatory role in the substance use behavior caused or increased by stress [123,142].

Clinical data exist suggesting that the impact of stress on substance use is regulated by CRH. Central administration of CRH causes a continuous increase and sensitization in the d-amphetamine locomotor response. It has been reported that treatment with a CRH antagonist blocks the sensitization developed against d-amphetamine following the stress. Central administration of an "anti-CRH antibody", and giving the CRH receptor antagonist, "alpha-helical CRH", block the locomotor hyperactivity induced by cocaine. Alcohol and cocaine withdrawal, which causes similar behaviors and decreases exploratory behavior, is accompanied by a selective CRH increase in the hypothalamus and the amygdala. Previous administration of anti-CRH immunoserum or "anti-helical CRH" that blocks the effects of CRH prevents the development of similar behaviors related to withdrawal. In line with these observations, high levels of CSF have been detected in individuals suffering alcohol withdrawal. As the period of sobriety is prolonged and the symptoms of withdrawal disappear, CSF and CRH fall to normal or subnormal levels. Injection of CRH in the cerebrovascular area causes substance exploration in mice that were previously taught to use heroin during the remission period [142].

Many preclinical studies demonstrate that high CRH levels in the brain, particularly in the amygdala, increase all fear behaviors, especially the startle response. The anxiogenic effects of CRH may be precluded by CRH antagonists. CRH also functions as a mediator in the occurrence of the effects of substances, in relapses arising from stress and in withdrawal symptoms. Therefore, the high brain levels of CRH in PTSD mediate overstimulation symptoms and the increased risk of alcohol and/or substance abuse that occur in this disorder. High CRH levels enhance the euphoric effects of some substances, primarily stimulants, and aggravate any withdrawal symptoms, thereby causing relapse. On the other hand, the high brain CRH levels caused by alcohol and/or substance withdrawal exacerbate overstimulation symptoms and induce the occurrence of other PTSD symptoms, causing individuals to resume their use of alcohol and/or substances [123].

The Noradrenergic System in PTSD and Addiction

In chronic stress, norepinephrine turnover increases in some areas of the brain such as the locus ceruleus, hypothalamus, hippocampus, amygdala and cortex. In PTSD patients, the 24-hour excretion of epinephrine and norepinephrine increases, the number of platelet alpha 2 adrenergic receptors decreases, and the 24-hour level of plasma norepinephrine increases. An exaggerated cardiovascular and 3-methoxy-4-hydroxyphenylglycol (MHPG; a norepinephrine metabolite) response occurs upon intravenous administration of yohimbine. Balance disorder also occurs in the noradrenergic system during alcohol withdrawal. In alcohol withdrawal, norepinephrine, plasma MHPG and CSF MHPG levels increase, and the number of platelet alpha 2 adrenergic receptors decreases. A directly proportional relation was detected between the severity of alcohol withdrawal symptoms and the MHPG concentration in the CSF. Findings indicative of noradrenergic balance disorder during opiate withdrawal are the high plasma and brain MHPG concentrations detected in humans and animals. The severity of the symptoms in opiate withdrawal is also directly proportional to the noradrenergic activity level. These findings led to the use of some alpha 2 adrenergic receptor agonists in the treatment of PTSD and opiate withdrawal [123,142].

Interaction between Noradrenergic Systems and the HPA Axis

According to Koob, the CRH–noradrenaline interaction functions as a feed-forward system. When an individual is exposed to trauma, it causes an ever-increasing stress reaction that is typical for PTSD. This phenomenon, also referred to as kindling, is the basis of both PTSD and alcohol and/or substance abuse disorders. Stress, including that related to alcohol and/or substance use or withdrawal, increases CRH release in the locus ceruleus. The locus ceruleus is activated and releases norepinephrine into the cortex, which in turn increases the release of CRH in the locus ceruleus. The interaction between these two systems is probably the underlying cause of the overstimulation symptoms observed in PTSD. PTSD patients are liable to use CSF depressants. They may use these agents to repress the activity in the locus ceruleus and stop the feed-forward mechanism [124,142]

Treatment

It is clear that the pathophysiological mechanisms in individuals with comorbid PTSD and alcohol/substance addiction cause overlapping or worsening of the symptoms of both disorders. For example, substance abuse (particularly alcohol, sedative-hypnotic and opiate withdrawal) may aggravate PTSD symptoms. Paranoia, hypervigilance, sleep disorders and autonomic arousal may be triggered by cocaine use. The anxiety resulting from the use of alcohol and sedative hypnotics and from opiate withdrawal also results from overstimulation of neurons in the locus ceruleus. As is known, the locus ceruleus plays an essential role in the pathogenesis of PTSD. It is still not known whether the common pathophysiological mechanism of the two disorders is a facilitating or aggravating factor in treatment [123,128].

Little is known about the efficient treatment of PTSD and comorbid alcohol/substance abuse. While multimodal approaches are usually recognized for the treatment of PTSD, pharmacotherapy is becoming increasingly more prominent. One of the most important targets of pharmacotherapy is to diminish the key symptoms of PTSD; thus, the individuals will be able to cope with traumatic events without using any other substances.

In double-blind placebo-controlled studies, TCA and MAOIs were reported to decrease the reexperiencing and depressive symptoms that are characteristic of PTSD [143]. The reports that carbamazepine, beta blockers, benzodiazepine and lithium have a positive effect are not based on controlled studies. Recently, placebo-controlled large-scale research has demonstrated that SSRIs, in particular, sertraline, fluoxetine and paroxetine, can be quite effective in PTSD treatment [21,128,144,145]. In a pilot study conducted in patients with PTSD and comorbid alcohol abuse disorder, it was demonstrated that sertraline improved PTSD symptoms and produced a decrease in alcohol use [146].

What has attracted most attention in the last few years has been the use of psychotherapy in patients with PTSD and alcohol and/or substance abuse disorders. In the conventional approach, the substance abuse was treated first, and the treatment of PTSD symptoms was postponed. One of the problems that occurred with this method was the fact that some of the PTSD symptoms (e.g., sleep disorder, thoughts of reexperiencing) might cause a relapse. Today, in psychotherapy targeting comorbid alcohol and/or substance abuse, treatments involving exposure, group therapy and cognitive-behavioral methods have proven to be successful and satisfactory. However, it is evident that further research and method development is needed [147,148].

Generalized Anxiety Disorder (GAD)

The leading causes of GAD are anxiety, motor tension, an increase in autonomous functions and a state of cognitive stimulation. Anxiety rises to excessive levels and negatively affects the patient's usual activities. The usual signs of tension are headache, discomfort and hand tremor. Patients sometimes express their discomfort by saying that their body "is shaking inside". The symptoms of increased autonomous function are frequently manifested by difficulty in breathing, excessive sweating, palpitation and various gastrointestinal complaints. The state of cognitive stimulation may cause irritability and an excessive startle response. Furthermore, such individuals check their environment continually for possible threats. Such chronic and generalized anxiety causes disability, and the signs of depression may occur at different levels to various extents [149].

Epidemiology

When the results from all centers in a World Health Organization multicenter study that investigated psychological problems in primary healthcare services were evaluated, GAD (7.9%) was placed second among the most commonly occurring psychological disorders following depression (10.4%). In the "Turkey's Mental Health Profile" study conducted by interviewing 7479 people 18 years of age or older, representing the adult population of Turkey, the prevalence of GAD, defined in terms of ICD-10, was 0.7% [150]. In another study, data from 330 patients in four primary healthcare centers indicated that the prevalence of GAD was 10%. In another study, 6.4% of primary care patients satisfied all the GAD criteria, and 12% satisfied some of these criteria [151].

In these studies, it was reported that another concurrent psychiatric disorder was diagnosed in GAD cases in prevalence rates of up to 90%. In the ECA study conducted in the USA, it was reported that a 58–65% prevalence of comorbidity was found in GAD, the most common codiagnoses being panic disorder and major depression [19]. Further, abuse or addiction with alcohol or anxiolytics may be seen in approximately a quarter of GAD patients. This may have been more frequent in cases where GAD was recognized but not treated. The social and occupational problems and high stress level caused by alcohol and/or substance addiction may subsequently exacerbate the anxiety symptoms. As with all comorbid cases, it is known that loss of function is more evident and the suicide risk is higher [152].

In alcohol abuse/addiction and GAD comorbidity, patients use alcohol in order to relieve their anxiety symptoms, even though alcohol addiction may also cause anxiety. It has been observed that the association between GAD and the state of withdrawal experienced by alcohol-addicted patients is stronger than the association between alcohol abuse disorder and GAD [83]. In patients with a comorbid diagnosis, GAD occurs after alcohol use; otherwise, it appears that alcohol is more frequently used to relieve symptoms in social anxiety disorder and agoraphobia. Contrary to common belief, recent studies have shown that alcohol addiction causes GAD. Results from the National Epidemiologic Survey on Alcohol and Related Conditions showed that men with GAD had significantly higher rates of comorbid alcohol and drug use disorders, nicotine dependence and antisocial personality disorder. Women with GAD had significantly higher rates of comorbid mood disorders (except bipolar disorder) and anxiety disorders (except social anxiety disorder). Men with GAD reported a greater use of alcohol and drugs to help relieve their GAD symptoms [153].

A review of the literature indicated that the studies conducted so far were limited to those on alcohol abuse disorder comorbidity in GAD, and GAD comorbidity in alcohol addiction. The alcohol addiction comorbidity rate for GAD cases has been reported as ranging from 9% to 25%, and the GAD comorbidity rate among alcohol addicts is from 8.3% to 56.2%. However, there are only a limited number of studies that have been conducted to explain the relation between GAD and alcohol addiction [7,8,19,26,43,83,113,154,155].

Fisher and Goethe investigated whether the signs of anxiety in depressive cases affected the pattern of alcohol and/or substance abuse differently for women and men. Even though men outnumber women in their abuse of drugs and alcohol, anxiety in depressive women increases the risk of alcohol and/or substance abuse [156]. Other research reminds us that the strongest link between anxiety and alcohol use is associated with phobia rather than with panic disorder and GAD [26].

In a study of patients with GAD and alcohol addiction, whereas 36% of these patients had anxiety before they started using alcohol, 64% had no anxiety prior to their becoming involved with alcohol. These data were interpreted to imply that alcohol use may play a role in the occurrence of anxiety symptoms, which increase to pathological levels in alcohol addicts diagnosed with GAD [157]. In the same study, the average age at which the consumption of alcohol begins in alcohol addiction and GAD comorbidity cases was 17, the average age of being diagnosed with alcohol addiction was 32, and the average age at which patients resorted to treatment for their alcohol addiction was 36. In the USA, the most common age range during which alcohol consumption begins is between 12 and 17 years. Problems associated with alcohol use develop from 20 to 35 years of age, and treatment is sought around the age of 40 [22]. Therefore, it is seen that the age at which treatment was sought decreased from the 40s to 36. This clear decrease in the age at which treatment is sought may be related to the fact that GAD, which may have been present for 1–10 years previously, may have finally become evident. In other words, GAD that is comorbid with alcohol addiction causes patients to resort to treatment four to five years earlier, thus confirming the hypothesis that alcohol addiction causes GAD development.

In a study that focused on GAD and particularly substance abuse/addiction comorbidity, Massion et al. interviewed 357 patients with panic disorder or GAD. Eighteen percent of these patients were diagnosed with GAD only, whereas 11% of the patients who were diagnosed with only GAD were also diagnosed with abuse of substances other than alcohol [158]. In another study, Milby et al., who examined opiate addicts and cocaine addicts receiving maintenance treatment with methadone, found GAD rates of 21% and 8%, respectively [47]. In some studies, GAD rates of 1.4% in opiate addicts [82] and 20.5% in inhalant addicts [81] were obtained.

Etiology

Kushner et al. suggested that alcohol addiction, contrary to the pattern observed in panic and phobic disorders (coping, self-treatment), was the cause, rather than the effect, when a specific GAD diagnosis was being considered [113]. The remission and maintenance of remission in anxious alcohol addiction patients is far more difficult than in nonanxious alcohol addiction patients, as a result of causes such as more severe signs of withdrawal, more frequent relapses and a greater level of disability. The diagnosis of patients with GAD using alcohol and/or substance should be differentiated when they are being treated [159].

Some hypotheses suggest that in terms of their etiological relation, GAD in alcohol addicts is different from GAD in cases that do not involve alcohol addiction. It is known that the gamma-aminobutyric acid (GABA)-benzodiazepine (BZD) receptor system is effective in GAD etiopathogenesis [160]. It has been reported that in alcohol addiction, as well, GABAergic dysfunction rather than anxiolytic activity causes the initial anxiogenesis [161]. Within this context, it is considered that alcohol intake by addicts decreases panic disorder comorbidity by preventing acute anxiety attacks such as panic disorder. However, this may cause chronic anxiety and the development of GAD as a result of GABAergic dysfunction that develops over time. These hypotheses support the suggestion that alcohol addiction causes GAD development.

Withdrawal, a characteristic feature of GAD caused by free-floating anxiety, alcohol, sedative hypnotics and opiates, is similar to a great extent to the anxiety observed in intoxication. Although most individuals with substance abuse disorder report similar anxiety symptoms to those observed in GAD, since the etiology of these symptoms is not known for certain, they may not satisfy most of the GAD criteria. In alcoholics, it is not possible to differentiate between GAD symptoms and alcohol withdrawal symptoms [162]. The same problems may occur when trying to differentiate between the withdrawal symptoms caused by sedative hypnotics, benzodiazepines and opiates and those of GAD.

Treatment

It is quite difficult to treat GAD and comorbid alcohol and/or substance abuse disorders. Many pharmacological agents, such as TCAs, SSRIs, venlafaxine and anticonvulsants, can be used effectively in the treatment of GAD patients without substance abuse. The use of benzodiazepines in alcohol and/or substance addicts is controversial, although they are efficient and beneficial in GAD. Apart from these agents, buspirone is an anxiolytic with no abuse potential. In a double-blind, placebo-controlled study involving 61 alcohol addicts, Kranzler et al. showed that attendance for treatment occurred for longer periods and that there was a greater decrease in anxiety, a longer period of time before resuming heavy alcohol drinking and a decrease in the number days on which the patients used alcohol during the follow-up period [163]. In other studies conducted with buspirone on populations who consumed alcohol, more complicated and controversial results were obtained [65]. McRae et al., in their placebo-controlled study, found that buspirone decreased anxiety to a considerable extent in 28 patients receiving maintenance treatment with methadone [164]. The data are controversial because only a limited number of studies have been conducted in this field. However, buspirone still seems to be a good option in cases with comorbid GAD and alcohol and/or substance abuse disorders, since the potential for abuse is low.

As with panic disorder, nonpharmacological treatments are also quite effective in GAD. Relaxation techniques, developing coping skills and cognitive-behavioral techniques can be used efficiently in the treatment of GAD [165,166]. It is considered appropriate to use pharmacotherapy and psychotherapy together to obtain optimum results. The use of psychotherapeutic strategies, accompanied to some extent by pharmacotherapeutic interventions, should be encouraged [101].

REFERENCES

[1] Westphal C: Die agoraphobie, Eine nueropathische Erscheinung. [The agoraphobia, a neuropathic phenomenon] *Arch Psychiatr Nervenkr* 1872; 3:138–161. (German)

[2] Marks I: Fears, *Phobias and Rituals.* London, Oxford University Press, 1987.

[3] Wilson GT: Alcohol and anxiety. *Behav Res Ther* 1988; 26:369–381.

[4] Wesner RB: Alcohol use and abuse secondary to anxiety. *Psych Clin North Am* 1990; 13:699–791.

[5] Conger JJ: Alcoholism: Theory, problem and challenge. II. Reinforcement theory and the dynamics of alcoholism. *Quarterly J Stud Alcohol* 1956; 17:296–305.

[6] Schuckit MA, Monterio MG: Alcoholism, anxiety and depression. *Br J Addiction* 1988; 83:1373–1380.

[7] Kushner MG, Sher KJ, Beitman BD: The relation between alcohol problems and the anxiety disorders. *Am J Psychiatry* 1990; 147:685–695.

[8] Schuckit MA, Irwin M, Brown SA: The history of anxiety symptoms among 171 primary alcoholics. *J of Studies on Alcohol* 1990; 51:34–41.

[9] Ludenia K, Donham GW, Holzer PD, Sands MA: Anxiety in an alcoholic population: A normative study. *J Clin Psychology* 1984; 40:356–358.

[10] Johnston AL, Thevos AK, Randal CL, Anton RF: Increased severity of alcohol withdrawal in in-patient alcoholics with a co-existing anxiety diagnosis. *Br J Addiction* 1991; 86:719–725.

[11] Schuckit MA, Hesselbrock VM, Tipp J, Nurnberger JI Jr, Anthenelli RM, Crowe RR: The prevalence of major anxiety disorders in relatives of alcohol dependent men and women. *J Stud Alcohol* 1995; 56:309–317.

[12] George DT, Zerby A, Noble S, Nutt DJ: Panic attacks and alcohol withdrawal: Can subjects differentiate the symptoms? *Biol Psych* 1988; 24:240–243.

[13] Hofmann SG, Richey JA, Kashdan TB, McKnight PE: Anxiety disorders moderate the association between externalizing problems and substance use disorders: Data from the National Comorbidity Survey—Revised. *J Anxiety Disord* 2009; 23:529–534.

[14] Flensborg-Madsen T, Mortensen EL, Knop J, Becker U, Sher L, Grønbaek M: Comorbidity and temporal ordering of alcohol use disorders and other psychiatric disorders: Results from a Danish register-based study. *Compr Psychiatry* 2009; 50:307–314.

[15] Bibb J, Chambless DL: Alcohol use and abuse among diagnosed agoraphobics. *Behav Res Ther* 1986; 24:49–58.

[16] Smail P, Stockwell T, Canter S, Hodgson R: Alcohol dependence and phobic anxiety states. I. A prevalence study. *Br J Psychiatry* 1984; 144:53–57.

[17] Samarasinghe DS, Tilley S, Marks IM: Alcohol and sedative drug use in neurotic outpatients. *British J Psychiatry* 1984; 145:45–48.

[18] Schuckit MA: Alcohol related disorder. In: HI Kaplan, BJ Sadock (editors): *Comprehensive Textbook of Psychiatry.* Baltimore, Williams &Wilkins, 1995, pp 773–778.

[19] Regier DA, Myer JK, Kramer M, Robins LN, Blazer DG, Hough RL, Eaton WW, Locke BZ: The NIMH Epidemiologic Catchment Area Program: Historical context, major objectives and study population characteristics. *Arch of Gen Psychiatry* 1984; 41:934–941.

[20] Regier DA, Farmer ME, Rae DS, Locke BS, Keith SJ, Judd LL, Godwin FK: Comorbidity of mental disorders with alcohol and other drug abuse: Results from the Epidemiologic Catchment Area (ECA) study. *JAMA* 1990; 264:2511–2518.

[21] Marshall RD, Beebe KL, Oldham M, Zaninelli R: Efficacy and safety of paroxetine treatment for chronic PTSD: A fixed-dose, placebo-controlled study. *Am J Psychiatry* 2001; 158:1982–1988.

[22] Miller NS: *Comprehensive Handbook of Drug and Alcohol Addiction.* 3rd edition, New York, Marcel Dekker Inc., 1991.

[23] Araujo L, Goldberg P, Eyma J, Madhusoodanan S, Buff DD, Shamim K, Brenner R: The effect of anxiety and depression on completion/withdrawal status in patients admitted to substance abuse detoxification program. *Subst Abuse Treat* 1996; 13:6–16.

[24] Verheul R, Kranzler H, Poling J, Tennen H, Ball S, Rounsaville BJ: Axis I and axis 2 disorders in alcoholics and drug addicts: Fact or artifact? *J Study Alcohol* 2000; 61:101–111.

[25] Khantzian EJ: The self-medication hypothesis of addictive disorders: Focus on heroin and cocaine dependence. *Am J Psychiatry* 1985; 142:1259–1264.

[26] Merikangas KR, Stevens DE, Fenton B, Stolar M, O'Malley S, Woods SW, Risch N: Co-morbidity and familial aggregation of alcoholism and anxiety disorder. *Psychol Med* 1998; 28:773–778.

[27] Sher L: The role of the endogenous opioid system in the pathogenesis of anxiety disorders. *Med Hypothesis* 1998; 50:473–474.

[28] Helzer JE, Pryzbeck T: The co-occurrence of alcoholism with other psychiatric disorders in the general population and its impact on treatment. *J Stud Alcohol* 1988; 49:219–224.

[29] Himle JA, Hill EM: Alcohol abuse and the anxiety disorders: Evidence from the Epidemiologic Catchment Area survey. *J Anxiety Disord* 1991; 5:237–245.

[30] Kessler RC, Crum RM, Warner LA, Nelson CB, Schulenberg J, Anthony JC: Lifetime co-occurrence of DSM-III-R alcohol abuse and dependence with other psychiatric disorders in the National Comorbidity Survey. *Arch Gen Psychiatry* 1997; 54:313–321.

[31] Thyer BA, Curtis GC: The effects of ethanol intoxication on phobic anxiety. *Behav Res Ther* 1984; 22:599–610.

[32] Cameron OG, Liepman MR, Curtis GC, Thyer BA: Ethanol retards desensitization of phobias in non-alcoholics. *Br J Psychiatry* 1987; 150:845–849.

[33] Meyer RE: How to understand the relationship between psychopathology and addictive disorders: Another example of the chicken and the egg. In: RE Meyer (editor): *Psychopathology and Addictive Disorders.* New York, Guilford Press, 1986, pp 3–16.

[34] Anthony JC: Epidemiology of drug dependence and illicit drug use. *Current Opinion Psychiatry* 1991; 4:435–439.

[35] Kushner MG, Sher KJ: Comorbidity of alcohol and anxiety disorders among college students: Effects of gender and family history of alcoholism. *Addict Behav* 1993; 18:543–552.

[36] Guillem E, Pelissolo A, Vorspan F, Bouchez-Arbabzadeh S, Lépine JP: Sociodemographic profiles, addictive and mental comorbidity in cannabis users in an outpatient specific setting. *Encephale* 2009; 35:226–233. (French)

[37] American Psychiatric Association: *Diagnostic and Statistical Manual of Mental Disorders.* 4th edition, Washington DC, American Psychiatric Press, 1994.

[38] Slaap BR, den Boer JA: The prediction of nonresponse to pharmacotherapy in panic disorder: A review. *Depress Anxiety* 2001; 14:112–122.

[39] Weismann MM, Bland RC, Canino GJ, Greenwald S, Hwu H, Lee CK, Newman SC, Oakley-Browne MA, Rubio-Stipec M, Wickramaratne PJ, Wittchen HU, Eng-kung Y: The cross national epidemiology of obsessive compulsive disorder. *J Clin Psychiatry* 1994; 55(suppl. 3):5–10.

[40] Horwath E, Weissman MM: Anxiety disorders: Epidemiology. In: BJ Sadock, VA Sadock (editors): *Kaplan and Sadock's Comprehensive Textbook of Psychiatry.* Vol. 1, 7th edition, Philadelphia, Lippincott, Williams & Wilkins, 2000, p 448.

[41] Rezaki MS, Ozgen G, Kaplan I, Gürsoy BM, Sağduyu A, Oztürk OM: Results from the Ankara Center. In: TB Ustun, N Sartorius (editors): *Mental Illness in General Health Care.* West Sussex, John Wiley & Sons, 1995, pp 39–56.

[42] Markowitz JS, Weissman MM, Ouellette R, Lish JD, Klerman GL: Quality of life in panic disorder. *Arch Gen Psychiatry* 1989; 46:984–992.

[43] Ross HE, Glasser FB, Germanson T: The prevalence of psychiatric disorders in patients with alcohol and other drug problems. *Arch Gen Psych* 1988; 45:1023–1031.

[44] Reich J, Chaudry D: Personality of panic disorder alcohol abusers. *J Nerv Ment Disease* 1987; 175:224–228.

[45] Otto MW, Pollack MK, Sachs GS, O'Neil CA, Rosenbaum JF: Alcohol disorder in panic disorder patients. *J Psychiatr Res* 1992; 26:29–38.

[46] Myrick DH, Brady KT: Social phobia in cocaine-dependent individuals. *Am J Addict* 1996; 6:99–104.

[47] Milby JB, Sims MK, Khuder S, Schumacher JE, Huggins N, McLellan AT, Woody G, Haas N: Psychiatric comorbidity: Prevalence in methadone maintenance treatment. *Am J Drug Alcohol Abuse* 1996; 22:95–107.

[48] Rosen MI, Kosten T: Cocaine-associated panic attacks in methadone maintained patients. *Am J Drug Alcohol Abuse* 1992; 18:57–62.

[49] Cox DJ, Ballenger JC, Laraia M, Hobbs WR, Peterson GA, Hucek A: Different rates of improvement of different symptoms in combined pharmacological and behavioural treatment of agoraphobia. *J Behav Ther Exp Psychiatry* 1988; 19:119–126.

[50] Rounsaville BJ, Anton SF, Carroll K, Budde D, Prusoff BA, Gawin F: Psychiatric diagnoses of treatment-seeking cocaine abusers. *Arch Gen Psychiatry* 1991; 48:43–51.

[51] Brooner RK, King VL, Kidorf M, Schmidt CW Jr, Bigelow GE: Psychiatric and substance use comorbidity among treatment-seeking opioid abusers. *Arch Gen Psychiatry* 1997; 54:71–80.

[52] Chen C, Tsai S, Su L, Yang T, Tsai C, Hwu H: Psychiatric co-morbidity among male heroin addicts: differences between hospital and incarcerated subjects in Taiwan. *Addiction* 1999; 94:825–832.

[53] Matthew L, Hiller ML, Knight K, Simpson DD: Prison based substance abuse treatment, residential aftercare and recidivism. *Addiction* 1999; 94:833–842.

[54] Moran C: Depersonalisation and agoraphobia associated with marijuana use. *Br J Med Psychol* 1986; 59:187–196.

[55] Aronson TA, Craig TJ: Cocaine precipitation of panic disorder. *Am J Psychiatry* 1986; 143:643–645.

[56] Louie AK, Lannon RA, Ketter TA: Treatment of cocaine-induced panic disorder. *Am J Psychiatry* 1989; 146:40–44.

[57] Price WA, Giannini AJ: Phencyclidine and "crack" precipitated panic disorder. *Am J Psychiatry* 1987; 144:686–687.

[58] Lydiard RB, Brawman-Mintzer O, Ballenger JC: Recent developments in the psychopharmacology of anxiety disorders. *J Consult Clin Psychol* 1996; 64:660–668.

[59] den Boer JA: Pharmacotherapy of panic disorder: Differential efficacy from a clinical viewpoint. *J Clin Psychiatry* 1998; 59(suppl. 8):30–36.

[60] Brady KT, Verduin ML: Pharmacotherapy of comorbid mood, anxiety, and substance use disorders. *Subst Use Misuse* 2005; 40:2021–2041, 2043–2048.

[61] den Boer JA, Slaap BR: Review of current treatment in panic disorder. *Int Clin Psychopharmacol* 1998; 13(suppl. 4):25–30.

[62] Gorelick DA: Serotonin uptake blockers and the treatment of alcoholism. *Recent Dev Alcohol* 1989; 7:262–281.

[63] Pettinati HM, Volpicelli JR, Kranzler HR, Luck G, Rukstalis MR, Cnaan A: Sertraline treatment for alcohol dependence: Interactive effects of medication and alcoholic subtype. *Alcohol Clin Exp Res* 2000; 24:1041–1049.

[64] Posternak MA, Mueller TI: Assessing the risks and benefits of benzodiazepines for anxiety disorders in patients with a history of substance abuse or dependence. *Am J Addict* 2001; 10:48–68.

[65] Malcolm R, Anton RF, Randall CL, Johnston A, Brady K, Thevos A: A placebo controlled trial of buspirone in anxious inpatients alcoholics. *Alcohol Clin Exp Res* 1992; 16:1007–1013.

[66] Post RM: Cocaine psychoses: A continuum model. *Am J Psychiatry* 1975; 132:225–231.

[67] Barlow DH. *Anxiety and its disorders: The nature and treatment of anxiety and panic.* New York, Guilford Press, 1988.

[68] Barlow DH, Lehman CL: Advances in the psychosocial treatment of anxiety disorders: Implications for national health care. *Arch Gen Psychiatry* 1996; 53:727–735.

[69] Jansson L, Ost LG: Behavioural treatments for agoraphobia: An evaluative review. *Clin Psychol Rev* 1982; 2:311–336.

[70] Bowen RC, D'Arcy C, Keegan D, Senthilselvan A: A controlled trial of cognitive behavioral treatment of panic in alcoholic inpatients with comorbid panic disorder. *Addict Behav* 2000; 25:593–597.

[71] Kessler RC, McGonagle KA, Zhao S, Nelson CB, Hughes M, Eshleman S, Wittchen H-U, Kendler KS: Lifetime and 12-month prevalence of DSM-III-R psychiatric disorders in the United States: Results from the National Comorbidity Survey. *Arch Gen Psychiatry* 1994; 51:8–19.

[72] Schneir, FR, Johnson J, Horning CD, Liebowitz MR, Weisman MM: Social phobia: Comorbidity and morbidity in an epidemiologic sample. *Arch Gen Psychiatry* 1992; 49:282–288.

[73] Quitkin FM, Rifkin A, Kaplan J, Klein DF: Phobic anxiety syndrome complicated by drug dependence and addiction. *Arch Gen Psychiatry* 1972; 27:159–162.

[74] Mullaney JA, Trippett CJ: Alcohol dependence and phobias: Clinical description and relevance. *Br J Psychiatry* 1979; 135:565–573.

[75] Evren EC, Can S, Evren B, Cakmak D: Yatarak tedavi gören erkek alkol bağımlılarında aleksitiminin depresyon, anksiyete ve erektil işlev bozukluğu ile ilişkisi: *Bir kontrollü çalışma*. [The relationship between alexithymia and depression, anxiety and erectile dysfunction in a sample of male alcoholic inpatients: A controlled study.] Klinik Psikofarmakoloji Bülteni 2002; 12:165–73. (Turkish)

[76] Magee WJ, Eaton WW, Wittchen HU, McGonagle KA, Kessler RC: Agoraphobia, simple phobia, and social phobia in the National Comorbidity Survey. Arch Gen Psychiatry 1996; 53:159–168.

[77] Lepine JP, Pelissolo A: Comorbidity of social phobia: Clinical and epidemiological issues. *Int Clin Psychopharmacol* 1996; 11(suppl. 3):35–41.

[78] Rieger DA, Rae DS, Narrow WE, Kealber CT, Schatzberg AF: Prevalence of anxiety disorders and their comorbidity with mood and addictive disorders. *Br J Psychiatry Suppl* 1998; 34:24–28.

[79] Page RM: Shyness as a risk factor for adolescent substance use. *J Sch Health* 1989; 59:432–435.

[80] Evren C, Barut T, Saatcioglu O, Cakmak D: Axis I psychiatric comorbidity among adult inhalant dependents seeking treatment. *J Psychoactive Drugs* 2006; 38:57–64.

[81] Evren EC, Er FO, Erkıran M, Çakmak D: Tedavi arayışında olan eroin bağımlılarında i. Eksen psikiyatrik komorbidite: *Sosyodemografik ve madde kullanım özellikleri ile ilişkisi* [Axis I psychiatric co-morbidity among treatment-seeking heroin dependents: its relation with socio-demographic and substance use properties]. Klinik Psikiyatri 2002; 5:92–104. (Turkish)

[82] Kushner MG, Sher KJ, Erickson DJ: Prospective analysis of the relation between DSM-III anxiety disorders and alcohol use disorders. *Am J Psychiatry* 1999; 156:723–732.

[83] Bradlyn AS, Strickler DP, Maxwell WA: Alcohol expectancy and stress: Methodological concerns with the expectancy design. *Addict Behav* 1981; 6:1–8.

[84] O'Hare TM: Alcohol expectancies and social anxiety in male and female undergraduates. *Addict Behav* 1990; 15:561–566.

[85] Stockwell T, Smail P, Hodgson R: Alcohol dependence and phobic anxiety states. II. A retrospective study. *Br J Psychiatry* 1984; 144:58–63.

[86] Mannuzza S, Schneier FR, Chapman TF, Liebowitz MR, Klein DF, Fyer AJ: Generalized social phobia: Reliability and validity. *Arch Gen Psychiatry* 1995; 52:230–237.

[87] Morgenstern J, Langenbucher J, Labouvie E, Miller KJ: The comorbidity of alcoholism and personality disorders in a clinical population: Prevalence rates and relation to alcohol typology. *J Abnorm Psychol* 1997; 106:74–84.

[88] Stravynski A, Lamontagne Y, Lavallée YJ: Clinical phobias and avoidant personality disorder among alcoholics admitted to an alcoholism rehabilitation setting. *Can J Psychiatry* 1986; 31:714–719.

[89] Crum R, Pratt LA: Risk of heavy drinking and alcohol use disorders in social phobia: A prospective analysis. *Am J Psychiatry* 2001; 158:1693–1700.

[90] Naftolowitz DF, Vaughn BV, Ranc J, Tancer ME: Response to alcohol in social phobia. *Anxiety* 1994; 1:96–99.

[91] Himle JA, Abelson JL, Haghightgou H, Hill EM, Nesse RM, Curtis GC: Effect of alcohol on social phobic anxiety. *Am J Psychiatry* 1999; 156:1237–1243.

[92] Allen JP, Litten RZ, Fertig JB: NIDA-NIAAA workshop: Efficacy of therapies in drug and alcohol addiction: Strategies for treatment of alcohol problems. *Psychopharmacol Bull* 1995; 31:665–669.

[93] Stockwell T, Hodgson R, Rankin H: Tension reduction and the effects of prolonged alcohol consumption. *Br J Addict* 1982; 77:65–73.

[94] Munjack KJ, Moss HB: Affective disorder and alcoholism in families of agoraphobics. *Arch Gen Psychiatry* 1981; 38:869–871.

[95] Cudrin JM: Social phobia and agoraphobia in alcoholism. *Am J Psychiatry* 1991; 148:1096. (letter)

[96] Wittchen HU, Stein MB, Kesler RC: Social fears and phobia in a community sample of adolescents and young adults: Prevalence, risk factors and co-morbidity. *Psychol Med* 1999; 29:309–23.

[97] Sonntag H, Wittchen HU, Höfler M, Kessler RC, Stein MB: Are social fears and DSM-IV social anxiety disorders associated with smoking and nicotine dependence in adolescents and young adults? *Eur Psychiatry* 2000; 15:67–74.

[98] Breslau N, Kilbey M, Andreski P: DSM-III-R nicotine dependence in young adults: Prevalence, correlates and associated psychiatric disorders. *Addiction* 1994; 89:743–754.

[99] Breslau N: Psychiatric comorbidity of smoking and nicotine dependence. *Behav Gen* 1995; 25:95–101.

[100] Lepine JP, Pelissolo A: Social phobia and alcoholism: A complex relationship. *Affective Disorders* 1998; 50:532–528.

[101] Myrick H, Brady KT: The use of divalproex in the treatment of addictive disorders. *Psychopharmacol Bull* 2003; 37(suppl. 2):89–97.

[102] Thevos AK, Johnston AL, Latham PK, Randall CL, Adinoff B, Malcolm R: Symptoms of anxiety in inpatient alcoholics with and without DSM-III-R anxiety diagnoses. *Alcohol Clin Exp Res* 1991; 15:102–151.

[103] Heimberg RG, Dodge CS, Hope DA, Kennedy CR, Zollo LJ, Becker RE: Cognitive-behavioural group treatment of social phobia: Comparison to a credible placebo control. *Cognit Ther Res* 1990; 14:1–23.

[104] Heimberg RG, Salzman DG, Holt DC, Blendell KA: Cognitive-behavioural group treatment for social phobia. *Cognit Ther Res* 1993; 4:325–339.

[105] Randall CL, Thomas S, Thevos AK: Concurrent alcoholism and social anxiety disorder: A first step toward developing effective treatments. *Alcohol Clin Exp Res* 2001; 25:210–220.

[106] Schade A, Marquenie LA, van Balkom AJ, Koeter MW, de Beurs E, van den Brink W, van Dyck R: The effectiveness of anxiety treatment on alcohol-dependent patients with a comorbid phobic disorder: A randomized controlled trial. *Alcohol Clin Exp Res* 2005; 29:794–800.

[107] Lydiard RB, Falsetti SA: Treatment options for social phobia. *Psychiatr Ann* 1995; 25:570–576.

[108] Pande AC, Davidson JR, Jefferson JW, Janney CA, Katzelnick DJ, Weisler RH, Greist JH: Sutherland SM: Treatment of social phobia with gabapentin: A placebo controlled study. *J Clin Psychopharmacol* 1999; 19:341–348.

[109] Randall CL, Johnson MR, Thevos AK, Sone SC, Thomas SE, Willard SL, Brady KT, Davidson JR: Paroxetine for social anxiety and alcohol use in dual-diagnosed patients. *Depress Anxiety* 2001; 14:255–462.

[110] Kasvikis YG, Tsakiris F, Marks IM: Past history of anorexia nervosa in women with obsessive-compulsive disorder. *Int J Eat Disorders* 1986; 5:1069–1075.

[111] Rasmussen SA, Tsuang MT: Clinical characteristics and family history in DSM-III obsessive-compulsive disorder. *Am J Psychiatry* 1986; 143(3):317–322.

[112] Eisen JE, Rasmussen SA: Coexisting obsessive compulsive disorder and alcoholism. *J Clin Psychiatry* 1989; 50:96–98.

[113] Kushner MG, Abrams K, Borchardt C: The relationship between anxiety disorders and alcohol use disorders: A review of major perspectives and findings. *Clin Psychol Rev* 2000; 20:149–171.

[114] Crum RM, Anthony JC: Cocaine use and other suspected risk factors for obsessive-compulsive disorder: A prospective study with data from the Epidemiologic Catchment Area surveys. *Drug Alcohol Depend* 1993; 31:281–295.

[115] Brady KT, Lydiard RB, Malcolm R, Ballenger JC: Cocaine-induced psychosis. *J Clin Psychiatry* 1991; 52:509–512.

[116] Senjo M: Obsessive-compulsive disorder in people that abuse codeine. Acta Psychiatr Scand 1989; 79:619–620.

[117] Leonard HL, Rapoport JL: Relief of obsessive-compulsive symptoms by LSD and psilocybin. *Am J Psychiatry* 1987; 144:1239–1240.

[118] Myrick H, Brady KT, Malcolm R: New developments in the pharmacotherapy of alcohol dependence. *Am J Addict* 2001; 10(suppl.):3–15.

[119] Fals-Stewart W, Marks AP, Schafer J: A comparison of behavioural group therapy and individual behavioural therapy in treating obsessive-compulsive disorder. *J Nerv Ment Dis* 1993; 181:189–193.

[120] van Oppen P, Arntz A: Cognitive therapy for obsessive-compulsive disorder. *Behav Res Ther* 1994; 32:79–87.

[121] Breslau N: Outcomes of PTSD. *J Clin Psychiatry* 2001; 62(suppl. 17):55–59.

[122] Gabbard GO: Anxiety disorders: Psychodynamic aspects. In: BJ Sadock, VA Sadock (editors): *Kaplan and Sadock's Comprehensive Textbook of Psychiatry,* Vol. 1, 7th edition, Philadelphia, Lippincott, Williams & Wilkins, 2000, pp 1472–1473.

[123] Jacobsen LK, Southwick SM, Kosten TR: Substance use disorders in patients with posttraumatic stress disorder: A review of the literature. *Am J Psychiatry 2001*; 158:1184–1190.

[124] Kessler RC, Sonnega A, Bromet E, Hughes M, Nelson CB, Breslau N: Epidemiological risk factors for trauma and PTSD. *Arch Gen Psych* 1995; 52:1048–1060.

[125] Green BL, Lindy JD, Grace MC, Gleser GC: Multiple diagnosis in PTSD: The role of war stressors. *J Nerv Ment Dis* 1989; 177:329–335.

[126] Helzer JE, Robins LN, McEvoy L: PTSD in the general population: Findings from the ECA survey. *New England J Medicine* 1987; 317:1630–1634.

[127] Cottler LB, Compton WM III, Mager D, Spitznagel EL, Janca A: PTSD among substance abusers from the general population. *Am J Psychiatry* 1992; 149:664–670.

[128] Brady KT, Cathleen T, Killeen Terese K, Brewerton T, Lucerini S: Comorbidity of psychiatric disorders and PTSD. *J Clinical Psychiatry* 2000; 61(suppl. 7):22–32.

[129] Keane TM, Gerardi RJ, Lyons JA, Wolfe J: The interrelationship of substance abuse and PTSD. In: M Galauter (editor): *Epidemiological and clinical considerations: Recent developments in alcoholism.* New York, Plemen, 1988, pp 27–48.

[130] McFall ME, Mackay PW, Donovan DM: Combat-related PTSD and psychosocial adjustment problems among substance abusing veterans. *J Nerv Ment Dis* 1991; 179:33–38.

[131] Kovach J: Incest as a treatment issue for alcoholic women. *Alcohol Treat Quarterly* 1986; 3:1–15.

[132] Kilpatrick DG, Resnick HS: PTSD associated with exposure to criminal victimisation in clinical and community populations. In: JRT Davidson, EB Foa (editors): *PTSD: DSM-IV and beyond.* Washington DC, American Psychiatric Press, 1992, pp 113–143.

[133] Brady KT, Killeen T, Saladin ME, Dansky B, Becker S: Comorbid substance abuse and PTSD: Characteristics of women in treatment. *Am J Addict* 1994; 3:160–164.

[134] Grice DE, Brady KT, Dustan LR, Malcolm R, Kilpatrick DG: Comorbidity of PTSD and substance abuse. *145th APA (American Psychiatric Association) Meeting,* Washington DC, 1992; p 245.

[135] Triffleman EG, Marmar CR, Delucchi KL, Ronfeldt H: Childhood trauma and posttraumatic stress disorder in substance abuse inpatients. *J Nerv Ment Dis 1995;* 183:172–176.

[136] Saladin ME, Brady KT, Dansky BS, Kilpatrick DG: Understanding comorbidity between PTSD and substance use disorders: Two preliminary investigations. *Addict Behav* 1995; 20:643–655.

[137] Evren C, Can S, Evren B, Saatcioglu O, Cakmak D: Lifetime posttraumatic stress disorder in Turkish alcohol-dependent inpatients: Relationship with depression, anxiety and erectile dysfunction. *Psychiatry Clin Neurosci* 2006; 60:77–84.

[138] Berk E, Black J, Locastro J, Wickis J, Simpson T, Penk W: Traumatogenicity: Effects of self-reported noncombat trauma on MMPIs of male Vietnam combat and noncombat veterans treated for substance abuse. *J Clin Psychol* 1989; 45:704–708.

[139] Najavits LM: Clinicians' views on treating posttraumatic stress disorder and substance use disorder. *J Subst Abuse Treat* 2002; 22:79–85.

[140] Breslau N, Davis GC, Andreski P, Peterson E: Traumatic events and PTSD in an urban population of young adults. *Arch Gen Psych* 1991; 48:216–222.
[141] Chilcoat HD, Breslau N: Investigations of causal pathways between PTSD and drug use disorders. *Addict Behav* 1998; 23:827–840.
[142] Shaham Y, Funk D, Erb S, Brown TJ, Walker CD, Stewart J: Corticotropin releasing factor, but not corticosterone, is involved in stress-induced relapse to heroin-seeking in rats. *J Neuroscience* 1997; 17:2605–2614.
[143] Davidson J: Drug therapy of posttraumatic stress disorder. *Br J Psychiatry* 1992; 160:309–314.
[144] Davidson JR, Rothbaum BO, van der Kolk BA, Sikes CR, Farfel GM: Multicenter, double-blind comparison of sertraline and placebo in the treatment of posttraumatic stress disorder. *Arch Gen Psychiatry* 2001; 58:485–492.
[145] van der Kolk BA, Dreyfuss D, Michaels M, Shera D, Berkowitz R, Fisler R, Saxe G: Fluoxetine in posttraumatic stress disorder. *J Clin Psychiatry* 1994; 55:517–522.
[146] Brady KT, Sonne SC, Roberts JM: Sertraline treatment of comorbid posttraumatic stress disorder and alcohol dependence. *J Clin Psychiatry* 1995; 56:502–505.
[147] Brady KT, Dansky BS, Back SE, Foa EB, Carroll KM: Exposure therapy in the treatment of PTSD among cocaine-dependent individuals: Preliminary findings. *J Subst Abuse Treat* 2001; 21:47–54.
[148] Schäfer I, Najavits LM: Clinical challenges in the treatment of patients with posttraumatic stress disorder and substance abuse. *Curr Opin Psychiatry* 2007; 20:614–618.
[149] Thayer JH, Friedman BF, Borcovec TD: Autonomic characteristics of generalised anxiety disorder and worry. *Biol Psychiatry* 1996; 39:255–266.
[150] Goldberg DP, Lecrubier Y: Form and frequency of mental disorders across centers. In: TB Üstün, N Sartorius (editors): Mental Illness in General Health Care: *An International Study*. New York, John Wiley & Sons, 1995, pp 323–334.
[151] Blazer DG, Hughes D, George LK, Swartz M, Boyer R: Generalized anxiety disorder. In: LN Robins, DA Regier (editors): Psychiatric Disorders in America: *The Epidemiologic Catchment Area Study*. New York, The Free Press, 1991, pp 180–203.
[152] Jaffe JH: Substance related disorder: Introduction and overview. In: BJ Sadock, VA Sadock (editors): *Kaplan and Sadock's Comprehensive Textbook of Psychiatry*. Vol. 1, 7th edition, Philadelphia, Lippincott, Williams & Wilkins, 2000, pp 924–952.
[153] Vesga-López O, Schneier FR, Wang S, Heimberg RG, Liu SM, Hasin DS, Blanco C: Gender differences in generalized anxiety disorder: Results from the National Epidemiologic Survey on Alcohol and Related Conditions (NESARC). *J Clin Psychiatry* 2008; 69:1606–1616.
[154] Yonkers KA, Dyck IR, Warshaw M, Keller MB: Factors predicting the clinical course of generalized anxiety disorders. *Br J Psychiatry* 2000; 176:545–550.
[155] Yonkers KA, Warshaw MG, Massion AO, Keller MB: Phenomenology and course of generalized anxiety disorder. *Br J Psychiatry* 1996; 168:308–313.
[156] Fisher EH, Goethe JW: Anxiety and alcohol abuse in patients in treatment for depression. *Am J Drug Alcohol Abuse* 1998; 24:453–463.
[157] Orhan S: Genelleşmiş anksiyete bozukluğu: Alkol bağımlılığı eş tanısı olan ve olmayan olguların karşılaştırılması, *Uzmanlık Tezi*. [Comparison of comorbidity of generalized

anxiety disorder with and without alcohol dependents. Thesis.] **Bakırköy Ruh Sinir Hastalıkları Eğitim ve Araştırma Hastanesi, Istanbul, 2001.** (Turkish)

[158] Massion AO, Warshaw MG, Keller MB: Quality of life and psychiatric morbidity in panic disorder and generalized anxiety disorder. *Am J Psychiatry* 1993; 150:600–607.

[159] Howell HB, Brawman-Mintzer O, Monnier J, Yonkers KA: Generalized anxiety disorder in women. *Psych Clin North Am* 2001; 24:165–176.

[160] Jetty VP, Charney SD, Goddard AW: Neurobiology of generalized anxiety disorder. *Psych Clin North Am* 2001; 24:75–92.

[161] Sher KJ: Street response dampening in psychological theories of drinking and alcoholism. In: HT Blane, KE Leonard (editors): *Psychological theories of drinking and alcoholism.* New York, Guilford Press, 1987, pp 227–271.

[162] Chambless DL, Cherney J, Caputo GC: Anxiety disorders and alcoholism: A study with inpatient alcoholics. *J Anxiety Disord* 1987; 18:29–40.

[163] Kranzler HR, Burleson JA, Del Boca FK, Babor TF, Korner P, Brown J, Bohn M: Buspirone treatment of anxious alcoholics: A placebo controlled trial. *Arch Gen Psychiatry* 1994; 51:720–731.

[164] McRae AL, Sonne SC, Brady KT, Durkalski V, Palesch Y: A randomized, placebo-controlled trial of buspirone for the treatment of anxiety in opioid-dependent individuals. *Am J Addict* 2004; 13:53–63.

[165] Butler G, Fennel M, Robson P, Gelder M: Comparison of behaviour therapy and cognitive behaviour therapy in the treatment of generalised anxiety disorder. *J Consult Clin Psychol* 1991; 59:167–175.

[166] Blowers C, Cobb J, Mathews A: Generalized anxiety: A controlled treatment study. *Behav Res Ther* 1987; 25:493–502.

In: Suicidal Behavior in Alcohol and Drug Abuse... ISBN: 978-1-60876-919-3
Editors: L. Sher, A. Vilens, pp. 83-99

Chapter 6

CO-OCCURRENCE OF SUBSTANCE USE DISORDERS WITH ANXIETY DISORDERS: EPIDEMIOLOGY, PSYCHOBIOLOGY, CLINICAL FEATURES, AND TREATMENT

A. Ender Altintoprak, Sebnem Pirildar and Ozlem Kuman
Ege University School of Medicine, Izmir, Turkey

ABSTRACT

Symptoms of anxiety and anxiety disorders commonly co-occur with substance use disorders (SUDs). The interaction between these disorders is bidirectional: anxiety disorders may contribute to the development of SUDs and modify the presentation and the outcomes of treatment for SUDs; on the other hand, SUDs may modify the manifestation of anxiety disorders. Anxiety symptoms are also accompanied with intoxication or withdrawal symptoms. Studies in clinical samples and community surveys have demonstrated high rates of co-occurrence of anxiety disorders with alcohol and drug use disorders. In National Epidemiologic Survey on Alcohol and Related Conditions, 17.71% of respondents with any 12 month substance use disorder had at least one independent anxiety disorder and 14.96% of respondents with any 12-month anxiety disorder had at least one substance use disorder, during the same 12-month period. Despite the high prevalence rates, anxiety disorders are frequently under-diagnosed in substance abuse settings. However, it is clinically important while the outcome for each type of disorder is worse across clinical and psychosocial domains than for the disorders without comorbidity. Integrated treatment strategies including medications and psychosocial treatment perspectives are needed for co-occurring anxiety and substance disorders to improve outcome.

INTRODUCTION

Comorbidity is the rule than the exception with substance use disorders as the other mental disorders. Identifying mechanisms involved in the development of this mutuality is an important public health concern, whereas comorbidity is associated with considerable disability, poor quality of life, inadequate treatment and generating social costs. People with dual diagnosis are non-compliant with medication, and more likely to experience psychosocial problems, suicidal behavior, rehospitalisation, higher family burden and relapsing risk [1,2,3].

Three epidemiological surveys are crucial about the prevalence of anxiety and SUD comorbidity: the National Epidemiological Survey on Alcohol and Related Conditions (NESARC) [4], the National Institute of Mental Health Epidemiologic Catchment Area (ECA) Study [5] and the National Comorbidity Study (NCS) [6]. The most recent and largest epidemiological survey, NESARC (n=43093 response rate=81%) pointed out that the 12-month prevalence of independent anxiety, any substance, any alcohol, and any drug use disorders are 11.08%, 9.35%, 8.46%, and 2.00%, respectively. 17.71% of respondents with any substance use disorder had at least one independent anxiety disorder during the same 12-month period [4]. A study using NESARC data indicated the prevalence of anxiety disorder in the drug-only group as 24%, in the drug and alcohol group as 26.5% and in the alcohol-only group as 15.6% [7]. Grant and colleges using the same data reported that among the respondents with anxiety disorder in the past 12-month, 14.96% had at least one SUD. Respondents with panic disorder with agoraphobia and generalized anxiety disorder were more likely than those with other anxiety disorders to have a substance use disorder. All the independent anxiety disorders were consistently more strongly related to alcohol and drug dependence than to drug abuse; besides, the relationship between anxiety disorders and drug use disorders (OR 2.8) was stronger than the relationship between anxiety and alcohol use disorders (OR 1.7) [4]. Marijuana use disorders were the most common drug use disorder among individuals with anxiety disorders (15.1%), followed by cocaine (5.4%), amphetamine (4.8%), hallucinogen (3.7%), and sedative (2.6%) use disorder [8].

In the ECA survey, the anxiety disorder group had about 50% increase in the odds of being diagnosed with an alcohol disorder (OR=1.52) and 70% increase in the odds of being diagnosed with any substance use disorder (OR=1.7), as compared to the rest of the sample [5].

Assessment of data from two independent community survey; NCS (n=5877, response rate= 82.4%) and the Ontario Health Survey - Mental Health Supplement (OHS; n=8116, response rate=67.4%), showed a significant association between any anxiety disorder diagnosis and lifetime stimulant, cocaine and hallucinogen use [9]. In both surveys, approximately one-third of individuals with lifetime use of stimulants, cocaine or hallucinogens had at least one lifetime anxiety disorder diagnosis. A stronger association was found between an anxiety disorder with heroin use (OR =3.0) than the association of an anxiety disorder with stimulant, cocaine or hallucinogen use (OR =2.0).

RELATIONSHIP BETWEEN ANXIETY AND ALCOHOL AND SUBSTANCE USE DISORDERS

A review of studies, examining alcohol use disorders and anxiety disorders, concluded that anxiety disorders and alcohol use disorders appear to influence each other, whereas having either an anxiety disorder or a substance use disorder may increase the risk of developing another disorder [10]. A recent study about the mutual relationship between two disorders indicated that anxiety disorders do precede the onset of alcohol dependence [11]. Several investigators have also proposed that anxiety sensitivity may be an important mediating factor for the susceptibility of drug-taking behavior [12]. Moreover, anxiety sensitivity is associated with poor coping skills that may result in an increased propensity to use drugs or alcohol [13].

Comorbid mental and substance use disorders may occur coincidentally and successively. Coincidental comorbidity occurs when two or more disorders are present at the same time. Successive comorbidity occurs when disorders occur at different times in a person's life and they may or may not causally relate to each other [14]. Although prevalence of comorbid substance use and anxiety disorders is well established, the causal mechanism underlying this relationship is less in agreement. Some investigators propose that anxiety disorders may lead to substance dependence through a process of self-medication to avoid symptoms of anxiety disorder [15,16]. Three possible explanations are proposed to clarify the co-occurrence of these disorders [17]:

1) Some investigators have suggested that substance use disorders directly induce anxiety and other mental disorders or, vice versa, the anxiety disorder may lead to substance dependence through a process of self-medication to avoid the symptoms of anxiety (direct causal model);
2) Presence of one disorder increases an individual's risk of developing the second disorder (indirect causal model);
3) The other possibility is that comorbidity between substance use and anxiety disorders may arise from common causes which may be a manifestation of a shared genetic, neurobiological or social predisposing. Common factors may expose an individual to risk for developing both disorders. A common diathesis with a shared vulnerability factor, explain mutual relationship.

The first model comprises self-medication hypothesis explicated that individuals having a primary anxiety disorder develop SUD in order to avoid distressing symptoms of anxiety. Self-medication is not a diagnosable SUD; substances are used to reduce anxiety or the other symptoms of mental disorder, but ineffective to treat the disorder and it is common in male [16,18]. Previous prevalence rate estimates for self-medication among anxiety disorders have generally come from clinical samples. Such samples may produce a selection bias, while prevalence rates increase [16]. Results from the NCS indicated lower prevalence rates for self-medication [15].

Motivational models of alcohol use propose that individuals are motivated to drink alcohol in order to reach a particular goal. Drinking motives are principal reasons underlying alcohol use and are believed to serve as the final "common pathway" through which secondary factors (depression and anxiety) carry out their influence [19]. Cooper proposed four classes of drinking motives: 1) enhancement ("because you like the feeling") 2) social ("because it makes social gatherings more enjoyable") 3) coping ("to forget about worries") 4) conformity ("to fit with a group you like"). The negative reinforcement motives of coping and conformity are associated with utilizing alcohol to avoid negative consequences such as negative affect or social censure and criticism. The positive reinforcement motives of enhancement and social entail using alcohol to increase positive affect. This model suggests that drinking for negatively reinforcing motives may mediate the relationship between anxiety disorders and problematic drinking and helps to explain the comorbidity [20]. Although alcohol improves mood in short term as a form of self-medication, it often turns out badly in the long term and produces dependence.

Comorbidity of Alcohol and Substance Use Disorders with Anxiety Disorders and Attachment Theory

Many persons with alcohol use-related problems also experience problems in establishing healthy interpersonal relationships [21,22] and in regulating their emotions [23]. Attachment theory [24] might be involved in the psychophysiology of alcohol and substance addiction and especially on comorbidity with other psychiatric problems such as anxiety, depression, and personality disorders. In a recent study, individuals with alcohol use disorders (AUDs) demonstrated an impaired attachment system manifesting itself in the incapacity to develop secure interpersonal relationships and problems with affect regulation [25]. This study also proved that the more impaired an alcoholic inpatient's attachment system and the more severe the trait anxiety and the depressive symptoms. It is also suggested that the disruption of the attachment system exists before the alcohol use problem, which can be defined as a developmental disturbance and might be helpful to understand the comorbidity of SUDs and anxiety.

Rewarding and Anxiolytic Effects of Alcohol

People commonly like to drink alcohol or use substance due to emotion altering effects. Alcohol induces euphoria, relaxation, disinhibition; reduces stress and anxiety and produces rewarding and anxiolytic effect [26,27]. Although alcohol and substance use have these well-known effects, the effect of alcohol on human brain circuits involved in reward, emotion and anxiety, has rarely been explored.

Alcohol might have a strengthening effect in the circuitry which regulates positive affect. Although a variety of non-imaging human studies have attempted to experimentally alter emotional states while administering alcohol, these studies have not demonstrated a specific anxiolytic interaction. Ventral striatum is a critical area which is recruited by reward-predictive stimuli [28]. Primary, as well as secondary rewards and drugs of abuse activate also this circuit [29]. PET studies indicated that striatal glucose metabolism is increased in response to alcohol [30,31]. Consequently, mesolimbic reward circuit has an important role in the development and maintenance of addiction.

The amygdala is critical for the requirement of an immediate behavioral response, such as fight or flight [32]. In a recent study, Gilman and colleagues (2008) reported that alcohol mediated anxiolysis may result from disruption of threat detection circuitry [33]. The increase of risk-taking behavior by alcohol intake might be related to disrupting the amygdala-mediated differentiation between threatening and non-threatening stimuli, whereas it may increase approach and decrease avoidance and facilitate social interaction. Visual and limbic brain regions are sensitive to the effects of alcohol and alcohol may attenuate the increased sensitivity of the visual and limbic areas to emotionally threatening stimuli which could account for the anxiolytic effect of alcohol. The reinforcing effects of alcohol most likely involve multiple neurotransmitter systems including dopaminergic, opioidergic, glutamatergic, GABAergic and serotonergic systems which are also included in the etiopathogenesis of anxiety disorders [33,34].

Obsessive Compulsive Disorder and Substance Use Disorders

Obsessive compulsive symptoms have been commonly reported among alcohol dependent patients [35]; on the other hand, in the National Comorbidity Survey Replication Study, Obsessive Compulsive Disorder (OCD) was found to be negatively correlated with alcohol use disorders [36]. In other studies, the prevalence of OCD among treatment seeking alcoholics ranges between 2.7-12% [37]. Clinical studies, comparing prevalence of smoking in OCD with that in anxiety disorders [38] and all psychiatric disorders [39] reported lower prevalence for OCD. Noteworthy, nicotine administration decreases some form of compulsive behaviors and obsessive thoughts [38]. By using ECA study results, the risk of developing OCD was estimated to be 5.6 times higher for individuals using both cocaine and marijuana, compared to individuals using no illicit substances [40].

The development of the obsessive compulsive drinking scale [41] indicates the existence of mutual relationship of OCD and substance use disorders. Understanding comorbidity appears especially relevant to OCD because there is evidence that certain substances (e.g. cocaine or methamphetamine) may exacerbate OCD symptoms while others (e.g. opiates) may alleviate OCD symptoms [42,43].

The symptoms of OCD often go undetected in patients with SUDs whereas only half of the patients seek treatment for their OCD symptoms [44]. In a recent study it is demonstrated that alcohol use disorders comorbid with OCD has specific clinical features and deserve special attention especially because of increased risk for suicide [45]. Furthermore juvenile onset of OCD and comorbidity with borderline personality disorder demonstrated increased risk for substance use disorders [46]. A comprehensive assessment of lifetime history of substance use is necessary, while patients with comorbid diagnosis require treatment for a longer duration and additional interventions.

Social Anxiety Disorder and Substance Use Disorders

Most research on anxiety disorders and SUDs comorbidity has focused on social phobia and panic disorder. In NCS, approximately 25% of individuals with alcohol dependence in the community met criteria for social anxiety disorder (SAD) and the risk for women was higher for both conditions than men, rates were 30.3% and 19.3% respectively [6]. Almost 20% of individuals with SAD met criteria for an alcohol use disorder and the lifetime prevalence of an AUD with SAD (48%) found to be much higher than the prevalence of AUD without lifetime SAD. In both NCS and NESARC, SAD was found more likely to be associated with increased risk of alcohol dependence than alcohol abuse [6,47]. NCS indicated that, there is a 4.2% lifetime prevalence rate for cannabis dependence in the general population and among individuals with SAD, the prevalence rate of cannabis dependence is elevated to 29.0%, which is more than twice that of any other anxiety disorder [48]. SAD was found to be associated with increased rates of cannabis dependence, but not abuse [48]. Consistent with the self- medication hypothesis, in most of the studies SAD preceded the onset of SUDs [49]. With regard to age of onset of two disorders, it is reported that social anxiety disorder serves as a risk factor for subsequent alcohol and substance use disorder [50,51]. A longitudinal cohort study of approximately 14 years, reported that, among the anxiety disorders, SAD appears to be unique as a risk factor for subsequent cannabis and alcohol dependence, but not abuse [52].

For nicotine, some studies have failed to demonstrate a relationship [53]; on the other hand, some showed an association [54,55]. One study showed that the association with nicotine dependence is also significant among those with social fears and subtreshold expressions of SAD [54]. In NESARC, lifetime prevalence of SAD was found to be 13%, 21%, 10% in individuals with opioid use disorder, dependence and abuse respectively, all higher than general population [8]. Myrick and Brady (1997) found lifetime prevalence of SAD in a cocaine dependent population to be 13.9%, with SAD preceding the onset of cocaine dependence, in nearly all cases [56].

Although little is known about the specificity of the relationship between SAD and SUDs, comorbid conditions are related with a more severe impairment [51]. Alcohol and substance use disorders in patients with social anxiety might be related to co-occurring mood pathology [57] whereas the individuals may believe that they need these substances to cope with negative affective states related to social anxiety. Consequently, adaptive coping strategies cannot be ameliorated and they are getting ever more addicted to substances to regulate affective states. It is reported that using alcohol in order to regulate emotions is associated with the dependence symptoms [52,58,59].

In a recent study it is suggested that dissociation and social anxiety are interrelated among alcohol-dependent men and demonstrated that the relationship between dissociation and social anxiety may have implications for prevention and treatment of alcohol dependency at least in a subgroup of alcohol-dependent men [60].

PANIC DISORDER-GENERALIZED ANXIETY DISORDER AND SUBSTANCE USE DISORDER

Research has suggested that having a history of panic attacks is a good indicator of having other psychiatric disorders, including posttraumatic stress disorder (PTSD), depression, attention deficit, substance abuse, as well as other mental health disorders [61]. In NESARC, among the anxiety disorders, panic disorder (PD) with agoraphobia was most strongly associated with SUDs (ORs, 1.9-10.5) [4]. 1.46% and 2.86% of the respondents with any SUD had PD with and without agoraphobia, respectively during the same 12-month period; while, among all respondents, the prevalence of PD with and without agoraphobia was 0.56% and 1.58% respectively. The risk of a comorbid SUD in patients with PD found to be 2.4 times higher than that in the general population, in the ECA study [5]. In a recent review of the literature published from 1960 to 2006, the risk of PD in presence of alcohol use disorder was found to be 2-4 times higher than in the absence of alcohol use disorder [62]. In NESARC study, individuals with PD had elevated 12 month prevalence rates of nicotine dependence [63].

In NESARC, generalized anxiety disorder (GAD) was more strongly related to dependence than abuse for alcohol and drug disorders, with strongest associations for drug dependence [64]. Higher rates of smoking have been observed among individuals with GAD [63]. The lifetime prevalence of GAD among individuals with opioid use disorder, opioid dependence, opioid abuse was 11%, 24% and 10%; whereas it was 4.1% among all respondents [8].

Although some research indicated that panic and social phobia are predictors of subsequent alcohol problems among adolescents and young adults [65] some other reports that patients with GAD and PD are less likely to use alcohol and substances as self-medication whereas illicit substances can precipitate physiological arousal sensations that cause intense fear in individuals with panic disorder. Intense worries about health and illness of individuals with GAD could also be a protective factor for these patients and may decrease alcohol and substance use disorders [59,66] whereas patients with PD might avoid cannabis owing to anxiogenic effects [67].

Contrary to these reports, higher prevalence rates of self-medication with drugs and alcohol in individuals with PD has also been proposed [16], self-medication was perceived as an effective coping strategy among patients with PD with agoraphobia. Among individuals with co-occurring PD or GAD and SUDs, the age of onset of PD and GAD is later than onset of SUDs [9,68,69]. Furthermore, some illicit drugs may trigger panic attacks. Cannabis dependence is reported as a risk factor for the development of panic [68]. Cocaine may also be responsible for the onset of panic and self-medication behavior might develop subsequently [70].

Posttraumatic Stress Disorder and Substance Use Disorders

For the prevalence of PTSD in SUD group there are different results; Peirce and colleagues (2008) [71] pointed out that PTSD occurs in community-based substance using individuals at rates (8%) similar to the rate found in non-substance-using samples [72,73]; but have much higher rates in treatment-seeking samples ranging between 25% and 43% [74,75,76].

In SUD populations, rates of 30–58% for lifetime PTSD and 20–38% for current PTSD have been reported by the studies made in USA and UK [77,78,79].

In NCS, individuals with PTSD were 2-4 times more likely to have a SUD than the individuals without PTSD [73]. Using the data from ECA study, Cottler and colleagues (1992) found that female cocaine/opiate users were most likely to report a PTSD-qualifying traumatic event (43%) [80].

There are some studies reporting high rates of childhood sexual abuse (54–90%), childhood physical abuse (42–50%) in SUD patients, and sexual assault (33–70%) in male and female AUD patients [81,82]. Over two-thirds of people seeking treatment for SUD have one or more traumatic life events [74,75,76]. It should be considered that symptoms of PTSD and unprocessed feelings about the past trauma could be masked by substance use and might exacerbate with continued abstinence. [83]. While abstinence from the substance does not mean resolving of the PTSD symptoms patients should be addressed to treatment for PTSD [84-85].

More recently, a series of studies have reported conflicting evidence about the relationship between alcohol use and PTSD, whereas potential mechanisms could explain this link between alcohol use and symptom development. As mentioned above, the first mechanism could be self-medication. Consistent with the self-medication hypothesis, individuals with PTSD reported significantly greater use of substances in response to negative situations such as unpleasant emotions and physical discomfort as compared to individuals without PTSD [86]. On the other hand, alcohol use at the time of the trauma may have a protective pharmacological effect. Alcohol enervates noradrenergic activation in the amygdala and locus coeruleus [87] and ordinate the fear conditioning. It has been hypothesized that alcohol may provide some protective function by modulating the neurobiological systems in the immediate and aftermath of the trauma, thereby reducing the likelihood of subsequent PTSD. Accordingly, it is important to consider both alcohol use prior to, at the time of the traumatic event, and in the aftermath, whereas moderate consumption might have a protective role against the development of posttraumatic anxiety, depression and PTSD symptoms [88].

TREATMENT OF ANXIETY DISORDERS WITH CONCURRENT SUBSTANCE USE DISORDERS

While patients with comorbid diagnosis suffer relapses and recurrences, the treatment warrants special attention. Although psychiatric disorders and SUDs can have devastating personal and social effects, limited practice guideline currently exists. Failure to treat a concurrent psychiatric disorder reduces the efficacy of treatment for SUD. The untreated comorbid diagnosis is directly associated with a shorter time to relapse [3]. Hence, integrated treatment for co-occurring anxiety and substance use disorders may include medications and psychosocial treatment perspectives. Pharmacotherapy and cognitive behavioral therapies (CBTs) for specific anxiety disorders can be combined with the usual treatments for SUDs [85]. Providing education about the anxiety and substance use disorders and about the effects the disorders have on each other, is also important [85]. It is important to pay attention to potential toxic interactions between the prescribed and illicit drugs and alcohol in case of relapse. It is also important to use the agent with the least abuse potential [89].

The beginning stage of treatment is the acute phase (6-12 weeks) which is marked by initiation of treatment until achieving remission. Subsequent maintenance phase (4-9 months) is characterized by perpetuating the acute phase treatment at the same dosage. Anxiety and depressive symptoms are common in alcohol and substance dependent patients which may be related to acute intoxication or substance withdrawal and consequently, alleviate in time. According to APA guideline, at least 3 weeks of permission is essential to decide using pharmacological treatment [90]. The presence of severe anxiety symptoms, the history of an affective or anxiety disorder or a family history indicates the need of earlier treatment. The compliance of the patient is essential to start with pharmacotherapy due to intoxication, drug-drug interactions and unwanted synergy, drug seeking behavior, overdose and abuse potential of medications. Multiple agents including antidepressants (SSRI, TCA, SNRI), benzodiazepines, anticonvulsants, have proved in the treatment of anxiety disorders [91,92]. The SSRIs, escitalopram, fluoxetine, paroxetine and sertralinc as well as SNRIs duloxetine and venlafaxine are indicated for specific anxiety disorders such as GAD, panic disorder, social phobia, and obsessive compulsive disorder [91,93]. Adverse effects of prescribed drugs such as seizure risk of bupropion during alcohol withdrawal syndrome should be considered [89] Mirtazapine -noradrenergic and specific serotonergic antidepressant (NaSSA) agent- has been suggested to be effective in the treatment of anxiety disorders (including post-traumatic stress disorder, panic disorder and social anxiety disorder, obsessive-compulsive disorder) [94]; it is also effective and well tolerated in abstinent patients with alcohol dependence [95]. Thus, it could be a suitable agent for comorbid patients. Desipramine was used to treat patients with PD that developed during or shortly after cocaine exposure and found to have a good effect [96]. The patients with cocaine–induced PD had substantial symptom improvement after treatment with carbamazepine or clonazepam also [97]. The medication with benzodiazepines should be limited to acute episode due to safety, toxicity, abuse liability and patients with SUDs should be closely monitored during benzodiazepine medication [85]. Buspirone appears to be an alternative attractive medication to traditional benzodiazepines due to its low addictive potential and lack of lethality [98]. One of two studies of buspirone in alcoholics with GAD found significant improvement [99,100].

It is very important to take into consideration that risk of relapse is high in the patients with SUDs. APA guideline and NICE guideline recommend a combination of psychosocial interventions (motivational enhancement therapy, CBT, 12-step programs, psychodynamic therapy/interpersonal therapy, self-help manuals, behavioral self-control, brief interventions, case management, and group, family and marital therapies) to improve outcome [85,90,101].

Patients with comorbid SUDs and anxiety disorder require long-term care in regard to preventing relapse and recurrence [3].

Conclusion

SUDs are commonly comorbid with other mental disorders. The relation between anxiety symptoms and SUDs is complex. Untreated co-occurring psychiatric and substance use disorders cause significant poor health, disability, poor quality of life, inadequate treatment and generating social costs. Comorbid disorders have always bidirectional relationship and require close follow-up. While relapse and recurrence are more common among individuals with comorbid psychiatric diagnosis, long-term follow up is also very important. Comorbidity has important implications for treatment. For example, in persons for whom alcohol dependence is a cause of depression, treatment of alcohol disorder may alleviate symptoms of depression. If, however, a person's alcohol dependence is the result of self-medicating depression, in that case, the treatment of depression is important for a good outcome. Treatment of comorbid anxiety disorder in the acute phase requires careful and comprehensive consideration.

References

[1] Drake RE, Mueser KT, Clark RE, Wallach MA: The course, treatment, and outcome of substance disorder in persons with severe mental illness. *Am J Orthopsychiatry* 1996; 66:42-51.

[2] Ormel J, Petukhova M, Chatterji S, Guilar-Gaxiola S, Alonso J, Angermeyer MC, Bromet EJ, Burger H, Demytenaere K, de Haro GG, Hwang JM, Kararm E, Kawakami N, Lepine JP, Medina-Mora ME, Posada-Villa J, Sampson N, Scott K, Ustun TB, Von KM, Williams DR, Zhang M, Kessler RC: Disability and treatment of specific mental and psychiatric disorders across the world. *Br J Psychiatry* 2008:368-375.

[3] Kushner MG, Abrams K, Thuras P, Hanson KL, Brekke M, Sletten S: Follow-up study of anxiety disorder and alcohol dependence in comorbid alcoholism treatment patients. *Alcohol Clin Exp Res* 2005; 29:1432-1443.

[4] Grant BF, Stinson FS, Dawson DA, Chou SP, Dufour MC, Compton W, Pickering RP, Kaplan K: Prevalence and co-occurrence of substance use disorders and independent mood and anxiety disorders: results from the National Epidemiologic Survey on Alcohol and Related Conditions. *Arch Gen Psychiatry.* 2004; 61:807-816.

[5] Regier DA, Farmer ME, Rae DS, Locke BZ, Keith SJ, Judd LL, Goodwin FK: Comorbidity of mental disorders with alcohol and other drug abuse. Results from the Epidemiologic Catchment Area (ECA) Study. *JAMA.* 1990; 264:2511-2518.

[6] Kessler RC, Crum RM, Warner LA, Nelson CB, Schulenberg J, Anthony JC: Lifetime co-occurrence of DSM-III-R alcohol abuse and dependence with other psychiatric disorders in the National Comorbidity Survey. *Arch Gen Psychiatry.* 1997; 54:313-321.

[7] Stinson FS, Grant BF, Dawson DA, Ruan WJ, Huang B, Saha T: Comorbidity between DSM-IV alcohol and specific drug use disorders in the United States: Results from the National Epidemiologic Survey on Alcohol and Related Conditions. *Drug Alcohol Depend.* 2005; 80:105-16.

[8] Conway KP, Compton W, Stinson FS, Grant BF: Lifetime comorbidity of DSM-IV mood and anxiety disorders and specific drug use disorders: results from the National Epidemiologic Survey on Alcohol and Related Conditions. *J Clin Psychiatry* 2006; 67:247-257.

[9] Sareen J, Chartier M, Paulus MP, Stein MB: Illicit drug use and anxiety disorders: findings from two community surveys. *Psychiatry Res.* 2006; 142:11-7.

[10] Kushner MG, Abrams K, Borchardt C: The relationship between anxiety disorders and alcohol use disorders: a review of major perspectives and findings. *Clin Psychol Rev.* 2000; 20:149-171.

[11] Marquenie LA, Schadé A, van Balkom AJ, Comijs HC, de Graaf R, Vollebergh W, van Dyck R, van den Brink W: Origin of the comorbidity of anxiety disorders and alcohol dependence: findings of a general population study. *Eur Eddict Res.* 2007; 13:39-49.

[12] Stewart SH, Kushner MG: Introduction to the special issue on "Anxiety Sensitivity and Addictive Behaviors". Addict Behav. 2001; 26:775-785.

[13] Kushner MG, Thuras P, Abrams K, Brekke M, Stritar L: Anxiety mediates the association between anxiety sensitivity and coping-related drinking motives in alcoholism treatment patients. *Addict Behav.* 2001; 26:869-885.

[14] Hall W, Degenhardt L, Teesson M: Understanding comorbidity between substance use, anxiety and affective disorders: Broadening the research base. *Addict Behav.* 2009; 34:526-530.

[15] Bolton J, Cox B, Clara I, Sareen J: Use of alcohol and drugs to self-medicate anxiety disorders in a nationally representative sample. *J Nerv Ment Dis.* 2006; 194:818-25.

[16] Robinson J, Sareen J, Cox BJ, Bolton J: Self-medication of anxiety disorders with alcohol and drugs: Results from a nationally representative sample. *J of Anxiety Disord.* 2009; 23: 38-45.

[17] Kraemer HC, Stice E, Kazdin A, Offord D, Kupfer D: How do risk factors work together? Mediators, moderators, and independent, overlapping, and proxy risk factors. *Am J Psychiatry.* 2001; 158:848-856.

[18] Bolton JM, Robinson J, Sareen J: Self-medication of mood disorders with alcohol and drugs in the National Epidemiologic Survey on Alcohol and Related Conditions. *J Affect Disord.* 2009; 115: 367-375.

[19] Cooper ML: Motivations for alcohol use among adolescents: Development and validation of a four-factor model. *Psychological Assessment* 1994; 6:117-128.

[20] Cooper ML, Frone MR, Russell M, Mudar P: Drinking to regulate positive and negative emotions: A motivational model of alcohol use. *J Pers Soc Psychol.* 1995; 69:990-1005.

[21] Dumbrava AN: The attachment style as a possible determinant of the addictive behaviour in alcoholism. *International Journal of Psychology* 2000; 35:357.

[22] Flores PJ (2001) Addiction as an attachment disorder: implications for group therapy. *Int J Group Psychother* 51:63–81.

[23] Evren C, Sar V, Dalbudak E, Oncu F, Cakmak D: Social anxiety and dissociation among male patients with alcohol dependency. *Psychiatry Res.* 2009; 165:273-80.

[24] Fonagy P, Leigh T, Steele M et al (1996) The relation of attachment status, psychiatric classification and response to psychotherapy. *J Consult Clin Psychol* 64:22–31

[25] De Rick A, Vanheule S, Verhaeghe P: Alcohol addiction and the attachment system: an empirical study of attachment style, alexithymia, and psychiatric disorders in alcoholic inpatients. *Subst Use Misuse* 2009; 44:99-114.

[26] Blanchard RJ, Magee L, Veniegas R, Blanchard DC: Alcohol and anxiety: ethopharmacological approaches. *Prog Neuropsychopharmacol Biol Psychiatry.* 1993; 17:171-182.

[27] Da Silva GE, Vendruscolo LF, Takahashi RN: Effects of ethanol on locomotor and anxiety-like behaviors and the acquisition of ethanol intake in Lewis and spontaneously hypertensive rats. *Life Sci. 2005*; 77:693-706

[28] Bjork JM, Knutson B, Fong GW, Caggiano DM, Bennett SM, Hommer DW: Incentive-elicited brain activation in adolescents: similarities and differences from young adults: *J Neurosci* 2004; 24:1793-1802.

[29] Knutson B, Cooper JC: Functional magnetic resonance imaging of reward prediction. *Curr Opin Neurol.* 2005; 18:411-417.

[30] Schreckenberger M, Amberg R, Scheurich A, Lochmann M, Tichy W, Klega A, Siessmeier T, Grunder G, Buchholz HG, Landvogt C, Stauss J, Mann K, Bartenstein P, Urban R: Acute alcohol effects on neuronal and attentional processing: striatal reward system and inhibitory sensory interactions under acute ethanol challenge. *Neuropsychopharmacology* 2004; 29:1527-1537.

[31] Boileau I, Assad JM, Pihl RO, Benkelfat C, Leyton M, Diksic M, Tremblay RE, Dagher A: Alcohol promotes dopamine release in the human nucleus accumbens. *Synapse* 2003; 49:226-231

[32] LeDeux J: The emotional brain, fear, and the amygdala: *Cell Mol Neurobiol* 2003; 23:727-738.

[33] Gilman JM, Ramchandani VA, Davis MB, Bjork JM, Hommer DW: Why we like to drink: a functional magnetic resonance imaging study of the rewarding and anxiolytic effects of alcohol. *J Neurosci.* 2008; 28:4583-4591.

[34] Pierce RC, Kumaresan V: The mesolimbic dopamine system: the final common pathway for the reinforcing effect of drugs of abuse? *Neurosci Biobehav Rev* 2006; 30:215-238.

[35] Lima AF, Pechansky F, Fleck MP, De Boni R: Association between psychiatric symptoms and severity of alcohol dependence in a sample of Brazilian men. *J Nerv Ment Dis.* 2005; 193:126-130.

[36] Kessler RC, Chiu WT, Demler O, Merikangas KR, Walters EE: Prevalence, severity, and comorbidity of 12-month DSM-IV disorders in the National Comorbidity Survey Replication. *Arch Gen Psychiatry.* 2005; 62:617-627.

[37] Kushner MG, Sher KJ, Beitmen BD: The relation between alcohol problems and the anxiety disorder. *Am J Psychiatry* 1990; 147:685-695

[38] Morissette SB, Tull MT, Gulliver SB, Kamholz BW, Zimering RT: Anxiety, anxiety disorders, tobacco use, and nicotine: a critical review of interrelationships. *Psychol Bull.* 2007; 133:245-272.
[39] Bejerot S, Humble M: Low prevalence of smoking among patients with obsessive-compulsive disorder. *Compr Psychiatry.* 1999; 40:268-272.
[40] Crum RM, Anthony JC: Cocaine use and other suspected risk factors for obsessive-compulsive disorder: a prospective study with data from the Epidemiologic Catchment Area surveys. *Drug Alcohol Depend.* 1993; 31:281-295.
[41] Anton RF, Moak DH, Latham PK: The obsessive compulsive drinking scale: a new method of assessing outcome in alcoholism treatment studies. *Arch Gen Psychiatry* 1996; 53:225-231.
[42] Satel SL, McDougle CJ. Obsessions and compulsions associated with cocaine abuse. *Am J Psychiatry.* 1991; 148:947.
[43] Koran LM, Aboujaoude E, Bullock KD, Franz B, Gamel N, Elliott M: Double-blind treatment with oral morphine in treatment-resistant obsessive compulsive disorder. *J Clin Psychiatry.* 2005; 66:353-359.
[44] Mayerovitch JI, du Fort GG, Kakuma R, Bland RC, Newman SC, Pinard G: Treatment seeking for obsessive-compulsive disorder: role of obsessive compulsive disorder symptoms and comorbid psychiatric diagnoses. *Compr Psychiatry.* 2003; 44:162-168.
[45] Gentil AF, de Mathis MA, Torresan RC, Diniz JB, Alvarenga P, do Rosário MC, Cordioli AV, Torres AR, Miguel EC: Alcohol use disorders in patients with obsessive-compulsive disorder: The importance of appropriate dual diagnosis. *Drug Alcohol Depend* 2009; 100:173-177.
[46] Mancebo MC, Grant JE, Pinto A, Eisen JL, Rasmussen SA: Substance use disorders in an obsessive compulsive disorder clinical sample. *J Anxiety Disord.* 2009; 23:429-435.
[47] Grant BF, Hasin DS, Blanco C, Stinson FS, Chou SP, Goldstein RB, Dawson DA, Smith S, Saha TD, Huang B: The epidemiology of social anxiety disorder in the United States: Results from the National Epidemiologic Survey on Alcohol and Related Conditions. *J Clin Psychiatry* 2005; 66:1351-1361.
[48] Agosti V, Nunes E, Levin F: Rates of psychiatric comorbidity among U.S. residents with lifetime cannabis dependence. *Am J Drug Alcohol Abuse.* 2002; 28:643-652.
[49] Brady KT, Verduin ML. Pharmacotherapy of comorbid mood, anxiety, and substance use disorders. *Subst Use Misuse.* 2005; 40:2021-2041.
[50] Randall CL, Thomas S, Thevos AK: Concurrent alcoholism and social anxiety disorder: a first step toward developing effective treatments. *Alcohol Clin Exp Res.* 2001; 25:210-220
[51] Schneier FR, Martin LY, Liebowitz MR, Gorman JM, Fyer Aj: Alcohol abuse in social phobia. *J Anxiety Disord.*1989; 3:15–23
[52] Buckner JD, Schmidt NB, Lang AR, Small JW, Schlauch RC, Lewinsohn PM: Specifity of social anxiety disorder as a risk factor for alcohol and cannabis dependence. *J Psychiatr Res.* 2008; 42:230-239.
[53] Johnson JG, Cohen P, Pine DS, Klein DF, Kasen S, Brook JS: Association between cigarette smoking and anxiety disorders during adolescence and early adulthood. *JAMA.* 2000; 284:2348-2351.

[54] Sonntag H, Wittchen HU, Höfler M, Kessler RC, Stein MB: Are social fears and DSM-IV social anxiety disorder associated with smoking and nicotine dependence in adolescents and young adults? *Eur Psychiatry.* 2000; 15:67-74.

[55] Wittchen HU, Stein MB, Kessler RC: Social fears and social phobia in a community sample of adolescents and young adults: prevalence, risk factors and comorbidity. *Psychol Med* 1999; 29:309-23.

[56] Myrick H, Brady KT: Social phobia in cocaine-dependent individuals. *Am J Addict.* 1997; 6:99-104.

[57] King SM, Lacono WG, McGue M: Childhood externalizing and internalizing psychopthology in the prediction of early substance use. *Addiction* 2004; 99:1548-1559.

[58] Buckner JD, Eggleston AM, Schmidt NB: Social anxiety and problematic alcohol consumption: the mediating role of drinking motives and situations. *Behav Ther.* 2006; 37:381-391.

[59] Buckner JD, Schmidt NB: Understanding social anxiety as a risk for alcohol use disorders: fear of scrutiny, not social interaction fears, prospectively predicts alcohol use disorders *J Psychiatr Res.* 2009; 43:477-483.

[60] Evren C, Evren B, Dalbudak E, Ozcelik B, Oncu F: Childhood abuse and neglect as a risk factor for alexithymia in adult male substance dependent inpatients. *J Psychoactive Drugs* 2009; 41:85-92.

[61] Reed V, Wittchen HU: DSM-IV panic attacks and panic disorder in a community sample of adolescents and young adults: how specific are panic attacks? *J Psychiatr Res.* 1998; 32:335-345.

[62] Cosci F, Schruers KR, Abrams K, Griez EJ: Alcohol use disorders and panic disorder: a review of the evidence of a direct relationship. *J Clin Psychiatry.* 2007; 68:874-880.

[63] Grant BF, Hasin DS, Chou SP, Stinson FS, Dawson DA: Nicotine Dependence and Psychiatric Disorders in the United States: Results From the National Epidemiologic Survey on Alcohol and Related Conditions. *Arch Gen Psychiatry.* 2004; 61:1107-1115.

[64] Grant BF, Hasin DS, Stinson FS, Dawson DA, June Ruan W, Goldstein RB, Smith SM, Saha TD, Huang B: Prevalence, correlates, co-morbidity, and comparative disability of DSM-IV generalized anxiety disorder in the USA: results from the National Epidemiologic Survey on Alcohol and Related Conditions. *Psychol. Med.* 2005; 35:1747-1759.

[65] Zimmermann P, Wittchen HU, Höfler M, Pfister H, Kessler RC, Lieb R: Primary anxiety disorders and the development of subsequent alcohol use disorders: a 4-year community study of adolescents and young adults. *Psychol Med.* 2003; 33:1211-1222.

[66] Craske MG, Rapee RM, Jackel L, Barlow DH: Qualitative dimensions of worry in DSM-III-R generalized anxiety disorder subjects and nonanxious controls. *Behav Ther.* 1989; 27:397-402.

[67] Szuster RR, Pontius EB, Campos PE: Marijuana sensitivity and panic anxiety. *J Clin Psychiatry.* 1988; 49:427-429.

[68] Zvolensky MJ, Bernstein A, Sachs-Ericsson N, Schmidt NB, Buckner JD, Bonn-Miller MO: Lifetime associations between cannabis, use, abuse, and dependence and panic attacks in a representative sample. *J Psychiatr Res.* 2006; 40:477-486.

[69] Kessler RC, Andrade LH, Bijl RV, Offord DR, Demler OV, Stein DJ: The effects of co-morbidity on the onset and persistence of generalized anxiety disorder in the ICPE

surveys. International Consortium in Psychiatric Epidemiology Psychological Medicine. *Psychol Med.* 2002; 32:1213-1225.

[70] Katerndahl DA, Realini JP: Relationship between substance abuse and panic attacks. *Addict Behav.* 1999; 24:731-736.

[71] Peirce JM, Kindbom KA, Waesche MC, Yuscavage AS, Brooner RK: Posttraumatic stress disorder, gender, and problem profiles in substance dependent patients. *Subst Use Misuse.* 2008; 43:596-611.

[72] Cottler LB, Nishith P, Compton WM: Gender differences in risk factors for trauma exposure and post-traumatic stress disorder among inner-city drug abusers in and out of treatment. *Compr Psychiatry.* 2001; 42:111-117.

[73] Kessler RC, Sonnega A, Bromet E, Hughes M, Nelson CB: Post-traumatic stress disorder in the national co-morbidity survey. *Arch. Gen. Psychiatry.* 1995; 52, 1048–1060.

[74] Back S, Dansky BS, Coffey SF, Saladin ME, Sonne S, Brady KT: Cocaine dependence with and without post-traumatic stress disorder: a comparison of substance use, trauma history and psychiatric comorbidity. *Am J Addict.* 2000; 9:51-62.

[75] Clark HW, Masson CL, Delucchi KL, Hall SM, Sees KL: Violent traumatic events and drug abuse severity. *J Subst Abuse Treat.* 2001; 20:121-127.

[76] Wasserman DA, Havassy BE, Boles SM: Traumatic events and post-traumatic stress disorder in cocaine users entering private treatment. *Drug Alcohol Depend.* 1997; 46:1-8.

[77] Triffelman EG, Marmar CR, Delucchi KL, Ronfeldt H: Childhood trauma and post-traumatic stress disorder in substance abuse inpatients. *J. Nerv. Ment. Dis.*1995; 183: 172–176.

[78] Najavits LM., Gastfriend DR., Barber J., Reif S, Muenz LR, Blaine J, Frank A, Crits-Christoph P, Thase M, Weiss RD: Cocaine dependence with and without PTSD among subjects in the National Institute on Drug Abuse Collaborative Cocaine Treatment Study. *Am. J. Psychiatr.* 1998; 155,214–219.

[79] Reynolds M, Mezey G, Chapman M, Wheeler M, Drummond C, Baldacchino A: Co-morbid post-traumatic stress disorder in a substance misusing clinical population. *Drug Alcohol Depend.* 2005; 77:251-258.

[80] Cottler LB, Compton WM 3rd, Mager D, Spitznagel EL, Janca A: Posttraumatic stress disorder among substance users from the general population. *Am J Psychiatry.* 1992; 149:664-670.

[81] Porter S: Assault experiences among drug users. *Subst Misuse Bull.* 1995; 8:1-2.

[82] Moncrieff J, Drummond DC, Candy B, Chesinski K, Farmer R: Sexual abuse in people with alcohol problems: a study of the prevalence of sexual abuse and its relationship to drinking behaviour. *Br J Psychiatr.* 1996; 169:355-360

[83] Najavits LM: Clinicians' views on treating posttraumatic stress disorder and substance use disorder. *J Subst Abuse Treat.* 2002; 22:79-85.

[84] Kofoed L, Friedman MJ, Peck R. Alcoholism and drug abuse in patients with PTSD. *Psychiatr Q.* 1993; 64:151-171.

[85] Kleber HD, Weiss RD, Anton RF Jr, George TP, Greenfield SF, Kosten TR, O'Brien CP, Rounsaville BJ, Strain EC, Ziedonis DM, Hennessy G, Connery HS, McIntyre JS, Charles SC, Anzia DJ, Cook IA, Finnerty MT, Johnson BR, Nininger JE, Summergrad P, Woods SM, Yager J, Pyles R, Cross CD, Peele R, Shemo JP, Lurie L, Walker RD,

Barnovitz MA, Gray SH, Saxena S, Tonnu T, Kunkle R, Albert AB, Fochtmann LJ, Hart C, Regier D; Work Group on Substance Use Disorders; American Psychiatric Association; Steering Committee on Practice Guidelines Treatment of patients with substance use disorders, second edition. American Psychiatric Association. *Am J Psychiatry.* 2007; 164 (suppl 4):5-123.

[86] Waldrop AE, Back SE, Verduin ML, Brady KT: Triggers for cocaine and alcohol use in the presence and absence of posttraumatic stress disorder. *Addict Behav.* 2007; 32:634-639.

[87] Shirao I, Tsuda A, Ida Y, Tsujimaru S, Satoh H, Oguchi M, Tanaka M, Inanaga K: Effect of acute ethanol administration on noradrenaline metabolism in brain regions of stressed and nonstressed rats. *Pharmacol Biochem Behav.* 1988; 30:769-773.

[88] McFarlane AC, Browne D, Bryant RA, O'Donnell M, Silove D, Creamer M, Horsley K: A longitudinal analysis of alcohol consumption and the risk of posttraumatic symptoms. *J Affect Disord.* 2009; 19.

[89] Waldrop AE, Hartwell KJ, Bardy KT: Co-occuring Addiction and Anxiety disorders. In: *Principles of Addiction Medicine.* Fourth Edition. Edited by Ries RK, Fiellin DA, Miller SC, Saitz R. Philadelphia, Lippincott Williams&Wilkins, 2009, pp:1183-1192.

[90] American Psychiatric Association. *Practice Guideline for the treatment of patients with substance use disorders.* 2nd edition. New York, NY: American psychiatric Association; 2006.

[91] American Psychiatric Association. *Practice Guideline for the Treatment of Patients with Panic Disorder.* 2nd edition. New York, NY: American psychiatric Association; 2009.

[92] McIntosh A, Cohen A, Turnbull N, Esmonde L, Dennis P, Eatock J, Feetam C, Hague J, Hughes I, Kelly J, Kosky N, Lear G, Owens L, Ratcliffe J, Salkovskis P: *Clinical Guidelines and Evidence Review for Panic Disorder and Generalised Anxiety Disorder.* Sheffield: University of Sheffield/London: National Collaborating Centre for Primary Care; 2004.

[93] Brady KT: Evidence based pharmacotherapy for mood and anxiety disorders with concurrent alcoholism. *CNS Spectr* 2008; 13(suppl 6):7-9.

[94] Croom KF, Perry CM, Plosker GL: Mirtazapine: a review of its use in major depression and other psychiatric disorders. *CNS Drugs.* 2009; 23:427-452.

[95] Altintoprak AE, Zorlu N, Coskunol H, Akdeniz F, Kitapcioglu G: Effectiveness and tolerability of mirtazapine and amitriptyline in alcoholic patients with co-morbid depressive disorder: a randomized, double-blind study. *Hum Psychopharmacol.* 2008; 23:313-319.

[96] Bystritsky A, Ackerman DL, Pasnau RO: Low dose desipramine treatment of cocaine-related panic attacks. *J Nerv Ment Dis.* 1991; 179:755-758.

[97] Louie AK, Lannon RA, Rutzick EA, Browne D, Lewis TB, Jones R. Clinical features of cocaine-induced panic. *Biol Psychiatry.* 1996; 40:938-940.

[98] Khouzam HR, Emes R: The use of buspirone in primary care. *J Psychosoc Nurs Ment Health Serv.* 2002; 40:34-41.

[99] Malcolm R, Anton RF, Randall CL, Johnston A, Brady K, Thevos A: A placebo-controlled trial of buspirone in anxious inpatient alcoholics. *Alcohol Clin Exp Res.* 1992; 16:1007-1013.

[100] Tollefson GD, Montague-Clouse J, Lancaster SP: Buspirone in comorbid alcohol dependency and generalized anxiety disorders. *Drug Therapy* 1990; 20:35–50.

[101] Schatzberg AF: Achieving remission and favorable outcomes in patients with depression/anxiety and substance use disorders. *CNS Spectr.* 2008; 13(suppl 6):10-12.

In: Suicidal Behavior in Alcohol and Drug Abuse... ISBN: 978-1-60876-919-3
Editors: L. Sher, A. Vilens, pp. 101-115

Chapter 7

ALCOHOL DEPENDENCE AND PTSD COMORBIDITY

Małgorzata Dragan
University of Warsaw, Poland

ABSTRACT

Epidemiological and cinical studies that have been conducted for at least last twenty years usually report high rates of comorbidity between alcohol use disorders and posttraumatic stress disorder. Although this problem was recognized as important and potentially disturbing to treatment, the comorbidity of disorders is still underdiagnosed and actually rarely addressed during the treatment. This chapter includes a review of the literature on comorbidity of both disorders as well as their consequences. Theoretical models explaining this phenomenon, also on biological levels, were described. Moreover, an issue of increased risk of suicidal behaviors among individuals presenting symptoms of both comorbid disorders was discussed in the light of the available literature.

INTRODUCTION

Post-traumatic stress disorder (PTSD) is an anxiety disorder comprising a characteristic set of symptoms that may develop after exposure to an event involving actual or threatened serious injury or death, or a threat to the physical integrity of the self or others (criterion A) [1]. Such events are described as traumatic if they are experienced with fear, helplessness, or horror. Thus, exposure to potentially traumatic event constitutes a necessary, but not sufficient, factor in the etiology of disorder. The three groups of symptoms include reexperiencing the traumatic event (criterion B), avoidance of reminders of the trauma as well as emotional numbing (criterion C), and increased physiological arousal (criterion D). A PTSD diagnosis requires that symptoms be present for more than one month (criterion E) and that the disturbance cause clinically significant distress or impairment in important areas of functioning (criterion F).

PTSD is a disabling disorder and commonly follows a chronic course. It is also a relatively common psychiatric disorder. The National Comorbidity Survey (NCS) [2] data set estimated lifetime prevalence of PTSD to be 7.8% in the general adult population, with women twice as likely as men to have PTSD at some point in their lives (10% versus 5%, respectively). The most recent NCS Report [3] estimated lifetime prevalence of PTSD among adult Americans at 6.8%. Research also shows [4] that experiences of traumatic events are definitely not a random phenomena. Even up to 90 percent of the U.S. population might have experienced at least one trauma, most frequently such as assaultive violence (physical or sexual), natural disaster, car or motor vehicle accident, or other kinds of serious accidents. However, research has also shown that experiencing trauma does not necessarily lead to psychopathology. Many people are able to cope with traumatic experiences and do not suffer from prolonged consequences. Different risk factors were identified for development of the disorder, such as gender (female), type of trauma, preexisting disorders, childhood history of physical abuse. For example, a review of literature revealed that the experience of severe trauma of interpersonal origins (i.e. rape and sexual assault, child physical or sexual abuse or neglect) heighten the risk for PTSD in the majority of victims [4-5]. Research also show that rates of co-occurance of PTSD with other psychiatric disorders (particularly major depression) are so high that it can be stated that this is a rule rather than exeption.

RESEARCH ON PTSD AND ALCOHOL USE DISORDERS COMORBIDITY

Epidemiological and clinical research has documented high rates of comorbidity of PTSD with other psychiatric disorders [4]. The results show that substance use disorders are among dominant comorbid disorders with PTSD. In the beginning, research on PTSD and substance use disorders comorbidity was conducted mainly on combat veterans, particularly Vietnam veterans. The first observations of high comorbidity were then verified in empirical studies. In a widely known, large epidemiological study of Vietnam veterans [6] 73% of veterans who met the criteria for PTSD were also diagnosed with alcohol abuse or dependence. Rates of alcohol use disorders comorbidity in the group of combat veterans qualified for a PTSD diagnosis range from 64 to 85% [7].

Studies on the general population report also confirm high rates of comorbidity between PTSD and substance use disorders. Chilcoat and Menard [8] performed a detailed metaanalysis of available research. It is worth summarizing the data from the main epidemiological studies on PTSD and alcohol use disorders comorbidity. The Epidemiologic Catchment Area study [9] assessed the prevalence of PTSD among a sample of 2,943 participants. The lifetime prevalence of PTSD was estimated to be 1%. The relative risk of alcoholism among respondents (odds ratios) was 1.6 (1.9 for men and 2.8 for women). In the widely quoted the National Comorbidity Survey [2], based on a representative sample of 5,877 men and woman, the odds ratio for an alcohol disorder, among those with PTSD, was 2.06 for men and 2.48 for women. In the Early Adulthood Research Project [10] conducted on 384 adolescents, the odds ratio for lifetime alcohol dependence diagnosis was 4.25 for those with a lifetime PTSD diagnosis, in a comparison with those with no trauma exposure. The odds ratio estimate for lifetime alcohol dependence for those with trauma exposure alone, compared with those with no exposure, was 2.30. Odds ratio estimate for current alcohol dependence, comparing individuals with lifetime PTSD with those with no trauma exposure, was 3.23. Exposure to trauma in the past year was related to a twofold increase in odds of current alcohol dependence. The majority of respondents reported that PTSD onset was prior to the onset of alcohol dependence. In the National Survey of Adolescents [11], conducted on a national sample of 4,023 adolescents, alcohol use disorders were associated with PTSD and such adverse experiences as familial alcohol problems, physical and sexual assault history and witnessed violence. Despite the findings regarding the order of onset of comorbid disorders were not presented, the authors examined the onset of alcohol use in relation to victimization status. In a comparison of the average age of nonexperimental alcohol use, the difference in ages of onset for victimized and nonvictimized adolescents appeared to be statistically significant (14.4 versus 15.1, respectively).

The other types of studies are those conducted on clinical samples. Comorbidity of substance abuse may be tested among trauma or PTSD patients, or comorbidity of PTSD may be tested among treatment-seeking substance misusers. These studies are vulnerable to self-selection bias, because the presence of a comorbid disorder increase the likelihood that individual with another disorder will seek treatment [8]. Prevalence rates of comorbid PTSD in alcohol and other drugs misuse groups range from 30 to 58% for lifetime PTSD, and from 20 to 38% for current PTSD [12-15]. However, the majority of these studies are related to patients with polysubstance use disorders, for example cocaine and alcohol misusers. Polysubstance users or mixed groups of patients with different substance problems are included. Only a few studies were conducted on patients with alcohol use disorders only. They showed similarly high rates of comorbidity, although lower than for illicit drug abuse and dependence. For example, Clark and Jacob [16] found that 27% of an examined sample of 30 adolescents meeting DSM-III-R criteria for alcohol dependence were diagnosed with current PTSD. In the study conducted in Turkey [17], prevalence of lifetime (not current) PTSD was found to be 27% among 82 alcohol-dependent male inpatients who met DSM-IV criteria for alcohol dependence. Dragan and Lis-Turlejska [18] conducted the study on a bigger sample of alcohol dependent patients (N = 458). From this sample, 67% of patients reported having experienced at least one criterion A traumatic event, and 60% of them reported multiple traumas. Approximately 25% to even 41% of them met the criteria for current PTSD, depending on the diagnostic scale used. Interestingly, the only significant difference between the PTSD and non-PTSD groups was abuse / dependence of other psychoactive substances, even though only 12% of the whole sample reported comorbid misuse. However, patients reporting physical assaults committed by a non-stranger reported more frequent PTSD diagnosis, more extensive symptomatology, more conflicts with the law and more physical injuries due to drinking. Odds ratio of PTSD diagnosis among these patients, compared with those with no experiences of this type of trauma, was 2.4. These results suggest that physical assault may be specific type of trauma of particular importance among risk factors for alcohol use disorders.

Stewart in her extensive metaanalysis [19], including different types of studies, concluded that there is much empirical evidence attesting to an important relationship between exposure to traumatic events alone and increased alcohol misuse. Evidence shows that exposure to a wide variety of trauma frequently leads to the development of alcohol abuse. Moreover, the data suggest that trauma severity may be positively associated with the degree of abusive alcohol consumption. Thus, exposure to severe trauma may lead to the development of alcohol use disorders, abuse or dependence. However, it also appears that

PTSD may be more highly associated with alcohol misuse than exposure to trauma alone or even the severity of trauma exposure. Some of the latest research also confirms these conclusions [20, 21], but casual associations between trauma and both disorders are still being explored, suggesting more complex picture of this type of comorbidity.

Despite quite high rates of PTSD and alcohol use disorders comorbidity found in different types of studies, attention should also be paid to some studies that do not confirm suggested association between both disorders. For example, in the Australian National Survey of Mental Health and Well-Being [22] conducted on a large sample of 10,641 people, the prevalence rate of current PTSD for individuals who met the criteria for alcohol use disorders was only 5%. The highest rate (33%) was found in individuals with opioid use disorders. However, among those with PTSD, an alcohol use disorder was the most common substance use disorder (24%). Findings from a longitudinal epidemiologic study of young adults in Michigan (N = 899) [23] also did not confirm an association between exposure to trauma, PTSD and alcohol use disorders, even for women (the possibility that trauma exposure predicted an increased risk for alcohol misuse in women was only suggested in the retrospective data from this study). Such association was confirmed only in cases of other drug abuse or dependence and nicotine dependence.

Consequences of PTSD and Alcohol Use Disorders Comorbidity

The high incidence of comorbidity between PTSD and alcohol and other substance use disorders has implications for the treatment and management of patients. In general, complex cases that present comorbidity of psychiatric disorders are associated with poorer treatment prognosis than cases with the presence of symptoms of one disorder [24]. Thus, alcohol use disorders reduce the effectiveness of PTSD treatment and, vice versa, PTSD influences the treatment of alcohol use disorders. Research confirm that patients who suffer from comorbid PTSD and substance use disorders experience more severe levels of psychopathology, poorer general functioning and higher health care utilization in relation to patients with either PTSD or substance use disorder alone [22, 25]. However, findings from one of the studies [26] suggest that it is not PTSD per se, but the frequent co-occurrence of PTSD and other psychopathology that may largely account for the severity of substance use disorder in patients with comorbid disorders.

Studies show that patients with comorbid PTSD and substance use disorders are at high risk of dropping out of treatment early. For example, in the study including a sample of women with PTSD and mixed substance dependence (alcohol or other drugs, or both), more than 60% of the patients completed only one-fourth of the cognitive-behavioral treatment sessions [27]. Riggs, Rukstalis, Volpicelli, Kalmanson and Foa [28] examined the demographic and social adjustment characteristics of a sample seeking treatment for comorbid PTSD and alcohol dependence. Results indicated that compared to the PTSD alone and alcohol dependence alone samples, a greater percentage of the comorbid sample was unemployed, with low income and living without the support of a spouse or intimate partner. Further, participants in the comorbid sample were less likely than those with the PTSD alone to have received more than a high school education, although the comorbid and alcohol dependence samples were comparable on education level. Authors suggested that poor social adjustment may place comorbid patients at greater risk of premature termination of therapy, particularly when that treatment is focused on alleviating PTSD symptoms.

Some researchers pay attention to the specific situation of drinking women. For example, Simpson [29] investigated whether a history of childhood sexual abuse or current PTSD was associated with alcohol-related expectancies and recalled the effects of drinking reported by women in substance use treatment. The results indicate that women currently manifesting PTSD were more likely than those without PTSD to report greater alcohol-related expectancies of tension reduction and having experienced greater positive enhancement from drinking. Interesting results were found in the study that examined differences in substance abuse severity, trauma history, PTSD symptomatology and psychiatric comorbidity in the sample of treatment-seeking women (N= 74) with PTSD and either comorbid cocaine or alcohol dependence [30]. Women in the cocaine/PTSD group, compared with the alcohol/PTSD group, demonstrated greater occupational impairment, more legal problems, and greater social impairment. Rates of exposure to serious accidents, other situations involving serious injury, and other stressful life events were higher among the alcohol/PTSD group. Women from this group evidenced also higher rates of major depression and social phobia. Moreover, they scored higher on the avoidance, hyperarousal, and total posttraumatic symptoms subscale scores.

Expert guidelines recommend screening patients with substance use disorders for comorbid disorders [31]. Ouimette, Moss and Brown [32] postulate that patients with substance use disorders should be regularly assessed for traumatic stress experiences as well as PTSD, and if needed referred for concurrent treatment. However, some studies show that clinicians who treat patients with substance use disorders do not routinely assess them for PTSD. For example, Dansky, Roitzsch, Brady, and Saladin [33] have found that a research interview identified 40% more PTSD cases than did chart diagnosis in the case of patients assessed for a substance abuse treatment. In our research conducted on 458 alcohol dependent patients [18] no differences were found on posttraumatic symptoms in relation to the length of treatment, suggesting that the issue of traumatization is not or is rarely addressed during alcohol dependence therapy.

Models of Association between PTSD and Alcohol Use Disorders

At least three hypotheses had been proposed in the literature to explain high rates of PTSD and substance use disorders comorbidity. Similarly to the comorbidity of substance use and other psychiatric disorders, one model explaining this phenomenon does not exist. The relation between comorbid disorders is complex and influenced by other factors, many of which are still not been identified. For example, much research shows that the association between PTSD and alcoholism is influenced by gender. The association between disorders is particularly strong for women. The rates for comorbid PTSD and substance use disorders are higher for females than males [8, 19]. This association may be explained by the fact that the risk of PTSD development is generally higher for women or by the fact that women's increased risk for this type of comorbidity is related to their higher incidence of childhood sexual abuse. Females are much more likely to be sexually abused than males, and because the risk of developing PTSD after this type of trauma is very high, consequently the symptoms of PTSD are more common for female than male substance misusers.

The most popular hypothesis that explains high rates of comorbidity is a self-medication hypothesis [34]. It proposes that addiction to psychoactive substances results from their use to control or relieve symptoms of underlying psychiatric disorder. This hypothesis has been also applicated to alcohol use and PTSD. It is assumed that there is a functional relation between PTSD and alcohol use disorders and that PTSD causes alcohol abuse or dependence. Studies on the relation between alcohol consumption and emotional responses show that alcohol, among others, usually selectively reduces distress through producing attenuation of negative affect by enabling one to set aside worries [35]. Jacobsen, Southwick and Kosten [36] draw attention to patients reporting on PTSD symptoms improvement by central nervous system (CNS) depressants, such as alcohol, cannabis, opioids, and benzodiazepines. These substances are used particularly to manage of hyperarousal and intrusion symptoms [37]. Patients with PTSD report also that the onset and severity of substance abuse runs parallel to the onset and escalation of PTSD symptoms [38]. Moreover, it is suggested that the choice of substances of abuse (CNS depressants versus CNS stimulants) may stem from the particular constellation of PTSD symptoms that patients experience. For example, some investigations [39] show that PTSD patients with alcohol dependence exhibit significantly more arousal symptoms that do PTSD patients with cocaine dependence. Newer findings [37] suggest that self-medication is a conscious, controlled process in the initial stages of substance use disorder development. At later stages, more automatic processes, including cue reactivity, play crucial role in maintenance of disorders.

It is worth taking into consideration conclusions made by McFarlane [40] who have mentioned in his metaanalysis that PTSD can lead to an increase, but also to a decrease in alcohol consumption. Although in the large majority of comorbid cases in retrospective, and also prospective studies, PTSD develop before the substance use disorder [21], findings on the self-medication process through alcohol after trauma among PTSD afflicted individuals should be regarded as inconsistent. They suggest more complex relationship between exposure to trauma and both disorders. Also research examining temporal relationships between PTSD and, specifically, alcohol use disorders in comorbid cases, have generated contradictory findings [41-42]. However, some research even show that (moderate) alcohol consumption prior to and following the trauma predicted lower levels of subsequent psychological distress, suggesting self-medication in a subgroup of survivors [43].

According to the high-risk hypothesis [8, 44] substance use is a high-risk behavior that increases individuals' risk of exposure to traumatic events. In this case, substance abuse precedes PTSD. Jacobsen, Southwick and Kosten [36] noticed that some substance abusers repetitively place themselves in dangerous situations to sustain their habit, thus experiencing high levels of trauma. For example, some research show that alcohol use is related to higher risk of experiencing accidents and physical and sexual abuse [45]. Moreover, chronic substance use can lead to higher levels of arousal and anxiety as well as to sensitization of neurobiological stress systems, resulting in a higher level of vulnerability to development of PTSD after exposure to trauma. This third pathway of explaining high rates of comorbidity was named as the susceptibility hypothesis [44].

Stewart, Pihl, Conrod and Dongier [7] described two other pathways to explain high incidence of substance abuse and PTSD comorbidity. First of all, substance use can worsen

PTSD symptoms or to extend them due to failure of habituation to traumatic memories or trauma processing. The use of alcohol or other depressant drugs could interfere with recovery from PTSD by interfering with the integration of the traumatic experience into a contextually based system of memories and beliefs [37]. According to the second pathway described by the authors, withdrawal symptoms can act as trauma reminders, leading to increase in the symptoms of arousal and, on the cognitive level, to increase the motivation to further use of the substance. Jacobsen, Southwick and Kosten [36] similarly drew attention to the hypothesis that the physiological arousal resulting from substance withdrawal may have an additive effect with arousal symptoms stemming from PTSD. The resulting hyperarousal may serve as a conditioned reminder of traumatic events and thus precipitate an increase in symptoms of trauma re-experiencing. Authors suggested that this process of PTSD symptoms exacerbation may then prompt relapse to substance use in an attempt to self-medicate.

Stewart and Conord [21] proposed that functional relations to explain comorbidity of PTSD and substance use disorders do not necessarily involve causality in terms of one disorder leading to the initial development of the other. According to them, functional relations may pertain to the maintenance of the symptoms. For example, on the one hand PTSD could serve to maintain substance use disorder symptoms through the process of self-medication. On the other hand, substance misuse could maintain or prolong the PTSD symptoms, for example by interfering with habituation to the trauma. Authors emphasize that there is also another possibility, that both of disorders operate in a vicious circle. The hypothesis specify that PTSD symptoms promote and maintain substance misuse through attempts to control them, and substance misuse in turn maintain and prolong or exacerbate PTSD symptoms, which in turn promote further substance misuse.

In addition to models explaining the PTSD and substance use disorders comorbidity, described in the literature, attention should be paid to biological models which assume common vulnerability to both disorders increasing the risk of their development. Despite this, little is still known about biological vulnerability, some interesting results were found in research conducted within behavior genetics and molecular psychiatry paradigms. For example, Segman et al. [46] examined the association of the dopamine transporter 3'UTR variable number tandem repeat (VNTR) polymorphism with PTSD. According to the authors' statement, this polymorphism was chosen given the previous findings of abnormal dopamine function in PTSD, and given the putative effect of dopamine neurotransmission in shaping the responses to stress in animals. Significant excess of 9 repeat allele was observed among patients with PTSD. An excess of 9 repeat homozygous genotype was also observed in PTSD. Interestingly, the same gene variant is associated with more severe effects of alcohol withdrawal [47] and is more frequent among patients with second type of alcoholism according to Cloninger's categorization [48].

The most popular pathway that was proposed in the literature to explain a self-medication hypothesis on biological level is endorphin compensation hypothesis [49]. It is based on animal and human studies that have confirmed that traumatic events can increase endorphin activity; research also show that trauma reminders in PTSD patients activate the endorphin system [49]. According to this hypothesis, drinking of alcohol compensates for deficiencies in endorphin activity following a traumatic experience. Usually, within minutes of exposure to a traumatic event there is an increase in the level of endorphins in the brain. During the time of the trauma, endorphin levels remain elevated and help numb the emotional and physical pain. However, chronic stimulation of the stress response during traumatic experiences leads to two compensatory responses. First, adrenocorticotropic hormone (ACTH) tends to inhibit the further release of corticotropin-releasing hormone (CRH). Second, chronic stimulation of opioid receptors leads to an increase in system that has anti-opioidlike effects. This opposing system gets stronger over time and leads to a lessening or habituation of the endorphin system.

After the trauma is over, endorphin levels gradually decrease and this may lead to a initial period of endorphin withdrawal that can last from hours to days. This period of endorphin withdrawal may produce emotional distress and contribute to symptoms of PTSD. Alcohol use can increase endorphin activity, like traumatic events, thus leading to compensation for the endorphin withdrawal and avoidance of associated emotional distress. Some people, most probably those who either experienced several traumatic events or continually reexperience the same event, as in chronic PTSD, may drink to reproduce the numbing effects experienced with increased levels of endorphins. PTSD symptoms may become associated with the state of withdrawal, during which the craving for alcohol increases. For some of the patients, alcohol use began after the onset of PTSD symptoms and continues to increase as symptoms of PTSD increase.

Early Childhood Trauma and Risk for Alcohol Misuse

The relation between early childhood traumatic experiences, such as childhood maltreatment, and substance use disorders in adolescence and adult life deserve more attention due to findings confirming their frequent comorbidity. For example, in our study that examined the lifetime exposure to traumatic events among 458 alcohol dependent patients, 42% reported experiencing childhood physical assault or abuse [18]. Moreover, these experiences were associated with higher rates of current PTSD diagnosis and higher levels of posttraumatic symptoms, and with higher rates of physical injuries due to drinking and conflicts with the law. Exposure to physical assault in childhood was also linked to generally earlier onset of alcohol-related problems. In our opinion, these results may indicate that physical assault experienced in childhood is a risk factor for poorer adult functioning with reference to both PTSD and some aspects of alcohol dependence symptomatology, or, alternatively, other important factors are mediators of this relationship, such as other comorbidities or genetic susceptibility. One of the possible mediators that remains largely unstudied, may be the symptoms of complex PTSD, asscociated with childhood trauma, and highly co-occuring in patients with comorbid substance use disorders and PTSD [50].

Some authors suggest that childhood abuse history is particularly important in the case of drinking women due of high incidence of early sexual abuse experiences. Reported estimates of lifetime history of physical and sexual abuse for women with alcohol and other drugs problems range from 55% to 99%, depending on the population studied and the method of data collection used [51]. Simpson [29] describes the studies indicating that women with histories of childhood sexual abuse are two to three times more likely to have a substance use problem than women without such histories. When compared with those without childhood sexual abuse histories, women with substance use-associated problems and childhood sexual abuse histories have been found to be more likely to use alcohol in order to facilitate sexual situations. In addition, women and girls with childhood abuse histories more frequently report using alcohol and drugs to deal with pain and discomfort, to escape family problems as well as to handle such symptoms as shakes and tremors.

De Bellis [52], in his metaanalysis of the studies in developmental traumatology, demonstrated that early childhood trauma is associated with an enhanced risk of adolescent and adult alcohol and substance use disorders. Studies that examined biological indicators of stress (mainly, levels of stress hormones in salivary, urine or plasma) show that maltreated children and adolescents manifest deregulation of major biological stress response systems (the hypothalamic–pituitary–adrenal [HPA] axis and "the catecholamine" system) including adverse influences on brain development. According to conclusions made by this author, the deregulation of biological stress response systems may lead to an enhanced vulnerability to psychopathology, particularly PTSD and depression. These negative affect disorders may put a child at increased risk for adolescent or young adult onset of substance use disorders.

Childhood trauma is usually related to persistent stress-induced changes in the HPA axis [5, 52-54]. Symptoms of PTSD and comorbid depression may be associated with chronic hyperactivity of central CRH. Elevations of catecholamines and central CRH during development may, in turn, enhance one's risk of an alcohol or other substances use disorder in the future. Traumatic childhood experiences probably interact with genetic vulnerability and other factors in the ability of an individual's biological stress response systems to either maintain homeostasis in the face of chronic and severe stress or to permanently change in response to stressors. Deregulation of these biological stress response systems can maintain negative affect symptoms, which in turn lead to an increased risk for self-medicating with alcohol and substances in later life. Thus, maltreatment experiences in childhood and adolescence may increase the probability of alcohol and other substances abuse through attempts to use them to reduce posttraumatic symptoms, and to dampen the effects of deregulated biological stress response systems. Further deregulation of these systems caused by increasing plasma cortisol levels in adolescent onset of alcohol and substance use disorders leads to further maintanence of their symptoms.

On the one hand, changes in biological stress response systems associated with childhood trauma can render one vulnerable to primary psychiatric disorders and thus lead to self-medicating with alcohol and other substances. However, on the other hand, deregulated biological stress response systems can be associated with maturation failures in the frontal and prefrontal cortex, which may lead to failures in self-regulation and a greater incidence of impulsive behaviors. DeBellis noticed that the increased cortisol levels during development may be neurotoxic to the hippocampus [53]. Furthermore, elevated levels of catecholamines and cortisol may lead to general adverse brain development through the mechanisms of accelerated loss (or metabolism) of neurons, delays in myelination, abnormalities in developmentally appropriate pruning or by inhibiting neurogenesis. A stress-related adverse brain development mechanism may contribute to maturation failures in the frontal and prefrontal cortex. For example, in maltreated children and adolescents with PTSD, as compared to non-maltreated control group, lower N-acetylaspartate/creatine ratios were found, suggesting neuronal loss in the anterior cingulate region of the medial prefrontal cortex [54]. These stress-induced mechanisms may lead to failures in executive function and self-regulation and, thus, to a greater incidence of impulsive behaviors, i.e. alcohol and other substances abuse.

SUICIDAL BEHAVIORS AND COMORBIDITY OF PTSD AND ALCOHOL USE DISORDERS

Suicidal behaviors are common and an important problem among alcohol abusing or dependent patients. Different risk and protective factors for suicidal behaviors in individuals with alcohol use disorders were identified [55]. Review of the literature reveals that exposure to trauma, particularly childhood physical or sexual trauma, and PTSD may be among the most important risk factors for suicidal behaviors in this group of patients.

Exposure to trauma per se and even PTSD alone are significant risk factors for suicidal behaviors. Wilcox, Storr and Breslau [56] reviewed the literature and noticed that exposure to traumatic events, especially sexual trauma during childhood, is associated with an increased risk of attempted suicide. However, according to them, no information is available as to whether the increased risk of attempted suicide is related primarily to PTSD following traumatic experiences or it applies also to individuals who experienced trauma but did not develop PTSD. Results of the study conducted by these authors to raise this question revealed that PTSD was associated with increased risk of a subsequent suicide attempt and, moreover, PTSD was an independent predictor of attempted suicide. However, exposure to traumatic events without PTSD was not associated with a later suicide attempt.

A smaller number of studies were conducted on suicidal behaviors in patients with comorbid substance use disorder and PTSD. In our study conducted on 458 individuals diagnosed with alcohol dependence [18], analysis of suicidal behaviors was made on the basis of one question on the presence of current thoughts about suicide. Analysis revealed that patients classified as having possible PTSD (41%) showed significantly higher scores on this item ($t = 18.50$, $df = 431$, $p < 0.001$). Langeland, Draije and van den Brink [57] emphasized that childhood abuse is an important factor that allows for an understanding of clinical impairment in treated alcoholics, regarding also comorbid PTSD and suicidality. The authors conducted the study on treatment-seeking alcoholics (men and women). The results showed that severity of childhood abuse was associated with PTSD and suicide attempts, but only in females. Other studies also confirm that childhood physical or sexual abuse may be among major predictors for suicidal behaviours in patients with alcohol use disorders [58]. Roy and Janal [59] investigated the study that was designed to examine risk factors for attempting suicide in 499 alcohol dependent patients. Results showed that those who had attempted suicide ($N = 198$) were more likely to be female, reported a family history of suicidal behavior, more childhood trauma, and greater levels of aggressive behavior, began heavy drinking earlier, and were more likely to receive antidepressant medication. Gender, family history, and childhood sexual abuse history made significant and, moreover, independent contributions to the risk of a suicide attempt. In the authors' opinion, all of these risk factors may differentiate alcohol dependent patients who have attempted suicide from those who have not. Somewhat in opposition to these results are findings from the Australian National Survey of Mental Health and Well-Being [22]. According to them, more than half of individuals identified as having comorbid substance use disorders and PTSD had ever thought about suicide and 17% had a lifetime history of attempted suicide. However, they were no more or less likely to have ever considered or attempted suicide than those with substance use disorder or PTSD alone.

Conclusion

A review of the literature shows that rates of PTSD and alcohol use disorders comorbidity obtained in different types of studies are in majority of cases relatively high. Despite the fact that not all of the studies confirm the existence of a causal association between exposure to these disorders, this problem is still important from the practical point of view. Patients with comorbid PTSD and alcohol use disorders, particularly those who experienced childhood physical or sexual trauma, usually present poorer functioning at different dimensions and are at higher risk for dropping out of therapy. The fact that this group of patients may represent significant proportion of alcohol misusing individuals emphasizes the importance of integrated treatment that may be needed to address their specific needs. Moreover, many authors underline the importance of routine assessment of childhood trauma and possible trauma-related disorders in individuals seeking alcohol use disorders treatment. Significant problem related to comorbidity of disorders, concerning this group of patients, is an elevated risk for suicidal behaviors.

References

[1] American Psychiatric Association: *Diagnostic and statistical manual of mental disorders* (4th ed., text revised). Washington, DC, APA, 2000.

[2] Kessler RC., Sonnega A, Bromet E, Hughes M, Nelson CB: Posttraumatic stress disorder in the National Comorbidity Survey. *Arch Gen Psychiatry* 1995; 52:1048-1060.

[3] Kessler RC, Chiu WT, Demler O, Merikangas KR, Walters EE: Prevalence, severity, and comorbidity of 12-month DSM-IV disorders in the National Comorbidity Survey Replication. *Arch Gen Psychiatry* 2005; 62:617-27.

[4] Breslau N: Epidemiologic studies of trauma, posttraumatic stress disorder, and other psychiatric disorders. *Can J Psychiatry* 2002; 47:923-929.

[5] Heim C, Nemeroff CB: The role of childhood trauma in the neurobiology of mood and anxiety disorders: preclinical and clinical studies. *Biol Psychiatry* 2001; 49:1023-1039.

[6] Kulka RA, Schlenger WE, Fairbank JA, Hough RL, Jordan BK, Marmar CR, Weiss DS: Trauma and the Vietnam War generation: *Report on findings from the National Vietnam Veterans Readjustment Study*. New York, Brunner/Mazel, 1990.

[7] Stewart SH, Pihl RO, Conrod PJ, Dongier M: Functional associations among trauma, PTSD, and substance-related disorders. *Addict Behav* 1998; 23:797-812.

[8] Chilcoat HD, Menard Ch: Epidemiological investigations: comorbidity of posttraumatic stress disorder and substance use disorder. Edited by Ouimette P, Brown PJ. Trauma and substance abuse. Washington, DC, *American Psychological Association,* 2003, pp 9-28.

[9] Helzer JE, Robins LN, McEvoy L: Post-traumatic stress disorder in the general population. *N Engl J Med* 1987; 317:1630-1634.

[10] Giaconia RM, Reinherz HZ, Hauf AC, Paradis AD, Wasserman MS, Langhammer DM: Comorbidity of substance use and post-traumatic stress disorders in a community sample of adolescents. *Am J Orthopsychiatry* 2000; 70:253-262.

[11] Kilpatrick DG, Acierno R, Saunders BE, Resnick HS, Best CL, Schnurr PP: Risk factors for adolescent substance abuse and dependence: data from a national sample. *J Consult Clin Psychol* 2000: 68:19-30.

[12] Triffleman EG, Marmar CR, Delucchi KL, Ronfeldt H: Childhood trauma and posttraumatic stress disorder in substance abuse inpatients. *J Nerv Ment Dis* 1995; 183:172-176.

[13] Brown PJ, Recupero PR, Stout RL: PTSD substance abuse comorbidity and treatment utilization. *Addict Behav* 1995; 20:251-254.

[14] Mills K, Lynskey M, Teesson M, Ross J, Darke S: Post-traumatic stress disorder among people with heroin dependence in the Australian Treatment Outcome Study (ATOS): prevalence and correlates. *Drug Alcohol Depend* 2005; 77:243-249.

[15] Reynolds M, Mezey G, Chapman M, Wheeler M, Drummond C, Baldacchino A: Co-morbid post-traumatic stress disorder in a substance misusing clinical population. *Drug Alcohol Depend* 2005; 77:251–258.

[16] Clark DB, Jacob RG: Anxiety disorders in 30 adolescents with alcohol abuse and dependence. *Alcohol Clin Exp Res* 1992; 16:371.

[17] Evren C, Can S, Evren B, Saatcioglu O, Cakmak D: Lifetime posttraumatic stress disorder in Turkish alcohol-dependent inpatients: relationship with depression, anxiety and erectile dysfunction. *Psychiatry Clin Neurosci* 2006; 60:77-84.

[18] ***Dragan*** M, ***Lis***-Turlejska M. Prevalence of posttraumatic stress disorder in alcohol dependent patients in Poland. **Addict Behav** 2007; 32:902-911.

[19] Stewart SH: Alcohol abuse in individuals exposed to trauma: a critical review. *Psychol Bull* 1996; 120:83-112.

[20] Kishore V, Theall KP, Robinson W, Pichon J, Scribner R, Robertson E, Johnson S: Resource loss, coping, alcohol use, and posttraumatic stress symptoms among survivors of Hurricane Katrina: a cross-sectional study. *Am J Disaster Med* 2008; 3:345-357.

[21] Stewart SH, Conord PJ: Psychosocial models of functional associations between posttraumatic stress disorder and substance use disorder. Edited by Ouimette P, Brown PJ. Trauma and substance abuse. Washington, DC, *American Psychological Association,* 2003, pp 29-56.

[22] Mills KL, Teesson M, Ross J, Peters L: Trauma, PTSD, and substance use sisorder: findings from the Australian National Survey of Mental Health and Well-Being. *Am J Psychiatry* 2006; 163:651-658.

[23] Breslau N, Davis GC, Schultz LR: Posttraumatic stress disorder and the incidence of nicotine, alcohol, and other drug disorders in persons who have experienced trauma. *Arch Gen Psychiatry* 2003; 60:289-294.

[24] ***Kranzler*** HR, ***Rosenthal*** RN: Dual diagnosis: alcoholism and comorbid psychiatric disorders. *Am J Addict* 2003; 12:S26-S40.

[25] Brown PJ, Stout RL, Mueller T: Substance use disorder and posttraumatic stress disorder comorbidity: addiction and psychiatric treatment rates. *Psychol Addict Behav* 1999; 13:115-122.

[26] Cacciola JS, Koppenhaver JM, Alterman AI, McKay JR: Posttraumatic stress disorder and other psychopathology in substance abusing patients. *Drug Alcohol Depend* 2009; 101:27-33.

[27] Najavits LM, Weiss RD, Shaw SR, Muenz LR: "Seeking Safety": outcome of a new cognitive-behavioral psychotherapy for women with posttraumatic stress disorder and substance abuse. *J Trauma Stress* 1998; 11:437-456.

[28] Riggs DS, Rukstalis M, Volpicelli JR, Kalmanson D, Foa EB: Demographic and social adjustment characteristics of patients with comorbid posttraumatic stress disorder and alcohol dependence: potential pitfalls to PTSD treatment. *Addict Behav* 2003; 28:1717–1730.

[29] Simpson TL: Childhood sexual abuse, PTSD, and the functional roles of alcohol use among women drinkers. *Subst Use Misuse* 2003; 38: 249-270.

[30] Back SE, Sonne SC, Killeen T, Dansky BS, Brady KT: Comparative profiles of women with PTSD and comorbid cocaine or alcohol dependence. *Am J Drug Alcohol Abuse* 2003; 29:169-189

[31] American Psychiatric Association: *Practice guidelines for the treatment of patients with substance use disorders* (2nd edition). Washington, DC, APA, 2006.

[32] Ouimette P, Moos RH, Brown PJ: Substance use disorder–posttraumatic stress disorder comorbidity: a survey of treatments and proposed practice guidelines. Edited by Ouimette P, Brown PJ. Trauma and substance abuse. Washington, DC, *American Psychological Association,* 2003, pp 91-110.

[33] Dansky BS, Roitzsch JC, Brady KT, Saladin ME: Posttraumatic stress disorder and substance abuse: use of research in a clinical setting. *J Trauma Stress* 1997; 10:141-148.

[34] Khantzian EJ: The self-medication hypothesis of addictive disorders: focus on heroin and cocaine dependence. *Am J Psychiatry* 1985; 142:1259-1264.

[35] Lang AR, Patrick CJ, Stritzke WGK: Alcohol and emotional response: a multidimensional-multilevel analysis. Edited by Leonard KE, Blane HT. *Psychological theories of drinking and alcoholism.* Second edition. London, Guilford Press, 1999, pp 328-371.

[36] Jacobsen LK, Southwick SM, Kosten TR: Substance use disorders in patients with posttraumatic stress disorder: a review of the literature. *Am J Psychiatry* 2001; 158:1184-1191.

[37] Conrod PJ, Stewart SH: Experimental studies exploring functional relations between posttraumatic stress disorder and substance use disorder. Edited by Ouimette P, Brown PJ. Trauma and substance abuse. Washington, DC, *American Psychological Association,* 2003, pp 57-72.

[38] Bremner JD, Southwick SM, Darnell A, Charney DS: Chronic PTSD in Vietnam combat veterans: course of illness and substance abuse. *Am J Psychiatry* 1996; 153:369–375.

[39] Saladin ME, Brady KT, Dansky BS, Kilpatrick DG: Understanding comorbidity between PTSD and substance use disorders: two preliminary investigations. *Addict Behav* 1995; 20:643-655.

[40] McFarlane AC: Epidemiological evidence about the relationship between PTSD and alcohol abuse: the nature of the association. *Addict Behav* 1998; 23:813-825.

[41] Cottler LB, Compton WM, Mager D, Spitznagel EL, Janca A: Posttraumatic stress disorder among substance users from the general population. *Am J Psychiatry* 1992; 149:664-670.

[42] ***Davidson J, Swartz M, Storck M, Krishnan RR, Hammett E:*** A diagnostic and family study of posttraumatic stress disorder. *Am J Psychiatry* 1985; 142:90-93.

[43] McFarlane AC, Browne D, Bryant RA, O'Donnell M, Silove D, Creamer M, Horsley K: A longitudinal analysis of alcohol consumption and the risk of posttraumatic symptoms. *J Affect Disord* in press; doi:10.1016/j.jad.2009.01.017.

[44] Brown PJ, Wolfe J: Substance abuse and post-traumatic stress disorder comorbidity. *Drug Alcohol Depend* 1994; 35:51-59.

[45] Murdoch D, Pihl R, Ross D: Alcohol and crimes of violence: present issues. *Int J Addict* 1990; 25:1065-1081.

[46] ***Segman*** RH, Cooper-Kazaz R, Macciardi F, Goltser T, Halfron Y, Dobroborski T, Shalev AY: Association between the dopamine transporter gene and posttraumatic stress disorder. *Mol* ***Psychiatry 2002; 7:903-907.***

[47] Schmidt LG, Harms H, Kuhn S, Rommelspacher H, Sander T: Modification of alcohol withdrawal by the A9 allele of the dopamine transporter gene. *Am J Psychiatry* 1998; 155:474-479.

[48] Samochowiec J, Kucharska-Mazur J, Grzywacz A, Jabłoński M, Rommelspacher H, Samochowiec A, Sznabowicz M, Horodnicki J, Sagan L, Pełka-Wysiecka J: Family-based and case-control study of DRD2, DAT, 5HTT, COMT genes polymorphisms in alcohol dependence. *Neurosci Lett* 2006; 410:1-5.

[49] Volpicelli J, Balarman G, Hahn J, Wallace H, Bux D: The role of uncontrollable trauma in the development of PTSD and alcohol addiction. *Alcohol Res Health* 1999; 23:256-262.

[50] Ford JD, Smith SF. Complex posttraumatic stress disorder in trauma-exposed adults receiving public sector outpatient substance abuse disorder treatment. *Addiction Res Theory* 2008; 16:193–203.

[51] Najavits LM, Weiss RD, Shaw SR: The link between substance abuse and posttraumatic stress disorder in women: A research review. *Am J Addict* 1997; 6:273-283.

[52] De Bellis MD: Developmental traumatology: a contributory mechanism for alcohol and substance use disorders. *Psychoneuroendocrinol* 2002; 27:155-170.

[53] De Bellis MD, Clark DB, Beers SR, Soloff P, Boring AM, Hall J, Kersh A, Keshavan MS: Hippocampal volume in adolescent onset alcohol use disorders. *Am J Psychiat* 2000; 157:737–744.

[54] De Bellis MD, Keshavan MS, Spencer S, Hall J: N-acetylaspartate concentration in the anterior cingulate in maltreated children and adolescents with PTSD. *Am J Psychiat* 2000; 157:1175–1177.

[55] Sher L: Risk and protective factors for suicide in patients with alcoholism. *Scientific World Journal* 2006; 6:1405-1411.

[56] Wilcox HC, Storr CL, Breslau N: Posttraumatic stress disorder and suicide attempts in a community sample of urban american young adults. *Arch Gen Psychiatry* 2009; 66:305-311.

[57] Langeland W, Draijer N, van den Brink W: Psychiatric comorbidity in treatment-seeking alcoholics: the role of childhood trauma and perceived parental dysfunction. *Alcohol Clin Exp Res* 2004; 28:441-447.

[58] Petersen ChB, Grønbaek MN, Rask MB, Nielsen B, Nielsen AS: Suicidal behaviour among alcohol-dependent Danes attending outpatient treatment. *Nord J Psychiatry* 2009; 63:209-216.

[59] Roy A, Janal MN: Risk factors for suicide attempts among alcohol dependent patients. *Arch Suicide Res* 2007; 11:211-217.

In: Suicidal Behavior in Alcohol and Drug Abuse...
Editors: L. Sher, A. Vilens, pp. 117-133
ISBN: 978-1-60876-919-3

Chapter 8

COMORBIDITY OF BIPOLAR DISORDER WITH ALCOHOL AND/OR DRUG ABUSE

***Ho-Jun Seo*[1], *Chi-Un Pae*[1,2]**

[1]The Catholic University of Korea College of Medicine, Seoul, Republic of Korea;
[2]Duke University Medical Center, Durham, North Carolina, USA

ABSTRACT

A high prevalence of comorbidity with alcohol dependence (AD) and/or substance use disorder (SUD) has been proposed in patients with bipolar disorders. While bipolar disorder and AD or SUDs are strongly associated, the exact relationship among these disorders is complex. A number of studies have demonstrated a negative impact of comorbid AD and SUD on clinical outcomes in patients with bipolar disorder, resulting in poorer response to treatment, more functional impairment, higher rate of suicide and more hazardous public health costs. Although a limited number of studies have addressed treatment of bipolar disorder comorbid with AD and/or SUD, there is a significant need for further clinical research, particularly double-blind trials, focused on treatment of co-occurring bipolar disorder and such disorders. An integrative and evidence-based etiological and treatment model will enhance the treatment outcome in bipolar patients comorbid with AD and/or SUD.

INTRODUCTION

Bipolar disorder is a common, serious, and burdensome mental illness. It affects 1.3 % of the population and is characterized by impaired judgment and a great deal of high risk behavior that is experienced as beyond one's control [1],[2]. Substance use disorders (SUDs) are also common and occur in the general population at a rate of 17% for alcohol use disorder and 6% for other drug use disorders; however, co-occurrence of SUDs with other psychiatric disorders is even more common [3]. Indeed, bipolar disorder is the most prominent Axis I disorder that is comorbid with SUDs [3,4]. In recent decades, many studies have been performed to elucidate the clinical meanings of this comorbidity, and, to date, several significant results have been reported. However, there are still many controversies concerning the characteristics of this comorbidity, and few studies have provided an empirically-based treatment strategy. These problems may be worsened by the fact that many clinical trials include substance abuse among the exclusion criteria for the study. In this chapter, we review the previous studies related to comorbid bipolar disorder and SUDs, especially those that have recently published data, as well as the results of clinical trials. In this chapter, we will discuss the Epidemiology of the SUD-bipolar disorder comorbidity, the Relationship between SUDs and bipolar disorder, the Impact of SUDs on bipolar disorder, and treatment.

EPIDEMIOLOGY

There has been much evidence from large population studies demonstrating an overrepresentation of substance use disorders (SUDs) among individuals with bipolar disorder. The Epidemiologic Catchment Area (ECA) study evaluated the prevalence of psychiatric disorders among 20,291 persons in community settings [3]. Compared to individuals with other Axis I disorders, individuals with bipolar I disorder had the highest lifetime history of drug or alcohol use disorder (41% and 46%, respectively). In patients with bipolar II disorder, 39% had a lifetime history of an alcohol use disorder, and 21% had a lifetime history of drug use disorder. Of the psychiatric illnesses, only anti-social personality disorder had a higher lifetime prevalence rate of any SUD (61 % for bipolar I disorder, 48% for bipolar II disorder, 84% for anti-social personality disorder, 27.2% for major depressive disorder, 47% for schizophrenia, and 17% for the general population).

In the National Comorbidity Survey (NCS), Kessler et al. found that individuals with mania were 8.2 times more likely to exhibit drug dependence and 9.7 times more likely to be alcohol dependent, as compared to the general population during the previous 12 months [5]. They also found that most patients with mood disorders reported their mood symptoms as occurring before or concurrently with the beginning of their SUDs. Furthermore, men and women who had experienced lifetime alcohol dependence were 12.0 and 5.3 times more likely to have a comorbid lifetime diagnosis of mania, respectively [4].

Recently, a large study was conducted as part of the National Epidemiologic Survey on Alcohol and Related Conditions (NESARC) [6]. The NESARC examined the prevalence and co-occurrence of DSM-IV substance, mood, and anxiety disorders in a representative sample of 43,093 respondents in the US. In this study, the 12-month prevalence of any SUD was 28% in those with a history of mania, 27% in those with hypomania, and 19% in those with major depressive disorder. In subjects with bipolar I disorder, 58% had a lifetime history of an alcohol use disorder, and 38% had a lifetime history of any SUDs. The 12-month prevalence for mania and hypomania remained virtually unchanged when persons with substance-induced mania or hypomania were excluded. The odds ratio of drug abuse was 3.7 for persons with mania and 1.7 for persons with hypomania, whereas the odds ratio for drug dependence was 13.9 for persons with mania and 4.4 for persons with hypomania. The epidemiological findings are presented in Table 1.

Table 1. Epidemiological findings of substance use disorders (SUDs) in bipolar disorder

Epidemiological Study	Subjects	lifetime prevalence of comorbid SUDs in bipolar I disorder	lifetime prevalence of comorbid SUDs in other diseases
Epidemiologic Catchment Area Study (ECA; 1980-1985)	Community sample (n=20,291)	alcohol use disorder: 46.2% other SUDs: 40.7% any SUDs: 60.7%	In general population alcohol use disorder: 13.5% other SUDs: 6.1% In bipolar II disorder alcohol use disorder: 39.2% other SUDs: 21.0% In major depressive disorder alcohol use disorder: 16.5% other SUDs: 18.0% In any anxiety disorder alcohol use disorder: 17.9% other SUDs: 11.9%
National Comorbidity Survey (NCS; 1990-1992)	Community sample (n=8,098)	alcohol use disorder: 64.2% other SUDs: 46.1% any SUDs: 71.0%	In major depressive disorder alcohol use disorder: 35.5% other SUDs: 22.0% In any anxiety disorder alcohol use disorder: 31.8% other SUDs: 20.1%
National Epidemiologic Survey on Alcohol and Related Conditions (NESARC; 2001-2002)	Community sample (n=43,093)	- lifetime prevalence; alcohol use disorder :58.0% other SUDs: 37.5% - 12-month prevalence; alcohol use disorder :23.8% other SUDs: 12.1%	- 12-month prevalence; In general population alcohol use disorder: 8.5% other SUDs: 1.1% In bipolar II disorder alcohol use disorder: 24.0 % other SUDs: 7.4 % In major depressive disorder alcohol use disorder: 16.4% other SUDs: 6.6% In any anxiety disorder alcohol use disorder: 13.0% other SUDs: 4.6%

There have been two major first episode mania studies that reported results regarding co-occurring SUDs and bipolar disorder. In the University of Cincinnati First-Episode Mania Study, which followed over a hundred patients who initially presented with a first manic or mixed episode within the previous five years, Strakowski et al. found the lifetime prevalence of alcohol and cannabis use disorders was 42% and 46%, respectively, among 144 bipolar patients [7, 8]. From the same data, Patel et al. found that patients in the typical onset group were more likely to have a SUD (41%), as compared to patients in the early onset group (24%) [9]. However, they suggested that this finding may be affected by the higher percentage of mixed episode presentations in the early onset group, because mixed patients were significantly less likely to have any co-occurring SUD.

Additionally, the McLean-Harvard First-Episode Mania Study followed up a hundred patients for 2–4 years who initially presented with a manic or mixed episode. Baethge et al. found that 33% of the patients had a SUD at the index manic episode. At the end of the 24 month follow up period, 31 out of the 80 remaining patients (39%) had a current SUD [10]. The most common SUD was alcohol use disorder, followed by cannabis and then cocaine use disorders. Anxiety disorder was also frequently observed in patients with SUDs (30% vs. 13%)

High rates of comorbidity of SUDs and bipolar disorder have also been documented in various studies based on clinical settings. Brown et al. [11] reviewed fourteen studies conducted with bipolar patients in both inpatient and outpatient psychiatric settings and reported that the lifetime rates of drug abuse or dependence for patients with bipolar disorder ranged from 14%–65%, compared with rates of 6%–12% in the general population.

Thus, both community and clinical data suggest that SUDs are highly prevalent in patients with bipolar disorder. Additionally, the prevalence of SUD in this population may be greater in patients with bipolar disorder than in the general population or among those with other major psychiatric disorders, including schizophrenia and major depression. Among the bipolar spectrum disorders, bipolar I disorder has been shown to have consistently higher rates of SUD comorbidity than other types of bipolar disorder. Alcohol and cannabis are most often abused, followed by cocaine and then opioids, which reflects the general availability of these compounds, rather than a diagnosis-specific selection [12].

Recently, Brown reviewed community based studies and commented that the data were more strongly associated with substance dependence than with substance abuse in patients with bipolar disorder, and suggested the presence of more severe and disabling effects of SUDs in these patients [11]. He also suggested that though a person with bipolar disorder is more likely to develop an alcohol-related disorder than a drug-related disorder, the relative risk of developing a drug-related disorder is greater than the risk of developing an alcohol-related disorder when compared to the general population [11].

Relations between SUDs and Bipolar Disorder

As mentioned above, most studies have addressed the strong association between SUDs and bipolar disorder. To explain this association, there have been three possible hypotheses: (1) SUDs could affect the development of bipolar disorder, (2) bipolar disorder could affect the development of SUDs, and (3) SUDs and the bipolar disorder could share common pathophysiologic factors [13].

Several studies have reported that substance abuse commonly precedes the onset of bipolar disorder [14, 15, 16]. Strakowski et al also found in their research of patients with a first manic episode that 75% of 77 hospitalized patients reported onset of substance abuse as having occurred at least 1 year before their first manic episode [17]. Although this temporal ordering seems to occur in many patients with both SUDs and bipolar disorder, it does not provide much support for the hypothesis that substance abuse may cause bipolar disorder. A substantial number of patients have bipolar disorder that precedes their SUD [6, 11]. Grant et al. reported that there was still a high prevalence of SUDs in patients with bipolar disorder after careful exclusion of the case of substance-induced mood disorder [18]. A conflicting hypothesis might seem to be persuasive, because the seeking out of pleasurable activities, impulsivity, and poor judgment in bipolar patients may lead to increased exposure to substance use. Bolton et al. found, from data of the National Epidemiologic Survey on Alcohol and Related Conditions, that a large percentage of patients with bipolar disorder used alcohol or other drugs for self-medication purposes [19]. Bipolar disorder could also lead to substance use through psychosocial changes, such as boarding homes. However, such theories neglect the fact that a relative minority of patients began abusing substances after the onset of bipolar disorder. Several studies found that more patients began abusing substances before the onset of bipolar disorder [14, 15]. The onset of each disorder is frequently in the adolescent period, though determining the onset of bipolar disorder can be extremely challenging. Childhood mania is frequently misdiagnosed as a disruptive behavioral disorder, including ADHD, conduct disorder, and oppositional defiant disorder, because of the overlapping characteristic features (mixed episode, hyperactivity, severe irritability impulsive behavior and anger). In such patients, co-occurring substance use may contribute to diagnosis of a disruptive behavioral disorder rather than to bipolar disorder [2, 20, 21]. The similarity of symptoms secondary to substance use and those of bipolar spectrum disorder could result in some patients being misdiagnosed or under-diagnosed, especially in substance abuse treatment settings [22,23]. The effect of mood symptoms on substance use in bipolar patients is also controversial. Healey et al. [24] performed a study focused on the reasons for substance use in patients with bipolar disorder and found that reasons for substance use were idiosyncratic, including both mood-related and mood-unrelated. Bizzarri et al. [25] also failed to find a difference for the motivations for substance use between bipolar patients with SUDs and patients with only SUDs.

Several studies have attempted to investigate the differences in the clinical features of bipolar disorder according to sequence of onset of two disorders. Strakowski et al divided subjects who experienced a first episode of a manic or mixed state into two groups, one in which SUDs preceded bipolar disorder and one in which bipolar disorder preceded SUD [7, 8]. Compared to patients with a preceding alcohol use disorder (n= 27), patients with preceding bipolar disorder (n=33) showed more affective symptoms, earlier onset of bipolar disorder, and a slower recovery from their affective symptoms [7]. In a comparison of patients with a preceding cannabis use disorder (n= 33) with those having a preceding bipolar disorder (n=36), there was no significant difference in all measured clinical variables after controlling for covariates [8]. Previously, Winokur et al. had tried to use the same distinction in patients with bipolar disorder and alcohol use disorder. They reported that patients with a preceding alcohol use disorder (n=34) had significantly fewer episodes of affective disorder during a five year follow up period than patients with a preceding bipolar disorder (n=30) [15]. Recently, Pacchiarotti et al. examined the clinical course and outcome of patients with bipolar disorder I or II whose bipolar onset was preceded by substance/alcohol use [26]. They found that patients with preceding substance/alcohol use disorder (n=145) showed less severe psychopathology than patients with a preceding bipolar disorder (n=144), exemplified by fewer total hypomanic and depressive episodes. However, patients with preceding substance/alcohol disorder had poor compliance to treatment. Though derived from a small sample, these results suggest that the patients for whom SUDs precede BDP may form a subgroup of bipolar patients that develop a relatively milder form of affective illness that is expressed only after exposure to alcohol abuse [12].

There is also inconclusive evidence supporting the hypothesis that SUDs and bipolar disorder could share common pathophysiologic factors. There has not been consistent data concerning the hypothesis that genetic factors can cause increased rates of substance use disorders in individuals with bipolar disorder [15, 21, 27, 28]. Strakowski et al. reported data that call this hypothesis into question: that first-degree relatives of persons with bipolar disorder had elevated rates of bipolar disorder, but not SUDs [29].

IMPACT OF SUDs ON BIPOLAR DISORDER

Recent research has focused on examining the effects that co-occurring SUDs have on illness course and treatment outcomes in bipolar disorder. A volume of data suggests that SUDs are associated with a poor prognosis in bipolar disorder. There have been several studies that have reported the characteristics of bipolar patients with SUDs compared with those without the disorder. Patients with both conditions have been shown to undergo an increased number of psychiatric hospitalizations, [30-34] increased treatment noncompliance, [35-38] a poorer response to acute treatment, [39] a slower remission rate from acute manic episodes, [5, 37, 39] increased episodes of depression,[17], a greater time with subsyndromal depressive and manic symptoms, [39] an increased total number of manic symptoms, [40] and increased aggression and violent behavior [40, 41]. Recently, there have been studies that have reported the association between comorbid SUDs and antidepressant-induced mania, [42] overweight/obesity, [43] and medical comorbidity in bipolar patients [44].

In a recent prospective study of first-episode mania, Strakowski et al. found that bipolar patients with SUDs had increased treatment noncompliance compared to those without any co-occurring SUD; they also showed delayed onset of symptomatic recovery even after adjusting for noncompliance [45]. In addition, the duration of alcohol abuse during the follow up was positively correlated with the duration of depression, and the duration of cannabis abuse was positively correlated with the duration of mania [46].

Weiss et al. examined the clinical characteristics and outcome of bipolar patients with co-occurring SUDs using data from 1000 patients enrolled in the Systematic Treatment Enhancement Program for Bipolar Disorder (STEP-BD) [47]. Of the 437 patients with past or current SUDs and the 480 with no history of a SUD, patients with SUDs had lower functioning and quality of life and were less likely to have the clinical status of recovery compared to those without substance use disorder [48]. Martinez et al. reported, with analysis of same data, that co-occurrence of SUDs was significantly associated with the development of serious adverse event during prospective study periods [49].

Recently, Hoblyn et al. evaluated the risk of psychiatric hospitalization for 2,963 veterans diagnosed as having bipolar disorder [50]. They found that 20% of the patients were hospitalized psychiatrically during the one-year study period, and patients diagnosed as having both alcohol use disorder and polysubstance dependence had a 100% risk of psychiatric hospitalization.

Mazza et al. examined clinical and psychopathological features of BP with and without comorbid SUDs among 131 patients with bipolar spectrum disorders for one year [51]. They found that patients with comorbid SUDs were significantly more impaired in social functioning and had a higher prevalence of personality disorder. However, these patients were less likely to have severe manic symptomatology.

Several studies have shown the association between co-occurring SUDs in bipolar patients and the increased risk of suicides. Weiss et al. found a higher number of lifetime suicide attempts in bipolar patients with co-occurring SUDs than those without from analysis of STEP-BD data [48].

The clinical and familial relationships between comorbid alcoholism and attempted suicide in affectively ill relatives of probands with bipolar I disorder was also found, in this study of 337 subjects with bipolar I disorder and their families, the odds of attempting suicide were 2.3 for individuals with comorbid bipolar disorder and alcohol dependence compared to those without alcohol dependence [52]. It was suggested that comorbid alcoholism was associated with a higher rate of attempted suicide and that there could be potential genetic traits of impulsivity that lead to this feature.

In a study [53] examining predictors of suicide attempts in attempters and non-attempters among 336 subjects with a diagnosis of bipolar I, bipolar II, or bipolar type schizoaffective disorder, a lifetime co-morbid substance use disorder was a significant predictor of suicide attempts. The odds ratio of lifetime attempted suicide was 2.09 in bipolar subjects with co-morbid substance use disorders compared to those without substance use issues.

Swann et al. investigated the relationships among suicidal behavior, potential predictors of eventual suicide, and measured impulsivity in patients with bipolar disorder [54]. They found that subjects with past suicidal behavior had more impulsive errors and shorter response latencies in immediate memory/delayed memory tasks and that a history of alcohol abuse was associated with an increased probability of a suicide attempt.

Recently, Sublette et al. investigated differences between bipolar subtypes with regard to SUDs as a risk factor for suicidal behavior among 96 bipolar I patients and 42 bipolar II patients [55]. They found that SUDs were associated with suicide attempts in bipolar I disorder, but not bipolar II disorder and that higher suicide attempts were associated with higher aggression scores. The presence of both alcohol use disorder and other SUDs increased the odds of suicide attempt exponentially, such that 97% of bipolar I patients who also had a substance use disorder had attempted suicide.

There have been several studies suggesting that the presence of other Axis I illnesses may be associated with SUDs in patients with bipolar disorder [56]. Specifically, comorbid anxiety disorders have been focused on as a significant risk factor for SUDs comorbidity in bipolar patients. A previous study examined the association between comorbid anxiety disorders and SUDs among 260 patients with severe affective disorders including major depression and bipolar disorder [57]. Among all subjects, cocaine (odds ratio (OR) = 5.9), stimulant (OR = 5.1), sedative (OR = 5.4), and opioid use disorders (OR = 13.9) were significantly more common in patients with anxiety disorders compared with those without. Of the 33 patients with bipolar disorder, especially patients with panic attacks, there was an increased likelihood of disorders of cocaine use (OR = 10.0), sedative use (OR = 25.0), and stimulant use (OR = 10.0) compared to bipolar patients without panic attacks.

In the study of 90 bipolar patients with SUDs, Kolodziej et al. found that a higher prevalence of lifetime cocaine and amphetamine use disorder in patients with lifetime Posttraumatic stress disorder (PTSD) compared to those without PTSD [58]. In this study, most PTSD patients were women with sexual abuse as the index trauma, which developed before the onset of drug use. They could not find an association between lifetime alcohol use disorder and lifetime PTSD.

The Axis I and II comorbidity of the 166 bipolar patients with SUDs was compared with the relative rates of comorbidity according to different substances [59]. In such study, about 80% of subjects had at least one comorbid anxiety disorder, which is nearly three times the value reported in the general bipolar population [60]. Generalized anxiety disorder and current depressed mood were significantly more common in bipolar patients with alcohol dependence than bipolar patients with cocaine dependence. Those with cocaine dependence had significantly higher rates of posttraumatic stress disorder. They suggested that cocaine dependence and alcohol dependence were associated with different clinical features and comorbid disorders in bipolar patients.

Recently, the prevalence rate of anxiety comorbidity in bipolar subjects with (n= 213) and without alcohol use disorders (n=137) was evaluated [61]. In this study, OCD and specific phobias were significantly less prevalent in patients with alcohol use disorders compared to those without, whereas PTSD was significantly more prevalent among women with alcohol use disorder than those without.

Goldstein et al. examined whether comorbid substance use disorders (SUDs) in bipolar I disorder were more prevalent among persons with versus those without comorbid anxiety disorders and the independent contribution of these comorbidities to the burden of bipolar disorder using data from the National Epidemiologic Survey on Alcohol and Related Conditions [62]. They found that among females only, the lifetime prevalence of SUDs was significantly greater among those with lifetime anxiety disorders (OR = 1.41). Anxiety disorders were independently associated with mixed episodes, prolonged depressive episodes, 12-month prevalence of depression, more mental health service utilization, and poorer functioning. SUDs were independently associated with mixed episodes among females, 12-month prevalence of depression among males, and with forensic history among both males and females.

Gao et al. examined the association among bipolar subtype, comorbid substance use, and comorbid anxiety disorders among 566 rapid cycling bipolar patients [63]. They found that there was no significant difference in comorbid anxiety disorder among patients without a lifetime SUD history. However, among patients with a lifetime SUD history, rapid cycling bipolar I patients had a significantly higher risk for generalized anxiety disorder (OR=3.29) and panic disorder (OR=2.95), but not OCD than those with bipolar II disorder.

Several studies have examined the possible association between mood state in bipolar disorder and substance use pattern. However, results have not been consistent, and there is still controversy concerning this association. Ringen et al. reported that patients with bipolar disorder had higher rates of alcohol consumption, while patients with schizophrenia more often used non alcoholic drugs, especially stimulating agents [64]. A subsequent study also reported a trend toward greater abuse of drugs during mania than during depression [65]. Some previous studies suggested that mixed mania may be more strongly associated with substance use than is euphoric mania [14, 66].

More alcohol use during the manic phase, but more cocaine use during the depressed phase was reported [56]. Similarly, Brown et al. reported from their two clinical trials, positive associations between changes in cocaine use or craving and changes in depressive symptoms than changes in manic symptoms, whereas changes in alcohol-related outcomes were more associated with changes in manic symptoms rather than depressive symptoms [11, 67, 68]. However, contradictory finding is also available. Strakowski et al. examined associations between affective symptoms and alcohol and cannabis use disorders among 50 new-onset bipolar patients and found that the duration of alcohol abuse during follow-up was associated with the time patients experienced depressive mood and that of cannabis abuse was associated with the duration of mania [46].

There have been three recent studies that have showed an association between the clinical features of bipolar disorder and substance use pattern. Mitchell et al. examined the relative rates of comorbidity, mood states, and diagnosis of bipolar spectrum disorder among 166 bipolar patients with dependence on different substances [59]. They found that current depressed mood was significantly more common in bipolar patients with alcohol dependence than those with cocaine dependence, whereas mixed mood state was more common in patients with cocaine dependence than in those with alcohol.

The difference in clinical variables between type I and II rapid cycling bipolar disorders comorbid with SUDs was assessed [69]. Of the 191 bipolar I patients and 53 bipolar II patients, they found a significantly higher rate of panic disorder (odds ratio=3.72) and a significantly higher psychiatric composite score on the Addiction Severity Index (ASI) in patients with rapid-cycling bipolar I disorder than bipolar II disorder. There were no significant differences between the subtypes in lifetime abuse or dependence history of specific drugs and the number of SUDs. There were also no significant differences in mood episodes in the last 12 months, the rates of previous hospitalization or suicide attempt, or early childhood verbal, physical, or sexual abuse history.

Jaffee et al. examined the association between alcohol use and depression among 115 patients with co-occurring bipolar disorder and substance use disorder for eight months [70]. They found that days of alcohol use and an increase in days of alcohol use each significantly predicted the presence of a depressive episode in the subsequent month when controlling for current depression and current drug use.

Treatment

Although a large number bipolar patients have comorbid SUDs, a fact which has complex implications for symptom outcome in bipolar disorder, there have been only a few controlled trials in this specific population.

In one study, the efficacies of lithium was compared with placebo for six weeks in 25 adolescent patients with affective disorder who were comorbid with SUDs, in which the lithium group showed a significantly greater improvement in both the symptoms of affective disorder and SUDs than placebo group [71].

Salloum et al. examined the efficacy of valproate in decreasing alcohol use and stabilizing mood symptoms in acutely ill patients with bipolar disorder and alcoholism [72]. Fifty-nine patients with bipolar I disorder and alcohol dependence who were treated with lithium and psychosocial interventions were randomly assigned to valproate or placebo for 24 weeks of treatment. It was shown that the valproate group had a significantly lower proportion of heavy drinking days and fewer drinks per heavy drinking and per drinking day, though affective symptoms improved equally in both groups. Improved alcohol use outcomes were correlated with serum valproate concentration.

Recently, Brown et al. evaluated the efficacy of quetiapine in decreasing alcohol use and improving mood symptoms in patients with bipolar disorder comorbid with alcohol use disorder [73]. In this study, patients were randomly assigned to quetiapine (titrated to 600 mg/day) add-on therapy or placebo for 12 weeks. One hundred two participants were used in the random regression analysis. No significant between-group differences were found in alcohol use and craving and manic symptoms during the study periods, though the quetiapine group showed a greater decrease in depressive symptoms. Authors suggested that the negative results of this study on alcohol use and craving may have been a result of relatively low levels of baseline alcohol use.

Table 2. Clinical outcome studies for SUDs in bipolar disorder

	Treatment	Duration	Subjects	Findings
Geller et al.	Lithium vs. Placebo	6-week	25 adolescent patients (12 with bipolar I, 5 with bipolar II, 8 with recurrent MDD) alcohol and marijuana dependence were most frequent	Improvement in affective and SUD symptoms
Salloum et al.	Lithium+valproate vs. Lithium+placebo	24-week	59 patients with bipolar I and alcohol dependence	Improvement in SUD but not affective symptoms
Brown et al.	prior medication + quetiapine* vs. prior medication + placebo	12- week	102 patients (50 with bipolar I and 52 with bipolar II; 99 with alcohol dependence and 3 with alcohol abuse) 50% of quetiapine group and 68% of placebo group used no concomitant medication	No improvement in SUD and manic symptoms Only improvement in depressive symptoms

There have been several uncontrolled trials in patients with bipolar disorder and SUDs, which may guide the possible use and further research of medication. O'Connell et al. [32] and Kusalic and Engelsmann [74] followed up the bipolar patients for years and found that comorbid SUDs predicted poor response to lithium. In addition to the controlled trial of bipolar patients with alcoholism, Salloum et al. found a significant improvement in mood symptoms and cocaine use disorder associated with divalproex use in bipolar patients [75]. Brown and his colleagues have studied various medications for the treatment of bipolar patients with SUDs. They assessed the effectiveness of aripiprazole for treatment of bipolar patients with SUDs including alcohol, cannabis, cocaine, and opioid dependence, and found improvement in mood symptoms and some positive results in substance use [76]. In addition, they found that bipolar patients with alcohol dependence showed significant improvements in mood symptoms and alcohol use and cravings with adjunctive use of naltrexone [77]. They also found that bipolar patients with cocaine dependence showed significant improvement both in mood symptoms and cocaine use, as well as craving associated with lamotrigine augmentation [68, 78]. Rubio et al. also reported positive results that support the effect of lamotrigine in mood symptoms, as well as alcohol use and craving [79]. However, these results have the limitation that they could not exclude the effects of mood symptom changes on improvement of SUDs.

Psychotherapeutic approaches have also been examined in much of the research for bipolar disorder and SUDs. Drake et al. followed up 51 bipolar patients with SUDs for three years providing 'assertive community treatment' or 'standard case management', both of which provided integrated mental health and substance abuse treatments in the state mental health system [80]. In this study, patients had significant remission from substance abuse and substantial improvements in functioning and quality of life, though psychiatric symptoms improved only modestly.

Cognitive behavioral therapy (CBT) approach specifically designed for bipolar patients with substance abuse has been developed and evaluated in clinical trials. In such trials, forty six patients were randomly assigned to medication or medication plus CBT for 12 weeks [81]. There were no differences in substance related outcomes between the two groups, though the CBT group reported significantly fewer days of manic or depressive symptoms and better medication compliance.

Weiss et al. developed an integrated group therapy for bipolar patients with SUDs, which is a CBT-based relapse-prevention treatment, and evaluated its efficacy in 45 patients for six months [82]. They found that patients who received integrated group therapy had significantly better outcomes in terms of drug abstinence and drug use severity than those with no experimental therapy.

Conclusion

Epidemiologic results from both community and clinical sample have consistently shown the extremely high comorbidity of bipolar disorder and SUDs. Although there have been several hypotheses for this strong association and trials to determine the sequence of onset of these two disorders, the reasons for this association are not well understood and could be affected by several confounding factors. Studies to determine the effects of SUDs on the illness course of bipolar disorder have consistently shown its negative outcome on various areas, such as psychiatric hospitalization, treatment compliance, remission and recurrence of mood episode, and aggression and other behavioral problems. Many studies have also reported the increased risk of suicides and comorbidity with other Axis I disorders in this population, especially anxiety disorders. Much research has been performed to examine the association between the mood state of bipolar disorder and substance use patterns. Although a few studies have reported some interesting findings, much of results are not consistent and there is still controversy concerning this issue. Until now, there have only been a few prospective, randomized controlled trials to test the effective treatment of this population. Although many results have provided a possible role for and guidance concerning the use of several medications in this comorbidity, such research is limited by the open label design, and the small sample size, and short duration of treatment in these patients. In the future, more controlled trials that include both pharmacotherapy and psychotherapeutic approaches are needed to support the evidence of effective treatment in this population.

Acknowledgments

This work was supported by a grant from the Medical Research Center, Korea Science and Engineering Foundation, Republic of Korea (R13-2002-005-04001-0).

References

[1] Kessler RC, McGonagle KA, Zhao S, Nelson CB, Hughes M, Eshleman S, Wittchen HU, Kendler KS. Lifetime and 12-month prevalence of DSM-III-R psychiatric disorders in the United States. Results from the National Comorbidity Survey. *Arch Gen Psychiatry* 1994;51(1):8-19.

[2] Biederman J, Faraone S, Mick E, Wozniak J, Chen L, Ouellette C, Marrs A, Moore P, Garcia J, Mennin D, Lelon E. Attention-deficit hyperactivity disorder and juvenile mania: an overlooked comorbidity? *J Am Acad Child Adolesc Psychiatry* 1996;35(8):997-1008.

[3] Regier DA, Farmer ME, Rae DS, Locke BZ, Keith SJ, Judd LL, Goodwin FK. Comorbidity of mental disorders with alcohol and other drug abuse. Results from the Epidemiologic Catchment Area (ECA) Study. *JAMA* 1990;264(19):2511-2518.

[4] Kessler RC, Crum RM, Warner LA, Nelson CB, Schulenberg J, Anthony JC. Lifetime co-occurrence of DSM-III-R alcohol abuse and dependence with other psychiatric disorders in the National Comorbidity Survey. *Arch Gen Psychiatry* 1997;54(4):313-321.

[5] Kessler RC, Nelson CB, McGonagle KA, Edlund MJ, Frank RG, Leaf PJ. The epidemiology of co-occurring addictive and mental disorders: implications for prevention and service utilization. *Am J Orthopsychiatry* 1996;66(1):17-31.

[6] Grant BF, Stinson FS, Hasin DS, Dawson DA, Chou SP, Ruan WJ, Huang B. Prevalence, correlates, and comorbidity of bipolar I disorder and axis I and II disorders: results from the National Epidemiologic Survey on Alcohol and Related Conditions. *J Clin Psychiatry* 2005;66(10):1205-1215.

[7] Strakowski SM, DelBello MP, Fleck DE, Adler CM, Anthenelli RM, Keck PE, Jr., Arnold LM, Amicone J. Effects of co-occurring alcohol abuse on the course of bipolar disorder following a first hospitalization for mania. *Arch Gen Psychiatry* 2005;62(8):851-858.

[8] Strakowski SM, DelBello MP, Fleck DE, Adler CM, Anthenelli RM, Keck PE, Jr., Arnold LM, Amicone J. Effects of co-occurring cannabis use disorders on the course of bipolar disorder after a first hospitalization for mania. *Arch Gen Psychiatry* 2007;64(1):57-64.

[9] Patel NC, Delbello MP, Keck PE, Jr., Strakowski SM. Phenomenology associated with age at onset in patients with bipolar disorder at their first psychiatric hospitalization. *Bipolar Disord* 2006;8(1):91-94.

[10] Baethge C, Baldessarini RJ, Khalsa HM, Hennen J, Salvatore P, Tohen M. Substance abuse in first-episode bipolar I disorder: indications for early intervention. *Am J Psychiatry* 2005;162(5):1008-1010.

[11] Brown ES. Bipolar disorder and substance abuse. *Psychiatr Clin North Am* 2005;28(2):415-425.

[12] Cerullo MA, Strakowski SM. The prevalence and significance of substance use disorders in bipolar type I and II disorder. *Subst Abuse Treat Prev Policy* 2007;2:29.

[13] Levin FR, Hennessy G. Bipolar disorder and substance abuse. *Biol Psychiatry* 2004;56(10):738-748.

[14] Feinman JA, Dunner DL. The effect of alcohol and substance abuse on the course of bipolar affective disorder. *J Affect Disord* 1996;37(1):43-49.

[15] Winokur G, Coryell W, Akiskal HS, Maser JD, Keller MB, Endicott J, Mueller T. Alcoholism in manic-depressive (bipolar) illness: familial illness, course of illness, and the primary-secondary distinction. *Am J Psychiatry* 1995;152(3):365-372.

[16] Hahesy AL, Wilens TE, Biederman J, Van Patten SL, Spencer T. Temporal association between childhood psychopathology and substance use disorders: findings from a sample of adults with opioid or alcohol dependency. *Psychiatry Res* 2002;109(3):245-253.

[17] Strakowski SM, Sax KW, McElroy SL, Keck PE, Jr., Hawkins JM, West SA. Course of psychiatric and substance abuse syndromes co-occurring with bipolar disorder after a first psychiatric hospitalization. *J Clin Psychiatry* 1998;59(9):465-471.

[18] Grant BF, Stinson FS, Dawson DA, Chou SP, Dufour MC, Compton W, Pickering RP, Kaplan K. Prevalence and co-occurrence of substance use disorders and independent mood and anxiety disorders: results from the National Epidemiologic Survey on Alcohol and Related Conditions. *Arch Gen Psychiatry* 2004;61(8):807-816.

[19] Bolton JM, Robinson J, Sareen J. Self-medication of mood disorders with alcohol and drugs in the National Epidemiologic Survey on Alcohol and Related Conditions. *J Affect Disord* 2009;115(3):367-375.

[20] Kuperman S, Schlosser SS, Kramer JR, Bucholz K, Hesselbrock V, Reich T, Reich W. Developmental sequence from disruptive behavior diagnosis to adolescent alcohol dependence. *Am J Psychiatry* 2001;158(12):2022-2026.

[21] Moss HB, Lynch KG. Comorbid disruptive behavior disorder symptoms and their relationship to adolescent alcohol use disorders. *Drug Alcohol Depend* 2001;64(1):75-83.

[22] Sherwood Brown E, Suppes T, Adinoff B, Rajan Thomas N. Drug abuse and bipolar disorder: comorbidity or misdiagnosis? *J Affect Disord* 2001;65(2):105-115.

[23] Albanese MJ, Clodfelter RC, Jr., Pardo TB, Ghaemi SN. Underdiagnosis of bipolar disorder in men with substance use disorder. *J Psychiatr Pract* 2006;12(2):124-127.

[24] Healey C, Peters S, Kinderman P, McCracken C, Morriss R. Reasons for substance use in dual diagnosis bipolar disorder and substance use disorders: a qualitative study. *J Affect Disord* 2009;113(1-2):118-126.

[25] Bizzarri JV, Sbrana A, Rucci P, Ravani L, Massei GJ, Gonnelli C, Spagnolli S, Doria MR, Raimondi F, Endicott J, Dell'Osso L, Cassano GB. The spectrum of substance abuse in bipolar disorder: reasons for use, sensation seeking and substance sensitivity. *Bipolar Disord* 2007;9(3):213-220.

[26] Pacchiarotti I, Marzo SD, Colom F, Sanchez-Moreno J, Vieta E. Bipolar disorder preceded by substance abuse: A different phenotype with not so poor outcome? *World J Biol Psychiatry* 2007:1-8.

[27] DelBello MP, Strakowski SM, Sax KW, McElroy SL, Keck PE, Jr., West SA, Kmetz GF. Familial rates of affective and substance use disorders in patients with first-episode mania. *J Affect Disord* 1999;56(1):55-60.

[28] Dunner DL, Hensel BM, Fieve RR. Bipolar illness: factors in drinking behavior. *Am J Psychiatry* 1979;136(4B):583-585.

[29] Strakowski SM, DelBello MP. The co-occurrence of bipolar and substance use disorders. *Clin Psychol Rev* 2000;20(2):191-206.

[30] Himmelhoch JM, Garfinkel ME. Sources of lithium resistance in mixed mania. *Psychopharmacol Bull* 1986;22(3):613-620.

[31] Tohen M, Waternaux CM, Tsuang MT. Outcome in Mania. A 4-year prospective follow-up of 75 patients utilizing survival analysis. *Arch Gen Psychiatry* 1990;47(12):1106-1111.

[32] O'Connell RA, Mayo JA, Flatow L, Cuthbertson B, O'Brien BE. Outcome of bipolar disorder on long-term treatment with lithium. *Br J Psychiatry* 1991;159:123-129.

[33] Haywood TW, Kravitz HM, Grossman LS, Cavanaugh JL, Jr., Davis JM, Lewis DA. Predicting the "revolving door" phenomenon among patients with schizophrenic, schizoaffective, and affective disorders. *Am J Psychiatry* 1995;152(6):856-861.

[34] Cassidy F, Ahearn EP, Carroll BJ. Substance abuse in bipolar disorder. *Bipolar Disord* 2001;3(4):181-188.

[35] Maarbjerg K, Aagaard J, Vestergaard P. Adherence to lithium prophylaxis: I. Clinical predictors and patient's reasons for nonadherence. *Pharmacopsychiatry* 1988;21(3):121-125.

[36] Keck PE, Jr., McElroy SL, Strakowski SM, West SA, Sax KW, Hawkins JM, Bourne ML, Haggard P. 12-month outcome of patients with bipolar disorder following hospitalization for a manic or mixed episode. *Am J Psychiatry* 1998;155(5):646-652.

[37] Goldberg JF, Garno JL, Leon AC, Kocsis JH, Portera L. A history of substance abuse complicates remission from acute mania in bipolar disorder. *J Clin Psychiatry* 1999;60(11):733-740.

[38] Manwani SG, Szilagyi KA, Zablotsky B, Hennen J, Griffin ML, Weiss RD. Adherence to pharmacotherapy in bipolar disorder patients with and without co-occurring substance use disorders. *J Clin Psychiatry* 2007;68(8):1172-1176.

[39] Gaudiano BA, Uebelacker LA, Miller IW. Impact of remitted substance use disorders on the future course of bipolar I disorder: findings from a clinical trial. *Psychiatry Res* 2008;160(1):63-71.

[40] Salloum IM, Cornelius JR, Mezzich JE, Kirisci L. Impact of concurrent alcohol misuse on symptom presentation of acute mania at initial evaluation. *Bipolar Disord* 2002;4(6):418-421.

[41] Scott H, Johnson S, Menezes P, Thornicroft G, Marshall J, Bindman J, Bebbington P, Kuipers E. Substance misuse and risk of aggression and offending among the severely mentally ill. *Br J Psychiatry* 1998;172:345-350.

[42] Manwani SG, Pardo TB, Albanese MJ, Zablotsky B, Goodwin FK, Ghaemi SN. Substance use disorder and other predictors of antidepressant-induced mania: a retrospective chart review. *J Clin Psychiatry* 2006;67(9):1341-1345.

[43] McIntyre RS, McElroy SL, Konarski JZ, Soczynska JK, Bottas A, Castel S, Wilkins K, Kennedy SH. Substance use disorders and overweight/obesity in bipolar I disorder: preliminary evidence for competing addictions. *J Clin Psychiatry* 2007;68(9):1352-1357.

[44] Kemp DE, Gao K, Ganocy SJ, Caldes E, Feldman K, Chan PK, Conroy C, Bilali S, Findling RL, Calabrese JR. Medical and substance use comorbidity in bipolar disorder. *J Affect Disord* 2008.

[45] Strakowski SM, Keck PE, Jr., McElroy SL, West SA, Sax KW, Hawkins JM, Kmetz GF, Upadhyaya VH, Tugrul KC, Bourne ML. Twelve-month outcome after a first hospitalization for affective psychosis. *Arch Gen Psychiatry* 1998;55(1):49-55.

[46] Strakowski SM, DelBello MP, Fleck DE, Arndt S. The impact of substance abuse on the course of bipolar disorder. *Biol Psychiatry* 2000;48(6):477-485.

[47] Sachs GS, Thase ME, Otto MW, Bauer M, Miklowitz D, Wisniewski SR, Lavori P, Lebowitz B, Rudorfer M, Frank E, Nierenberg AA, Fava M, Bowden C, Ketter T, Marangell L, Calabrese J, Kupfer D, Rosenbaum JF. Rationale, design, and methods of the systematic treatment enhancement program for bipolar disorder (STEP-BD). *Biol Psychiatry* 2003;53(11):1028-1042.

[48] Weiss RD, Ostacher MJ, Otto MW, Calabrese JR, Fossey M, Wisniewski SR, Bowden CL, Nierenberg AA, Pollack MH, Salloum IM, Simon NM, Thase ME, Sachs GS. Does recovery from substance use disorder matter in patients with bipolar disorder? *J Clin Psychiatry* 2005;66(6):730-735; quiz 808-739.

[49] Martinez JM, Marangell LB, Simon NM, Miyahara S, Wisniewski SR, Harrington J, Pollack MH, Sachs GS, Thase ME. Baseline predictors of serious adverse events at one year among patients with bipolar disorder in STEP-BD. *Psychiatr Serv* 2005;56(12):1541-1548.

[50] Hoblyn JC, Balt SL, Woodard SA, Brooks JO, 3rd. Substance use disorders as risk factors for psychiatric hospitalization in bipolar disorder. *Psychiatr Serv* 2009;60(1):50-55.

[51] Mazza M, Mandelli L, Di Nicola M, Harnic D, Catalano V, Tedeschi D, Martinotti G, Colombo R, Bria P, Serretti A, Janiri L. Clinical features, response to treatment and functional outcome of bipolar disorder patients with and without co-occurring substance use disorder: 1-year follow-up. *J Affect Disord* 2009;115(1-2):27-35.

[52] Potash JB, Kane HS, Chiu YF, Simpson SG, MacKinnon DF, McInnis MG, McMahon FJ, DePaulo JR, Jr. Attempted suicide and alcoholism in bipolar disorder: clinical and familial relationships. *Am J Psychiatry* 2000;157(12):2048-2050.

[53] Dalton EJ, Cate-Carter TD, Mundo E, Parikh SV, Kennedy JL. Suicide risk in bipolar patients: the role of co-morbid substance use disorders. *Bipolar Disord* 2003;5(1):58-61.

[54] Swann AC, Dougherty DM, Pazzaglia PJ, Pham M, Steinberg JL, Moeller FG. Increased impulsivity associated with severity of suicide attempt history in patients with bipolar disorder. *Am J Psychiatry* 2005;162(9):1680-1687.

[55] Elizabeth Sublette M, Carballo JJ, Moreno C, Galfalvy HC, Brent DA, Birmaher B, John Mann J, Oquendo MA. Substance use disorders and suicide attempts in bipolar subtypes. *J Psychiatr Res* 2009;43(3):230-238.

[56] Sonne SC, Brady KT, Morton WA. Substance abuse and bipolar affective disorder. *J Nerv Ment Dis* 1994;182(6):349-352.

[57] Goodwin RD, Stayner DA, Chinman MJ, Wu P, Tebes JK, Davidson L. The relationship between anxiety and substance use disorders among individuals with severe affective disorders. *Compr Psychiatry* 2002;43(4):245-252.

[58] Kolodziej ME, Griffin ML, Najavits LM, Otto MW, Greenfield SF, Weiss RD. Anxiety disorders among patients with co-occurring bipolar and substance use disorders. *Drug Alcohol Depend* 2005;80(2):251-257.

[59] Mitchell JD, Brown ES, Rush AJ. Comorbid disorders in patients with bipolar disorder and concomitant substance dependence. *J Affect Disord* 2007;102(1-3):281-287.

[60] McElroy SL, Altshuler LL, Suppes T, Keck PE, Jr., Frye MA, Denicoff KD, Nolen WA, Kupka RW, Leverich GS, Rochussen JR, Rush AJ, Post RM. Axis I psychiatric

comorbidity and its relationship to historical illness variables in 288 patients with bipolar disorder. *Am J Psychiatry* 2001;158(3):420-426.

[61] Levander E, Frye MA, McElroy S, Suppes T, Grunze H, Nolen WA, Kupka R, Keck PE, Jr., Leverich GS, Altshuler LL, Hwang S, Mintz J, Post RM. Alcoholism and anxiety in bipolar illness: differential lifetime anxiety comorbidity in bipolar I women with and without alcoholism. *J Affect Disord* 2007;101(1-3):211-217.

[62] Goldstein BI, Levitt AJ. The specific burden of comorbid anxiety disorders and of substance use disorders in bipolar I disorder. *Bipolar Disord* 2008;10(1):67-78.

[63] Gao K, Tolliver BK, Kemp DE, Verduin ML, Ganocy SJ, Bilali S, Brady KT, Shim SS, Findling RL, Calabrese JR. Differential interactions between comorbid anxiety disorders and substance use disorder in rapid cycling bipolar I or II disorder. *J Affect Disord* 2008;110(1-2):167-173.

[64] Ringen PA, Lagerberg TV, Birkenaes AB, Engn J, Faerden A, Jonsdottir H, Nesvag R, Friis S, Opjordsmoen S, Larsen F, Melle I, Andreassen OA. Differences in prevalence and patterns of substance use in schizophrenia and bipolar disorder. *Psychol Med* 2008;38(9):1241-1249.

[65] Estroff TW, Dackis CA, Gold MS, Pottash AL. Drug abuse and bipolar disorders. *Int J Psychiatry Med* 1985;15(1):37-40.

[66] Himmelhoch JM, Mulla D, Neil JF, Detre TP, Kupfer DJ. Incidence and signficiance of mixed affective states in a bipolar population. *Arch Gen Psychiatry* 1976;33(9):1062-1066.

[67] Brown ES, Nejtek VA, Perantie DC, Bobadilla L. Quetiapine in bipolar disorder and cocaine dependence. *Bipolar Disord* 2002;4(6):406-411.

[68] Brown ES, Nejtek VA, Perantie DC, Orsulak PJ, Bobadilla L. Lamotrigine in patients with bipolar disorder and cocaine dependence. *J Clin Psychiatry* 2003;64(2):197-201.

[69] Gao K, Verduin ML, Kemp DE, Tolliver BK, Ganocy SJ, Elhaj O, Bilali S, Brady KT, Findling RL, Calabrese JR. Clinical correlates of patients with rapid-cycling bipolar disorder and a recent history of substance use disorder: a subtype comparison from baseline data of 2 randomized, placebo-controlled trials. *J Clin Psychiatry* 2008;69(7):1057-1063.

[70] Jaffee WB, Griffin ML, Gallop R, Meade CS, Graff F, Bender RE, Weiss RD. Depression precipitated by alcohol use in patients with co-occurring bipolar and substance use disorders. *J Clin Psychiatry* 2009;70(2):171-176.

[71] Geller B, Cooper TB, Sun K, Zimerman B, Frazier J, Williams M, Heath J. Double-blind and placebo-controlled study of lithium for adolescent bipolar disorders with secondary substance dependency. *J Am Acad Child Adolesc Psychiatry* 1998;37(2):171-178.

[72] Salloum IM, Cornelius JR, Daley DC, Kirisci L, Himmelhoch JM, Thase ME. Efficacy of valproate maintenance in patients with bipolar disorder and alcoholism: a double-blind placebo-controlled study. *Arch Gen Psychiatry* 2005;62(1):37-45.

[73] Brown ES, Garza M, Carmody TJ. A randomized, double-blind, placebo-controlled add-on trial of quetiapine in outpatients with bipolar disorder and alcohol use disorders. *J Clin Psychiatry* 2008;69(5):701-705.

[74] Kusalic M, Engelsmann F. Predictors of lithium treatment responsiveness in bipolar patients. A two-year prospective study. *Neuropsychobiology* 1998;37(3):146-149.

[75] Salloum IM, Douaihy A, Cornelius JR, Kirisci L, Kelly TM, Hayes J. Divalproex utility in bipolar disorder with co-occurring cocaine dependence: a pilot study. *Addict Behav* 2007;32(2):410-415.

[76] Brown ES, Jeffress J, Liggin JD, Garza M, Beard L. Switching outpatients with bipolar or schizoaffective disorders and substance abuse from their current antipsychotic to aripiprazole. *J Clin Psychiatry* 2005;66(6):756-760.

[77] Brown ES, Beard L, Dobbs L, Rush AJ. Naltrexone in patients with bipolar disorder and alcohol dependence. *Depress Anxiety* 2006;23(8):492-495.

[78] Brown ES, Perantie DC, Dhanani N, Beard L, Orsulak P, Rush AJ. Lamotrigine for bipolar disorder and comorbid cocaine dependence: a replication and extension study. J *Affect Disord* 2006;93(1-3):219-222.

[79] Rubio G, Lopez-Munoz F, Alamo C. Effects of lamotrigine in patients with bipolar disorder and alcohol dependence. *Bipolar Disord* 2006;8(3):289-293.

[80] Drake RE, Xie H, McHugo GJ, Shumway M. Three-year outcomes of long-term patients with co-occurring bipolar and substance use disorders. *Biol Psychiatry* 2004;56(10):749-756.

[81] Brown ES, Gorman AR, Hynan LS. A randomized, placebo-controlled trial of citicoline add-on therapy in outpatients with bipolar disorder and cocaine dependence. *J Clin Psychopharmacol* 2007;27(5):498-502.

[82] Weiss RD, Griffin ML, Greenfield SF, Najavits LM, Wyner D, Soto JA, Hennen JA. Group therapy for patients with bipolar disorder and substance dependence: results of a pilot study. *J Clin Psychiatry* 2000;61(5):361-367.

PART III. TREATMENT OF ALCOHOL AND DRUG ABUSE AND DEPENDENCE

In: Suicidal Behavior in Alcohol and Drug Abuse... ISBN: 978-1-60876-919-3
Editors: L. Sher, A. Vilens, pp. 137-168

Chapter 9

PHARMACOLOGICAL TREATMENT OF ALCOHOL, TOBACCO AND SUBSTANCE USE

A. Ender Altintoprak
Ege University School of Medicine, Izmir, Turkey

ABSTRACT

Alcohol and drug dependencies are chronic diseases. They often follow the course of relapsing and remitting pattern. Addictive disorders represent a significant burden to the individual who suffers from them and to society. Although multiple medications have been investigated for treating addictions, only a few have shown acceptable safety and efficacy and are approved. On the other hand, for a successful treatment outcome and a long remitting period, rehabilitation and prevention programs must be added to treatment process. In many societies the people suffering from dependence are still stigmatized and have no access to treatment and rehabilitation. However, dependencies are preventable and treatable diseases, and effective prevention and treatment interventions are available.

INTRODUCTION

Because of the relapsing patern of the addictions, clinicians face both intoxication and withdrawal syndromes frequently. Sufficient medical managements may prevent medical/psychiatric complications and, it may serve for initiation to quit alcohol/drug use and, increase the compliance to psychosocial treatments, which are needed for longer remissions also. In the past decades scientific evidence indicates that the development of the disease is a result of a complex multi-factorial interaction between repeated exposure to alcohol/drugs and biological and environmental factors. The neurological changes in the motivation pathways in the brain must be taken into account especially for pharmacological treatments. On the other hand, maintenance treatments improve health, decrease communicable disease and criminal behavior, and improve social and occupational functioning.

The pharmacological treatments for intoxication and withdrawal syndromes and maintenance therapies of alcohol and most using addictive drugs-tobacco, cannabis, psychostimulants, opoioids, sedative-hypnotics, ecstasy and hallusinogens- are reviewed below.

1. ALCOHOL

Alcohol consumption may result acute (e.g. intoxication symptoms, traffic accidents, injuries) or chronic (e.g. alcohol abuse/dependence, medical or mental illness) consequences that need to be treated. Alcohol dependence is a treatable disorder when efficacious medicines are added to enhance the effects of psychosocial treatment [1].

1.1. Management of Alcohol Intoxication

The clinical manifestations of alcohol intoxication relate to blood alcohol levels. The management of alcohol intoxication and overdose is supportive. Patients should be evaluated for respiratory depression and pulmonary aspiration related to vomiting should be prevented. All patients with impaired consciousness should be treated with intravenous glucose and thiamine. It is also important to assess whether the patient has ingested other drugs in addition to alcohol, because this may alter the approach towards the treatment. If large amount of alcohol has been ingested within the last 30-60 minutes, or other drug ingestion is suspected, gastric lavage may be useful. In extreme cases hemodialysis can be used, but supportive care is usually sufficient for most of the cases. There is no reversing agent that is effective as an alcohol antagonist in alcohol intoxication. For only very agitated and violent patient, short-acting benzodiazepines (such as lorezepam) or/and an antipsychotic agent (such as haloperidol) can be administered attentively [2].

1.2. Management of Alcohol Withdrawal Syndrome and Delirium Tremens

Alcohol withdrawal syndrome (AWS) usually developes within 6–24 h after the last drink and can be a life-threatening condition affecting some alcohol-dependent patients who too suddenly discontinue or decrease their alcohol consumption [3]. It manifests from light to moderate forms, symptoms include increase in blood pressure and pulse rate, tremors, hyper-reflexia, irritability, anxiety and depression [3]. The symptoms of severe AWS may progress to more complicated forms characterized by delirium tremens [4], seizures [5] and coma [6]. In these forms, cardiac arrest and death may occur in 5–10% of patients [7,8]. Hence, AWS requires rapid and effective medical treatment.

Supportive care and repletion of nutrient, fluid or mineral deficiencies play a very important role in the treatment of AWS [9]. Supplementation, especially of B vitamins including thiamine to prevent the development of Wernicke-Korsakoff syndrome, is recommended [9,10]. Magnesium should be provided in cases of hypomagnesemia [9]. The major aims of pharmacotherapy are sedation of patients to control increased excitability manifested by agitation, anxiety and related symptoms and prevention of cardiovascular complications due to high blood pressure and pulse rate [9, 11]. Hence, beta-adrenergic blockers may be of value in patients with persistent hypertension in AWS [9].

Results from placebo-controlled studies suggest that benzodiazepines (BZDs), Beta-adrenergic receptor antagonists, calcium channel blockers, anticonvulsants, and clonidine reduce withdrawal symptoms [10,12].

Worldwide, benzodiazepines (BZDs) are the drugs of first choice in the treatment of AWS since they have proven their efficacy in ameliorating symptoms and decreasing the risk of seizures and delirium tremens [9, 11, 13]. BZDs act via allosteric effects at the GABA receptor and are cross-tolerant with alcohol, where carbamazepine and divalproate are also believed to have their main actions [14, 15]. There is good empirical evidence from a number of placebo-controlled studies of the clinical efficacy of BZDs. They are also superior to many other drugs for this indication [12]. Besides, BZDs are found to be more effective than antipsychotics in reducing the duration of delirium and mortality risk [16].

The most commonly used BZDs are diazepam, chlordiazepoxide, oxazepam, lorazepam and alprazolam. It is controversial whether short or long-acting BZDs are preferable. Many clinicians favour the long-acting agents because they provide a smoother course of withdrawal, may require less frequent dosing, and are more forgiving of a missed dose [17]. For patients who have severe hepatic disease, are elderly, or have delirium, dementia or another cognitive disorder, short-acting BZDs like lorazepam and oxazepam [9, 18] are preferred by some clinicians and appear to be efficacious [19].

In most cases, oral treatment with BZDs is sufficient and effective in the treatment of AWS. In severely disturbed or physically ill patients, especially those with delirium tremens, intravenous administration of, e.g., diazepam may be preferred [9]. Some authors suggest a single oral loading dose of 200-400 mg chlordiazepoxide or 20-40 mg diazepam, or as needed may be used [10]. Orally administered chlordiazepoxide (50 mg every 2-4 hours), diazepam (10 mg every 2-4 hours), oxazepam (60 mg q2h), and lorezepam (1mg q2h) are commonly used [10]. Another approach is to take the total dose necessary to suppress central nervous system (CNS) irritability and autonomic hyperactivity in the first 24 hours and give it in four divided doses on the following day. Then the dose can usually be tapered over 3-5 days with monitoring for the emergence of symptoms [20]. Some patients may require up to 10 days of treatment before benzodiazepines can be completely withdrawn [10].

However, the use of BZDs is associated with increased risk of excess sedation, memory deficits and respiratory depression in patients with liver impairment [17]. Besides, benzodiazepines have abuse and dependence liability [21, 22] which limits their use in subjects affected by substance use disorder [17].

In Europe, clomethiazole (also called chlormethiazole) is also widely used in the therapy of AWS [17]. It acts as a CNS depressant, causing sedation and sleep [23]. A major disadvantage of clomethiazole is its potentially lethal interaction with alcohol, causing respiratory depression and arrest [23]. Recent findings show that pharmacotherapy with clomethiazole may positively influence the risk of premature discharge. This might be a consequence of the psychoactive properties of the drug which leads to positive reinforcement [24].

Barbiturates have also been used in the treatment of AWS [25]. Although they have been proposed as an option in the treatment of alcohol delirium tremens [16], there are major disadvantages in using barbiturates. In fact, barbiturates have a narrow therapeutic window and can interfere with the clearance of many drugs using hepatic metabolism, thus creating the potential for multiple drug interactions [26].

New Non-benzodiazepine Medications in the Treatment of AWS

Due to their abuse liability, pharmacological interaction with alcohol, and adverse cognitive and psychomotor effects, BZDs have some limitations in clinical use. Hence, non-BZD drug alternatives are being investigated in AWS rigorously. New non-BZD GABAergic compounds represent promising medications in the treatment of alcohol-dependent patients [27]. Their particular mechanism of action may be useful in treating the various phases that an alcohol dependent experiences during and after treatment [27] particularly thanks to its mild side effects and no known addictive properties [21].

Anticonvulsants are suggested that they provide safe alternatives to benzodiazepines for the treatment of alcohol withdrawal in a number of studies [10, 22]. They appear to have comparable efficacy in preventing seizures during AWS as benzodiazepines [28]. However, the prophylactic use of anticonvulsants such as phenytoin is not generally recommended except in individuals with a co-occuring seizure disorder who have stopped their anticonvulsant drug while drinking [10]. Carbamazepine, oxcarbazepine, valproic acid and its derivates; vigabatrin tiagabine, topiramate and gabapentin are tested in AWS, and most of them seem as a promising treatment in the AWS (for more detail, see: Leggio et al. 2007]. However, antiepileptics face some limitations as a treatment for alcohol withdrawal: they have mostly been studied in patients undergoing mild or moderate withdrawal; some may interact with other drugs; some produce hepatic and hematological toxicities [29].; finally, some antiepileptics are currently available only in oral forms, which is a drawback for patients who are experiencing nausea, vomiting, or seizures. However, their efficacy in the treatment of alcohol withdrawal, low abuse potential, minimal interactions with alcohol, and possible efficacy in reducing alcohol intake make them good candidates for the treatment of withdrawal in alcohol-dependent patients [30].

Gamma-hydroxybutyrate (GHB) has been approved for the treatment of alcohol in some European countries. However, because of its potential for abuse, GHB is a Schedule III Controlled Substance in US [31], and has been approved only for cataplexy in narcoleptic patients by the Food and Drug Administration (FDA) [32]. It is not recommended to treat alcohol withdrawal or dependence.

Baclofen is a stereoselective gamma-aminobutyric acid-B receptor agonist with an approved indication to control spasticity [33]. In recent years, clinical trials suggested that it is potentially a promising and unique pharmacotherapy for the treatment of AWS and post-withdrawal [34, 35, 36, 37]. Baclofen was generally well tolerated and had no apparent abuse liability. Adverse events, none of which were serious, consisted of nausea, vertigo, transient sleepiness and abdominal pain [34].

1.3. Management of Relapse Prevention

The medications that have been evaluated in the treatment of alcoholism include disulfiram, naltrexone, ondansetron, acamprosate, anticonvulsants, and others. Currently, four agents are approved by the FDA for alcohol dependence treatment: disulfiram, acamprosate, oral naltrexone, and the once-monthly injectable, extended-release naltrexone [38]. An exciting development in the field of alcohol dependence is the potential use of antiepileptic medications for the treatment of alcoholism [30].

Disulfiram has been used for more than half a century in the treatment of alcoholism [39]. It inhibits aldehyde dehydrogenase, the enzyme that transforms acetaldehyde into acetate during alcohol metabolism. When a person drinks alcohol while taking disulfiram, the resulting acetylaldehyde accumulation causes an aversive reaction (flushing, sweating, headache, nausea, tachycardia, palpitations, arterial hypotension, hyperventilation) which discourages further drinking [1]. Serious side effects also have been reported, including hepatitis, hepatotoxicity, depression, and psychotic reactions [39]. Despite its widespread use, disulfiram has a limited and largely negative documentation for efficacy [40]. Disulfiram has no significant effect on craving for alcohol. Hence, patients must be highly motivated to maintain disulfiram treatment, whereas those who wish to drink can simply stop taking the medication. The efficacy of disulfiram is generally limited to those who are highly compliant or who receive their medication under supervision — i.e., the type of alcohol- dependent individuals who are likely to abstain on their own without adjunctive pharmacotherapy. Including a supportive spouse or partner in a disulfiram treatment plan helps to improve outcome [1, 40].

Naltrexon and nalmefene are opiate receptor antagonists. Naltrexon is most widely studied medication for the treatment of alcoholism [41; 42; 43]. Nalmefene has also been shown to reduce alcohol consumption [44; 45; 46] In 1994, the Food and Drug Administration (FDA) approved naltrexone for the treatment of alcohol dependence [1]. There are three forms of natrexon is available: oral, once-monthly injectable, extended-release forms. Naltrexone has been found to be efficacious in a number of well-controlled single-site studies [41], whose positive results have been confirmed in several meta-analyses [42,. 43]. Studies suggested that naltrexone can reduce craving for alcohol as well as its consumption; however, these effects appear to be more readily demonstrable among individuals with a positive family history for the disease and individuals with strong cravings for alcohol [1].

Nausea is the most reported adverse effect with naltrexon [47]. It's because of the rapid rise in plasma levels following initial doses of oral naltrexone [1]. Therefore, new technologies that aim to improve compliance by delivering naltrexone in depot form might possess a therapeutic advantage to the oral formulation. In addition, naltrexone has been reported to cause reversible, mild-to-moderate liver toxicity in some patients when administered at doses of 150 mg/d or higher [48, 49]

Acamprosate is an antagonist drug of NMDA glutamate receptors, which restores the balance between excitatory and inhibitory neurotransmission and modulates glutamate neurotransmission dysregulated following chronic alcohol consumption [50] Clinical trials in detoxified alcohol-dependent patients have shown the efficacy of acamprosate in lengthening time to relapse, reducing drinking days and maintaining abstinence [51, 52]. However, there are conflicting results in terms of craving. While some authors have reported a significantly favorable effect of acamprosate on craving [53], others have failed to observe any significant effects at 12 months of treatment [54].

Studies have also shown that acamprosate is relatively safe, with the most important adverse events being diarrhea, nervousness and fatigue, especially at a relatively high [55; 56] dose (3 g/day). Since acamprosate is excreted unchanged in the kidneys, there is no risk of hepatotoxicity, but it should be used with caution in those with renal impairment [55; 56].

Acamprosate has no significant clinical interaction with alcohol. It has been approved by the FDA in the treatment of alcohol dependence in 2004 [1]. From the European studies, acamprosate appears to benefit alcohol-dependent individuals with increased levels of anxiety, physiological dependence, negative family history, late age of onset and female gender [57] The results of U.S. studies have been disappointing that there was no overall clinical evidence that acamprosate was superior to placebo [1]. Future studies are needed to delineate more clearly what type of alcohol-dependent individual can benefit the most from acamprosate treatment [1]

2. TOBACCO

Tobacco use was introduced to Europe from the Indians by early Spanish explorers having reached to the New World. There, Jean Nicot was an early importer and cultivator of a plant he called *Nicotiana tabacum* (after himself). Although known since the end of the 18th century, nicotine was first isolated from tobacco in 1828 [58]. Nicotine is a major pharmacologically active substance in tobacco, accounting for less than 10% of the dry weight of the plant [59].

Although cigarette smoking peaked in many western countries in 1940s and 1950s, since then it has declined significantly in response to concerted public health campaigns and legislation. [60]. However, in 2000 about 5 million people died of tobacco-caused diseases and an estimated 10 million tobacco-related deaths are expected to occur by 2030 [61].

2.1. Management of Intoxication

Most people smoke cigarettes because of its relaxation, anxiolytic effects and to improve their concentration. Toxic levels of nicotine are very rare in smokers, nausea and headedness may occur, and it does not need to be treated generally [60].

2.2. Management of Withdrawal and Relaps Prevention

Nicotine withdrawal is defined as occurring where abrubt cessation of nicotine use, or reduction in the amount of nicotine used, is followed within 24 h by ≥4 of the following symptoms or signs: dysphoria, insomnia, irritability, frustration or anger, anxiety, difficulty in concentrating, restlessness, decreased heart rate, increased appetite or weight gain [60].

In addition to behavioral therapies, various pharmacologic strategies have been developed for nicotine dependence. First-line therapies include nicotine replacement, bupropion and varenicline. Second-line treatments include clonidine and nortriptyline. Additional treatment strategies with less proven efficacy include monoamine oxidase inhibitors, selective serotonin reuptake inhibitors, opioid receptor antagonists, bromocriptine, anti-anxiety drugs, nicotinic receptor antagonists (e.g. mecamylamine) and glucose tablets. Various approaches under investigation include inhibitors of the hepatic P450 enzyme (e.g.

methoxsalen), cannabinoid-1 receptor antagonists (e.g. rimonabant), and nicotine vaccines [62] (for more details, see: Firshman 2006; 2009)[58, 62].

Nicotine Replacement Therapies (NRT) are the most effective and commonly available pharmacotherapies for nicotine withdrawal and dependence therapy. Nicotine replacement therapy (NRT) has become the standard pharmacological treatment for tobacco dependence due to its well-proven effectiveness, benign side effect profile and easy availability through pharmacy and general sales points [63]. To date FDA has approved five nicotine replacement products: nicotine gum, nicotine patch, nicotine lozenge, nicotine nasal spray and nicotine inhaler. Innovative nicotine replacement formulations under investigation to facilitate rapid alkaloid delivery and ease in patient use include nicotine straws, nicotine wafers, nicotine lollipops, nicotine solution drops, buccal adhesive nicotine tablets, rapid-release nicotine gum, and a pulmonary delivery nicotine inhaler [64]. The dose and duration of NRT treatment should be based on the patient's subjective need for relief of withdrawal symptoms and support for smoking abstinence [65]. Some pharmaceutical companies are currently developing nicotine vaccines for human use [58].

Bupropion is an atypical antidepressant that has dopaminergic and adrenergic actions [66]. The mechanism of action of bupropion does not rely on the drug's antidepressant effects as the studies have shown bupropion to be equally efficacious in smokers with or without a history of depression [67]. It is a first-line therapy like the nicotine patch and gum, and should be offered depending on the patient's preference [58]. For patients interested in reducing but not quitting smoking, bupropion can help sustain reduction during the course of treatment, reduce the time to the next attempt at cessation, and increase short-term abstinence rates [68]. Bupropion can also be combined with nicotine replacement therapy with greater effects on smoking cessation than either treatment alone [69]. Side effects of bupropion include insomnia headache and dry mouth. Insomnia can be managed by taking the evening dose more than 4 hours before bedtime. Clinicians should consider the risk of seizure at high dosages (more then 300 mg) [58]. Bupropion should also not be used in combination with monoamine oxidase inhibitors or in patients with schizophrenia. Bupropion has been assigned a class B category for pregnancy by the FDA [70].

Varenicline is an orally administered small molecule with partial agonist activity at the alpha4beta2 nicotinic acetylcholine receptor. Varenicline was approved by both the US FDA and the European Medicines Agency of the EU in 2006 as an aid to smoking cessation. Subsequently, varenicline has been approved in over 80 other countries [71].

It was found out that Varenicline significantly reduces craving and the rewarding effects of smoking [72, 73]. It appears to have greater efficacy than bupropion SR or placebo [74].Varenicline improves quit rates and reduces background urge [75, 76]. However, adverse events associated with varenicline therapy have been reported in post-marketing surveillance, including neuropsychiatric events such as depressed mood, agitation, changes in behaviour, suicidal ideation and suicide. Currently, it is unclear whether the association of varenicline therapy with these adverse events is causal, coincidental or related to smoking cessation. Although available clinical-trial data support its use as an effective and generally well-tolerated therapy for smoking cessation in healthy adult smokers, there is a need for further efficacy and safety evaluation in the general population, particularly among those with comorbid conditions [77].

3. Cannabis

Cannabis sativa is the source of a number of products known collectively as cannabis [78] The term cannabis includes *marijuana*, the term for the cut and dried tops, leaves and stems of the plant; *sinsemilla*, derived from the buds and flowering tops of the plant; and *hashish*, the resin that coats the plant [79]. Tablets containing THC (Tetrahydrocannabinol, the main active ingredient in cannabis) can also be used.

Cannabis is typically smoked or eaten. The primary psychoactive compound in cannabis is D9-tetrahydrocannabional (THC), a highly lipophilic molecule that readily crosses the blood-brain barrier and has both sedative and hallucinogenic effects [78, 80]. THC has been shown to increase dopamine release in the nucleus accumbens like the other addictive substances [81]. While cannabinoids have been shown to interact with a number of neurotransmitter systems, including the GABAergic, glutamatergic, and cholinergic systems, its interactions with this dopaminergic system and with the opioid system is thought to be of primary importance in facilitating dependence [82].

3.1. Management of Intoxication

The initial and desired psychological effects of marijuana intoxication include relaxation, euphoria, slowed time perception, altered (often intensified) sensory perception, increased awareness of the environment, and increased appetite. The physiologic effects of marijuana intoxication include conjunctival injection ('red eye'), tachycardia (sometimes with palpitations), orthostatic hypotension (sometimes resulting in syncope), and dry mouth. [83]. Higher doses, repeated use, or a stressfull setting are associated with adverse effects such as hypervigilance, anxiety, paranoia, derealization and depersonalization (commonly associated with altered time sense), acute panic (associated with anxiety), illusions or hallucinations (usually auditory or visual), psychosis or delirium [84].

Adverse effects of marijuana intoxication tend to be self-limited and often can be managed without medication. The patient should be kept in a quiet environment and offered supportive reassurance. Benzodiazepines are recommended for severe agitation or anxiety, and low doses of second generation of antipsychotic are recommended for psychosis. Recently, rimonabant, a cannabinoid receptor-1 antagonist, has been shown to block the acute psychologic and cardiovascular effects of marijuana [85].

3.2. Management of Withdrawal and Relapse Prevention

For a long time, cannabis has been perceived as a "soft drug" causing questionable dependence. However, not only is D9-THC reinforcing, but there is also a well-characterized withdrawal state demonstrated by dependent individuals, especially by heavier users, when the drug is removed. The withdrawal syndrome of cannabis is characterized by anxiety, irritability, decreased mood and food intake, muscle pain, chills, disrupted sleep, and craving [86, 87, 88]. Furthermore, recent studies have indicated that cannabis smoking may precipitate psychosis in susceptible individuals and it may bring about serious physical and psychiatric consequences [89, 90]. The medical, legal and psychiatric impairment associated with cannabis dependence appears roughly comparable to that of cocaine dependence [91]

Despite high prevalence of cannabis use and its severe health and psychiatric consequences, very little research has focused on the treatment of cannabis withdrawal and/or relapse prevention and, most of these researches are carried out in small samples.

The treatment of cannabis withdrawal would be effective in countering anger, anxiety, aggression, anorexia, weight loss, irritability, nervousness, anxiety, restlessness and sleep disorders (and/or strange dreams) (for more details, see: Benyamina 2008) [92].

To date, there is not any recommended pharmacotherapy in marijuana withdrawal yet. It may be that a medication with stimulant side effects, such as bupropion [93], is not suited to treat marijuana withdrawal characterized by irritability, disrupted sleep and decreased food intake. Nefazodon[95], naltrexon [96] and divalproex [94] have shown several undesirable effects more than beneficial effects during marijuana withdrawal. Mirtazapine [98] was associated with improved mood ratings and well tolerated in withdrawal. Oral THC [94,97] between 30-90mg/d doses and the combination of lofexidine and oral THC [99] have shown some promise in the treatment of marijuana withdrawal and dependence.

Rimonabant, is a CB1-selective cannabinoid receptor antagonist, may be a useful medication in maintaining abstinence, but this result has not been confirmed in further studies yet. [100].

Clinical studies showed that oral THC in higher [97] doses was more effective than low doses [101] in alleviating cannabis withdrawal and, consequently, may be more effective in maintaining cannabis abstinence.

In a clinical study, the effect of *divalproex* maintenance on marijuana use was compared with placebo. All participants had CBT also. Marijuana craving and quantity of marijuana use and irritability reduced in both groups, although no significant differences between two groups were shown [102].

The result of the study on *buspiron* is promising. It was statistically significant decreased anxiety, craving and irritability and, marijuana use was reduced also with any adverse effect. [103].

Atomoxetine is a drug indicated in the treatment of adult attention deficit syndrome. It was found to be effective in decreasing cannabis use despite the high incidence of mild to moderate gastointestinal adverse effects. These adverse effects seem to limit the treatment acceptability [104].

4. PSYCHOSTIMULANTS

Most known psychostimulants include cocaine, amphetamine, amphetamine-like stimulants (Amphetamin sulfate, crystalline metamphetamine [ice, crystal, meth], methamphetamine base [paste], 3-4 methylendioxymethamphetamine [MDMA, ecstasy, E], paramethoxyamphetamine [PMA]) and benzylpiperazine. They are typically sympathomimetics, acting like noradrenaline to increase cardiovascular tone and activity and central nervous system arousal [105].

The demand for treatment of cocaine dependence did not change from 1992 to 2005, while the demand for treatment of amphetamine dependence increased about eight-fold [106].

In 2007, the United States had 1.16 million people dependent on cocaine during the past year [107] and the United Nations estimated about 14 million users globally [108].

4.1. Management of Intoxication

At the stage of desired effects of psychostimulant use (increased energy, alertness, and sociability; elation; euphoria; decreased fatigue, need for sleep, and appetite) users do not seek or need treatment [109]. However, the symptoms such as anxiety, irritability, interpersonal sensitivity, hypervigilance, suspiciousness, grandiosity, impaired judgment, stereotyped behavior, and psychotic symptoms such as paranoia and hallucinations require treatment. In such cases, patients should be evaluated for an acute neurologic lesion (e.g.; intracranial bleeding), a preexisting neuropsychiatric (e.g.; panic or bipolar disorder) or medical (e.g.; hypothyroidism, hypoglisemia) condition [84].

The initial treatment approach includes observing the patient in a quite environment with a minimal sensory stimulation; accepting immediate needs of patient (such as pain relief or use of bathroom) and reassuring the patient that the condition will dissipate in few hours [84, 105]. Patients should be monitorized closely for blood pressure, body temperature, pulse and respiratory rate; rehydration and electrolyte disturbances must be corrected (especially in the use of MDMA and PAM) [105]. The patients with chest pain should be monitorized with serial ECGs, cardiac enzymes and troponin levels for myocardial infarction; the risk is highest in the first hour of psychostimulant intoxication [105].

As far as possible, clinicians should avoid physical restraints, because it can increase the risk of hyperthermia and rhabdomyolysis, resulting in severe medical complications. Acidification of urine, e.g. with ammonium chloride may accelerate the excretion of amphetamines and amphetamine-like stimulants [105]. There is no specific antidote for psychostimulant toxicity [105]. If medication is needed, most clinicians prefer benzodiazepines (*diazepam* 10-30 mg PO or 2-10 mg IM or IV, typically dose required 60-80 mg in the first day; *midazolam* 2,5-10 mg IV or IM, maximum dose 20 mg or *lorazepam* 2-4 mg PO, IM, or IV) rather than antipsychotic drugs to control severe agitation, anxiety, or psychotic symptoms [84, 105, 111]. Parenteral benzodiazepine dosing may be repeated every 5-10 minutes until light sedation is achieved. In the case of psychosis, the high potent antipsychotics with low anticholinergic activity such as droperidol, haloperidol (5 to 10 mg PO, IM, or IV) or risperidon (2-4 mg PO) is recommended to avoid the delirium or hyperthermia [84].

4.2. Management of Withdrawal and Relaps Prevention

Psychostimulant withdrawal symptoms, including dysphoric mood, fatigue, sleep disturbance, appetite changes, and irritability, anhedonia, contribute to many dependent patients' difficulties quitting the drug [112, 113]. The initial period of intense symptoms is commonly termed "crash" but most symptoms are mild and self-limited, resolving within 1 to 2 weeks without treatment [84].

Simple and uncomplicated withdrawal may be managed in supportive home environment. However, severely dependent patients with medical or psychiatric complication are best managed in hospital. A supportive safe, quite and non-threatening environment is essential for rest and sleep. Nutritional supplement or well balanced diet rich in monoamine precursors, namely, phenylalanine, tyrosine or l-tryptophan, e.g pumpkin seeds, chocolate, marmite or vegemite, bananas may speed up the recovery [105, 114]. Short-term benzodiazepines may be administered for insomnia and agitation, e.g diazepam or lorezepam [84, 105]. It is important to recognize and treat the co-morbid psychiatric disorders; especially the patients with depression have increased risk for suicide [84, 105]. Severe and persistent depression symptoms may require antidepressant therapy. Tricyclic antidepressants (TCAs) and SSRIs appear to be effective in comorbid depressive syndrome, however TCAs treatment may be risky in the suicidal patient, and SSRIs may cause serotonin syndrome if combined with stimulants [105].

To date there are no widely accepted and evidence-based pharmacotherapy for the treatment of stimulant withdrawal or maintenance therapy. There are several drugs such as methylphenidate, d-amphetamine mazindol, levodopa (L-dopa) and carbidopa, amantadine, selegiline, disülfiram, adrogolide, ecopipam, bromocriptine, valproic acid, topiramate, tiagabine, baclofen, gabapentin, progesterone, adrenoceptor antagonists, vasodilators, oral formulations of cocaine, antipsychotic drugs and immunotherapies, that have been tested in psychostimulant dependence (for more details, see: Sofuoglu 2005 [115]; Kampman 2008 [116], Elkashef et al. 2008 [117]). The search for medications to treat amphetamine and methamphetamine dependence started much more recently than that for cocaine treatment medications. Consequently, fewer medications have been tested. Similarities between the mechanisms of action of amphetamine and methamphetamine and those of cocaine suggest that the same medications may help with both dependencies. Hence, several of the medications that have been discussed are under study for methamphetamine dependence.

The new and promising drug opportunities are described below

Modafinil is the most promising medication for abstinence initiation. It is a newer stimulant that increases daytime alertness in narcoleptic patients [118]. Preclinical assessment suggests that the stimulatory action of modafinil is nondopaminergic [119]. Modafinil has been shown to block the euphoric effects of cocaine in human laboratory studies [120, 121, 122]. As a mild stimulant, it may reduce cocaine withdrawal symptoms [123]. Clinical studies of modafinil showed low abuse liability [124, 125, 126], beneficial effects on craving [127, 128] and improving effect on cocaine abstinence rates [128, 129]. Modafinil was also found to be an effective drug in the treatment of methamphetamine dependence [130]. Although the modafinil was safe and well tolerated in phase I interaction studies with cocaine [131,123], it must be kept in the mind that it promotes wakefulness and may cause insomnia. Hence, clinicians are advised to avoid its use in patients with bipolar disorder or psychosis, as it may exacerbate symptoms of mania and psychosis. Besides, it should not be used in patients with left ventricular hypertrophy or mitral valve prolapsus, as patients with these conditions developed potentially serious adverse effects in clinical trials [116]. In summary, modafinil is a promising pharmacotherapy choice for cocaine and synthetic stimulant dependence.

Disulfiram is known as the drug that inhibits aldehyde dehydrogenase, hence it is marketed as a medicine for alcohol dependence for over fifty years. Disulfiram also inhibits dopamine beta-hydroxylase, the enzyme that transforms dopamine into norepinephrine. Such inhibition would increase dopamine levels and decrease norepinephrine levels in the nervous system. This effect is considered to be therapeutic for cocaine dependence. In addition, a disulfiram metabolite may block glutamatergic receptors [132]. Clinical trials have demonstrated that disulfiram reduces cocaine use in cocaine-dependent patients: Carroll et al., 1998 [133] and Higgins et al., 1993 [134] (cocaine- and alcohol-dependent patients); Carroll et al., 2004 [135] (patients dependent on cocaine only); George et al., 2000 [136] (cocaine- and opiate-dependent patients); Petrakis et al., 2000 [137] (cocaine- and opiate-dependent patients). Recently, beneficial effect of high dose disulfiram along with CBT was reported on alcohol and cocaine use in outpatients abusing both cocaine and alcohol [138]. In human laboratory studies, disulfiram inhibits cocaine metabolism increasing cocaine plasma levels, when the two are administered together [139] and subjects receiving disulfiram reported dysphoria, anxiety, and paranoia after cocaine administration [140]. Disulfiram is generally well-tolerated, although it may cause side effects, including sedation, headache, or a metallic taste in the mouth. Disulfiram is contraindicated in patients who have severe myocardial disease or coronary occlusion, psychoses; and those who are receiving/have recently received metronidazole, paraldehyde, alcohol, or alcohol-containing products. On the other hand, both cocaine and the disulfiram–alcohol interaction can produce severe cardiovascular effects. Hence, a patient who relapsed to cocaine and/or alcohol use while taking disulfiram might be at risk for serious, perhaps life-threatening, adverse events. This might limit the use of disulfiram in patients who are highly motivated for abstinence, have an active social support network for early detection of relapse and are in good cardiovascular health [141].

Propranolol is a beta blocker. Beta blockers reduce anxiety by reducing the impact of the neurotransmitter adrenaline. Hence, it suggested being effective in cocaine withdrawal symptoms. Along with potential efficacy against withdrawal-related anxiety, propranolol may lessen some of cocaine's rewarding properties and more uncomfortable symptoms of craving. Clinical trials have suggested that propranolol may help patients with severe cocaine addiction to remain in treatment and to establish initial abstinence [142, 143, 144]. Carvediol, another beta-blocker, was also found to be effective in reducing cocaine self-administration [145]. Propranolol is usually well-tolerated. The main side effect is sedation. However, beta blockers are best avoided in patients with a history of cocaine-induced cardiac ischemia. Patients who have applied to a medical facility with complaints of chest pain associated with cocaine use have been excluded from all clinical trials of propranolol for cocaine dependence and should not be treated with propranolol [116].

Dextroamphetamine (d-amphetamine) promotes to release dopamine and norepinephrine. Agonist replacement therapies are effective for managing substance abuse disorders including nicotine and opioid dependence. The results of preclinical laboratory studies and clinical trials indicate that agonist replacements like d-amphetamine may be a viable option for managing cocaine and methamphetamine dependence [146, 147, 148, 149, 150]. The model of opioid maintenance treatment has been adopted for amphetamine users in the U.K. using dexamphetamine and it has also been tried in Australia [117].

TA-CD Vaccine is another promising relapse prevention therapy currently being explored. TA-CD works by stimulating the production of cocaine-specific antibodies that bind to cocaine molecules and prevent them from crossing the blood–brain barrier, thereby blunting the drug's euphoric and reinforcing effects. Preclinical [151] and clinical studies supported this hypothesis [152, 153]. Either two doses or three doses of vaccinations were well tolerated and reduced the euphoric effects of cocaine [152, 153].

Baclofen is a GABA-B receptor agonist. Studies showed that baclofen significantly reduced cocaine craving and cocaine self-administration in cocaine-dependent subjects [154, 155, 156]. Preliminary evidence suggested that baclofen has some anxiolytic [157] and antidepressant [158] effects, hence it may have clinical utility beyond any anti addiction effect in cocaine-dependent patients who have psychiatric comorbidity.

Tiagabine, vigabatrin and topiramate are anticonvulsant drugs that increase GABA neurotransmission. Studies showed the efficacy of tiagabine in reducing cocaine use [159, 160, 161]. Tiagabine may have clinical utility beyond its antiaddiction effect. There is clinical evidence that it may be an anxiolytic agent [162]. Topiramate reduced the cocaine use also in the preclinical and clinical studies. [163, 164]. Topiramate seems as another promising agent. According the clinical studies, vigabatrin (gamma-vinyl GABA; GVG) was well tolerated and associated with substantial drug abstinence in cocaine- and/or methamphetamine dependent outpatients, albeit with about a 50% dropout rate [165, 166, 167]. Vigabatrin is not marketed in some countries (e.g. USA) because of concern over ophthalmological side-effects, but none were observed during these short-term studies [167].

Bupropion has stimulant-like effects in animals and is a weak inhibitor of the presynaptic dopamine transporter, but the mechanism of its therapeutic action is unclear. Although most of the studies have shown bupropion to be ineffective in treating cocaine dependence, a recent clinical trial suggested that bupropion, in combination with behavioral group therapy, may have promise for methamphetamine dependence [168]. Bupropion is fairly well-tolerated. Common side effects include insomnia, agitation, dry mouth, and nausea. This medication is contraindicated in patients with seizure disorders, current or prior diagnoses of bulimia or anorexia nervosa, or concurrent treatment with monoamine oxidase inhibitors. Bupropion should not be used in patients detoxifying from alcohol or sedatives [116].

Antipsychotic drugs blocks dopamine receptors, this may be a plausible therapeutic approach for cocaine dependence because cocaine acts directly on the dopaminergic system. Conventional (first-generation) antipsychotic, which act mainly as dopamine D2 receptor antagonists, are not effective in reducing cocaine use in patients with major psychiatric comorbidity (e.g. schizophrenia) [169]. Although olanzapine was reported as a effective drug for cocaine craving in two cases without psychiatric comorbidity [170], it was found noneffective in a double-blind placebo controlled trial [171]. Risperidon [172] and aripiprazol [173] was also found ineffective for cocaine dependence. A previous study also indicated that aripiprazole may have clinical utility in treating stimulant dependence [174]. Quetiapine was found effective in reducing the cravings and, improved some aspects of cocaine dependence [175]. Newer second-generation neuroleptics are currently being evaluated.

In summary, development of pharmacotherapies for psychostimulants is an area of active research. GABA medications including tiagabine, topiramate and baclofen have shown promise in early clinical trials. Because of its dopaminergic effects, disulfiram has demonstrated efficacy in a number of clinical trials.

Propranolol may also be effective in cocaine users with high withdrawal severity. Agonist replacement, like d-amphetamine, may be a viable option for managing cocaine and methamphetamine dependence. Some of the anticonvulsants and antipsychotics have shown promising effects. Finally, a cocaine vaccine holds promise for future treatment, especially for relapse prevention in combination with psychotherapy or medication treatments. It is hoped that effective pharmacological treatments for stimulant dependence will soon become available.

5. Opioids

Commonly abused opioids include heroin, hydromorphone hydrochloride, oxycodone, propoxyphene, opium, meperidine, and codeine [176]. All these drugs are associated with intoxication and withdrawal syndromes.

5.1. Management of Intoxication

Features of opioid intoxication include drooping eyelids, constricted pupils, sedation, reduced respiratory rate, head nodding, itching and scratching (due to histamine release) [177]. Generalized seizures may accompany petidine overdose; confusional state with agitation and rarely psychosis may accompany morphine overdose [178].

Patients with opioid overdose should be treated if the respiratory rate is less than 10 per minute or if they are hypoxic on pulse oxymetry (oxygen saturation <92%). In managing opioid overdoses, the primary concern should always be respiration and oxygenation. Typically, adequate respiration will resume within 30 seconds of naloxone administration. Naloxone is a non-selective, short-acting opioid receptor antagonist [177, 179]. It has been used as an effective antidote for overdoses of short-acting opiates such as heroin. A standard dose for the treatment of suspected heroin overdose is 400 mcg intramuscularly or 800 mcg subcutaneously, repeated 2 minutes later, if necessary. Initial use of high naloxone doses (>2 mg) can induce severe withdrawal, with the risk of vomiting and aspiration; very high doses (>10 mg) may even be life threatening [180].

Overdoses with opioids that are long-acting (such as methadone) or more potent (such as fentanyl) are more difficult to manage. They may require repeated boluses of naloxone or naloxone infusions [181]. Clinicians should be aware of precipitating withdrawal symptoms that may result angry and difficult behavior [178, 179]. Ideally, the patient who can mobilize as usual, have oxygen saturation on room air of >92%, have a respiratory rate between 10-20 breaths/minute, have a temperature between 35.0^{0}C and 37.5^{0}C, have heart rate between 50-100 beats/minute and, Glasgow Coma Scale score of 15 beats/minute may be discharged [182].

5.2. Management of Withdrawal and Detoxification Treatments

Physical dependency is the core component of the withdrawal symptoms. Hence, mild to severe withdrawal symptoms occur when the drug can not be used and often prompt to continuation of opiate use. However, some opiate users may intend to quit their opiate use in a safer and comfortable way in a detoxification treatment.

Features of opioid withdrawal include yawning, anxiety, muscle aches, abdominal cramps, headache, dilated pupils, difficulty in sleeping, vomiting, diarrhoea, piloerection (gooseflesh), agitation, myoclonic jerks, restlessness, delirium, seizures and elevated respiratory rate, blood pressure and pulse [177, 178, 179]. Generally these symptoms are not life-threatening (unlike alcohol withdrawal syndrome). The onset and the duration of these withdrawal symptoms depend on the amount and type of the opiate abused. According to the half-life of the drug, withdrawal symptoms may occur within hours of cessation of opiates. The withdrawal symptoms peak within 18-72 hours for heroin, 3-4days for methadone, 5 days for buprenorphine [178] and 8-12 hours for petidine [179]. It is not necessary for an opioid user to complete withdrawal from opioids before commencing opioid maintenance treatment [178].

Several detoxification protocols have been developed to assist patients through a safer and comfortable opioid withdrawal. Whichever of protocol is chosen; general supportive measures, such as reassurance, rest, hydration and good nutrition are useful [178, 179]

In the "tapering opioid replacement therapy", buprenorphine is given 4-8 mg in the first day, and then it is increased to 10-12 mg/day by 2-4 mg daily additional doses; later reduced by 0.4-2 mg/day to zero. Also methadone can be chosen for this option. In this case, 30 mg methadone is given in the first day, then it is reduced by 5 mg/day to zero [178]. Clinical trials showed that buprenorphine therapy is more effective than methadon or clonidine in reducing withdrawal symptoms [179].

In the "symptomatic treatment", BZDs are used for insomnia, anxiety and restlessness in 5-10 mg nocte or qid for 3-4 days, then taper off over 2-3 days; hyoscine butylbromide 20 mg qid for abdominal cramps; metoclopramide 10 mg tds for nausea and vomiting; loperamide or atropine sulphate for diarrhoe and antihistamines to help with insomnia. Alpha-2 adrenergic agonists' clonidine, lofexideine, guanfacine or guanabenz acetate is also used to reduce opioid withdrawal symptoms. Clonidine is the most used drug for this aim. It seems to be most effective in suppressing autonomic sign and symptoms of withdrawal but less effective in subjective symptoms [183], thus it may require adjuvant therapies (e.g.;BZDs, NSADs, antiemetics, anti diarrhoetics) [184]. While using alfa-2 adrenergic agonists, because of their hypotensive properties, close monitorization is needed. Lofexidine induces less postural hypotension than clonidine [177, 178] and therefore it is currently being studied in clinical trials for the medical management of withdrawal [179].

In "ultra rapid opioid detoxification", naltrexone is administered to induce opioid withdrawal under general anesthesia and in "rapid detoxification" it is administered under light sedation. Hence, detoxification period is shortened. Naltrexon is given for maintenance therapy, then. As it is associated with greater risks than conventional therapies, they are not standard practices [178, 179].

In the course of managing opioid withdrawal, clinicians also need to evaluate the medical problems such as acute bacterial infections, HIV and hepatitis C [179].

5.3. Maintenance Treatment in Opioid Dependence

Opioid Agonists Medications

Methadone is the major pharmacotherapeutic agent for the management of opiate dependence and is an orally active, long-acting synthetic opiate [185]. Investigators also reported that methadone doses ranging between 80–120 mg/day blocked the effects of intravenously administered heroin, hydromorphone, and methadone [185]; however 60-90 mg/day is sufficient for many patients to relieve withdrawal symptoms [178]; hence dosing should be individualized. Clinical trials using a variety of designs showed a benefit of methadone to reduce opiate use and retain patients in treatment. These studies also showed a collateral benefit to reduce recidivism, criminal activity, morbidity and mortality [177].

Methadone has the greatest risk of over sedation, but this risk can be reduced with lower doses (<20 mg) [177]. Methadone is included in Schedule I of the Single Convention in Narcotic Drugs, 1961.

Levomethadyl acetate (LAAM) is the alpha-acetyl congener of methadone. It was approved by Food and Drug Administration (FDA) in 1993 for opiate dependence [186], but FDA issued a "black box" warning for LAAM because of postmarketing surveillance reports of QTc prolongation in ECGs, with several reports of torsades de pointes, a polymorphic life-threatening ventricular arrhythmia [187].

Buprenorphine is a mu-opiate partial agonist [188] that was originally marketed as an analgesic product. The partial activity of buprenorphine means that it does not induce tolerance to opioids to the same extent as methadone. Its high receptor affinity means that buprenorphine can block the effects of additional opioid use without inducing the same degree of tolerance as methadone [177]. Buprenorphine 8mg /day was found to be effective to reduce craving and illicit opioid use [179]. The sublingual route was preferable to oral dosing because of high first pass effect [185]. Subsequent to the study by Ling et al.[1998], it was decided to develop a sublingual tablet and to add naloxon, an opioid antagonist, to the formulation[189]. In 2002, FDA approved sublingual buprenorphine tablets and buprenorphine/naloxone tablets for the management of opiate dependence [190]. Buprenorphine is included in Schedule III of the Convention on Psychotropic Substances, 1971. Clinical research over the past 15 years has established that buprenorphine (and buprenorphin with naloxon) is a safe and effective alternative to methadone and LAAM for opioid maintenance treatment [177, 179].

The main adverse effect of buprenorphine is headache. Besides, buprenorphine can cause significant respiratory depression when used in combination with other sedatives, including benzodiazepines, alcohol, tricyclic antidepressants, sedating antihistamines and major tranquilizers [177].

Opioid Antagonist Medications

Naltrexone is an orally active opioid antagonist, with an effective duration of action of 24–48 hours, making it suitable for once a day usage. It has a very high affinity for opioid receptors and will displace heroin, methadone in minutes and buprenorphine in 1–4 hours. It is used clinically after opioid withdrawal to prevent relapse to opioid dependence [191]. It should be initiated after at least a 5 to 7 days of opioid-free period for the short acting opioids and 7 to 10 days period for the long-acting agents [192]. A meta-analysis of multiple studies did not provide strong support for naltrexon treatment of opioid dependence [193]. Nevertheless, for some patients (such as health care professionals, business executives, or probation referrals) for whom there is an external incentive to comply with naltrexon therapy and to remain opioid abstinent, naltrexon has been very effective [194]. Injectable and long-acting form may be available for noncompliant patients. Depot formulation was found to reduce opiate use and reinforcement [195, 196]

6. Sedative-Hypnotics

Although, alcohol and marihuana are classified as sedative-hypnotics pharmacologically, in this chapter the term 'sedative-hypnotics' used only for prescription medications that are manufactured by pharmaceutical companies for treatment of medical disorders.

The most known drugs in this class are methaqualone, glutethimide, phenobarbital, temazepam, nitrazepam, lorazepam, alprazolam and triazolam. Sedative-hypnotics have been widely used, both therapeutically and sometimes illicitly.

6.1. Management of Intoxication

The patient with mild to moderate toxicity presents with slurred speech, ataxia and uncoordination, similar to that seen with alcohol intoxication. On occasion, particularly in the older adults, a paradoxical agitated confusion and even delirium may be produced. At more severe stages, stupor and coma may develop [197]. On the other hand, benzodiazepines rarely lead to death. The few that have occured all involves alprozolam and triazolam [198] or administration of benzodiazepines by an intravenous route. However, benzodiazepines in combination with alcohol, major tranquilizers, antidepressants, or opiates, can be fatal [199].

Treatment of intoxication involves gastric lavage, activated charcoal, and careful monitoring of vital signs and CNS activity. Vomiting should be induced. If a patient is comatose, the clinician must establish an intravenous fluid line, monitor the patient's vital signs, insert an endotracheal tube to maintain a patent airway, and provide mechanical ventilation if necessary [197, 200].

Flumazenil is a competitive benzodiazepine receptor antagonist with very weak agonist properties. It can reverse sedative effects of benzodiazepines, but cannot reverse the other sedative agents or alcohol effects. The effect of flumazenil is short, hence the symptoms may return in 30 to 60 minutes. Moreover if it is admistered rapidly in large amounts, seizures and cardiac arrhythmias may occur [201].

6.2. Management of Withdrawal

Sedative-hypnotic withdrawal syndromes resemble acute alcohol withdrawal syndrome in many ways. This resemblance is related to the properties of the binding site in the brain (the GABA receptor) [197]. Withdrawal severity has been related to dose and duration of treatment, and the withdrawal onset latency is related to the elimination half-life [202].

Benzodiazepine withdrawal manifests with many symptoms such as anxiety, sleep disturbance, restlessness, agitation, irritability, muscle tension, nausea, diaphoresis, aches and pains, letargy, depressed mood, depersonalisation, derealisation; besides delirium, seizures and death also occur in severe withdrawal syndrome [197, 203].

The current management of benzodiazepine withdrawal syndrome consists of: adequate treatment of continuing symptoms of depression or anxiety; utilization of a gradual taper schedule; and switching the patient to an equivalent dose of a long half-life benzodiazepines (e.g. chlordiazepoxide or clonazepam) or phenobarbital, if difficulty is encountered in tapering-off therapy with short half-life benzodiazepines [197, 204].The most common clinical recommendation for reducing benzodiazepines, withdrawal and improving clinical outcome involves the use of a gradual taper schedule [205]. Benzodiazepines should not be withdrawn abruptly because there is a risk of epileptic fits or confusion or experiencing paranoid psychosis [203].

Chlordiazepoxide, clonazepam and phanobarbital are the most widely used substitution agents [203]. If impaired hepatic function or elevated liver tests are present, then oxazepam may be a good substitute [206]. Lorezepam could be considered, but its abuse liability is much higher than that of oxazepam [207].

Clinical studies showed that carbamazepine 600mg/d may be an effective intervention for benzodiazepine gradual taper discontinuation. However, larger controlled studies are needed to confirm carbamazepine's potential benefit, to assess adverse effects and to identify when its clinical use might be most indicated [208].

Sodium valproat, gabapentine, topiramat and lamotrigine have been tried. More studies are needed to confirm their effectiveness in the sedative-hypnotic withdrawal symptoms Propranolol can be used in doses 60-120 mg/d as an adjunctive to one of the aforementioned withdrawal methods. Trazodone can be used to improve sleep during benzodiazepine tapering [197].

Flumazenil is a useful drug in acute intoxication. It is not useful as an adjunct to tapering. Because of its weak agonist properties, it may be useful to reduce cravings after the tapering is completed [209].

7. Ecstasy

Ecstasy (3,4-methylenedioxymethamphetamine [MDMA]) is an amphetamine derivative. It has hallucinogenic and sympathomimetic properties. Because of its stimulant and psychoactive effects, MDMA is used recreationally [210]. Characteristic intoxication symptoms include enhanced physical activity, sweating, mental confusion, trismus, bruxism, agitation, hyperreflexia, hyperthermia, shivering, rhabdomyolysis, metabolic acidosis, myoclonus, tremor, and nystagmus [211]. There are no clear guidelines for treatment. Gastric lavage with activated charcoal within the first hour after ingestion may be helpful [110]. Serotonin reuptake inhibiting antidepressants may offer a possible treatment for subjects. Exploring the use of paroxetine and the atypical antipsychotic drugs, olanzapine and clozapine, in human MDMA toxicity is indicated. Nantenine is a naturally occurring plant alkaloid that has been shown to block the behavioral and physiological effects of MDMA in mice [212]. Its safety and efficacy has not been documented in humans.

During the first few days of cessation the withdrawal of MDMA resembles a mild form of psychostimulants, heart rate and blood pressure may incraese [110]. It resolves without any treatment usually.

8. Hallucinogens

Most known hallucinogens are LSD, psilocybin, mescaline, DOM and STP. Different hallucinogens have different intoxication symptoms; most common symptoms are disorientation, impaired memory, depressed or elaveted mood, confusion, hallucinations, delusions, bizarre or suicidal behavior, violence, poor judgment. Physical symptoms such as dizziness, paresthesias, headache, nausea, or tremor may occure. Complications that require treatment are rare in the absence of over dose [213]. Initial treatment of hallusinogens is nonpharmacologic. Patients should be placed a quiet environment and observed because of the risk of self-injury or suicide. Clinicians should avoid the restraints if it is not necessary because of the rhabdomylosis risk [214]. If the patient do not respond the reassurance alone, PO or IM benzodiazepines (e.g. diazepam or lorezepam) may be effective. If the benzodiazepines are insufficient, a high potency antipsychotic (e.g. haloperidol) can be used [110]. There is no evidence to suggest a clinically significant hallucinogen withdrawal syndrome [215].

Conclusion

Addictions are major public health problem and resemble, in many ways, other chronic relapsing medical conditions. Hence, clinicians face both intoxication and withdrawal syndromes to manage frequently. Solid evidence available today is that pharmacological treatments can improve clinically relevant outcomes in addictions. The development of safe, effective treatments for addictive disorders is a high public health priority because addictive disorders represent a significant burden to the individual who suffers from them and to society. Although multiple medications have been investigated for treating addictions, only a few have shown acceptable safety and efficacy and are approved. Medical interventions also serve for initiation to alcohol/drug quit and, increase the compliance to psychosocial treatments, which are needed for longer remissions.

References

[1] Johnson BA.Update on neuropharmacological treatments for alcoholism: scientific basis and clinical findings. *Biochem Pharmacol.* 2008;75(1):34-56.

[2] Mayo-Smith MF. Managemant of Alcohol Intoxication and withdrawal. In: *Principles of Addiction Medicine.* Fourth Edition. Edited by Ries RK, Fiellin DA, Miller SC, Saitz R. Philadelphia, Lippincott Williams&Wilkins, 2009, pp:559-572.

[3] Kosten TR, O'Connor PG. Management of drug and alcohol withdrawal. *N Engl J Med* 2003;348:1786–95.

[4] Fiellin DA, O'Connor PG, Holmboe ES, Horwitz RI. Risk for delirium tremens in patients with alcohol withdrawal syndrome. *Subst Abuse* 2002;23:83–94.

[5] Pieninkeroinen IP, Telakivi TM, Hillbom ME. Outcome in subjects with alcohol-provoked seizures. *Alcohol Clin Exp Res* 1992;16:955–9.

[6] Morton WA, Laird LK, Crane DF, Partovi N, Frye LH. A prediction model for identifying alcohol withdrawal seizures. *Am J Drug Alcohol Abuse* 1994;20:75–86.

[7] Lerner WD, Fallon HJ. The alcohol withdrawal syndrome. *N Engl J Med* 1985;313:951–2.

[8] Schuckit MA. Alcoholism acute treatment. In: Schuckit MA, editor. Drug and alcohol abuse. *A clinical guide to diagnosis and treatment.* New York–London: Plenum Medical Book Co; 1995. p. 97–117.

[9] Soyka M, Kranzler HR, Berglund M, Gorelick D, Hesselbrock V, Johnson BA, Möller HJ; WFSBP Task Force on Treatment Guidelines for Substance Use Disorders. World Federation of Societies of Biological Psychiatry (WFSBP) Guidelines for Biological Treatment of Substance Use and Related Disorders, Part 1: Alcoholism. *World J Biol Psychiatry.* 2008;9:6-23.

[10] Kleber HD, Weiss RD, Anton RF Jr, George TP, Greenfield SF, Kosten TR, O'Brien CP, Rounsaville BJ, Strain EC, Ziedonis DM, Hennessy G, Connery HS, McIntyre JS, Charles SC, Anzia DJ, Cook IA, Finnerty MT, Johnson BR, Nininger JE, Summergrad P, Woods SM, Yager J, Pyles R, Cross CD, Peele R, Shemo JP, Lurie L, Walker RD, Barnovitz MA, Gray SH, Saxena S, Tonnu T, Kunkle R, Albert AB, Fochtmann LJ, Hart C, Regier D; Work Group on Substance Use Disorders; American Psychiatric Association; Steering Committee on Practice Guidelines Treatment of patients with substance use disorders, second edition. American Psychiatric Association. *Am J Psychiatry.* 2007; 164 (suppl 4):5-123.

[11] Leggio L, Kenna GA, Swift RM. New developments for the pharmacological treatment of alcohol withdrawal syndrome. A focus on non-benzodiazepine GABAergic medications.*Prog Neuropsychopharmacol Biol Psychiatry.* 2008;32:1106-17.

[12] Berglund M, Thelander S, Jonsson E. *Treating alcohol and drug abuse. An evidence based review.* 2003, Weinheim: Wiley-VCH.

[13] Saitz R. Clinical practice. Unhealthy alcohol use. *N Engl J Med* 2005;352:596–607.

[14] Lejoyeux M, Solomon J, Ades J. Benzodiazepine treatment for alcohol-dependent patients. *Alcohol Alcohol* 1998;33:563- 75.

[15] Nutt D. Alcohol and the brain: pharmacological insights for psychiatrists. *BrJ Psychiatry* 1999;175:114-9.

[16] Mayo-Smith MF, Beecher LH, Fischer TL, Gorelick DA, Guillaume JL, Hill A, et al. Management of alcohol withdrawal delirium. An evidence-based practice guideline. *Arch Intern Med* 2004;164:1405–12.

[17] Mayo-Smith MF. Pharmacological management of alcohol withdrawal: a meta analysis and evidence-based practice guideline: American Society of Addiction Medicine Working Group on Pharmacological Management of Alcohol Withdrawal. *JAMA* 1997;278:144–51.

[18] Bird RD, Makela EH. Alcohol withdrawal: what is the benzodiazepine of choice? *Ann Pharmacother.* 1994;28:67-71.

[19] D'Onofrio G, Rathlev NK, Ulrich AS, Fish SS, Freedland ES.Lorazepam for the prevention of recurrent seizures related to alcohol. *N Engl J Med.* 1999;340:915-9.

[20] Bradley KA.Management of alcoholism in the primary care setting. *West J Med.* 1992;156:273-7.

[21] Malcolm RJ. GABA systems, benzodiazepines, and substance dependence. *J Clin Psychiatry* 2003;64:36–40.

[22] Ait-Daoud N, Malcolm Jr RJ, Johnson BA. An overview of medications for the treatment of alcohol withdrawal and alcohol dependence with an emphasis on the use of older and newer anticonvulsants. *Addict Behav* 2006;31:1628–49.

[23] Williams D, McBride AJ. The drug treatment of alcohol withdrawal symptoms: a systematic review. *Alcohol Alcohol.* 1998;33:103-15.

[24] Hillemacher T, Weinland C, Heberlein A, Wilhelm J, Bayerlein K, Kornhuber J, Frieling H, Bleich S. Treatment with Clomethiazole is Associated with Lower Rates of Premature Discharge during Alcohol Withdrawal. *Pharmacopsychiatry* 2008; 41: 134-137.

[25] Murray TD, Berger A. Alcohol withdrawal. *Va Med Q* 1997;124:184–7 189.

[26] Blondell RD. Ambulatory detoxification of patients with alcohol dependence. *Am Fam Phys* 2005;71:495–502.

[27] Johnson BA, Swift RM, Addolorato G, Ciraulo DA, Myrick H. Safety and efficacy of GABAergic medications for treating alcoholism. *Alcohol Clin Exp Res* 2005;29:248–54.

[28] Ntais C, Pakos E, Kyzas P, Ioannidis JP. Benzodiazepines for alcohol withdrawal. *Cochrane Database Syst Rev.* 2005 Jul 20;(3):CD005063.

[29] Malcolm R, Myrick H, Brady KT, Ballenger JC. Update on anticonvulsants for the treatment of alcohol withdrawal. *Am J Addict.* 2001;(10 Suppl):16-23.

[30] Johnson BA, Swift RM, Ait-Daoud N, DiClemente CC, Javors MA, Malcolm RJ Jr. Development of novel pharmacotherapies for the treatment of alcohol dependence: focus on antiepileptics. *Alcohol Clin Exp Res.* 2004;28(2):295-301.

[31] Tunnicliff G, Raess BU. Gamma-hydroxybutyrate (orphan medical). *Curr Opin Investig Drugs* 2002;3:278–83.

[32] Pardi D, Black J. Gamma-hydroxybutyrate/sodium oxybate: neurobiology, and impact on sleep and wakefulness. *CNS Drugs* 2006;20:993–1018.

[33] Davidoff RA. Antispasticity drugs: mechanisms of action. *Ann Neurol* 1985;17:107–16.

[34] Addolorato G, Caputo F, Capristo E, Domenicali M, Bernardi M, Janiri L, et al. Baclofen efficacy in reducing alcohol craving and intake: a preliminary double-blind randomized controlled study. *Alcohol Alcohol* 2002;37:504–8.

[35] Flannery BA, Garbutt JC, Cody MW, Renn W, Grace K, Osborne M, et al. Baclofen for alcohol dependence: a preliminary open-label study. *Alcohol Clin Exp Res* 2004;28:1517–23.

[36] Addolorato G, Leggio L,AgabioR,Colombo G, Gasbarrini G. Baclofen: a new drug for the treatment of alcohol dependence. *Int J Clin Pract* 2006;60:1003–8.

[37] Knapp DJ, Overstreet DH, Breese GR.Modulation of ethanol withdrawal-induced anxiety-like behavior during later withdrawals by treatment of early withdrawals with benzodiazepine/gamma-aminobutyric acid ligands. *Alcohol Clin Exp Res* 2005;29:553–63.

[38] Garbutt JC. The state of pharmacotherapy for the treatment of alcohol dependence. *J Subst Abuse Treat.* 2009;36(1):S15-23; quiz S24-5.

[39] Suh JJ, Pettinati HM, Kampman KM, O'Brien CP The status of disulfiram: a half of a century later. *Journal of Clinical Psychopharmacology* 2006;26: 290–302.

[40] Heilig M &, Egli M. Pharmacological treatment of alcohol dependence: Target symptoms and target mechanisms. *Pharmacol Ther* 2006; 111: 855–876.

[41] Anton RF, Swift RM. Current pharmacotherapies of alcoholism: a U.S. perspective. *Am J Addict.* 2003;12:S53–S68.

[42] Streeton C, Whelan G. Naltrexone, a relapse prevention maintenance treatment of alcohol dependence: a meta-analysis of randomized controlled trials. *Alcohol Alcohol.* 2001;36:544–552.

[43] Kranzler HR, Van Kirk J. Efficacy of naltrexone and acamprosate for alcoholism treatment: a meta-analysis. *Alcohol Clin Exp Res.* 2001;25:1335–1341.

[44] Mason BJ, Ritvo EC, Morgan RO, et al. A double-blind, placebo- controlled pilot study to evaluate the efficacy and safety of oral nalmefene HC1 for alcohol dependence. *Alcohol Clin Exp Res.* 1994;18:1162–1167.

[45] Mason BJ, Salvato FR, Williams LD, et al. A double-blind, placebo-controlled study of oral nalmefene for alcohol dependence. *Arch Gen Psychiatry.* 1999;56:719–724.

[46] Drobes DJ, Anton RF, Thomas SE, et al. A clinical laboratory paradigm for evaluating medication effects on alcohol consumption: naltrexone and nalmefene. *Neuropsychopharmacology.* 2003; 28:755–764.

[47] Croop RS, Faulkner EB, Labriola DF. The safety profile of naltrexone in the treatment of alcoholism. Results from a multicenter usage study. The Naltrexone Usage Study Group. *Arch Gen Psychiatry* 1997;54:1130–5.

[48] Kim SW, Grant JE, Adson DE, et al. Double-blind naltrexone and placebo comparison study in the treatment of pathological gambling. *Biol Psychiatry.* 2001;49:914–921.

[49] Berg BJ, Pettinati HM, Volpicelli JR. A risk-benefit assessment of naltrexone in the treatment of alcohol dependence. *Drug Saf.* 1996;15:274–282.

[50] De Witte, P.; Bachteler, D.; Spanagel, R. Acamprosate: preclinical data. In: Spanagel, R.; Mann, KF., editors. *Drugs for relapse prevention of alcoholism.* Basel, Switzerland: Birkhäuser Verlag; 2005. p.73-83.

[51] Bouza C, Angeles M, Munoz A, Amate JM. Efficacy and safety of naltrexone and acamprosate in the treatment of alcohol dependence: a systematic review. *Addiction* 2004;99:811–28.

[52] Mason BJ, Goodman AM, Dixon RM, Hameed MH, Hulot T, Wesnes K, et al. A pharmacokinetic and pharmacodynamic drug interaction study of acamprosate and naltrexone. *Neuropsychopharmacology* 2003;27:596–606.

[53] Chick J, Anton R, Checinski K, et al. A multicentre, randomized, double-blind, placebo-controlled trial of naltrexone in the treatment of alcohol dependence or abuse. *Alcohol Alcohol.* 2000;35:587–593.

[54] Gual A, Lehert P. Acamprosate during and after acute alcohol withdrawal: a double-blind placebo-controlled study in Spain. *Alcohol Alcohol.* 2001;36:413-8.

[55] Johnson BA, O'Malley SS, Ciraulo DA, Roache JD, Chambers RA, Sarid-Segal O, et al. Doseranging kinetics and behavioral pharmacology of naltrexone and acamprosate, both alone and combined, in alcohol-dependent subjects. *J Clin Psychopharmacol* 2003;23:281–93.

[56] Mason BJ, Goodman AM, Dixon RM, Hameed MH, Hulot T, Wesnes K, et al. A pharmacokinetic and pharmacodynamic drug interaction study of acamprosate and naltrexone. *Neuropsychopharmacol* 2002;27:596–606.

[57] Verheul R, Lehert P, Geerlings PJ, Koeter MW, van den Brink W. Predictors of acamprosate efficacy: results from a pooled analysis of seven European trials including 1485 alcohol-dependent patients. *Psychopharmacology* 2005;178:167–73.

[58] Frishman WH, Mitta W, Kupersmith A, Ky T. Nicotine and non-nicotine smoking cessation pharmacotherapies. *Cardiol Rev.* 2006;14:57-73.
[59] LeHouezec J, Benowitz NL. Basic and clinical psychopharmacology of nicotine. *Clin Chest Med.* 1991;12:681- 699.
[60] Latt N, Conigrave K, Saunders JB, Marshall EJ, Nutt D. Tobacco. In: *Oxford Specialist Handbooks Addicition Medicine.* Oxford Uni. Press, 2009a, NY.pp:143-166.
[61] Ezzati M, Lopez AD. Estimates of global mortality attributable to smoking in 2000. *Lancet.* 2003;362(9387):847-52.
[62] Frishman WH. Smoking cessation pharmacotherapy. *Ther Adv Cardiovasc Dis.* 2009;3:287-308.
[63] Stapleton JA, Watson L, Spirling LI, Smith R, Milbrandt A, Ratcliffe M, Sutherland G. Varenicline in the routine treatment of tobacco dependence: a pre-post comparison with nicotine replacement therapy and an evaluation in those with mental illness. *Addiction.* 2008;103:146-54.
[64] Foulds J, Burke M, Steinberg M, et al. Advances in pharmacotherapy for tobacco dependence. *Exp Opin Emerg Drugs.* 2004;9:39 –53.
[65] Hurt RD, Ebert OJ, Hays JT. Pharmacologic Intervantions for Tobacco Dependence. In: *Principles of Addiction Medicine.* Fourth Edition. Edited by Ries RK, Fiellin DA, Miller SC, Saitz R. Philadelphia, Lippincott Williams&Wilkins, 2009, pp:723-734.
[66] Ascher JA, Cole JO, Colin J, et al. Bupropion: a review of its mechanism of antidepressant activity. *J Clin Psychiatry.* 1995;56:395–401.
[67] Hayford KE, Patten CA, Rummans TA, et al. Efficacy of bupropion for smoking cessation in smokers with a former history of major depression or alcoholism. *Br J Psychiatry.* 1999;174:173–178.
[68] Hatsukami DK, Rennard S, Patel MK, et al. Effects of sustained-release bupropion among persons interested in reducing but not quitting smoking. *Am J Med.* 2004;116:151–157.
[69] Jorenby DE, Leischow SJ, Nids MA, et al. A controlled trial of sustained release bupropion, a nicotine patch, or both for smoking cessation. *N Engl J Med.* 1999;340:685- 691.
[70] Aubin H-J. Tolerability and safety of sustained-release bupropion in the management of smoking cessation. *Drugs.* 2002;(suppl 2):45–52.
[71] Jiménez-Ruiz C, Berlin I, Hering T. Varenicline: a novel pharmacotherapy for smoking cessation. *Drugs.* 2009;69:1319-38.
[72] West R, Baker CL, Cappelleri JC, Bushmakin AG. Effect of varenicline and bupropion SR on craving, nicotine withdrawal symptoms, and rewarding effects of smoking during a quit attempt. *Psychopharmacology (Berl)* 2008;197:371-7.
[73] 2008 PHS Guideline Update Panel, Liaisons, and Staff. Treating tobacco use and dependence: 2008 update U.S. Public Health Service Clinical Practice Guideline executive summary. *Respir Care.* 2008;53:1217-22.
[74] Cahill K, Stead L, Lancaster T. Nicotine receptor partial agonists for smoking cessation. *Cochrane Database Syst Rev* 2007:CD006103.
[75] Gonzales D., Rennard S. I., Nides M., Oncken C., Azoulay S., Billing C. B. et al. for the Varenicline Phase 3 Study Group. Varenicline, an alpha4beta2 nicotinic acetylcholine receptor partial agonist, vs sustained-release bupropion and placebo for smoking cessation: a randomized controlled trial. *JAMA* 2006; 296: 47–55.

[76] Jorenby, D. E., Hays, J. T., Rigotti, N. A., Azoulay, S., Watsky, E. J., Williams, K. E., et al. Efficacy of varenicline, an alpha4beta2 nicotinic acetylcholine receptor partial agonist, vs placebo or sustainedrelease bupropion for smoking cessation: A randomized controlled trial.*Journal of the American Medical Association,* **2006;296: 56–63.**
[77] Garrison GD, Dugan SE. Varenicline: a first-line treatment option for smoking cessation. *Clin Ther.* 2009;31:463-91.
[78] MacFadden W, Woody G. Cannabis-related disorders. In: Sadock BJ, Sadock VA, eds. *Kaplan and Sadock's Comprehensive Textbook of Psychiatry.* 7th ed. Philadelphia, Pa.: Lippincott Williams &Wilkins; 2000:990–999.
[79] Nordstrom BR, Levin FR. Treatment of cannabis use disorders: a review of the literature. *Am J Addict.* 2007;16:331-42.
[80] Iverson LL. *The Science of Marijua*na. New York, NY: Oxford University Press; 2000.
[81] Tanda G, Pontieri FE, Di Chiara G. Cannabinoid and heroin activation of mesolimbic dopamine transmission by a common mu1 opioid receptor mechanism. *Science.* 1997;276:2048–2050.
[82] Tanda G, Goldberg SR. Cannabinoids: reward, dependence, and underlying neurochemical mechanisms—a review of recent preclinical data. *Psychopharmacology.* 2003;169:115–134.
[83] Grotenhermen F.The toxicology of cannabis and cannabis prohibition.*Chem Biodivers.* 2007;4:1744-69.
[84] Wilkins JN, Danovitch I, Gorelick DA. Management of Stimulant, Hallusinogen, Marijuana, Phencyclidine, and Club Drug Intoxication and Withdrawal. In: *in Principles of Addiction Medicine*. Fourth Edition. Edited by Ries RK, Fiellin DA, Miller SC, Saitz R. Philadelphia, Lippincott Williams&Wilkins, 2009, pp:607-628.
[85] Huestis MA, Boyd SJ, Heishman SJ, Preston KL, Bonnet D, Le Fur G, Gorelick DA. Single and multiple doses of rimonabant antagonize acute effects of smoked cannabis in male cannabis users. *Psychopharmacology* (Berl). 2007;194:505-15.
[86] Kouri EM, Pope HG Jr. Abstinence symptoms during withdrawal from chronic marijuana use. *Exp Clin Psychopharmacol.* 2000;8:483-92.
[87] Budney AJ, Hughes JR, Moore BA, Vandrey R. Review of the validity and significance of cannabis withdrawal syndrome.*Am J Psychiatry* 2004;161(11):1967-77.
[88] Elkashef A, Vocci F, Huestis M, Haney M, Budney A, Gruber A, el-Guebaly N. Marijuana neurobiology and treatment. *Subst Abus.* 2008;29:17-29.
[89] Arseneault L, Cannon M, Witton J, Murray RM. Causal association between cannabis and psychosis: examination of the evidence. *Br J Psychiatry.* 2004;184:110-7.
[90] Henquet C, Murray R, Linszen D, van Os J.The environment and schizophrenia: the role of cannabis use. *Schizophr Bull.* 2005;31:608-12.
[91] Budney AJ, Radonovich KJ, Higgins ST, Wong CJ.Adults seeking treatment for marijuana dependence: a comparison with cocaine-dependent treatment seekers. *Exp Clin Psychopharmacol.* 1998;6:419-26.
[92] Benyamina A, Lecacheux M, Blecha L, Reynaud M, Lukasiewcz M. Pharmacotherapy and psychotherapy in cannabis withdrawal and dependence. *Expert Rev Neurother.* 2008;8:479-91.
[93] Haney M, Ward AS, Comer SD, Hart CL, Foltin RW, Fischman MW. Bupropion SR worsens mood during marijuana withdrawal in humans. *Psychopharmacology* 2001;155:171–171.

[94] Haney M, Hart CL, Vosburg SK, Nasser J, Bennett A, Zubaran C, Foltin RW.. Marijuana withdrawal in humans: effects of oral THC or divalproex. *Neuropsychopharmacology* 2004; 29:158-70.

[95] Haney M, Hart CL, Ward AS, Foltin RW. Nefazodone decreases anxiety during marijuana withdrawal in humans. *Psychopharmacology* 2003;165:157–157.

[96] Haney M, Bisaga A, Foltin RW. Interaction between naltrexone and oral THC in heavy marijuana smokers. *Psychopharmacology.* 2003;166:77-85.

[97] Budney AJ, Vandrey RG, Hughes JR, Moore BA, Bahrenburg B.Oral delta-9-tetrahydrocannabinol suppresses cannabis withdrawal symptoms. *Drug Alcohol Depend.* 2007 Jan 5;86:22-9.

[98] Frewen A, Baillie A, Rea F. The role of Mirtazapine in cannabis withdrawal. In: *Collage of Problems on Drug Dependence.* 2007.Quebec, Canada.

[99] Haney M, Hart CL, Vosburg SK, Comer SD, Reed SC, Foltin RW. Effects of THC and lofexidine in a human laboratory model of marijuana withdrawal and relapse.*Psychopharmacology* 2008;197:157-68.

[100] Huestis MA, Gorelick DA, Heishman SJ, Preston KL, Nelson RA, Moolchan ET, Frank RA. Blockade of effects of smoked marijuana by the CB1-selective cannabinoid receptor antagonist SR141716. *Arch Gen Psychiatry.* 2001;58:322-8.

[101] Hart CL, Haney M,Ward AS, Fishman MW, Foltin RW. Effects of oral THC maintenance on smoked marijuana self-administration *Drug Alcohol Depend.*2002;67: 301-309.

[102] Levin FR, McDowell D, Evans SM et al. Pharmacotheraphy for marijuana dependence: a double-blind, placebo controlled pilot study of divalproex sodium. *Am J. Addict* 2004;13: 21-32.

[103] McRae AL, Brady KT, Carter RE. Buspirone for treatment of marijuana dependence: a pilot study. *Am J Addict.* 2006;15:404.

[104] Tirado CF, Goldman M, Lynch K, Kampman KM, Obrien CP. Atomoxetine for treatment of marijuana dependence: a report on the efficacy and high incidence of gastrointestinal adverse events in a pilot study. *Drug Alcohol Depend.* 2008;94:254-7.

[105] Latt N, Conigrave K, Saunders JB, Marshall EJ, Nutt D. Psychostimulants. In: Oxford *Specialist Handbooks Addicition Medicine.* Oxford Uni. Press, 2009, NY.pp:239-270.

[106] Substance Abuse and Mental Health Services Administration, Office of Applied Studies, 2006. Treatment Episode Data Set (TEDS): 1994-2004. *National Admissions to Substance Abuse Treatment Services*, DASIS Series: S-33, DHHS Publication No. (SMA) 06-4180, Rockville, MD: Substance Abuse and Mental Health Services Administration.

[107] Substance Abuse and Mental Health Services Administration, 2008. *Results from the 2007 National Survey on Drug Use and Health: National Findings.* Office of Applied Studies, NSDUH Series H-34. DHHS Publication No. SMA 08-4343.Rockville, MD.

[108] United Nations Office on Drugs and Crime, 2007. World Drug Report 2007. United Nations: New York, NY, pp. 82.

[109] Romanelli F, Smith KM. Clinical effects and management of methamphetamine abuse. *Pharmacotherapy.* 2006;26:1148-56.

[110] Wilkins JN, Danovitch I, Gorelick DA. Management of Stimulant, Hallusinogen, Marijuana, Phencyclidine, and Club Drug Intoxication and Withdrawal. In: *in*

Principles of Addiction Medicine. Fourth Edition. Edited by Ries RK, Fiellin DA, Miller SC, Saitz R. Philadelphia, Lippincott Williams&Wilkins, 2009, pp:607-628.
[111] Mokhlesi B, Garimella PS, Joffe A, Velho V. Street drug abuse leading to critical illness. *Intensive Care Med.* 2004;30:1526-36.
[112] Coffey SF, Dansky BS, Carrigan MH, Brady KT.Acute and protracted cocaine abstinence in an outpatient population: a prospective study of mood, sleep and withdrawal symptoms.*Drug Alcohol Depend.* 2000;59:277-86.
[113] McGregor C, Srisurapanont M, Jittiwutikarn J, Laobhripatr S, Wongtan T, White JM. The nature, time course and severity of methamphetamine withdrawal. *Addiction.* 2005;100:1320-9.
[114] Ling W, Rawson R, Shoptaw S, Ling W. Management of methamphetamine abuse and dependence. *Curr Psychiatry Rep.* 2006;8:345-54.
[115] Sofuoglu M, Kosten TR. Novel approaches to the treatment of cocaine addiction. *CNS Drugs.* 2005;19:13-25.
[116] Kampman KM. The search for medications to treat stimulant dependence. *Addict Sci Clin Pract* 2008;4:28-35.
[117] Elkashef A, Vocci F, Hanson G, White J, Wickes W, Tiihonen J. Pharmacotherapy of methamphetamine addiction: an update. *Subst Abus.* 2008;29:31-49.
[118] Moldofsky H, Broughton RJ, Hill JD: A randomized trial of longterm continued efficacy and safety of modafinil in narcolepsy. *Sleep Med* 2000;1:109–116.
[119] Ferraro L, Antonelli T, O'Connor WT, Tanganelli S, Rambert FA, Fuxe K: Modafinil: an antinarcoleptic drug with a different neurochemical profile to d-amphetamine and dopamine uptake blockers. *Biol Psychiatry* 1997; 42:1181–1183.
[120] Dackis CA, Lynch KG, Yu E, Samaha FF, Kampman KM, Cornish JW, Rowan A, Poole S, White L, O'Brien CP. 2003. Modafinil and cocaine: A double-blind, placebo-controlled drug interaction study. *Drug Alcohol Depend.* 2003;70:29-37.
[121] Malcolm R, Swayngim K, Donovan JL, DeVane CL, Elkashef A, Chiang N, Khan R, Mojsiak J, Myrick DL, Hedden S, Cochran K, Woolson RF. Modafinil and cocaine interactions. *Am J Drug Alcohol Abuse.* 2006;32:577-87.
[122] Hart CL, Haney M, Vosburg SK, Rubin E, Foltin RW. Smoked cocaine self-administration is decreased by modafinil. *Neuropsychopharmacology.* 2008;33:761-8.
[123] Dackis C, O'Brien C. Glutamatergic agents for cocaine dependence. *Ann N Y Acad Sci.* 2003;1003:328-45.
[124] Rush CR, Kelly TH, Hays LR, Baker RW, Wooten AF: Acute behavioral and physiological effects on modafinil in drug abusers. *Behav Pharmacol* 2002;13:105–115 62.
[125] Jasinski DR: An evaluation of the abuse potential of modafinilusing methylphenidate as a reference. *J Psychopharmacol* 2000;14:53–60.
[126] Warot D, Corruble E, Payan C, Weil JS, Peuch AJ: Subjective effects of modafinil: a new central adrenergic stimulant in healthy volunteers: a comparison with amphetamine, caffeine, and placebo. *Eur Psychiatry* 1993;8:201–208.
[127] Malcolm R, Book SW, Moak D, DeVane L, Czepowicz V: Clinical applications of modafinil in stimulant abusers: low abuse potential. *Am J Addict* 2002;11:247–249.
[128] Anderson AL, Reid MS, Li SH, Holmes T, Shemanski L, Slee A, Smith EV, Kahn R, Chiang N, Vocci F, Ciraulo D, Dackis C, Roache JD, Salloum IM, Somoza E, Urschel

HC 3rd, Elkashef AM. Modafinil for the treatment of cocaine dependence. *Drug Alcohol Depend.* 2009;104:133-9.

[129] Dackis CA, Kampman KM, Lynch KG, Pettinati HM, O'Brien CP. A double-blind, placebo-controlled trial of modafinil for cocaine dependence. *Neuropsychopharmacology.* 2005;30:205-11.

[130] Shearer J, Darke S, Rodgers C, Slade T, van Beek I, Lewis J, Brady D, McKetin R, Mattick RP, Wodak A. A double-blind, placebo-controlled trial of modafinil (200 mg/day) for methamphetamine dependence. *Addiction.* 2009;104:224-33.

[131] Donovan, J.L., DeVane, C.L., Malcolm, R.J., Mojsiak, J., Chiang, C.N., Elkashef, A., Taylor, R.M., Modafinil influences the pharmacokinetics of intravenous cocaine in healthy cocaine-dependent volunteers. *Clin. Pharmacokinet.* 2005;44:753–765.

[132] Ningaraj N, Chen W, Schloss J, Faiman M, Wu J-Y. S-Methyl-N,N-diethylthiocarbamate sulfoxide elicits neuroprotective effect against N-methyl-D-aspartate receptor-mediated neurotoxicity. *Journal of Biomedical Science* 2001;8:104–113.

[133] Carroll KM, Nich C, Ball SA, McCance E, Rounsavile BJ. Treatment of cocaine and alcohol dependence with psychotherapy and disulfiram. *Addiction*1998;93:713–727.

[134] Higgins ST, Budney AJ, Bickel WK, Hughes JR, Foerg F: Disulfiram therapy in patients abusing cocaine and alcohol (letter). *Am J Psychiatry* 1993; 150:675–676.

[135] Carroll KM, Fenton LR, Ball SA, Nich C, Frankforter TL, Shi J, Rounsaville BJ. Efficacy of disulfiram and cognitive behavior therapy in cocaine-dependent outpatients: A randomized placebo-controlled trial. *Arch Gen Psychiatry.* 2004;61:264-72.

[136] George TP, Chawarski MC, Pakes J, Carroll KM, Kosten TR, Schottenfeld RS.. Disulfiram versus placebo for cocaine dependence in buprenorphine-maintained subjects: A preliminary trial. *Biol Psychiatry.* 2000;47:1080-6.

[137] Petrakis IL, Carroll KM, Nich C, Gordon LT, McCance-Katz EF, Frankforter T, Rounsaville BJ. Disulfiram treatment for cocaine dependence in methadone-maintained opioid addicts. *Addiction.* 2000;95:219-28.

[138] Grassi MC, Cioce AM, Giudici FD, Antonilli L, Nencini P. Short-term efficacy of Disulfiram or Naltrexone in reducing positive urinalysis for both cocaine and cocaethylene in cocaine abusers: a pilot study. *Pharmacol Res.* 2007;55:117-21.

[139] Baker JR, Jatlow P, McCance-Katz EF. Disulfiram effects on responses to intravenous cocaine administration. *Drug Alcohol Depend.* 2007;87:202-9.

[140] McCance EF, Kosten TR, Jatlow P: Chronic disulfiram treatment effects on intranasal cocaine administration. *Biol Psychiatry* 1998; 43:540–543.

[141] Karila L, Gorelick D, Weinstein A, Noble F, Benyamina A, Coscas S, Blecha L, Lowenstein W, Martinot JL, Reynaud M, Lépine JP. New treatments for cocaine dependence: a focused review. *Int J Neuropsychopharmacol.* 2008;11:425-38.

[142] Kampman KM, Rukstalis M, Ehrman R, McGinnis DE, Gariti P, Volpicelli JR, Pettinati H, O'Brien CP. Open trials as a method of prioritizing medications for inclusion in controlled trials for cocaine dependence. *Addict Behav.* 1999;24:287-91.

[143] Kampman KM, Alterman AI, Volpicelli JR, Maany I, Muller ES, Luce DD, Mulholland EM, Jawad AF, Parikh GA, Mulvaney FD, Weinrieb RM, O'Brien CP. Cocaine withdrawal symptoms and initial urine toxicology results predict treatment

attrition in outpatient cocaine dependence treatment. *Psychol Addict Behav.* 2001;15:52-9.
[144] Kampman KM, Dackis C, Lynch KG, Pettinati H, Tirado C, Gariti P, Sparkman T, Atzram M, O'Brien CP. A double-blind, placebo-controlled trial of amantadine, propranolol, and their combination for the treatment of cocaine dependence in patients with severe cocaine withdrawal symptoms. *Drug Alcohol Depend.* 2006;85:129-37.
[145] Sofuoglu M, Brown S, Babb DA, Pentel PR, Hatsukami DK. Carvedilol affects the physiological and behavioral response to smoked cocaine in humans. *Drug Alcohol Depend.* 2000;60:69-76.
[146] Negus SS, Mello NK.Effects of chronic d-amphetamine treatment on cocaine- and food-maintained responding under a progressive-ratio schedule in rhesus monkeys. *Psychopharmacology* (Berlin) 2003;167:324–332.
[147] Grabowski J, Rhoades H, Schmitz J, Stotts A, Daruzska LA, Creson D, Moeller FG Dextroamphetamine for cocaine-dependence treatment: a double-blind randomized clinical trial. *Journal of Clinical Psychopharmacology* 2001;21:522–526.
[148] Grabowski J, Rhoades H, Stotts A, Cowan K, Kopecky C, Dougherty A, Moeller FG, Hassan S, Schmitz J. Agonist-like or antagonist-like treatment for cocaine dependence with methadone for heroin dependence: two double-blind randomized clinical trials. *Neuropsychopharmacology* 2004;29, 969–981.
[149] Shearer J, Wodak A, van Beek I, Mattick RP, Lewis J. Pilot randomized double blind placebo-controlled study of dexamphetamine for cocaine dependence. *Addiction* 2003;98:1137–1141.
[150] Rush CR, Stoops WW, Hays LR. Cocaine effects during d-amphetamine maintenance: A human laboratory analysis of safety, tolerability and efficacy. *Drug Alcohol Depend.* 2009;99:261-71.
[151] Kantak KM, Collins SL, Lipman EG, Bond J, Giovanoni K, Fox BS. Evaluation of anti-cocaine antibodies and a cocaine vaccine in a rat self- *Psychopharmacology* (Berl). 2000;148:251-62.
[152] Kosten TR, Rosen M, Bond J, Settles M, Roberts JS, Shields J, Jack L, Fox B.Human therapeutic cocaine vaccine: Safety and immunogenicity. *Vaccine* 2002; 20:1196-1204.
[153] Martell BA, Mitchell E, Poling J, Gonsai K, Kosten TR Vaccine pharmacotherapy for the treatment of cocaine dependence. *Biol Psychiatry.* 2005;58:158-64.
[154] Brebner K, Childress AR, Roberts DCS: A potential role for GABA(B) agonists in the treatment of psychostimulant addiction. *Alcohol Alcohol* 2002; 37:478–484.
[155] Haney M, Hart CL, Foltin RW Effects of baclofen on cocaine self-administration: opioid- and nonopioid-dependent volunteers. *Neuropsychopharmacology.* 2006;31:1814-21.
[156] Shoptaw S, Yang X, Rotherman-Fuller EJ, Hsieh YC, Kintaudi PC, Charuvastra YC, Ling W: Randomized placebo-controlled trial of baclofen for cocaine dependence: preliminary effects for individuals with chronic patterns of cocaine use. *J Clin Psychiatry* 2003; 64:1440–1448.
[157] Drake RG, Davis LL, Cates ME, Jewell ME, Ambrose SM, Lowe JS. Baclofen treatment for chronic posttraumatic stress disorder. *Ann Pharmacother.* 2003;37:1177-81.

[158] Krupitsky EM, Burakov AM, Ivanov VB, Krandashova GF, Lapin IP, Grinenko AJa, Borodkin YuS. Baclofen administration for the treatment of affective disorders in alcoholic patients. *Drug Alcohol Depend.* 1993;33:157-63.

[159] Winhusen TM, Somoza EC, Harrer JM, Mezinskis JP, Montgomery MA, Goldsmith RJ, Coleman FS, Bloch DA, Leiderman DB, Singal BM, Berger P, Elkashef A. A placebo-controlled screening trial of tiagabine, sertraline and donepezil as cocaine dependence treatments. *Addiction.* 2005;(Suppl 1):68-77.

[160] Gonzalez G, Sevarino K, Sofuoglu M, Poling J, Oliveto A, Gonsai K, George TP, Kosten TR. Tiagabine increases cocaine-free urines in cocaine-dependent methadone-treated patients: results of a randomized pilot study. *Addiction.* 2003;98:1625-32.

[161] González G, Desai R, Sofuoglu M, Poling J, Oliveto A, Gonsai K, Kosten TR. Clinical efficacy of gabapentin versus tiagabine for reducing cocaine use among cocaine dependent methadone-treated patients. *Drug Alcohol Depend.* 2007;23;87:1-9.

[162] Schwartz TL, Nihalani N. Tiagabine in anxiety disorders. *Expert Opin Pharmacother.* 2006;7:1977-87.

[163] Johnson BA Recent advances in the development of treatments for alcohol and cocaine dependence: focus on topiramate and other modulators of GABA or glutamate function. *CNS Drugs* 2005;19:873-96.

[164] Kampman KM, Pettinati H, Lynch KG, Dackis C, Sparkman T, Weigley C, O'Brien CP. A pilot trial of topiramate for the treatment of cocaine dependence. *Drug Alcohol Depend.* 2004;75:233-40.

[165] Brodie JD, Figueroa E, Dewey SL Treating cocaine addiction: from preclinical to clinical trial experience with gamma-vinyl GABA. *Synapse*2003;50: 261–265.

[166] Brodie JD, Figueroa E, Laska EM, Dewey SL. Safety and efficacy of gamma-vinyl GABA (GVG) for the treatment of methamphetamine and/or cocaine addiction. *Synapse* 2005;55:122–125.

[167] Fechtner R, Khouri A, Figueroa E, Ramirez M, Federico M, Dewey S, Brodie JD Short-term treatment of cocaine and/or methamphetamine abuse with vigabatrin: ocular safety pilot results. *Archives of Ophthalmology* 2006;124:1257–1262.

[168] Elkashef AM, Rawson RA, Anderson AL, Li SH, Holmes T, Smith EV, Chiang N, Kahn R, Vocci F, Ling W, Pearce VJ, McCann M, Campbell J, Gorodetzky C, Haning W, Carlton B, Mawhinney J, Weis D. Bupropion for the treatment of methamphetamine dependence. *Neuropsychopharmacology.* 2008;33:1162-70.

[169] Green AI. Schizophrenia and comorbid substance use disorder: effects of antipsychotics. *J Clin Psychiatry.* 2005;(Suppl 6):21-6.

[170] Longo LP. Olanzapine for cocaine craving and relapse prevention in 2 patients. *J Clin Psychiatry.* 2002;63:595-6.

[171] Hamilton JD, Nguyen QX, Gerber RM, Rubio NB. Olanzapine in cocaine dependence: a double-blind, placebo-controlled trial. *Am J Addict.* 2009;18:48-52.

[172] Loebl T, Angarita GA, Pachas GN, Huang KL, Lee SH, Nino J, Logvinenko T, Culhane MA, Evins AE. A randomized, double-blind, placebo-controlled trial of long-acting risperidone in cocaine-dependent men. *J Clin Psychiatry.* 2008;69:480-6.

[173] Stoops WW, Lile JA, Lofwall MR, Rush CR. The safety, tolerability, and subject-rated effects of acute intranasal cocaine administration during aripiprazole maintenance. *Am J Drug Alcohol Abuse.* 2007;33:769-76.

[174] Stoops WW. Aripiprazole as a potential pharmacotherapy for stimulant dependence: human laboratory studies with d-amphetamine. *Exp Clin Psychopharmacol.* 2006;14:413-21.

[175] Kennedy A, Wood AE, Saxon AJ, Malte C, Harvey M, Jurik J, Kilzieh N, Lofgreen C, Tapp A. Quetiapine for the treatment of cocaine dependence: an open-label trial. *J Clin Psychopharmacol.* 2008;28:221-4.

[176] Chang G.Kosten TR. Detoxification. In: *Substance Abuse,* 4th Edition. Editors: Lowinson, Joyce H.; Ruiz, Pedro; Millman, Robert B.; Langrod, John G. Lippincott Williams & Wilkins. 2005. pp:579-587.

[177] WHO 2009: Guidelines for the psychosocially assisted pharmacological treatment of opioid dependence. WHO Press, Geneva, Switzerland] To Access: http://www.who.int/substance_abuse/publications/Opioid_dependence_guidelines.pdf

[178] Latt N, Conigrave K, Saunders JB, Marshall EJ, Nutt D. Opioids. In: *Oxford Specialist Handbooks Addicition Medicine*. Oxford Uni. Press, 2009, NY.pp:199-238.

[179] Tetrault JM&O'Connor PG. Managemant of Opioid Intoxication and Withdrawal.In: *Addiction Medicine.* Editors: Reis RK, Fiellin DA, Miller SC, Saitz R.. Lippincott Williams & Wilkins. Philedelphia PA, USA. 2009. pp:589-606.

[180] van Dorp EL, Yassen A and Dahan A. Naloxone treatment in opioid addiction: the risks and benefits. *Expert Opinion in Drug Safety* 2007;6:125-132.

[181] Lo Vecchio F, Pizon A, RileyB et al. Onset of symptoms after methadone overdose. *Am J Emerg Med* 2007; 25:57-59.

[182] Christenson J, Etherington J, Grafstein E, et al. Early discharge of patients with presumed opioid overdose: development of a clinical prediction rule. *Acad Emerg Med* 2000; 7:1110-1118.

[183] Rosen MI, McMahon TJ, Hameedi FA, et al. Effect of clonidine pretreatment on naloxon-precipitated opiate withdrawal. *J Parmachol Exp Ther* 1996;276:1128-1135.

[184] O'Connor PG, Carroll KM, Shi JM, et al. Three methods of opioid detoxification in a primary care settings. A randomized trial. *Ann Intern Med* 1997;127:526-530.

[185] Vocci FJ, Acri J, Elkashef A. Medication Development for Addictive Disorders: *The State of the Science Am J Psychiatry* 2005; 162:1432–1440.

[186] Fudala PJ, Vocci F, Montgomery A, Trachtenberg AI: Levomethadyl acetate (LAAM) for the treatment of opiate dependence: a multisite, open label study of LAAM safety and an evaluation of the product labeling and treatment regulations. *J Maint Addict* 1997; 1:9–39.

[187] Kreek MJ, Vocci FJ: History and current status of opioid maintenance treatments: blending conference session. *J Subst Abuse Treat* 2002; 23:93–105.

[188] Martin WR, Eades CG, Thompson JA, Huppler RE, Gilbert PE: The effects of morphine- and nalorphine-like drugs in the nondependent and morphine-dependent chronic spinal dog. *J Pharmacol Exp Ther* 1976; 197:517–532.

[189] Ling W, Charuvastra C, Collins JF, Batki S, Brown LS Jr, Kintaudi P, Wesson DR, McNicholas L, Tusel DJ, Malkerneker U, Renner JA Jr, Santos E, Casadonte P, Fye C, Stine S, Wang RI, Segal D: Buprenorphine maintenance treatment of opiate dependence: a multicenter, randomized clinical trial. *Addiction* 1998; 93:475–486.

[190] US Food and Drug Administration Center for Drug Evaluation and Research Drug Information: *Subutex (buprenorphine hydrochloride) and Suboxone tablets*

(buprenorphine hydrochloride and naloxone hydrochloride).(To access: http://www.fda.gov/cder/drug/infopage/subutex_suboxone/default.htm)

[191] Kim S, Wagner HN, Jr., Villemagne VL, Kao PF, Dannals RF, Ravert HT, Joh T, Dixon RB and Civelek AC Longer occupancy of opioid receptors by nalmefene compared to naloxone as measured in vivo by a dual-detector system. *Journal of Nuclear Medicine* 1997; 38:1726-1731.

[192] Stine SM and Kosten TR. Pharmacological Interventions for Opioid Dependence. In: In: *Addiction Medicine*. Editors: Reis RK, Fiellin DA, Miller SC, Saitz R. Lippincott Williams & Wilkins. Philedelphia PA, USA.2009. pp:651-669.

[193] Minozzi S, Amato L, Vecchi S et al. Oral naltrexon maintenance treatment for opioid dependence. *Cochrane Database Syst Rev* 2006; 25;(1):CD001333.

[194] Washton AM, Gold MS, Pottash AC. Naltrexon in addicted physicians and business executives. *NIDA Res Monogr* 1984; 55:185-190.

[195] Comer SD, Collins ED. Depot naltrexon: long-lasting antagonism of the effects of heroin in humans. *Psychopharmacology* (Berl) 2002;159: 351-360.

[196] Comer SD, Sullivan MA, Yu E, et al. Injectable, sustained-release naltrexon for the treatment of opioid dependence: a randomized placebo controlled trial. *Arch Gen Psychiatry* 2006;63:210-218.

[197] Dickinson WE, Eickelberg SJ. Management of Sedative-Hypnotic Intoxication and Withdrawal. In: *Principles of Addiction Medicine*. Fourth Edition. Edited by Ries RK, Fiellin DA, Miller SC, Saitz R. Philadelphia, Lippincott Williams&Wilkins, 2009, pp:573-587.

[198] Epstein FB Fatal benzodiazepine toxicity? *Am J Emerg Med.* 1987 Sep;5(5):472-3.

[199] Charlson F, Degenhardt L, McLaren J, Hall W, Lynskey M. A systematic review of research examining benzodiazepine-related mortality. *Pharmacoepidemiol Drug Saf.* 2009;18:93-103

[200] Latt N, Conigrave K, Saunders JB, Marshall EJ, Nutt D. Sedative Hypnotics. In: *Oxford Specialist Handbooks Addicition Medicine*. Oxford Uni. Press, 2009, NY.pp:167-186.

[201] Ngo AS, Anthony CR, Samuel M, Wong E, Ponampalam R.Should a benzodiazepine antagonist be used in unconscious patients presenting to the emergency department? *Resuscitation.* 2007;74:27-37.

[202] Woods JH, Katz JL, Winger G. Benzodiazepines: use, abuse, and consequences. *Pharmacol Rev.* 1992;44:151-347.

[203] Lader M, Tylee A, Donoghue J. Withdrawing benzodiazepines in primary care. *CNS Drugs.* 2009;23:19-34.

[204] Schweizer E, Rickels K, Case WG, Greenblatt DJ. Carbamazepin treatment in patients discontinuing long-term benzodiazepine therapy. Effects on withdrawal severity and outcome. *Archives of General Psychiatry* 1991;48:448–52.

[205] Schweizer E, Rickels K, Case WG, Greenblatt DJ. Long-term use of benzodiazepines. Effects of gradual taper. *Archives of General Psychiatry* 1990;47:908–15.

[206] Smith DE, Landry MJ. Benzodiazepine dependency discontinuation: focus on the chemical dependency detoxification setting and benzodiazepine-polydrug abuse. *J Psychiatr Res.* 1990;24 (Suppl 2):145-56.

[207] Griffiths RR, Wolf B Relative abuse liability of different benzodiazepines in drug abusers. *J Clin Psychopharmacol.* 1990;10:237-43.

[208] Denis C, Fatséas M, Lavie E, Auriacombe M. Pharmacological interventions for benzodiazepine mono-dependence management in outpatient settings. *Cochrane Database Syst Rev.* 2006 Jul 19;3:CD005194.

[209] Gerra G, Zaimovic A, Giusti F, Moi G, Brewer C. Intravenous flumazenil versus oxazepam tapering in the treatment of benzodiazepine withdrawal: a randomized, placebo-controlled study.*Addict Biol.* 2002;7:385-95.

[210] Doyon S. The many faces of ecstasy. *Curr Opin Pediatr.* 2001;13:170-6.

[211] El-Mallakh RS, Abraham HD. MDMA (Ecstasy). *Ann Clin Psychiatry.* 2007;19:45-52.

[212] Fantegrossi WE, Kiessel CL, Leach PT, et al.: Nantenine: An antagonist of the behavioral and physiological effects of MDMA in mice. *Psychopharmacol* (Berl) 2004; 173:270–277.

[213] Frecska E, Luna LE.The adverse effects of hallucinogens from intramural perspective. *Neuropsychopharmacol Hung.* 2006;8:189-200.

[214] Miller PL, Gay GR, Ferris KC, Anderson S. Treatment of acute, adverse psychedelic reactions: "I've tripped and I can't get down". *J Psychoactive Drugs.* 1992;24:277-9.

[215] Khantzian EJ, McKenna GJ. Acute toxic and withdrawal reactions associated with drug use and abuse. *Ann Intern Med.* 1979;90:361-72.

In: Suicidal Behavior in Alcohol and Drug Abuse... ISBN: 978-1-60876-919-3
Editors: L. Sher, A. Vilens, pp. 169-190

Chapter 10

PHARMACOTHERAPY FOR ALCOHOL DEPENDENCE

József Nagy
Gedeon Richter Plc., Budapest, Hungary

ABSTRACT

Alcohol use disorders represent an extensive public health problem all over the world affecting more than 2 billion alcohol users worldwide. According to the recent facts reported by the WHO, alcohol causes 1.8 million deaths (3.2% of total) and 58.3 million (4% of total) of Disability-Adjusted Life Years (DALYs) and estimated to cause about 20-30% of oesophageal or liver cancer, liver cirrhosis, epilepsy, accidents, homicide and suicide.

Given the harmful effects of alcohol on the concerned individuals as well as the society as a whole, there is an increasing urge for efficient therapies. Due to the extensive research on the machinery causal for the actions of ethanol in the central nervous system that has been ongoing for more than a century, by now there is increasing amount of information available about the mechanisms by which alcohol exerts its effects. In recent years, scientists discovered evidence that alcohol acts on several neurotransmitter systems in the brain to create its tempting effects. Besides altering the release of neurotransmitters like dopamine, ethanol alters the function of a number of neurotransmitter receptors and transporters as well. When ethanol is consumed in larger amounts and used for a longer period of time, changes in these specific neurotransmitter functions may occur possibly leading to the development of alcohol dependence. Therefore, modulators of these targets of ethanol can be used as pharmacotherapeutic approaches for the treatment of alcohol related disorders.

This chapter focuses on the pharmacotherapies used for the treatment of alcohol dependence and summarizes the pharmacologically most relevant targets and agents currently available or would be accessible in the near future.

INTRODUCTION

According to a recent World Health Report published by the WHO, alcohol consumption is one of the top hazards to health worldwide. Around 15% to 20% of the worldwide population is considered problem drinkers and alcohol became the biggest menace to health also in the developing countries leaving behind such main risk factors like high blood pressure, obesity or tobacco use characteristic for rich nations. Nevertheless alcohol is a top health risk in the wealthy countries as well [1]. Altogether, WHO recently reported that alcohol causes almost 2 million deaths (3.2% of total) and 60 million (4% of total) Disability-Adjusted Life Years (DALYs) worldwide [2].

Alcoholism is usually divided into two general categories: abuse and dependence. An abuser is not yet physically addicted to alcohol, but an alcohol dependent person absolutely must consume alcohol. By now, according to most experts and medical practitioners in this field, alcoholism is considered as a disease. The underlying symptom of this disease is a need for alcohol that can be as strong as the need for food or water. A person afflicted with alcoholism will continue to consume alcohol even though he or she ends up experiencing extreme emotional, mental, physical, inter-personal and legal problems. Consequently the four aggravating primary symptoms of alcoholism are 1) the craving for alcohol, 2) loss of control over alcohol use, 3) development of tolerance and finally 4) physical dependence upon alcohol. Affective disorder is the most common psychiatric disorder, followed by alcohol misuse.

Comorbidity of disorders greatly increases risk of suicide [3]. Suicide may be the end point of a long term drinking career with gradual social isolation and depression, but it may also be the solution to the child or the wife of an alcohol abuser seeing no other way to escape from insecurity, isolation, neglect, and violence. Hence, alcohol abuse may not only increase the risk of suicide in the drinker, but also increase the risk of suicide in his spouse or children [4]. Alcohol misuse, particularly dependence, is strongly associated with suicide risk [5]. According to the view of Menninger "Alcoholism is a chronic form of suicide" [6]. In line with different reports, 5% to 27% of all deaths of alcoholics are directly related to suicide [6, 7]. Whereas the lifetime risk for suicide is 1% in the general population, it is 15% among alcoholics [8]. On the other hand, the incidence of alcoholism among persons who commit suicide ranges from 6% to 30% (~20% most frequently cited) [7, 9]. Thus, on the basis of individual level studies the findings are quite consistent with respect to an excess mortality by suicide in alcohol abusers, and an elevated proportion of alcohol abusers and alcohol intoxicated persons in samples of suicides [10].

Along with the recent developments in drug abuse research across the areas of molecular genetics, cell biology, animal behavior, and human brain imaging studies, the widely held elderly view about drug abuse and addiction – i.e. that the problem of drug abuse would go away if only the abuser or addict could change their behavior – tends to be displaced by novel conceptions. The theory is based on the hypothesis that the administration of a drug acutely "unbalances" the neurochemical poise of the brain. In order to overcome this "unbalanced" status the brain introduces a homeostatic mechanism, i.e. an "opposing neuron-adaptation" that balances the effect of the drug. While the drug is present in the brain, the system remains in relative balance (i.e. tolerance develops). However, removal of the drug unsettles this delicate balance, resulting in functional disturbances underlying the emergence of a negative emotional and disturbed physiological state (i.e. withdrawal symptoms). To overwhelm this depressing situation desire develops to seek for and take the drug, leading to the loss of control over drug use (i.e. dependence develops) [11, 12]. Collier's modification of this hypothesis of Himmelsbach was to propose that, since drugs act on receptors in the brain, a primary mechanism for neuron-adaptation to drugs would be to regulate the numbers of those receptors [13]. This type of adaptation would reduce the effects of the drug, but would also cause alterations when the drug left the brain because the natural transmitters inside the brain also use the same receptors [14].

Main Targets of Ethanol

The early hypothesis on ethanol's action, i.e. it has non-specific effects on biological membranes, has been challenged by data demonstrating that definite subunit compositions and/or even certain amino-acid residues of sensitive receptors may be crucial for the modulatory effect of ethanol [15-18]. Nowadays, it is well known that ethanol can influence the function of several neurotransmitters and their receptors.

The most important targets for the acute effects of alcohol are the main inhibitory, i.e. the GABA-ergic, and the main excitatory, i.e. the glutamatergic neurotransmitter systems. Up to now a large body of evidence has been collected implicating that these neurotransmitter systems are extremely sensitive for ethanol, and play a central role in the adaptive transformation of the CNS caused by chronic alcohol experience. It turned out that potentiation of the GABAergic inhibitory functions by ethanol in concert with its inhibitory effect on the excitatory glutamatergic circuitry may underlie the acute sedative effects of alcohol. Consequently, during long term exposure a compensatory down-regulation of the GABA-ergic [19] and an up-regulation of the glutamatergic system [20, 21] arise resulting in development of alcohol dependence [22]. These changes reset the acute effects of ethanol, so the CNS can function as normally as possible, even in the presence of depressant amounts of alcohol. However, when alcohol is abruptly withdrawn, the CNS is left in a state of hyper-excitability, perceived by the subject as a disagreeable state of arousal, anxiety and sleeplessness. This is what is behind the negative affective state, which the alcoholic patient wants to avoid with continuation of alcohol intake. These plastic changes in brain functions may explain the persistence of craving during alcohol withdrawal, and difficulties to achieve stable abstinence after acute detoxification.

Recently Used Medications

The treatment of alcohol dependence requires a two-step approach that includes withdrawal and detoxification followed by further interventions to maintain abstinence. There is considerable uncertainty about the best treatment strategies for patients in the post-detoxification stage. Some advocate a "drug-free" 12-step approach developed by Alcoholics Anonymous (AA), while others assert that the 12-step approach or other psychosocial approaches combined with appropriate non-addictive pharmacotherapies may improve treatment outcomes.

Pharmaceutical agents that have been historically or are presently used in the treatment of alcoholism are the aversive agent disulfiram, some opiate antagonists like naltrexone and nalmefene, several serotonergic agents such as ondansetron, buspirone, and selective serotonin reuptake inhibitors (SSRIs, such as citalopram, fluoxetine, paroxetine, sertraline, etc.) or the mood stabilizer lithium. Among these possibilities, disulfiram and naltrexone, in particular, are mainstream agents in use in the United States nowadays.

Disulfiram (Antabuse®) has been used to treat alcohol dependence since the 1940s. The objective of disulfiram treatment is to create an aversion to alcohol, rather than to modulate its neurochemical effects. This drug (and the related calcium carbimide) inhibits the activity of the enzyme aldehyde-dehydrogenase, this way it prevents the metabolism of alcohol and causes an accumulation of acetaldehyde in the blood. Subsequently upon alcohol intake, it triggers unpleasant symptoms like increased blood pressure and heart rate, flushing and vomiting. Although, it was supposed to reduce the number of days dependent patients drink, there is still no evidence from clinical trials for this drug to increase the rate of abstinence. In addition, this kind of aversive therapy can be dangerous for certain patients and should be closely supervised.

Naltrexone (Revia®) and its 6-methylene analogue nalmefene (Revex®) are non-selective opioid receptor antagonists. Initially naltrexone was used in the therapy of heroin addiction, but Volpicelli et al. [23] initiated its use in alcoholism as well, and the FDA approved its use in this field in 1994. It is an anti-craving medication that has been shown to reduce the effects of alcohol and to reduce the amount of alcohol consumed when used in parallel with behavioral therapies. In short-term studies naltrexone was reported to cut the occurrence of relapse in half. It is a well tolerated drug; nausea was reported only by around 10% of patients treated [24-26].

Another anticraving medication is acamprosate (Campral®); which was shown to improve the outcome in rehabilitation of alcohol-dependent patients without serious side effects. It is believed to maintain abstinence by blocking the negative craving that alcohol-dependent patients experience in the absence of alcohol. Accordingly, it is suggested to be used primarily as a relapse-prevention medication. The exact mechanism of action of acamprosate, originally developed as a GABA analogue, is still a matter of debate. Early studies indicated that acamprosate interacts with the GABA-ergic system [27] to affect behaviors related to ethanol consumption. However, it was observed that acamprosate did not bind to recombinant or native $GABA_A$ receptors or enhance chloride currents [28]. Later on, it was suggested that it has an inhibitory effect on the NMDA-receptors and/or voltage-sensitive Ca^{2+} channels [29-31]. Indeed, acamprosate effectively reduced both the enhanced glutamate-induced calcium entry and neurotoxicity in ethanol pre-treated primary cultures of organotypic hippocampal [32] or neocortical neurons from rats in a concentration-dependent manner [33, 34]. However, its protective effects against glutamate-induced neurotoxicity could be detected in ethanol-withdrawn cultures only. Furthermore, although it significantly reduced the calcium entry caused by glutamate or K^+ in control and ethanol-exposed cultures, its neuroprotective effect did not correlate with its efficacy on calcium entry, making a direct effect on the glutamate binding site of the NMDA receptor or the receptor-operated calcium channel unlikely. This idea was further confirmed by studies founding no direct effects of acamprosate on NMDARs [33-37]. However, Al Qatari et al. [38] showed that the effect of acamprosate on NMDARs depends on the experimental conditions arguing that acamprosate, at least partly, acts as a `partial agonist' at the NMDA receptor. According to the observations of Harris et al., acamprosate displaced [^{3}H]-glutamate but did not compete with NMDA for [^{3}H]-glutamate binding sites in membrane preparations from the cortex, cerebellum or and hippocampus of rats. Furthermore acamprosate displayed total competition with trans-ACPD (1-aminocyclopentane-trans-1,3-dicarboxylic acid) an agonist at both group I and II metabotropic glutamate receptors and similarly to SIB-1893, a non-competitive antagonist at the mGluR5 receptor, it was neuroprotective against trans-ACPD induced neurotoxicity that likely results from mGluR mediated potentiation of NMDARs [39]. Also, in the CA1 region of ethanol pre-treated organotypic hippocampal slices in culture, where neurotoxicity was observed after a 24-hr withdrawal period, acamprosate, as well as SIB-1893, MK-801, and staurosporine had a neuroprotective effect. In this ethanol pre-treated slice culture preparation the polypeptide levels of mGluR5 receptors were found to be increased [40], similarly as in case of NR1 and NR2B subunits of NMDARs in other neuronal cultures after long-term ethanol exposure [30, 41]. Considering these observations, acamprosate is thought to act on the mGluR5 receptors reducing its positive feedback control over the NMDARs [42]. This glutamatergic hypothesis may help to explain many of the effects of acamprosate in human alcohol dependence, especially in the acquisition of cue-elicited drinking behaviors [33, 43-48].

Novel generation of antidepressants, like selective serotonin reuptake inhibitors (SSRIs), is proved to be useful in a variety of seemingly diverse disorders. In addition to major depressive disorder, several of them have received FDA approval for other disorders such as generalized anxiety disorder (venlafaxine), bulimia nervosa (fluoxetine), obsessive-compulsive disorder (fluvoxamine, paroxetine, sertraline, and fluoxetine), social phobia (paroxetine), panic disorder (sertraline, paroxetine), and posttraumatic stress disorder (sertraline). In controlled studies, these agents have also shown value in premenstrual dysphoric disorder, borderline personality disorder, obesity, smoking cessation, and alcoholism [49, 50]. Recent studies have shown that acute co-administration of fluoxetine with a 5-HT1A receptor antagonist (p-MPPI) alleviates the diminished interest in brain stimulation reward observed during withdrawal from either nicotine or amphetamine in rats [51]. These findings suggest that the combination of selective antagonism at 5-HT1A receptors and selective inhibition of the 5-HT transporter may be a useful approach in preventing relapse to drug-seeking behavior. Interestingly, compounds with combined serotonin reuptake inhibitor and 5HT1A agonist activity are also claimed useful for the treatment of cocaine and alcohol addiction [52].

Unfortunately, currently used pharmacological agents have shown only limited efficacy and reliability in pharmacological approaches for the treatment of alcoholism [53]. Hence, taking into account the huge costs associated with drug abuse and drug-related diseases for the society and recognizing that our knowledge on the field of alcohol related neuronal changes has evolved substantially in the past 10 years, development of new medications with improved, long-term efficacy and more reduced side effects should be in the focus of drug research. Understanding the common mechanisms by which drugs of abuse modify neurotransmitter systems is critically important for this point of view making it possible to develop new therapeutic strategies.

Future Medications

Based on the novel hypothesis of Collier accepted by many neuropharmacologists today, new opportunities are emerging for the pharmacotherapy of drug dependence. Hereunder, recent approaches targeting some of the main neurotransmitter systems are summarized.

GABA-ergic System

$GABA_A$ receptors are thought to play a central role in both the short- and long-term effects of ethanol in the CNS [54]. These receptors are pentameric structures with a high degree of homology with nicotinic receptors [55, 56]. $GABA_A$ receptors are built up of several different types of subunits, including six α, four β, three γ, two ρ, and one-one δ, ε, θ and π subunits [57]. The subunits are arranged in a radial fashion forming a central ion pore. Upon GABA binding, the ion channel opens and the influx of chloride ions shifts the postsynaptic membrane potential further away from its firing threshold resulting in membrane hyperpolarization. Thus, GABA is classified as an inhibitory amino acid neurotransmitter. The $GABA_A$ receptors not only bind their neurotransmitter ligands, but can also interact with a number of other compounds that usually bind at other; allosteric sites on the protein modulating the actions of GABA [58, 59]. These modulatory agents like benzodiazepines, barbiturates, neurosteroids and anesthetics enhance the actions of GABA and have sedative or hypnotic effects.

Similarly to the above mentioned compounds, the anxiolytic or sedative effects of ethanol are associated with its GABA facilitating effect at the $GABA_A$ receptors [60]. The ethanol induced potentiation of GABA actions generally occurs in a pharmacologically relevant range of concentrations (below 100 mM). Although, this issue is somewhat controversial, since some laboratories report no effect of alcohols at $GABA_A$ receptors, and the range of concentrations at which effects are seen also seems to vary [61-63]. The efficacy of ethanol on $GABA_A$ receptors seems to be dependent on the subunit composition of the receptor. A study using α1β2γ2 receptors showed ethanol potentiation, but only in those receptors in which a particular splice variant of the γ2 subunit was present [64]. The "long" version of γ2 (γ2L) - so-called because of the presence of an extra 8 amino acids in the intracellular loop - was considered necessary for the potentiation to occur. However, other laboratories have been unable to reproduce this finding and have shown that the effects of ethanol appear to be independent of the type of γ2 subunit [65]. Altogether, there appears to be no subunit dependence with respect to the effects of ethanol on $GABA_A$ receptors [66] with the exception of the α4β1δ combination, which seems to be more sensitive to ethanol than other subtype compositions tested [67].

One of the most commonly prescribed groups of psychoactive drugs acting on $GABA_A$ receptors is the group of benzodiazepines. Benzodiazepines and benzodiazepine-like compounds act by increasing the probability of channel opening, thus leading to a greater hyperpolarization of the postsynaptic membrane and a further decrease in neuronal excitability than what would be seen with activation by GABA alone. These compounds are used to treat anxiety, convulsions, muscle tension and insomnia. They can reverse many of the behavioral effects that are associated with alcohol withdrawal [68-70]. Increasing GABA levels in the synaptic cleft is another possibility to reduce psychostimulant-induced increase of DA in the nucleus accumbens, thereby reducing the reinforcing properties of the stimulant [71]. Accordingly, enhancing the levels of GABA can be an alternative for restoring the overbalance of the excitatory system taking place under withdrawal. This hypothesis is supported by studies showing that gabapentin, which increases the release of GABA by acting at P/Q-type of voltage-gated Ca^{2+} channels [72] significantly reduces craving for cocaine [73] and can be used as an add-on medication to a standard detoxification regime in heroin addicts undergoing opiate withdrawal treatment [74]. In addition, gabapentin as well as gamma-vinyl GABA (vigabatrin) [75] appear to reduce alcohol withdrawal symptoms too, in preclinical and open-label clinical trials [76-78] while lacking the undesirable side-effects of e.g. carbamazepine or divalproex. Vigabatrin, a selective and irreversible GABA-transaminase inhibitor [79] greatly increases whole-brain levels of GABA and effectively attenuates the ethanol induced elevation of extracellular DA levels in nucleus accumbens of freely moving rats. Thus, vigabatrin - currently used for the treatment of epilepsy and infantile spasms – could be also a potential pharmacotherapeutic agent against alcohol addiction. GABA analogues like the salts of γ-hydroxybutiric acid (GHB) also proved to be effective both in the treatment of the syndrome of abstinence from alcohol and in reducing the desire for and addiction to alcohol [80]. The amides of GHB show similar or even better neuropharmacological activity compared to that of GHB [81]. They cause excitatory effects at lower doses and have longer duration. Therefore, these amides claimed to be useful in the treatment of drug addictions, such as heroin, cocaine, and in particular, in the treatment of alcoholism: in reduction of chronic alcoholics' desire for and habit of consuming alcoholic drinks as well as in the treatment of abstinence syndrome.

Glutamatergic System

In the past years, there has been increasing evidence that behavioral, neurophysiological and pathological effects of ethanol are mediated primarily through the glutamatergic neurotransmitter system [82-85]. Besides α-amino-3-hydroxy-5-methyl-4-isoxazole-propionic acid (AMPA) receptors, especially the N-methyl-D-aspartate (NMDA) types of ionotropic glutamate receptors (NMDARs) seem to be important sites of ethanol's action [86-88]. As mentioned before, the sedative and anxiolytic effects of ethanol are associated mainly with inhibition of the NMDA glutamate receptors [89, 90]. Neuroadaptation studies of chronic ethanol exposure indicate a significant role of increased function of these receptors in the development of alcohol dependence as well as in the expression of withdrawal symptoms and associated neuronal damage. Initial *in vivo* experiments showed that seizures evoked by withdrawal of ethanol in alcohol dependent animals were exacerbated by administration of NMDA at doses that are not convulsant in control animals, and attenuated by NMDAR antagonists. Accordingly, it has been hypothesized that increased NMDA neurotransmission following removal of ethanol blockade mediates ethanol withdrawal seizures [91-93]. It was also shown that systemic administration of NMDAR antagonists stimulates the release of dopamine (DA) in the nucleus accumbens [94]. Correspondingly, it was suggested that glutamate exerts a tonic inhibitory action on DA release via mainly NMDARs [95, 96]. According to the model of Fadda et al. [97], ethanol by blocking NMDARs releases dopaminergic neurons from the tonic inhibitory action of GABA-ergic interneurons possessing NMDARs. In addition, when alcohol is withdrawn, DA release is decreased in the limbic forebrain areas [98] due to the increased activity of GABA-ergic interneurons in consequence of increased NMDAR function, resulting in decreased firing rate of dopaminergic neurons [99]. This inhibitory effect of ethanol withdrawal on the dopaminergic neurotransmitter system is suggested to constitute a neurobiological correlate of the dysphoric and depressive symptoms of withdrawal. All these findings strongly support the hypothesis that increased NMDAR functions may underlie both the physical signs (seizures, tremor etc.) and the affective or emotional disturbances occurring under alcohol withdrawal. Therefore, modulators of these receptors are suggested useful in the pharmacotherapy for alcohol dependence and withdrawal symptoms [34, 100].

Since the early 90s, numerous animal studies and preliminary clinical observations proved that NMDA receptor antagonists are indeed excellent candidates for the treatment of alcohol dependence, inasmuch as these compounds may attenuate not only the physical but also the affective and motivational components of dependence. A novel low-affinity non-competitive NMDA receptor antagonist with rapid blocking/unblocking kinetics and strong voltage dependence is under development for the treatment of Alzheimer's disease, cerebral ischemia, chronic pain and alcohol dependence. This compound called neramexane is a novel analogue of memantine (Merz) [101]. Although neramexane was found effective in the treatment of alcohol withdrawal symptoms in combination with benzodiazepine [102], no difference in efficacy between neramexane and placebo was detected in a randomized, double-blind, placebo-controlled international multicentre trial [103]. However, memantine was found effective in a recent 12-week open-label study investigating its efficacy as a treatment for cognitive and behavioral problems in patients with probable alcohol-related dementia improving global cognition, quality of life and behavioral symptoms [104].

In response to chronic blockade of NMDARs, differential up-regulation of NMDAR subunits like NR1, NR2A and NR2B was observed in the cortex and/or hippocampus of rats or mice in association with sustained ethanol administration [105-107]. Similarly, studies on ethanol treated primary neuronal cultures showed increased protein levels of NR2A, NR2B [108] and NR1 subunits [107, 109]. Furthermore, in these cultures ethanol as well as several NR2B subunit-selective antagonists (SSNAs) had enhanced inhibitory effects on NMDARs [41]. Considering these results, it is not surprising, that NR2B SSNAs - like the prototype compounds ifenprodil and eliprodil - have received considerable attention in recent years, since they have shown positive effects in animal models of ischemic neuronal damage [110], hyperalgesia [111-114], Parkinson disease [115] and were reported to inhibit alcohol withdrawal induced audiogenic seizure in mice and rats [116, 117]. The recently found new NR2B SSNAs are known to have a much more preferable side-effect profile due to their high selectivity towards the NR2B subunit compared with the former non-subunit selective (MK-801) NMDA antagonists [118].

Dopaminergic System

Among the many neurotransmitters involved in alcohol's action, dopamine seems to play a significant role both in tolerance to and in withdrawal from alcohol (for review, see ref. [119]). Early behavioral evidences that i) microinjection of ethanol into the ventral tegmental area (VTA) of the midbrain supports ethanol self-administration, ii) ethanol dose-dependently increases DA release in the nucleus accumbens (NAc) in rats self-administering ethanol, and iii) interference with DA transmission by microinjection of pharmacological agents into VTA or NAc reduces ethanol-reinforced responding have provided direct support for a role of DA in the reinforcing actions of ethanol. Manipulations of DA receptor gene expression and receptor knockout (KO) methodologies have also supported this opinion [120-124].

Consequently to the role of DA in ethanol's action, it has been also hypothesized that subjects with impaired dopaminergic activity may compensate for this deficiency by the use of alcohol and other substances that increase DA levels in the brain [125,126]. Whether this deficiency plays a role in some of the symptoms observed during withdrawal is still controversial, but the hypothesis of a reduced dopaminergic activity in the mesocorticolimbic reward pathway responsible for negative mood states after alcohol cessation is an attractive theory [127], and modulators of this system acting either on the different dopamine receptors or transporters are thought to be useful in the therapy of alcohol dependence [128].

Neuroleptics like haloperidol, olanzapine, and tiapride have all demonstrated various degrees of efficacy reducing craving, alcohol consumption or increasing abstinence [129]. The widely used DA receptor antagonist compound haloperidol has been shown to moderate the effects of alcohol on craving. Another agent olanzapine acting at the D2 dopamine and 5-HT2 serotonin receptors, although did not influence the rewarding effects of alcohol but did attenuate the effects of alcohol cues and an alcohol challenge on urge to drink [130, 131]. Tiapride - a selective D2 receptor antagonist - increased abstinence and reduced alcohol consumption in two placebo-controlled clinical trials as an adjunct to psychotherapy for long-term rehabilitation [132]. However, another trial evaluating the effect of flupenthixol decanoate [133] - a non subtype selective DA receptor antagonist - demonstrated a significant reduction in the proportion of patients remaining abstinent after 6 months of treatment (14.8% on active treatment compared with 34.5% on placebo). Negative results have also been obtained in a pilot randomized controlled trial with amisulpride, a D2/D3 receptor antagonist [134]. Although, given the potential undesirable effects of chronic therapy with the available DA receptor antagonists [135-137], such as tardive dyskinesia, there are several novel patents claiming compounds acting on this type of dopamine receptors.

The atypical neuroleptic aripiprazole acting as a partial dopamine agonist and also on 5-HT1A/2A receptors has fewer limiting side effects compared to the above mentioned typical neuroleptics. It causes only few extrapyramidal side effects, lacks strong histamine activity suspected of causing sedation, causes relatively little elevation in prolactin levels or QTc prolongation, has no propensity for weight gain, and the risk of agranulocytosis is no greater than for the typical neuroleptics. Besides its tolerable side effect profile, it shows significant effects reducing alcohol use in both animals and humans. Because of its potential as a treatment for alcohol dependence, Bristol-Myers Squibb completed a double-blind placebo controlled trial using this drug for the treatment of alcohol-dependence resulting in no difference between aripiprazole and placebo in the percentage of days abstinent over 12 weeks possibly because of dose-related attrition. However, aripiprazole-treated subjects reported more positive subjective treatment effects and less overall severity of alcohol dependence than placebo-treated subjects suggesting that further study of aripiprazole for treatment of alcohol dependence may be warranted at lower doses [129, 138, 139].

Several clinically available monoamine-reuptake inhibitors (e.g. bupropion, imipramine, desipramine and fluoxetine), have been also tested for their effectiveness in psychostimulant abuse. So far, robust therapeutic effects have not been reported, although future studies in genetically or psychiatrically defined populations might identify particularly sensitive populations. Several types of compounds like piperidinol derivatives [140], and 4′,4-substituted 3alpha-(diphenylmethoxy) tropane [141] or 1-(substituted-phenyl)-3-azabicyclo[3.1.0]hexane analogs (e.g. DOV-216303) [142] are recently patented for treating alcohol addiction. This later group of compounds inhibits not only the dopamine, but the norepinephrine and serotonin transporters as well [143].

Serotonergic System

Serotonin (also known as 5-hydroxytryptamine or 5-HT) dysfunction probably contributes to the development of alcoholism [144]. It is known that receptors for serotonin contribute to the development of alcohol dependence in animals, as alcohol increases the basal levels of 5-HT receptors. Of the seven distinct families of 5-HT receptors, three are described to take part in alcohol induced alterations: 5-HT1A receptors might be associated with alcohol consumption and the development of tolerance, 5-HT2 receptors with reward and 5-HT3 receptors with the development of reinforcement. Whereas the acute administration of some drugs of abuse typically increases levels of monoamines by blocking their presynaptic reuptake, chronic drug abuse leads to down regulation of monoamine systems [145]. Indeed, withdrawal-induced depression and drug craving might be linked to this down regulation and it is hypothesized that pharmacotherapeutic approaches augmenting serotonin levels would reduce the reinforcing efficacy of drugs of abuse and alleviate drug abstinence symptomatology, dysphoria and craving. The most widely known biological marker of alcoholism and suicide is serotonin. Low serotonin levels are thought to be common in depression, suicide and alcoholism. Asberg, in a study of 68 depressed patients found low 5-hydroxyindoleacetic acid (5-HIAA, a break-down product of 5-HT) levels in the CSF in patients who attempted suicide [146]. In addition, the lowest levels of 5-HIAA were observed in suicides by the most violent means. Alcoholics with depression have been found to have higher risk for suicide. The ratio of tryptophan, the amino acid the body uses to make serotonin, over the other amino acid levels was also associated with depression [147]. Low tryptophan levels observed in alcoholics may be connected to the increased rate of suicide. Based on all these observations, serotonergic agents might be useful for pharmacotherapy of alcohol related depression. Unfortunately, up to now several serotonergic drugs have been examined, but with inconsistent results [144]. Presently, some serotonergic drugs like sertraline or ondansetron appear to show some promise with certain subtypes of alcoholic patients and fluoxetine with depressed alcoholics.

Other Neurotransmitter Systems

Interactions between ethanol and the opioid system have been in focus of neurobiological research on alcohol addiction. It was shown that ethanol stimulates the release of endogenous opioid peptides within the reward circuitry of the brain, and both nonselective opioid receptor antagonists and antagonists selective for μ- or δ-opioid receptors (MORs and DORs) reduce ethanol consumption and reinforced responding in animal models (for review, see refs [148] and [149]). These findings led to the testing and subsequent FDA approval of the opioid receptor antagonist naltrexone (ReVia) as a pharmacologic treatment for alcoholism. Although this compound has been useful, its efficacy has been hampered by compliance problems and its toxic effects on the liver. Besides the currently in use naltrexone, its 6-methylene analogue, nalmefene that has been available for several years as Revex(TM) for reversing opioid effects and for opioid overdose has also shown promising activity in studies on alcohol dependent animals. Besides the previous observations, that nalmefene is 28 times more potent than naloxone and also somewhat more potent than naltrexone in precipitating withdrawal from opiate dependence in rats [150], Sinclair et al. [151] described that nalmefene effectively decreased the alcohol consumption in chronically alcohol dependent AA rats [152]. A clinical trial with nalmefene (10-40 mg/d) performed on 21 randomized subjects to placebo and 2 nalmefene dosage showed significantly lower relapse rate in the high-dosage nalmefene group [153, 154]. In addition, extensive research has indicated that nalmefene is safe for human use and there is currently no evidence of side-effects or adverse reactions that would limit its use with alcoholics. In addition, nalmefene has no abuse potential of its own, and its subjective effects are minimal: e.g. according to a study on feeding [155] reported only a slight increase in self-rated alertness and decreases in ratings of both tiredness and elation.

Strong evidence suggests that β2 nicotinic acetylcholine receptors (nAChRs) play a prominent role in the effects of nicotine on DA neurons, including DA release in the nucleus accumbens and nicotine self-administration [156]. SSR 591813 (Dianicline), developed by Sanofi-Aventis is a novel selective partial agonist at the α4-β2 nAChRs [157] and thought to be effective in the treatment or prevention of cognitive impairments, and claimed to prevent symptoms due to withdrawal from various substances inducing alcohol, cocaine and cannabis. The bungarotoxin sensitive nACHRs composed of α7 subunits are believed to be involved in many important biological processes in the central nervous system, including learning and memory. They are localized both pre- and post synaptically and are highly permeable also to Ca^{2+} ions [158]. This type of nAChRs is suggested to be involved in modulation of synaptic transmission; therefore it is of interest to develop novel compounds acting as ligands on this subunit of nAChRs. α7 nAChR agonists expected to be useful for the treatment of a variety of cognitive disorders, neurodegeneration associated with stroke and ischemia, nicotine addiction and even of alcohol withdrawal syndrome [159, 160].

Research on the role of cannabinoids on brain reward function has developed significantly when D9-tetrahydro-cannabinol, the major psychoactive component of the hemp plant was isolated, the central CB1 cannabinoid receptor was cloned, and the selective CB1 receptor antagonist SR141716 (Rimonabant) [161] was characterized [162]. A growing body of evidence has shown that D9-tetrahydrocannabinol acts on brain reward systems similarly to non-cannabinoid addictive drugs [163]. This might partly explain the efficacy of Rimonabant in blocking the reinforcing properties of heroin [164], morphine [165], ethanol [166], cocaine [167] and nicotine [168], suggesting that activation of the endogenous cannabinoid system participates in the motivational and DA-releasing effects of several drugs of abusc [71]. Rimonabant has been shown to block voluntary ethanol intake in rats and mice [169]. Rimonabant is under development by Sanofi-Synthelabo and is currently under clinical investigations for smoking cessation and alcohol addiction. Sanofi-Synthelabo is also developing another selective CB1 receptor antagonist, SR-147778 (Surinabant) [170]. This compound is in Phase I trials for smoking cessation, obesity and alcohol dependence.

Acute administration of most drugs of abuse like alcohol, nicotine and tetrahydrocannabinoids activates the hypothalamic-pituitary-adrenal axis (HPA) as measured by an increase in adrenocorticotropic hormone (ACTH) and corticosterone secretion. Furthermore, chronic administration of cocaine, benzodiazepines, nicotine and possibly alcohol, but not opioid drugs, can lead to a sustained increase in basal activity of the HPA axis in animals. In addition, drug withdrawal syndrome resembles both physiological and behavioral changes associated with responses to stressors that are linked to brain CRF activation [171], and exposure to stressors is associated with increased drug-taking behavior and relapse to drugs in both humans and laboratory animals [172]. These findings, together with data on the effect of selective CRF1 receptor antagonists on cocaine self-administration, drug withdrawal from several drug classes and stress-induced relapse to heroin-, cocaine-, and alcohol-seeking in rats [173, 174], provide a rationale for the use of CRF1 receptor antagonists in the treatment of compulsive drug use in humans [71, 175].

Conclusion

Drug addiction is a chronically deteriorating disorder, which involves a complex neurocircuitry underlying drug reinforcement, drug craving and compulsive drug-seeking and drug-taking behaviors despite adverse consequences as physical or psychological deterioration. Since addiction, especially at the stage of withdrawal is generally accompanied by sadness, depression, and even by suicide, there might be some correlation or some common intervening mechanisms underlying these joint symptoms. As a result of advances in the understanding of the neural mechanisms of alcohol dependence, more and more possibilities may arise for potential therapeutic intervention. Investigating medications blocking the reinforcing affects of alcohol, reducing craving or inhibiting the manifestation of withdrawal symptoms by affecting multiple neuronal systems may initiate new, alternative solutions in therapy for the whole complex problem. Data acquired from clinical trials have provided clear evidence for the utility of pharmacotherapy in rehabilitation from alcohol dependence [176]. Although, pharmacotherapy should be used in association with appropriate psychosocial support, a combined complex treatment regime could provide answers for these psychiatric comorbidities.

References

[1] Hawton K and Heeringen K: Suicide. *Lancet* 2009, 373: 1372–1381.

[2] http://www.who.int/substance_abuse/facts/alcohol/en/index.html

[3] Cavanagh JTO, Carson AJ, Sharpe M, Lawrie SM: Psychological autopsy studies of suicide: a systematic review. *Psychol Med* 2003; 33: 395–405.

[4] Norström T: A time series analysis of the Swedish suicide rare 1915-1968 Edited by Bergryd U and Janson CG. *Sociological Miscellary Essays in Honour of Gunnar Boalt,* 1987, pp 142-159.

[5] Menninger KA: *Man against Himself.* 1938, New York: Harcourt, Brace.

[6] Rushing WA: Individual behavior and suicide. Edited by Gibbs JP, *Suicide,* 1968, pp 96-121.

[7] Berglund M: Suicide in alcoholism: a prospective study of 88 suicides. I. The multidimensional diagnosis at first admission. *Arch. Gen. Psychiatry* 1984, 41: 888-891.

[8] Frances RJ, Franklin J, Flavin DK: Suicide and alcoholism. *Ann N Y Acad Sci.* 1986, 487:316-326.

[9] Beck AT, Weissman A and Kovacs M: Alcoholism, hopelessness and suicidal behavior. *J. Studies Alcohol* 1976, 37: 66-76.

[10] Rossow I: Alcohol and suicide-beyond the link at the individual level. *Addiction 1996,* 91(10):1413-1416.

[11] Himmelsbach CK: The morphine abstinence syndrome: its nature and treatment, *Annals of Internal Medicine* 1941, 15:829–843.

[12] Koob GF, Le-Moal M: Drug addiction, dysregulation of reward, and allostasis. *Neuropsychopharmacology.* 2001, 24(2): 97-129.

[13] Collier HOJ: A general theory of the genesis of drug dependence by the induction of receptors. *Nature* 1965, 205:181–182.

[14] Littleton J: Receptor regulation as a unitary mechanism for drug tolerance and physical dependence—not quite as simple as it seemed! *Addiction* 2001, 96:87–101.

[15] Allgaier C: Ethanol sensitivity of NMDA receptors. *Neurochem. Int.* 2002, 41(6): 377-382.

[16] Mihic SJ, Ye Q, Wick MJ, Koltchine VV, Krasowski MD, Finn SE, Mascia MP, Valenzuela CF, Hanson KK, Greenblatt EP, Harris RA, Harrison NL: Sites of alcohol and volatile anaesthetic action on GABA(A) and glycine receptors. *Nature* 1997, 389(6649): 385-389.

[17] Kumari M, Ticku MK: Regulation of NMDA receptors by ethanol. *Prog. Drug Res.* 2000, 54: 152-189.

[18] Ueno S, Lin A, Nikolaeva N, Trudell JR, Mihic SJ, Harris RA, Harrison NL: Tryptophan scanning mutagenesis in TM2 of the GABA(A) receptor alpha subunit: effects on channel gating and regulation by ethanol. *Br. J. Pharmacol.* 2000, 131(2): 296-302.

[19] Davies M: The role of GABAA receptors in mediating the effects of alcohol in the central nervous system. *J Psychiatry Neurosci* 2003, 28(4): 263-274.

[20] Krystal JH, Petrakis IL, Mason G, Trevisan L, D'Souza DC: N-methyl-D-aspartate glutamate receptors and alcoholism: reward, dependence, treatment, and vulnerability. *Pharmacology & Therapeutics* 2003, 99: 79–94.

[21] Nagy J, László L: Increased sensitivity to NMDA is involved in alcohol-withdrawal induced cytotoxicity observed in primary cultures of cortical neurones chronically pre-treated with ethanol. *Neurochem. Int.* 2002, 40: 585-591.

[22] Mann K: Pharmacotherapy of Alcohol Dependence. A Review of the Clinical Data. *CNS Drugs* 2004, 18(8): 485-450.

[23] Volpicelli JR, O'Brien CP, Alterman AI, Hayshida M: Naltrexone and the Treatment of Alcohol-Dependence: Initial Observations. Edited by Reid LD. *Opioids, Bulimia, and Alcohol Abuse and Alcoholism,* 1990, 195- 214.

[24] Volpicelli JR, Alterman AI, Hayashida M, O'Brien CP: Naltrexone in the treatment of alcohol dependence. *Arch. Gen. Psychiatry* 1992, 49: 876–880.

[25] O'Malley SS, Jaffe AJ, Chang G, Schottenfeld RS, Meyer RE, Rounsaville B: Naltrexone and coping skills therapy for alcohol dependence. A controlled study. *Arch. Gen. Psychiatry* 1992, 49: 881–887.

[26] Tempesta E, Janiri L, Bignamini A, Chabac S, Potgieter A: Acamprosate and relapse prevention in the treatment of alcohol dependence: a placebo-controlled study. *Alcohol & Alcoholism* 2000, 35(2): 202–209.

[27] Boismare F, Daoust M, Moore N, Saligaut C, Lhuintre JP, Chretien P, Durlach J. A homotaurine derivative reduces the voluntary intake of ethanol by rats: are cerebral GABA receptors involved? *Pharmac. Biochem. Behav.* 1984, 21: 787-789.

[28] Zieglgansberger W, Hauser C, Putzke J, Spanagel R, Wetzel C: The enhanced excitability of central neurons following chronic alcohol intake is reduced by acamprosate. *Alcohol Alcohol.* 1995, 30: 5524-5526.

[29] Allgaier C, Franke H, Sobottka H, Scheibler P: Acamprosate inhibits Ca2+ influx mediated by NMDA receptors and voltage-sensitive Ca2+ channels in cultured rat mesencephalic neurones. *Naunyn Schmiedebergs Arch. Pharmacol.* 2000, 362(4-5): 440-443.

[30] Rammes G, Mahal B, Putzke J, Parsons C, Spielmanns P, Pestel E, Spanagel R, Zieglgansberger W, Schadrack J: The anti-craving compound acamprosate acts as a weak NMDA-receptor antagonist, but modulates NMDA-receptor subunit expression similar to memantine and MK-801. *Neuropharmacology* 2001, 40(6): 749-760.

[31] Spanagel R, Zieglgansberger W: Anti-craving compounds for ethanol: new pharmacological tools to study addictive processes. *Trends Pharmacol. Sci.* 1997, 18(2): 54-59.

[32] Mayer S, Harris BR, Gibson DA, Blanchard JA, Prendergast MA, Holley RC, Littleton J. Acamprosate, MK-801, and ifenprodil inhibit neurotoxicity and calcium entry induced by ethanol withdrawal in organotypic slice cultures from neonatal rat hippocampus. *Alcohol. Clin. Exp. Res.* 2002, 26(10): 1468-1478.

[33] alQatari M, Khan S, Harris B, Littleton J: Acamprosate is neuroprotective against glutamate-induced excitotoxicity when enhanced by ethanol withdrawal in neocortical cultures of fetal rat brain. *Alcohol. Clin. Exp. Res.* 2001, 25(9): 1276-1283.

[34] Nagy J, Horvath C, Farkas S, Kolok S, Szombathelyi Z: NR2B subunit selective NMDA antagonists inhibit neurotoxic effect of alcohol-withdrawal in primary cultures of rat cortical neurones. *Neurochem. Int.* 2004, 44(1): 17-23.

[35] Spanagel R, Holter SM, Allingham K, Landgraf R, Zieglgansberger W: Acamprosate and alcohol: I. Effects on alcohol intake following alcohol deprivation in the rat. *Eur. J. Pharmacol.* 1996, 305(1-3): 39-44.

[36] Popp RL, Lovinger DM. Interaction of acamprosate with ethanol and spermine on NMDA receptors in primary cultured neurons. *Eur. J. Pharmacol.* 2000, 394(2-3): 221-231.

[37] Mayer S, Harris B, Gibson DA, Blanchard J, Prendergast MA, Holley RC, Littleton J: Acamprosate has no effect on NMDA-induced toxicity but reduces toxicity induced by spermidine or by changing the medium in organotypic hippocampal slice cultures from rat. *Alcohol. Clin. Exp. Res.* 2002, 26(5): 655-662.

[38] alQatari M, Bouchenafa O, Littleton J: Mechanism of action of acamprosate. Part II. Ethanol dependence modifies effects of acamprosate on NMDA receptor binding in membranes from rat cerebral cortex. *Alcohol. Clin. Exp. Res.* 1998, 22(4): 810-814.

[39] Harris BR, Prendergast MA, Gibson DA, Rogers DT, Blanchard JA, Holley RC, Fu MC, Hart SR, Pedigo NW, Littleton JM. Acamprosate inhibits the binding and neurotoxic effects of trans-ACPD, suggesting a novel site of action at metabotropic glutamate receptors. *Alcohol Clin Exp Res.* 2002, 26(12): 1779-1793.
[40] Harris BR, Gibson DA, Prendergast MA, Blanchard J.A., Holley RC, Hart SR, Scotland RL, Foster TC, Pedigo NW, Littleton JM: The neurotoxicity induced by ethanol withdrawal in mature organotypic hippocampal slices might involve cross-talk between metabotropic glutamate type 5 receptors and N-methyl-D-aspartate receptors. *Alcohol Clin. Exp. Res.,* 2003, 27(11): 1724-1735.
[41] Nagy J, Kolok S, Dezső P, Boros A, Szombathelyi Z: Differential alterations in the expression of NMDA receptor subunits following chronic ethanol treatment in primary cultures of rat cortical and hippocampal neurones. *Neurochem. Int.* 2003, 42(1): 35-43.
[42] De Witte P, Littleton J, Parot P, Koob G: Neuroprotective and abstinence-promoting effects of acamprosate: elucidating the mechanism of action. *CNS Drugs* 2005, 19(6): 517-537.
[43] Dahchour A, De Witte P, Bolo N, Nedelec JF, Muzet M, Durbin P, Macher JP: Central effects of acamprosate: part 1. Acamprosate blocks the glutamate increase in the nucleus accumbens microdialysate in ethanol withdrawn rats. *Psychiatry Res.* 1998, 82(2): 107-114.
[44] Bolo N, Nedelec JF, Muzet M, De-Witte P, Dahchour A, Durbin P, Macher JP: Central effects of acamprosate: part 2. Acamprosate modifies the brain in-vivo proton magnetic resonance spectrum in healthy young male volunteers. *Psychiatry Res.* 1998, 82(2): 115-127.
[45] Heyser CJ, Schulteis G, Durbin P, Koob GF: Chronic acamprosate eliminates the alcohol deprivation effect while having limited effects on baseline responding for ethanol in rats. *Neuropsychopharmacology* 1998, 18(2): 125-133.
[46] Hölter SM, Landgraf R, Zieglgansberger W, Spanagel R: Time course of acamprosate action on operant ethanol self-administration after ethanol deprivation. *Alcohol Clin. Exp. Res.* 1997, 21(5): 862-868.
[47] Lhuintre JP, Daoust M, Moore ND, Chretien P, Saligaut C, Tran G, Boismare F, Hillemand B: Ability of calcium bis acetyl homotaurine, a GABA agonist, to prevent relapse in weaned alcoholics. *Lancet* 1985, 1: 1014-1016.
[48] Lhuintre JP, Moore N, Tran G, Steru L, Langrenon S, Daoust M, Parot P, Ladure P, Libert C, Boismare F, Hillemand B: Acamprosate appears to decrease alcohol intake in weaned alcoholics. *Alcohol Alcohol.* 1990, 25: 613-622.
[49] Schatzberg AF: New indications for antidepressants. *J Clin Psychiatry* 2000, 61 Suppl 11: 9-17.
[50] Upadhyaya HP, Brady KT, Sethuraman G, Sonne SC, Malcolm R: Venlafaxine treatment of patients with comorbid alcohol / cocaine abuse and attention-deficit/hyperactivity disorder: a pilot study. *J Clin Psychopharmacol* 2001, 21(1): 116-118.
[51] Harrison AA, Liem YT, Markou A: Fluoxetine combined with a serotonin-1A receptor antagonist reversed reward deficits observed during nicotine and amphetamine withdrawal in rats. *Neuropsychopharmacology* 2001, 25(1): 55-71.
[52] Zhao R, Tran M, Mewshaw RE, Stack GP, *WO03010169A1,* 2003.

[53] Krystal JH, Cramer JA, Krol WF, Kirk GF, Rosenheck RA: Naltrexone in the treatment of alcohol dependence. *N Engl J Med.* 2001, 345(24):1734-1739.

[54] Grobin AC, Matthews DB, Devaud LL, Morrow AL: The role of GABAA receptors in the acute and chronic effects of ethanol. *Psychopharmacology (Berl)* 1998, 139(1-2): 2-19.

[55] Nayeem N, Green TP, Martin IL, Barnard EA: Quaternary structure of the native GABAA receptor determined by electron microscopic image analysis. *J Neurochem* 1994, 62(2): 815-818.

[56] Barnard EA, Bateson AN, Darlison MG, Glencorse TA, Harvey RJ, Hicks AA, Lasham A, Shingai R, Usherwood PN, Vreugdenhil E: Genes for the GABAA receptor subunittypes and their expression. *Adv Biochem Psychopharmacol* 1992, 47: 17-27.

[57] Bonnert TP, McKernan RM, Farrar S, le Bourdelles B, Heavens RP, Smith DW, Hewson L, Rigby MR, Sirinathsinghji DJ, Brown N, Wafford KA, Whiting PJ: Theta, a novel γ-aminobutyric acid type A receptor subunit. *Proc Natl Acad Sci U S A* 1999, 96(17): 9891-9896.

[58] Olsen RW: Drug interactions at the GABA receptor-ionophore complex. *Ann Rev Pharmacol Toxicol* 1982, 22: 245-277.

[59] Sieghart W: GABAA receptors: ligand-gated Cl- ion channels modulated by multiple drug-binding sites. *Trends Pharmacol Sci* 1992, 13(12): 446-450.

[60] Davies M: The role of GABAA receptors in mediating the effects of alcohol in the central nervous system. *J Psychiatry Neurosci* 2003, 28(4): 263-274.

[61] Siggins GR, Pittman QJ, French ED: Effects of ethanol on CA1 and CA3 pyramidal cells in the hippocampal slice preparation: an intracellular study. *Brain Res* 1987, 414: 22-34.

[62] Marszalec W, Kurata Y, Hamilton BJ, Carter DB, Narahashi T. Selective effects of alcohols on gamma-aminobutyric acid A receptor subunits expressed in human embryonic kidney cells. *J Pharmacol Exp Ther* 1994, 269(1): 157-163.

[63] Frye GD, Fincher AS, Grover CA, Griffith WH: Interaction of ethanol and allosteric modulators with GABAA-activated currents in adult medial septum/diagonal band neurons. *Brain Res* 1994, 635(1-2): 283-292.

[64] Wafford KA, Whiting PJ: Ethanol potentiation of GABAA receptors requires phosphorylation of the alternatively spliced variant of the gamma 2 subunit. *FEBS Lett* 1992, 313(2): 113-117.

[65] Zhai J, Stewart RR, Friedberg MW, Li C: Phosphorylation of the GABAA receptor γ2L subunit in rat sensory neurons may not be necessary for ethanol sensitivity. *Brain Res* 1998, 805(1-2): 116-122.

[66] Mihic SJ, Whiting PJ, Harris RA: Anaesthetic concentrations of alcohols potentiate GABAA receptor-mediated currents: lack of subunit specificity. *Eur J Pharmacol* 1994, 268(2): 209-214.

[67] Sundstrom-Poromaa I, Smith DH, Gong QH, Sabado TN, Li X, Light A, Wiedmann M, Williams K, Smith SS: Hormonally regulated α4β2δ GABAA receptors are a target for alcohol. *Nat Neurosci* 2002, 5(8): 721-722.

[68] Frye GD, Breese GR: GABAergic modulation of ethanol-induced motor impairment. *J Pharmacol Exp Ther.* 1982, 223(3): 750-756.

[69] Liljequist S, Engel J: Effects of GABAergic agonists and antagonists on various ethanol-induced behavioral changes. *Psychopharmacology (Berl).* 1982, 78(1): 71-75.

[70] Teuber L, Larsen JS: WO2004087690A2 and WO2004087690A3, 2004.
[71] Heidbreder CA, Hagan JJ: Novel pharmacotherapeutic approaches for the treatment of drug addiction and craving. *Current Opinion in Pharmacology* 2005, 5:107–118.
[72] Dooley DJ, Donovan CM, Meder WP, Whetzel SZ: Preferential action of gabapentin and pregabalin at P/Q-type voltage-sensitive calcium channels: inhibition of K+-evoked [3H]-norepinephrine release from rat neocortical slices. *Synapse.* 2002, 45(3): 171-190.
[73] Raby WN, Coomaraswamy S: Gabapentin reduces cocaine use among addicts from a community clinic sample. *J Clin Psychiatry* 2004, 65: 84-86.
[74] Martinez-Raga J, Sabater A, Perez-Galvez B, Castellano M, Cervera G: Add-on gabapentin in the treatment of opiate withdrawal. *Prog Neuropsychopharmacol Biol Psychiatry* 2004, 28: 599-601.
[75] Dewey SL, Brodie JD, *Ashby CR Jr.:* US 6828349, 2004.
[76] Watson WP, Robinson E, Little HJ: The novel anticonvulsant, gabapentin, protects against both convulsant and anxiogenic aspects of the ethanol withdrawal syndrome. *Neuropharmacology.* 1997, 36(10): 1369-1375.
[77] Bonnet U, Banger M, Leweke FM, Specka M, Muller BW, Hashemi T, Nyhuis PW, Kutscher S, Burtscheidt W, Gastpar M: Treatment of acute alcohol withdrawal with gabapentin: results from a controlled two-center trial. *J Clin Psychopharmacol.* 2003, 23(5): 514-519.
[78] Book SW, Myrick H: Novel anticonvulsants in the treatment of alcoholism. *Expert Opin Investig Drugs.* 2005, 14(4): 371-376.
[79] Saletu B, Grunberger J, Linzmayer L, Schwartz JJ, Haegele KD, Schechter PJ: Psychophysiological and psychometric studies after manipulating the GABA system by vigabatrin, a GABA-transaminase inhibitor. *Int. J.Psychophysiol.* 1986, 4(1): 63-80.
[80] Addolorato G, Caputo F, Capristo E, Stefanini GF, Gasbarrini G: Gamma-hydroxybutyric acid efficacy, potential abuse, and dependence in the treatment of alcohol addiction. *Alcohol.* 2000, 20(3): 217-222.
[81] Cacciaglia, R., Loche, A., Perlini, V., Guano, L: US6436998, 2002.
[82] Tsai G, Gastfriend DR, Coyle JT: The glutamatergic basis of human alcoholism. *Am. J. Psychiatry* 1995, 152(3): 332-340.
[83] Tsai G, and Coyle JT: The role of glutamatergic neurotransmission in the pathophysiology of alcoholism. *Annu. Rev. Med.* 1998, 49: 173-184.
[84] Di Chiara G, Tanda G, Cadoni C, Aquas E, Bassareo V, Carboni E: Homologies and differencesin the action of drugs of abuse and a conventional reinforcer (food) on dopamine transmission: an interpretative framework of the mechanism of drug dependence. *Adv. Pharmacol.* 1998, 42: 983-987.
[85] Dodd PR, Beckmann AM, Davidson MS, Wilce PA: Glutamate-mediated transmission, alcohol, and alcoholism. *Neurochem. Int.* 2000, 37: 509-533.
[86] Grant KA, Lovinger DM: Cellular and behavioral neurobiology of alcohol: receptor-mediated neuronal processes. *Clin. Neurosci.* 1995, 3(3): 155-164.
[87] Krystal JH, Tabakoff B: Ethanol Abuse, Dependence, And Withdrawal: Neurobiology And Clinical Implications. Edited by Davis KL, Charney DS, Coyle JT, Nemeroff C, *Neuropsychopharmacology: A Fifth Generation of Progress.* 2002, 1425-1443.

[88] Chandler LJ: Ethanol and brain plasticity: receptors and molecular networks of the postsynaptic density as targets of ethanol. *Pharmacology & Therapeutics* 2003, 99: 311–326.
[89] Hoffman PL, Rabe CS, Moses F, Tabakoff B: N-methyl-D-aspartate receptors and ethanol: inhibition of calcium flux and cyclic GMP production. *J. Neurochem.* 1989, 52: 61937-61940.
[90] Lovinger DM, White G, Weight FF: Ethanol inhibits NMDA-activated ion current in hippocampal neurons. *Science* 1989, 243: 1721-1724.
[91] Grant KA, Valverius P, Hudspith M, Tabakoff B: Ethanol withdrawal seizures and the NMDA receptor complex. *Eur. J. Pharmacol.* 1990, 176: 289-296.
[92] Gulya K, Grant KA, Valverius P, Hoffman PL, Tabakoff B: Brain regional specificity and time-course of changes in the NMDA receptor-ionophore complex during ethanol withdrawal. *Brain Res.* 1991, 547(1): 129-134.
[93] Gonzalez LP, Veatch LM, Ticku MK, Becker HC: Alcohol withdrawal kindling: Mechanisms and implications for treatment. *Alcohol Clin. Exp. Res.* 2001, 25: 197S-201S.
[94] Zhang J, Chiodo LA, Freeman AS: Electrophysiological effects of MK-801 on rat nigrostriatal and mesoaccumbal dopaminergic neurons. *Brain-Res.* 1992, 590(1-2): 153-163.
[95] Hoffman PL, Tabakoff B: Alcohol dependence: a commentary on mechanisms. *Alcohol Alcohol.* 1996, 31(4): 333-340.
[96] Kretschmer BD. Modulation of the mesolimbic dopamine system by glutamate: role of NMDA receptors. *J. Neurochem.* 1999, 73(2): 839-848.
[97] Fadda F, Rossetti ZL: Chronic ethanol consumption: from neuroadaptation to neurodegeneration. *Prog-Neurobiol.* 1998, 56(4): 385-431.
[98] Rossetti ZL, Melis F, Carboni S, Diana M, Gessa GL: Alcohol withdrawal in rats is associated with a marked fall in extraneuronal dopamine. *Alcohol Clin. Exp. Res.* 1992, 16(3): 529-532.
[99] Diana M, Pistis M, Carboni S, Gessa GL, Rossetti ZL: Profound decrement of mesolimbic dopaminergic neuronal activity during ethanol withdrawal syndrome in rats: electrophysiological and biochemical evidence. *Proc. Natl. Acad. Sci.* USA. 1993, 90(17): 7966-7969.
[100] Bisaga A, Popik P: In search of a new pharmacological treatment for drug and alcohol addiction: N-methyl-D-aspartate (NMDA) antagonists. *Drug Alcohol Depend.* 2000, 59(1): 1-15.
[101] Parsons CGR, Kalvinsh I, Kauss V, Jirgensons A, Gold M, Danysz W: US 6071966, 2000.
[102] Sengul C, Dilbaz N, Okay T, Balci Sengul M: The effectiveness of memantine in alcohol withdrawal syndrom *18th Congr Eur Coll Neuropsychopharmacol* (ECNP) (Oct 22-Oct 26, Amsterdam) 2005, Abst P.6.011
[103] Wiesbeck GA: 2007 ESBRA 2007, 10th Congress of the European Society for Biomedical Research on Alcoholism, Canterbury, UK, 23-26 September 2007. *Alcohol Alcohol* 2007, 42: i1-i66
[104] Cheon Y, Park J, Joe KH, Kim DJ: The effect of 12-week open-label memantine treatment on cognitive function improvement in patients with alcohol-related dementia. *Int. J. Neuropsychopharmacol.* 2008, 11(7): 971-983.

[105] Faingold CL, N'Guemo P, Riaz A: Ethanol and neurotransmitter interactions - from molecular to integrative effects. *Progress in Neurobiol.* 1998, 55: 509-535.

[106] Trevisan L, Fitzgerald LW, Brose N, Gasic GP, Heinemann SF, Duman RS, Nestler EJ. Chronic ingestion of ethanol up-regulates NMDAR1 receptor subunit immunoreactivity in rat hippocampus. *J Neurochem.* 1994, 62(4): 1635-1638.

[107] Kalluri HS, Mehta AK, Ticku MK: Up-regulation of NMDA receptor subunits in rat brain following chronic ethanol treatment. *Brain Res. Mol. Brain Res.* 1998, 58(1-2): 221-224.

[108] Follesa P, Ticku MK. Chronic ethanol-mediated up-regulation of the N-methyl-D-aspartate receptor polypeptide subunits in mouse cortical neurons in culture. *J. Biol. Chem.* 1996, 271(23): 13297-13299.

[109] Follesa P, Ticku MK. NMDA receptor upregulation: molecular studies in cultured mouse cortical neurons after chronic antagonist exposure. *J Neurosci.* 1996, 16(7): 2172-2178.

[110] Kew JN, Trube G, Kemp JA: State-dependent NMDA receptor antagonism by Ro 8-4304, a novel NR2B selective, non-competitive, voltage-independent antagonist. *Br J Pharmacol.* 1998, 123(3): 463-472.

[111] Boyce S, Wyatt A, Webb JK, O'Donnell R, Mason G, Rigby M, Sirinathsinghji D, Hill RG, Rupniak NM. Selective NMDA NR2B antagonists induce antinociception without motor dysfunction: correlation with restricted localisation of NR2B subunit in dorsal horn. *Neuropharmacology* 1999, 38(5): 611-623.

[112] Kocsis P, Kovacs G, Farkas S, Horvath C, Szombathelyi Z, Tarnawa I. NR2B receptors are involved in the mediation of spinal segmental reflex potentials but not in the cumulative motoneuronal depolarization in vitro. *Brain Res Bull.* 2004, 64(2): 133-138.

[113] Fillhard JA: The effects of CI-1041 in two tests of analgesia: acetic acid-induced writing test and formalin foot pad test. *Soc. Neurosci. Abstr.* 2000, 26: 617.4.

[114] Chizh BA: Novel approaches to targeting glutamate receptors for the treatment of chronic pain: Review article. *Amino Acids* 2002, 23: 169-176.

[115] Wright JL, Gregory TF, Kesten SR, Boxer PA, Serpa KA, Meltzer LT, Wise LD, Espitia SA, Konkoy CS, Whittemore ER, Woodward RM: Subtype-selective N-methyl-D-aspartate receptor antagonists: synthesis and biological evaluation of 1-(heteroarylalkynyl)-4-benzylpiperidines *J. Med. Chem.* 2000, 43: 3408-3419.

[116] Kotlinska J, Liljequist S. Oral administration of glycine and polyamine receptor antagonists blocks ethanol withdrawal seizures. *Psychopharmacology (Berl).* 1996, 127(3): 238-244.

[117] Narita M, Soma M, Mizoguchi H, Tseng L-F, Suzuki T. Implications of the NR2B subunit-containing NMDA receptor localized in mouse limbic forebrain in ethanol dependence. *Eur J Pharmacol.* 2000, 401(2): 191-195.

[118] Nikam SS, Meltzer LT: *NR2B Selective NMDA Receptor Antagonists Current Pharmaceutical Design* 2002, 8: 845-855.

[119] McBride WJ, Li TK: Animal models of alcoholism: neurobiology of high alcohol-drinking behavior in rodents. *Crit-Rev-Neurobiol.* 1998, 12(4): 339-369.

[120] El-Ghundi M, George SR, Drago J, Fletcher PJ, Fan T, Nguyen T, Liu C, Sibley DR, Westphal H, O'Dowd BF: Disruption of dopamine D1 receptor gene expression attenuates alcohol-seeking behavior. *Eur-J-Pharmacol.* 1998, 353(2-3): 149-158.

[121] Phillips TJ, Brown KJ, Burkhart-Kasch S, Wenger CD, Kelly MA, Rubinstein M, Grandy DK, Low MJ: Alcohol preference and sensitivity are markedly reduced in mice lacking dopamine D2 receptors. *Nat-Neurosci.* 1998, 1(7): 610-615.

[122] Cunningham CL, Howard MA, Gill SJ, Rubinstein M, Low MJ, Grandy DK: Ethanol-conditioned place preference is reduced in dopamine D2 receptor-deficient mice. *Pharmacol-Biochem-Behav.* 2000, 67(4): 693-699.

[123] Risinger FO, Freeman PA, Rubinstein M, Low MJ, Grandy DK. Lack of operant ethanol self-administration in dopamine D2 receptor knockout mice. *Psychopharmacology-(Berl).* 2000, 152(3): 343-350.

[124] Risinger FO, Freeman PA, Greengard P, Fienberg AA. Motivational effects of ethanol in DARPP-32 knock-out mice. *J-Neurosci.* 2001, 21(1): 340-348.

[125] Koob GF, Roberts AJ, Schulteis G, Parsons LH, Heyser CJ, Hyytia P, Merlo-Pich E, Weiss F: Neurocircuitry targets in ethanol reward and dependence. *Alcohol Clin Exp Res* 1998, 22: 3–9.

[126] Nestler EJ, Aghajanian JK: Molecular and cellular basis of addiction. *Science 1997,* 278: 58–63.

[127] Roy A, De Jong J, Lamparski D, George T, Linnoila M: Depression among alcoholics. *Arch Gen Psychiat* 1991, 48: 428–432.

[128] Heidbreder CA, Hagan JJ: Novel pharmacotherapeutic approaches for the treatment of drug addiction and craving. *Current Opinion in Pharmacology* 2005, 5:107–118.

[129] Kenna GA: Rationale for use of aripiprazole for alcohol dependence treatment. *Drugs Future* 2003, 28: 1227–1235.

[130] Beasley CM Jr., Chakrabarti JK, Hotten TM, Tupper DE: US 5817657, 1998.

[131] Hutchison KE, Swift R, Rohsenow DJ, Monti PM, Davidson D, Almeida A: Olanzapine reduces urge to drink after drinking cues and a priming dose of alcohol. *Psychopharmacology-(Berl).* 2001, 155(1): 27-34.

[132] Peters DH, Faulds D: Tiapride: a review of its pharmacology and therapeutic potential in the management of alcohol dependence syndrome. *Drugs* 1994, 47: 1010-1032.

[133] Wiesbeck GA, Weijers JG, Lesch OM, Glaser T, Toennes PJ, Boening J: Flupenthixol decanoate and relapse prevention in alcoholics: results from a placebo-controlled trial. *Alcohol Alcohol* 2001, 36: 329-334

[134] Marra D, Warot D, Berlin I, Hispard E, Notides C, Tilikete S, Payan C, Lépine JP, Dally S, Aubin HJ.: Amisulpride does not prevent relapse in primary alcohol dependence: results of a pilot randomized, placebo-controlled trial. *Alcohol Clin Exp Res* 2002, 26: 1545-1552

[135] Sherer MA, Kumor KM, Jaffe JH: Effects of intravenous cocaine are partially attenuated by haloperidol. *Psychiatry Res.* 1989, 27: 117–125.

[136] Ohuoha DC, Maxwell JA, Thomson LE, Cadet JL, Rothman RB: Effect of dopamine receptor antagonists on cocaine subjective effects: a naturalistic case study. *J. Subst. Abuse Treat.* 1997, 14: 249–258.

[137] Evans SM. Walsh SL, Levin FR, Foltin RW, Fischman MW, Bigelow GE: Effect of flupenthixol on subjective and cardiovascular responses to intravenous cocaine in humans. *Drug Alcohol Depend.* 2001, 64: 271–283.

[138] Anton RF, Kranzler H, Breder C, Marcus RN, Carson WH, Han J: A randomized, multicenter, double-blind, placebo-controlled study of the efficacy and safety of

aripiprazole for the treatment of alcohol dependence. *J. Clin. Psychopharmacol.* 2008, 28(1): 5-12.

[139] Kenna GA. Pharmacotherapy of alcohol dependence: Targeting a complex disorder. *Drug Discovery Today* 2005, 2(1): 71-78.

[140] Wang S, Kozikowski A, Sakamuri S, Enyedy I, Johnson K: WO 200122964, 1999.

[141] Zemlan FP: US 2004142962, 2004.

[142] Beer B, Epstein JW: US 6204284, 2001.

[143] Kreek MJ: Drug addictions. Molecular and cellular endpoints. *Ann N Y Acad Sci.* 2001, 937: 27-49.

[144] Johnson BA. Role of the serotonergic system in the neurobiology of alcoholism: implications for treatment. *CNS Drugs* 2004, 18: 1105–1118.

[145] Johnson BA. The role of serotonergic agents as treatments for alcoholism. *Drugs Today* 2003, 39: 665–672.

[146] Asberg M, Traskma L, Thoren NP: 5-HIAA in the cerebrospinal fluid. A biochemical suicide predictor. *Arch. Gen. Psychiatry* 1976, 33: 1193- 1197.

[147] Branchely L, Branchesy M, Haw S, Lieber CS: Depression, suicide, and aggression in alcoholics and their relationship to plasma amino acids. *Psychiatry Res.* 1984, 12: 219-226.

[148] Herz A: Endogenous opioid systems and alcohol addiction. *Psychopharmacology-(Berl).* 1997, 129(2): 99-111.

[149] Gianoulakis C: Influence of the endogenous opioid system on high alcohol consumption and genetic predisposition to alcoholism. *J-Psychiatry-Neurosci.* 2001, 26(4): 304-318.

[150] Katovich MJ, Simpkins JW, Song IC, Bodor N, Tuttle R: A rapid, quantitative in vivo assay for narcotic antagonists. *Subst-Alcohol-Actions-Misuse.* 1984, 5(2): 87-95.

[151] Sinclair JD, Scheinin H, Lammintausta R: US5086058, 1992.

[152] Sinclair JD: Evidence about the use of naltrexone and for different ways of using it in the treatment of alcoholism. *Alcohol Alcohol.* 2001, 36(1): 2-10.

[153] Mason BJ, Ritvo EC, Morgan RO, Salvato FR, Goldberg G, Welch B, Mantero-Atienza E: A double-blind, placebo-controlled pilot study to evaluate the efficacy and safety of oral nalmefene HCl for alcohol dependence. *Alcohol-Clin-Exp-Res.* 1994, 18(5): 1162-1167.

[154] Williams SH: Medications for treating alcohol dependence. *Am Fam Physician.* 2005, 72(9):1775-80.

[155] Yeomans MR, Wright P, Macleod HA, Critchley JA: Effects of nalmefene on feeding in humans. Dissociation of hunger and palatability. *Psychopharmacology (Berl).* 1990, 100(3): 426-432.

[156] Zhou FM, Liang Y, Dani JA: Endogenous nicotinic cholinergic activity regulates dopamine release in the striatum. *Nat. Neurosci.* 2001, 4(12): 1224-1229.

[157] Galli F, Jegham S, Lochead A, Samson A: US6908927, 2005.

[158] Fucile S, Palma E, Mileo AM, Miledi R, Eusebi F. Human neuronal threonine-for-leucine-248 alpha 7 mutant nicotinic acetylcholine receptors are highly Ca2+ permeable. PNAS 2000, 97(7): 3643-3648.

[159] Tehim A, Xie W, Gauss CM: WO 2004029050, 2004.

[160] Herbert B, Nguyen TM, Tehim A, Hopper AT, Xie W: WO 2004019943, 2004.

[161] Barth F, Basellas P, Congy C, Martinez S, Rinaldi M: US 5462960, 1995.

[162] Barth F, Rinaldi-Carmona M: The development of cannabinoid antagonists. *Curr Med Chem* 1999, 6: 745-755.

[163] Tanda G, Pontieri FE, Di Chiara G: Cannabinoid and heroin activation of mesolimbic dopamine transmission by a common mu1 opioid receptor mechanism. *Science* 1997, 276: 2048-2050.

[164] Navarro M, Carrera MR, Fratta W, Valverde O, Cossu G, Fattore L, Chowen JA, Gomez R, del Arco I, Villanua MA, Maldonado R, Koob GF, Rodriguez de Fonseca F: Functional interaction between opioid and cannabinoid receptors in drug self-administration. *J Neurosci* 2001, 21: 5344-5350.

[165] Chaperon F, Soubrie P, Puech AJ, Thiebot MH: Involvement of central cannabinoid (CB1) receptors in the establishment of place conditioning in rats. *Psychopharmacology (Berl)* 1998, 135: 324-332.

[166] Freedland CS, Sharpe AL, Samson HH, Porrino LJ: Effects of SR141716A on ethanol and sucrose self-administration. *Alcohol Clin Exp Res* 2001, 25: 277-282.

[167] De Vries TJ, Shaham Y, Homberg JR, Crombag H, Schuurman K, Dieben J, Vanderschuren LJ, Schoffelmeer AN: A cannabinoid mechanism in relapse to cocaine seeking. *Nat Med* 2001, 7: 1151-1154.

[168] Cohen C, Perrault G, Voltz C, Steinberg R, Soubrie P: SR141716, a central cannabinoid (CB(1)) receptor antagonist, blocks the motivational and dopamine-releasing effects of nicotine in rats. *Behav Pharmacol* 2002, 13: 451-463.

[169] Arnone M, Maruani J, Chaperon F, Thiebot MH, Poncelet M, Soubrie P, Le-Fur G: Selective inhibition of sucrose and ethanol intake by SR 141716, an antagonist of central cannabinoid (CB1) receptors. *Psychopharmacology-(Berl).* 1997, 132(1): 104-106.

[170] Gessa GL, Serra S, Vacca G, Carai MAM, Colombo G: Suppressing effect of the cannabinoid CB1 receptor antagonist, SR147778, on alcohol intake and motivational properties of alcohol in alcohol-preferring sP rats. *Alcohol Alcohol* 2005, 40(1): 46.

[171] Weiss F, Ciccocioppo R, Parsons LH, Katner S, Liu X, Zorrilla EP, Valdez GR, Ben-Shahar O, Angeletti S, Richter RR: Compulsive drug-seeking behavior and relapse. Neuroadaptation, stress, and conditioning factors. *Ann N Y Acad Sci* 2001, 937: 1-26.

[172] Stewart J: Stress and relapse to drug seeking: studies in laboratory animals shed light on mechanisms and sources of long-term vulnerability. *Am J Addict* 2003, 12: 1-17.

[173] Shaham Y, Erb S, Leung S, Buczek Y, Stewart J: CP-154,526, a selective, non-peptide antagonist of the corticotropinreleasing factor1 receptor attenuates stress-induced relapse to drug seeking in cocaine- and heroin-trained rats. *Psychopharmacology (Berl)* 1998, 137: 184-190.

[174] Nie Z, Schweitzer P, Roberts AJ, Madamba SG, Moore SD, Siggins GR: Ethanol augments GABAergic transmission in the central amygdala via CRF1 receptors. *Science* 2004, 303: 1512-1514.

[175] Valdez GR, Roberts AJ, Chan K, Davis H, Brennan M, Zorrilla EP, Koob GF: Increased ethanol self-administration and anxiety-like behavior during acute ethanol withdrawal and protracted abstinence: regulation by corticotropin-releasing factor. *Alcohol-Clin-Exp-Res.* 2002, 26(10): 1494-1501.

[176] Mann K: Pharmacotherapy of Alcohol Dependence. A Review of the Clinical Data. *CNS Drugs* 2004, 18 (8): 485-450.

In: Suicidal Behavior in Alcohol and Drug Abuse... ISBN: 978-1-60876-919-3
Editors: L. Sher, A. Vilens, pp. 191-214

Chapter 11

MANAGEMENT OF ACUTE PSYCHIATRIC CONDITIONS IN A DUAL DIAGNOSIS UNIT

Raman Gopalakrishnan
Penn Presbyterian Medical Center, Philadelphia, Pennsylvania, USA

ABSTRACT

Dual Diagnosis Inpatient units specialize in the stabilization of concurrent psychiatric and substance use disorders. The high prevalence, complexity and severity of these disorders have been borne out in several national surveys. The temporal relationship between the disorders is unclear in most cases and therefore concurrent and integrated treatments are crucial to achieve optimal outcomes.

This chapter lists the common conditions encountered in the dual diagnosis unit. Given the scope of the subject, the list cannot be realistically expected to include all conditions. They are classified based on the nature of the symptoms. Under each symptom, the differential diagnoses and management strategies for each condition are discussed in some detail. Given the expertise, probably more weight is given to medical management; but enough cannot be said about the vital importance of psychosocial and aftercare services. A wide variety of resources are fortunately available for the intellectually curious.

INTRODUCTION

Dual diagnosis disorders refer to the co-occurrence of substance use disorders and one or more psychiatric disorders in a patient. Dual diagnosis units cater to this population when hospital level care is indicated. The indications [1] for hospitalization are 1) Patients with severe drug overdoses; 2) Patients at risk for severe or complicated substance withdrawal; 3) Patients with acute or chronic general medical conditions that complicates detoxification; 4) Patients severe substance abuse and psychiatric comorbid conditions who are at danger to self or others; and 5) Patients with documented history of non-compliance or non-response to less intensive levels of care.

Goals of Treatment

The ideal outcome for patients admitted with comorbid disorders is total cessation of drug use [19] and control and stabilization of their comorbid psychiatric condition. The goals of treatment [1] are: 1) Motivating change, 2) Establishing and maintaining a therapeutic framework and alliance, 3) Assessing safety and clinical status, 4) Managing intoxication, 5) Managing withdrawal, 6) Reducing the morbidity and sequelae of substance use disorders, 7) Facilitating adherence to a treatment plan and preventing relapse, 8) Providing education about dual diagnosis disorders and their treatment and 9) Facilitating access to services and coordinating resources among medical, psychiatric, drug treatment, and other services.

Prevalence

The National Comorbidity Survey (NCS) and Epidemiologic Catchment Area (ECA) studies [2,3] confirm that those with substance use disorders (38-51%) are substantially more likely to experience other mental disorders and those with mental disorders (51% of those with lifetime mental disorders) are considerably more likely to develop substance abuse.

Alcohol dependence occurs in approximately 10% of men and 3-5% of women, while alcohol abuse ranges from 20% for men and 10% for women. Among psychiatric patients the rate of alcohol abuse may reach 20-30%. Three psychiatric conditions viz. Schizophrenia, Bipolar Disorder and ASPD clearly increase the risk of subsequent alcohol related disorders [4]. Schizophrenia is associated with a high incidence of nicotine dependence [5]. Among patients with Major Depression, close to 25% have comorbid substance use disorders [6]. Patients with bipolar disorder have very high (>50%) prevalence rates for comorbid substance use disorders [3]. Likewise, there is a two-way correlation between substance use disorders and anxiety disorders [2].

Alcoholism increases the risk of concurrent substance use disorders like Sedative / Hypnotic / Anxiolytic dependence. Over 12-33% of alcoholics have concomitant use of Benzodiazepines (BZs). Similarly, substance use disorders are clearly associated with increased incidence of psychiatric disorders like depressive disorders [7], anxiety disorders [2-3] and personality disorders [8]; as well as increased severity and worse outcomes of bipolar disorders [9]. Opioid dependence is associated with significant psychiatric comorbidity with an estimated 24% lifetime prevalence of an Axis I disorder and 35% prevalence of an Axis II disorder.

Table 1. Diagnoses associated with class of substances

	Depen-dence	Abuse	Intoxi-cation	With-drawal	Intoxi-cation Delirium	With-drawal Delirium	Deme-ntia	Amnestic Disorder	Psychotic Disorders	Mood Disorders	Anxiety Disorders	Sexual Dysfunctions	Sleep Disorders
Alcohol	X	X	X	X	I	W	P	P	I/W	I/W	I/W	I	I/W
Amphetamines	X	X	X	X	I				I	I/W	I	I	I/W
Caffeine			X								I		I
Cannabis	X	X	X		I				I		I		
Cocaine	X	X	X	X	I				I	I/W	I/W	I	I/W
Hallucinogens	X	X	X		I				I*	I	I		
Inhalants	X	X	X		I		P		I	I	I		
Nicotine	X			X									
Opioids	X	X	X	X	I				I	I		I	I/W
Phencyclidine	X	X	X		I				I	I	I		
Sedatives, hypnotics, or anxiolytics	X	X	X	X	I	W	P	P	I/W	I/W	W	I	I/W
Polysubstance	X												
Other	X	X	X	X	I	W	P	P	I/W	I/W	I/W	I	I/W

* Also Hallucinogen Persisting Perception Disorder (Flashbacks).

Note: X, I, W, I/W, or P indicates that the category is recognized in DSM-IV. In addition, I indicates that the specifier With Onset During Intoxication may be noted for the category (except for Intoxication Delirium); W indicates that the specifier With Onset During Withdrawal may be noted for the category (except for Withdrawal Delirum); and I/W indicates that either With Onset During Intoxication or With Onset During Withdrawal may be noted for the category. P indicates that the disorder is Persisting.

From DSM IV: Diagnostic and Statistical Manual of Mental Disorders, ed. 4; American Psychiatric Association, Washington, DC, 1994.

Table 2. Differntial diagnosis – cognitive disorders

Causes	Salient features
Alcohol / BZ intoxication delirium	Modified by tolerance, polysubstance abuse
Alcohol / BZ induced amnesia	**"Blackout"**
Alcohol / BZ withdrawal delirium (Delirium Tremens)	3-5% of alcohol withdrawal occurring within 8-72 hours of abstinence - tremors, autonomic hyperactivity, confusion, sweating, tactile/visual hallucinations.
Post Alcohol / BZ withdrawal seizures	Seizures commonly referred to as Rum Fits.
Alcohol / BZ related persisting amnestic disorder – **Wernicke's encephalopathy**	Thiamine deficiency- Confusion, ataxia and 6th nerve (lateral rectus) palsy
Alcohol /BZ related persisting amnestic disorder – **Korsakoff's syndrome**	Often permanent- Pronounced anterograde and retrograde amnesia, apathy and impaired visuo-spatial or abstract learning; Personality change
Alcohol induced persisting dementia	Multifactorial-trauma, vitamin deficiencies, toxic effects of alcohol
Stimulant (Cocaine / Amphetamine / Methamphetamine / Substituted amphetamines) Intoxication Delirium	Agitation, Sweating, Rigidity, High blood pressure, Tachycardia
(Other substances) related intoxication Delirium	Cannabis / Hallucinogen / Inhalants / Steroids can all cause delirium
Inhalant-induced Persistent Dementia	Cerebral white matter abnormalities
PCP intoxication Delirium	HTN, Vertical Nystagmus, Rigidity, SZ
Opioid Intoxication Delirium	Miosis, drowsiness/ coma, slurring Meperidine – fatal Hyperthermia, SZ
Complicated Opioid withdrawal	In patients with debilitating illnesses
Severe Psychosis or Mania	Occasionally present with confusion and marked disorganization
Neuroleptic Malignant Syndrome	Confusion, Fever, Rigidity, Renal failure, death

Primary v/s Secondary Distinction

Comorbid psychiatric and substance use disorders were historically categorized as primary or secondary disorders based on the age of onset of one disorder in relation to the other. There is an increased likelihood of existence of a primary psychiatric disorder if there is 1) Strong family history of psychiatric disorder; 2) Psychiatric symptoms occur outside the context of drug use; 3) Clear evidence that the onset of the psychiatric disorder preceded the substance use and 4) Psychiatric symptoms are present during extended sobriety [1].

With a few exceptions, most other studies have determined no definite temporal relationships between comorbid disorders. The direction of causality is complex for most dually diagnosed patients. In view of the complex relationship between substance use disorders and psychiatric disorders, integrated treatment is essential in a dual diagnosis unit. Goals may need to be prioritized depending on the nature of presentation. For instance, severe psychiatric symptoms like psychosis or suicide require immediate interventions even while a patient is in detoxification. Once a patient's mental health condition is stabilized, a referral can be made to an appropriate drug treatment program. The comorbid psychiatric condition continues to be monitored and treated appropriately even in this setting.

Given below is a chart of DSM-IV Diagnosis associated with Class of Substances.

Table 3. Blood levels of alcohol and observed behavioral changes

Alcohol Level (grams/deciliter)	Symptoms
0.02-0.03	Behavioral changes, Elevated mood
0.03-0.08	Motor/cognitive ↓
0.08-0.1	Legal limit in most states
0.1-0.2	Incoordination, Labile mood, ↓↓ cognition
0.2-0.3	Slurred speech, blackouts, nystagmus
>0.3	Neuro-respiratory depression, Death

SUBSTANCE ABUSE AND COGNITIVE DISORDERS

Patients presenting to a dual diagnosis unit can present with diffuse or specific cognitive impairments. They are often referred from the ER or Crisis Centers with a broad diagnosis of "Change in Mental Status". They can account for certain medical emergencies on the inpatient unit. While most substance use disorders (except possibly nicotine or caffeine) can cause cognitive impairments, alcohol, PCP, cocaine and opiate related substance disorders perhaps warrant the most attention.

Clinical Features and Treatment

Alcohol intoxication manifests with sensorium worsening progressively with increasing levels of alcohol. The clinical picture may however be altered by patient tolerance, presence of other medical conditions or concomitant use of other substances.

Benzodiazepine Intoxication: BZ intoxication usually presents with sedation. It can occasionally present with severe disinhibition and manifest with aggression and hostility. Severe BZ intoxication can occur especially when used along with Alcohol or other sedative-hypnotic substances.

> *Treatment:* Most cases of mild to moderate alcohol/BZ intoxication can be treated by careful monitoring. Severe cases should be treated with cautious airway and respiratory management and administration of a specific BZ antagonist like Flumazenil (starting dose at 0.2 mg administered over 15 seconds and repeated as needed in minute intervals to a maximum of 1 mg).

Alcohol (Sedative/Hypnotic) withdrawals commonly present with anxiety, tremors, sweating, insomnia, nausea, or vomiting. Autonomic hyperactivity (Temperature/Pulse/Diastolic Blood Pressure >100) is a classic sign of alcohol/BZ withdrawal. When alcohol withdrawal manifests with severe agitation, confusion and extreme autonomic dysfunction it is classified as alcohol withdrawal delirium or delirium tremens. Rarely, patients may experience alcohol withdrawal- related seizures (Grand mal type). Patients may present to the dual-diagnosis unit in the post-ictal phase marked by confusion and disorganized behavior.

Alcohol/BZ Detoxification: Alcohol and Benzodiazepine withdrawals carry the risk of severe withdrawals, which if left untreated could lead to seizures and or withdrawal delirium. Once detoxification is completed and if patient's psychiatric symptoms resolve completely, there is no indication for continued prescription of any psychotropic medications. Persistent anxiety or insomnia is best addressed through lifestyle changes and behavior modifications.

Alcohol detoxification is usually carried out with Lorazepam (2-4 mg), Oxazepam (15-30 mg), Chlordiazepoxide (25-50 mg) or Diazepam (10-20 mg) mg given 4-6 times a day and gradually tapered by about 20% each day Physical signs like tremors, sweating; anxiety and vitals should be monitored to facilitate a smooth titration. Adjunct medications known to be valuable in withdrawal treatment include Clonidine (0.1-0.3 mg twice or thrice daily) and β blockers like Propranolol (60-120 mg in divided doses) or Atenolol (50-100 mg). They decrease craving and anxiety. In Delirium Tremens, a comprehensive work up should be carried out to rule out concomitant medical conditions. Thiamine, Alcohol detoxification protocol and Fluid/Electrolyte management should help manage most cases of DTs. 1:1 observation, antipsychotic agents like Haloperidol (5-20 mg), seclusion and rarely restraints may be required to help control agitation. Alcohol withdrawal seizures require comprehensive neurological management. Anticonvulsants like Valproic acid (Depakote 500-2000 mg daily) or Carbamazepine (Tegretol 200-1600 mg daily) can provide limited benefits.

Sedative/Hypnotic Detoxification: The keys to BZ detoxification are 1) stabilization on equivalent dose of a known BZ followed by 2) gradual taper at a rate of 10-25% every few days. Adjunctive therapy used in alcohol withdrawal can also prove valuable in BZ detoxification. Barbiturate Detoxification is usually carried out by 1) Pentobarbital challenge test to assess tolerance, stabilization, followed by gradual taper or 2) Phenobarbital loading doses to achieve stabilization and allowing self-taper.

Pharmacotherapy for Alcohol dependence: Disulfiram (250mg per day), Naltrexone (50mg per day) and Acamprosate (2000mg per day) could be initiated and may help suppress craving and maintain abstinence. Disulfiram should be avoided in patients with schizophrenia as it may worsen psychosis.

Alcohol induced Persisting Amnestic Disorder: While Wernicke's encephalopathy is preventable and can be rapidly reversed with thiamine and vitamin supplementation, the prognosis for Korsakoff's syndrome is not as good.

Treatment: Every patient with suspected or proven alcohol use should be treated with Thiamine 100 mg daily and multivitamins. Thiamine administration is recommended especially prior to any glucose administration to avoid precipitating Wernicke's encephalopathy. Korsakoff's syndrome is treated with 50-100 mg of Thiamine administered over several months. Management of Alcohol-induced persisting dementia would involve a detailed investigation into the cause and appropriate treatment of dementia in a setting that ensures sobriety.

Stimulant (Cocaine / Amphetamine / Methamphetamine / Substituted amphetamines) intoxication can be associated occasionally with toxic manifestations including elevated blood pressure, tachycardia, high fever, rigidity, rhabdomyolysis, renal damage, seizures, coma and death. Tachycardia and arrhythmias can be managed with α and β adrenergic antagonists.

Treatment: Haloperidol and Phenothiazines may have some role in the treatment of psychotic symptoms. Hyperpyrexia and muscle rigidity should be treated on the lines of Neuroleptic Malignant Syndrome (NMS) with cooling mechanisms, muscle relaxants like Dantrolene. Seizures might respond to Diazepam.

Inhalant intoxication (delirium) could be seen as a component of polysubstance dependence. Patients may present with mild to moderate inhalant intoxication characterized by behavioral changes like incoordination, slurred speech, unsteady gait, psychomotor retardation usually resolves spontaneously. Severe intoxication could be marked by airway constriction, cardiac arrhythmias, trauma and sometimes coma.

Treatment: Dextrose 50 mg (to treat presumed hypoglycemia) and Naloxone 0.8-2mg (to reverse Opioid intoxication) should be given to any comatose patient. Patients need to be maintained in a calm environment since agitation may precipitate arrhythmias. Benzodiazepines are contraindicated, as they may exacerbate inhalant intoxication delirium.

PCP intoxication is characterized by fluctuating symptoms with alternating delirium and psychosis. Occasionally, it can be complicated by cardio-vascular, neuromuscular and renal damage. In most cases recovery in noted in 24-72 hours. Cardinal signs of PCP intoxication are Hypertension or tachycardia, Vertical or Horizontal Nystagmus, Muscular Rigidity, Ataxia, Dysarthria, Seizures or Coma. It can lead to muscle breakdown (Rhabdomyolysis), Myoglobinuria and Acute Renal Failure. Behavioral manifestations include rage, panic and severe agitation.

Treatment: Patients should be closely monitored to ensure safety. Treatment focuses on reducing PCP levels through administration of activated charcoal. Behavioral management aims to minimize sensory stimulation by placing the patient in quiet isolation. Restraints should be judiciously used, as patients have been known to fight themselves to death (given the high incidence of rhabdomyolysis). Oral or intramuscular antipsychotics (preferably with low intrinsic anticholinergic activity like Haloperidol 5-20 mg) can help with sedation.

Opioid/Opiate intoxication is characterized by CNS depression and manifests with drowsiness or coma, slurred speech, and pupillary constriction. The presentations in prescription opiate intoxication can vary, often complicated by concomitant drug use and comorbid medical conditions. For instance, Meperidine (Demerol) can lead to severe toxicity, Seizures, Delirium, Hyperthermia and death when abused by those taking MAO-inhibitors and patients with impaired renal function.

Treatment: Severe Opioid intoxication requires emergency medical management. It includes airway protection, mechanical ventilation and administration of an Opioid antagonist like Naloxone (~0.8 mg initial dose repeated every few minutes), which usually reverses the intoxication.

Uncomplicated Opioid / Opiate withdrawal while unpleasant has a relatively benign course. It is commonly termed "cold turkey" and is characterized by craving, anxiety, yawning, rhinorrhea, lacrimation, itching, cold sweats, piloerection, muscle spasms, abdominal cramps, nausea, vomiting or diarrhea. Uncomplicated Opioid / Opiate withdrawal should not result in delirium; but it can happen in a setting of medical complications including infections, electrolyte disturbances and polysubstance abuse.

Treatment: Opioid Detoxification Protocol is recommended for most patients. Mild withdrawals can be managed by administration of non-Opioid agents. They usually include Clonidine (0.1-0.3 mg) for craving, NSAIDs like Ibuprofen (600-800 mg) for pain and cramps, anti-diarrheal agents, Dicyclomine (20 mg) for abdominal cramps and Diphenhydramine (25-50 mg) for itching / rhinorrhea / lacrimation. In severe withdrawal, 10-20 mg methadone (a long acting opiate) should be started depending on the severity of addiction. The methadone is then gradually tapered by 5 mg everyday. The only exception is where patients are already on methadone/buprenorphine maintenance in which case they are maintained on their prescribed dose of the opiate. Withdrawal symptoms experienced during the methadone taper is managed with support and non-Opioid medications. In the context of significant comorbidity seen in Opioid addicts, it is crucial to remember important drug interactions. For instance, agents like Dilantin, alcohol, and barbiturates can induce hepatic enzymes and lower methadone levels while erythromycin, ketoconazole and cimetidine can inhibit hepatic enzymes and elevate methadone levels.

SUBSTANCE ABUSE AND PSYCHOTIC DISORDERS

Table 4. Differential diagnosis – psychotic disorders

Alcohol intoxication including so called "Pathological alcohol intoxication"	Can present with irritability, violent outbursts and occasionally frank psychotic symptoms
Alcohol-induced Psychotic Disorder	Presentation includes "Othello's syndrome" or delusional jealousy
Stimulant (Cocaine / Amphetamine / Methamphetamine / Substituted amphetamines) Intoxication	Can be associated with tactile hallucinations called "cocaine bugs" or "formication"
Cannabis induced psychotic disorder	"Hemp insanity"
Hallucinogen (e.g. LSD) intoxication	Autonomic arousal, synesthesias
Hallucinogen induced psychosis	Euphoria, hyper religiosity, multimodal hallucinations
Hallucinogen Persisting Perception d/o	Aeropsia (seeing air) and Pareidolias (faces on walls and floor)
Inhalant induced Psychotic Disorder	Confusion, panic and agitation
PCP intoxication	Often associated with rage, violence
Schizophrenia	Slow onset teens-20s, patients experience more significant alcohol related problems.
Mood disorder/ Schizoaffective disorder	Severe mood d/o associated with Mood congruent/incongruent psychotic symptoms

Clinical Features and Treatment

Alcohol intoxication can be associated with disorganized behavior. This is particularly relevant in Pathological Alcohol Intoxication where extreme aggression may be seen following ingestion of relatively small amounts of alcohol. Patients usually experience amnesia to such unusual behaviors. Alcohol induced psychosis may present with delusional jealousy. These symptoms usually resolve with sustained abstinence.

Amphetamine and Cocaine use disorders are frequently associated with psychotic symptoms that stem from excessive dopaminergic activity. The phenomenon of "sensitization" has been speculated to play a role in these disorders as well in seizures. Sometimes, they are associated with vivid visual hallucinations and tactile hallucinations that are experienced as bugs crawling under the skin. This phenomenon is known variously as "Cocaine bug", "Formication" or "Crank Sores".

Besides abstinence from the agent, a short course of antipsychotics like Haloperidol (5-20mg) or phenothiazines like Chlorpromazine (50-200mg) may be needed to alleviate these symptoms.

Cannabis induced psychosis is not very common and is usually caused by using cannabis laced with PCP. Cannabis could exacerbate schizophrenia. Treating cannabis dependence is important because there is some evidence that Cannabis (like Nicotine) serves as a gateway drug.

Hallucinogen intoxication can be associated with Euphoria, Hyper-religiosity and Synesthesias (feeling sounds; hearing colors). These effects can be re-experienced after a long time and is termed as Hallucinogen Persisting Perception disorder.

Hallucinogen intoxication is treated with BZs like Diazepam (20 mg) and "talking down" the patient. A "Palm test" to rule out PCP intoxication is usually recommended since BZs can occasionally exacerbate PCP intoxication. Hallucinogen persisting perception disorder may respond to long-acting BZs and anticonvulsants. Hallucinogen induced psychosis may benefit from antipsychotics. Inhalant induced psychosis like PCP can be worsened by BZ use. Similar to PCP, it is treated with cautious isolation, reassurance and administration of Haloperidol (5-20 mg)

PCP induced psychosis can mimic all the symptoms of schizophrenia and persist for a long period of time. Antipsychotics are found to be of some use in management of psychotic symptoms. Most cases resolve in 24-72 hours; even in prolonged PCP-induced psychotic disorder, complete recovery can be expected in 4-6 weeks irrespective of antipsychotic use.

Schizophrenia is associated with an elevated risk of developing substance abuse and dependence (Buckley PF, 1998). Schizophrenic patients use nicotine, amphetamines and cocaine for their stimulant effects in order to alleviate their negative symptoms and/or side effects of antipsychotic medications. Substance abuse/dependence on the other hand may contribute to development of schizophrenia. The comorbid disorders can present with severe paranoia, florid delusions, hallucinations and agitation necessitating inpatient treatment.

Table 5. Signs and symptoms of schizophrenia

Delusions	Paranoid, grandiose, religious, disorganized, bizarre
Hallucinations	Usually auditory, commentary, critical or command Visual and Tactile Hallucinations may signify comorbid substance use disorder
Disorganized Thoughts	Incoherence, illogical thoughts, Derailment, Verbigeration, Neologisms, Flight of ideas, Loose associations, Th. Alienation
Disorganized Behavior	Mutism, Catatonia, Bizarre mannerisms, Stereotypy, Inappropriate affect, Echopraxia, Disinhibition, Poor self care
Catatonia	Catalepsy, Waxy flexibility, Stupor, Catatonic excitement, Negativism, Posturing, Mannerisms, Echolalia or Echopraxia
Negative Symptoms	Anhedonia, Avolition, Apathy, Asociality, Alogia, Flat affect

Management of Schizophrenia

Pharmacotherapy is the mainstay in the treatment of schizophrenia and schizoaffective disorder. The choice of antipsychotics is determined by past history of response, nature and severity of psychotic symptoms, side effect profile, medication compliance, cost and accessibility. Guidelines like the Texas Algorithm and American Psychiatric Association (APA) Practice Guidelines [1] are valuable tools in sequencing and planning medication regimens. The table below lists the antipsychotics commonly used in an inpatient unit. With the possible exception of Clozapine, antipsychotics generally share similar efficacy in the treatment of schizophrenia [10]

Adverse effects of Antipsychotics include Dystonia, Parkinsonism and Akathisia. Dystonia and Parkinsonism can be managed by choice of newer generation of antipsychotics, using lower doses of the medications and addition of Benztropine (2-4 mg), Diphenhydramine (25-100 mg), Hydroxyzine (25-100 mg) or BZs. Akathisia is treated with β blockers like Propranolol (30-90 mg) or BZs. Tardive Dyskinesia is often seen among chronic schizophrenics who have been treated with anti-psychotics for a long time. While no specific treatments are available, Clozapine has been known to improve and even prevent Tardive Dyskinesia.

Table 6. Pharmacotherapy of schizophrenia

Antipsychotics	Dosage	Benefits/ Disadvantages
Chlorpromazine	200-600mg	Sedation, Useful in acute agitation, EPS ++, TD+
Fluphenazine	2-20mg	↓ Sedation, EPS +++, TD +, Depot formulation available
Haloperidol	5-20mg	↓ Sedation, EPS +++, TD+, Depot formulation available
Risperidone	2-16mg	↓Sedation, ↓ EPS, Depot formulation available
Olanzapine	5-25mg	Sedation, No EPS, Useful in acute agitation, Weight Gain
Quetiapine	200-600mg	Sedation, No EPS, Useful in anxiety, Weight Gain
Clozapine	150-800mg	Sedation, No EPS, Weight Gain, Risk of Agranulocytosis

Table 7. Differntial diagnosis – mood disorders

Depression	
Alcohol / Sedative / Hypnotic induced depressive disorder	Recognized CNS depressants; Symptoms during alcohol use ~ 4 weeks into abstinence
Stimulant (Cocaine / Amphetamine / Methamphetamine) withdrawal	**"Cocaine Crash"**
Opioid induced mood disorder	Usually presents with mixed symptoms
Major Depression, Schizoaffective disorder	Risk of Suicide
Mania	
Stimulant (Cocaine / Amphetamine / Methamphetamine / Substituted amphetamines) intoxication	Elevated mood, talkativeness, racing thoughts, hypersexual behavior, ↑ **goal directed activity,** lack of fatigue, enhanced creativity, recklessness
Bipolar Mania; Schizoaffective disorder	Elevated risk of substance use disorders

Rarely, potential life threatening side effects of antipsychotics may be encountered in the form of Neuroleptic Malignant Syndrome. It is characterized by rigidity, fever, sweating, confusion, rhabdomyolysis, renal failure, seizures and even death. Management includes immediate discontinuation of neuroleptics and treatment with trials of Bromocriptine, Amantadine and Dantrolene.

Agitation stems from paranoia, hallucinations, involuntary commitment to treatment. It can be managed by a combination of high potency antipsychotics and BZs. In such situations, control of agitation takes precedence over concerns of long term BZ dependence.

Patients with schizophrenia and comorbid substance use disorders face daunting odds. Medication compliance is often an issue. Long acting antipsychotics (Haloperidol decanoate, Fluphenazine decanoate or Risperdal consta) are useful options and should be discussed and initiated during inpatient treatment.

Most rehabs and drug treatment programs exclude psychotic patient; schizophrenic patients thus have problems in access to drug treatment programs.

Substance Abuse and Mood Disorders

The co-occurrence of depression and substance abuse has far-reaching consequences, affecting physical well-being and social-occupational functioning. The comorbidity is associated with high severity, high costs, and poor functional prognosis. For instance, depressive symptoms typically predict increased alcohol use. Conversely, heavy drinking predicts poor response to depression treatment [11]

Clinical Features and Treatment

DSM –IV recognizes that virtually all substances (with the exception of caffeine, cannabis and nicotine) can precipitate or worsen depressive symptoms. [12]

Multiple causal factors and mechanisms probably underlie the association between alcoholism and depression. Alcohol as a CNS depressant has been frequently associated, with clinical depression occurring in over 80% of alcoholics. Alcohol induced mood disorder is diagnosed when patients experience intense mood symptoms during use and lasting several days up to 4 weeks into abstinence. Just about 5-10% meet criteria for a primary mood disorder. Since a significant majority of patients with alcohol use disorders, experience spontaneous resolution of their anxiety and depressive symptoms once they achieve sobriety; a critical question is when to initiate antidepressants?

Cocaine dependence is associated with increased incidence and severity of Major Depression. Patients with major depression attempt to self medicate their depression with cocaine and other stimulants. Stimulant withdrawal can present with severe depressive symptoms [13]. Cocaine withdrawal (Cocaine crash) can manifest with exhaustion, fatigue, hypersomnia and hyperphagia. Stimulant (Cocaine / Amphetamine) withdrawal is different from alcohol / sedative / BZ or Opioid withdrawals since the physiological symptoms don't warrant inpatient treatments. However it may be associated with severe depressive symptoms, suicidal behaviors and psychotic symptoms that merit inpatient dual-diagnosis treatment.

Major depression and substance use disorders commonly co-occur in clinical populations and in the community. Patients with Major Depression have high lifetime rates of substance use disorders [6]. Depression presents with persistent sadness of mood, neurovegetative symptoms like change in appetite / sleep / energy, loss of drive or motivation, anhedonia, guilt and ideas of worthlessness, hopelessness or helplessness. Psychosis may be present and is not uncommon with comorbid substance use. Patients often present to a dual-diagnosis unit with suicidal thoughts or after a suicide attempt. Depressed patients present challenges in the form of suicide risk, loss of motivation for change, social withdrawal and high relapse rates.

Patients with bipolar mania present with hyperexcitability, grandiosity, impulsitivity, impaired judgment and may use alcohol as a CNS depressant to self-regulate their mood. Patients with bipolar disorder carry a well-established risk for alcohol related disorders. Conversely, substance use disorders can worsen each episode of mania and worsen the overall course of the disorder [9]. Patients with stimulant intoxication can exhibit manic or mixed mood states. Hallucinogens, inhalants and PCP can all be associated with mood changes during intoxication. Anabolic Steroids, which are lately under growing scrutiny, can present with severe mood changes accompanied by rage, violence and occasionally homicidal tendencies. An initial focus in the inpatient unit will be to stabilize and treat the manic symptoms before drug rehabilitation can be considered. Manic patients present a unique challenge in dual diagnosis units. They can be entertaining, infectious, loud, disruptive, demanding, entitled, sarcastic and occasionally prone to violence. Severe mania can resemble delirium with marked confusion and disorganization.

Pharmacotherapy of Mood Disorders

As in Schizophrenia, substantial treatment options are available in the treatment of mood disorders seen in a dual diagnosis unit. For patients with no past history of depression, a 1-4 week delay of antidepressant therapy is advised to rule out substance induced depressive symptoms. In all other cases, depression treatment may be initiated concurrent with substance abuse treatment. Again, APA guidelines [1] or the Texas Algorithm [14] can be used in the planning or sequencing of different treatment options. Patients should always be assessed and monitored for risk of suicide.

Table 8. Commonly used antidepressants with salient features

Class	Antidepressants	Doses	Benefits/Disadvantages
TCAs	Imipramine, Amitryptiline Doxepin	75-300mg	Sedation, Anticholinergic side effects, Orthostasis, Overdose may be fatal, TCAs useful in pain disorder
SSRIs	Fluoxetine,	20-60mg	Arousal, Anxiety, Sexual side effects
	Citalopram	20-60mg	Usually well tolerated, minimal interactions
	Paroxetine	20-50mg	Sedation, Anticholinergic S/E, Withdrawals
	Sertraline	50-200mg	Nausea, vomiting, diarrhea, Sexual S/Es
SNRIs	Venlafaxine	75-300mg	Resistant Depression, GI Distress, Hypertension
	Duloxetine	20-60mg	Resistant Depression, Useful in pain disorder
Dopamine	Bupropion	75-300mg	Insomnia, Agitation, No Sexual S/Es, SZ risk
Others	Mirtazapine	15-30mg	Sedation, weight gain, No Sexual S/Es
	Trazodone	75-300mg	Sedation, Anxiolytic, Priapism

Table 9. Commonly used mood stabilizers with salient features

Mood Stabilizers	Doses	Benefits/Disadvantages
Lithium	600-1800mg	Acute mania, bipolar depression, toxicity, therapeutic levels,↓ Thyroid fns.
Valproate	250-3000mg	Dysphoric/ mixed / Rapid cycling, SZ benefit, GI / Liver S/E
Carbamazepine	400-1600mg	GI distress, Liver toxicity, SZ benefit, ↓ CBC, Teratogenic
Clonazepam	1.5-4mg	Acute mania, Control of agitation, Sedation
Lamotrigine	50-200mg	SZ benefit, Bipolar Depression, Steven-Johnson's syndrome
Olanzapine	5-25mg	Acute mania, Bipolar Depression, Sedation, Weight gain
Risperdal	2-16mg	Acute mania, Low side effects, ↑ Prolactin
Quetiapine	200-800mg	Bipolar Depression, Anxiety benefits, Sedation, Weight gain
Abilify	15-30mg	Few side effects
Topiramate	50-400mg	Bipolar Depression, Few side effects

Non-pharmacological Interventions

A wide variety of therapeutic options are available in the treatment of depression. They are well studied and are useful in 1) Remission of symptoms, 2) Prevention of Relapse and 3) Psychosocial rehabilitation. The different therapies available in the treatment of mood disorders are

1. Interpersonal therapy
2. Cognitive Behavioral therapy
3. Behavioral management
4. Supportive psychotherapy
5. Psychodynamic psychotherapy
6. Psychoeducation
7. Electroconvulsive therapy
8. Group therapy
9. Family and Couple therapy

Substance Abuse and Anxiety Disorders

Dual diagnosis treatment is critical in treatment of patients with substance abuse and comorbid anxiety since residual symptoms of one condition could interfere with treatment of the other. A primary anxiety disorder is associated with a more chronic course of substance use disorders. Patients with anxiety disorders especially panic disorder and generalized anxiety disorders are likely to depend on downers or anxiolytics like alcohol, BZs, Opiates or Barbiturates as opposed to stimulants like amphetamines or cocaine [15]. Withdrawals from these substances are usually associated with worsening anxiety symptoms, which, if left un-addressed can interfere with patient participation in recovery. Physicians often encounter competing goals of substance detoxification and anxiety relief. Additionally, panic attacks and agoraphobia can interfere with patient participation in group therapy. The optimal goal should be remission of anxiety symptoms and abstinence from psychoactive substances with addictive potential.

Etiology

1. Self Medication Hypothesis: Patients with psychiatric disorders preferentially use psychotropic substances to treat their dysphoric states.
2. Genetic Predisposition: Both anxiety disorders and substance use disorders tend to cluster in families and may have a common genetic predisposition.
3. Similar Neurobiological abnormalities like hyperactive noradrenergic pathways are observed in substance withdrawals and anxiety disorders.

Table 10. Differential diagnosis – anxiety

Alcohol / Sedative / Hypnotic/ Opioid withdrawal	Craving commonly presents with anxiety
Stimulant (Cocaine / Amphetamine / Methamphetamine) intoxication	Panic attacks; sometimes associated with tics and stereotyped behaviors
Cannabis induced anxiety disorder	
Panic Disorder, PTSD, GAD, Social phobia	Flashbacks, Agitation, Avoidance

Treatment

Research studies have demonstrated that effective treatment of anxiety disorders and addictive disorders is also cost effective with significant savings in total health care costs.

1 In Alcohol, Sedative and Opiate dependence, initial stabilization of anxiety requires supervised detoxification since substance withdrawal can worsen anxiety. Controlled administration of equivalent doses of the drug (e.g. BZs) or cross-tolerant agents (BZs like Clonazepam, lorazepam, oxazepam or temazepam to treat alcohol withdrawal or sedative withdrawal; methadone in opiate withdrawal) is usually followed by gradual taper. It may be prudent to rely on physical signs like temperature, pulse, blood pressure and tremors to adjust the dosing of these agents.

2 Judicious use of other anxiolytics like Clonidine, beta-blockers or anticonvulsants is recommended to suppress craving and withdrawal anxiety.

3 Supportive therapy, reassurance, education and specific behavior therapies like Deep Breathing, Deep Muscle Relaxation, Guided imagery, Graded Exposure and Desensitization can address comorbid anxiety symptoms.

4 Lifestyle modifications include reducing caffeine and nicotine consumption.

5 Cognitive Behavior therapy can help address distortions in thinking patterns that initiate and exacerbate anxiety symptoms.

6 Psychoeducation is key and patients have to be reassured that while anxiety symptoms may worsen in the short run, they will gradually improve over time.

7 The recommended treatments for comorbid panic disorder [16] as well as other anxiety disorders are SSRIs and integrated psychosocial treatment (Center for substance abuse treatment [17]. Despite their addiction potential, BZs remain effective medications for treating severe anxiety like acute panic. One should however carefully weigh the potential for abuse when used for long term treatment of anxiety in dually diagnosed patients.

8 For long-term treatment of anxiety, anxiolytics medications with little or no potential for abuse are preferred. They include SSRIs, TCAs, buspirone, trazodone, antihistamines (diphenhydramine or hydroxyzine) and beta-blockers. They are listed in Table 11.

Table 11. Commonly used anti-anxiety agents

Anxiolytic Agents	Examples and Dosing	Notes
Benzodiazepines	Lorazepam 2-10mg Oxazepam 30-120mg Clonazepam 1.5-4mg	Potential for abuse
SSRIs	Fluoxetine 20-60mg; Sertraline 50-200 mg; Citalopram 20-60 mg; Paroxetine 20-40 mg	Fluoxetine associated with ↑anxiety. Paxil withdrawal associated with anxiety. Safe in overdose.
TCAs	Doxepin 75-300 mg Imipramine 75-300 mg Clomipramine 75-300 mg	Sedation; benefits in depression, panic, OCD and PTSD. Risky in overdose
Trazodone	25mg – 200 mg	Safe; low abuse potential, priapism
Anti-histamines	Diphenhydramine 25-100 mg Hydroxyzine 25-100 mg	Sedation; additional benefits in opiate withdrawal
Buspirone	15-60mg in 4 divided doses	~ 4-6 weeks for benefits; GAD
β-blockers	Propranolol 15-60 mg	↓ abuse potential, Social phobia
Neuroleptics	Risperidone 2-4 mg; Olanzapine 5-20 mg; Quetiapine 100-200 mg	Effective in anxiety with delirium, psychosis, mood disorder and PTSD
Naltrexone Acamprosate	50-100 mg daily 666 mg thrice daily	Anti-alcohol treatments may reduce alcohol craving and related anxiety
Methadone and Buprenorphine	Methadone 40-60 mg usually Buprenorphine 16-32 mg	Reduce Opioid craving and withdrawal anxiety; Opioid use in patients with chronic pain

SUBSTANCE ABUSE AND PERSONALITY DISORDERS

Conduct disorder and Antisocial Personality Disorder (ASPD) represent independent additional risk factors for addictive disorders [15]. The NCS data indicated that conduct disorder without adult ASPD increased the odds of drug dependence 5-fold while adult ASPD further increased those odds 10-14 fold. The rate of lifetime substance use disorder reaches 50-60% for those with co-occurring personality disorder (82% among those with lifetime diagnosis of conduct disorder or ASPD). Patients with Substance Use disorders and Borderline Personality Disorder or ASPD have greater Risk-taking Behaviors, higher risk of suicide and poorer treatment outcomes [18].

Presentation and Management

It is best to establish a personality disorder diagnosis after patients achieve sustained remission, because many of the drug-seeking behaviors can be seen as personality defects. Prejudging patients can lead to counter-transference reactions on the unit, failure of therapeutic alliances and subsequent treatment failure. That being said, patients with Axis II disorders especially Narcissistic and Borderline Personality Disorders can be quite disruptive in the unit, manipulating patients and staff to their own advantage. Staff should be on alert to detect and manage Staff Splitting. This is best handled through staff education and teamwork. Behavior therapy appears to work best in such situations. For patients who malinger/ doctor shop/ feign symptoms, coordination with institutions and insurance companies tend to discourage a "revolving-door" phenomenon. Few of these patients may even try to sneak in drugs through manipulation; patient / relative checks for contraband may be required in such cases.

TREATMENT CONSIDERATIONS

1. General Medical Conditions and Physical Examination

All patients admitted to a dual-diagnosis unit should have a detailed history and complete physical examination. Table 12 illustrates the broad range of medical problems encountered in Dual-Diagnosis Settings. Based on the findings, appropriate medical consultations should be requested.

Other (or Unknown) Substance-Related Disorders

Nitrite inhalants referred to as "poppers" are used among adolescents and homosexual men for smooth muscle relaxation and to enhance orgasms. Nitrous Oxide, which is a common anesthetic is commonly abused in the health care population can be associated with B-12 deficiency related symptoms including pernicious anemia and neuropathies.

Table 12. Substance use related medical conditions

System	Findings
Cardiovascular	Hypertension, arrhythmias, MI, Cardiomyopathy, Shock
Respiratory	Respiratory failure, pulmonary edema, pneumonia, COPD, Tuberculosis
CNS	Encephalopathy, Seizures, Head injuries, CVA, Dementia, Neuropathies
Endocrine	Diabetes, Thyroid abnormalities
Gastrointestinal	Gastric ulcers, Gastritis, Ascites, Cancer
Nutritional	Obesity, Vitamin deficiencies, Lipid abnormalities
Hepatobiliary	Hepatitis, Cirrhosis, Pancreatitis, Hepatic Encephalopathy, Cancer
Hematological	Anemia, Thrombocytopenia, Infections and sepsis, Pernicious anemia
Metabolic	Dehydration, Electrolyte imbalances, Renal Failure
Musculoskeletal	Hyperthermia, Rhabdomyolysis, Fractures, Trauma
Infections	Endocarditis, Septicemia, Hepatitis B/C; HIV (especially in IVDA); STDs
Neonatal / Fetal	IUGR, Congenital malformations, Crack baby, Mental Retardation
Obstetric	Spontaneous abortions, Premature rupture of membranes

2. Lab Investigations and Rationale

i. Blood alcohol level (or Breathalyzer) and Urine Drug Screen should be mandatory for every patient admitted to the dual-diagnosis unit. Where use of other addictive substances (e.g. prescription painkillers) is suspected, a comprehensive drug panel may be required to detect metabolites of those drugs.
ii. HCG – pregnant women with substance use disorders have an elevated risk of STDs, complicated pregnancy and impaired fetal development. Mood stabilizers like Lithium, Carbamazepine and Valproate are associated with significant teratogenic effects.
iii. CBC – nutritional deficiency anemia, HIV related leucopoenia Carbamazepine related Agranulocytosis.
iv. Metabolic Profile is critical in delirium and severe withdrawal.
v. Liver Function Tests – Alcohol/ Inhalant cause liver dysfunction. IV drug abuse is often associated with Hepatitis C/ HIV. Mood stabilizers like Valproate / CBZ can also cause liver dysfunction.
vi. Serum Amylase and Lipase: Alcohol related pancreatitis
vii. Serum Ammonia Levels: Cognitive impairment, r/o alcohol related hepatic encephalopathy.
viii. Thyroid function tests: Thyroid abnormalities associated with anxiety and depression; Lithium can depress thyroid functions.
ix. Lipid Profile: Long term antipsychotic treatment, Obesity.
x. STD screen, Hepatitis B/C screen and HIV screen in high-risk patients.
xi. EKG – Stimulant use could be associated with significant cardio-vascular toxicity, arrhythmias, myocardial infarctions and cardiac failure. Alcohol can cause cardiomyopathy.
xii. Radiological investigations including X-ray Chest and CT Scan or MRI of the brain are suggested in appropriate situations.

3. Medication Issues

Sleep disturbances, anxiety and craving are often seen in substance withdrawal. Insomnia is a strong predictor of relapse [20]. They should be sensitively addressed with education, sleep hygiene, lifestyle modifications, relaxation therapy and non-addictive medications like Trazodone, Diphenhydramine or Hydroxyzine. Management of anxiety, insomnia or mood changes should be dictated by the severity and functional impairment caused by the symptoms. Medication Seeking Behavior is often seen in patients with severe craving, personality disorders like ASPD and malingering. BZs should be recommended solely for physiological withdrawals, severe agitation or severe anxiety. When in doubt, it is prudent to manage alcohol/ BZ / Opioid withdrawal by relying on objective signs like vital signs and pupillary dilatation.

4. Smoking Privileges

Nicotine dependence is the most common co-occurring substance use disorder ranging from 60-95% of all inpatients [21]. Patients with nicotine dependence are more likely to have comorbid psychiatric and conversely, patients with psychiatric disorders are twice as likely to smoke as the general population [22, 23]. It is well known that this gateway drug substantially lowers blood levels of several first-generation antipsychotics. Despite all that, smoking is perceived as very relaxing by most patients. Smoking privileges are often powerful motivators in positive patient behavior. Smoking privileges are lately becoming an issue as more and more hospitals go smoke-free. The pros and cons need to be evaluated in instituting smoking privileges. Nicotine Replacement therapy and Smoking Cessation treatments should always be offered in dual diagnosis units to maximize treatment benefits.

5. Suicide, Agitation and Aggressive Behaviors

There is a substantially greater risk of suicide among patients with comorbid psychiatric and substance use disorders. There is an elevated risk of suicide in patients with substance use disorders when associated with Major Depression [24], Bipolar Disorder [25] and Cluster B Personality Disorder [18]. It is commonly associated with impulsivity and heavy drinking [26,27]. Other predictors include early onset of substance disorder, more severe substance disorder, polysubstance dependence, panic symptoms, being separated or divorced and diagnosis of substance induced psychiatric disorder [28]. Suicide risk should be routinely assessed in every patient admitted to a dual diagnosis unit. A useful measure is the Columbia Suicide Risk Severity Scale [29].

Patients with comorbid disorders often demonstrate poor impulse control, agitation, impaired reality testing and aggressive acting out behaviors. Stimulant and PCP intoxication, alcohol / BZ / Sedative / Hypnotic intoxication/withdrawal, hallucinogens, inhalants and anabolic steroids are commonly associated with aggression [30].

Patients will need 1:1 observation and close monitoring especially during the initial part of the treatment. For safety purposes, it would be prudent to maintain every admission on a 15-minute check in the unit for at least the first 24 hours. Aggression and Suicidal Behaviors must be addressed with preventive measures, behavioral management, cognitive therapy, supportive, group and milieu therapy.

6. Court Commitments and Legal Issues

While internal motivation and voluntary admission are desirable, often times, inpatient admissions to a dual diagnosis unit are under involuntary commitment and legally enforced. Common involuntary admission diagnoses include severe psychosis, agitation, threat or assault and impaired reality testing leading to poor self- care from and/or medical decompensation. Elopement precautions and safety precautions are required in such patients to prevent danger to self or others. The goal in such situations would be to develop a therapeutic alliance, stabilize the patient adequately enough to change to a voluntary treatment status consistent with allowing the least restrictive level of care. Legal problems often abound among dual diagnosis clients and can serve as a powerful motivational tool to improve treatment adherence. It is important to coordinate their treatment with appropriate legal counsel (e.g. probation officers) to facilitate recovery. Patient confidentiality and respect for autonomy should be adhered to at all times.

7. Non-pharmacological Treatments

Individual psychotherapy can play a useful role in psychotic patients and patients with mood disorders who cannot tolerate or participate in groups. Most patients respond well to supportive therapy that should focus on providing encouragement/support, education, improving medication/treatment compliance and social skills training. Motivational Enhancement Therapy and Motivational interviewing are effective brief therapies lasting 1-4 sessions aimed at maximizing intrinsic desire for change and enhancing adherence to intensive and extended treatments [31]

Group therapy is the mainstay in inpatient dual diagnosis treatment. Treatment groups are often unstructured because of psychiatric diversity in the population. They are open ended because of rolling admissions. The emphasis is often on educating patients about their illness, confronting their substance use patterns, providing support and enhancing motivation for further recovery in Rehabilitation programs and psychiatric aftercare programs.

Family Interventions: Families play a significant role in the life of dually diagnosed patients. At a biological level, several psychiatric disorder and addictions (especially alcohol dependence) run in families. Family dysfunctions noted in the families of addicts include parental loss, absent or distant parent, over-protection or over control by the other parent, symbiotic relationships, pseudo-independence and co-dependence. Families could appear to deal with addictive members through denial and sometimes frank enabling. Despite the negative roles played by the family, it is believed that families often provide crucial support and reinforcement of drug abstaining behaviors. It includes providing collateral sources of information; providing essential support to recovering patient, monitoring the patient's progress and helping to boost treatment compliance. Often times, alcoholics minimize their alcohol use and obtaining collateral information from the family becomes very critical.

9. Post-Discharge Treatment Options

Five stages of patient motivation for substance recovery are proposed. They include Pre-Contemplation, Contemplation, Preparation, Action and Maintanence. Available resources for treatment can be broadly divided into 4 major programs: Drug-free outpatient; Methadone Maintanence; Short term Residential (Chemical Dependency) and Long-term Residential (Therapeutic Community). The DATOS (Drug Abuse Treatment Outcome Study) showed significant 1-year remission outcomes among those who participated in short term inpatient programs and those who stayed at least 3 months in the outpatient drug-free programs [32].

Once stable, patients discharged from hospitals need to be matched with aftercare services. American Society of Addiction Medicine (ASAM) placement criteria [33], or those derived from it (e.g. Pennsylvania Criteria for Placement of Adult Clients or PCPC) can be used to match patients with an appropriate level of care. The commonly available options are:

1) Partial Hospitalization Programs: Usually involve more than 20 hours/week of treatment and therapy. They often serve as a "Step Down" for patients discharged from inpatient treatment. They usually provide a combination of individual and group therapy, family meetings, medical and psychiatric supervision. Services usually also include Vocational Rehabilitation, Educational Counseling, Skills Training, Assertiveness Training, Relapse Prevention and Random Urine Testing.
2) Intensive Outpatient Programs: While offering similar services as a partial hospitalization program, it is not as intense as partial hospitalization programs (~9hours/week). Additionally, the schedule can be modified to accommodate regular working patients.
3) Residential Treatment Programs: It is recommended for patients who need a greater level of structure to stay stabilize their psychiatric symptoms and maintain sobriety. Residential programs provide pharmacological and psychological treatments, psycho-education, relapse prevention, self-help groups, social skills training, and vocational / occupational rehabilitation. For patients with pervasive behavioral problems, Long-Term Structured Rehabilitation and Nursing homes are recommended though the waiting period for such programs can sometimes be prohibitive.
4) Therapeutic Communities: Patients with chronic substance use and psychiatric disorders can benefit from long-term residential therapeutic communities. These are organized along strict hierarchies. Supportive confrontation of maladaptive behaviors and denial, either individually or in groups constitutes a fundamental method of treatment. They provide individual, social and vocational rehabilitation through social learning methods.
5) Community Residential Facilities: Patients getting out of a dual diagnosis unit can be supported in Transitional / Halfway / Recovery Houses. These drug free housing units offer more structure and supervision to patients who are at a risk of relapse on their own. Also belonging to this category are Cooperative apartments, Personal care Boarding Homes, Foster Care homes and Shelters. Certain facilities remain opposed to any kind of medication treatment. Medication philosophies should be considered before dual diagnosis patients are referred to such facilities.
6) Outpatient therapy and rehabilitation: Patients in these programs are typically higher functioning and offer medication management, CBT (Relapse prevention/ social skills training), MET (Motivational Enhancement Therapy), Behavioral Therapies, Psychotherapy and Self Help Groups. They can be combined with 12 Step Facilitation (TSF) programs and AA/NA that offer additional support for patients through groups and mentorship [34].
7) Methadone Maintanence programs have been proven to significantly reduce Opioid use, minimize drug seeking and criminal behaviors, promote recovery and social rehabilitation [35]. They are appropriate for patients with a prolonged history of Opioid dependence (>1 year). They have also helped reduce other substance dependence like cocaine when combined with reward programs. Buprenorphine

Maintanence programs allow treatment of Opioid dependence in an office setting. Buprenorphine is prescribed in the range of 16-32 mg daily.

8) Case Management: They serve to coordinate treatments and social services available to the patient with a goal of minimizing relapse and improving overall outcomes. It typically involves a case manager and / or mobile teams that go out into the community and help patients with medications, encourage compliance, transportation, housing, income and advocacy services.

CONCLUSION

Patients with Comorbid Psychiatric and Substance Use disorders constitute a discreet population who require specialized management. Comorbid disorders are complex in their etiology and presentation. Different levels of care are available for this population. Dual diagnosis units constitute probably the most crucial of the treatment settings given the acuity and severity of symptoms encountered in its clients. Sound evidence based treatment and integrated care offered in a dual diagnosis unit sets the stage for further drug/psychiatric treatment and psychosocial rehabilitation.

REFERENCES

[1] Practice Guideline for the Treatment of Patients With Substance Use disorders, *Second Edition: Supplement to the American Journal of Psychiatry,* 164 (4) (2007).

[2] Kessler RC, Nelson CB, McGonagle KA, Liu J, Swartz M, Blazer DG: Comorbidity of DSM-III-R major depressive disorder in the general population: results from the US National Comorbidity Survey. *Br J Psychiatry* (1996); 30 (Jun Suppl): 17-30.

[3] Regier DA, Farmer ME, Rae DS, Locke BZ, Keith SJ, Judd LL, Goodwin FK: Comorbidity of mental disorders with alcohol and other drug use: Results from the Epidemiologic Catchment Area (ECA) study. JAMA (1990); 264: 2511-2518.

[4] Schuckit M in Alcohol Related Disorders: *Kaplan and Sadock's Comprehensive Textbook of Psychiatry* (7th edition). Lippincott, Williams & Wilkins, Philadelphia, PA 2000.

[5] Tidey JW, Rosenhow DJ, Kaplan GB, Swift RM: Cigarette smoking topography in smokers with schizophrenia and matched non-psychiatric controls. *Drug Alcohol Depend* (2005); 80: 259-265.

[6] Kessler RC, Berglund P, Demler O, Jin R, Koretz D, Merikangas KR, Rush AJ, Walters EE, Wang PS: The epidemiology of major depressive disorder: results from the National Comorbidity Survey Replication (NCS-R). *JAMA* 2003; 289: 3095-3105.

[7] Brook DW, Brook JS, Zhang C, Cohen P, Whiteman M: Drug use and the risk of major depressive disorder, alcohol dependence and substance use disorders. *Arch Gen Psychiatry* (2002); 59: 1039-1044.

[8] Nace EP: Substance abuse and personality disorder. *J Chem Depend Treat* (1990); 3: 183-198.

[9] Salloum IM, Thase ME: Impact of substance abuse on the course and treatment of bipolar disorder. *Bipolar Disord* (2000); 2: 269-280.

[10] Lieberman JA, Stroup TS, McEvoy JP, Swartz MS, Rosenheck RA, Perkins DO, Keefe RS, Davis SM, Davis CE, Lebowitz BD, Severe J, Hsiao JK: Effectiveness of antipsychotic drugs in patients with chronic schizophrenia. *N Engl J Med* (2005); 353: 1209-1223.

[11] Gopalakrishnan R, Ross J, O'Brien C and Oslin D: Course of Late-Life Depression with Alcoholism following Combination Therapy. *J of Studies on Alcohol and Drugs* (2009); 70 (2): 237-241.

[12] DSM IV: Diagnostic and Statistical Manual of Mental Disorders. Ed. 4. *American Psychiatric Association,* Washington DC, 1994.

[13] Coffey SF, Dansky BS, Carrigan MH, Brady KT: Acute and protracted cocaine abstinence in an outpatient population: a prospective study of mood, sleep and withdrawal symptoms. *Alcohol Depend* (2000); 59: 277-286.

[14] Suppes T, Dennehy EB, Hirschfeld RM, Altshuler LL, Bowden CL, Calabrese JR, Crismon ML, Ketter TA, Sachs GS, Swann AC: The Texas implementation of medication algorithms: update to the algorithms for treatment of bipolar I disorder. Texas Consensus Conference Panel on Medication Treatment of Bipolar Disorder. *Clin Psychiatry.*(2005); 66(7): 870-86.

[15] Jaffe HJ: Introduction and Overview of Substance Related Disorders: *Kaplan and Sadock's Comprehensive Textbook of Psychiatry* (7th edition). Lippincott, Williams & Wilkins, Philadelphia, PA, 2000.

[16] Practice Guidelines for Treatment of Patients with Panic Disorder, Second Edition, *American Journal of Psychiatry* (2009); 166: Issue 1: Supplemental Data.

[17] Center for Substance Abuse Treatment: Substance Abuse Treatment for Persons with Co-occurring Disorders: *Treatment Improvement Protocol* (TIP) Series No.42. DHHS Publication (SMA) 05-3922. Rockville, Md, Substance Abuse and Mental Health Services Administration, 2005.

[18] Darke S, Williamson A, Ross J, Teesson M, Lynskey M: Borderline personality disorder, antisocial personality disorder and risk-taking among heroin users: findings from the Australian Treatment Outcome Study (ATOS): *Drug Alcohol Depend 2004;* 74: 77-83.

[19] Vaillant GE: A 60-year follow up of alcoholic men. *Addiction* (2003); 98 1043-1051.

[20] Brower KJ, Aldrich MS, Robinson EA, Zucker RA, Greden JF: Insomnia, self-medication, and relapse to alcoholism. *Am J Psychiatry* (2001); 158: 399-404.

[21] Ziedonis DM, Williams JM: Addressing tobacco in mental health and addiction settings. *Psychiatr Ann* (2003); 22: 425-426.

[22] Lasser K, Boyd JW, Woolhandler S, Himmelstein Du, McCormick D, Bor DH: Smoking and Mental Illness: a population based prevalence study. *JAMA* (2000); 284: 2606-2610.

[23] Patkar AA, Gopalakrishnan R, Lundy A, Leone FT, Certa KM, Weinstein SP: Relationship between tobacco smoking and positive and negative symptoms in schizophrenia. *J Nerv Ment Dis.* 2002; 190(9): 604-10.

[24] Arsenault-Lapierre G, Km C, Turecki G: Psychiatric Diagnosis in 3275 suicides: a meta-analysis: *BMC Psychiatry* (2004); 4: 37.

[25] Garno JL, Goldberg JF, Ramirez PM, Ritzler BA: Bipolar Disorder with comorbid cluster B personality disorder features: impact of suicidality. *J Clin Psychiatry* (2005); 66: 339-345.

[26] Cornelius JR, Salloum M, Day NL, Thase ME, Mann JJ: Patterns of suicidality and alcohol use in alcoholics with major depression. *Alcohol Clin Exp Res* (1996); 20: 1451-1455.

[27] Sullivan LE, Fiellin DA, O'Connor PG: The prevalence and impact of alcohol problems in Major Depression: a systematic review. *Am J Med* (2005); 118: 330-341.

[28] Preuss UW, Schuckit MA, Smith TL, Danko GP, Bucholz KK, Hesselbrock MN, Hesselbrock V, Kramer JR: Predictors and correlates of suicide attempts over 5 years in 1237 alcohol-dependent men and women. *Am J Psychiatry* 2003; 160: 56-63.

[29] Posner K, Oquendo MA, Gould M, Stanley B, Davies M: Columbia Classification Algorithm of Suicide Assessment (C-CASA): Classification of Suicidal Events in the FDA's Pediatric Suicidal Risk Analysis of Antidepressants.: *Am J Psychiatry* (2007); 164: 1035-1043.

[30] Hoaken PN, Stewart SH: Drugs of abuse and the elicitation of aggressive behavior. *Addic Behav* (2003); 28: 1533-1554.

[31] Dunn C, Deroo L, Rivara FP: The use of brief interventions adapted from motivational interviewing across behavioral domains: a systematic review. *Addiction* (2001); 96: 1725-1742.

[32] Simpson DD, Joe GW, Brown BS: Treatment Retention and follow up outcomes in the Drug Abuse Treatment Outcome Study (DATOS). *Psychol Addict Behav* (1997); 11: 294.

[33] ASAM Patient Placement Criteria: *Principles of Addiction Medicine* (3rd edition). Eds. Graham AW, Schulz TK, Mayo-Smith MF, Ries RK and Wilford BB. American Society of Addiction Medicine Inc; Chevy Chase, Md , 2003.

[34] Humphreys K, Wing S, McCarty D, Chappel J, Gallant L, Haberle B, Horvath AT, Kaskutas LA, Kirk T, Kivlahan D, Laudet A, McCrady BS, McLellan AT, Morgenstern J, Townsend M, Weiss R: Self-help organizations for alcohol and drug problems: towards evidence-based practice and policy. *J Subst Abuse Treat* (2004); 26: 151-158.

[35] Ball JC, Ross A: *The Effectiveness of Methadone Maintenance Treatment: Patients, Programs, Services and Outcome.* New York, Springer Verlag, 1991.

Part IV. Substance Use Disorders and Self-Injurious Behaviour

In: Suicidal Behavior in Alcohol and Drug Abuse... ISBN: 978-1-60876-919-3
Editors: L. Sher, A. Vilens, pp. 217-236

Chapter 12

SELF-INJURIOUS BEHAVIOR IN INDIVIDUALS WITH ALCOHOL AND DRUG ABUSE AND DEPENDENCE

Cuneyt Evren
Bakirkoy State Hospital for Psychiatric and Neurological Diseases, Istanbul, Turkey

ABSTRACT

Self-injurious behavior (SIB) is frequently seen in the clinical practice and negatively effect the course of the treatment and the attitude of the caregivers. Nevertheless a basic understanding of SIB, including its classification, diagnosis, and treatment, is still lacking. Although SIB is an explicit part of the DSM-IV diagnostic criteria for borderline personality disorder and impulse control disorder not otherwise specified, SIB is also quite frequently seen in other personality disorders (i.e. antisocial or borderline personality disorder) and Axis I disorders (i.e. eating disorders, dissociative disorders, substance use disorders and occasionally in depressive disorders and posttraumatic stress disorder). Since substance use disorders also have high comorbidity with mentioned disorders, in which SIB is common, it is obvious that SIB is an important issue to focus attention in individuals with alcohol and /or drug abuse. Although this relationship between substance use and SIB is generally accepted, there are few studies conducted within alcohol and /or drug abusing populations, and most of them included only males. These studies found that SIB is related with younger age, childhood physical abuse, suicide attempt history, having a personality disorder and drug dependency in heterogeneous group of substance dependents, whereas it was related with younger age, childhood abuse, early onset of alcoholism, suicide attempt history, dissociative taxon membership, hostility, negative affect (i.e. anxiety and depression) in homogeneous groups of alcohol dependents. Predominate function of SIB in opiate dependents were both affect-regulation and than secondly self-punishment, although other functions (i.e. anti-suicide, anti-dissociative and anti-hostility) for SIB may also have their place in alcohol and /or drug dependents. Findings suggest that a history of SIB may alert clinicians to patients with difficult and complex psychopathology who may have more severe and chronic illness. By identifying factors that have led to the SIB in alcohol and/or alcohol use disorders, these adults can obtain appropriate psychotherapy and/or pharmacotherapy and deal in a more productive and beneficial manner with the pain that underlies their self-injurious impulses.

Definition, Types and Classification of Self-Injurious Behavior

Self-injurious behavior (SIB) is an act that is performed by oneself towards oneself, which is physically violent, intentional and purposeful, but not suicidal [1-4]. It can be defined as intentional, direct damage to one's body tissue without intent to die [5,6]. In fact, defining self-injury (SI) is not a simple task, because it has not been widely defined as a syndrome and acts of SI vary greatly and depend on the imagination of the person with SIB.

Although SIB is the most commonly used term, researchers and counseling professionals have not agreed on one term for acts of self-inflicted injury. Indeed SI may hold the record for the most names for a single phenomenon: Ross and McKay listed more than 30 names for SI, including their own label of "self-mutilation" [7]. Other names for this behavior include deliberate self-harm [8], superficial-moderate self-mutilation [9], self-injurious behavior [5], self-destructive behavior [10], self-cutting [11], self-wounding [12], and parasuicide [13]. Nevertheless clinicians agree that the SIB involves the intentional infliction of physical damage upon one's own body, and that this physical damage is not sanctioned by one's identified culture. Most body modification (such as piercing, tattoos, and ritual scarification) is considered culturally sanctioned and therefore not SIB [2]. Cultural influences are proposed to explain some of the ethnic variations in rates, nature and presentation of SIB within any one country and across countries [14].

SIB typically starts in adolescence, between ages 14 and 24, involves numerous episodes and a variety of methods, and continues over many years, with repetitive episodes [15,16]. Research suggests that the most common form of SI is skin-cutting, scratching, occurring in between 70 and 97% of individuals with SIB, followed by banging or hitting (21%–44%) and burning (15%–35%) [17]. Nevertheless, most of these individuals use more than one method [15,16]. Since the term SI includes a wide range of behaviors and people engaging in SI are a heterogeneous group, caution is needed when generalizing about SI.

In attempt for classification of SI, Favazza [2] explained this phenomenon in three different classes as; 1- major SI (infrequent acts such as eye enucleation and castration), 2- stereotypic SI (such acts as head banging and self-biting) and 3- superficial/moderate SI (compulsive acts such as trichotillomania and skin picking and such episodic acts as skin-cutting and burning). There are several case reports regarding self-enucleation related with drug-induced (cannabis, amphetamines, solvent abuse and PCP) psychosis [18]. But the subject of the present chapter is superficial/moderate SIB.

Mental health professionals have long been concerned with SI because of the behavior's robust association with psychopathology and suicide [19]. As a symptom, SI has typically been regarded as a manifestation of borderline behavior and misidentified as a suicide attempt [2]. Indeed, the disorder most frequently associated with SIB is borderline personality disorder (BPD), which is the only DSM-IV disorder for which SI is a diagnostic criterion [20]. Although research findings are consistent with the idea that SIB is an important symptom of BPD, studies have also indicated that SIB occurs across a variety of diagnoses, as well as in nonclinical subjects. In DSM-IV, SIB is most often associated with mood, anxiety, eating, dissociative and personality disorders.

SIB also is an explicit part of the DSM-IV diagnostic criteria for impulse control disorder not otherwise specified [20]. According to Pattison and Kahan SIB meets the 3 essential features of DSM, Third Edition category of "disorders of impulse control not elsewhere classified": (a) failure to resist an impulse; (b) increasing tension before committing the act; and (c) experience of pleasure, gratification, or release at the time of committing the act [21]. Some authors even suggested that the field of clinical psychology may benefit from adopting a deliberate SI syndrome as a distinct disorder in light of the behavior's clinical significance and presence across multiple disorders [22]. The most important objection against the proposal of a distinct syndrome is the lack of convincing research data. At present, a basic understanding of SI, including its classification, diagnosis, and treatment, is still lacking.

Finally, some authors [23] consider SIB—together with other disorders such as obsessive-compulsive disorder, substance abuse disorder, eating disorder, kleptomania, pyromania and others—as a symptom of an underlying spectrum of disorders with varying degrees of obsessive compulsive and impulsive traits.

Comorbidity and Prevalence

SI is encountered frequently in psychiatric hospitals [16] and also in outpatient settings [11]. Rate of SIB was approximately 21.4% in adult clinical populations [8]. Also comorbid psychiatric disorders are commonly found among those with SIB. Those with SIB had more symptoms of several personality disorders than those without SIB, and their performance across measures suggested that anxiety plays a prominent role in their psychopathology [8]. There appears to be high rates of major depression, anxiety, post traumatic stress disorder (PTSD) [24], schizophrenia [25,26] impulse control disorders [3], dissociative disorders [1], eating disorders [25,27], last but not the least substance abuse [4,28-30]. SI may also be present among patients with different personality disorders [30], especially anti-social personality disorder [3] and BPD [4,10,31]. Indeed as a symptom, SIB has typically been regarded as a manifestation of borderline behavior [2]. It was suggested that multiple causal factors, including biological, psychological, and social risks, influence thresholds for SIB in patients with BPD [31]. Nevertheless, deliberate SI occurs in nonclinical populations as well. Lifetime rates appear to be particularly high in adolescents and young adults, where approximately 14–35% report a history of SIB [32,33]. Finally, the prevalence of SIB was found as 4% in general population [1].

There are also studies conducted among patients with alcohol and/or drug use disorder. The survey of 50 women attending an alcoholic-treatment unit explored the prevalence of 26% for SIB [28]. The rates of SI in studies ranged between 33.0% and 34.6% among treatment-seeking patients who were substance dependents [34,35], ranged between 13.0% and 34.0% among male inpatients who were only dependent to alcohol [28,30,34-37] and was found to be 49% in homogeneous group of opioid dependents [38]. In two studies which compared heterogeneous group of drug dependents with homogeneous group of alcohol dependents found that SIB was more prevalent in drug dependents. In the first study risk of SIB was 3.5 times higher in drug-dependent (n=40, 55%) than alcohol-dependent (n=96,

26%) patients [34]. In the second study this risk was 8.1 times higher in drug dependents (n=56, 53.6%) than alcohol dependents (n=56, 12.5%). In this later study drug dependency even predicted SIB [35]. When considering the rate of 4% for SI in the general population [1] these rates for SI are higher in alcohol and/or drug dependents than other clinical and general populations. Thus, it is an important issue in these populations since SIB have been linked to negative outcomes, including increased risk for successful suicide [39,40] and significant problems in therapeutic and interpersonal relationships [2].

Functions of Self-Injurious Behavior

To date, studies have provided evidence for several functions of SIB, including that SI is a means of regulating negative affect, self-punishment, influence others, terminate the discomfort of dissociative episodes, resisting urges to attempt suicide, and sensation-seeking [1,2,5,9,41-45]. Findings from past research suggest that the theory of tension relief and reducing anxiety might be at least a partial explanation for SI [1,8,46]. Following the act, the individual usually reports feeling himself better and relieved [1,5] and there is physiological evidence that those with SIB experience a reduction in tension after an episode of SI [47]. A review of the literature suggests that evidence from 18 studies provide converging evidence for an affect-regulation function (coping with feelings), strong support for a self-punishment function, and modest evidence for the other functions such as anti-dissociation (to feel real again) [17,48]. SIB can often relieve any or a combination of these problems simultaneously [49].

Results of previous studies indicate that SI is associated with improvements in affective valence and decreases in affective arousal. Specifically, participants tended to feel overwhelmed, sad, and frustrated before SI, and relieved and calm after SI. Further, these affective changes predict lifetime frequency of SI, suggesting that they reinforce the behavior [45]. Specifically, three types of evidence support an affect-regulation function: (a) most participants who self-injure report that they do so to reduce negative affect; (b) self-report and laboratory studies suggest that negative affect precedes SI and that affect improves following SI; and (c) proxies for SI performed in laboratory settings cause reductions in negative affect [45].

Alexithymia, which is defined as the inability to identify and use language to describe feelings, reflects a deficit in regulation of emotions, and alexithymic individuals are prone to outbursts of weeping, anger or rage [50]. Among male alcoholics, alexithymia was common and severity of alexithymia was related with emotional disturbance and interpersonal difficulties related with this emotional disturbance [51]. Alexithymia was found to be associated with a primitive defense style [52] and with anxiety, depression, anger and somatization [50,52]. Similar with alexithymic patients, the individual with SIB might be emotionally and cognitively restricted, unable to differentiate his feelings, verbalize them and solve the problem. Perhaps the persons with SIB has difficulty verbalizing or articulating their feelings [53,55]. Briere and Gil state that SI may serve to distract the individual away from internally experienced emotional distress [1]. It was found that individuals with SIB displayed a greater degree of alexithymia than those without and alexithymia was associated with SIB [56]. Consistent with these alexithymia (difficulty in identifying feelings and difficulty in describing feelings components of alexithymia) was higher in self-injurious group in alcohol dependents [34]. In a recent study conducted among opiate dependents, patients with SIB had higher scores on "difficulty in identifying feelings" subscale of alexithymia, also higher scores on this subscale predicted SIB in this study [38]. Results of these two studies conducted among alcohol and opiate dependents are consistent with the affect-regulation function of SIB and Wheeler and Braod's [57] suggestion that SIB fulfils the function of expressing tensions and managing intense negative feelings in the absence of self-soothing and interpersonal capacities characterized by alexithymia.

An affect-regulation model of self-injury requires evidence that the affective improvements subsequent to self-injury encourage or reinforce the behavior [45]. Also, it is unclear how to reconcile evidence for multiple functions. Although different functions may co-occur or overlap conceptually, some functions may be more common or fundamental than others [44]. Several studies have reported that a majority of participants endorsed both affect-regulation and self-punishment reasons [1,42,45]. However, in one of these studies conducted in young adults, although reasons for SI was related to both affect-regulation (e.g., to release emotional pressure that builds up inside of me) and self-punishment (e.g., to express anger at myself) were endorsed by a majority of participants, affect-regulation reasons were overwhelmingly rated as primary and self-punishment reasons as secondary [45]. Thus, SIB may have more than one function, even potential effect of these functions on the SIB may differ for the same individual. Also different functions in different clinical samples and among individuals without psychopathology can be expected. In the study of Oyefeso et al. [38], both including males and females, it was suggested that predominate function of SIB in homogeneous group of opiate dependents were both affect-regulation (84%) and than secondly self-punishment (68%). Similarly, the majority (92%) reported two or more reasons for SIB and the majority of SIB patients (61%) endorsed both the affect-regulation and self-punishment functions of SIB.

Dissociation

There is increasing understanding and acceptance that SIB is a response to profound emotional pain. It is a way of dealing with distress and of getting relief from feelings of self-hatred, anger, sadness, depression and so on. By engaging in SIB people may alter their state of mind so that they feel better able to cope with the other pain they are feeling [58]. Dissociation is considered to serve as a defense mechanism against intolerable, trauma-associated memories and feelings, and results from a disintegration of consciousness, memory, identity and perception [59]. According to Paris [31], one of the functions of SI is to help to cope with dissociative states in BPD, which has high comorbidity with dissociative disorder [60]; also among alcohol and/or drug dependent inpatients [61]. Several studies have indicated a close link between SI and dissociation [62,63]. Favazza [2] suggested that SI could best be understood as a morbid self-help effort providing rapid but temporary relief from feelings of depersonalization which is a symptom of dissociative disorder.

Studies provide modest evidence for anti-dissociative function of SIB [17]. It has been hypothesized that SI terminates the discomfort of dissociative experiences, in particular, deadness and depersonalization [4]. Indeed, many patients report feeling numb and 'dead' prior to injure themselves [64]. They often claim not to experience pain during SI and report a sense of relief and feeling himself better afterwards [2,64,65], which was supported by physiological evidence [66]. Levenkron [55] even classified SI into non-dissociative and dissociative types, considering dissociative type to represent a more severe form than non-dissociative type. Consistent with these findings, in recently detoxified alcohol dependents, dissociative taxon membership predicted SI and among DES-Taxon items "auditory verbal hallucinations" was predictor of SI in this population. Authors suggested that there is a complex relationship between dissociation, alcohol use, and SIB [36].

SELF-INJURIOUS BEHAVIOR AND SUBSTANCE USE DISORDERS

Most of the time, individuals with SIB repeat this behavior on regular basis. One of the most striking aspects of repeated SI is the apparently addictive quality of the behavior, and this goes together with the frequent coexistence of SI with other impulsive behaviors such as drug addiction or alcohol abuse [67]. Multiple lines of evidence suggest that endogenous opioids are involved in the pathogenesis of SI [68]. An alternative hypothesis emphasizes that pain associated with SIB results in release of brain endorphins and draws a parallel between such endogenous release of endorphins and addiction to an exogenous substance [69].

A release of endorphins after the physical damage that contributes to the feeling of relief supports an addictive maladaptive coping cycle of pain [3,70]. The addiction hypothesis suggests that there exists an essentially normal endogenous opioid system that has been chronically over-stimulated by frequent SIB for the purpose of relieving dysphoria. The individual develops a tolerance to the outpouring of endogenous opioids, cyclically suffers a withdrawal reaction, and is driven to further endogenous opioid system stimulation by means of impulsive SIB [71].

SIB has numerous characteristics that also have been identified in the self-destructive behavior of addiction; these characteristics include similarities in origin, in emotions experienced, in family structure and in the repetitive nature of tension-release responses [72]. SI as addictive behavior has been mentioned in a case study of a girl with narcissistic BPD, who undertook multiple, repetitive self-injurious acts. Authors emphasized the evaluation of repetitive SIB by applying criteria for addictive and dependence disorders, in order to achieve additional adequate strategies for treating patients showing this behavior [73]. Another study which aimed to emphasize the addictive features of SIB in adolescents reported that more than 90%, "the behavior occurs more often and/or severity of SI has increased" and "SI continues despite recognizing it is harmful" and more than 80% "tension levels reoccur if SI is discontinued" and "SI urges are upsetting but not enough to stop" [74]

SI is often considered similar to other apparently SIBs such as substance abuse (i.e. intoxication and liver dysfunction in alcoholics, using of needles for injection of heroine), although these behaviors are all indirect forms of SIB. Ross and McKay [7] proposed that the ingestion of drugs and alcohol itself is an act of SI and that a drug–induced state may actually trigger SI because of impaired judgment, reduced pain perception, and fantasy stimulation. The association between alcohol misuse and SI may reflect the disinhibiting role of alcohol [75]. Among adolescents moderate/severe injurers were more likely than minor injurers to report to have used alcohol or drugs during SI (26.5% v. 3.4%) [76]. Also there is a trend towards greater use of alcohol and violent methods at the time of the SI attempt, especially in females, and of comorbid substance misuse in both sexes [77]. A large international study suggested that intoxication is significantly related to the association between alcohol consumption and SIB in adolescents [78]. In two different studies conducted among alcohol dependents, 86.8% and 88.2% of inpatients reported that they were intoxicated with alcohol during SIB [36,37]. Question is; in patients with alcohol and/or drug abuse, do motivations of SIB and comorbid psychopathology differ according to being intoxicated or not during the SIB.

Nock and Prinstein recently developed and evaluated a comprehensive theoretical model including 4 primary functions of SIB that differ along 2 dichotomous dimensions: contingencies for SIB that are automatic (within the self) vs social and reinforcement that is positive (followed by a favorable stimulus) vs negative (followed by the removal of an aversive stimulus) [32].

- Automatic negative reinforcement refers to the use of SIB to achieve a reduction in negative affective states (i.e., to reduce feelings of anger, sadness, etc).
- Automatic-positive reinforcement refers to the use of SIB to create a desirable (physiological) state (i.e., to feel something).
- Social-negative reinforcement refers to the use of SIB to escape from interpersonal demands (i.e., to avoid punishment, schoolwork).
- Social-positive reinforcement refers to the use of SIB to gain attention from others or gaining access to materials (i.e., to ask for attention).

Similarly, alcohol and drug abuse/dependence may be maintained by both of these automatic negative and positive reinforcements [79]. SIB provides rapid but temporary relief from range of negative affective experiences. As such, it may operate directly and/or indirectly: the conversion of invisible emotional pain into visible physical pain may serve as self-medication. Finding that those who experience the greatest affective benefits were the ones who had most often cut themselves, indicate that the affective changes associated with SI may provide reinforcement and increase the chances that the behavior will be repeated [45]. Any positive feeling, however, are soon replaced by guilt, embarrassment, self-hatred, and anger-fueling the next cycle. This reminds the substance dependent person waking in the morning and regretting that he/she had used substance again and using substance to relieve this negative feeling. Adolescents with SIB differed from other adolescents in terms of coping strategies they reported employing when faced with difficulties, showing less focus on problems and more avoidant behaviors [80]. One of the poor problem-solving skills and maladaptive coping may be abusing substance and this is supported by the self-medication hypothesis. Substances of abuse may help these individuals to relieve painful affects or to experience or control emotions when they are absent or confusing [81].

Mixed results have been found regarding the associations between SIB and substance abuse. Several studies have reported associations between substance abuse and SIB [4,28-30], but at least one study has not confirmed this relationship [82]. This association was found among inpatients at university psychiatric hospital [29], in a sample of women incest survivors [30] and in a sample of general psychiatric outpatients [4], whereas no association was found among inpatients with BPD [82]. Thus this shows that relationship of SIB and substance use disorders may differ according to the population that is studied.

Most common diagnosis in those with SIB is BPD, which is also a common comorbid personality disorder diagnosis in substance use disorders. Thus it is not surprising that other frequently reported co-occurring diagnoses with SIB are alcohol and substance abuse [83]. In adolescents heavy alcohol use and other substance misuse is associated with SIB [84,85] and they frequently co-occur with SIB [86]. Drug and alcohol abuse are reported to be common concomitants of SIB, and lack of social support appears temporally related [21]. Alcohol misuse is a risk factor for depressed mood, suicidal ideation and SIB. A vicious cycle can be set up between depression and increasing alcohol use if people use alcohol to cope with low mood. Alcohol may trigger SIB by increasing impulsivity, impairing judgement and increasing the pain threshold. The negative consequences of substance abuse accumulate in a vicious circle of diminishing social support and increased exposure to life events, subsequent affective disorder and increased SI risk.

In a study conducted among patients with SIB, those with alcohol dependency were older and more often male, living alone, unemployed, sick, disabled, or with a past history of SIB [87]. In recent studies conducted among alcohol/substance dependents gave some information about sociodemographic characteristics of those with SIB. The rates of being single [34,35,37] and being unemployed [34,37] were higher in these subgroups, whereas age at time of the evaluation [34-37], age at regular alcohol and/or substance use [34,36,37] and education level [35,37] were lower in these subgroups with SIB. In a general population survey Briere and Gil [1] found that one of the variables that showed a link to SI was younger age. Consistent with this, age even predicted SIB in substance dependents [34].

The most frequent types of SI were self-cutting (n = 25), hitting one's head or extremities to the wall or another hard surface (n = 19), and self-burning (n = 7) in alcohol dependents [36]. In the other study among alcohol dependents, most frequent types of SI were as follows; self-cutting (n=26, %16.7), cigarette and other burns (n=5, %3.2), hitting hard palaces with fist or head (n=18, %11.5) and more than one type (n=4, %2.5) [37]. Finally, the most frequently reported SIB types were cutting (74%), nail biting (51%), chewing inside mouth (44%), and self-beating (36%) in opiate dependents [38]. The mean (± SD) numbers of SI episodes were 4.7 ± 4.6 (range, 1 to 15) and 2.74±1.93 (range, 1 to 10), whereas mean (± SD) age at first SI was 25.2 ± 9.6 years (range, 11.0- 48.0 years) and 24.64±8.26 in alcohol dependent male inpatients [36,37].

There are few studies that evaluated SI among alcohol and substance dependent populations. In previous studies evaluating SI in heterogeneous group of male subjects with substance dependency, determinants of SI were younger age [34], childhood physical abuse [34,35], suicide attempt history [34,35] and having a personality disorder [35] and drug dependency [35]. In homogeneous groups of male alcohol dependents younger age [36], childhood abuse [36], early onset of alcoholism [36,37], suicide attempt history [37] and dissociative taxon membership [36], hostility [36,37] and negative affect (i.e. anxiety and depression) [37] predicted SI. It must be remembered that these studies included only male patients, although the absence of gender differences in the prevalence and pattern of SIB has been previously reported by Briere and Gil [1] in their general population and clinical population study and in homogeneous group of opiate dependents [38]. In this later study, sexual harassment and "difficulty identifying feelings" of alexithymia were the only independent significant predictors of SIB [38]. Main limitation of these studies was that they were in cross-sectional design, thus it is impossible to draw conclusions about the direction of causality between SIB and substance dependency. Secondly, samples that were studied were restricted to a treatment seeking populations, and therefore it is not possible to generalize the findings to non-treatment groups.

TRAUMA HISTORY

Zlotnick et al. [88] found that a majority of the substance abusing subjects (74%) reported at least one traumatic event in their life and that these subjects were at higher risks for SIB. It has been suggested that [54] the act of SI seems to be associated with difficult and distressing life experiences often beginning in childhood and that SI may have its roots in a history of childhood abuse [1,2,10,88,89]. Individuals with a history of childhood trauma may be repeatedly exposed to high levels of arousal, but are unable to cope properly with those situations or experiences. Thus, later in life SI may be an attempt to gain a sense of control over oneself during high arousal states [10]. SI may also allow individuals to inflict onto themselves trauma that they experienced from others [2], and thus gain more subjective control over experiences that were perceived as out of their control.

Gender may play an important role in this relationship. Findings from the study of Zweig-Frank et al. [89] showed that childhood sexual abuse and physical abuse were risk factors for SI in female patients, whereas in another study of Zweig-Frank et al. [90] childhood sexual abuse and physical abuse did not discriminate between male personality disordered subjects with SIB and those without. Adults who have been chronically traumatized in childhood might be using SIBs as ways of modulating interpersonal relationship [91]. Briere and Gil pointed out that although many experiences may predispose a person to SI, the etiological factor that has the most statistically powerful association is childhood sexual and physical abuse [1]. Meta-analysis of Klonsky and Moyer [92] did not support theories that childhood sexual abuse has a central or causal role in the development of SIB. Instead, it appears that the two are modestly related because they are correlated with the same psychiatric risk factors. Thus it is logical to suggest that not just one type of trauma, but all the types are important in relation with SIB. In substance dependent male inpatients, rates of physical abuse [34], sexual abuse [34,35], emotional abuse and neglect history [35] were higher in those with SIB, whereas physical abuse history predicted SIB [34] in this population. In alcohol dependent populations' mean of any trauma history was higher [37] and any childhood abuse predicted SIB [36]. Also sexual harassment predicted SIB in opiate dependents [38]. Therapists working with clients with SIB should be prepared to deal with past issues of childhood trauma as well as the effects of such experiences on current life [10]. Clearly, there is an urgent need for studies on how alcohol and /or substance dependent patients can be taught to cope with negative childhood experiences without engaging in SIB in adult life.

AXIS I DISORDERS, PERSONALITY DISORDERS AND SELF-INJURIOUS BEHAVIOR

Studies of self-injurers who present to hospitals that used standard diagnostic criteria have shown that more than 90% of these people had at least one psychiatric disorder, most commonly depression, followed by substance abuse and anxiety disorders [26,93]. Zlotnick et al. [4] found that axis I disorders of substance abuse, PTSD, and intermittent explosive disorder were significantly related to SIB, independent of personality disorders in a sample of general psychiatric outpatients. Klonsky et al. [8] reported that while both depression and anxiety scores were higher in military recruits with history of SI than in non-self-injurers, anxiety maintained a substantial unique relationship to SI over and above depression. Although many studies of psychiatric patients have found higher levels of depression in those with SI [1,30,65,94], two studies that included only female subjects did not find self-injurers to be more depressed than comparison subjects [29,63]. Similarly, a study in which 79% of the participants were women did not show an association between anxiety and SI [83]. In a study conducted among patients with SIB, those with alcohol dependency 92.5% had comorbid psychiatric disorder, this being depression in three-quarters of those cases [87]. Study conducted among male substance dependents did not show any significant difference between those with SIB and those without in terms of axis I diagnosis. But severity of depressive and anxiety symptoms were higher in group with SIB [35]. In another study severity of anxiety and depression symptoms even predicted SIB in alcohol dependents [37]. These findings suggest that alcohol and/or substance dependents with SI may be depressed and anxious, and that SIB may be a coping mechanism for depression and anxiety for these subjects, as Nixon et al. [95] reported in their sample of depressed self-injurers. Briere and Gil state that SI may serve to distract the individual from internally experienced emotional distress and may reduce anxiety and depression [1]. Thus, treatment of self-injurious patients with alcohol and /or substance disorders should include the treatment of any comorbid anxiety and depressive illness [87].

Among Axis I disorders posttraumatic stress disorder (PTSD) has a special place in alcohol and substance dependents with high rates of PTSD ranging between 36–52% in western countries [96] and between 26.8-31.0% in Turkey [97,98]. Compared to patients with alcohol use solely, those with both alcohol use and PTSD respond to treatment less favorably, relapse faster, take more alcohol during drinking days, and experience more heavy drinking days in post-treatment period [99]. PTSD patients are one of the highest risk groups for SI [24,100]. A study showed that, among other diagnosis, outpatients with substance abuse or PTSD may be at risk for SIB independent of BPD [4]. A recent study found that in a sample of male veterans with PTSD, half of them had SIB, whom were younger and reported higher severity of PTSD, depression, hostility, and impulsivity compared to those who did not engage in SIB [24]. Similarly, rate of PTSD was higher in those with SIB in the alcohol dependents, half of the patients with PTSD had SIB and hostility predicted SIB alone in alcohol dependent patients with PTSD comorbidity [37].

Findings from the literature suggest that SI is most often performed to cope with acute negative affect. Because high negative affect is a feature of numerous disorders, it follows that SI can be found in a variety of psychiatric disorders, including personality, mood, anxiety, eating, psychotic, and substance disorders [4,19,26,87]. At the same time, because affective lability and dysregulation are central features of BPD, it follows that SI disproportionately occurs in this disorder [45]. One consistent finding in literature is that BPD is related with SI. For example, SI is a DSM-IV diagnostic criterion for BPD [1,4], and researches have shown that up to 80% of patients with BPD report histories of SI [101]. Dulit et al. [82] found this rate as 18.6% for infrequent SI (fewer than 5 lifetime events) and 31.5% for frequent SI (5 or more lifetime events) among inpatients with BPD. In a recent study, it was suggested that SI does not usually imply suicidal intent for patients with BPD, but instead, serves other functions, including regulation of dysphoric affect, communication of distress, expression of emotions, and coping with dissociative states [31]. Klonsky et al.'s [8] results supported the DSM-IV classification of SI as a symptom of BPD but also indicated that SI may be present in individuals with other personality disorders. In the study conducted among substance dependent inpatients, the rate of personality disorder was 64.9% among those with SIB [35]. Also, risk of SI was 8.8 times higher among those with any personality disorder and 12.1 times higher among those with antisocial personality disorder. Having any personality disorder diagnosis even predicted SI in substance dependents [35]. An unexpected finding in this study was that, there were no significant differences in terms of other personality disorders, especially for BPD. One of the reasons for this could be that, the rates of other personality disorders including BPD were rather low in this study, which could be due to the study sample's consisting only of male subjects. Nevertheless, Leichsenring et al. [102] suggested that antisocial personality disorder is the equivalent of BPD in male sample of imprisoned violent offenders. Finally, a study evaluating the relationship of SIB with temperament and character dimensions in substance dependents showed that self-directedness was lower in those with SIB, which suggests the higher probability of personality disorders. Nevertheless, SIB was not explained by specific dimensions within Cloninger's model of personality in this population [34].

Possible link between SIB and anger and hostility have been implicated in previous studies [103,104]. In the study among adolescent students, prior to SI feelings of both hostility and anxiety were described, which indicated support for the hostility model of SI [105]. In a recent study conducted among male veterans with PTSD found that veterans reporting SIB also reported higher levels of PTSD, depression, hostility, and impulsivity compared to the body-focused repetitive behaviors, such as nail biting, hair pulling, and teeth grinding, all of which have been considered to be repetitive and automatic, and no-habit groups [24]. In a study conducted among patients with SIB, those with alcohol dependency had higher scores on measures of anger, aggression, and impulsivity [87]. Finally hostility was the predictor of SI in alcohol dependent inpatients in two different studies [36,37]. Hostility as a predictor of SI in these studies may be pointing to an inner tension for impulsive tendencies due to anger and a need to control these strong emotions.

Suicide Attempt History and Self-injurious Behavior

As a symptom, SI has typically been misidentified as a suicide attempt [2]. There is some disagreement between the lethality of SI, whether repetitive self-injurers are at higher risk of suicide [2] or at low risk for eventual suicide [1]. Despite the fact that up to 10% of this population commits suicide, the purpose of suicidal behavior in SI has been described as not "genuinely" suicidal or life-threatening [106] but primarily attention seeking and manipulative. With the term "parasuicide", which refers to any intentionally self –inflicted physical damage that does not result in death, the distinction between suicidal and non-suicidal SIB began to blur. Similarly "attempted suicide" is also used for nonlethal SIB [107]. However, many individual who engage in SIB also have a history of suicide attempts, and they report that their SIB and suicide attempts are qualitatively distinct [94], in that SIB helps them stay alive [108]. As the saying goes, suicide is a permanent solution to a temporary problem. SI may be conceptualized as just the opposite - a temporary solution to a permanent problem.

Although SI is often conflated with suicidal ideation, researchers suggest that these are different in intent and function. It has been hypothesized that the difference between attempted suicide and SI is that in a suicide attempt the person truly wants to die while in the case of SI the person merely wants to feel better [2]. SI is considered distinct from suicidal behavior in its intent of ideation, lethality and repetition but share common experimental qualities [94]. Suicide attempters with SIB have history of childhood abuse and personality disorders, which are factors that increase the risk of suicide and suicide attempts. SIB is linked with suicide, since 25-50% of those committing suicide have previously self-injured [109]. Approximately 55%-85% of self-injurers have made at least one suicide attempt [94]. This rate ranged between 53.2% and 67.6% [34,35] in previous studies conducted among substance dependents and between 39.6% and 41.2% among alcohol dependents [36,37]. The high co-occurrence of suicidal behavior and SIB suggests that they may share a common biology; i.e. endogenous opioids may be involved in the pathophysiology of both behaviors [68].

The anti-suicide model views SI function as a coping mechanism for resisting urges to attempt suicide, such that SI serves as a replacement for or compromise with the desire to commit suicide [17]. In previous studies SI was related to suicide attempt history [109] and suicide attempt history predicted SI in substance dependents [34,35], alcohol dependents [36,37] and among male inmates [110]. Consistent with this, male gender and substance use disorders are significant risk factors for later suicide in patients with SI [40]. Among outpatient women, PTSD or substance dependence contributed to SIB and suicidal behavior [83].

Treatment

Establishing a trusting relationship appears to be the most critical component of assessing and treating the client with SIB. One of the psychoanalytic literature on SI and substance abuse, which is limited to a case report, has proposed that the initial ego support, therapeutic boundary setting, the continuous analysis of the transference and the counter-transference and to explore the frequent and mutual interpersonal / intrapsychic acting out is essential [111]. Psychotherapy and psychotropic medications, though not specific to SI, remain the most compelling treatment options [112]. The two most frequently studied psychotherapeutic approaches to SI are cognitive – behavioral therapy [113] and dialectical behavior therapy (DBT) [114]. For most of the self-injurers, it appears that SI is usually performed to cope with acute negative affect and arousal. For these patients treatment should seek to reduce negative affect and foster the development of alternative strategies for affect-regulation. For example, DBT was designed in part to improve skills for regulating intense and labile emotions, and has been shown to reduce SI [114]. Linehan, in her DBT encourages the client to develop a strong dependent relationship on the therapist, which may include telephone contact out of hours, but only if SIB has not just occurred [114]. Supplementary interventions that specifically help patients manage negative affective arousal, such as relaxation training and progressive muscle relaxation, may also help patients avoid SI [45].

Winchel and Stanley reviewed data suggesting that serotonergically, opiatergically, and /or dopaminergically mediated processes may be implicated in SIB [115]. Although no form of treatment has yet been demonstrated to be general benefit, data suggest that treatment with dopamine antagonists, serotonin reuptake inhibitors, and opiate antagonists may be of value. In general, the individual's underlying disorder should inform the selection of psychiatric medication. The mainstay of treatment is the use of antidepressants, particularly fluoxetine [116] mood stabilizers and, when appropriate, small doses of antipsychotics [117]. The opiate antagonist naltrexone, which is an anticraving agent for alcohol and heroin, has been used for SIB with some success in adults [68], although the behavior often returns upon discontinuation of the medication [118]. Support for SI which occurs alongside alcohol and/or drug dependency should be provided via, or in close connection with, the specialist alcohol/substance services.

Conclusion

A basic understanding of SI, including its classification, diagnosis, and treatment, is still lacking [8]. To improve clinical practice, it is important to increase our knowledge of SI in alcohol and/or substance use disorders. There is a need for more detailed psychological as well as psychiatric investigation of a representative samples of SIB in order to ascertain more adequately what treatments may be most appropriate [75].

Patients who self-injure themselves and have alcohol and/or drug problems present a considerable challenge for clinical services [87]. Complications of SIB include social rejection and condemnation as a response both to the behavior or the resulting disfigurement [112]. SI is a common clinical problem, but it is poorly understood and arouses ambivalent feelings in health professionals. In psychiatric settings, patients who engage in SIB tend to be both terrifying and infuriating for mental health professionals. The unsettling nature of SI tends to raise anxieties for clinical staff which, if poorly contained, can result in strong reactions and adversely influence treatment outcome [119]. It is common for therapists to become frustrated or upset by a patient's SI, and many therapists have to manage their own reactions even as they attempt to manage the SIB of their patients [8]. With good general management and the minimum of stigmatization it is possible to help even the most entrenched and self injurious patients towards rehabilitation, and it is to be hoped that in future a more humane and less punitive attitude will emerge towards this disadvantaged group of patients.

Gaining a better sense of the meaning of these behaviors and the functions they serve for the patients could be beneficial to the clinician in helping to decrease them. Results of previous studies conducted among alcohol and/or drug dependent populations may support several SI models; affect regulation, self-punishment, anti-suicide, anti-dissociative and hostility model. This suggests that there is no single explanation for SI in alcohol and/or drug dependents and all these models might be at least a partial explanation for this act in these populations. Nevertheless, at the minimum, findings suggest to the clinician that a history of SI may alert clinicians to patients with difficult and complex psychopathology who may have more severe and chronic illness. Clinicians working with alcohol and/or drug dependent patients may consider specifically assessing for and treating SIB because this subgroup of patients may warrant special attention in management of their clinical condition.

SI is more common in drug dependents than alcohol dependents [35]. Among substance dependents SI might be related to presence of personality disorder, PTSD, hostility, anxiety and depression [35,37]. Studies suggests that wherever SIB is present, there, childhood abuse and neglect must be evaluated in substance dependents [34,35]. Also, alcohol/drug dependents with SIB must be evaluated for suicide attempts and suicidal ideation for future suicide attempts [34-37]. Finally young drug users, particularly those with "difficulty in identifying feelings" could be the target population to prevent SIB [34,38]. Inability to manage negative emotional states may be a predictor of SIB. Thus, teaching these individuals emotion management and an emotional vocabulary to properly express their feelings in a positive environment may help curb the need to express feelings through SIB [120].

The advanced clinician can utilize knowledge of the processes of SIB and addiction to assist unit staff in understanding potential needs of these particular clients and provide resource information to the staff, which may assist in resolving some of the fear and frustration in interacting with self-injurious clients [72]. By identifying factors that have led to the SI in alcohol and/or drug use disorders, adults can obtain appropriate psychotherapy and deal in a more productive and beneficial manner with the pain that underlies their self-injurious impulses [121]. With continuing research on this subject in substance dependents, better therapeutic interventions for the person engaging in these acts will be possible.

REFERENCES

[1] Briere J, Gil E: Self-mutilation in clinical and general population samples: prevalence, correlates, and functions. *Am J Orthopsychiatry* 1998;68:609-620.

[2] Favazza AR: The coming of age of self-mutilation. *J Nerv Ment Dis* 1998;186:259-268.

[3] Taiminen TJ, Kallio-Soukainen K, Nokso-Koivisto H, Kaljonen A, Helenius H: Contagion of deliberate self-harm among adolescent inpatients. *J Am Acad Child Adolesc Psychiatry* 1998;37:211-217.

[4] Zlotnick C, Mattia JI, Zimmerman M: Clinical correlates of self-mutilation in a sample of general psychiatric patients. *J Nerv Ment Dis* 1999;187:296-301.

[5] Herpertz S, Steinmeyer SM, Marx D, Oidtmann A, Sass H: The significance of aggression and impulsivity for self-mutilative behavior. *Pharmacopsychiatry* 1995;28 (Suppl 2):64-72.

[6] Muehlenkamp JJ: Self-injurious behavior as a separate clinical syndrome. *Am J Orthopsychiatry* 2005;75:324-333.

[7] Ross RR, McKay HB: *Self-mutilation.* Lenxington, MA:DC Health Company, 1979.

[8] Klonsky ED, Oltmanns TF, Turkheimer E: Deliberate self-harm in a nonclinical population: prevalence and psychological correlates. *Am J Psychiatry* 2003;160:1501-1508.

[9] Favazza AR, Rosenthal RJ: Diagnostic issues in self-mutilation. *Hosp Community Psychiatry* 1993;44:134-140.

[10] van der Kolk BA, Perry JC, Herman JL: Childhood origins of self-destructive behavior. *Am J Psychiatry* 1991;148:1665-1671.

[11] Suyemoto KL, MacDonald ML: Self-cutting in female adolescents. *Psychotherapy* 1995;32:162-171.

[12] Tantam D, Whittaker J: Personality disorder and self-wounding. *Br J Psychiatry* 1992;161:451-464.

[13] Ogundipe LO: Suicide attempts v. deliberate self-harm. *Br J Psychiatry* 1999;175:90.

[14] Bhui K, McKenzie K, Rasul F: Rates, risk factors & methods of self harm among minority ethnic groups in the UK: a systematic review. *BMC Public Health* 2007;19:336.

[15] Favazza AR, Conterio K: Female habitual self mutilator. *Acta Psychiatr Scand* 1989;79:283–289.

[16] Favazza AR: Why patients mutilate themselves. *Hosp Community Psychiatry* 1989;40: 137–145.

[17] Klonsky ED: The functions of deliberate self-injury: a review of the evidence. *Clin Psychol Rev* 2007;27:226-239.

[18] Bergua A, Sperling W, Küchle M: Self-enucleation in drug-related psychosis. *Ophthalmologica* 2002;216:269-271.

[19] Skegg K: Self-harm. *Lancet* 2005;366:1471-1483.

[20] American Psychiatric Association: *Diagnostic and statistical manual of mental disorders:* DSM-IV-TR. Washington, DC: Author, 2000.

[21] Pattison EM, Kahan J: The deliberate self-harm syndrome. *Am J Psychiatry* 1983;140:867-872.

[22] Muehlenkamp JJ: Self-injurious behavior as a separate clinical syndrome. *Am J Orthopsychiatry* 2005;75:324-333.

[23] Hollander E, Stein D: *Impulsivity and aggression.* Chichester, UK; John Wiley; 1995.

[24] Sacks MB, Flood AM, Dennis MF, Hertzberg MA, Beckham JC: Self-mutilative behaviors in male veterans with posttraumatic stress disorder. *J Psychiatr Res* 2008;42:487-494.

[25] Romans SE, Martin JL, Anderson JC, Herbison GP, Mullen PE: Sexual abuse in childhood and deliberate self-harm. *Am J Psychiatry* 1995;152:1336-1342.

[26] Haw C, Hawton K, Houston K, Townsend E: Psychiatric and personality disorders in deliberate self-harm patients. *Br J Psychiatry* 2001;178:48-54.

[27] Farber SK: Self-medication, traumatic reenactment, and somatic expression in bulimic and self-mutilating behavior. *Clinical Social Work Journal* 1997;25:87-106.

[28] Evans C, Lacey JH: Multiple self-damaging behaviour among alcoholic women. A prevalence study. *Br J Psychiatry* 1992;161:643-647.

[29] Langbehn DR, Pfohl B: Clinical correlates of self-mutilation among psychiatric inpatients. *Ann Clin Psychiatry* 1993;5:45-51.

[30] Turell SC, Armsworth MW: Differentiating incest survivors who self-mutilate. *Child Abuse Negl* 2000;24:237-249.

[31] Paris J: Understanding self-mutilation in borderline personality disorder. *Harv Rev Psychiatry* 2005;13:179-185.

[32] Nock MK, Prinstein MJ: Contextual features and behavioral functions of self-mutilation among adolescents. *J Abnorm Psychol* 2005;114:140-146.

[33] Zoroglu SS, Tuzun U, Sar V, Tutkun H, Savas HA, Ozturk M, Alyanak B, Kora ME: Suicide attempt and self-mutilation among Turkish high school students in relation with abuse, neglect and dissociation. *Psychiatry Clin Neurosci* 2003;57:119-126.

[34] Evren C, Evren B: Self-mutilation in substance-dependent patients and relationship with childhood abuse and neglect, alexithymia and temperament and character dimensions of personality. *Drug Alcohol Depend* 2005;80:15-22.

[35] Evren C, Kural S, Cakmak D: Clinical correlates of self-mutilation in Turkish male substance-dependent inpatients. *Psychopathology* 2006;39:248-254.

[36] Evren C, Sar V, Evren B, Dalbudak E: Self-mutilation among male patients with alcohol dependency: the role of dissociation. *Compr Psychiatry* 2008;49:489-495.

[37] Evren C, Dalbudak E, Cetin R, Durkaya M, Evren B: Relationship of self-mutilation with posttraumatic stress disorder in male alcohol dependents. *Psychiatry Res* 2010 (in press)

[38] Oyefeso A, Brown S, Chiang Y, Clancy C: Self-injurious behaviour, traumatic life events and alexithymia among treatment-seeking opiate addicts: prevalence, pattern and correlates. *Drug Alcohol Depend* 2008;98:227-234.

[39] Cooper J, Kapur N, Webb R, Lawlor M, Guthrie E, Mackway-Jones K, Appleby L: Suicide after deliberate self-harm: a 4-year cohort study. *Am J Psychiatry* 2005;162: 297–303.

[40] Suominen K, Isometsa E, Haukka J, Lonnqvist J: Substance use and male gender as risk factors for deaths and suicide-a 5-year follow-up study after deliberate self-harm. *Soc Psychiatry Psychiatr Epidemiol* 2004;39:720-724.

[41] Favazza AR: Repetitive self-mutilation. *Psychiatr Annals* 1992;22:60-63.

[42] Brown MZ, Comtois KA, Linehan MM: Reasons for suicide attempts and nonsuicidal self-injury in women with borderline personality disorder. *J Abnorm Psychol* 2002;111:198-202.

[43] Nock MK, Prinstein MJ: A functional approach to the assessment of self-mutilative behavior. *J Consult Clin Psychol.* 2004;72:885-890.

[44] Kemperman I, Russ MJ, Shearin E: Self-injurious behavior and mood regulation in borderline patients.*J Pers Disord* 1997;11:146-157.

[45] Klonsky ED: The functions of self-injury in young adults who cut themselves: Clarifying the evidence for affect-regulation. *Psychiatry Res* 2009;166:260-268.

[46] Yaryura-Tobias JA, Neziroglu FA, Kaplan S: Self-mutilation, anorexia, and dysmenorrhea in obsessive compulsive disorder. *Int J Eat Disord* 1995;17:33-38.

[47] Brain KL, Haines J, Williams CL: The psychophysiology of self-mutilation: evidence of tension reduction. *Arch Suicide Res* 1998;4:227-242.

[48] Klonsky ED: Non-suicidal self-injury: an introduction. *J Clin Psychol* 2007;63:1039-1043.

[49] Suyemoto KL: The functions of self-mutilation. *Clin Psychol Rev* 1998;18:531–554.

[50] Taylor GJ, Bagby RM, Parker JDA: Disorders of affect regulation: *Alexithymia in medical and psychiatric illness.* Cambridge. Cambridge University Press, 1997.

[51] Cecero JJ, Holmstrom RW: Alexithymia and affect pathology among adult male alcoholics. *J Clin Psychol* 1997;53:201-208.
[52] Kooiman CG, Spinhoven P, Trijsburg RW, Rooijmans HG: Perceived parental attitude, alexithymia and defense style in psychiatric outpatients. *Psychother Psychosom* 1998;67:81-87.
[53] Farber SK: Self-medication, traumatic reenactment, and somatic expression in bulimic and self-mutilating behavior. *Clinical Social Work Journal* 1997;25:87-106.
[54] Arnold L, Babiker G: Counselling People who self-injure. In Zetta Bear (Ed) *Good Practice in Counselling People Who Have Been Abused 133-146.* Bristol, Pennsylvania: Jessica Kingsley Publishers, 1998.
[55] Levenkron S: Cutting: *Understanding and Overcoming Self-Mutilation.* New York: W.W. Norton and Company, 1998.
[56] Zlotnick C, Shea MT, Pearlstein T, Simpson E, Costello E, Begin A: The relationship between dissociative symptoms, alexithymia, impulsivity, sexual abuse, and self-mutilation. *Compr Psychiatry* 1996;37:12-16.
[57] Wheeler K, Braod R: Alexithymia and overeating. *Perspect Psych Care* 1994;30:7–10.
[58] Mental Health Foundation. *Truth hurts: report of the National Enquiry into self-harm among young people.* London: Mental Health Foundation, 2006.
[59] Tutkun H, Savas HA, Zoroglu SS, Esgi K, Herken H, Tiryaki N: Relationship between alexithymia, dissociation and anxiety in psychiatric outpatients from Turkey. *Isr J Psychiatry Relat Sci* 2004;41:118-124.
[60] Sar V, Akyuz G, Kugu N, Ozturk E, Ertem-Vehid H: Axis-I dissociative disorder comorbidity of borderline personality disorder and childhood trauma reports. *J Clin Psychiatry* 2006;67:1583-1590.
[61] Evren C, Sar V, Karadag F, Tamar-Gurol D, Karagoz M: Dissociative Disorders among Alcohol-Dependent Inpatients. *Psychiatry Res* 2007;152:233-241.
[62] Lipschitz DS, Kaplan ML, Sorkenn J: Childhood abuse, adult assault, and dissociation. *Compr Psychiatry* 1996; 37: 261-266.
[63] Brodsky BS, Cloitre M, Dulit RA: Relationship of dissociation to self-mutilation and childhood abuse in borderline personality disorder. *Am J Psychiatry* 1995;152:1788-1792.
[64] Akyuz G, Sar V, Kugu N, Dogan O: Reported childhood trauma, attempted suicide and self-mutilative behavior among women in the general population. *Eur Psychiatry* 2005;20:268-273.
[65] Herpertz S: Self-injurious behaviour. Psychopathological and nosological characteristics in subtypes of self-injurers. *Acta Psychiatr Scand* 1995;91:57-68.
[66] Brain KL, Haines J, Williams CL: The psychophysiology of self-mutilation: evidence of tension reduction. *Arch Suicide Res* 1998;4:227-242.
[67] Lacey JH, Evans CD: The impulsivist: a multi-impulsive personality disorder. *Br J Addict* 1986;81:641-649.
[68] Sher L, Stanley BH: The role of endogenous opioids in the pathophysiology of self-injurious and suicidal behavior. *Arch Suicide Res* 2008;12:299-308.
[69] Cataldo MF, Harris J: The biological basis for self-injury in the mentally retarded. *Analysis and Intervention in Developmental Disabilities* 2:21–39, 1982.
[70] Hicks KM, Hinck SM: Concept analysis of self-mutilation. *J Adv Nurs* 2008;64:408-413.

[71] Richardson JS, Zaleski WA: Endogenous opiates and self-mutilation. *Am J Psychiatry* 1986;143:938–940.

[72] Faye P: Addictive characteristics of the behavior of self-mutilation. *J Psychosoc Nurs Ment Health Serv* 1995;33:36-39.

[73] Karwautz A, Resch F, Wöber-Bingöl C, Schuch B: Self-mutilation in adolescence as addictive behaviour. *Wien Klin Wochenschr* 1996;108:82-84.

[74] Patel S: *Self-Injurious Behaviour (SIB) in Adolescents: an Important Consideration as a Risk Factor for Suicide,* Penn State College of Medicine, 2003.

[75] Hawton K, Harriss L, Simkin S, Bale E, Bond A: Self-cutting: patient characteristics compared with self-poisoners. *Suicide Life Threat Behav* 2004;34:199-208.

[76] Lloyd-Richardson EE, Perrine N, Dierker L, Kelley ML: Characteristics and functions of non-suicidal self-injury in a community sample of adolescents. *Psychol Med* 2007 ;37:1183-1192.

[77] Hawton K, Harriss L, Hall S, Simkin S, Bale E, Bond A: Deliberate self-harm in Oxford, 1990-2000: a time of change in patient characteristics. *Psychol Med* 2003; 33: 987–95.

[78] Rossow I, Ystgaard M, Hawton K, Madge N, van Heeringen K, de Wilde EJ, DeLeo D, Fekete S, Morey C: Cross-national comparisons of the association between alcohol consumption and deliberate self-harm in adolescents.Suicide Life *Threat Behav* 2007;37:605-615.

[79] Koob G, Kreek MJ: Stress, dysregulation of drug reward pathways, and the transition to drug dependence. *Am J Psychiatr* 2007;164: 1149–1159.

[80] Evans E, Hawton K, Rodham K: In what ways are adolescents who engage in self-harm or experience thoughts of self-harm different in terms of help-seeking, communication and coping strategies? *J Adolesc* 2005;28:573-587.

[81] Khantzian EJ: The self-medication hypothesis of substance use disorders: a reconsideration and recent applications. *Harv Rev Psychiatry* 1997;4:231-244.

[82] Dulit RA, Fyer MR, Leon AC, Brodsky BS, Frances AJ: Clinical correlates of self-mutilation in borderline personality disorder.*Am J Psychiatry* 1994;151:1305-1311.

[83] Harned MS, Najavits LM,Weiss RD: Self-harm and suicidal behavior in women with comorbid PTSD and substance dependence. *Am J Addict* 2006;15:392–395.

[84] Brunner R, Parzer P, Haffner J, Steen R, Roos J, Klett M, Resch F: Prevalence and psychological correlates of occasional and repetitive deliberate self-harm in adolescents. *Arch Pediatr Adolesc Med* 2007;161:641–649.

[85] Haavisto A, Sourander A, Multimäki P, Parkkola K, Santalahti P, Helenius H, Nikolakaros G, Moilanen I, Kumpulainen K, Piha J, Aronen E, Puura K, Linna SL, Almqvist F: Factors associated with ideation and acts of deliberate self-harm among 18-year-old boys. A prospective 10-year follow-up study. *Soc Psychiatry Psychiatr Epidemiol* 2005;40:912–921.

[86] Sinclair J, Hawton K: Suicide and deliberate self-harm. In: Lloyd GG, Guthrie E, eds. *Handbook of liaison psychiatry*. Cambridge: Cambridge University Press, 2007.

[87] Haw C, Houston K, Townsend E, Hawton K: Deliberate self-harm patients with alcohol disorders: characteristics, treatment, and outcome. *Crisis* 2001;22:93-101.

[88] Zlotnick C, Shea MT, Recupero P, Bidadi K, Pearlstein T, Brown P: Trauma, dissociation, impulsivity, and self-mutilation among substance abuse patients. *Am J Orthopsychiatry* 1997;67:650-654.

[89] Zweig-Frank H, Paris J, Guzder J: Psychological risk factors and self-mutilation in male patients with BPD. *Can J Psychiatry* 1994;39:266-268.
[90] Zweig-Frank H, Paris J, Guzder J: Psychological risk factors for dissociation and self-mutilation in female patients with borderline personality disorder. *Can J Psychiatry* 1994;39: 259-264.
[91] Saxe GN, Chawla N, Van der Kolk B: Self-destructive behavior in patients with dissociative disorders. *Suicide Life Threat Behav* 2002;32:313-320.
[92] Klonsky ED, Moyer A: Childhood sexual abuse and non-suicidal self-injury: meta-analysis. *Br J Psychiatry* 2008;192:166-170.
[93] Suominen K, Henriksson M, Suokas J, Isometsa E, Ostamo A, Lonnqvist J: Mental disorders and comorbidity in attempted suicide. *Acta Psychiatr Scand* 1996; 94**:** 234–40.
[94] Stanley B, Gameroff MJ, Michalsen V, Mann JJ: Are suicide attempters who self-mutilate a unique population? *Am J Psychiatry* 2001;158:427-432.
[95] Nixon MK, Cloutier PF, Aggarwal S: Affect regulation and addictive aspects of repetitive self-injury in hospitalized adolescents. *J Am Acad Child Adolesc Psychiatry* 2002;41:1333-1341.
[96] Kessler RC, Sonnega A, Bromet E, Hughes M, Nelson CB: PTSD in the National Comorbidity Survey. *Arch. Gen. Psychiatry* 1995;52:1048–1060.
[97] Kural S, Evren EC, Can S, Cakmak D: PTSD among substance dependents and its relationship with sociodemographic and clinical characteristics. *Klinik Psikofarmakoloji Bülteni* 2004;14:1-8.
[98] Evren C, Can S, Evren B, Saatcioglu O, Cakmak D. Lifetime posttraumatic stress disorder in Turkish alcohol-dependent inpatients: relationship with depression, anxiety and erectile dysfunction. *Psychiatry Clin Neurosci* 2006;60:77-84.
[99] Read JP, Brown PJ, Kahler CW: Substance use and posttraumatic stress disorder: Symptom interplay and effects on outcome. *Addict Behav* 2004;29:1665–1672.
[100] Gupta MA, Lanius RA, Van der Kolk BA: Psychologic trauma, posttraumatic stress disorder, and dermatology. *Dermatol Clin* 2005;23:649-656.
[101] Shearer SL, Peters CP, Quaytman MS, Wadman BE: Intent and lethality of suicide attempts among female borderline inpatients. *Am J Psychiatry* 1988;145:1424-1427.
[102] Leichsenring F, Heike K, Jurgen H: Borderline personality organization in violent offenders: Correlations of identity diffusion and primitive defense mechanisms with antisocial features, neuroticism, and interpersonal problems. *Bull Menninger Clin* 2003;67:314-327.
[103] Soloff PH, Lis JA, Kelly T, Cornelius J, Ulrich R: Risk factors for suicidal behavior in borderline personality disorder. *Am J Psychiatry* 1994;151:1316-1323.
[104] Herpertz S, Sass H, Favazza A: Impulsivity in self-mutilative behavior: psychometric and biological findings. *J Psychiatr Res* 1997;31:451-465.
[105] Ross S, Heath NL: Two models of adolescent self-mutilation. *Suicide Life Threat Behav* 2003;33:277-287.
[106] Bongar B, Peterson LG, Golann S, Hardiman JJ: Self-mutilation and the chronically suicidal patient: an examination of the frequent visitor to the psychiatric emergency room. *Ann Clin Psychiatry* 1990;2:217-222.
[107] Hawton K, Simkin S, Fagg J: Deliberate self-harm in alcohol and drug misusers: patient characteristics and patterns of clinical care. *Drug Alcohol Rev* 1997;16:123-129.

[108] Connors RE: *Self-injury: psychotherapy with people who engage in self-inflicted violence.* Northvale, NJ: Aronson, 2000.

[109] Hawton K, James A: Suicide and deliberate self harm in young people. *BMJ* 2005;330:891-894.

[110] Matsumoto T, Yamaguchi A, Chiba Y, Asami T, Iseki E, Hirayasu Y: Self-burning versus self-cutting: patterns and implications of self-mutilation; a preliminary study of differences between self-cutting and self-burning in a Japanese juvenile detention center. *Psychiatry Clin Neurosci* 2005;59:62-69.

[111] Waska RT: Self-mutilation, substance abuse and the psychoanalytic approach: four cases. *Am J Psychother* 1998;52:18-27.

[112] Dallam SJ: The identification and management of patients with SI in primary care. *Nurse Pract 1997;*22:151-153, 159-165.

[113] Evans K, Tyrer P, Catalan J, Schmidt U, Davidson K, Dent J, Tata P, Thornton S, Barber J, Thompson S: Manual-assisted cognitive-behaviour therapy (MACT): a randomized controlled trial of a brief intervention with bibliotherapy in the treatment of recurrent deliberate self-harm. *Psychol Med* 1999;29:19-25.

[114] Linehan MM, Schmidt H 3rd, Dimeff LA, Craft JC, Kanter J, Comtois KA: Dialectical behavior therapy for patients with borderline personality disorder and drug-dependence. *Am J Addict* 1999;8:279-292.

[115] Winchel RM, Stanley M: Self-injurious behavior: a review of the behavior and biology of self-mutilation. *Am J Psychiatry* 1991;148:306-317.

[116] Velazquez L, Ward-Chene L, Loosigian SR: Fluoxetine in the treatment of self-mutilating behavior. *J Am Acad Child Adolesc Psychiatry* 2000;39:812-814.

[117] Hough DW: Low-dose olanzapine for self-mutilation behavior in patients with borderline personality disorder. *J Clin Psychiatry* 2001;62:296-297.

[118] Roth AS, Ostroff RB, Hoffman RE: Naltrexone as a treatment for repetitive self-injurious behaviour:an open-label trial. *J Clin Psychiatry* 1996;57:233-237.

[119] Allen C: Helping with deliberate self-harm; some practical guidelines. *J Mental Health* 1995;4:243-250.

[120] Polk E, Liss M: Psychological characteristics of self-injurious behavior. *Pers Individ Dif* 2007;43:567–577.

[121] Makhija N, Sher L: Childhood abuse, adult alcohol use disorders and suicidal behaviour. *QJM* 2007;100:305-309.

Part V. Substance Use Disorders and Suicide: Epidemiology, Pathophysiology, Clinical Aspects

In: Suicidal Behavior in Alcohol and Drug Abuse... ISBN: 978-1-60876-919-3
Editors: L. Sher, A. Vilens, pp. 239-253

Chapter 13

EPIDEMIOLOGICAL EVIDENCE FOR THE LINK BETWEEN SUICIDE AND SUBSTANCE USE, ABUSE AND DEPENDENCE

Gillian W. Smith[1], Colette Corry[2] and James E. Houston[1]
[1]Nottingham Trent University, Nottingham, UK
[2]University of Ulster, Londonderry, UK

ABSTRACT

Suicidal behaviors remain prevalent globally; however, rates of suicide for those with substance abuse are in excess of those in the general population. This chapter presents epidemiological evidence for the link between suicide and substance use, abuse and dependence including polydrug use with a particular focus on the US and European trends. Risk factors presented include both distal and proximal associates with substance abuse, spanning demographic, psychosocial, psychiatric and situational factors. Given the complex interplay of substance use, abuse and dependence with these risk factors, prevention efforts to prevent substance use behaviors may play a key role in reducing suicide rates.

INTRODUCTION

This chapter will firstly present the evidence for the link between substance abuse and suicidal behaviors. However, a simple statement of the associations cannot fully conceptualize the link. To develop a true understanding of substance abuse in suicidality it is important to contextualize its role as both a predictor of, and as a means to engage in the behavior. On this premise the chapter will begin with an overview of suicide statistics in Europe and the United States, followed by a review of recent epidemiologic evidence supporting the link. This chapter will also assess the role of proximal factors (which are temporally close to any suicidal behaviors) and distal factors (which are more distant from the suicidal behavior) noting that these factors can sometimes be both [1]. Finally, the chapter will conclude with a cautionary note in relation to under-reporting of estimates of suicidality and how these affect the epidemiological evidence, as well as the role of psychological autopsies and the implications of the evidence on the prevention of suicidal behaviors. Note that substance abuse, in this instance refers to the range of alcohol and drug, use, abuse and dependence. Abuse as a clinical disorder will be referred to only with the substance named, for example alcohol abuse.

The World Health Organization (WHO) reports that approximately one million people die from suicide each year whilst acknowledging that these figures are compromised by underreporting. This represents a global mortality rate of 16 deaths per 100,000 of the population, or one death every 40 seconds. Suicide has increased by 60% over the last 45 years and is now one of the three leading causes of death in those aged 15-44 years of both sexes worldwide. Furthermore, suicide attempts are estimated to be up to 20 times more frequent than completed suicides, this figure once again possibly compromised by underreporting. By 2020 it is estimated that completed suicide will represent 2.4% of the total global burden of disease in countries with market economies. Suicides among young people have escalated to such an extent that they are now the group at most risk in a third of both developed and developing countries. Mental disorders are associated with more than 90% of completed suicides, in particular depression and substance abuse disorders. Highlighting the need for public health awareness of the complex factors influencing suicidality, the Centre for Disease Control and Prevention [2] emphasized the critical role of substance use in suicidal behaviors.

Embedded in this assertion is the belief that periods of socioeconomic, family and individual crisis situations are also indicators of the behavior. Approximately 33,000 deaths each year in the United States are attributed to suicide, in comparison to 60,000 each year in Europe. Using dedicated data from the WHO mortality database, Ajdacic-Gross et al [3] sought to compile the first comprehensive international comparison of suicide methods. Overdose was prevalent in female suicides in both Europe and the United States, whilst American males had a tendency towards firearms, European males were more likely to use overdose as their preferred method. Subpopulations with particular characteristics exist within all countries that are at higher risk for suicide, such as veterans, the homeless and prisoners in correctional facilities. Immigration, particularly in the EU, is emerging as an area requiring further research owing to the high levels of substance use and suicidal gestures within the global migrant population. The same additional risk factors and complex interactions apply to this section of the population, including gender, age, socio-economic status and psychopathology. As findings from the US and the EU demonstrate consistency with regard to prevalence, method and precipitation, the current chapter will use a combined approach to assess the contribution of substance use, abuse and dependence to the phenomenon of suicidal behavior.

Evidence for a Link between Substance Abuse and Suicidal Behaviors

Epidemiological studies provide clear associations of substance use, abuse and dependence with suicidal behaviors. Figures from SAMHSA's Drug Abuse Warning Network in 2005 [4] illustrate that there were almost 133,000 visits to emergency rooms due to alcohol and drug related suicide attempts. Additionally, data collected on adolescents aged between

12 and 17 years old suggest a similarly strong association with 21,584 emergency room visits for substance abuse suicide attempts (on average 1.7 drugs related to each attempt). This may well be a conservative estimate, as not all hospitals were included (including Children's hospitals). In a study of deliberate self harm (suicide attempts) admissions to hospital conducted in Oxford, UK, Hawton et al. [5] found 10% of males and 7% of females in the sample were either alcohol dependent, or illustrated physical alcohol dependence symptomatology. The authors also found 12% of males and 6% of females presenting for deliberate self harm were drug users. However, it is likely that these drug users may also have been alcohol users. Typically, three quarters of these drug users had previously attempted suicide compared with approximately half of those who misused alcohol alone and one third of those that were not considered to be related to substance abuse. This suggests that drug users may well be more likely to attempt suicide again. In the year follow up from the initial contact, 33% of drug users attempted again, compared with 17% of alcohol users and 11% of those not related to substance abuse. Moreover, Kolves, Varnik, Tooding, and Wasserman [6] found in a sample of 427 individuals who had committed suicide, that over half met a diagnosis for alcohol dependence, confirming this strong link.

Completed rates for suicide in substance abusers are typically in excess of the rates of prevalence in the general population. In a review of the literature, Modesto-Lowe, Brooks and Ghani [7] concluded the lifetime risk of suicide was 7% for those without alcohol dependence to 15% for those with alcohol dependence. Furthermore, the authors note that retrospective post-mortem studies of suicide show that 25-35% may have been alcohol dependent; however, this is noted to be in the context of polydrug use (in particular cocaine and opioid use). Those diagnosed with alcohol dependence had a suicide risk of 60-120 times that of those without psychiatric illness [8]. Harris and Barraclough [9] found for alcohol dependent patients that the standardized mortality rate was 14 times higher than expected for the general population. Wilcox, Conner and Caine [10] used the estimates from this study and 22 later published studies to determine the standardized mortality rate (SMR) for specific substance use disorders (completed suicides only). The SMR for heavy alcohol use was 351 (95%CI=251-478) and for alcohol disorders was 979 (95%CI=898-1065) i.e. three and nine fold increase in the observed number of suicides to expected respectively. This indicates that severity in alcohol use involvement relates to a higher risk of suicide. Estimates of rates for drug use were consistently higher than for alcohol use. For general drug use the SMR was 1685 (95%CI=1473-1920), for intravenous drug users 1373 (95%CI=1029-1796), for opiate use 1351 (95%CI=1047-1715), and for amphetamine abuse 1136 (369-2652) illustrating a considerably higher risk of completed suicide for those who engage in illegal drug use.

However, the link with alcohol use (and indeed polydrug use) is not limited to those with diagnoses of either abuse or dependence. Stack [11] assessed the correlation between alcohol use and suicide rates and found that almost 62% of the 89 studies assessed from 17 countries found an association between increases in per capita alcohol consumption with increased suicide rates. However, the broad harm (including suicidal behaviors) associated with alcohol consumption has been demonstrated to be better predicted by patterns of use, than aggregate or average measures [13,14]. In a European study, Ramstedt [14] found the association to be stronger in dry drinking cultures compared to both moderate and wet cultures, a distinction which considers both drinking levels and drinking patterns. Dry cultures are typically Northern European with low per capita consumption, heavy weekend drinking, and restrictive alcohol policies, with wet cultures being consistently high per capita consumption and evenly distributed during the week with less restriction in policy and typical of Southern Europe. This suggests that heavier drinking on occasion may play a larger role in suicidal behaviors.

Examining the impact of substance use on multiple suicide attempts, Roy [15] assessed 214 cocaine dependent patients in a substance abuse treatment program and found that 39% had attempted suicide in their lifetime, with a mean number of attempts 2.1 (range 1-9 attempts). In a replication of this study [16], a different set of 449 drug dependent patients in the same substance abuse program found a broadly identical rate of lifetime attempts. In this sample 39% had attempted suicide with a mean number of attempts of 1.8 and a slightly wider range of number of attempts (from 1 to 14). In a similar study assessing 280 alcohol dependent patients [17] found 43% had lifetime attempts, with a mean of 2.2 attempts (range of 1-13) suggesting a slightly higher rate for alcohol dependent patients compared to drug dependent patients. Borges, Walters and Kessler [18] also assessed the contribution of substance specific dependence on the prediction of first suicide attempt in a large epidemiological study of the US (NCS). The specific substance dependence with the highest association was inhalant dependence (Odds Ratio (OR=6.8) followed by alcohol dependence (OR=5.9), stimulant dependence (OR=4.0), sedative dependence (OR=3.4) and cannabis dependence (OR=2.7). The relationship with substance specific abuse was highest for heroin (OR=34) and inhalants (OR=10) with approximate odds ratios in the region of 3-4 for all other substances, however, stimulant abuse was not a significant predictor of first suicide attempt. Substance specific use (without abuse or dependence) also predicted first suicide attempt. Odds ratios ranged from 1.7 for cocaine to 3.5 for heroin use, but all 10 substances had an elevated risk (in the region of 2, alcohol, analgesics, sedatives, tranquillizers, stimulants, cannabis, inhalants, and hallucinogens). This broadly suggests that the strength of the relationship of a given used substance in predicting first suicide attempt varies as a function of the extent of the use whether it is use, abuse or dependence. They also assessed the relationship between the individual polydrug use and their transition between suicidal behaviors. Using a continuous variable of number of substances used compared to those who did not use, numbers of drugs used were significant predictors (with increasing odds ratios for increased number of substances used) for first subsequent suicide attempt, suicide ideation and an unplanned attempt among ideators without a plan. A suicide plan without an attempt was only related the use of 6 or 7 substances. The number of drugs used did not significantly predict planned attempts among ideators. Broadly speaking Borges and colleagues [18] conclude that the number of drugs used is more important than the specific substances being used. This is contrary to previous research which focuses on alcohol and tranquillizers.

The literature on alcohol use is considerably more established than drug use [10]. Partly, this is considered to be due to considerable polydrug use found within those who use illegal drugs (which may include legal or other illegal substances). However, polydrug use is also common in alcohol abuse, even if the levels of other drug consumption do not reach levels which warrant a diagnosis of either abuse or dependence. It is therefore difficult to isolate which drug (or combinations of drugs) is particularly implicated in suicidal behaviors. Both the literature on alcohol and drug abuse would benefit from better methods to control for the effects of polydrug use in single substances research, as in many cases (e.g. [15]) the primary drug of abuse is chosen as the focus, in essence ignoring the potentially contributory effect of polydrug use.

SUBSTANCE USE, ABUSE AND DEPENDENCE AS DISTAL FACTORS FOR SUICIDAL BEHAVIORS

Relationship with other Mental Health Disorders

From an epidemiological perspective, associations of co-morbidity (substance use disorders and mental health disorders) and suicide are well established [16,19]. Alone, mental health disorders increase the risk of suicidal behaviors. The most frequently associated disorders include major depression, with rates of suicide at around 59-87%, schizophrenia, with around 10-12%, and substance use disorders with similar rates to those of schizophrenia [20]. As the combination of disorders is likely to increase the risk, it is important to account for co-morbidity when assessing the epidemiological relationship of substance abuse on suicidal behaviors. Borges, Walters and Kessler [18] found controlling for mental health comorbidity and other drug use considerably decreases the odds ratio of a first suicide attempt. The association of alcohol use, abuse and dependence with subsequent first suicide attempt compared to no alcohol use was 2.8, 6.1 and 17.6 respectively. Controlling for just mental health co-morbidity reduced the magnitude of the odds ratios to 2.2, 3.3 and 5.9 respectively. The magnitude decreased further when additionally controlling for illegal drug use, abuse or dependence to odds of 1.8, 2.1 and 3.3 times more likely than no alcohol use respectively. A similar situation exists when assessing the association of lifetime drug use, abuse and dependence with odds ratios of 3.3, 7.8 and 12.7 times respectively. These decrease to odds ratios of 2.3, 3.8 and 5.3 times respectively compared to non-users when controlling for co-morbid mental health disorders and to 2.0, 2.7 and 3.5 respectively compared to non-drug users when controlling for mental health and alcohol use, abuse or dependence.

Modesto-Lowe, Brooks and Ghani [7] in a review of the literature suggested that personality, panic disorder, anxiety and depressive disorders are most frequently co-morbid with suicidal behavior and alcohol use disorders. The risk of suicidal behaviors is considered to be attenuated with increased numbers of disorders [21]; however, this does not hold with suicidal behaviors which include a plan. Concerns are also expressed regarding risk of suicide after discharge from psychiatric care. Christiansen and Jensen [22] in a study of 3037 cases in Oslo found a significantly high peak in risk of suicide attempts in the first few weeks following discharge, regardless of demographic profile. This effect was further compounded by findings that risk of further attempt was positively correlated with an increasing number of previous hospitalizations, suggesting this as a time of increased vulnerability in those with co-morbid substance abuse disorders.

It could be suggested that substance use disorders are one of the strongest predictors of suicidal behavior in a range of mental disorders. Borges, Nock, Medina-Mora, Benjet, Lara, Chiu and Kessler [23] in a study of 5782 Mexican respondents found the strongest temporally prior lifetime psychiatric disorder which predicted the first onset of suicide ideation was drug abuse. Furthermore, substance use disorders had the strongest association with transitions from plan to attempt. The presence of three or more psychiatric disorders was associated with increased odds of attempts compared with those with no disorders. However, co-morbidity should be expected in the relationship between substance abuse and suicide although others [24] note that mood disorders can increase substance use, but also that chronic substance use can lead to mood disorders. Consequently, with the frequency of comorbidity it is difficult to assess causation of the substance abuse, the mental health disorder or indeed the suicidal behaviors.

Trauma and Life Stress

The use of alcohol or drugs can contribute to adverse life events (either major trauma or life stress, or both), the subsequent stress of which may be a catalyst for a range of suicidal behaviors. Alternatively, experiences of this nature may lead to self medication; in turn leading to suicidal behavior. Pirkola, Isometsa, Heikkinen and Lonnqvist [25], for example assessed the alcohol use of adult suicides, finding that 35% of those surveyed were alcohol users. In this group however, these individuals were most likely to have experienced current unemployment, or divorce/separation (also likely to be both male and young). Additionally, current unemployment or marital breakdown (separation/divorce) can distinguish between those with an alcohol disorder with and without suicide attempts[26].

An interesting area of suicide research in relation to stress concentrates on residential change and integration (given the high levels of resettlement between EU countries) [27,28]. Many immigrants demonstrate lower-level education and participation in the labour market in comparison to natives; low SES and minority status creates additional stressors when attempting to resettle in an unfamiliar environment [29]. One such study of immigration was conducted in Germany which has approximately 6.7 million inhabitants of foreign origin. While female immigrants were found to be more likely to engage in substance abuse than natives, male immigrants were more likely to complete suicide than their German born counterparts. Suicide mortality was significantly higher shortly after residential change. These findings were attributable to external causes including psychoactive substance use, and highlighted difficulties in successful integration [30].

With regard to major trauma, evidence from population-based studies has found that childhood physical abuse significantly increased the risk of past year alcohol abuse or dependence [31], and furthermore that victims of childhood physical abuse were more likely than non victims to have problems related to alcohol and drugs [32]. Similarly, alcoholics who had engaged in suicidal behaviors had increased childhood trauma questionnaire scores for emotional, physical, or sexual abuse, emotional and physical neglect and family history of suicidal behavior compared to those who had not [16]. Interestingly, these findings were replicated in a sample of 449 drug dependent patients [16]. In a further study, Lloyd, Ricketts, Havens, Cornelius, Bishai, Huettner, Latkin, and Strathdee [33] studied a sample of needle exchange program attendees and found that more than 25% of the sample had suicidal ideation. They further reported that emotional and sexual abuse were related to suicide ideation in their sample, as those drug users who had experienced emotional abuse were over twice as likely to have suicidal ideation, and those who had experienced sexual abuse were over four times more likely to have suicidal ideation. In fact different types of trauma have been associated with drug and alcohol use, for example, in the wake of the terrorist attacks in the United States of America, Vlahov, Galea, Resnick, Ahern, Boscarino, Bucuvalas, Gold, and Kilpatrick [34] found a 30% overall increase in substance use, a 25% increase in alcohol intake, and a dramatic increase in the sales of alcohol, tobacco and prescription drugs.

SUBSTANCE USE, ABUSE AND DEPENDENCE AS PROXIMAL RISK FACTORS FOR SUICIDAL BEHAVIORS

The Role of Acute Intoxication

Acute intoxication episodes may also play a key role in suicides for some individuals. If the substance being used is absent, the idea of engaging in any of the suicidal behaviors from ideation to completed attempt may not be considered. The disinhibition effect of alcohol in particular can make a key contribution, particularly given how frequently it is used within most populations. However, alcohol can additionally promote depressive mood states, hopelessness and aggression [35]. It may also be more difficult for intoxicated individuals to generate alternative problem solving solutions to challenges arising prior, during or after the intoxication episode [6].

It is of note that *current* substance use is a better predictor of suicidal behaviour than *previous* use of substance use [18]. This lends support for the role of the intoxication episode whether inside or outside the context of clinically relevant substance specific abuse or dependence. Toxicology reports also provide key evidence for a substance abuse and suicide link. Recent toxicology reports from the National Violent Death Reporting System suggest that those who successfully committed suicide in 13 US states were found to have consumed alcohol in 33.3% of cases, opiates in 16.4%, cocaine in 9.4%, marijuana in 7.7%, and amphetamines in 3.9% of cases [36]. These percentages may reflect considerable polydrug use, in particular alcohol use with other illicit substances. Furthermore, this data is supported by others, for example in Finland, where detectable blood alcohol was found in 36% of completed suicides [37].

However, the role of acute intoxication episodes can play a role in the context of distal factors. Considerable psychosocial impairments and comorbidity were found in a psychological autopsy study of completed Finnish adolescent suicides where there was a diagnosis of either DSM-III-R alcohol use disorders or sub-threshold alcohol misuse [38]. Those with this pattern of substance use were also more likely to be intoxicated at the time of death than others in the cohort who did not have either DSM-III-R alcohol use disorder or sub-threshold alcohol misuse. Volkow [39] notes that substance abuse has common predisposing factors which are attenuated by the neurological effects of drugs such as mood states. Consequently, it is difficult to ascertain which factors relate to the substance use and which do not.

Impulsivity, Aggression and other Personality Factors

Not all of those engaged in substance use, regardless of substance(s) used or the level of use will engage in suicidal behaviors, as personality traits may well mediate the vulnerability to engage in behavior of this nature. Aggression and impulsivity in particular are associated with suicidal behaviors, and other self-destructive behaviors more generally. The risk may therefore be attenuated in the presence of substance use, abuse or dependence [40]. Impulsivity and lack of inhibition as a consequence of intoxication may promote suicidal ideation and increase the likelihood of suicide attempt with low survival probability [35].

Modesto-Lowe, Brooks and Ghani [7] also found these traits amongst those with alcohol dependence who had engaged in suicidal behaviors. These traits are also found with substance use and suicidal behaviors in adolescent populations [41].

Other personality characteristics may include anxiousness or irritability, for example Pompili and colleagues [42] sought to examine the relationship between substance use, temperament and suicide risk in an Italian sample of two matched groups of psychiatric outpatients with and without substance abuse. Those with substance abuse differed in temperament between the groups, with higher anxiety, irritability, impulsivity and aggressive traits and suicide risk compared to those who did not abuse substances. It was also reported that a high level of substance abusers met criteria for bipolar disorders type II in relation to the control group, which may also contribute to suicide risks.

In a similar study of prisoners in Italy, Cuomo et al [43] reported increased psychoticism, neuroticism, violent behavior, hostility, and impulsivity in a population of prisoners, with 21% reporting substance abuse and a history of one or more suicide attempts, establishing them as a group with a particularly high risk of eventual completed suicide. Roy [15] also found higher neuroticism, introversion and psychoticism in drug dependent patients in substance abuse treatment who had attempted suicide, a finding broadly supported in a similar study of alcohol dependent patients in substance abuse treatment who had also attempted suicide [17]. In a study focusing on cocaine as the primary drug of dependence, Roy [15] found lower extraversion, and higher neuroticism, but no relationship with either hostility or impulsivity in those who had attempted suicide compared to those who had not.

Demographic Risk Factors

Murphy suggests that alcoholic women are less likely to attempt suicide than alcoholic males, despite the illness perhaps having a stronger effect on women and the loss of protective factors commonly found for women in the general population as a broad consequence of illness [44,45]. The author cites the ratio for the general population of males to females in terms of suicide attempts as 2.3:1 whereas for those with alcohol dependence is 5.2:1. However, there is some evidence to suggest that the relationship may vary as a function of the primary substance abused. Wilcox, Conner and Caine [10] in a review of the literature found the standardized mortality ratio (SMR) was higher for females at 1690 (95%CI=1246-2241) than males 483 (95%CI=444-524) for those with alcohol disorders. The SMR for opiates was conversely higher for males 756 (95%CI=440-1210) than females 357 (95%CI=9-1990) although the authors noted some of the studies cited in overall rates were not broken down by gender. The absence of gender breakdown is a common issue, SMR's for intravenous drug use, general drug use, and heavy alcohol use were difficult to determine due to the lack of gender breakdown in cited studies. Roy [15] in a study of cocaine dependent patients engaged in a substance abuse treatment program found attempters were more likely to be female with an earlier onset of cocaine dependence and higher scores on the addiction severity index. Subsequent studies in both alcohol dependent patients [17] and drug dependent patients [16] engaged in substance abuse treatment found that younger females were more likely to attempt suicide. However, it is difficult to conclusively assess whether these substance specific differences hold for those who have not engaged with treatment.

Alcohol in particular may also vary as a function of patterns of consumption. Ramstedt [14] found an increased relationship with suicide for men in Northern Europe where dry consumption patterns are likely. For females, the relationship between suicide and alcohol use was highest in Northern and Central Europe where dry to medium consumption patterns are evident. Age was also related. Younger individuals were more likely to engage in suicidal behaviors in Northern and Central Europe in Dry and Medium drinking cultures respectively, but not Southern European countries, which have a typically wet drinking culture.

Some studies have constructed typical typologies of substance abusers who have engaged with suicidal behaviors. Modesto-Lowe, Brooks and Ghani [7] suggest that the typical case (with respect to alcohol) is an older, male Caucasian, with high levels of psychological loss, and a long drinking career. However, some note that similarly profiled females are also at risk [46]. Cottler, Campbell, Krishna, Williams and Abdallah [47] suggest drug dependent suicide attempters are typically younger than those with alcohol use disorders. A Collaborative Study in the Genetics of Alcoholism investigation [48] of 3190 alcohol dependent individuals concluded that those who had attempted suicide were more likely to be female with an early onset of alcohol dependence, severe disorder, social problems including aggression, with co-morbid disorders (including other drug use) compared to those who had not attempted suicide.

Underreporting

The reliability of suicide classification and associated underreporting remains important in establishing the epidemiological link with substance abuse. Problems include incomplete or absent evidence, procedural deficiencies, cultural definitions of suicide and discrepancies in determination of intent. Owing to differences in death certification practices, official suicide mortality data should be interpreted with caution [49]. If it was assumed that all undetermined deaths were suicides, it is estimated that the official rate may be underestimated by at least 22% [50]. For example, a certification of suicide can be issued by a general practitioner without a police investigation in Germany, whereas all suspected suicides are subject to police investigation and a coroner's inquest in the United Kingdom. Interpretation of suicide varies widely among countries, with cultural differences affecting classification of cause of death. This interpretation has been consolidated by findings that cause of death for immigrants in their host country may differ from those of similar cases in their country of origin [51]. The accuracy of mortality data attributed to suicide remains a contentious area. Missing information at time of death has been suggested as a cause of random error, while cultural stigma relating to suicide has been implicated as a source of random bias [52]. As such, disparities continue to exist among coroners in suicide verdicts. Differences in classification have also been observed with regard to gender, age and race; Cooper and Milroy [53] suggest that mortality statistics in the UK are distorted due to underreporting of suicides and cause of death. In their retrospective study of coroner's files in Yorkshire from 1985 to 1991, only 60% of 536 deaths with the clinical characteristics of suicide were issued a death certificate confirming suicide as cause of death. Male deaths were more frequently classified as suicide relative to females, while a higher proportion of younger females were classified as suicide in comparison to older females. Reported method of death and subsequent interpretation were highlighted as possible confounding factors in classification, most notably poisoning, drowning, self-immolation and jumping from a height. Phillips and Ruth [54] reported similar findings with regard to females and groups with typically low suicide rates such as black Americans. Racial disparities indicated a greater susceptibility for misclassification of black suicides than white with an emphasis on substance use, as well as deficits in black female classification relative to black males. European research has shown that suicide rates are higher when classification is determined by health criteria rather than legal requirements [55]. Due to high level of specificity required to facilitate a judgment of death by suicide, death due to substance use is often recorded as 'undetermined' and therefore subject to the possible confounding factors associated with official interpretation. Additionally, many substance users also have a co-morbid psychiatric diagnosis; while death may not involve ingestion, the suicidal act may be in response to behavior prompted by substance use [52]. It is easy to see where the boundaries become blurred and misclassification could result in such cases.

Psychological Autopsy

It is impossible to accurately identify which event or series of events have led to such an extreme, irreversible expression of despair. Often, those closest to the deceased react with shock and disbelief as the individual gave no indication of their intentions. Retrospective analysis in the form of psychological autopsy provides a unique opportunity to examine events prior to the suicide. This reconstruction gathers information from personal documents, police reports, medical and coroner's records, and conducts interviews with those who had contact with the person before the death, such as families and friends. Psychological autopsy studies have identified addictive and affective disorders in more than 90% of suicide victims [56,57], with alcohol abuse or dependence identified in up to 56% of victims [24]. The ultimate aim of the psychological autopsy is to uncover information which can then be used to inform future intervention and prevention strategies targeted towards those at risk. From the perspective of substance disorders and suicide, valuable information can be compiled about demographic and other factors which may have prompted the development of substance abuse and the eventual suicidal act, such as gender and age, stressors, life events and prior help-seeking behavior. In turn, these can be used to inform policy and assist in the evaluation of risk for individuals with similar profiles. Toxicological evidence of any direct contribution of alcohol inebriation or other substance ingestion during the final act of suicide would also be important.

Implications for Prevention

It is difficult to detect imminent suicide, however, an awareness of the epidemiologically determined risk factors are useful in particular for primary and secondary prevention efforts[2]. Understanding the links between substance abuse and suicidal behavior will make it easier to tailor suicide prevention efforts, improve treatment, and ensure targeted information for substance users that may be able to make a difference. Clinicians play a key role at the point of access to treatment, with an opportunity to ascertain ideation history, severity of substance use involvement, interpersonal stress and coping factors, the presence of polydrug use, in addition to protective factors such as ethnicity, religious belief, and attitudes to suicide [7]. Links between substance use and mental health treatment providers may also help. More widely, the reduction of stigma attached to help seeking for mental health problems, substance use or suicidal behaviors may also play a role, as it may be likely that reduction in mental health or substance use disorder symptomatology could reduce suicidal behavior [2].

Compelling results highlighting the immediacy of need for assessment, intervention and prevention of suicidal behavior have prompted a direct response from the United States and many countries within the European Union. The World Health Organisation's [58] statement on suicide prevention highlighted the need for adequate treatment of suicide risk in people with mental illness, among these substance disorders. Specific country and specific continent steps are driving forward primary, secondary, and tertiary prevention strategies at both universal population level and to targeted populations including substance abusers. In addition, epidemiological studies are also playing their part in better monitoring and exploration of the interplay between substance abuse and suicide with the SAMHSA's [4] National survey asking about depression and suicide from the 2008 wave onward. However, it must be noted that not all suicides can be prevented, and that for some the choice to engage in the behavior, despite best efforts of health professionals, relatives, friends and colleagues, cannot be stopped. Sher [59] notes "if suicide is difficult to predict, then prevention is even more difficult to detect", (pp.679) illustrating that the challenge for prevention strategies is great.

CONCLUSION

The role of substance abuse in suicidal behaviors has been well documented; however, evidence presented suggests that it may not be necessary or sufficient for suicidal behaviors. Individuals who attempt, or are successful in committing suicide are not always dependent on, or abusing substances, and those who are dependent or are abusing substances do not always display suicidal behavior. It appears to be through a complex interaction with other risk factors including co-morbidity, adverse life events, trauma, personality traits, acute intoxication and other socio-demographic variables which makes substance abuse a key aspect in a wider constellation of cause for suicidal behaviors. Prevention efforts therefore must take into consideration the role of substance abuse in suicide. Finally, epidemiological evidence presented may be compromised by under-reporting, which may vary between country and even between individuals. Psychological autopsy permits examination of background factors and events leading up to death. Through analysis of this type, in combination with toxicological findings, it may be possible to generate various profiles for those particularly at risk for the behavior. These findings could inform policy and assist in the development of appropriate intervention and prevention strategies. However, the area of suicidality can only be adequately addressed through examination of the complex myriad of interconnecting factors which both mediate and moderate the behavior. Research of this type will depend on government support and as such will remain at the forefront of mental health agendas worldwide.

REFERENCES

[1] Brady J: The association between alcohol misuse and suicidal behavior. *Alcohol Alcohol* 2006; 41:473-478.

[2] Center for Substance Abuse Treatment: *Substance Abuse and Suicide Prevention: Evidence and Implications*- A white paper. Rockville, MD: Substance Abuse and Mental Health Services Administration: 2008.

[3] Ajdacic-Gross V, Weiss MG, Ring M, Hepp U, Bopp M, Gutzwiller F, Rössler W: Methods of suicide: international suicide patterns derived from the WHO mortality database. *Bull World Health Organ* 2008; 86:726–732.

[4] Ball J, Albright V: Drug Abuse Warning Network, 2005: *Area Profiles of Drug-Related Mortality.* Rockville, MD: Substance Abuse and Mental Health Services Administration, 2009.

[5] Hawton K: Trends in deliberate self-harm in Oxford, 1985-1995. Implications for clinical services and the prevention of suicide. *Brit J Psychiatry* 1997; 171:556-560.

[6] Kolves K, Varnik A, Tooding LM, Wasserman D: The role of alcohol in suicide: a case-control psychological autopsy study. *Psychol Med* 2006; 36(7):923-30.

[7] Modesto-Lowe V, Brooks D, Ghani M: Alcohol Dependence and suicidal behavior from research to clinical challenges. *Harv Rev Psychiat* 2006; 14:241-248.

[8] Murphy GE, Wetzel RD: The lifetime risk of suicide and alcoholism. *Arch Gen Psychiatry* 1990; 47:383-392.

[9] Harris EC, Barraclough B: Suicide as an outcome for mental disorders. A meta-analysis. *Brit J Psychiatry* 1997; 170:205–228.

[10] Wilcox HC, Conner KR, Caine ED: Association of alcohol and drug use disorders and completed suicide: an empirical review of cohort studies. *Drug Alcohol Depend* 2004; 76S:S11-S19.

[11] Stack S: Suicide: a 15-year review of the sociological literature Part I: cultural and economic factors, *Suicide Life Threat Behav* 2000; 30:145–162.

[12] Nordentoft M: Prevention of suicide and attempted suicides in Denmark. *Dan Med Bull* 2007; 54:306-369.

[13] Smith GW, Shevlin M: Patterns of alcohol consumption and related behavior in Great Britain: A latent class analysis of the Alcohol Use Disorder Identification Test (AUDIT). *Alcohol Alcohol* 2008; 43:590-594.

[14] Ramstedt M: Per capita alcohol consumption and liver cirrhosis mortality in 14 European countries. *Addiction* 2001; 96:S19–S34.

[15] Roy A: Characteristics of cocaine dependent patients who attempt suicide. *Am J Psychiat* 2001; 158:1215-1219.

[16] Roy A: Characteristics of drug addicts who attempt suicide. *Psychiatry Res* 2003; 121:99-103.

[17] Roy A: Distal risk factors for suicidal behavior in alcoholics: Replications and new findings. *J Affect Disord* 2003; 77:267-271.

[18] Borges G, Walters EE, Kessler RC: Association of substance use, abuse and dependence with subsequent suicidal behavior. *Am J Epidemiol* 2000; 151:781-789.

[19] Zweben JE: Severely and persistently mentally ill substance abusers: Clinical and policy issues. *J Psychoactive Drugs* 2000; 32:383-389.

[20] Rihmer Z, Kiss K: Bipolar disorders and suicide risk. *Bipolar Disord* 2002; 1: 15–21.

[21] Borges G, Angst J, Nock MK, Ruscio AM, Kessler RC: Risk factors for the incidence and persistence of suicide related outcomes: A 10 year follow up study using the NCS. *J Affect Disord* 2008; 105:25-33.

[22] Christiansen E, Jensen BF: A nested case-control study of the risk of suicide attempts after discharge from psychiatric care: the role of co-morbid substance use disorder. *Nord J Psychiatry* 2009; 63:132-139.

[23] Borges G, Nock MK, Medina-Mora ME, Benjet C, Lara C, Chiu WT, Kessler RC: The epidemiology of suicide related outcomes in Mexico. *Suicide Life Threat Behav* 2007; 37:627-640.

[24] Cherpitel CJ, Borges GLG, Wilcox HC: Acute alcohol use and suicidal behavior: A review of the literature. *Alcohol Clin Exp Res* 2004; 28:S18-S25.

[25] Pirkola SP, Isocmetsa ET, Heikkinen ME, Lonnqvist, JK: Suicides of alcohol misusers and non-misusers in a nationwide population. *Alcohol Alcohol* 2000; 35:70-75.

[26] Preuss UW, Schuckit MA, Smith TL, Danko GP, Bucholz KK, Hesselbrock MN, Hesselbrock V, Kramer JR: Comparison of 3190 alcohol-dependent individuals with and without suicide attempts. *Alcohol Clin Exp Res* 2002; 26:471-477.

[27] Bollini P, Siem H: No real progress towards equity: health of migrants and ethnic minorities on the eve of the year 2000. *Soc Sci Med* 1995; 41:819-828.

[28] Bhugra D, Jones P: Migration and mental illness. *Adv Psychiatr Treat* 2001; 7:216-223.

[29] Frick JR: Integration of migrants in Germany on the basis of comparable national and international representative microdata. Im Auftrage des Sachverstandigenrats fur Zuwanderung und Immigration. cited in Ott JJ, Winkler V, Kyobutungi C, Laki J, Becher H: Effects of residential changes and time patterns on external-cause mortality in migrants: Results of a German cohort study. *Scand J Public Health* 2008; 36:524-531.

[30] Ott JJ, Winkler V, Kyobutungi C, Laki J, Becher H: Effects of residential changes and time patterns on external-cause mortality in migrants: Results of a German cohort study. *Scand J Pub Health* 2008; 36:524-531.

[31] Kilpatrick D G, Acierno Saunders B, Resnick HS, Best CL, Schnurr PH: Risk Factors for Adolescent Substance Abuse and Dependence: Data from a National Sample. *J Consult Clin Psychol* 2004; 68:1-12.

[32] Duncan RD, Saunders BE, Kilpatrick DG, Hanson RF, Resnick HS: Childhood physical assault as a risk factor for PTSD, depression, and substance abuse: Findings from a national survey. *Am J Orthopsychiatry* 1996; 66:437–448.

[33] Lloyd JJ, Ricketts EP, Havens JR, Cornelius LJ, Bishai D, Huettner S, Latkin C, Strathdee SA: The Relationship Between Lifetime Abuse and Suicidal Ideation in a Sample of Injection Drug Users. *J Psychoactive Drugs* 2007; 39:159–166.

[34] Vlahov D, Galea S, Resnick H, Ahern J, Boscarino JA, Bucuvalas M, Gold J, Kilpatrick D: Increased use of cigarettes, alcohol, and marijuana among Manhattan residents after the September 11th terrorist attacks. *Am J Epidemiol* 2002; 555:988-996.

[35] Hufford MR: Alcohol and suicidal behavior. *Clin Psychol Rev* 2001; 21:797-811.

[36] Karch D, Crosby A, Simon T: Toxicology testing and results for suicide victims-13 States, 2004. *Morb Mortal Wkly Rep* 2006; 55:1245-8.

[37] Ohberg A, Vuori E, Ojanpera I, Lonngvist J: Alcohol and drugs in suicides. *Brit J Psychiatry* 1996; 169:75-80.

[38] Pirkola SP, Martunnen MJ, Henriksson MM, Isometsa ET, Heikkinen ME, Lonnqvist JK: Alcohol related problems among adolescent suicides in Finland. *Alcohol Alcohol* 1999; 34:320-329.

[39] Volkow ND: Drug Abuse and Mental Illness: Progress in Understanding Comorbidity. *Am J Psychiatry* 2001; 158:1181-1183.

[40] Koller G, Preuss UW, Bottlender M, Wenzel K, Soyka M: Impulsivity and aggression as predictors of suicide attempts in alcoholics. *Eur Arch Psychiatry Clin Neurosci* 2002; 252:155-60.

[41] Goldston DB: Conceptual issues in understanding the relationship between suicidal behavior and substance use during adolescence. *Drug Alcohol Depend* 2004; 76:S79-S91.

[42] Pompili M, Innamorati M, Lester D, Akiskal HS, Rihmer Z, Del Casale A, Amore M, Girardi P, Tatarelli R: Substance Abuse, Temperament and Suicide Risk: Evidence from a Case-Control Study. *J Addict Dis* 2009; 28:13-20.

[43] Cuomo C, Sarchiapone M, Di Giannantonio M, Mancini M, Roy A: Aggression, Impulsivity, Personality Traits and Childhood Trauma of Prisoners with Substance Abuse and Addiction. *Am J Drug Alcohol Abuse* 2008; 34:339-345.

[44] Murphy GE: Psychiatric Aspects of Suicidal Behavior: Substance Abuse. In *The International Handbook of Suicide and Attempted Suicide*. Edited by Hawton K and van Heerigen K. Chichester: Wiley Blackwell, 2000.

[45] Murphy GE: *Suicide in Alcoholism.* Oxford: Oxford University Press, 1992.

[46] Wilsnack SC, Wilsnack RW, Kristjanson AF, Vogeltanz-Holm ND, Windle M: Alcohol use and suicidal behavior in women: Longitudinal patterns in a U.S. national sample. *Alc Clin Exp Res* 2004: 29:S38-S47.

[47] Cottler LB, Campbell W, Krishna VAS, Williams RMC, Abdallah AB: Predictors of high rates of suicidal ideation among drug users. *J Nerv Ment Dis* 2005; 193(7):431–437.

[48] Preuss UW, Schuckit MA, Smith TL, Danko GP, Bucholz KK, Hesselbrock MN, Hesselbrock V, Kramer JR: Predictors and correlates of suicide attempts over 5 years in 1,237 Alcohol-Dependent men and women. *Am J Psychiat* 2003; 160:56-63.

[49] De Leo D, Evans R: *International suicide rates and prevention strategies*. Cambridge: Hogrefe & Huber, 2004.

[50] Sainsbury P, Jenkins JS: The accuracy of officially reported suicide statistics for purposes of epidemiological research. *J Epidemiol Community Health* 1982; 36:43-48.

[51] Hjern A, Allebeck P: Suicide in first- and second-generation immigrants in Sweden: A comparative study. *Soc Psychiatry Psychiatr Epidemiol* 2002; 37:423–429.

[52] Mohler B, Earls F: Trends in Adolescent Suicide: Misclassification Bias? *Am J Pub Health* 2001; 91:150-153.

[53] Cooper PN, Milroy CM: The coroner's system and under-reporting of suicide. *Med Sci Law* 1995; 35:319-326.

[54] Philips DP, Ruth TE: Adequacy of official statistics for scientific research and public policy. *Suicide Life Threat Behav* 1993; 23:307-319.

[55] Baume P, McTaggart P: Suicides in Australia, in *Suicide Prevention: The Global Context*. Edited by Kosky RJ, Eshkevari HS, Goldney R, Hassan R. New York: Plenum Press, 1998.
[56] Brent DA, Perper JA, Kolko D, Zelenak J: The psychological autopsy: Methodological considerations for the study of adolescent suicide. *J Am Acad Child Adolesc Psychiatry* 1998; 27:362-366.
[57] Foster T, Gillespie K, McClelland R: Mental disorders and suicide in Northern Ireland. *Brit J Psychiatry* 1997; 170:447–452.
[58] Fleischmann A: WHO Statement. World Suicide Prevention Day, 10th September 2008. Retrieved June 11, 2009 from http://www.who.int/mental_health/prevention/suicide.
[59] Sher L: Preventing Suicide. *Quarterly Journal of Medicine* 2004; 97:677-680.

In: Suicidal Behavior in Alcohol and Drug Abuse...
Editors: L. Sher, A. Vilens, pp. 255-269
ISBN: 978-1-60876-919-3

Chapter 14

EPIDEMIOLOGY OF SUICIDAL BEHAVIOR IN INDIVIDUALS WITH ALCOHOL AND/OR DRUG ABUSE

Tamás Zonda[1], Csilla Csoboth[2] and Károly Bozsonyi[3]
[1]Hungarian Association for Suicide Prevention, Budapest, Hungary; [2]Semmelweis University, Institute of Behavioral Sciences, Budapest, Hungary; [3]Pázmány Péter Catholic University, Institute of Sociology, Budapest, Hungary

ABSTRACT

The authors summarize the data derived from an extensive literature search regarding the relationship between alcoholism and suicide.

Individual-level studies, which are mainly retrospective, show the frequency and characteristics of suicides and the extent of suicidal behavior among individuals with alcohol-related disorders. The studies show a clear and strong relationship between the two aberrant behaviors. This does not prove an unambiguous causal connection but provides further evidence for the possibility of a link. It seems that Durkheim's concept regarding the connection between the two phenomena has not stood the test of time. In the last decade, the relationship between alcoholism and suicide has been studied at the population-level, including time-series analyses, which have found sharp cultural differences between alcohol-consumption and suicide (different suicide rates in the "dry" and "wet" drinking cultures). The effects of restrictive governmental alcohol policies are examined. It is difficult to judge the relationship between drug abuse and suicidal behavior because of the lack of objective data and the frequent co-morbid conditions associated with drug abuse. However, at the individual level, a strong connection between the two deviant behaviors has been demonstrated.

Introduction

Both alcohol consumption and the intention to regulate it on a social level date back several thousand years. Beginning around 2500 B.C., manuscripts report problems resulting from the over-consumption of wine. During the history of mankind, alcohol consumption has played different roles in various periods and cultures. Its most traditional purpose was to augment *celebrations or sacral events* [1]. From the 16th century, when beer or wine consumption was just about the only form of fluid intake due to widespread contamination of drinking water, alcohol became a *complement to meals*, and because of its high energy content, it often became a *substitute for meals* [2].

Suicide has also been present as long as man has lived but in the great ancient cultures (Mesopotamia, Egypt, India) its considerable social significance has not been demonstrated. Suicide became more frequent in the Greek and Roman Empires, and was judged in heated social and philosophical polemics. In early European history, specifically in the English and Norwegian codes of law, we can read about strict prohibition of alcohol and penalties for those who did consume alcoholic beverages. The Catholic Church gradually became more judgmental of suicide, until the unambiguous and still standing prohibition of suicide arose [3].

Despite early historical evidence of disapproval of excessive alcohol use, alcohol-consumption only appeared as a *social problem* in the 18th century, which can be explained not only by the very high level of consumption, but primarily by capitalism and the development of industrial societies, which demanded the maintenance of the efficiency of workforce from both employer's and employee's points of view. The formulation of alcohol as a problem is attached to Temperance Movement-type campaigns from the 1830s, which appeared both in Europe and North-America: They regarded alcohol consumption primarily as an *ethical/moral issue*, and promoted *full abstinence*.

The medicalization of alcoholism appeared in the middle of the 19th century. Jellinek was the first who formulated that "alcoholism is an illness", a concept which implies that the solution to the problem is exclusively medical [4]. The beginning of *sociological research* on the alcohol problem can be traced to the late 1930s and the early 1940s.

In recent years *the manner and the cultural embedment of drinking* has been studied and regarded as a determinant in the development of related problems [5, 6]. According to this approach, researchers and alcohol-policy should concentrate not on alcohol consumption in general, but *on dangerous consumption manners and situations* [7]. Alcoholism did not play a significant role in the interpretation of changes in suicide rates until the early 1980s. It might be explained by Durkheim's[8] view that alcoholism is not a relevant variable in studying suicide, as he found it exclusively a psychiatric and also an individual factor and not a sociological category. However, his arguments about the relationship between alcoholism and suicide are not even theoretically convincing in the mirror of thorough examination, and his data needed revision [9, 10]. Nowadays, several empirical facts – epidemiological and psychiatric –show the close connection between alcoholism and suicide. According to a relatively new summary, the frequency of alcoholism among completed suicide is 9.8 % [11]. It is also widely recognized that alcoholism rates and suicide rates vary strongly across cultures and within cultures over time [3, 12, 13, 14].

The suicide-inducing effect of alcoholism can be realized through two mechanisms. First, in the case of *acute intoxication*, the victim who has previous suicidal intentions "drinks courage", as the well-known expression says. The acute alcohol intoxication sets the personality free from its inhibitions and its obstacles socialized and learned to different degrees; the victim chooses an "easy" tragic behavior (auto- or heteroaggressivity) to end his/her life.

Second, a specific paradox complicates the judgment of alcohol-consumption: moderate alcohol-consumption can solve different anxiety conditions. However, it is already school-book data that moderate alcohol intake also positively influences the development of cardiovascular diseases, but both types of alcohol consumption can potentially lead to the development of addiction.

Another suicide-inducing mechanism of alcoholism is that *chronic alcohol-consumption leads to irreversible health damage*. Extensive and serious physical injuries (liver and pancreatic cirrhosis, cardiomyopathy, etc.) themselves can also cause suicidal intention. However, the damages to the central nervous system are even more serious: cognitive deterioration, dementia, depression, and impotence. Paranoid conditions and aggressiveness, consequences of chronic alcoholism, can both be reasons for suicidal behavior. As a result of all these, serious social tapering, backsliding, solitude, marginalization, disorganization of social relationships (family, workplace) can occur, which latter ones are perhaps the most common causes of suicidal death in chronic alcoholics. Also, the chronic alcoholic's behavior can often induce suicide of family members.

CONNECTION BETWEEN ALCOHOL CONSUMPTION AND SUICIDE

There are two main trends in detection of a connection between alcohol consumption and suicide. The first one is the empirical investigation *on an individual level*, while the other method is to study the data on an *aggregate level* (time series studies).

Empirical studies on an individual level can be divided further in to two groups: the occurrence of suicide behavior (committed and/or attempted suicide) among alcohol-using persons, and to study the occurrence of alcohol use (abuse, bring drinking) in connection with suicides. Several studies are available in the literature and in the following we will only summarize the most important findings of these studies.

Suicide among Alcoholic Individuals

Information about how often alcoholics commit suicide can be gathered from follow-up studies that report how many deaths were due to suicide in a *sample of alcoholics*, or by studying the *suicides in the general population* and to find out how many alcoholics were among them. There have been a range of efforts to review follow-up studies. Miles [15] reviewed 15 follow-up studies that report the incidence of suicide among alcoholics. He estimated that 15% of alcoholics die by committing suicide. Roy and Linnoila [16] reported data from 21 follow-up studies, all published in the year 1986, and found significant mortality by suicide in samples of alcohol abusers in treatment, ranging from 2% to 25%. During the same time period, Murphy and Wetzel [17] reviewed the epidemiological literature and emphasize that "current estimates of the lifetime risk of suicide in alcoholism (11% to 15%) are shown statistically to be untenable". They found the lifetime risk of suicide among individuals with alcohol dependence treated in out- and in-patient settings was 2.2% and 3.5% for the USA, UK and other English-speaking countries. However, one study showed that individuals with alcoholism have a 60-120 times greater suicide risk than the non-psychiatrically ill population, while others found that the risk is almost six times greater than expected [18].

A literature review [19] of the period 1991-2001 summarized associations between *acute alcohol use* and suicidal behavior and a wide range of alcohol-positive cases were found for both completed suicide (10%-69%) and suicide attempts (10% -73%). Suokas et al. [20] investigated the subgroup of suicide attempters with post-mortem evidence of long-term alcohol misuse (n=1018). At the end of the follow-up period, after 14 years, 222 (22.7%) died and of these, 85 individuals (38.5%) showed clear post-mortem evidence of long-term alcohol misuse. High rates of *attempted* suicide among persons with alcohol use disorders have also been reported [21, 22, 23, 24].

A population-based investigation [25] of a sample (22,804) of men aged 40 to 79 years was conducted in Japan. In the 7 years follow-up period, 73 participants committed suicide. There was a statistically significant positive and linear association between the amount of alcohol consumption and the risk of suicide.

There are a few studies regarding *suicides among the elderly* and alcoholism. Although suicide is a significant and persistent health problem among older adults, the computed data of geriatric suicides (aged 65-74 years) of 34 European countries and the per capita alcohol consumption has shown a positive correlation between suicide rates of old males and the per capita consumption of alcohol, but only with spirits, not for beer and wine. There was no connection between suicide and alcohol consumption in females [26].

There are a few studies which detect the suicide behaviors in Hungary among alcoholics. In a Hungarian sample of 326 suicides (aged 65 and older) 10.2% of victims were related to alcohol disorders [27]. Twenty-one percent of hospitalized alcoholics attempted suicide in their life [28]. One-third of hospitalized alcoholics have given suicide ideation answers in the T.A.T. test [29].

Alcoholism among Suicide Attempters and Completers

There are abundant studies which investigate the quantity and quality of alcohol use (abuse, heavy drinking etc.) among suicides and/or suicide attempters. We mention only a few studies from the literature to show evidence of the close relationship between alcohol use and suicide behavior on an individual level.

Table 1. Findings about alcohol-related suicides in Hungary

Source	Year	No	BAC positive victims >1.5 ‰ (%)	Percentage of alcoholics
Harsányi et al. [33]	1976	816	16.6	36.6
Zonda & Gubacsi [34]	1999	1600	28.6	46.3
Szappanos [35]	1989	799	33.0	16.1
Jegesy et al. [36]	1995	798	M:30.2 F: 13.0	45.1
Zonda [37]	1997	1490	M: 83.2 F:5.6	36.7
Gubacsi [38] (attempts)	1984	441	59.0	39.4
WHO/EURO(attempts) [39]	1990	1158	M:18.7 F:7.5	12.0
Zonda [40]	2006	100	33.0	

M: male; F: female.

Suicide attempters and completers have more severe alcoholism compared with individuals with alcoholism but without a history of suicidal behavior [30]. Alcoholism was detected in 14.6% of males and 4.2% of females who attempted suicide. The risk of further attempts was considerably greater among alcoholics [16]. Among all suicides recorded in Finland (229 victims), 43% had alcohol dependence (34% dependent, 9 % abuser) [31]. In Sweden, 56% of the suicides among men from urban areas and 27 % of the suicides among men from rural areas were found to be in connection to alcohol dependence [32]. The individual-level studies performed and published in Hungary are shown in Table 1.

Time-series, Aggregate Level Studies

In the last two decades a couple of time-series *population-level* analyses have appeared which have raised several unexplored questions regarding the trans-cultural aspects of suicide, and have served as a basis for the creation of governmental alcohol-policies in certain populations and countries. There are several theoretical reasons for expecting an aggregate level relationship between alcohol and suicide. First, the higher the aggregate consumption in a culture, the more frequently people are under the influence of alcohol, and hence the higher the risk that latent suicidal impulse may be triggered. Second, it is well-established that the higher the overall level of consumption in a culture, the larger the number of chronic abusers [5, 12]. Heavy drinking is known to increase the risk for depression and weakened social relations [41], and since depression and weak social relations increase the risk for suicide, a high per capita consumption level ought to produce more suicides.

A paper by Wasserman [42] reported that the prohibition period in the US produced a decrease in suicide rates. Another study also [43] examined whether the effects of per capita consumption on rates of suicide in subsequent years are influenced by other aggregate factors, particularly including unemployment rates, per capita income, and divorce rates. Bivariate association between alcohol consumption and suicide rates was not significant. However, when unemployment was included in the model, increases in per capita alcohol consumption were significantly related to increases in suicide overall, for men and women, and for the young (under 40 years) and middle-aged [40-59 years) but not for those over age 60. A Canadian study [44] showed that the total suicide rate in Canada increased significantly (by around 4%) as alcohol consumption increased by one liter per capita (annually), suggesting that approximately 25-30% of Canadian suicides were related to alcohol. The relationship was stronger for women than for men. Internationally, the relationship for women was somewhat weaker than in Sweden and Norway, but larger than in Finland, the USA and the Southern European countries. Norström [45] made a comparative time series analysis in the Scandinavian countries for the years between 1930 and 1980. He reported a significant effect of per capita alcohol consumption on male suicide mortality for Norway (16%) and Sweden (15%). In contrast to expectations, the alcohol effect in Finland and Denmark was not significant. That Danish situation was analyzed again by Scog [46] on data reported between 1911 and 1924. During this time the alcoholic beverage sales decreased dramatically, from about 10 liters per capita during the period between 1911 and 1915, to 2.2 liters in 1918. The number of suicides also dropped overall by 19%, and more than 50% among alcohol drinkers. They also found that a decrease of each liter of alcohol consumption (per year), the total suicide rate decreased by 2.5%. This finding was also repeated in Finnish research [47]. The results of the new analysis of the time series of 1950-91 years has shown that the suicide rate of Finnish men in age groups 15-34 years and 35-49 years is associated with per capita alcohol consumption, while no connection could be established among the elder groups. It was found that a 1-liter change in per capita/year consumption should be followed by approximately a 10% change in the suicide rate of *men aged 15-49 years.*

Another comparative time-series analysis [7] was performed on Swedish and French data and the estimated alcohol effect was markedly stronger in Sweden (13 % per liter annually) than in France 3%. The same low connection has been found in Portugal (1931-89). A study [48] showed that an increase in per capita alcohol consumption of one liter (annually) is accompanied by a simultaneous increase in the male suicide rate of 1.9%.

The first Central Eastern European time-series study of this subject [49] was performed in Hungary, a country with high rates of suicide and mortality of alcoholic liver cirrhosis. Trends in per capita alcohol consumption and the overall suicide rate in Hungary during the period 1950-1990 were detected. The trends are very highly correlated (r= 0.981). The results suggested that an increase in alcohol consumption of 1 liter annually brings about a 10% increase of suicide rate, but the authors suggested on the basis of other data that the true figure might be closer to the lower end of the confidence interval, which was 5%. Hence, changes in alcohol consumption predict changes in suicide rate in the following year. A time-series analysis [50] of annual data for the period 1950-1990 was not able to support a relationship between alcohol consumption and suicide rate in Switzerland. Another country in Central Europe with high suicide and alcohol consumption rates is Slovenia. In 1997, the annual rate of alcohol consumption was more than 14 liters per adult and the unregistered consumption was also high. Research showed that 13% of Slovenian adults are heavy drinkers. In another study [51], 74% of suicide victims were under the influence of alcohol. In 2003, the Slovenian Government has created a new alcohol policy aiming to decrease alcohol consumption. In the years between 2003 and 2005, there was a 12% reduction in registered alcohol consumption, with a 12% decrease in alcohol-related traffic accidents. The number of suicides decreased by 10% among men; the new alcohol policy led to immediate and permanent changes.

After the recent fundamental political and economic changes in the Soviet Union, the prospect of accessing the morbidity and mortality data, which were classified earlier as top secret, improved. At the height of Gorbachev's reforms, information held by the State Statistical Committee became accessible. Multiple studies were performed and the data of these studies was replicated. After a large restrictive anti-alcohol campaign was initiated in the first year of *perestroika*, there was a dramatic decrease among all alcohol-related harms [52]. A significant decline (34.5%) in the suicide rate occurred between 1984 and 1988 throughout the USSR. Regression analysis showed that suicide and alcohol consumption were positively correlated among males [53, 54]. The same efforts were seen among women in the Baltic Countries (Lithuania, Latvia, Estonia), in the three Slavic Countries (Russia, Belarus, Ukraine) and in two Central Asian Republics (Kazakhstan, Kirgizstan). Everywhere, suicide, alcohol consumption, and violent death were positively correlated. However, alcohol seems to have a lower explanatory value for female suicide compared with male suicides. Female suicide rate decreased by 19% in the whole former Soviet Union between 1984 and 1990, and varied in order of magnitude from one Republic to another [54].

The relationship between alcohol toxicity (psychoses, alcohol poisoning) also showed a close connection in Belarus in the period of 1970-2005 [55, 56]. Nemtsov [57] studied the total Russian suicide rate and alcohol consumption in the years 1965-1999, and has found an overall 12% decline of total suicides per liter of alcohol during strong anti-alcohol campaign (1985-87) (13% for male and 6% for women). His results were strengthened by a much longer time-series study in Russia [58]. In his study Nemtsov [57] has showed that changes in the number of BAC (blood-alcohol-concentration) -negative suicides were not related to changes in consumption. Another notable observation about the effect of decrease of alcohol consumption and suicide: it seems that a restrictive alcohol policy does not significantly change the suicide rate of non-alcoholics. Värnik [59] and co-workers examined the blood alcohol concentration among Estonian suicides before the time of the major Soviet anti-alcohol campaign (1981-84), during the campaign (1986-88) and after the campaign (1989-92). They studied 5054 suicide cases (76% males, 24% females). During the campaign, annual per capita alcohol consumption in Estonia fell from 10.9 to 6.6 liters. Blood alcohol levels were found in 47.9% of victims before the campaign, 35.1% of victims during the campaign, and 40.9% of victims after the campaign. During alcohol restriction, the alcohol-positive suicides decreased by 39.2% for men and 41.4% for females, but the number of suicides without blood-alcohol changed only modestly. After the campaign, the suicide rate started to rise. The rigorous alcohol restriction caused a decrease only among the BAC-positive suicides in both sexes, so the authors suggest that the major soviet natural experiment "does not demonstrate convincingly that the fall in the suicide rate was due specifically to the decrease in alcohol use as such."

An analysis [60] was made on the data of annual suicide mortality rates and per capita consumption for the post-war period from 7 Eastern European countries, which were divided into two groups, i.e., "spirits countries" ("dry-drinking") (Russia, Belarus, Poland) and "non-spirits" ("wet-drinking") countries (Hungary, Bulgaria, the former Czechoslovakia and the former German Democratic Republic). All countries showed positive alcohol effect correlation estimates. The effects in the 'spirits countries' was stronger: a 1-liter increase in per capita annual consumption was associated with an increase in overall suicide rates of 5.7-7.5 % (pooled 6.6%); among 'non-spirits' countries the effects were only 2.7-4.7 %. The estimates for males were larger, the female numbers were smaller and did not differ between the two groups. Another study [61] about alcohol and suicide in 14 European countries showed that the countries can be pooled into low-, medium-, and high-consumption countries. A stronger absolute alcohol effect for men was found only in Northern Europe; also, the suicide rates in younger age groups were more often significantly related to per capita consumption. The study stated that the population-level association between alcohol and suicide is conditioned by cultural factors, and suggests that suicide and alcohol consumption is more closely connected in "dry" cultures than in "wet" cultures.

Our study-group performed a rank-correlation of 46 European (and Middle-Asian) countries using 2009 WHO data [62] about "chronic liver diseases and cirrhosis", "suicide and self-inflicted injury", "homicide and intentional injury" (all ages per 100,000) and "pure alcohol consumption" in annual liters per capita. (Table 2 shows the results).

Hungarian Situation

We have already mentioned the analysis of trends in alcohol consumption and suicide (1950-1990) with Granger's [49] causal analysis, which showed a strong correlation between the two trends: a one year delay was observed between changes in the rates of alcohol consumption and suicide. Another study [10] analyzed the trends in deaths caused by the cirrhosis of the liver and by suicide between 1920 and 1990 in Hungary. The cross-correlation analysis of datelines was significant in the case of a 4-year retardation (R^2= 0.68; $p< 0.05$). Consequently, the correlation between society's inclination to alcohol consumption and suicide is very strong.

The present authors studied the possible connection between suicide rates and per capita alcohol consumption in the time interval of 1960-2000 [under review for publication]. The interpretation of the relation is the following: if the per capita alcohol consumption increases by one liter in the base-line year, the male suicide rates will prospectively increase by 3 per 100,000 compared to the previous year. As shown in Figure 1, the lines of alcohol consumption and of suicides run parallel till 2000, and thereafter the alcohol consumption *began to increase* again, while the decrease in the suicide rates (which began in 1988) continued. (Figure 1).

Table 2. Rank-correlations of suicide, homicide, chronic liver disease and cirrhosis (per 100.000) and absolute alcohol consumption per capita/year in 47 European countries

Pearson correlation	**Alcohol**	**Liver**	**Suicide**	**Homicide**
Alcohol	1	- 0.124	**0.315***	- 0.20
Liver	-0.214	1	0.265	**0.538****
Suicide	0.315*	0.265	1	**0.570****
Spearman correlation				
Alcohol	1.000	-0.053	**0.356***	**-0.428****
Liver	-0.053	1.000	**0.320***	**0.537****
Suicide	0.356*	0.320*	1.000	0.278

* Correlation is significant at the 0.05 level (2-tailed).

** Correlation is significant at the 0.01 level (2-tailed).

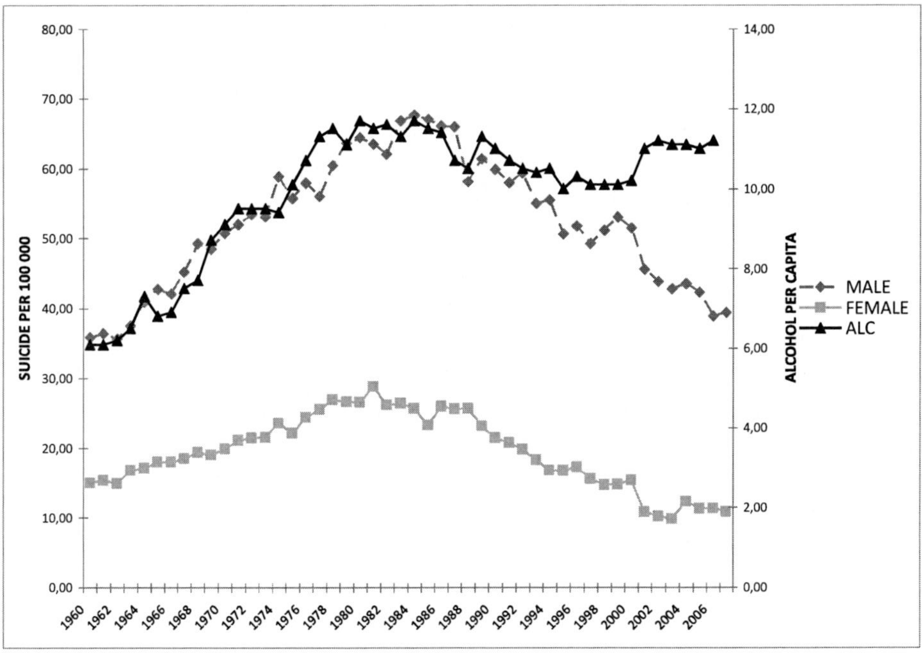

Figure 1. Suicide rate by gender and alcohol consumption 1960-2007

Suicidal Behavior among Youth

Discussion of the most serious problem, which is one of the greatest health and social problems in all parts of the world, has been kept for the end of this chapter, namely the issue of the increase in numbers of self-damaging and deviant behaviors among the young. Suicide is the second or third leading cause of death for teenagers between the ages of 15 and 24 years [63].

Numerous reports [64, 65] suggest that early use of *inhalants* increases the likelihood of progression to more severe drug-taking behaviors. In a study of youth on probation [66], inhalant users reported significantly more lifetime thoughts of suicide and suicide attempts. Kirmayer [67] and colleagues found that youth who had used solvents at some time in their past were more likely to attempt suicide. There are few publications [68] on the association between *marijuana* use and suicide ideation/attempts and it seems that marijuana use is not an important risk factor for suicidal thoughts and behaviors. Kung [69] found, after adjusting for socio-demographic factors, that marijuana was associated with suicide deaths in the 1993 National Mortality Followback Survey (NMFS) that included youth and young adults.

A study [70] investigated the relationship between *cannabis* use on depression, suicidal ideation, and suicide attempts in a cohort of young Norwegians. 2033 individuals were followed up over a 13-year period, from their teens to their late twenties. The finding suggests that exposure to cannabis by itself does not lead to depression but that it may be associated with later suicidal thoughts and attempts.

Another study [71] examined the prevalence and correlations of self-medication of anxiety disorders with alcohol and drugs in a nationally representative sample (N = 5877). Frequencies of self-medication ranged from 7.9% to 35.6%. Self-medication behavior remained significantly associated with an increased likelihood of suicidal ideation as well as suicide attempts.

387 heroin users were interviewed about suicide attempts at baseline, and after 1, 2, and 3 years. Across the follow-up period, 11.6% attempted suicide. Independent predictors of a suicide attempt during the follow-up period were lifetime suicide history, baseline suicidal ideation, social isolation, and extent of baseline multi-drug use [72].

In Hungary, we have not found definitive data showing a connection between suicide behavior and illicit drug use or substance dependence. Yearly there are approximately 100-120 deaths among legal and illegal drug users in Hungary, but the precise number of suicides is not possible to assess exactly.

Finally, we cite in detail the summary of the large European "Child and Adolescent Self harm in Europe" (CASE) study [73], which allows us to explore self-reported suicidal behavior among adolescents more exactly. In the representative school-based community study an anonymous, self-reported questionnaire was conducted with 4408 (males: 2388, females: 2020) 15 and 16 year-old pupils. Out of the 4408 adolescents, 7.8% (males: 4.6%, females: 11.6%) reported former suicide attempt, 1.6% of the boys and 3.6% of the girls reported more than one suicide attempts. According to the statistical analysis the suicidal group differs greatly from the non-suicidal one. Suicidal adolescents were more likely to use alcohol, drugs or nicotine than their non-suicidal peers. Drug abuse was four times more common among suicidal boys, and five times more common among suicidal girls than in the non-suicidal group. 30% of the boys and 13% of the girls used more than one kind of drug. The use of ecstasy, sedatives, and hypnotic drugs showed the most spectacular difference between suicidal and non-suicidal teenagers in both genders. Suicidal behavior frequently appeared with addictive problems.

In addition we note the following discouraging observation [21]: "Adolescent suicide is a major public health problem. In the general population, about 2.000 adolescents in the United States die by suicide each year. The suicide rate has more than doubled during the period from 1956 to 1993, and the increasing suicide rate has been blamed on the increase of adolescent alcohol abuse. These words not only apply to the USA; the problem is growing around the world. Future studies of psychological, sociological, and neurobiological mechanisms of suicidality in adolescents with alcohol and/or substance abuse are merited".

Conclusion

The *epidemiological* study of the connection between alcohol consumption and suicide has many pitfalls. The biggest problem is how to measure the alcohol consumption of a given country or population. Per capita alcohol consumption itself is an estimated value, which is first of all based on production and selling statistics, and is calculated on the basis of *official data sources*. These data cannot give information about the so-called *"not-registered alcohol consumption"*. The official alcohol sales statistics do not include some important data. To emphasize this gap in data, we have picked out some examples from the WHO's publication of 1999 [74]. According to this report, not-registered alcohol consumption increases the per capita alcohol consumption by 20% in Denmark, 25% in Finland, one-third in Norway, 7,5 liters per capita annually in Russia and 7-8 liters per capita annually in Slovenia. According to a survey [75] made in the ex-member states of the former USSR, for example in the Moldavian Republic, not-registered per capita annual alcohol consumption exceeds the official data of nearly 12 liters by another 12 liters. The associations calculated from aggregated data depend strongly on the culture and demographic situations of specific countries (age group, sex, region, minority status, unemployment, etc.), therefore it is justified to manage the results of aggregate level studies (time-series investigations) with caution.

Sociologists often assert that the co-incidence of the two phenomena proves neither the directness nor the exclusiveness of the connection between them. The opinion is also justified that the two deviances can be responses to the same causes, and it depends on the culture and personality of an individual which determines what form of self-harm one chooses and in which direction it will be drifted.

On the basis of the unanimous opinions of the great number of *individual-level studies,* we ourselves accept unambiguously that alcoholism is associated with a high risk for suicidal behavior and approximately 40% of alcohol-related persons attempt suicide at some time and around 7% of them end their lives by committing suicide.

The epidemiological study of legal and illegal drug users and suicide stands on an even more unstable ground, because – apart from a very few exceptions – it cannot be verified whether the death-causing overdose was accidental or intentional (voluntary), therefore all studies regarding this issue should be handled with reservations. It is a fact that the number of suicide attempts is higher among drug users, but because of high co-morbidity there are scarcely any possibilities for separated study.

Finally, we make a skeptical comment. Despite a sea of studies, data, connections, and theories, the real reasons for suicide remain concealed from us. Even today, we cannot answer the great question: from the 100 people who suffer from *the same* sorrow, pain, loss, crises, why do only 3 or 8 choose suicide while the others struggle further? Why, for example, do 3 people commit suicide in Southern Europe and why 8 in the Eastern part of Europe? Why does one person react to an unbearable situation with the quick and final way of suicide and why do others choose different forms of deviance? There are clear *trends*, which we can explore on the basis of the large numbers of suicides; we know several psychological working methods, suicidal typologies, the complicated interaction of biogenic amines in the genotype; but even today we know very little about the complicated and specific road to suicide of the individual, the phenotype. We must cite the great psychiatrist-philosopher, Karl Jaspers's hardly deniable thought again: "The real origin and cause of suicide remains the incommunicable secret of the individual."

REFERENCES

[1] Kelemen G: Az alkoholprobléma kezeléstörténetének rövid vázlata in: Kelemen G. *Az addikciók széles spektruma* OAI Budapest 1994. p: 114-157.

[2] Mäkela, P. The Use of Alcohol and Their Cultural Regulation. *Acta Sociologica* 1983; (26), 1:21-31.

[3] Zonda T: A*z öngyilkosság kultúrtörténete* (Cultural history of suicide) Budapest, 1991 Végeken Alapítvány Pgs.233.

[4] Fillmore KM: *Alcohol Problems from a Sociological Perspective Alcoholism: Origins and Outcome.* Ed: Robert M., Rose and James Barett. Raven Press Ltd New York 1988.

[5] Skog OJ: The collectivity of drinking cultures A theory of the distribution of alcohol consumption. *Brit J Addict.* 1985; 80:83-99.

[6] Mäkela P, Mustonen H: Harm as a function of the frequency of drinking different amounts of alcohol: further views on the preventive paradox. *29th Annual alcohol Epidemiology Symposium of the Bruun Society* June 2003. Krakow.

[7] Norström T: Alcohol and suicide: a comparative analysis of France and Sweden. *Addiction* 1995; 90:1463-9.)

[8] Durkheim E: Suicide. *A study in sociology.* 1992/1897. London, Routlegde.

[9] Skog OJ: Alcohol and suicide - Durkheim revisited. *Acta Sociologica* 1991;34:193-206.

[10] Paksi B, Bozsonyi K, Kó J: Az alkoholfogyasztás és az öngyilkosság összefüggésének vizsgálata.(in Hungarian) (Analysis of the relation between alcohol consumption and suicide. *Szenvedélybetegségek* 1995; III.6:404-410.

[11] Bertolote JM, Fleischmann A, De Leo D, Wasserman D. Psychiatric diagnoses and suicide: revisiting the evidence. *Crisis,* 2004; 25/4: 147-155.

[12] Popham RE: *Indirect methods of alcoholism prevalence estimation: A critical evaluation, in Alcohol and Alcoholism* Edited by Popham RE, Toronto, University of Toronto Press 1970.

[13] Zonda T: *Öngyilkos nép-e a Magyar?* (Are Hungarians a suicide nation?) Budapest, 1995 Végeken Alapítvány. Pgs. 26o.

[14] Rossow I. Alcohol and suicide - beyond the link at the individual level. *Addiction.Editoral.* 1996; 91(10):1413-1416.

[15] Miles CP: Conditions predisposing to suicide: a review. *J Nerv Ment Dis* 1979; 164:231-46.

[16] Roy A, Linnoila M: Alcoholism and suicide. *Suic Life Threat Behav* 1986; 16:244-273.

[17] Murphy G, Wetzel RD: The lifetime risk of suicide in alcoholism. *Arch Gen Psychiatry* 1990, 47:383-392.

[18] Harris C, Barraclough B: Suicides as an outcome for mental disorders. *Brit J Psychiat* 1997; 170: 205-228.

[19] Cherpitel CJ, Borges GL, Wilcox HC: Acute alcohol use and suicidal behaviour: a review of the literature. *Alcohol Clin Exp Res* 2004 May; 28(5 Suppl): 18S-28S.

[20] Suokas J, Suominen K, Lönquist J: Chronic alcohol problems among suicide attempters - post-mortem findings of a 14-year follow-up. *Nord J Psychiatry* 2005;59(1):45-50.

[21] Sher L, Zalsman G: Alcohol and adolescent suicide. *Int J Adolesc Med Health.* 2005 Jul-Sep; 17(3): 197-203.

[22] Weissman MM, Myers JK, Harding PS: Prevalence and psychiatric heterogeneity of alcoholism in a United States urban community. *J Stud Alcohol* 1980; 41: 672-681.

[23] Suominen K, Isometsa E, Haukka J, Lonnquist J: Substance use and male gender as risk factors for deaths and suicide - a 5-year follow-up study after deliberate self- harm. *Soc Psychiatry Psychiatr Epidemiol* 2004 Sep; 39(9):720-4.

[24] Roy A, Janal MN: Risk factors for suicide attempts among alcohol dependent patients *Arch Suicide Res* 2007; 11(2):211-7.

[25] Nakaya N, Kikuchi N, Shimazu T, Ohmori k, Kakizaki M, Sone T, Awata S, Kuiyama S, Tsuji I: Alcohol consumption and suicide mortality among Japanese men: the Ohsaki Study. *Alcohol* 2007; Nov; 41(7): 513-510.

[26] Sher L: Relation between rates of geriatric suicide and consumption of alcohol beverages in European countries. *Scientific World Journal* 2006 Mar 27; 6: 383-7.

[27] Zonda T: Az idősek öngyilkossági jellemzői egy megye 25 éves eseményeinek elemzése alapján (l97o-1994) *LAM* 1999;2: 136-141 (Suicide among old people in a Hungarian county).

[28] Elekes Zs: The relationship between the regional differences of alcoholism and suicide. *Research Review* 1989;1:21-26 Budapest Edited: Münnich I, Kolozsi B.

[29] Andorka R, Buda B, Cseh-Szombathy L, Hegedűs I, Kiss J, Simon Gy: Az alkoholizmus kifejlődésének tényezői. 1972. *Budapest Central Statistical Bureau pg.* 202-203.

[30] Sher L: Alcoholism and suicidal behavior: a clinical overview. *Acta Psychiatr Scand* 2006; 113:13-22.

[31] Henriksson MM, Aro HM, Marttunen MJ, Heikkinen ME, Isometsä ET, Kimmo IK, Lönnquist JK. Mental disorders and comorbidity in suicide. *Am J Psychiatry* 1993; 150: 935-9406.

[32] Beskow J. Suicide and mental disorder is Swedish men. *Acta Psychiatr Scand* 1989; Suppl. 277:1-138.

[33] Harsányi L, Jobb S, Miltényi K, Nemskéri J, Szuchovszky Gy: Budapesti öngyilkosok vizsgálata 1972. (Suicides in Budapest 1972) *Scientific Research Institue Budapest,* 1976.

[34] Zonda T, Gubacsi L: Bács-Kiskun és Nógrád 199o-1994 között történt öngyilkossági eseményeinek elemzése. *LAM* 1999; 9/10: 800-804.

[35] Szappanos M: Befejezett öngyilkosságok Bács-Kiskun megye északi részén 1989. *(Committed suicides in county Bács-Kiskun* 1979-83).

[36] Jegesy A, Harsányi L, Angyal M: Alkoholism és öngyilkosság. (Alcoholism and suicide in county Baranya) *Szenvedélybetegségek* 1995; II.2:91-96.

[37] Zonda, T.1999): Suicide in Nógrád County, *Hungary Crisis* 1999; 2o:2.64-70.

[38] Gubacsi L: Öngyilkossági kísérletek Bács-Kiskun megyében Kecskemét 1984. (*Suicide attempts in county Bács-Kiskun)*

[39] Jessen G., Jensen BF., Arensman E., Bille-Brahe U., Crepet P, De Leo, D., Hawton K., Harong C., Hjelmeland H., Michel K., Ostamo A., Salander- Renberg, E., Schmidtke A., Temesvary B., Wasserman, D. Attempted suicide and major public holidays in Europe: findings from the WHO/EURO Multicentre Study on Parasuicide. *Acta Psych Scand* 1999; 99(6): 397-8.

[40] Zonda T . One-hundred Cases of Suicide in Budapest (A case-controlled psychological autopsy Study) *Crisis* 2006; 27(3): 125-129.

[41] Murphy,G.: *Suicide and Alcoholism* Oxford University Press 1992.

[42] Wasserman JM: The effects of war and alcohol consumption patterns on suicide: United States 1910-1933. *Social Forces,* 1989; 68: 513-530.

[43] Cases F, Harford T: Time series analysis of alcohol consumption and suicide mortality in United States, 1934-1987. *J. Stud Alcohol 1*998 Jul; 59(!):455-61.

[44] Ramstedt M. Alcohol and suicide at the population level -the Canadian experience *Drug and Alcohol Review,* 2005, 24: 203-208

[45] Norström T: Alcohol and suicide in Scandinavia. *British J of Addiction;* 1988; 83:553-559.

[46] Skog OJ: Alcohol and suicide in Denmark 1911-24 - experiences from a natural experiment. *Addiction* 1993; 88, 1189-1193).

[47] Mäkelä P. Alcohol consumption and suicide mortality by age among Finnish men, 1950-1991. *Addiction,* 1996; 91(1) 101-112.

[48] Skog, O-J, Teixeira Z., Barrias,J., Moreira,R.: Alcohol and suicide - the Portuguese experience. *Addiction* 1995; 90: 1053-1061.

[49] Skog OJ, Elekes Zs: Alcohol and the 1950-90 suicide trend - is there a causal connection. *Acta Sociologica* 1993; 36;33-46.

[50] Gmel G, Rehm J, Ghazinouri A: Alcohol and suicide in Switzerland - an aggregate-level analysis. *Drug Alcohol Rev* 1998; 17(1): 27-37.

[51] Pridemore WA, Snowden AJ. Reduction in suicide mortality following a new national alcohol policy in Slovenia: an interrupted time-series analysis. *Am J of Pub Health* 2008;99, 5: 915-920.

[52] Nemtsov A. Alcohol-related harm and alcohol consumption in Moscow before, during and after a major anti-alcohol campaign. *Addiction,* 1998; 93(10): 1501-1510.

[53] Wasserman D, Värnik A, Eklund G: Male suicides and alcohol consumption in the former USSR. *Acta Psych Scand* 1994; 89:306-313).

[54] Wasserman D, Värnik A, Eklund G: Female suicides and alcohol consumption during *perestroika* in the former USSR in: Värnik, A: Suicide in the Baltic countries and in the former republics of the USSR. *Stockholm Gotab*1997. pg.157-165.

[55] Razvodovszky YE: Suicide and alcohol psychoses in Belarus 1970-2005. *Crisis;* 2007.28(2):61-66.

[56] Razvodovsky YE: Suicide and alcohol poisoning in Belarus between 1970 and 2005. *Addiciones.* 2007; 19(3): 297-303.

[57] Nemtsov A. Suicides and alcohol consumption in Russia, 1965-1999. *Drug and alcohol dependence.* 2003; 71: 161-168.

[58] Pridemore WA, Chamlin MB: A time series analysis of the effects of heavy drinking on homicide and suicide rates in Russia 1956-2002- *Addiction. 2006.*101: 1719-1729

[59] Värnik A, Kõlves A,Väli M, Tooding LM, Wasserman D: Do alcohol restrictions reduce suicide mortality? *Addiction 2007;* 102: 251-6.

[60] Landberg J: Alcohol and suicide in Eastern Europe. *Drug and Alcohol Review 2008.*July; 27:361-373.

[61] Ramstedt M. Alcohol and suicide in 14 European countries. *Addiction. 2001;* 96 (Suppelment 1) S59-S75.

[62] WHO (http://data.euro.who.int/alcohol/Default.aspx?TabID=4936)

[63] Galaif ER, Sussman S, Newcomb MD, Locke TF: Suicidality, depression, and alcohol use among adolescents: a review of empirical findings. *Int J Adolesc Med Health.* 2007 Jan-Mar; 19(1): 27-35.

[64] Schulz CG, Chilcoat HD, Anthony JC: The association between sniffing inhalants and injections. *Compr Psychiat* 1994;35(2):99-105.

[65] Compton WM, Cottler LB, Dinwiddie SH, Spitznagel EL, Mager DE, Asmus G: *Inhalants and Predictors American Journal on Addiction 1994;* 3: 263-72.

[66] Freedenthal S, Michael GV, Jenson JM, Howard MO: Inhalant use and suicidality among incarcerated youth. *Drug Alcohol Depend 2007* Sep 6; 90(1): 81-88.

[67] Kirmayer LJ, Malus M, Boothroyd LJ: Suicide attempts among Inuit youth: a community suicide and risk factors. *Acta Psychatr Scand 1996;* 96(1): 8-17.

[68] Wilcox HC: Epidemiological evidence on the link between drug use and suicidal behaviors among adolescents. *Can Child Adolesc Psychiatr Rev.* 2004 May; 13(2):27-30.

[69] Kung HC, Pearson JL, Liu X: Risk factors for male and female suicide decedents ages 15-64 States. Results from the 1993 National Mortality Followback Survey. *Soc Psychiatry 2003* Aug; 38(8): 419-26.

[70] Pedersen W: Does cannabis use lead to depression and suicidal behavior? A population-based longitudinal study. *Acta Psychiatr Scand 2009 May*; 119(5):411.

[71] Bolton J, Cox B, Clara I, Sareen J: Use of alcohol and drugs self-mediate anxiety disorders in a nationally representative simple. *J Nerv Ment Dis 2006* Nov;194(11): 818-25.

[72] Darke S, Ross J, Williamson A, Mills KL, Havard A, Teesson M**:** Patterns and correlates of attempted suicide by heroin users over a 3-yar-period: findings from the Australian treatment outcome study. *Drug Alcohol Depend.* 2007 Mar 16:87(2-3): 146-152.

[73] Vörös V, Fekete S, Hewitt A, Osváth P. [Suicidal behavior in adolescents--psychopathology and addictive comorbidity] *Neuropsychopharmacol Hung.* 2005 Jun; 7 (2):66-71.

[74] Globals Status Report on Alcohol (1999). *Substance Abuse Department, Social Change and Mental health*, WHO.

[75] Pomerleau J, McKee M, Rose R, Haerpfer ChW, Rotman D, Tumanov S: Drinking in the Commonwealth of independent states - evidence from eight countries *Addiction, 2005;*100:1647-1668.

[76] Jaspers K: *Einführung in die Philosophie.* R.Pieper and Co.Verlag, München 1953.

In: Suicidal Behavior in Alcohol and Drug Abuse... ISBN: 978-1-60876-919-3
Editors: L. Sher, A. Vilens, pp. 271-284

Chapter 15

SUBSTANCE USE DISORDERS AND RISK OF COMPLETED SUICIDE

Barbara Schneider
Johann Wolfgang Goethe-University, Frankfurt am Main, Germany

ABSTRACT

Substance use disorders are among the most frequent psychiatric disorders found in suicides. In psychological autopsy studies between 19 % and 63 % of all suicides suffered from substance use disorders, mostly from alcohol use disorders. Suicide risk is highly increased in substance use disorders, particularly in alcohol use disorders, and in co-morbid alcoholism and depression. Alcohol use disorders were identified as risk factors for suicide in controlled psychological autopsy studies and in cohort studies. So far, some risk factors for suicide have been identified in alcoholism. Opioid use disorders and mixed drug use were also associated with highly increased suicide risk. Nevertheless, various questions about the relationship between substance use disorders and suicide remain open, which implicate the directions to future research.

INTRODUCTION

Suicide is an enormous problem in public health. Up to 100 % [1] of all suicides are associated with mental disorders, mostly with mood disorders and schizophrenia, but also with substance use disorders, in particular alcohol use disorders [2]. The treatment of these three disorders most frequently found in association with suicide, would reduce suicide rates by 20.5% from 15.1 per 100,000 to 12 per 100,000 [3]. Suicide is one important cause for premature mortality in alcohol, tobacco, and illegal drug use. Use of alcohol, tobacco, and illegal drugs is very common: In the U.S., 12-month prevalence of DSM-IV alcohol use disorder in males was 12.4 %, while only 4.9 % of females met DSM-IV criteria for alcohol use disorder; 1.2 % of all women and 2.8 % of all men fulfilled criteria for any drug use disorder; 14.1 % of men had DSM-IV nicotine dependence and 11.5 % of women [4].

Reviews of cohort studies [5, 6] and psychological autopsy studies [7] have shown that substance use disorders are strongly associated with suicide. However, results of cohort studies are limited: Cohorts were usually based on clinically treated (i.e. more severe ill) samples; this fact could inflate risk estimates. Sample sizes of psychological autopsy studies are often limited; therefore, they only provide information about the associations of the broad category of all substance-related disorders and suicide and of alcohol use disorders and suicide. Moreover, controlled psychological autopsy studies and cohort studies have several general methodological limitations, each, which have already been comprehensively reported [6, 8].

The present article gives an up-to-date overview of cohort studies and psychological autopsy studies regarding substance use disorders and suicide. Cohort studies and (controlled) psychological autopsy studies, which were published in English language, were checked for presenting associations between substance use disorders and suicide. These results are presented in the following review. Furthermore, some detailed information about factors associated with suicide risk in specific substance use disorders is given.

Substance Use Disorders in General

In psychological autopsy studies, which were carried out mostly in Northern Europe and in the U.S., a high proportion of suicides suffered from substance-related disorders, however with a wide range of percentages in the different studies (see Table 1). Evidence for an association of suicide with substance use disorders and individual substance use disorders is based upon retrospective and prospective cohort studies and controlled postmortem psychological autopsy studies. In controlled psychological autopsy studies, substance use disorders were associated with an increased suicide risk (see Table 1; [OR {odds ratio} = 3.3 {Ref. No. 18}; OR = 7.0 {Ref. No. 16}]), in younger and in older age groups (Table 1). Dependence from any substance was associated with highly increased suicide risk (OR = 3.6 [37]; OR = 8.5 [18]).

In psychological autopsy studies, about one third of all male and about 15 % of all female suicides had substance use disorders – with wide ranges of percentages [9, 10, 15, 16, 18, 21 – 23, 26, 27, 29, 38 – 40]. The percentage of suicides with substance use disorders was higher in younger than in elderly suicides (Table 1); even within cohorts rates of substance use disorders were lower in elderly than in middle aged or young suicides [14, 23, 40 – 42]. In adolescents and young adults, the proportion of suicides who suffered from substance use disorders increased with increasing age [27]. Only one controlled psychological autopsy study assessed the association of age and suicide risk in substance use disorders: Substance use disorders were associated with higher increased risk in middle-aged than in elderly suicides [42].

Table 1. Substance use disorders in psychological autopsy studies (1 reference per study)

Author(s)	No. of suicides	Country	Age group	S vs. C
Robins et al. 1959# [9]	134	USA	-	28 %
Barraclough et al. 1974 [10]	100	UK	-	19 %
Chynoweth et al. 1980 [11]	135	Australia	-	34 %
Rich et al. 1986 [12]	283	USA	-	51 %
Duberstein et al. 1994 [13]	52	USA	-	19 %.
Conwell et al. 1996 [14]	141	USA	-	63 %
Cheng 1995 [15]	116	Taiwan	-	45 % vs. 25 %
Foster et al. 1999 [16]	117	UK	-	44 % vs. 13 %*
Vijayakumar and Rajkumar 1999 [17]	100	India	-	36 % vs. 8 %*
Schneider et al. 2006 [18]	163	Germany	-	41 % vs. 17 %*
Cavanagh et al. 1999 [19] ‡	45	UK	-	31 % vs. 25 %
Conner et al. 2003b [20]	193	New Zealand	-	36% vs. 6%
Beskow 1979 [21, only men]	271	Sweden	-	37 %
Asgard 1990 [22, only women]	104	Sweden	-	12 %
Henriksson et al. 1993 [23] †	229	Finland		58 %
Marttunen et al. 1991 [24]	53	Finland	13 – 19	26 %
Runeson 1989 [25]	58	Sweden	15 – 29	47 %
Lesage et al. 1994 [26, only men]	75	Canada	18 – 35	57 % vs. 16 %
Shaffer et al. 1996 [27]	119	USA	< 20	35 % vs. 5 %*
Shafii et al. 1988 [28]	21	USA	11 – 19	62 %vs. 29 %*
Brent et al. 1999 [29]	140	USA	13 – 19	66 % vs. 4 %*
Brent et al. 1996 [30]	58	USA	13 – 20	36 % vs. 6 %*
Appleby et al. 1999 [31]	84	UK	< 35	57 % vs. 11 %*
Brent et al. 1988 [32]	27	USA	≤ 19	37 % vs. 18 %
Houston et al. 2001 [33]	22	UK	15 – 24	9 % vs. 41 %
Conwell et al. 1991[34]	18	USA	≥ 50	44 %
Harwood et al. 2001 [35]	100	UK	≥ 60	4 % vs. 0 %
Waern et al. 2002 [36]	85	Sweden	≥ 65	27 % vs. 1 %*

- all age groups or no control group or no information.
*: "statistical significant difference" between suicides and controls according to the authors ($p < 0{,}05$).
#: reanalysis by Robins 1981.
S: suicides.
C: controls.
† randomized group.
‡ matched for psychiatric disorders.

Bukstein et al. [43] revealed risk factors for suicide among adolescent substance abusers in a controlled psychological autopsy study: Major Depression, current substance use, alcohol abuse, family history of substance use and affective disorder, particularly of Major Depression, conflicts with the law, and ownership of a weapon.

Table 2. Psychological autopsy studies: Suicide and alcoholism (1 reference per study)

Author(s)	No. of suicides	Age group/ **Comments	Alcohol abuse or alcohol dependence S vs. C
Barraclough et al. 1974 [10]	100	-	15 %
Arato et al. 1988 [39]	200	-	20 %
Robins et al. 1959# [9]	134	-	25 %
Dorpat and Ripley 1960 [5]	114	-	27 %
Conwell et al. 1996 [14]	141	-	56 %
Chynoweth et al. 1980 [11]	135	-	22 % (dependence)
Cheng 1995 [15]	116	-	17 % vs. 17 % (abuse); 28 % vs. 8 % (dependence)*
Foster et al. 1999 [16]	117	-	43 % vs. 11 %*
Vijayakumar and Rajkumar 1999 [17]	100	-	34 % vs. 8 %*
Schneider et al. 2006 [18]	163	-	22% vs. 7% * (15% vs. 2%, dependence)
Kõlves et al. 2006 [40]	427	-	51% vs. 14% (dependence); 10% vs. 7% (abuse)
Gururaj et al. 2004 [50]	269	-	35% vs. 9%
Zhang et al. 2004 [51]	66	-	15 % vs. 6 % (abuse)
Conner et al. 2003b [20]	193	-	20% vs. 5% (dependence)
Beskow 1979 [21]	271	Only men	31 %
Asgard 1990 [22]	104	Only women	7 %
Henriksson et al. 1993 [23]	229	Randomized sample	53 %
Lesage et al. 1994 [26]	75	Only men (18 – 35)	24 % vs. 5 % (dependence)*
Brent et al. 1996 [30]	58	13 – 20	33 % vs. 6 %*
Runeson 1989 [25]	58	15 – 29	31 %
Chiu et al. 2004 [52]	70	≥ 60	2.9 % vs. 0 % (dependence)
Waern 2003 [53]	85	≥ 65	35 % vs. 2 %*(men); 18 % vs.1 %* (women)

-: all age groups or no control group or no information.

*: "statistical significant difference" between suicides and controls according to the authors ($p < 0,05$).

#: reanalysis by Robins 1981.

C: population-based controls.

In the National Suicide Prevention Project in Finland, female suicide victims with dependence from psychoactive substances were significantly more often sexually misused, had more often dependence from prescribed medication and previous suicide attempts than male suicides [44]. Furthermore, psychoactive substance dependent female suicides were significantly younger and more likely to be alcohol-intoxicated at the time of death and used less violent methods than nondependent female suicides [45].

ALCOHOL USE DISORDERS

According to a meta-analysis of mortality studies, the lifetime risk for suicide is about 8% in alcohol dependence. Contrary to other psychiatric disorders, suicide risk of alcoholism remained constantly elevated over lifetime [46].

Alcohol use disorders were associated with a highly increased suicide risk as shown by meta-analyses of follow-up studies [5, 6, 47] and the large Danish Psychiatric Case Register study with a follow-up up to 20 years [48]. In their meta-analyses with a follow-up up to 30 years, which include a population of 45,000 people (90 % men) in 32 studies in eleven countries (Europe, Northern America, Japan), Harris & Barraclough [5, 47] found an about six times increased suicide risk in alcohol abuse and dependence (DSM-III-R) compared to the general population. The majority of studies showed an over-mortality by suicide in alcoholism between 5 and 10 in men and about 20 in women [5]. For alcohol use disorders, the mortality risk for suicide was about five times that expected for men, and 17 to 18 times that expected for women [6, 47]. A recent large population-based Danish cohort study has shown that individuals with alcohol use disorders were at significantly increased risk of committing suicide, with a crude hazard ratio (HR) of 7.98 compared to individuals without alcohol use disorders, with lower risk after adjustment for all psychiatric disorders (HR = 3.23 [49]). In the stratified sub-sample of individuals without psychiatric disorders, the risk of completed suicide was 9.69 among individuals with alcohol use disorder [49]. In the Danish Psychiatric Case Register, standardized mortality ratios (SMR) were raised for alcoholism (ICD-8) in men (SMR = 10.64) and in women (SMR = 15.86 [48]).

Table 3. Controlled psychological autopsy studies: Risk for suicide in alcohol use disorders

Author(s)	OR
Cheng 1995 [15]	abuse: 1.6; dependence: 5.5
Foster et al. 1999 [16]	8.4
Schneider et al. 2006 [18]	3.7 [dependence: 8.5]
Kõlves et al. 2006 [40]	dependence: 11.6; abuse: 6.8
Lesage et al. 1994 [26]	5.6
Waern 2003 [53]	18.4 (men); 9.5 (women)

In psychological autopsy studies, comprising all age groups and both genders, between 15% and 61% of all suicides suffered from alcohol use disorders (Table 2). In case-control studies using psychological autopsy method, alcohol-related disorders were repeatedly identified as risk factors for suicide, in spite of differences in diagnostic methodology, age groups, and proportion of males [15, 16, 18, 26, 40, 50, 53; Table 2]. Suicide risk was elevated for alcohol abuse and particularly highly elevated for alcohol dependence with an up to eleven-fold increased suicide risk (Table 3). Suicide risk associated with alcohol use disorders was particularly high in middle age [40, 42]. A Norwegian follow-up study found a higher relative risk for suicide in male alcohol abusers older than 40 years compared to younger ages [54].

Risk Factors for Suicide in Alcoholism

Although it has been established that alcoholism raises the risk for completed suicide, the knowledge about risk factors for suicide in alcoholism is limited. In controlled studies [18, 20, 55] several sub-acute and chronic risk factors for suicide in alcoholism were identified: Recent heavy drinking, talk/threat of suicide, little social support, major depressive disorder or mood disorders, being unemployed, living alone, being older, male, partner-relationship difficulties and other interpersonal life events, substance dependence, smoking more than 20 cigarettes per day, and low education. Co-morbid mood disorders obviously highly increased suicide risk [18, 20]. The association of alcohol dependence and suicide was amplified with increased age between 20 and 50 years; however, neither mood disorder nor gender moderated the relationship between alcohol dependence and suicide [56]. White male alcoholics who committed suicide had more of those risk factors than the living controls [55]. In inpatients with alcohol use disorders, in particular personality disorders and depressive diagnoses were associated with increased suicide risk [57]. Interestingly, violent behavior in the past year with alcohol misuse was less associated with suicide than violent behavior without alcohol use (suicides compared to accident victims; [58]).

Furthermore, some clues for difference between suicides with alcoholism and suicides without alcoholism were found in psychological autopsy studies: In the National Suicide Prevention Project in Finland 1987 [59], alcohol misusers were younger, more often male, divorced or separated, had more often worked, but were recently unemployed, had more often recent adverse life events, were far more likely to be alcohol-intoxicated at the time of suicide, and tended to die from drug overdose. Several characteristics of these predominantly male alcohol misusers indicated better earlier lifetime psychosocial adjustment compared to the non-misusers, but more adverse life events close to suicide [59]. The tendency of employed alcohol misusers to commit suicide during weekends has been partly explained by the direct effect of alcohol intoxication [60]. Compared to non-alcoholic depressive suicides, suicides with alcoholism had more often interpersonal loss/conflict, male sex, unemployment, lack of recent somatic illness, and financial trouble during the last three months [61]. Adolescent suicides with alcohol use disorders or diagnostically sub-threshold alcohol misuse differed from other adolescent suicides in characteristics like more co-morbid psychiatric disorders, antisocial behavior, disturbed family backgrounds, life events, and severe psychosocial impairment [62]. Compared to depressed 13- to 19-year old suicides, interpersonal separations, difficulties regarding discipline or the law and unstable earlier family history, and weakened parental support during the previous year were common recent stressors among the alcohol abuse victims of the same age [63].

Suicides over age 65, who suffered from alcoholism, used significantly more often a non-violent suicide method, had proof of alcohol post-mortem, and had less often a severe physical illness than suicides without alcoholism; however, there were no significant differences in several other factors such as former suicide attempts or co-morbid affective disorder [53]. Men with alcohol dependence over 50 years, who had committed suicide, had significantly more often affective disorders, serious medical problems, and less often separation and unemployment than younger alcohol dependent male suicides [64].

The acute effects of alcohol intake have been implicated in suicidal behavior as much as the chronic effects of alcohol misuse. Acute use of alcohol can increase psychological distress and aggressiveness and the likelihood of unplanned suicidal behavior [65, 66]. A wide range of alcohol-positive cases were found for completed suicides (10 – 69%: [67]). The risk of suicidal behavior might also be associated with the amount of alcohol consumed [68]. The increased suicide risk in alcoholism has a neurobiological basis: HPA and serotonergic dysregulation may contribute to both alcohol abuse and suicidal behavior [69 – 72] and other transmitters systems such as norepinephrine and dopamine might be involved in suicidal behavior in alcoholism, too [73, 74]. Furthermore, alcohol could damage the brain in many ways and might contribute to suicidal behavior in persons with alcohol dependence or abuse [75, 76].

SUICIDE AND SUBSTANCE USE DISORDERS OTHER THAN ALCOHOL

These results were almost exclusively obtained by cohort studies. Nine studies carried out in five countries including more than 7,500 people with opiate use (DSM-III-R) revealed a standard mortality ratio of 14.0 [5]. Wilcox et al. [6] identified additionally to Harris and Barraclough [5] three more studies. In their meta-analysis, the overall SMR for opioid use was 13.51. The corresponding sex-specific SMR estimates were 3.57 (from five studies) for females and 7.56 (from six studies) for males. Results on the association between opiate use disorders and suicide might be particularly biased by misclassification of suicides as non-intentional overdoses or vice versa, as overdose deaths are common in opiate use disorders and other i.v. drug use. Female gender, depression, and psychopathology were associated with suicide among heroin users [77].

Consumption of sedatives, hypnotics, and anxiolytics (DSM-III-R) resulted in a SMR of 20.34 [5]. Although benzodiazepines play an important role in substance use in the elderly, there are no studies about the association of benzodiazepines and suicide in the elderly.

In their meta-analysis for mixed drug use, Harris and Barraclough [5] included four studies obtained a SMR of 19.23. Wilcox et al. [6] identified four additional studies, resulting in an estimated SMR of 16.85. The SMR for general drug abuse was 3.29 for men, including two studies [78, 79], and 10.00 for women [79]. Young men with Cannabis consumption had a suicide risk of 3.85 times higher than that of the general population in a follow-up of 15 years [80].

Smoking is not an obvious cause of suicide. However, despite of differences in the definition of smoking (e.g. number of smoked cigarettes), age groups, or focus on special professional groups, smoking was associated with an about twofold increased suicide risk, in women and in men [5, 47]. This link between cigarette smoking and suicide has been reported in more recent epidemiological studies [81 – 83], especially in young men [84]; moreover, a dose-dependent relationship between smoking and suicide was reported [85 – 91]. In contrast to current smokers, suicide risk was not raised in former smokers [86, 88, 89, 90]. The significant associations between smoking and suicide were observed in studies that controlled for potential confounders, such as socioeconomic position, ethnicity, previous illness, age, and education, and several others [88 – 90, 92]. Hemmingsson & Kriebel [83] found that after adjustment for other factors, such as psychiatric diagnosis, medication for nervous problems, heavy alcohol consumption, drug use, and education, smoking was not longer a risk factor for suicide. However, their analysis was possibly overadjusted [93]. Furthermore, in two controlled psychological autopsy studies [94 [working female nurses], 95] smoking was also associated with increased suicide risk, even after adjustment for psychiatric disorders [95]. Unfortunately, definitions of smoking were rough in most of the cited literature.

Co-morbidity in Substance Use Disorders

It is estimated that about 60 % of all depressive episodes in alcoholics might be substance-induced [96]. Correspondingly, several studies revealed a close association between depression, alcoholism, and suicide.

Foster et al. [97] reported that 89 % of all suicides with alcohol dependence had co-morbidity with other axis I-disorders. In the National Suicide Prevention Project in Finland, 7 % of all suicide victims had co-morbidity of alcohol dependence and Major Depression [23 [random sample]]; among the suicides with Major Depression, 24 % had alcohol dependence and 4 % alcohol abuse and among victims with alcohol dependence, 22 % had Major Depression and 26 % depressive disorder not otherwise specified [23]. In Conwell et al.'s [14] study, 14 % of all suicides had co-morbidity of substance dependence and Major Depression and 43 % of all suicides with substance use disorders suffered from mood disorders. In subjects with active substance use disorders, older age was related to co-morbid affective illness [14]. Suicides with a co-morbid condition had most often major depression with substance use disorders (43 %), followed by double depression with substance use disorders (26 % [15]). Co-morbidity of depression and substance use disorders revealed the highest risk for suicide [15]. Co-morbidity of substance abuse and affective disorders was also related to highly elevated risk for suicide in adolescents [98]. Conner et al. [56] found that co-morbidity of depressive disorder and alcohol dependence increased suicide risk about 4.5 times in 20-year olds and about 83 times in 50-year olds.

In a random sample of 229 suicides in Finland, 14% had co-morbidity of alcohol dependence and personality disorder [23]. In this sample, 61 % of all suicides with personality disorders suffered from psychoactive substance use disorder and 39 % suffered from both, psychoactive substance use disorder and depressive syndromes [99]. In the Taiwanese psychological autopsy study, among suicides with substance dependence 74 % had co-morbid personality disorder (controls: 67 %; [37]).

CONCLUSION

Literature on alcohol use disorders and suicide is large; however, the number of reports about the association of suicide and other specific substance-related disorders is only moderate. Cohort studies and controlled psychological autopsy studies have repeatedly revealed the strong association between alcohol use disorders and suicide. Furthermore, opioid use disorders were associated with highly increased suicide risk in cohort studies.

Despite of a lot of well designed studies addressing the association between substance use disorders and suicide, there are still challenges for future more specific research. (1) Studies about the complicated association between suicide and substance use disorders in different age groups and gender are still missing, (2) the influence of substance-related disorders on the suicide risk of relatives of substance dependent people have not been assessed by now, and (3) the knowledge of risk constellations in the various substance use disorders is scarce. Therefore, further studies are needed to discover this specific information for use in prevention, in terms of identifying subjects at risk and recognizing preventable and treatable risk factors.

REFERENCES

[1] Dorpat TL, Ripley HS: A study of suicide in the Seattle area. *Compr Psychiatry* 1960; 1: 349-359.

[2] Bertolote MJ, Fleischmann A: *World Psychiatry* 2002; 1: 181-185.

[3] Bertolote JM, Fleischmann A, De Leo D, Wasserman D: Psychiatric diagnoses and suicide: revisiting the evidence. *Crisis* 2006; 25: 147-155.

[4] Grant BF, Hasin DS, Chou SP, Stinson FS, Dawson DA: Nicotine dependence and psychiatric disorders in the United States. Results from the National Epidemiologic Survey on Alcohol and Related Conditions. *Arch Gen Psychiatry* 2004, 61: 1107-1115.

[5] Harris EC, Barraclough B: Suicide as an outcome for mental disorders: a meta-analysis. *Br J Psychiatry* 1997; 170: 205-228.

[6] Wilcox HC, Conner KR, Caine ED: Association of alcohol and drug use disorders and completed suicide: an empirical review of cohort studies. *Drug Alcohol Depend.* 2004; 76 (Suppl): S11-19.

[7] Cavanagh JTO, Carson AJ, Sharpe M, Lawrie SM: Psychologcial autopsy studies of suicide: a systematic review *Psychol Med* 2003; 33: 395-405.

[8] Isometsä ET: Psychological autopsy studies – a review. *Eur Psychiatry* 2001; 16: 379-385.

[9] Robins E, Murphy GE, Wilkinson RH, Gessner F, Kayes J: Some clinical considerations in the preventions of suicide based on a study of 134 successful suicides. *Am J Public Health* 1959; 49: 888-899.

[10] Barraclough BM, Bunch J, Nelson B, Sainsbury P: A hundred cases of suicide: clinical aspects. *Br J Psychiatry* 1974; 125: 355-373.

[11] Chynoweth R, Tonge JI, Armstrong J: Suicide in Brisbane – a retrospective psychosocial study. *Aust N Z J Psychiatry* 1980; 14: 37-45.

[12] Rich CL, Young, D, Fowler RC: San Diego Suicide Study. I. Young vs old subjects. *Arch Gen Psychiatry* 1986; 43: 577-582.

[13] Duberstein PR, Conwell Y, Caine ED: Age differences in the personality characteristics of suicide completers: preliminary findings from a psychological autopsy study. *Psychiatry* 1994; 57: 213-224.

[14] Conwell Y, Duberstein PR, Cox C, Herrmann JH, Forbes NT, Caine ED: Relationship of age and axis I diagnoses in victims of completed suicide: a psychological autopsy study. *Am J Psychiatry* 1996; 153: 1001-1008.

[15] Cheng ATA: Mental illness and suicide. A case-control study in East Taiwan. *Arch Gen Psychiatry* 1995; 52: 594-603.

[16] Foster T, Gillespie K, McClelland R, Patterson C: Risk factors for suicide independent of DSM-III-R Axis I disorder. Case-control psychological autopsy study in Northern Ireland. *Br J Psychiatry* 1999; 175: 175-179.

[17] Vijayakumar L, Rajkumar S: Are risk factors for suicide universal? A case-control study in India. *Acta Psychiatr Scand* 1999; 99: 407-411.

[18] Schneider B, Georgi K, Weber B, Schnabel A, Ackermann H, Wetterling T: Risikofaktoren für Suizid bei Störungen im Zusammenhang mit psychotropen Substanzen [Risk factors for suicide in substance-related disorders]. *Psychiatr Prax* 2006; 33: 81-87.

[19] Cavanagh JTO, Owens DGC, Johnstone EC: Life events in suicide and undetermined death in south-east Scotland: a case-control study using the method of psychological autopsy. *Soc Psychiatry Psychiatr Epidemiol* 1999; 34: 645-650.

[20] Conner KR, Beautrais AL, Conwell Y: Risk factors for suicide and medically serious suicide attempts among alcoholics: analyses of Canterbury Suicide Project Data. *J Stud Alcohol* 2003a; 64: 551-554.

[21] Beskow J: Suicide and mental disorder in Swedish men. *Acta Psychiatr Scand* 1979; 277 (Suppl): 1-138.

[22] Asgard U: A psychiatric study of suicide among urban Swedish females. *Acta Psychiatr Scand* 1990; 82: 115-124.

[23] Henriksson MM, Aro HM, Marttunen MJ, Heikkinen ME, Isometsä ET, Kuoppasalmi KI, Lönnqvist JK: Mental disorders and comorbidity in suicide. *Am J Psychiatry* 1993; 150: 935-940.

[24] Marttunen MJ, Aro HM, Henriksson MM, Lönnqvist JK: Mental disorders in adolescent suicide: DSM-III-R Axes I and II diagnoses in suicides among 13- to 19-year-olds in Finland. *Arch Gen Psychiatry* 1991; 48: 834-839.

[25] Runeson B: Mental disorder in youth suicide. DSM-III-R Axes I and II. *Acta Psychiatr Scand* 1989; 79: 490-497.

[26] Lesage AD, Boyer R, Grunberg F, Vanier C, Morissette R, Menard-Buteau C, Loyer M: Suicide and mental disorders: a case-control study of young men. *Am J Psychiatry* 1994; 151: 1063-1068.

[27] Shaffer D, Gould MS, Fisher P, Traufman P, Moreau D, Kleinman M, Flory M: Psychiatric diagnosis in child and adolescent suicide. *Arch Gen Psychiatry* 1996; 53: 339-348.

[28] Shafii M, Steltz-Lenarsky J, Derrick AM, Beckner C, Whittinghill JR: Comorbidity of mental disorders in the post-mortem diagnosis of completed suicide in children and adolescents. *J Affect Disord* 1988; 15: 227-233.

[29] Brent DA, Baugher M, Bridge J, Chen T, Chiappetta L: Age- and sex-related risk factors for adolescent suicide. *J Am Acad Child Adolesc Psychiatry* 1999; 38: 1497-1505.

[30] Brent DA, Bridge J, Johnson BA, Connolly J: Suicidal behaviour runs in families. A controlled family study of adolescent suicide victims. *Arch Gen Psych* 1996; 53: 1145-1152.

[31] Appleby L, Cooper J, Amos T, Faragher B: Psychological autopsy of suicides by people under 35. *Br J Psychiatry* 1999; 175: 168-174.

[32] Brent DA, Perper JA, Goldstein CE, Kolko DJ, Allan MJ, Allman CJ, Zelenak JP: Risk factors for adolescent suicide: a comparison of adolescent suicide victims with suicidal inpatients. *Arch Gen Psychiatr* 1988; 45: 581-588.

[33] Houston K, Hawton K, Sheppard R. Suicide in young people aged 15-24: a psychological autopsy study. *J Affect Disord* 2001; 63: 159-170.

[34] Conwell Y, Olsen K, Caine ED, Flannery C: Suicide in later life: psychological autopsy findings. *Int Psychogeriatr* 1991; 3: 59-66.

[35] Harwood D, Hawton K, Hope T, Jacoby R: Psychiatric disorder and personality factors associated with suicide in older people: a descriptive and case-control study. *Int J Geriatr Psychiatry* 2001; 16: 155-165.

[36] Waern M, Runeson BS, Allebeck P, Beskow J, Rubenowitz E, Skoog I, Wilhelmson K: Mental disorder in elderly suicides: a case-control study. *Am J Psychiatry* 2002; 159: 450-455.

[37] Cheng ATA, Chen THH, Chen CC, Jenkins R: Psychosocial and psychiatric risk factors for suicide. *Br J Psychiatry* 2000; 177: 360-365.

[38] Rich CL, Rickets JE, Fowler RC, Young D: Some differences between men and women who commit suicide. *Am J Psychiatry* 1988; 145: 718-722.

[39] Arato M, Demeter E, Rihmer Z, Somogyi E: Retrospective psychiatric assessment of 200 suicides in Budapest. *Acta Psychiatr Scand* 1988; 77: 454-456.

[40] Kõlves K, Värnik A, Tooding LM, Wasserman D: The role of alcohol in suicide: a case-control psychological autopsy study. *Psychol Med* 2006; 36: 923-933.

[41] Henriksson MM, Marttunen MJ, Isometsä ET, Heikkinen ME, Aro HM, Kuoppasalmi KI, Lönnqvist JK: Mental disorders in elderly suicide. *Int Psychogeriatr* 1995; 7: 275-286.

[42] Schneider B, Kõlves K, Blettner M, Wetterling T, Schnabel A, Värnik A: Substance use disorders as risk factors for suicide in an Eastern and a Central European city (Tallinn and Frankfurt/Main). *Psychiatry Res* 2009; 165: 263-272.

[43] Bukstein OG, Brent DA, Perper JA, Moritz G, Baugher M, Schweers J, Roth C, Balach L: Risk factors for completed suicide among adolescents with a lifetime history of substance abuse: a case-control study. *Acta Psychiatr Scand* 1993; 88: 403-408.

[44] Pirkola SP, Isometsä ET, Heikkinen ME, Henriksson MM, Lönnqvist JK: Female psychoactive substance-dependent suicide victims differ from male – results from a nationwide psychological autopsy study. *Compr Psychiatry* 1999a; 40: 101-107.

[45] Pirkola S: Alcohol and other substance misuse in suicide. *Academic dissertation,* Helsinki, Finland, Medical Faculty of the University of Helsinki, 1999.

[46] Inskip HM, Harris C, Barraclough B: Lifetime risk of suicide for affective disorder, alcoholism and schizophrenia. *Br J Psychiatry* 1998; 172: 35-37.

[47] Harris EC, Barraclough B: Excess mortality of mental disorder. *Br J Psychiatry* 1998; 173: 11-53.

[48] Hiroeh U, Appleby L, Mortensen PB, Dunn G: Death by homicide, suicide, and other unnatural causes in people with mental illness: a population-based study. *Lancet* 2001; 358 (9299): 2110-2112.

[49] Flensborg-Madsen T, Knop J, Mortensen EL, Becker U, Sher L, Grønbæk M: Alcohol use disorders increase the risk of completed suicide - irrespective of other psychiatric disorders. A longitudinal cohort study. *Psychiatry Res* 2009; 167: 123-130.

[50] Gururaj G, Isaac MK, Subbakrishna DK, Ranjani R: Risk factors for completed suicides: a case-control study from Bangalore, India. *Inj Control Saf Promotion* 2004; 11: 183-191.

[51] Zhang J, Conwell Y, Zhou L, Jiang C: Culture, risk factors and suicide in rural China: a psychological autopsy case control study. *Acta Psychiatr Scand* 2004; 110: 430-437.

[52] Chiu HF, Yip PS, Chi I, Chan S, Tsoh J, Kwan CW, Li SF, Conwell Y, Caine E: Elderly suicide in Hong Kong - a case-controlled psychological autopsy study. *Acta Psychiatr Scand* 2004; 109: 299-305.

[53] Waern M: Alcohol dependence and misuse in elderly suicides. *Alcohol alcohol* 2003; 38: 249-254.

[54] Rossow I, Amundsen A: Alcohol abuse and suicide: a 40-year prospective study of Norwegian conscripts. *Addiction* 1995; 90: 685-691.

[55] Murphy GE, Wetzel RD, Robins E, McEvoy L: Multiple risk factors predict suicide in alcoholism. *Arch Gen Psychiatry* 1992; 49: 459-463.

[56] Conner KR, Beautrais AL, Conwell Y: Moderators of the relationship between alcohol dependence and suicide and medically serious suicide attempts: analyses of Canterbury Suicide Project data. *Alcohol Clin Exp Res* 2003b; 27:1156-1161.

[57] Duffy J, Kreitman N: Risk factors for suicide and undetermined death among in-patient alcoholics in Scotland. *Addiction* 1993; 88: 757-766.

[58] Conner KR, Cox C, Duberstein PR, Tian L, Nisbet PA, Conwell Y: Violence, alcohol and completed suicide: a case-control study. *Am J Psychiatry* 2001; 158: 1701-1705.

[59] Pirkola S, Isometsä E, Heikkinen M, Lönnqvist J: Suicides of alcohol misusers and non-misusers in a nationwide population. *Alcohol alcohol* 2000; 35: 70-75.

[60] Pirkola S, Isometsä E, Heikkinen M, Lönnqvist J: Employment status influences the weekly patterns of suicide among alcohol misusers. *Alcohol Clin Exp Res* 1997; 21: 1704-1706.

[61] Heikkinen ME, Aro HM, Henriksson MM, Isometsä ET, Sarna SJ, Kuoppasalmi KI, Lönnqvist JK: Differences in recent life events between alcoholic and depressive nonalcoholic suicides. *Alcohol Clin Exp Res* 1994; 18: 1143-1149.

[62] Pirkola SP, Marttunen MJ, Henriksson MM, Isometsä ET, Heikkinen ME, Lönnqvist JK: Alcohol-related problems among adolescent suicides in *Finland Alcohol alcohol* 1999b; 34: 320-329.

[63] Marttunen MJ, Aro HM, Henriksson MM, Lönnqvist JK: Adolescent suicides with alcohol abuse compared with depressive adolescent suicides. *J Am Acad Child Adolesc Psychiatry* 1994; 39: 490-497.

[64] Conner KR, Duberstein PR, Conwell Y: Age-related patterns of factors associated with completed suicide in men with alcohol dependence. *Am J Addic*t 1999; 8: 312-318.

[65] Hufford MR: Alcohol and suicidal behavior. Clin Psychol Rev 2001; 21: 797-811.

[66] Swahn M, Bossarte R, Sullivent E: Age of alcohol use initiation, suicidal behaviour, and peer and dating violence victimization and perpetration among high-risk, seventh-grade adolescents. *Pediatrics* 2008; 121: 297-305.

[67] Cherpitel CJ, Borges GLG, Wilcox HC: Acute alcohol use and suicidal behavior: A review of the literature. *Alcohol Clin Exp Res* 2004; 28: 18S-28S.

[68] Borges G, Rosovsky H: Suicide attempts and alcohol consumption in an emergency room sample. *J Stud Alcohol* 1996; 57: 543-548.

[69] Gorwood P: Biological markers for suicidal behavior in alcohol dependence. *Eur Psychiatry* 2001; 16: 410-417.

[70] Sher L, Oquendo MA, Li S, Huang Y, Grunebaum MF, Burke AK, Malone KM, Mann JJ: Lower CSF: Homovanillic Acid levels in depressed patients with a history of alcoholism. *Neuropsychopharmacology* 2003; 28: 1712-1719.

[71] Sher L, Oquendo MA, Grunebaum MF, Burke AK, Huang Y, Mann JJ: CSF monoamine metabolites and lethality of suicide attempts in depressed patients with alcohol dependence. *Eur Neuropsychopharmacol* 2007; 17: 12-15.

[72] Sher L: The role of the hypothalamic-pituitary-adrenal axis dysfunction in the pathophysiology of alcohol misuse and suicidal behavior in adolescents. ***Int J Adolesc Med** Health* 2007; 19: 3-9.

[73] Oquendo MA, Mann JJ: The biology of impulsivity and suicidality. *Psychiatr Clin North Am* 2000; 23: 11-25.

[74] Tupala E, Tiihonen J: Dopamine and alcoholism neurobiological basis of ethanol abuse. *Prog Neuropsychopharmacol Biol Psychiatry* 2004; 28: 1221-1247.

[75] Oscar-Berman M, Marinković K: Alcoholism and the brain: an overview. *Alcohol Res Health* 2003; 27: 125-133.

[76] Oquendo MA, Friedman JH, Grunebaum MF, Burke A, Silver JM, Mann JJ: Suicidal behaviour and mild traumatic brain injury in major depression. *J Nerv Ment Dis* 2004; 192: 430-434.

[77] Darke S, Ross J: Suicide among heroin users: rates, risk factors and methods. *Addiction* 2002; 97: 1383–1394.

[78] Allebeck P, Allgulander C: Suicide among young men: psychiatric illness, deviant behaviour and substance abuse. *Acta Psychiatr Scand* 1990; 81: 565-570.

[79] Benson G, Holmberg MB: Drug-related mortality in young people. *Acta Psychiatr Scand* 1984; 70: 525-534.

[80] Andreasson S, Allebeck P: Cannabis and mortality among young men: A longitudinal study of Swedish conscripts. *Scand J Soc Med* 1990; 18: 9-15.

[81] Angst J, Clayton PJ: Personality, smoking and suicide: a prospective study. *J Affect Disord* 1998; 51: 55-62.

[82] Hemmingsson T, Kriebel D: Smoking at age 18-20 and suicide during 26 years of follow-up – how can the association be explained? *Int J Epidemiol* 2003; 32: 1000-1004.

[83] Tanskanen A, Tuomilehto J, Viinamaki H, Vartiainen E, Lehtonen J, Puska P: Smoking and the risk of suicide. *Acta Psychiatr Scand* 2000; 101: 243-245.

[84] Riala K, Alaräisänen A, Taanila A, Hakko H, Timonen M, Räsänen P: Regular daily smoking among 14-year-old adolescents increases the subsequent risk for suicide: the Northern Finland 1966 Birth Cohort Study. *J Clin Psychiatry* 2007; 68: 775-780.

[85] Davey Smith G, Phillips AN, Neaton JD: Smoking as "independent" risk factor for suicide: illustration of an artifact from observational epidemiology? *Lancet* 1992; 340(8821): 709-712.

[86] Hemenway D, Solnick SJ, Colditz GA: Smoking and suicide among nurses. *Am J Public Health* 1993; 83: 249-251.

[87] Tverdal A, Thelle D, Stensvold I, Leren P, Bjartveit K: Mortality in relation to smoking history: 13 years' follow-up of 68,000 Norwegian men and women 35-49 years. *J Clin Epidemiol* 1993; 46: 475-487.

[88] Leistikow BN, Martin DC, Samuels SJ: Injury death excesses in smokers: a 1990-95 United States national cohort study. *Inj Prev* 2000; 6: 277-280.

[89] Miller M, Hemenway D, Bell NS, Yore MM, Amoroso PJ: Cigarette smoking and suicide: a prospective study of 300,000 male active-duty army soldiers. *Am J Epidemiol* 2000a; 151: 1060-1063.

[90] Miller M, Hemenway D, Rimm E: Cigarettes and suicide: a prospective study of 50,000 men. *Am J Public Health* 2000b; 90: 768-773.

[91] Iwasaki M, Akechi T, Uchitomi Y, Tsugane S, JPHC Study Group: Cigarette smoking and completed suicide among middle-aged men: a population-based cohort study in Japan. *Ann Epidemiol* 2005; 15: 286-292.

[92] Davey Smith G, Phillips AN: "Cigarette smoking and suicide: a prospective study of 300,000 male active-duty army soldiers" [letter]. *Am J Epidemiol* 2001; 153: 308.

[93] Leistikow B: Commentary: Questionable premises, overadjustment, and a smoking/suicide association in younger adult men. *Int J Epidemiol* 2003; 32: 1005-1006.

[94] Hawton K, Simkin S, Rue J, Haw C, Barbour F, Clements A, Sakarovitch C, Deeks J: Suicide in female nurses in England and Wales. *Psychol Med* 2002; 32: 239-250.

[95] Schneider B, Schnabel A, Weber B, Frölich L, Maurer K, Wetterling T: Nicotine use in suicides: a case-control study. *Eur Psychiatry* 2005; 20: 129-136.

[96] Schuckit MA, Tipp JE, Bergman M, Reich W, Hesselbrock VM, Smith TL: Comparison of induced and independent major depressive disorders in 2,945 alcoholics. *Am J Psychiatry* 1997; 154: 948-957.

[97] Foster T, Gillespie K, McClelland R: Mental disorders and suicide in Northern Ireland. *Br J Psychiatry* 1997; 170: 447-452.

[98] Brent DA, Perper JA, Moritz G, Allman C, Friend A, Roth C, Schweers J, Balach L, Baugher M: Psychiatric risk factors for adolescent suicide: a case-control study. *J Am Acad Child Adolesc Psychiatry* 1993; 32: 521-529.

[99] Isometsä ET, Henriksson MM, Heikkinen ME, Aro HM, Marttunen MJ, Kuoppasalmi KI, Lönnqvist JK: Suicide among subjects with personality disorders. *Am J Psychiatry* 1996; 153: 667-673.

In: Suicidal Behavior in Alcohol and Drug Abuse... ISBN: 978-1-60876-919-3
Editors: L. Sher, A. Vilens, pp. 285-297

Chapter 16

PSYCHOSOCIAL RISK FACTORS FOR SUICIDE ATTEMPTS AMONG DRUG USERS

Elizabeth Maloney and Shane Darke
National Drug and Alcohol Research Centre, University of New South Wales, Sydney, Australia

ABSTRACT

Elevated rates of attempted suicide have been reported among substance dependent individuals compared to the general population. Attempted suicide is associated with substantial morbidity and significant risk of subsequent mortality, with this risk increasing for each attempt. Attempted suicide is clearly an issue deserving of clinical and research attention. To date, however, attempted suicide has received relatively limited research attention. The literature suggests that attempted suicide affects substance users in general, rather than being contained to a particular drug class. This review summarises the risk factors for suicide attempts among individuals with substance use disorders including sociodemographic factors, family dysfunction and childhood experiences, and comorbid psychopathology. This review also distinguishes self-mutilation as a distinct behaviour from attempted suicide with self-mutilation remaining a poorly understood and understudied phenomenon, and examines the prevalence and risk factors associated with self-mutilation among substance users. Additionally, the clinical characteristics associated with the co-occurrence of suicide attempts and self-mutilation are discussed, including what this may mean for treatment. Finally, the clinical implications associated with assessment and treatment of suicidal behaviours are discussed.

INTRODUCTION

Suicide is a major public health issue among the general population. It has been among the top ten causes of death for many years among the western world, with estimates suggesting that almost one million people die by suicide each year worldwide [1, 2]. While suicide is clearly an important issue among the general population, the fact that it affects sub-groups within the community at disproportionately high rates cannot be ignored.

Prevalence of Suicide among Substance Users

Research has increasingly recognised high rates of mortality among substance users [3, 4]. Overdose, disease (HIV, hepatitis, cirrhosis, for example), trauma (assault, motor vehicle accidents, for example) and suicide are consistently identified as the leading causes of death among drug users [3, 5, 6]. When the standardised mortality rates (SMR) for all causes of death are compared to suicide rates among this group the difference is striking [4, 7, 8]. The SMR for all causes of death among benzodiazepine users is 2.1 compared to 44.2 for suicide among this group, for example. Similar levels of overrepresentation for suicide among alcohol and opioid dependent individuals has been reported [4, 7].

Despite these figures, exploring suicidal behaviours has remained a low priority for research. It does, however, represent a major clinical issue for those treating individuals with substance use disorders, especially when we consider that a previous suicide attempt is a strong predictor of subsequent attempts and later mortality [9, 10]. Additionally, attempted suicide is associated with substantial morbidity including psychological distress and injury (with the severity of the injury largely dependent on the method chosen) [3]. Addressing and preventing attempted suicide in clinical settings is a core component to reducing the excess mortality among drug users.

Prevalence of Suicide Attempts among Substance Users

High rates of lifetime and recent suicide attempts among drug users have been consistently reported across studies and across countries (20% to 40%, and 6% to 10%, respectively). This is particularly evident when we consider that fewer than 5% of the general population have ever attempted suicide, and fewer than 2% have made a recent suicide attempt (preceeding year) [11]. Furthermore, the evidence suggests that individuals with substance use disorders are significantly more likely to report multiple attempts over their lifetime [12, 13]. The large majority of studies have focused on suicide attempts among individuals with a history of alcohol or opioid dependence; however, more recently studies have begun to examine suicidal behaviour among cocaine, cannabis and methamphetamine dependent individuals.

A number of studies have identified a strong association between lifetime suicidal behaviour and alcohol dependence [14]. The prevalence of lifetime suicide attempts among individuals with alcohol dependence is estimated to be between 20% and 30% [15]. Other studies have suggested that problem drinkers are twice as likely to report recent suicide attempts, and four times as likely to report lifetime suicide attempts, compared to individuals without drinking problems [16]. Additionally, studies have suggested that individuals with an alcohol use disorder (and a history of attempted suicide) have an elevated (approximately 5 to 6 times higher) risk for subsequent suicide attempts compared to others with a suicide attempt history [15].

A large body of research suggests that alcohol use can increase the distal and proximal risks associated with suicide attempts. While there is some debate, distal risk factors are generally considered to be those which increase the potential or predispose individuals to suicidal behaviour, whereas proximal risk factors are those which immediately precede, and often trigger, suicidal behaviour [17]. Research suggests that alcohol dependence on its own, and in combination with comorbid psychopathology, negative life events (the experience of childhood trauma, for example), a family history of suicide, and personality characteristics (introversion, for example) are distal risk factors for suicide attempts [17, 18]. Alcohol intoxication has been identified as a proximal risk factor for suicide attempts via multiple pathways, including the acute effects of alcohol on increasing an individual's psychological distress and/or level of aggression, and the effects of alcohol on limiting an individual's ability to employ appropriate coping strategies [17].

Studies across a number of countries (including US, UK and Australia) have estimated that 17% to 40% of opioid-dependent individuals have attempted suicide at least once in their lifetime, and between 6% and 10% have reported recent attempts (in the preceeding 12 months) [19-26].

The literature is still fairly limited on the relationship between cannabis use and increased risk of suicidal behaviour. While some studies have noted an association, others have shown little evidence [27, 28]. A twin study found that those who were cannabis dependent had odds of suicidal ideation and attempts 2.5 to 2.9 times higher than their non-dependent twin [29]. Additionally early onset of cannabis use (before age 17 years) was associated with elevated rates of subsequent suicide attempts, but not suicidal ideation [29].

Similarly, only a few studies have assessed suicide attempts among cocaine or methamphetamine dependent individuals. Among cocaine users the prevalence of attempted suicide has been estimated to be between 28% and 44% [30, 31], with 7% reporting an attempt in the preceding 12 months, and 16% reporting multiple lifetime attempts [30]. Cocaine injectors were more likely to report a lifetime suicide attempt, repeated attempts, and to report using a violent method to attempt suicide, compared to non-injecting cocaine users [30]. Likewise, the prevalence of lifetime suicide attempts among a methamphetamine dependent sample was estimated to be 29% [32].

RISK FACTORS FOR SUICIDE ATTEMPTS

While the above literature is limited in some respects, the evidence clearly shows that a history of attempted suicide is highly prevalent among individuals with a range of drug use disorders. This review will focus on the risk factors for suicide attempts among drug users in general many of whom could also be characterised as polydrug users [33]. Higher levels of polydrug use have been found to be associated with attempted suicide, and further, the number of drug classes has been shown to be a stronger predictor of suicide attempts than any individual drug class [34]. The risk factors for suicide attempts are discussed below and have been grouped into three broad areas: sociodemographic factors, family dysfunction, and comorbid psychopathology. While the focus here is on attempted suicide, the risk factors for completed suicide are essentially the same, with the exception of gender, which will be explored in more detail below [19].

Sociodemographic Factors

As indicated above gender is the only risk factor which appears to differ between attempted and completed suicide. This gender difference in suicide rates is consistent among drug users and the general population: males are more likely to complete suicide, and females are more likely to attempt suicide, and to make multiple attempts over their lifetime [19]. This gender difference has been reported consistently across drug types, including studies of opioid dependent [35-37], alcohol dependent [38], cocaine dependent [39] and methamphetamine dependent individuals [32].

Research also suggest female drug users make their first suicide attempt, on average, 2 to 6 years earlier than male drug users [24, 40]. Additionally, among heroin users studies have found that in over half of cases the initial suicide attempt preceded initiation into heroin use, with this being far more likely among females than males (18 times) [24]. An earlier age of onset of heroin use has also been reported as significantly more likely among those with a history of attempted suicide, compared to those with no history of suicide attempts [37, 41]. Similar findings have been reported for alcohol dependent individuals [15].

Being younger, less educated, unemployed, divorced or separated have all been found to be associated with suicide attempts among drug users [21, 36, 39, 40, 42]. Additionally, social isolation and disadvantage appear to increase the risk of suicidal behaviours. Specifically, a lack of social or family support, unemployment, living alone and homelessness have all been associated with an increased risk of suicidal behaviours among drug users [43, 44]. While some of these risk factors have also been reported for the general population, the occurrence of the risk factors appears to be greatly elevated among individuals with a substance use disorder [11, 21].

Family Dysfunction

A number of family characteristics and childhood experiences have been reported as increasing the risk of attempted suicide among substance users, including childhood trauma, parental factors, and family history of suicidal behaviour.

A history of childhood physical and/or sexual abuse is consistently reported as a risk factor for suicide attempts among substance users [21, 31, 36, 38, 39, 43, 45]. This is likely to be a result of the high rates of childhood abuse reported among this group [46]. After controlling for a range of sociodemographic and psychological variables, Heffernan and colleagues [47] found that opiate users were almost 3 times more likely to report a history of childhood abuse, compared to non-opiate users. While childhood sexual and physical abuse have received the most attention, limited reports suggest that childhood emotional abuse and neglect are also associated with suicidal behaviours among substance users [36, 48].

A number of parental factors have also been linked to increasing the risk of lifetime suicide attempts among substance users, including parental absence during childhood, and parental substance use or mental health problems [19, 21, 24, 49]. Additionally, numerous studies have reported that substance users (including studies on opioid, cocaine and alcohol dependent individuals) with a family history of attempted suicide were themselves significantly more likely to also have a history of attempted suicide [36-39].

Comorbid Psychopathology

Research suggests that a large majority of individuals who report a lifetime suicide attempt will also meet diagnostic criteria for at least one psychological disorder (90%) [50]. Additionally, the occurrence of comorbid mental disorders is common among individuals with a history of suicide attempts [51]. Numerous studies have found that the presence of a lifetime psychological disorder is associated with an increased risk of suicide attempts among substance users [32, 41, 48, 52]. Substance dependent individuals have one psychiatric disorder implicit within the definition of being 'substance-dependent'; it is therefore not surprising that comorbidity is high among this group and that it has been associated with an increased risk of suicide attempts. The literature examining suicide attempts among those with comorbid psychiatric and substance use disorders has focused on depression, Borderline Personality Disorder, Posttraumatic Stress Disorder, and polydrug use, each of which are discussed below.

Depression

Depression is a well documented risk factor for attempted suicide among the general population [4]. Substance dependent individuals, however, experience lifetime mood disorders at elevated rates compared to the general population (approximately twice the rate; 33% vs. 17%) [33, 53]. Additionally, studies have consistently reported higher rates of lifetime suicide attempts among individuals with a comorbid mood disorder and substance dependence, even when compared to individuals with either disorder alone [19, 32, 52, 54]. Research has also shown that among substance users high levels of depression remain even years after a suicide attempt, indicating the level of vigilance required to assess and treat comorbid depression and substance use in the absence of recent suicidal behaviour [19].

Personality Disorders

In clinical practice Borderline Personality Disorder (BPD) is the most commonly diagnosed personality disorder (15-25%), while only prevalent in a small percentage of the general population (2%) [55]. Research suggests that a large proportion of BPD patients have attempted suicide at least once in their lifetime (75%) (with multiple attempts common), and one in ten will ultimately die by suicide [56]. Numerous studies have reported elevated rates of BPD among substance dependent individuals (27%) [57], and an increased risk of suicidal behaviour among those with comorbid substance use disorder and BPD [48, 58-61]. It has been argued that the relationship between BPD and suicide attempts is an artefact of the "self-harm" criterion within the diagnosis. It is important to highlight, however, that studies which have removed this criterion from the analyses have still found BPD to be a significant predictor of suicide attempts [58, 62]. There is, however, little evidence of an association between substance use disorders, suicidal behaviour and other personality disorders, such as antisocial personality disorder (ASPD) [24].

Anxiety Disorders

The majority of the literature examining the relationship between anxiety disorders and suicidal behaviour among substance dependent individuals has focused on Posttraumatic Stress Disorder (PTSD). As with other psychiatric disorders, substance dependent individuals experience elevated levels of trauma and associated PTSD compared to the general population (37% vs. 7%) [53, 63]. Additionally, elevated rates (up to 6 times) of attempted suicide have been reported among substance dependent individuals with comorbid PTSD [48, 64, 65]. While a link between other anxiety disorders (including panic disorder and social phobia) and elevated rates of attempted suicide have received some support among the general population, the literature is limited and it yet to determine to what extent this applies to substance dependent individuals.

Polydrug Dependence

As reported earlier, research suggests that the number of drug classes an individual uses is a better predictor of suicide attempts than which drug type they use [34]. Polydrug use and dependence are common among substance users and although the research is limited, both have been linked to an increased risk of attempted suicide [19, 36, 42, 65]. This is not surprising when we consider that many drug types have independently been associated with suicide attempts, and therefore the cumulative effect of using multiple drug types increases the risk of suicidal behaviour even further [19]. This appears to be particularly evident among heroin dependent individuals, where concurrent alcohol and/or benzodiazepine use has been associated with increased risk of attempted suicide [19, 21, 34].

Distinguishing Suicide Attempts and Self Mutilation

Self-mutilation is a distinct behaviour from attempted suicide, but is worthy of discussion in this review as the two behaviours often co-occur [66]. Self-mutilation has been defined as the ***"deliberate, direct destruction** or alteration of body tissue without conscious suicidal* ***intent"*** [67]. While acts of self-mutilation vary greatly, they commonly include cutting and burning the skin, banging the head and limbs, picking at wounds, chewing fingers, needle-sticking, inserting objects under the skin and self-biting [67]. Self-mutilation has been identified as a clinically significantly problem, but remains poorly understood and understudied.

A number of studies have identified an association between self-mutilation and substance use disorders, with lifetime rates substantially elevated compared to the general population (10% to 46% vs. 2% to 4% respectively) [68-70]. In fact, one study found that those with a drug use disorder were over 3 times more likely to self-mutilate, compared to those with an alcohol use disorder [69]. It has been proposed that substance misuse may trigger self-mutilation by impairing judgement, reducing pain perception and diminishing psychological inhibition [69]. The risk factors for self-mutilation among substance dependent individuals are fairly consistent with those reported for attempted suicide and include being single, unemployed, a history of childhood physical or sexual abuse, comorbid PTSD, and a history of attempted suicide [69, 70].

While the literature has consistently identified links between attempted suicide and self-mutilation, little is known about the clinical characteristics associated with their co-occurrence. Recent research among an opioid-dependent sample found that while the two behaviours were distinct, their co-occurrence was associated with a more severe clinical profile (i.e. the presence of multiple substance use and mental health disorders), compared to those with a history of either behaviour alone [71]. The findings suggested that, like suicidal behaviours, self-mutilation should be routinely assessed by treatment services. If self-mutilation is disclosed a full assessment of underlying psychiatric disorders is required, as these will complicate clinical care. The treatment of comorbid disorders is often difficult as one disorder may drive the occurrence of other disorders and the associated self-harm behaviors. For example, childhood maltreatment is associated with risk for BPD; both are associated with risk for poor coping and problematic adult relationships which often drive both self-mutilation and suicide attempts.

Clinical Implications

This review has highlighted a number of important points. Attempted suicide effects substance users at disproportionately high rates compared to the general population. It is likely that of those entering a drug treatment program, one in three will have a history of attempted suicide, and up to one in ten will have attempted suicide in the preceding 12 months. Additionally, multiple lifetime attempts are common, and each attempt will increase the risk of eventually dying by suicide. We have also illustrated that attempted suicide is not a problem confined to a particular drug class, but rather it affects substance users more generally. An extensive range of risk factors for suicide attempts were highlighted including demographic characteristics (i.e. gender, unemployment), family dysfunction (i.e. childhood trauma, family history of suicide), and psychiatric comorbidity (i.e. depression, PTSD, BPD). While most of these risk factors have been documented among the general population, they are prevalent in excess levels among substance users.

The risk factors highlighted above not only occur in excess levels among substance users, but their co-occurrence is also common. This will impact substantially on psychiatric and substance use treatment. It is likely that the majority of individuals seeking treatment for a serious substance use problem will have at least one additional underlying psychiatric condition or childhood factor which will complicate treatment. It is unlikely that suicidal risk will be reduced if any underlining psychiatric conditions are not taken into account, and treated concurrently with substance misuse. Additionally, recent suicidal behaviour should not be the only marker for identifying current suicidal risk. As mentioned earlier, studies have shown that levels of depression, for example, remain high even in the absence of recent suicidal behaviour [19]. Furthermore, the importance of psychosocial support for all at risk clients should not be underestimated, as this may be a determining factor in the event of a crisis [44]. Monitoring of serious life events (i.e. relationship breakdown, incarceration, financial problems) should be an important component of any treatment plan as these may trigger suicidal behaviour among vulnerable individuals already at risk [17].

Research which has explored transitions from suicidal ideation to plans to attempts among substance users have found that almost all those who reported a history of attempted suicide, reported a history of ideation [72]. In addition, the risk of transitioning to a suicide attempt was higher among those reporting suicidal plans. Furthermore, a 3-year follow-up study of substance dependent individuals found that suicidal ideation and previous suicide attempts were strongly predictive of attempts during the follow-up period [73]. In fact, those with a history of attempted suicide were five times more likely to make an attempt during the follow-up period, and one in four of those who reported suicidal ideation at baseline reported an attempt during the follow-up period [73]. These findings suggest that regular brief screening is warranted among individuals with substance use problems and that there is value in focusing suicide prevention efforts on those who report suicidal ideation.

Recent studies have also suggested that there may be some value in assessing whether previous suicide attempts were impulsive or not (by assessing how long they had spent planning the attempt, for example). Impulsive suicide attempts have been found to predict both post-treatment relapse, and a shorter time to relapse [74]. These findings suggest individuals with a history of impulsive suicide attempts may require continued support and ongoing follow-up upon completing treatment.

Other research has found that individuals who reported consuming alcohol prior (preceding 6 hours) to their indexed suicide attempt were significantly more likely to be diagnosed with a substance use disorder [75]. Admission to hospital following a suicide attempt may present a unique opportunity for individuals who may otherwise not be motivated to seek treatment to be thoroughly assessed for underlying psychological conditions. The research suggests that if there is evidence of recent alcohol use extra attention should taken in assessing for a substance use disorders.

CONCLUSION

Suicide has been highlighted as a clinically significant issue among substance users that is associated with substantial morbidity and future risk of mortality. Considering the importance of this issue, it is surprising that it has received relatively limited clinical and research attention. It is important to acknowledge that many of the negative consequences of a substance dependent lifestyle are those which have been identified in this review as risk factors for suicide attempts, including limited social supports, unemployment, poor physical and mental health and the experience of traumatic events [76]. It is often an accumulation of such risk factors which will trigger a suicide attempt. Additionally, the risk factors are not necessarily related to substance use per se, but rather that substance users experience most of these risks at substantially elevated rates which in turn increases their risk and prevalence of suicidal behaviour [48]. The research suggests there is a need to routinely screen all individuals seeking treatment for substance misuse for suicidal risk. A thorough assessment of underlying psychological conditions is needed for at risk individuals. Additionally, the management and treatment of comorbid substance use and mental health problems needs to occur concurrently to lower suicidal risk. While the literature base has grown in recent years, more clinical and research attention is needed, particularly among the less studied drug dependent sub-groups including cocaine, cannabis and methamphetamine dependent individuals.

REFERENCES

[1] Baume P. *Epidemiological overview of suicide in Australia: Australian Institute for Suicide Research and Prevention,* Griffith University; 1997.

[2] Diekstra RFW. Parasuicide: is it a distinct phenomenon? In: Botsis AJ, Soldatos CR, Stefanis CN, eds. *Suicide: Biopsychosocial Approaches.* Amsterdam: Elsevier 1997:177-85.

[3] Darke S, Degenhardt L, Mattick R. *Mortality among illicit drug users: Epidemiology, causes and intervention.* Cambridge: Cambridge University Press 2006.

[4] Harris EC, Barraclough B. Suicide as an outcome for mental disorders: A meta-analysis. *The British Journal of Psychiatry.* 1997 March; 170(3):205-28.

[5] Bargagli AM, Sperati A, Davoli M, Forastiere F, Perucci CA. Mortality among problem drug users in Rome: An 18-year follow-up study, 1980-1997. *Addiction.* 2001; 96(10):1455-63.

[6] Hser YI, Hoffman V, Grella CE, Anglin D. A 33-Year follow-up of narcotics addicts. *Archives of General Psychiatry.* 2001 May; 58:503-8.

[7] Harris EC, Barraclough B. Excess mortality of mental disorder. *British Journal of Psychiatry.* 1998; 173:11-53.

[8] Wilcox HC, Conner KR, Caine ED. Association of alcohol and drug use disorders and completed suicide: an empirical review of cohort studies. *Drug and Alcohol Dependence.* 2004; 76 (Supplement 1):S11-S9.

[9] Hawton K, Fagg J, Platt S, Hawkins M. Factors associated with suicide after parasuicide in young people. *British Medical Journal.* 1993 June; 306(6893):1641-5.

[10] Kessler RC, Borges G, Walters EE. Prevalence of and risk factors for lifetime suicide attempts in the National Comorbidity Survey. *Archives of General Psychiatry.* 1999 July; 56(7):617-26.

[11] Weissman MM, Bland RC, Canino GJ, Greenwald S, Hwu HG, Joyce PR, Karam EG, Lee CK, Lellouch J, Lepine JP, Newman SC, Rubio-Stipec M, Wells JE, Wickramaratne PJ, Wittchen HU, Yeh EK. Prevalence of suicide ideation and suicide attempts in nine countries. *Psychological Medicine.* 1999; 29:9-17.

[12] Miranda R, Scott M, Hicks R, Wilcox HC, Munfakh JLH, Shaffer D. Suicide attempt characteristics, diagnoses, and future attempts: Comparing multiple attempters to single attempters and ideators. *Journal of the American Academy of Child and Adolescent Psychiatry.* 2008; 47(1):32-40.

[13] Pagura J, Cox BJ, Sareen J, Enns MW. Factors associated with multiple versus single episode suicide attempt in the 1990-1992 and 2001-2003 United States National Comorbidity Surveys. *The Journal of Nervous and Mental Disease.* 2008; 196(11):806-13.

[14] Bernal M, Haro JM, Bernert S, Brugha T, de Graaf R, Bruffaerts R, Lepine JP, de Girolamo G, Vilagut G, Gasquet I, Torres JV, Kovess V, Heider D, Neeleman J, Kessler RC, Alonso J. Risk factors for suicidality in Europe: Results from the ESEMED study. *Journal of Affective Disorders.* 2007; 101:27-34.

[15] Berglund M, Ojehagen A. The influence of alcohol drinking and alcohol use disorders on psychiatric disorders and suicidal behavior. *Alcoholism: Clinical and Experimental Research.* 1998; 22 (Supplement)(7):333S-45S.

[16] Innamorati M, Pompili M, Lester D, Tatarelli R, Girardi P. Recreational drug use and suicidality among italian young adults. *Journal of Addictive Diseases*. 2008; 27(4):51-9.
[17] Hufford MR. Alcohol and suicidal behavior. *Clinical Psychology Review*. 2001; 21(5):797-811.
[18] Roy A. Distal risk factors for suicidal behavior in alcoholics: replications and new findings. *Journal of Affective Disorders*. 2003; 77:267-71.
[19] Darke S, Ross J. Suicide among heroin users: Rates, risk factors and methods. *Addiction*. 2002; 97:1383-94.
[20] Johnsson E, Fridell M. Suicide attempts in a cohort of drug abusers: A 5-year follow-up study. *Acta Psychiatrica Scandinavica*. 1997; 96:362-6.
[21] Murphy SL, Rounsaville BJ, Eyre S, Kleber HD. Suicide attempts in treated opiate addicts. *Comprehensive Psychiatry*. 1983 January/February; 24(1):79-89.
[22] Rossow I, Lauritzen G. Shattered childhood: a key issue in suicidal behavior among drug addicts? *Addiction*. 2001; 96:227-40.
[23] Vingoe L, Welch S, Farrell M, Strang J. Heroin overdose among a treatment sample of injecting drug misusers: Accident or suicidal behaviour? *Journal of Substance Use*. 1999; 4:88-91.
[24] Darke S, Ross J. The relationship between suicide and heroin overdose among methadone maintenance patients in Sydney, Australia. *Addiction*. 2001; 96:1443-53.
[25] Allison M, Hubbard RL, Ginzburg HM. Indicators of suicide and depression among drug abusers. *1979-1981 TOPS Admission Cohorts*. Rockville, MD: US Department of Health and Human Services; 1985.
[26] Ravndal E, Vaglum P. Overdoses and suicide attempts: Different relations to psychopathology and substance abuse? A 5-year prospective study of drug abusers. *European Addiction Research*. 1999; 5:63-70.
[27] Moore THM, Zammit S, Lingford-Hughes A, Barnes TRE, Jones PB, Burke M, Lewis G. Cannabis use and risk of psychotic or affective mental health outcomes: a systematic review. *Lancet*. 2007; 370:319-28.
[28] Pedersen W. Does cannabis use lead to depression and suicidal behaviours? A population-based longitudinal study. *Acta Psychiatrica Scandinavica*. 2008; 118:395-403.
[29] Lynskey MT, Glowinski AL, Todorov AA, Bucholz KK, Madden PAF, Neslon EC, Statham DJ, Martin NG, Heath AC. Major depressive disorder, suicidal ideation, and suicide attempt in twins discordant for cannabis dependence and early-onset cannabis use. *Archives of General Psychiatry*. 2004; 61:1026-32.
[30] Darke S, Kaye S. Attempted suicide among injecting and noninjecting cocaine users in Sydney, Australia. *Journal of Urban Health*. 2004; 81(3):505-15.
[31] Roy A. Characteristics of cocaine dependent patients who attempt suicide. *Archives of Suicide Research*. 2009; 13:46-51.
[32] Glasner-Edwards S, Mooney LJ, Marinelli-Casey P, Hillhouse M, Ang A, Rawson R. Risk factors for suicide attempts in methamphetamine-dependent patients. *The American Journal on Addictions*. 2008; 17:24-7.
[33] Darke S, Ross J. Polydrug dependence and psychiatric comorbidity among heroin injectors. *Drug and Alcohol Dependence*. 1997; 48:135-41.

[34] Borges G, Walters EE, Kessler RC. Associations of substance use, abuse, and dependence with subsequent suicidal behavior. *American Journal of Epidemiology.* 2000; 151(8):781-9.

[35] Kosten TR, Rounsaville BJ. Suicidality among opioid addicts: 2.5 year follow-up. *American Journal of Drug and Alcohol Abuse*. 1988; 14(3):357-69.

[36] Roy A. Characteristics of opiate dependent patients who attempt suicide. *Journal of Clinical Psychiatry*. 2002 May; 63(5):403-7.

[37] Tremeau F, Darreye A, Staner L, Correa H, Weibel H, Khidichian F, Macher J. Suicidality in opioid-dependent subjects. *The American Journal on Addictions.* 2008; 17:187-94.

[38] Roy A, Janal MN. Risk factors for suicide attempts among alcohol dependent patients. *Archives of Suicide Research.* 2007; 11(2):211-7.

[39] Roy A. Characteristics of drug addicts who attempt suicide. *Psychiatry Research.* 2003; 121:99-103.

[40] Darke S, Williamson A, Ross J, Teesson M. Attempted suicide among heroin users: 12-month outcomes from the Australian Treatment Outcome Study (ATOS). *Drug and Alcohol Dependence*. 2005; 78:177-86.

[41] Kalyoncu A, Mirsal H, Pektas O, Tan D, Beyazyurek M. Heroin-dependent patients attempting and not attempting suicide: a comparison. *Acta Neuropsychiatrica.* 2007; 19:297-303.

[42] Preuss UW, Schuckit MA, Smith TL, Danko GP, Bucholz KK, Hasselbrock MN, Hesselbrock V, Kramer JR. Predictors and correlates of suicide attempts over 5 years in 1,237 alcohol-dependent men and women. *American Journal of Psychiatry.* 2003; 160:56-63.

[43] Klein H, Elifson KW, Sterk CE. Predictors of suicidal ideation among "at risk" cocaine-using African American women. *Suicide and Life-Threatening Behavior.* 2006; 36(3):336-48.

[44] Sher L. Alcoholism and suicidal behavior: a clinical overview. *Acta Psychiatrica Scandinavica.* 2006; 113:13-22.

[45] Bartholomew NG, Courtney K, Rowan-Szal GA, Simpson DD. Sexual abuse history and treatment outcomes among women undergoing methadone treatment. *Journal of Substance Abuse Treatment*. 2005; 29:231-5.

[46] Conroy E, Degenhardt L, Mattick RP, Nelson EC. Child maltreatment as a risk factor for opioid dependence: Comparison of family characteristics and type and severity of child maltreatment with a matched control group. *Child Abuse and Neglect* 2009; 33:343-52.

[47] Heffernan K, Cloitre M, Tardiff K, Marzuk PM, Portera L, Leon AC. Childhood trauma as a correlate of lifetime opioid use in psychiatric patients. *Addictive Behaviors.* 2000; 25(4):797-803.

[48] Maloney E, Degenhardt L, Darke S, Mattick RP, Nelson EC. Suicidal behaviour and associated risk factors among opioid dependent persons: A case-control study. *Addiction.* 2007; 102:1933-41.

[49] Chatham LR, Knight K, Joe GW, Simpson DD. Suicidality in a sample of methadone maintenance clients. *American Journal of Drug and Alcohol Abuse. 1995 August;* 21(3):345-62.

[50] Beautrais AL, Joyce PR, Mulder RT, Fergusson DM, Deavoll BJ, Nightingale SK. Prevalence and comorbidity of mental disorders in persons making serious suicide attempts: A case-control study. *American Journal of Psychiatry.* 1996 August; 153(8):1009-14.

[51] Suominen K, Henriksson M, Suokas J, Isometsa E, Ostamo A, Lonnqvist J. Mental disorders and comorbidity in attempted suicide. *Acta psychiatrica Scandinavica.* 1996; 94:234-40.

[52] Sher L, Stanley BH, Harkavy-Friedman JM, Carballo JJ, Arendt M, Brent DA, Sperling D, Lizardi D, Mann JJ, Oquendo MA. Depressed patients with co-occurring alcohol use disorders: A unique patient population. *Journal of Clinical Psychiatry.* 2008; 69(6):907-15.

[53] Kessler RC, Berglund P, Demler O, Jin R, Merikangas KR, Walters EE. Lifetime prevalence and age-of-onset distributions of DSM-IV disorders in the National Comorbidity Survey Replication. *Archives of General Psychiatry.* 2005 June; 62:593-602.

[54] Bolton JM, Belik S, Enns MW, Cox BJ, Sareen J. Exploring the correlates of suicide attempts among individuals with major depressive disorder: Findings from the National Epidemiological Survey on Alcohol and Related Conditions. *Journal of Clinical Psychiatry.* 2008; 69(7):1139-49.

[55] Gunderson JG. Borderline personality disorder: *A clinical guide.* Washington: American Psychiatric Publishing, Inc. 2001.

[56] Black DW, Blum N, Pfohl B, Hale N. Suicidal behavior in borderline personality disorder: prevalence, risk factors, prediction and prevention. *Journal of Personality Disorders.* 2004; 18(3):226-38.

[57] Trull TJ, Sher KJ, Minks-Brown C, Durbin J, Burr R. Borderline personality disorder and substance use disorders: A review and integration. *Clinical Psychology Review.* 2000; 20(2):235-53.

[58] Darke S, Williamson A, Ross J, Teesson M, Lynskey M. Borderline personality disorder, antisocial personality disorder and risk-taking among heroin users: findings from the Australian Treatment Outcome Study (ATOS). *Drug and Alcohol Dependence.* 2004; 74:77-83.

[59] Links PS, Heslegrave RJ, Mitton JE, van Reekum R, Patrick J. Borderline personality disorder and substance abuse: Consequences of comorbidity. *Canadian Journal of Psychiatry.* 1995 February; 40(1):9-14.

[60] Yen S, Shea TM, Pagano M, Sanislow CA, Grilo CM, McGlashan TH, Skodol AE, Bender DS, Zanarini MC, Gunderson JG, Morey LC. Axis I and Axis II disorders as predictors of prospective suicide attempts: Findings from the collaborative longitudinal personality disorders study. *Journal of Abnormal Psychology.* 2003; 112(3):375-81.

[61] Kolla NJ, Eisenberg H, Links PS. Epidemiology, risk factors and psychopharmacological management of suicidal behavior in borderline personality disorder. *Archives of Suicide Research.* 2008; 12:1-19.

[62] Maloney E, Degenhardt L, Darke S, Nelson EC. Impulsivity and borderline personality as risk factors for suicide attempts among opioid-dependent individuals. *Psychiatry Research.* 2009; 169:16-21.

[63] Mills K, Lynskey M, Teesson M, Ross J, Darke S. Post-traumatic stress disorder among people with heroin dependence in the Australian treatment outcome study (ATOS): Prevalence and correlates. *Drug and Alcohol Dependence.* 2005; 77:243-9.

[64] Clark WH, Masson CL, Delucchi KL, Hall SM, Sees KL. Violent traumatic events and drug abuse severity. *Journal of Substance Abuse Treatment.* 2001; 20:121-7.

[65] Darke S, Ross J, Lynskey MT, Teesson M. Attempted suicide among entrants to three treatment modalities for heroin dependence in the Australian Treatment Outcome Study (ATOS): Prevalence and risk factors. *Drug and Alcohol Dependence.* 2004; 73:1-10.

[66] Stanley B, Gameroff MJ, Michalsen V, Mann JJ. Are suicide attempters who self-mutilate a unique population? *The American Journal of Psychiatry.* 2001 March; 158(3):427-32.

[67] Favazza AR. The coming of age of self-mutilation. *The Journal of Nervous and Mental Disease.* 1998 May; 186(5):259-68.

[68] Cumming S, Covic T, Murrell E. Deliberate self-harm: Have we scratched the surface? *Behaviour Change.* 2006; 23(3):186-99.

[69] Evren C, Evren B. Self-mutilation in substance-dependent patients and relationship with childhood abuse and neglect, alexithymia and temperament and character dimensions of personality. *Drug and Alcohol Dependence.* 2005; 80:15-22.

[70] Harned MS, Najavitis LM, Weiss RD. Self-harm and suicidal behaviour in women with comorbid PTSD and substance dependence. *The American Journal on Addictions.* 2006; 15:392-5.

[71] Maloney E, Degenhardt L, Darke S, Nelson EC. Investigating the co-occurrence of self-mutilation and suicide attempts among opioid dependent individuals. *Suicide and Life-Threatening Behavior.* in press.

[72] Conner KR, Hesselbrock VM, Meldrum SC, Schuckit MA, Bucholz K, Gamble SA, Wines Jr. JD, Kramer J. Transitions to, and correlates of, suicidal ideation, plans, and unplanned and planned suicide attempts among 3,729 men and women with alcohol dependence. *Journal of Studies on Alcohol and Drugs.* 2007; 68:654-62.

[73] Darke S, Ross J, Williamson A, Mills KL, Havard A, Teesson M. Patterns and correlates of attempted suicide by heroin users over a 3-year period: Findings from the Australian treatment outcome study. *Drug and Alcohol Dependence.* 2007; 87:146-52.

[74] Wojnar M, Ilgen MA, Jakubczyk A, Wnorowska A, Klimkiewicz A, Brower KJ. Impulsive suicide attempts predict post-treatment relapse in alcohol dependent patients. *Drug and Alcohol Dependence.* 2008; 97:268-75.

[75] Lejoyeux M, Huet F, Claudon M, Fichelle A, Casalino E, Lequen V. Characteristics of suicide attempts preceded by alcohol consumption. *Archives of Suicide Research.* 2008; 12:30-8.

[76] Murphy GE. Psychiatric aspects of suicidal behaviour: Substance abuse. In: Hawton K, van Heeringen K, eds. *The International Handbook of Suicide and Attempted Suicide.* Chichester: John Wiley & Sons 2000:135-46.

In: Suicidal Behavior in Alcohol and Drug Abuse...
Editors: L. Sher, A. Vilens, pp. 299-311
ISBN: 978-1-60876-919-3

Chapter 17

LINKS BETWEEN PERSONALITY, ALCOHOL USE, AND SUICIDE IN EMERGING ADULTHOOD

Julie A. Patock-Peckham and Lindsey M. Backer
Baylor University, Waco, Texas, USA

ABSTRACT

Individual differences in personality play a significant role in the development of alcohol-related problems. Alcohol and other substance abuse disorders are known to be linked to suicide attempts and completions. This chapter will discuss both externalizing and internalizing pathways to alcohol-related problems in emerging adulthood as well as illustrate possible links to these mechanisms to suicide attempts. In the internalizing pathway to alcohol-related problems which may lead to suicide attempts, we will discuss one contributing mechanism, neuroticism, and one potentially protective mechanism, obsessive compulsive disorder. In the externalizing pathway to alcohol-related problems, we will explore antisocial personality disorder as a contributing mechanism to alcohol use, alcohol-related problems, suicide attempts, and suicide completions.

INTRODUCTION

The model of deviance proneness presumes that alcohol use disorders occur due to complex interactions between temperamental predispositions (i.e. genetics and variations in personality) and the environment (i.e. parental, peer, and romantic relationships) [1]. Temperament or personality usually is thought to be linked to alcohol use through either internalizing (e.g. depression, neuroticism, or obsessive compulsive disorder) or externalizing symptoms (e.g. impulsiveness, sensation seeking, behavioral under-control, criminal behavior, or antisocial personality disorder). In this chapter, we will explore two internalizing symptoms neuroticism and obsessive compulsive disorder discussed within the context of how alcohol use relates to suicide attempts and completions. In addition, we will explore the most serious of the externalizing symptoms or disorders, antisocial personality disorder, and its links to alcohol use, alcohol-related problems and suicide attempts and completions.

NEUROTICISM

In an 11 year longitudinal study, Jackson and Sher (2003) found that alcohol use disorders (AUDs) and the tendency to experience psychological distress (i.e. neuroticism and childhood stressors), were strongly linked [2]. Neuroticism denotes the tendency to experience negative affect [3, 4]. Individuals higher on neuroticism tend to feel tense, anxious, and worried. Eysenck and Eysenck (1985) suggest that individual differences in neuroticism are indicative of inherited physiological characteristics of the nervous system [5]. According to Steward and Devine (2000), neuroticism indicates a degree of instability in the autonomic nervous system [6]. Neurotics presumably have a high sensitivity and a greater degree of responsiveness to negative affect stimuli. These individuals are typically characterized as punishment avoidant folks who may be more likely to use alcohol for self-medicating reasons [7, See also, pp. 497; 6].

Neuroticism has been linked to psychological distress [2], co-morbid binge eating and alcohol abuse among women [8], hard drug use (e.g. amphetamine, barbiturate, hallucinogen, cocaine, and opiate) among convicted male offenders (17-21 years old) [9], and to individuals meeting diagnostic criteria for alcohol use and dependence [10, 11]. Reed and Conner (2006) observed that neuroticism was directly linked to alcohol related problems regardless of levels of alcohol use [12]. In addition, Stewart and Devine (2000) found that neuroticism was specifically linked to drinking to reduce tension [6]. More recently, Hussong (2003) found that "coping motives mediate the relationship between neuroticism and alcohol use and problem use" (p. 146) [13].

Tension reducing reasons for drinking were found to be stronger predictors of drinking problems among university students than were social facilitative reasons for drinking [14]. Previous investigators have shown that consumption of alcohol to cope with negative affect is associated with drinking alone, heavy drinking, alcohol-related problems, alcohol abuse [15, 3, 14, 16], and frequency of intoxication [17]. Hesselbrook, O'Brien, Weinstein, and Carter-Menendez (1987) reported a direct link between the greater amount of alcohol consumed and the importance of relief from unpleasant affect as a reason for drinking [18]. Moreover, Reese, Chassin and Molina (1994) found that problem drinkers are more likely to anticipate that alcohol will reduce aversive emotional states to a greater extent than non-problem drinkers [19]. This is important because the stress-reduction drinking motive takes increasing precedence over other drinking motives in post collegiate life [20].

NEUROTICISM AND DRINKING TO COPE (SELF-MEDICATION)

The pathways to drinking as a means of coping with stress are highly complex [21] and not well understood. The relationship between experiencing stress or anxiety on drinking behaviors is mixed. While some investigators have reported that stress and anxiety do not lead to increased alcohol consumption [22, 23] many other investigators suggest that stress is related to increases in drinking related behaviors. For instance, increased alcohol use has been linked to overall life stress [24, 25, 26, 27, & 28], negative affectivity [29], anxiety [30], and nervousness [31].

College students who suffer from poor mental health and depression report more instances of problematic drinking related outcomes [32, 33, & 34]. Apparently, college students often use alcohol to cope with negative affect [30, 35] as well as a means to deal with life stressors [24, 36]. It is possible that the link between drinking for tension reduction and alcohol related problems may be moderated by gender. In a recent longitudinal study, Rutledge and Sher (2001) found that stress was only positively linked to heavy drinking among males (age 21) with stronger tension reduction motives [37]. This is consistent with the finding of Kushner et al. (1994) who found that anxiety was more strongly associated with alcohol use among male college freshman who held stronger tension-reduction alcohol expectancies than among males with weaker tension-reduction expectancies [30]. This relationship was not found among college freshman women [30]. These findings are consistent with Patock-Peckham and Morgan-Lopez (2009) who found that neuroticism and pathological reasons for drinking mediated the impact of father authoritarianism on both alcohol use and alcohol-related problems but only among males [38]. Therefore, it is possible that males may be more susceptible to environmental factors that may be ripe for the development of a neurotic personality.

Neuroticism and Suicide Attempts

O'Boyle and Brandon (1998) found suicide attempters who had entered a substance abuse program had higher neuroticism and borderline personality scores than non-attempters (See pages 355-356) [39]. Moreover, suicide attempters had a history of abusing more substances than non-attempters [39]. This is consistent with Ward and Schuckit (1980) who found that among individuals who preferred depressant drugs there was a higher frequency of suicide attempts [40]. According to Statham and colleagues (1998) risk of persistent suicidal thoughts and suicide attempts may best be explained by a complex interplay of psychiatric history, neuroticism, traumatic life experiences (i.e. childhood sexual abuse, rape, or physical assaults) or status-loss (e.g. job loss, loss of property or home, divorce), genetic vulnerability, and socio-cultural factors [41]. Interestingly, neuroticism remained a significant predictor of suicidal thoughts even when psychiatric history was controlled for among Australian twins followed longitudinally [41]. Among Taiwanese college students, Shur-Fen Gau and colleagues (2008) found a positive linear trend between increased suicidal tendency (e.g. death wishes, suicidal ideations, and suicidal plans) and higher levels of neuroticism, harm avoidance, novelty seeking, psychopathology, and parenting styles of low affection, overprotection, and authoritarian controlling (See page 135) [42].

While it is clear that higher levels of neuroticism are linked to suicide attempts, Useda et al. (2007) reported that suicide completers (decedents) are actually lower in neuroticism and higher in conscientiousness than suicide attempters (who fail to complete the act) [43]. Thus, neuroticism may be more related to failed suicide attempts than completed acts and may serve as a way to relieve tension and draw attention to one's need for assistance from others. Regardless, it is very clear that neuroticism is linked to both increased suicidal thoughts and suicidal attempts [39, 41, & 42]. Nevertheless it is highly unlikely that there will be a suicide completion without individuals first experiencing some suicidal thoughts or attempting suicide. Therefore, neuroticism is an important variable to consider regarding overall suicide risk.

Obsessive Compulsive Personality Disorder

Obsessive compulsive symptoms reflect anxiety involving recurrent and intrusive thoughts that translate into subsequent compulsions used as a means to alleviate the distress [44, see also pp. 434; 45]. Obsessive Compulsive Disorder (OCD) has been associated with other anxiety disorders such as panic disorders and social phobias [46]. This is important because suicide risk is relatively high among individuals with co-morbid panic attacks and substance abuse [47]. OCD is co-morbid (i.e. co-varies; where one is found so is the other) with Body Dysmorphic Disorder (BDD), a preoccupation with an imagined physical anomaly such as having a scar or a perception of having a large nose, [48]. This may account for some of the development of social phobias among those with OCD.

Frost, Steketee, Williams, and Warren (2000) found that individuals with both OCD and hoarding symptoms had elevated anxiety, depression, and social dysfunction compared to individuals with OCD and no hording symptoms [49]. Individuals diagnosed with OCD are more likely to engage in compulsive buying behavior than controls [50]. Compulsive buying reflects the uncontrollable purchasing of items that are not needed which is often followed by disappointment once the items are obtained and is frequently seen among those who engage in hording behaviors. Individuals with both OCD and Compulsive Buying (CB) diagnoses are more likely to also be depressed and have been found to consume greater amounts of alcohol than those with just OCD [50].

Spinella (2005, see p. 433) found greater severity of obsession and compulsions were related to a greater degree of intensity regarding negative emotions or moods such as anger, tension, confusion, fatigue, and depression [45]. According to Gentil and colleagues (2009) among patients with comorbid OCD and Alcohol Use Disorders, 80% of those studies reported that their first obsessive compulsive symptoms occurred in childhood while evidence of alcohol misuse did not occur until emerging adulthood [51].

OCD May Protect against Suicide

OCD appears to be unrelated or even protective of incarcerations and suicides. In Tye and Mullen's (2006) investigation of mental disorders among female prisoners, they found 84% met criteria for a mental disorder [52]. Interestingly, women in prison were significantly more likely to meet a slew of diagnoses compared to women in the community such as drug use disorders (57% of the prison population), major depression (44% of the prison population), psychosis (24% of the prison population), and posttraumatic stress disorder (36% of the prison population) with the exception of OCD (see page 266; 52). Women in prisons do not seem to have OCD in greater rates than those in the community [52].

Khan, Leventhal, Khan, and Brown (2002) reported suicide risk was 10 times more likely in those with diagnosed anxiety disorder than those in the general population [see pp. 189; 53]. While OCD is often found co-morbid with a wide variety of issues related to suicide, OCD alone appears to be protective against suicide. For "although suicide ideation and depression symptoms are common in OCD adolescent inpatients, they seem protected against suicide attempts" [see pp. 75; 54].

Antisocial Personality Disorder and Psychopathology

Antisocial Personality Disorder or APD reflects the general disregard for the rights of others [see pp. 645; 55] and is highly resistant to treatment [56]. According to American Psychiatric Association (1994) criteria for being diagnosed with APD is that one must be at least 18 years old, and have evidence of conduct disorder or CD (i.e. the general disregard for the rights of others usually diagnosed in children and adolescents) before the age of 15 [55]. The occurrence of the behavior must not be during episodes of Schizophrenia or Mania. These individuals display at least three of the following behaviors: failure to conform to social norms regarding lawful behavior, deceitfulness, impulsivity or an inability to plan ahead, irritability or aggressiveness, reckless disregard for their own and others safety, consistent irresponsibility by not sustaining consistent work behavior or honoring financial obligations, and a lack of remorse [see pp. 649-650; 55].

The constructs of Psychopathy and Antisocial Personality Disorder (APD) are quite controversial and sometimes used interchangeably. However, Hare, Hart, and Harpur (1991) [57] called this practice into question and Hare (1996) concluded that psychopathy and APD are two different constructs [58]. Psychopathy was defined by the 2nd addition of the *Diagnostic and Statistical Manual of Mental Disorders* [59] as one being un-socialized, impulsive, selfish, guiltless, callous, and showing an antisocial personality. However, in the DSM-III, psychopathy was changed to antisocial personality disorder and had many of the criteria used today [60]. According to Hare (1996) the problem with the new definition of psychopathy/APD is the criteria consists of mostly behaviors that deviate from social norms and do not concern personality traits [58].

Hare, McPherson, and Forth (1988) observed that criminal psychopaths show a reduction in criminality approximately around the age of 35 or 40 regarding nonviolent offenses [61]. Nevertheless, their preference for aggression and violence is persistent throughout most of their lives [62]. Consistent with these ideas Harpur and Hare (1994) found socially deviant aspects in psychopaths decrease with age, while affective/ interpersonal aspects remain constant with age [63]. Psychopaths are more likely to return to their previous criminal habits due to their recidivate behavior (i.e. tendency to repeat criminal or antisocial behavior) [64]. The most dangerous psychopaths are those that are sexually aroused by violence [65]. This is important because sex offenders are known for being resistant to treatment [66].

Antisocial Personality Disorder and Conduct Disorder

Since the criteria for APD requires one to have Conduct Disorder (CD), the majority of patients with APD have had CD as a child [56]. Thirty to forty percent of children with CD are likely to develop APD [67, 68, 69]. Symptoms of APD are thought to appear in childhood and persist through adolescence and early adulthood [70]. Robins, Tipp and Przybeck (1991) found 80% of individuals with APD had their first symptom by age 11 [see pp. 264; 69].

Loeber et al. (2003) claimed there are three main childhood diagnoses involved in the development of APD in adulthood: Conduct Disorder (CD), Oppositional Defiant Disorder (ODD) and Attention Deficit-Hyperactivity Disorder (ADHD) [56]. ODD is defined as a pattern of negativistic, defiant and hostile behavior while ADHD is defined as symptoms of inattention, hyperactivity and impulsivity [55]. The factor most often associated with APD is childhood development of conduct disorder or CD [71, 72, & 73].

APD, Environment, Substance Use, and Deviant Behaviors

Moffitt's (1993) antisocial behavior model describes the observed behaviors in adolescence and the risks of these behaviors in adulthood [74]. Her model demonstrates individuals with persistent antisocial behavior experience the most continued problems in adulthood compared to antisocial behavior limited to adolescence. Moffitt (1993) additionally states antisocial behavior may possibly be worsened by poor parenting [74].

Problematic behaviors are likely to arise in adults with APD. Risk-taking behaviors, such as early use of alcohol and tobacco and being more likely to use illicit drugs are shown to be greater in individuals with APD [75]. According to Sher and Trull (1994) APD is a major risk factor for alcohol dependence [76]. People with APD experience higher rates of alcohol abuse than the general population [77]. Loeber, Burke and Lahey (2002) observed marijuana use, depression and callous/unemotional behaviors are a risk factor for APD [78].

Another problematic behavior associated with APD is the development of violent and criminal behaviors. Individuals with CD prior to the development of APD are likely to be more violent than those individuals with CD which did not advance into APD [78]. Hodgins and Cote (1993) examined that individuals with APD tend to have their first incarceration earlier than those without the personality disorder [79]. They have also observed these individuals tend to have more violent and nonviolent crime convictions. APD is more apt to develop in delinquents than in non-delinquents, but only a small proportion of delinquents are actually diagnosed with APD [80].

Males develop APD more than females [81, 82, & 83]. Childhood and adolescent mental disorders are thought to affect the development of APD [84]. Hodgins and Cote (1993) observed that inmates with APD are more likely to have a juvenile record (84.6% had an arrest) compared to those without the diagnosis of APD (37.6% had an arrest) [see pp. 123; 79]. They also measured APD inmates with mental disorders and without disorders and revealed that there was not a significant difference between these two groups [79].

Recall, Oppositional Defiant Disorder (ODD) is negative, deviant and hostile behavior while CD is children having a general disregard for the rights of others. Loeber, et al's (2003) Hierarchical Developmental Model described ODD as a precursor of CD which is thought to be a precursor of APD [56]. According to this model, there are a relatively large proportion of young males who experience ODD and only a small proportion of this group will develop CD. From this group of individuals with CD a small proportion will develop APD. A solution for decreasing the abundance of APD in the population is to begin by preventing ODD and then work on preventing CD [78].

APD, Anxiety, and Death

Interestingly, internalizing behaviors such as symptoms of depression may play a factor in the development of APD. [85, 78, 86, & 87]. For instance, Sourander et al. (2005) found depression in children was a predictor of APD [86]. However, anxiety disorders may act as a shield against APD [56]. This may be because these individuals feel anxious about carrying out or repeating risky or unsafe behaviors. On the other hand, individuals who lack anxiety may be more prone to APD because they present fearlessness and behavior disinhibition [88].

Males diagnosed with APD who were under the age of 40 have a significant increase in risk for an early death [89]. Martin, Cloninger, Guze, and Clayton (1985) observed that a significant amount of APD out-patients die at an early age [90]. The odds ratio for APD and death is 2.93 [see pp. 446; 91]. Thus, individuals diagnosed with APD are about 3 times as likely to die young than are individuals without an APD diagnosis.

According to numerous investigators, a relationship exists between APD and suicide [92, 93, & 91]. James and Taylor (2008) observed APD is associated with suicide threats, self-injurious behavior, and suicide attempts among women [94]. About 30-40% of suicides are committed by Axis II disorders (i.e. personality disorders and SUDs) and APD is an example of one which contributes to these cases [92]. APD in conjunction with SUDs are associated with suicide attempts and completions [91, 95].

Conclusion

Alcohol and substance abuse are highly associated with both suicide attempts and completions. Both internalizing and externalizing pathways to alcohol-related problems appear to have implications for suicide attempts as well as completions. In the internalizing pathway, it is clear that individuals higher in neuroticism may be more likely to use alcohol to cope or to escape from feelings of anxiety. These individuals may also be more likely to attempt suicide to escape unhappy feelings. However, there is evidence to suggest that while neuroticism is associated with suicidal thoughts and suicide attempts that it may not be as strongly associated with suicide completions. This may suggest that neurotics may be using a suicide attempt as a plea for help. On the other hand, OCD involves recurrent and intrusive thoughts which may lead to compulsive shopping or hording behaviors as well as alcohol misuse to self-medicate. Presumably, alcohol could be used as a negative reinforcer that may temporarily take away the intrusive thoughts. However, while OCD is predictive of alcohol use and suicide ideation, it appears to somehow be protective of individuals experiencing incarceration, actually attempting suicide, as well as suicide completions.

In this chapter we only explored one externalizing pathway through APD. APD has been linked to alcohol, tobacco, and illicit drug use, criminal, and violent behaviors. Patients diagnosed with APD are known to die at an early age (3 times the rate of others) in emerging adulthood [91]. When APD is found in conjunction with substance use disorders it has been strongly linked to not just suicide attempts but to suicide completions [91, 95]. This pathway is an important one to understand because individuals with APD are highly resistant to treatment and frequently drop out of treatment [96].

REFERENCES

[1] Sher K: *Children of alcoholics: A critical appraisal of theory and research.* Chicago: University of Chicago Press, 1991.

[2] Jackson KM, Sher KJ: Alcohol use disorders and psychological distress: A prospective state-trait analysis. *Journal of Abnormal Psychology* 2003; 112(4): 599-613.

[3] Cooper ML: Motivations for alcohol use among adolescents: Development and validation of a four-factor model. *Psychological Assessment* 1994; 6: 117-128.

[4] Costa Jr. PT, McCrae RR: NEO-PI-R: Professional manual. Odessa, Florida: *Psychological Assessment Resources,* 1992

[5] Eysenck HJ, Eysenck MW: *Personality and individual differences.* London: Plenum Press. 1985.

[6] Stewart SH, Devine H: Relations between personality and drinking motives in young adults. *Personality and Individual Differences* 2000; 29: 495-511.

[7] Gray JA: *The neuropsychology of anxiety: An inquiry into the functions of septo-hippocampal system.* Oxford: Oxford University Press, 1982.

[8] Benjamin L, Walfert E: Dispositional correlates of addictive behaviors in college women: Binge eating and heavy drinking. *Eating Behaviors* 2005; 6: 197-209.

[9] Cookson H: Personality variables associated with alcohol use in young offenders. *Personality and Individual Differences* 1994; 16(1): 179-182.

[10] 10. Trull T, Sher KJ: Relationship between the five-factor model of personality and AXIS-I disorders in a non-clinical sample. *Journal of Abnormal Psychology* 1994; 103: 350-360.

[11] Martin ED, Sher KJ: Family history of alcoholism, alcohol use disorders and five-factor model of personality. *Journal of Studies on Alcohol* 1994; 55: 81-90.

[12] Read JP, O'Connor RM: High-and low-dose expectancies as mediators of personality dimensions and alcohol involvement. *Journal of Studies on Alcohol* 2006; 67: 204-214.

[13] Hussong AM: Social influences in motivated drinking among college students. *Psychology of Addictive Behaviors* 2003; 17(2): 142-150.

[14] Cox WM, Hosier SG, Crossley S, Kendall B, Roberts KL: Motives for drinking, alcohol consumption, and alcohol-related problems among British secondary-school and university students. *AddictiveBehaviors* 2006; 31: 2147-2157.

[15] Carey KB, Correia CJ: Drinking motives predict alcohol-related problems in college students. *Journal of Studies on Alcohol* 1997; 58: 100-105.

[16] Windle M, Windle RC: Coping strategies, drinking motives, and stressful life events among adolescents: Associations with emotional and behavioral problems, and academic functioning. *Journal of Abnormal Psychology* 1996; 105: 551-560.

[17] Carpenter KM, Hasin DS: Reasons for drinking alcohol: Relationships with DSM-IV alcohol diagnoses and alcohol consumption in a community sample. *Psychology of Addictive Behaviors* 1998; 12(3): 168-184.

[18] Hesselbrock VM, O'Brien J, Weinstein MA, Carter-Menendez N: Reasons for drinking and alcohol use in young adults at high risk and at low risk for alcoholism. *British Journal of Addiction* 1987; 82: 1335-1339.

[19] Reese FL, Chassin L, Molina BSG: Alcohol expectancies in early adolescents: Predicting drinking behavior from alcohol expectancies and parental alcoholism. *Journal of Studies on Alcohol* 1994; 55: 276-284.

[20] Perkins HW: Stress-motivated drinking in collegiate and post collegiate young adulthood: Life course and gender patterns. *Journal of Studies on Alcohol* 1999; 60: 219-227.

[21] Park CL, Armeli S, Tennen H: The daily stress and coping process and alcohol use among college students. *Journal of Studies on Alcohol* 2004; 65: 126-135.

[22] Greeley J, Oei T: Alcohol and tension reduction. In: Leonard, K. E. and Blane, H. T. (Eds.). *Psychological theories of drinking and alcoholism,* 2nd edition, New York: Guliford Press, pp. 14-53, 1999.

[23] Pohorecky LA: Stress and alcohol interaction: An update of human research. Alcoholism: *Clinical and Experimental Research* 1991; 15: 438-459.

[24] Hutchinson GT, Patock-Peckham JA, Cheong J, Nagoshi CT: Irrational beliefs and behavioral mis-regulation in the role of alcohol abuse among college students, *Journal of Rational-Emotive & Cognitive -Behavior Therapy* 1998; 16(1): 61-74.

[25] McCreary DR, Sadava SW: Stress, drinking, and the adverse consequences of drinking in two samples of young adults. *Psychology of Addictive Behaviors 1998;* 12: 247-261.

[26] Newcomb MD, Harlow LL: Life events and substance use among adolescents: Mediating effects of perceived loss of control and meaninglessness in life. *Journal of Personality and Social Psychology* 1986; 51: 564-577

[27] Steptoe A, Wardle J, Pollard TM, Canaan L, Davies GJ: Stress, social support and health-related behaviors: A study of smoking, alcohol consumption and physical exercise. *Journal of Psychosomatic Research* 1996; 41: 171-180.

[28] Weidner G, Kohlmann C-W, Dotzauer E, Burns L R: The effects of academic stress on health behaviors in young adults. *Anxiety Stress Coping* 1996; 9: 123-133.

[29] Sher KJ, Walitzer KS, Wood PK, Brent EE: Characteristics of children of alcoholics: Punitive risk factors, substance use and abuse, and psychopathology. *Journal of Abnormal Psychology* 1991; 100: 427-448.

[30] Kushner MG, Sher KJ, Wood MD, Wood PK: Anxiety and drinking behavior: Moderating effects of tension-reduction alcohol outcome expectancies. *Alcoholism: Clinical and Experimental Research* 1994, 18: 852-860.

[31] Swendsen JD, Tennen H, Garney MA, Affleck G, Willard A, Hromi A: Mood and alcohol consumption: An experience sampling test of the self-mediation hypothesis. *Journal of Abnormal Psychology* 2000, 109: 198-204.

[32] Hussong AM, Hicks RE, Levy SA, Curran PJ: Specifying the relations between affect and heavy alcohol use among young adults. *Journal of Abnormal Psychology* 2001; 110: 449-461.

[33] Patock-Peckham JA, Morgan-Lopez AA: College drinking behaviors: Mediational links between parenting styles, parental bonds, depression, and alcohol problems. *Psychology of Addictive Behaviors* 2007; 21(3): 297-306.

[34] Weitzman ER: Poor mental health, depression, and associations with alcohol consumption, harm and abuse in a national sample of young adults in college. *The Journal of Nervous and Mental Disease* 2004, 192(4): 269-277.

[35] Wood MD, Nagoshi CT, Dennis DA: Alcohol norms and expectations as predictors of alcohol use and problems in a college student sample. *American Journal of Drug and Alcohol Abuse* 1992; 18: 461-476.

[36] Park CL, Levenson MR: Drinking to cope among college students: Prevalence, problems, and coping processes. *Journal of Studies on Alcohol* 2002; 63: 486-497.

[37] Rutledge PC, Sher KJ: Heavy drinking from the freshman year into early young adulthood: The role of stress, tension-reduction drinking motives, gender and personality. *Journal of Studies on Alcohol* 2001; 62: 457-466.

[38] Patock-Peckham JA, Morgan-Lopez AA: The gender specific mediational pathways between parenting styles, neuroticism, pathological reasons for drinking, and alcohol-related problems in emerging adulthood. *Addictive Behaviors* 2009; 34: 312-315.

[39] O'Boyle M, Brandon, EAA: Suicide attempts, substance abuse, and personality. *Journal of Substance Abuse Treatment* 1998; 15(4): 353-356.

[40] Ward NG, Schuckit MA: Factors associated with suicidal behavior in poly drug abusers. *Journal of Clinical Psychiatry* 1980; 41: 379-385.

[41] Statham DJ, Heath AC, Madden PAF, Bucholz KK, Bierut L, Dinwiddle SH, Slutske WS, Dunne,MP, Martin NG: Suicidal behavior: An epidemiological and genetic study. *Psychological Medicine* 1998; 28: 839-855.

[42] Shur-Fen Gua S, Chen Y-Y, Tsai F-J, Lee M-B, Chiu Y-N, Soong W-T, Hwu H-G: Risk factors for suicide in Taiwanese College students. *Journal of American College Health* 2008; 57(2): 135-142.

[43] Usesda JD, Duberstein PR, Conner KR, Beckman A, Franus N, Tu X, Convell Y: Personality differences in attempted suicide versus suicide in adults 50 years of age or older. *Journal of Consulting and Clinical Psychology* 2007; 75(1): 126-133.

[44] American Psychiatric Association: *Diagnostic and statistical manual of mental disorders*, (4th ed.). Washington, DC: American Psychiatric Association, 2000.

[45] Spinella M: Mood in relation to subclinical obsessive-compulsive symptoms. *International Journal of Neuroscience* 2005, 115: 433-443.

[46] Richter MA, Summerfeldt LJ, Antony MM, Swinson RP: Obsessive-compulsive spectrum conditions in obsessive-compulsive disorder and other anxiety disorders. *Depression and Anxiety* 2003; 18(3): 118-127.

[47] Lepine JP, Chignon JM, Teherani M: Suicide attempts in patients with panic disorder. *Arch. Gen. Psychiatry* 1993; 50: 144-149.

[48] Frare F, Perugi G, Ruffolo G, Toni C: Obsessive-compulsive disorder and body dysmorphic disorder: A comparison of clinical features. *European Psychiatry* 2004; 19: 292-298.

[49] Frost RO, Steketee O, Williams LF, Warren R: Mood personality disorder symptoms and disability in obsessive compulsive hoarders: A comparison with clinical and non-clinical controls. *Behavioral Research and Therapy* 2000; 38(1): 1071-1081.

[50] Lejoyeux M, Bailly F, Moula H, Loi S, Andes J: Study of compulsive buying inpatients presenting obsessive-compulsive disorder. *Comprehensive Psychiatry* 2005; 46: 105-110.

[51] Gentil AF, de Mathis MA, Torresau RC, Diniz JB, Alvarenga P, Conceicao de Rosario M, Cordioli AV, Torres AR, Miguel EC: Alcohol use disorders in patients with obsessive-compulsive disorder: The importance of appropriate dual diagnosis. *Drug and Alcohol Dependence* 2009; 100: 173-177.

[52] Tye CS, Mullen PE: Mental disorders in female prisoners. *Australian and New Zealand Journal of Psychiatry* 2006; 40: 266-271.

[53] Khan A, Leventhal RM, Khan S, Brown WA: Suicide risk in patients with anxiety disorders: A meta-analysis of the FDA database. *Journal of Affective Disorders* 2002; 68: 183-190.

[54] Apter A, Horesh N, Gothelf D, Zalsman G, Erlich Z, Soreni N, Weizman A: Depression and suicidal behavior in adolescent inpatients with obsessive compulsive disorder. *Journal of Affective Disorders* 2003; 75: 181-189.

[55] American Psychiatric Association: **Diagnostic and statistical manual of mental disorders** (4th ed.). Washington, DC: Author, 1994.

[56] Loeber R, Green SM, Lahey BB: Risk factors for adult antisocial personality. In DP Farrington & JW Coid (Eds.) *Early prevention of adult antisocial behaviour* (pp. 79-108). Cambridge, England: Cambridge University Press, 2003.

[57] Hare RD, Hart SD, Harpur TJ: Psychopathy and the DSM-IV criteria for antisocial personality disorder. *Journal of Abnormal Psychology* 1991; 100: 391-398.

[58] Hare RD: Psychopathy: A clinical construct whose time has come. *Criminal Justice and Behavior* 1996; 23: 25-54.

[59] American Psychiatric Association: **Diagnostic and statistical manual of mental disorders** (2nd ed.). Washington, DC: Author, 1968.

[60] American Psychiatric Association: **Diagnostic and statistical manual of mental disorders** (3rd ed.). Washington, DC: Author, 1980.

[61] Hare R.D, McPherson LE, Forth AE: Male psychopaths and their criminal careers. *Journal of Consulting and Clinical Psychology* 1998; 56: 710-714.

[62] Harris GT, Rice ME, Cormier CA: Psychopathy and violent recidivism. *Law and Human Behavior* 1991; 15: 625-637.

[63] Harpur TJ, Hare RD: The assessment of psychopathy as a function of age. *Journal of Abnormal Psychology* 1994; 103: 604-637.

[64] Quinsey VL, Harris GE, Rice ME, Lalumiere ML: Assessing treatment efficacy in outcome studies of sex offenders. *Journal of Interpersonal Violence* 1993; 8: 512-523.

[65] Rice ME, Harris GT, Quinsey VL: A follow-up of rapists assessed in a maximum security psychiatric facility. *Journal of Interpersonal Violence* 1990; 5(4): 435-448.

[66] Quinsey VL, Rice ME, Harris GT: Actuarial prediction of sexual recidivism. *Journal of Interpersonal Violence* 1995; 10: 85-105.

[67] Robins LN: *Deviant children grown up. Baltimore:* Williams & Wilkins, 1966.

[68] Robins LN: Conduct disorder. *Journal of Child Psychology and Psychiatry* 1991; 32: 193-212.

[69] Robins LN, Tripp J, Przybeck T: Antisocial personality. In L.N. Robins & D.A. Regier (Eds.), *Psychiatric disorders in America* (pp. 224-271). New York: Free Press, 1991.

[70] Frick PJ, O'Brien BS, Wootton JM, McBurnett K: Psychopathy and conduct problems in children. *Journal of Abnormal Psychology* 1994; 103(4): 700-707.

[71] Abramowitz CS, Kosson DS, Seidenberg M: The relationship between childhood attention deficit hyperactivity disorder and conduct problems and adult psychopathy in male inmates. *Personality and Individual Differences* 2004, 36: 1031-1047.

[72] Lahey BB, Loeber R: Attention-deficit/hyperactivity disorder, oppositional defiant disorder, conduct disorder, and adult antisocial behavior: A life span perspective. In D. M. Stoff, J. Breiling, & J. D. Maser (Eds.), *Handbook of antisocial behavior* (pp. 51-59). New York: Wiley, 1997.

[73] Moffitt TE, Caspi A, Rutter M, Silva PA: Sex differences in antisocial behaviour: *Conduct disorder, delinquency, and violence in the Dunedin Longitudinal Study. Cambridge,* England: Cambridge University Press, 2001.

[74] Moffitt TE: Adolescence-limited and life-course persistent antisocial behavior: A developmental taxonomy. *Psychology Review* 1993; 100: 674-701.

[75] Westermeyer J, Thuras P: Association of antisocial personality disorder and substance disorder morbidity in a clinical sample. *American Journal of Drug & Alcohol Abuse* 2005; 31: 93-110.

[76] Sher KJ, Trull TJ: Personality and disinhibitory psychopathology: alcoholism and antisocial personality disorder, *American Journal of Psychiatry* 1994; 130: 92-102.

[77] Schuckit MA: The clinical implicatons of primary diagnostic groups among alcoholics. *Archives of General Psychiatry* 1985; 42: 1043-1049.

[78] Loeber R, Burke JD, Lahey BB: What are the adolescent antecedents to antisocial personality disorder? *Criminal Behaviour & Mental Health* 2002; 12: 24-36.

[79] Hodgins S, Cote, G: The criminality of mentally disordered offenders. *Criminal Justice & Behavior* 1993; 20: 115-129.

[80] Patrick CJ, Zempolich KA, Levenston GK: Emotionality and violent behavior in psychopaths. In A. Raine, P.A. Brennan, D.P. Farrington and S.A. Mednick (eds.), *Biosocial Bases of Violence* (pp. 145-62). New York: Plenum, 1997.

[81] Fazel S, Danesh J: Serious mental disorder in 23,000 prisoners: A systematic review of 62 surveys. *Lancet* 2002, 359: 545-550.

[82] Kim-Cohen J, Caspi A, Moffitt TE, Harrington H, Milne BJ, Poulton, R: Prior juvenile diagnoses in adults with mental disorder: Developmental follow-back of a prospective-longitudinal cohort. *Archives of General Psychiatry* 2003; 60: 709-717.

[83] Lyons MJ, Jerskey BA: Personality disorders: Epidemiological findings, methods, and concepts. In MT Tsuang & M Tohen (Eds.) *Textbook in psychiatric epidemiology* (2nd ed., pp. 563-599). New York: Wiley-Liss, 2002.

[84] Washburn JJ, Romero EG, Welty LJ, Abram KM, Teplin LA, McClelland GM, Paskar L D: Development of antisocial personality disorder in detained youths: The predictive value of mental disorders. *Journal of Consulting and Clinical Psychology* 2007; 75(2): 221-231.

[85] Bardon AM, Moffitt T, Caspi A, Dickson N: Adult mental health and social outcomes of adolescent girls with depression and conduct disorder. *Development and Psychopathology* 1996; 8: 811-829.

[86] Sourander AM, Multimaki PM, Nikolakaros GM, Haavisto AM, Ristkari T.M, Helenius HM, Parkkola K, Piha J, Tamminen T, Moilanen I, Kumpulainen K, Almqvist F: Childhood predictors of psychiatric disorders among boys: A prospective community-based follow-up study from age 8 years to early adulthood. *Journal of the American Academy of Child & Adolescent Psychiatry* 2005; 44: 756-767.

[87] Kasen S, Cohen P, Skodol AE, Johnson JG, Smailes E, Brook JS: Childhood depression and adult personality disorder: Alternative pathways of continuity. *Archives of General Psychiatry* 2001; 58: 231-236.

[88] Frick PJ, Lilienfeld SO, Ellis M, Loney B, Silverthorn P: The association between anxiety and psychopathy dimensions in children. *Journal of Abnormal Child Psychology* 1999; 27: 383-392.

[89] Black DW, Baumgard CH, Bell SE, Kao C: Death rates in 71 men with antisocial personality disorder: A comparison with general population mortality. *Psychosomatics: Journal of Consultation Liaison Psychiatry* 1996; 37: 131-136.

[90] Martin RL, Cloninger CR, Guze SB, Clayton PJ: Mortality in a follow-up of 500 psychiatric outpatients. II. Cause-specific mortality. *Archives General Psychiatry,* 1985, 42: 58-66.

[91] Verona E, Sachs-Ericsson N, Joiner TE: Suicide attempts associated with externalizing psychopathology in an epidemiological sample. *American Journal of Psychiatry 2004,* 161: 444-451.

[92] Duberstein PR, Conwell Y: Personality disorders and completed suicide: A methodological and conceptual review. *Clinical Psychology: Science and Practice* 1997; 4(4): 359-376.

[93] Verona E, Patrick CJ, Joiner TE: Psychopathy, antisocial personality, and suicide risk. *Journal of Abnormal Psychology* 2001; 110(3): 462-470.

[94] James LM, Taylor J: Associations between symptoms of borderline personality disorder, externalizing disorders, and suicide-related behaviors. *Journal of Psychopathology and Behavioral Assessment* 2008; 30: 1-9.

[95] Hills AL, Cox BJ, McWilliams LA, Sareen J: Suicide attempts and externalizing psychopathology in a nationally representative sample. *Comprehensive Psychiatry* 2005; 46(5): 334-339.

[96] Fals-Stewart W, Leonard KE, Birchler GR: The occurrence of male-to-female intimate partner violence on days of men's drinking: The moderating effects of antisocial personality disorder. *Journal of Consulting and Clinical Psychology 2005;* 73(2), 239-248.

In: Suicidal Behavior in Alcohol and Drug Abuse...
Editors: L. Sher, A. Vilens, pp. 313-324
ISBN: 978-1-60876-919-3

Chapter 18

ACUTE ALCOHOL USE AND SUICIDE ATTEMPTS

Courtney L. Bagge and Julie A. Schumacher
University of Mississippi Medical Center, Jackson, Mississippi, USA

ABSTRACT

The aim of this chapter is to characterize the role of acute alcohol use within suicide attempts. Approximately 40% of suicide attempters drink surrounding their attempt and the prevalence is higher among men, adults between the ages of 26 and 50, and individuals with chronic alcohol use. There is empirical evidence that acute alcohol use substantially increases the risk for suicide attempt and some evidence suggests that it is a more important risk factor than habitual alcohol use. The majority of attempters who drink surrounding the attempt use alcohol for non suicide-related reasons (i.e., not to facilitate the attempt). The reason or purpose for consumption could potentially influence the types of mechanisms responsible for increased suicide risk. Methodological limitations include inconsistent assessment of intent to die, potential for inaccurate recording of acute alcohol use, and ascertainment of suicide attempters who only seek medical attention. It is essential for researchers to develop innovative approaches to study potential mechanisms that may underlie an observed acute alcohol-attempt association.

INTRODUCTION

In the United States, more than 32,000 individuals commit suicide each year [1] and it is estimated that for every death by suicide there are between 8 to 25 nonfatal suicide attempts [2]. In addition to the devastating loss of life, the adverse effects of suicide and suicide attempts on individuals and society are often severe and account for additional emotional and economic costs [3, 4]. Recognizing the importance of suicide and suicide attempts to the Nation's health, Healthy People 2010 [5] has listed as high priority goals to reduce, by more than half, completed suicide and suicide attempts.

Given the clinical and public health significance of suicide, there is considerable interest in identifying factors that increase the risk for suicide attempts. It is well recognized that drinking often surrounds suicide attempts [6]. As such, the aim of this chapter is to characterize the role of acute alcohol use within suicide attempts. The current chapter is organized in four sections. The first section reviews and evaluates the evidence on the association between acute alcohol use and suicide attempts. Specifically, we review the evidence for an acute alcohol-suicide attempt association among adults who are 18 years of age or older. Individuals interested in this association among adolescents are referred to Bagge & Sher [7]. The second section provides an overview of potential reasons for the consumption of alcohol on the day of an attempt as well as the current understanding of potential mechanisms of action underlying the acute alcohol-attempt association. The third section highlights methodological limitations of the literature to date, and the fourth section concludes with recommendations for future research.

The present review uses the most recent nomenclature for the study of suicide and suicide-related behaviors [8]. The nomenclature defines *suicide attempt* as a "self-inflicted, potentially injurious behavior with a nonfatal outcome for which there is evidence (either explicit or implicit) of intent to die" [8, p. 273]. *Undetermined suicide-related behavior* includes self-inflicted behavior where suicide intent is unknown (or not assessed). Studies which examine *self-harm* (evidence of no intent to die) will not be included in the present review. Thus, we will use a higher-order term, *suicide-related behavior*, to refer across studies of both suicide attempts and undetermined suicide-related behavior.

In terms of alcohol involvement, Menninger [9] and Koob and colleagues [10], have highlighted the importance of distinguishing between alcohol's acute and chronic effects on the brain and behavior. Thus, for the purposes of the present review, acute alcohol use refers to alcohol consumption on the day of the suicide attempt, while chronic alcohol use refers to drinking patterns and alcohol abuse/dependence symptoms.

EVALUATING THE EVIDENCE

Prevalence of Acute Alcohol Use Surrounding Suicide-Related Behavior

In this section, we review clinical studies of individuals with suicide-related behavior. These studies report the proportion of individuals who drank on the day this suicide-related behavior occurred. We review overall rates of acute alcohol use, as well as rates within demographic (i.e., gender and age) and chronic alcohol use (i.e., regular alcohol consumption and alcohol use disorders) subgroups. Importantly, such research is descriptive in nature and does not facilitate an evaluation of associations and possible causal mechanisms.

Overall Rates

A recent literature review of acute alcohol consumption and suicide-related behavior among adults [6] found that on average, 40% (median = 41%) of adults ingest alcohol prior to their suicide-related behavior. However, a wide range of percentages [10-73%) was observed, and the reasons for potential variability are numerous (e.g., differences in operalization of suicide attempt, purpose of study, measurement of acute alcohol use). These highly variable results make it difficult to draw conclusions about the true prevalence of acute alcohol use surrounding suicide-related behavior.

Gender

The overwhelming majority of studies find that men (ranging from 53%- 54%) consume alcohol more often than women (ranging from 33% to 47%) prior to suicide-related behavior [11-16] using both subjective and objective measures (self-report and breathalyzers) of alcohol consumption. When examining quantity of consumption, a number of studies [13, 16] demonstrate that women had significantly lower blood alcohol levels and were less likely to use alcohol as the "main substance" (i.e., substance most toxic in the amounts taken) [13] compared to men engaging in undetermined suicide-related behavior.

Age

Two independent large studies report similar patterns of acute alcohol use across the lifespan among adults with undetermined suicide-related behavior. Specifically, research [11, 16] suggests that the prevalence of acute alcohol use surrounding suicide attempts increases from ages 25 and under (prevalence ranging from 38% and 60%) to ages 26-35 (prevalence ranging from 48% and 72%), decreases slightly from ages 36-50 (prevalence ranging from 46% and 64%), and then drops dramatically among individuals 51 and older (prevalence ranging from 27% and 37%, respectively). However, this research is cross-sectional and longitudinal research is needed to determine if rates of acute alcohol use changes within individuals.

Chronic Alcohol Use

Finally, chronic alcohol use/abuse (i.e., regular alcohol consumption and alcohol use disorders) occurs more frequently among individuals who drank the day of their undetermined suicide-related behavior than those who did not consume alcohol. For instance, one study [17] demonstrates significantly greater frequency of past drinking days, frequency of intoxication, and number of drinks per drinking day among individuals who drank (vs. those who did not drink) on the day that undetermined suicide-related behavior occurred. When examining alcohol misuse, alcohol use proximal to undetermined suicide-related behavior occurred significantly more often among alcoholics (ranging from 43% to 90%) than non-alcoholics (ranging from 9% to 38%) [11, 12, 17], but not invariably so [18].

Summary

Overall, a significant proportion of individuals drink alcohol surrounding their suicide-related behavior. These rates are elevated among males, adults between the ages of 26 and 50, and individuals with chronic alcohol use. Unfortunately, the majority of studies sampled individuals with undetermined suicide-related behavior and did not specifically focus on rates of acute alcohol use among individuals where there is evidence of intent to die. Moreover, although rates of co-occurrence are seemingly high, these studies are descriptive in nature and do not provide estimates of the strength of the association between acute alcohol use and suicide-related behavior.

Strength of the Association

Unlike the studies mentioned above, which provide rates of alcohol use surrounding suicide-related behavior, in this section we review studies which examine whether the "occasion specific" rates of alcohol consumption are higher than would be expected in either non-attempters on comparable measurement occasions (case-controls) or higher than the same attempters on appropriately matched non-attempt occasions (case-crossover comparison).

Case-control Research

Two case-control studies have examined the strength of the association between acute alcohol use and suicide attempt. The first study [19], an emergency room-based case-control study, found that alcohol consumption prior to a suicide attempt appears to be a more important risk factor than habitual alcohol use. Specifically, suicide attempters (i.e., cases) were compared to patients with accidents, such as workplace and recreational accidents (i.e., controls) on both self-reported alcohol use within 6 hours of the event and alcohol use measured by an alcohol breath test. Results indicate that when controlling for demographics, acute alcohol use increases the risk for suicide attempt up to 58 times, in comparison with abstinence. Interestingly, the results differed as a function of the measurement of acute alcohol use. Self-report measurements of acute alcohol use indicated a dose-response effect, whereby the risk for suicide attempt increased with greater consumption. In comparison, breathalyzer results suggested a positive association between any acute alcohol use and suicide attempt, but provided no evidence for a dose-response effect (see *Measurement of Acute Alcohol Use* for further discussion of limitations of objective and subjective alcohol measures). Habitual alcohol consumption (quantity of consumption over the past 12 months) increased the risk for suicide attempt up to 3 times, an estimate which is considerably lower compared to acute alcohol use. However, it is impossible to determine whether estimates of acute and habitual alcohol consumption were significantly different since alcohol exposure variables were not included within the same statistical model.

The second study [20] is a population-based case-control study, which directly examined whether acute alcohol use increases risk for suicide attempt above and beyond chronic alcohol use. Cases consisted of nearly lethal suicide attempts presenting to emergency departments of three hospitals in Houston, while community controls from the same geographic area were sampled through random-digit dialing. Acute alcohol use within three hours of the event (odds ratio = 6.2, 95% confidence interval [CI]: 3.2, 11.8] was significantly associated with suicide attempts controlling for other alcohol-related exposures (e.g., past-year frequency of binge drinking, *ns* and alcoholism, *ns*). In addition, acute alcohol use was the only alcohol exposure variable to remain significantly associated with suicide attempts after controlling for demographics and numerous potential confounders (e.g., depression, exposure to suicide, relationship break-ups, and loss). However, it is important to note that these confounder variables were assessed for the past 12 months, rather than the three hours prior to the event. Thus, it remains unknown whether there is an acute-alcohol association after controlling for other proximal factors, such as mood and stressful life events.

Summary

These two case-control studies provide compelling evidence that acute alcohol use is associated with substantially increased risk for suicide attempt. They also suggest that acute alcohol use is a more important risk factor than habitual alcohol use, but did not examine whether acute alcohol use increases risk for suicide attempt above and beyond other proximal factors, which limits conclusions that can be drawn. In general, an important limitation to the case-control methodology is the appropriate selection of controls. Case and controls can differ on a number of factors, such as gender and mood disorder, and these differences when not accounted for can limit conclusions that can be drawn regarding the acute alcohol-suicide attempt relation.

Case-crossover

The epidemiologic case-crossover design [21], is a promising approach for researching the acute alcohol-suicide attempt relation. The case-crossover design was first developed to identify factors that trigger the onset of myocardial infarction [22, 23]. Case-crossover studies assess factors like alcohol use, which can change from day-to-day, at the time of a target period (e.g., 6 hours before a suicide attempt) and also at a control period (e.g., the same 6 hours a day earlier or the usual frequency of consumption in the past year) for each person. If alcohol is acutely related to suicide attempts, it would be expected that individuals would be more likely to drink during a period immediately prior to the attempt than during a similar time interval more distant from the attempt (or compared to their usual frequency of drinking in the past year). Given that individuals serve as their own controls in case-crossover studies, there is no variability in stable suicide attempt risk factors, such as gender and mood disorder. As such, the case-crossover design effectively controls for differences between people that might explain both their alcohol use and their suicide-related behavior. Lack of certainty about all the ways cases and controls may differ from one another have limited the conclusions drawn from case-control studies of the association between acute alcohol use and suicide attempts.

Although the case-crossover methodology has been used extensively to study the impact of alcohol on injury and violence-related injury in emergency departments [24-27], only one study [28] has used this methodology to characterize the role of acute alcohol use in suicide attempts. Findings indicated a large positive association between any alcohol use within 6 hours of the attempt and suicide attempts (relative risk [RR] = 9.6; 95% CI: 5.7, 16.3) among a group of 102 suicide attempters presenting to emergency rooms across four countries. The authors also examined whether the acute alcohol effect differed across subgroups such as men versus women or married versus unmarried individuals. The effect did not differ by demographic groupings (e.g., gender, age, marital status), but varied as a function of alcohol quantity-frequency typology. Specifically, even though infrequent drinkers had a lower prevalence of acute alcohol use surrounding the attempt, compared to chronic alcohol users, they held the highest acute alcohol-related risk for suicide attempt. Thus, since drinking on the day of thc suicide attempt was less "unusual" for moderate or high frequency drinkers compared with infrequent drinkers, acute alcohol use was less likely to serve as a triggering factor for suicide attempt among frequent drinkers.

Summary

The one case-crossover study to date of suicide-related behaviors identified a large positive association between acute alcohol use and suicide attempts. The study also provides preliminary evidence that this effect is strongest among infrequent drinkers. Although further research is needed, this finding highlights the clinical importance of acute alcohol use within suicide attempts among this subgroup, a group who might be less likely targeted for alcohol-suicide interventions. As with the case-control studies discussed previously, a limitation in this case-crossover study is that the impact of other potentially relevant proximal factors such as acute drug use and life events remains unknown. Moreover, these studies do not shed light on the potential underlying mechanisms of the acute alcohol-suicide attempt relation.

PURPOSE OF CONSUMPTION

Although there is strong evidence that alcohol is often used on the day of suicide attempts, attempters' reasons for consumption on the day of attempts have received far less research attention. It is well-established that alcohol is used for a variety of purposes [29], and suicide attempters may use alcohol the day of their attempt for suicide-related and non suicide-related reasons. Better understanding of the reason or purpose for consumption will likely enhance understanding of the mechanisms responsible for increased suicide risk.

Non Suicide-Related Alcohol Motives

Prevalence

Alcohol is most often consumed for a variety of non suicide-related purposes which include drinking for social (to be sociable), enhancement (to get high), and coping (to forget your worries) reasons [30]. Importantly, the limited research to date suggests that a large percentage of acute alcohol use on the day of suicide attempts is consumed for reasons not directly tied to suicide (e.g., to facilitate a suicide attempt or as part of the suicide method). Specifically, Baca-Garcia and colleagues [31] found that 67% of individuals who drank on the day of a suicide attempt acutely used alcohol for non-suicide related reasons. Among these individuals, 39% acknowledged impaired judgment secondary to alcohol use, whereas 61% reported that their acute alcohol use did not influence their attempt. Interestingly, in another study, the majority (82%) of depressed alcoholics who used alcohol on the day of their attempt endorsed drinking for non suicide-related reasons [32]. Their perception of alcohol's influence on their attempt was as follows: 57% acknowledged impaired judgment secondary to alcohol use, while 43% believed that there was no association between drinking and their suicide attempt.

Mechanisms

There are a number of potential underlying mechanisms relating acute alcohol use and suicide attempts [7, 33] when alcohol is initially consumed for non-suicide related reasons. These mechanisms may include alcohol increasing psychological distress, depressed mood and anxiety, aggressiveness, and/or impulsivity. Such processes can also be described at the neuropharmacological level by alcohol's effect on central brain such as increased GABA and serotonin [34]. In addition, cognitive constriction (narrowed attention which reduces perceived potential solutions to a dichotomy – immediate solution or suicide) is frequently observed prior to a suicide attempt [35]. Alcohol produces a similar effect on cognitive processing via a process termed alcohol myopia [36]. The extent to which appraisal of immediate stressors and possible solutions are altered by alcohol use prior to an attempt could play an important role in cognitive constrictions. This hypothesis is consistent with research showing that inhibition conflict (weighing pros and cons and identifying alternative solutions) mediates the relation between intoxication and behavior [37].

Suicide-Related Alcohol Motives

Prevalence

Although not typically considered, alcohol may be used specifically to facilitate a suicide attempt or to be used as part of the suicide method. Research to date suggests that a significant minority (between 18% and 33%) of suicide attempters who drank on the day of their attempt endorsed using alcohol to facilitate their attempt [31, 32]. Moreover, two studies found that 26% of individuals with unknown suicide intent perceived their alcohol use as part of their suicide-related behavior [11, 12].

Mechanisms

Consumption of alcohol for suicide-related reasons can be conceptualized into two categories: drinking to enable suicide by other means and drinking as part of the suicide method itself [7]. In the former, drinking may be used to facilitate a suicide attempt by removing psychological barriers by increasing courage and numbing fears, and by removing physiological barriers by anesthetizing the pain of dying. In the latter, alcohol is consumed with lethal intention (e.g., alcohol poisoning or an intentional interaction with medications or illicit drugs).

Summary

Research investigating the purpose of alcohol consumption surrounding a suicide attempt is in its nascent stage. The existing literature suggests a large percentage of individuals who drink surrounding a suicide attempt report using alcohol for non suicide-related reasons. Among these individuals, acute alcohol consumption may lead to an attempt by increasing psychological distress, negative affect, impulsivity, and cognitive constriction. For a significant minority of adults, alcohol plays a role in facilitating suicide attempts by other means (perhaps by increasing individuals' motivation to die), or by serving as part of the suicide method itself (e.g., alcohol poisoning or interaction with other substances). Additional research on the purpose of consumption on the day of an attempt will increase understanding of the mechanisms underlying the relation between acute alcohol use and suicide attempts.

Methodological Limitations

There are a number of general methodological considerations pertaining to assessment of intent to die, measurement of alcohol consumption, and sample selection, which limit conclusions to be drawn from the literature reviewed in this chapter.

Operalization of Suicide Attempt

First, the suicide-related behavior phenotype differed across studies included within this review. For example, some studies reported on undetermined suicide-related behavior, whereas others reported on suicide attempts. Studies of undetermined suicide-related behaviors include individuals who engage in self-harm with no intent to die as well as those who have engaged in self-inflicted behavior as part of a suicide attempt. Failure to separate these two types of behaviors, each of which has different correlates [38], can result in faulty inferences regarding the prevalence of acute alcohol use surrounding attempts and the mechanisms underlying the association between acute alcohol use and suicide attempts. Fortunately, the studies which reported the overall statistical association (rather than prevalence of acute alcohol use) sampled individuals with intent to die, which allows some degree of confidence in the conclusion about the overall statistical association. It is imperative for future researchers to include attempt-specific information on intention to accurately characterize alcohol's effect on suicide attempt.

Measurement of Acute Alcohol Use

In the studies reviewed, the assessment of alcohol consumption was based on either objective measures (e.g., breath test) or subjective measures (i.e., self-report). Each is subject to measurement inaccuracies. For instance, self-report is reliant on retrospective recall, which can lead to under- or over- reporting of acute alcohol use surrounding the attempt. There also may be differential recall of drinking, with more accurate recall more proximal to the event (e.g., the day of the attempt compared to the day before). In studies which utilize objective measures of alcohol intoxication, the time-frame from last sip to hospital arrival is varied and is often not reported. As alcohol metabolizes relatively quickly, undetermined intervals between the last drink and the time of measurement can contribute to unreliable objective estimates of the level of intoxication during the attempt. Moreover, lengthy intervals between last drink and the time of assessment can lead to an erroneous conclusion that no alcohol was consumed prior to the attempt, and this is particularly true for individuals who consume small quantities of alcohol surrounding the attempt.

Ascertainment of Suicide Attempters

All studies included in this review sampled individuals with suicide-related behavior who presented to the hospital. However, not all suicide attempters seek medical attention.

Attempters who present to the emergency department may differ from attempters who do not on a range of characteristics other than medical severity (e.g., greater help-seeking behavior, more severe pathology). Thus, clinical ascertainment may result in limited generalizability of results [39].

Summary

There are a number of methodological considerations which limit our understanding of the acute alcohol-suicide attempt relation. These include inconsistent assessment of intent to die, potential for inaccurate recording of acute alcohol use, and ascertainment of only suicide attempters who seek medical attention.

CONCLUSION

Although in its nascent stage, the literature reviewed in this chapter, provides compelling evidence that acute alcohol use is associated with suicide attempts. However, there are many questions that remain unanswered regarding this association and a number of important future directions for research in this area. First, in order to clarify the boundaries of this relation, researchers should consider determining whether a relation exists between acute alcohol consumption and suicide attempts, when controlling for various acute or transient risk factors (e.g., other drug use, affect, and life events). It will also be important to determine whether there are different mechanisms of action underlying the association between acute alcohol use and suicide attempts based on the attempter's purpose of consumption. Second, interactions between acute and chronic alcohol use in the prediction of suicide attempt is an area in need of further study. At least one study found that infrequent drinkers hold the highest acute alcohol suicide-related risk, highlighting the importance for frequent assessment of alcohol use across all individuals at risk for suicide. Third, investigators should evaluate whether drinking and suicide attempts are not causally related, but rather spuriously correlated due to a common third-variable influence which is antecedent to both. For instance, acute intoxication and suicide attempts may be spuriously related through a proximal stressful life event that causally influences both behaviors (e.g., relationship break up, sexual assault or bereavement) [40, 41]. Fourth, it is essential for future researchers to develop innovative approaches to study potential mechanisms that may underlie an observed acute alcohol-attempt association [7]. Such studies may include daily diary studies among very high risk groups and laboratory studies investigating the effect of drinking on cognitive processes which directly relate to suicidal thoughts and behavior. Employing a collection of approaches will place both researchers and clinicians in a much stronger position to understand this complex problem, and to ultimately aid preventative efforts.

References

Web-based Injury Statistics Query and Reporting System (WISQARS) on the National Center for Injury Prevention and Control, *Centers for Disease Control and Prevention website.* Available at: www.cdc.gov/ncipc/ wisqars Accessed July 9, 2009.

Moscicki EK: Epidemiology of completed and attempted suicide: Toward a framework for prevention. *Clin Neurosci Res* 2001; 1:310-323.

Corso PS, Mercy JA, Simon TR, Finkelstein EA, Miller TR: Medical costs and productivity losses due to interpersonal and self-directed violence in the United States. *Am J Prev Med* 2007; 32:474-482.

Miller TR, Covington K, Jensen A: *Measuring the burden of injury.* Edited by Mulder M, Van Beeck, EF. Amsterdam, ECOSA, 1999, pp 23-40.

Department of Health and Human Services: Healthy People 2010. *With understanding and improving health and objectives for improving health,* 2nd ed. Washington, DC, U.S. Government Printing Office, 2000.

Cherpitel CJ, Borges G, Wilcox HC: Acute alcohol use and suicidal behavior: A review of the literature. *Alcohol Clin Exp Res* 2004; 28:18-28.

Bagge CL, Sher KJ: Adolescent alcohol involvement and suicide attempts: Toward the development of a conceptual framework. *Clin Psychol Rev* 2008; 28:1283-1296.

Silverman MM, Berman AL, Sanddal ND, O'Carroll PW, Joiner TE: Rebuilding the Tower of Babel: a revised nomenclature for the study of suicide and suicidal behaviors. Part II: Suicide-related ideations, communications, and behaviors. *Suicide Life Threat Behav* 2007; 37:264-277.

Menninger KA*: Man against himself.* Oxford, Harcourt Brace, 1938.

Koob GF, Le Moal M: Drug abuse: Hedonic homeostatic dysregulation. *Science* 1997 ; 278:52-58.

Hawton K, Fagg J, McKeown SP: Alcoholism, alcohol and attempted suicide. *Alcohol* Alcohol 1989; 24:3-9.

Haw C, Hawton K, Casey D, Bale E, Shepherd A: Alcohol dependence, excessive drinking and deliberate self-harm: Trends and patterns in Oxford, 1989-2002. *Soc Psychiatry Psychiatr Epidemiol* 2005; 40:964-971.

Hovda KE, Bjornaas MA, Skog K, Opdahl A, Drottning P, Ekeberg O, Jacobsen D: Acute poisonings treated in hospitals in Oslo: A one-year prospective study (I): Patterns of poisoning. *Clin Toxicol* 2008; 46:35-41.

McMahon GT, McGarry K: Deliberate self-poisoning in an Irish county hospital. *Ir J Med Sci* 2001; 170:94-97.

Merrill J, Milner G, Owens J, Vale A: Alcohol and attempted suicide. *Br J Addict* 1992; 87:83-89.

Suokas J, Lonnqvist J: Suicide attempts in which alcohol is involved: A special group in general hospital emergency rooms. *Acta Psychiatr Scand* 1995; 91:36-40.

Lejoyeux M, Huet F, Claudon M, Fichelle A, Casalino E, Lequen V: Characteristics of suicide attempts preceded by alcohol consumption. *Arch Suicide Res* 2008; 12:30-38.

Peterson LG, Peterson M, O'Shanick GJ, Swann A: Self-inflicted gunshot wounds: Lethality of method versus intent. *Am J Psychiatry* 1985; 142:228-231.

Borges G, Rosovsky H: Suicide attempts and alcohol consumption in an emergency room sample. *J Stud Alcohol* 1996; 57:543-548.

Powell KE, Kresnow M, Mercy JA, Potter LB, Swann AC, Frankowski RF, Lee RK, Bayer TL: Alcohol consumption and nearly lethal suicide attempts. Suicide Life Threat Behav 2001; 32:30-41.

Maclure M, Mittleman MA: Should we use a case-crossover design? *Annu Rev Public Health* 2000; 21:193-221.

Maclure M: The case-crossover design: A method for studying transient effects on the risk of acute events. *Am J Epidemiol* 1991; 133:144-153.

Mittleman MA, Maclre M, Tofler GH, Sherwood JB, Goldberg RJ, Muller JE: Triggering of acute myocardial infarction by heavy physical exertion: Protection against triggering by regular exertion. Determinants of Myocardial Infarction Onset Study investigators. *N Engl J Med* 1993; 329:1677-1883.

Borges G, Cherpitel C, Mittleman M: The risk of injury after alcohol consumption: A case-crossover study in the emergency department. *Soc Sci Med* 2004; 58:1191-1200.

Borges G, Cherpitel C, Mondragon L, Poznyak V, Peden M, Gutierrez I: Episodic alcohol use and the risk of nonfatal injury. *Am J Epidemiol* 2004; 159:565-571.

Vinson DC, Mabe N, Leonard LL, Alexander J, Becker J, Boyer J, Moll J: Alcohol and injury: A case-crossover study. *Arch Fam Med* 1995; 4:505-511.

Vinson DC, Maclure M, Reidinger C, Smith GS: A population-based case-crossover and case-control study of alcohol and the risk of injury. *J Stud Alcohol* 2004; 64:358-366.

Borges G, Cherpitel CJ, Macdonald S, Giesbrecht N, Stockwell T, Wilcox HC: A case-crossover study of acute alcohol use and suicide attempt. *J Stud Alcohol* 2004; 65:708-714.

Kuntsche EN, Knibbe R, Gmel G, Engels R: Why do young people drink? A review of drinking motives. *Clin Psychol Rev* 2005; 25:841-861.

Cooper ML, Russell M, Skinner JB, Windle M: Development and validation of a three - dimensional measure of drinking motives. *Psychol Assess* 1992; 4:123-132.

Baca-Garcia E, Diaz-Sastre C, Basurte E, Prieto R, Ceverino A, Saiz-Ruiz J, de Leon J: A prospective study of the paradoxical relationship between impulsivity and lethality of suicide attempts. *J Clin Psychol* 2001; 62:560-564.

Cornelius JR, Salloum IM, Da NL, Thase ME, Mann JJ: Patterns of suicidality and alcohol use in alcoholics with major depression. *Alcohol Clin Exp Res* 1996; 20:1451-1455.

Hufford MR: Alcohol and suicidal behavior. *Clin Psychol Rev* 2001; 21:797-811.

Julien RM: *A primer of drug action,* 9th ed. New York, NY, Worth Publishers, 2001.

Shneidman E: *Definition of suicide.* New York: NY, Wiley, 1985.

Steele CM, Josephs RA: Alcohol myopia: Its prized and dangerous effects. *Am Psychol* 1990; 45:921-933.

Steele CM, Southwick L: Alcohol and social behavior: I. The psychology of drunken excess. *J Pers Soc Psychol* 1985; 48:18-34.

Nock MK, Kessler RC: Prevalence of and risk factors for suicide attempts versus suicide gestures: Analysis of the National Comorbidity Survey. *J Abnorm Psychol* 2006; 115:616 -623.

Kazdin AE: *Research design in clinical psychology,* 3rd ed. Needham Heights, MA, Allyn & Bacon, 1998.

Overholser J, Spirito A: *Evaluating and treating adolescent suicide attempters: From research to practice*. Edited by Spirito A, Overholser, JC. San Diego, CA, Academic Press, 2003, pp 19-41.

Volpicelli J, Balaraman G, Hahn J, Wallace H, Bux D: The role of uncontrollable trauma in the development of PTSD and alcohol addiction. *Alcohol Res Health* 1999; 23: 256-262.

In: Suicidal Behavior in Alcohol and Drug Abuse... ISBN: 978-1-60876-919-3
Editors: L. Sher, A. Vilens, pp. 325-339

Chapter 19

PREVENTION OF SUICIDAL BEHAVIOR IN INDIVIDUALS WITH ALCOHOL AND/OR DRUG ABUSE

Ioana Todor
University of Alba Iulia, Romania

ABSTRACT

Suicidal behavior has a complex and multidimensional etiology, being the product of a large spectrum of biological, psychological, socio-cultural, interpersonal and situational factors. Alcohol and/or drug abuse is one of the causal factors of suicidal behavior. Other significant risk factors include: depression and associated mental disorders, history of suicide attempt(s), the existence of suicidal ideation, plan or intent, impulsivity and aggression, severely disturbing physical illnesses, negative life events, unrestricted access to lethal means, demographic and situational variables. Because of the strong statistical association between the two conditions, it is recommended that all the patients with alcohol/drug abuse should be carefully assessed for suicidal risk in primary care units. The assessment of suicidal risk is only the first step in prevention. According to their estimated suicidal risk, these patients are followed up at home, they are hospitalized, or they are oriented towards rehabilitation centers, mental health institutions or psychiatric units. The second step in prevention of suicidal risk consists in the management of the risk factors, involving a wide range of techniques and strategies: from a non-harm contract and follow-up visits, enhanced psychosocial support, or counseling on specific problems, to individual or group psychotherapy, family therapy, and pharmacological treatment. The success of prevention depends on the collaborative efforts of family doctors, physicians with various specialties, psychiatrists, psychologists, social workers, educators, various health care professionals and community members.

INTRODUCTION

Alcohol or substance abuse problems are strongly associated with suicidal behavior [1, 2]. According to statistical data, the risk of suicide attempts in patients with alcohol and drug abuse disorders is estimated as 50% higher than in the general population [3, 4]. Approximately 25% to 35% of all suicide attempts from the general population are associated with alcohol abuse as a contributing factor [1, 5]. On the other hand, people who commit suicide under alcohol or drug consumption attempt to use means that leave them small chances of survival [6]. These data qualify people with alcohol or drug abuse as being at-risk, and justify the efforts of mental heath practitioners and related professionals to develop and implement evidence-based strategies to prevent suicide in this population.

In the World Health Organization documents [7, 8], suicide is conceptualized as a multidimensional disorder, the result a complex interaction of biological, psychological, sociological and environmental factors. Suicide prevention is a very complex task in the general population as well as alcohol or drug dependent individuals. It involves various activities ranging from a continuous preoccupation in communities to ensure a certain quality of life for their members – through effective diagnostic and treatment of psychiatric disorders –, to assessment of suicidal risk and implementation of specific preventive measures to reduce this risk (from the control of environmental factors and limitation of access to specific methods to commit suicide, to psychological interventions designated to improve problem solving abilities, coping skills or social adaptation). An effective strategy to prevent suicide requires the collaborative efforts of various persons and groups, including mental health professionals, general physicians, clinicians, counselors, social workers, educators, media communicators, families and communities [7].

From both the World Health Organization (WHO) and National Institute of Mental Health (NIMH) perspective, the concept of prevention in mental health goes beyond a set of actions taken before the initial onset of a disorder. The definition of prevention has been extended to integrate interventions addressed to the whole health-illness continuum: interventions designated to reduce the risk and incidence of a disorder, severity, duration, its relapses, the disability associated with it [9, 10]. In relationship with their aims, preventive strategies could be classified as: primary prevention (when the target is to reduce the number of new cases of a specific disorder), secondary prevention (which refers to interventions aiming to reduce the prevalence of the disorder), and tertiary prevention (interventions undertaken to diminish its consequences). From a cost-benefit analysis point of view (the cost, risk or discomfort of the preventive strategy versus its positive effects), prevention in mental health has been divided in the following three categories: universal prevention (targeting the general public or a whole population group, regardless of their risk to develop a mental disorder), selective prevention (targeting subgroups or individuals of the population whose risk of developing a mental disorder is estimated as significantly higher compared with the rest of the population), and indicated prevention (targeting persons at high risk of mental disorder) [9].

Primary Prevention

Primary prevention of suicide refers to measures directed at a large population in order to prevent the occurrence of new cases of suicidal acts. These measures include an effective control of alcohol and drug abuse problems and other psychiatric disorders (studies conducted in different countries have shown an overall prevalence of mental disorders situated around 90% in the cases of completed suicide; depression, alcohol and drug abuse and personality disorders are the most incriminated in this etiology) [4, 11].

At the same time, primary prevention can be accomplished through measures addressed to the environmental and individual factors, which non-specifically contribute to the etiology of suicide. I mention here all active measures to reduce social exclusion and social alienation, to control poverty and incurable physical illnesses, to improve peoples' quality of life, to help them to avoid and to change at-risk attitudes and behaviors. Such generous objectives are feasible through a wide range of activities starting with informational campaigns, counseling, guidance and training sessions in the communities, and leading to sustained social, economical and legislative measures.

Secondary Prevention

Secondary prevention of suicide refers to specific measures to reduce its incidence in vulnerable groups. Identification of the groups at risk represents a necessary step in secondary prevention, which allows the development and implementation of more adapted, reliable and efficient preventive strategies.

As mentioned earlier, available statistical data indicate that the individuals with substance abuse problems present a higher risk of suicidal behavior [3-5]. An accurate prediction of the occurrence of suicidal acts is still difficult to accomplish, since they are relatively infrequent events [11], even in these at-risk populations (the suicide rate among the people with alcohol abuse disorders has been estimated as 5% in the U. S. [2]). Alcohol or drug abuse is not the only risk factor for suicide attempts. In every particular case, the suicidal behavior is the outcome of complex psycho-physiological mechanisms, triggered by social, biological or various environmental influences [4, 12].

There is a certain difference between suicidal thoughts, suicide attempts and suicide completion. Practically, only some of the people who present suicidal ideation commit suicide. The overcautious assumption that every individual who reports suicidal ideation is at risk of suicide inevitably generates false positive predictions and may lead to unnecessary limitation of the patients' rights and liberties as well as a wasting of medical resources. On the other hand, the opposite extreme attitude, characterized by the underestimation of the patients' complains and suicidal thoughts, generates false negative predictions and may endanger the patients' safety [7].

Secondary prevention of suicide in individuals with alcohol and/or drug abuse implies the following main objectives/activities:

treating the primary psychiatric condition - alcohol or substance abuse;

an accurate evaluation of the imminent and short-term suicidal risk with the identification of the most vulnerable cases;

implementation of specific strategies in order to reduce the suicidal risk (treating the comorbide disorders, controlling depression and impulsivity, limitation of access to potentially lethal means, cognitive restructuring, enhancing social support and communication, etc.).

Assessment of the Risk Factors for Suicidal Behavior in Individuals with Alcohol and/or Drug Abuse

The relationship between alcohol or drug abuse and suicidal behavior is complex, being mediated by a number of independent and interrelated biological, psychological, social and situational variables, which in their turn represent other important risk factors for suicide (e. g. depressive mood, lack of family support, poor social insertion, financial problems, poor physical health, impulsivity, lack of control, inclination to engage in high risk behaviors). There are individual cases when some of these variables play a causal role for the addictive behavior; for example, a person can motivate his/her drinking behavior as a cure for his intense feelings of sadness or loneliness. On the other hand, the alcohol or drug consumption itself may lead to financial and social problems, depression, various somatic illnesses, impaired mental and behavioral control, etc (Figure 1). Suicide risk increases as other risk factors add to alcohol or drug consumption

In assessing the suicidal risk for the patients with alcohol or drug abuse, the clinician should carefully consider the following categories of factors: severity/history of abuse, depression and associated mental disorders, the existence of previous suicide attempts, suicidal ideation, plan or intent, impulsivity and aggression, the presence of physical illnesses, negative life events, and other significant situational variables. In each particular case, the suicidal risk is increased as more of these factors are added.

Depression, Severity of Substance Abuse, and Associated Mental Disorders

Studies conducted in the U. S. and Europe have indicated that over 90% of the people who committed suicide had an associated mental disorder, the most incriminated being clinical depression and substance abuse [2, 4, 6]. According to some estimations, suicide attempts are 20 times more probable in depressed patients compared with the general population [5], and the comorbid association of depression with alcoholism and/or substance abuse dramatically increases suicidal risk [3, 13, 14]. Hopelessness is the dimension of depression most frequently related to suicidal behavior in literature [6, 12].

Among alcohol dependent individuals, increased age, a long history of chronic refractory and severe alcoholism, or additional substance abuse are associated with greater suicidal risk [12, 15]. The comorbidity of major depression, alcoholism and cocaine abuse appears to be particularly associated with suicidal behavior [16, 17]. The positive correlation between alcohol or drug abuse, depression and suicide argues for the necessity of a comprehensive approach to suicide prevention, taking into consideration both the treatment of substance abuse and depression.

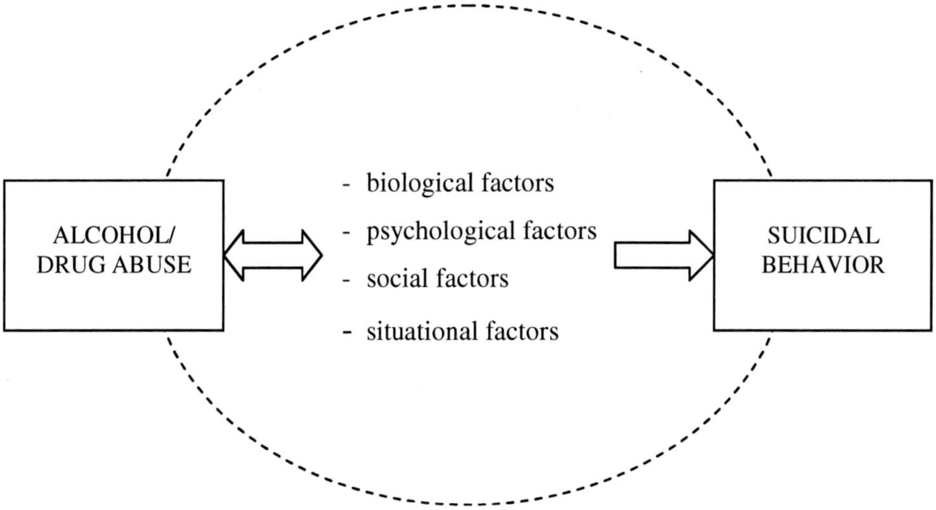

Figure 1. A multi-pathway description of the relationship between alcohol/drug abuse and suicidal behavior.

In fact, the relationship between alcoholism and depression has proved to be very robust and complex, being explained through various psychological, environmental, neurochemical or genetic mechanisms [18, 19]. Some studies argue for a common genetic condition that makes the individuals vulnerable to both depression and alcoholism [20], while others emphasize the role of vicarious learning in this comorbidity. For example, an individual who observes during childhood that his father drinks alcohol to feel better when he has problems or failures is prone to adopt the same behavior later in life when confronted with the same kind of obstacles. On the other hand, there are people who simply use alcohol or illicit drugs to solve their depressive states. According to a number of studies, this often leads to a vicious cycle because sustained heavy alcohol abuse may trigger neurochemical mechanisms that have significant depressant effects [12, 21].

Antisocial and borderline personality disorder, schizophrenia (especially during the remission periods), anxiety/panic disorder, bipolar disorder are other psychiatric conditions that clinicians need to efficiently diagnose and treat because they may increase the suicidal risk, especially when comorbid with depression and alcohol abuse.

History of Suicide Attempt(s)

According to statistical data, previous suicide attempts significantly increase the actual suicidal risk [4, 5]. The existence of previous suicide attempt(s) is considered by some authors one of the best predictors of actual suicidal risk in individuals with alcohol/substance abuse [15, 22]. It has been estimated that 20%-30% of the people who commit suicide have made a previous suicide attempt [5]. In the assessment interview, special attention should be given to the potential lethality of the method chosen by the patient, to the triggered events and to the circumstances in which past attempts occurred (depressive state, feelings of despair, hopelessness, guilt, loneliness, divorce or job loss).

Family history of suicide is also a risk factor for the suicidal behavior: empirical data shows that a significant proportion of alcohol dependent individuals who attempted suicide reported that a first- or second-degree relative had committed suicide [23].

Suicidal Ideation, Plan and Intent

It is true that not all people who have had suicidal thoughts commit suicide but especially in the case of individuals with alcohol or drug abuse this risk factor should not be ignored. All these individuals are recommended to be evaluated for suicidal ideation, especially when they have recently suffered a relapse, unemployment, separation or divorce, or if they present symptoms of depression. Studies have shown that a large number of people with alcohol or drug abuse report suicidal ideation, especially at the end of a binge or in the early phase of withdrawal [7, 22, 24].

The physician or mental health specialist has the role to establish a professional and trustful relationship with any patient at risk, and asses his/her suicidal ideation. There is a myth that people who talk about their suicidal intent rarely commit suicide; in reality, many of them give some clues or warning before passing on to action. Another myth is that by asking vulnerable patients about their suicidal intentions, the physician involuntarily suggests them a solution, which might provoke the suicidal act; in reality, many patients experience considerable relief and feel understood after discussing about their thoughts with a specialist. The suicidal intent is particularly difficult to asses in the cases when patients who have a firm intention to kill themselves deliberately deny their plans. An increased attention has also to be paid in cases when a patient at risk, who has been anxious and agitated for a period of time, unexpectedly looks calm and relaxed; this state could be the consequence of the difficult decision he/she has made to end his/her life [7].

The suicidal risk increases with the frequency, persistence and mental elaboration of suicidal ideation, in particular when suicidal ideation is associated with hopelessness or comorbide depression [22]. This risk is significantly higher when the patient has an established plan of actions and/or a suicidal intent.

Impulsivity and Aggression

In most cases, suicidal behavior may be considered an impulsive act of aggression oriented toward the self [22]. Impulsivity and aggression are major risk factors for suicide, in particular among the individuals with alcoholism, substance abuse and other psychiatric conditions [6, 22, 25]. A considerable amount of research demonstrates a strong correlation between alcohol or substance abuse and aggression-impulsivity traits (the comorbide constellation of aggression, impulsivity, alcoholism and/or substance abuse, found in many clinical studies, has been described as a "desinhibitory syndrome" [26, 27]). For example, alcohol consumption has been estimated to be involved in more than 50% of the crimes committed with violence and in 86% of all murders [27, 28]. According to Koller and his colleagues [29], alcohol-dependent individuals with a history of violent suicide attempts show an increased incidence of aggressive behavior during lifetime and higher scores on aggressive-impulsive traits. Compared with depressed patients without alcohol abuse, individuals with a history of alcohol abuse and comorbide depression have higher aggression and impulsivity, and more frequently report suicide attempts, childhood abuse or tobacco smoking [6, 12, 30]. Not only the chronic consumption of alcohol, but also acute alcohol use is associated with suicide; the blood tests performed to the people who have committed suicide frequently indicate the presence of alcohol (in approximately 33%-69% of the cases) [1, 2]. Probably due to its disinhibitory effects, associated with the rise of aggression and impulsivity, alcohol consumption may increase the suicidal risk even for the people with no previous psychiatric history [24].

Meta-analytical investigations conclude that the alcohol - aggression relationship is causal and not simply correlational [25, 31]. According to Pihl and Lemarquand [30] acute alcohol intoxication can lead to aggressive behavior by three possible pathways (behavioral effects): potentiation, disinhibition and disorganization, all of these effects being neurophysiologically mediated by serotonergic mechanisms. Potentiation refers to a facilitation of behavioral responses to cues of reward, and an inhibition of behavioral responses to cues of punishment, which promotes exploration of the environment and approach behavior, minimizing the possible danger or threats. At the same time, the potentiation effect of alcohol (as well as of other stimulants, like amphetamine or cocaine) consists in a direct enhancement of aggression. The disinhibition effect is related to anxiety: anxiety has an inhibitive effect on aggression; alcohol has an anxiolytic effect and disinhibits the learned responses of aggression. Third, alcohol consumption consists in a disorganization of the higher-order cognitive functions (especially executive functions), impairing the capacity of the individual to consider the future consequences of his/her acts, which directly increases the likelihood of impulsivity and aggressive behavior.

Serotonin activity (the neurotransmitter 5-HT being particularly involved) mediates the effects of alcohol on aggression [31, 32]. A number of studies demonstrate that acute alcohol consumption transiently increases central 5-HT functioning, while chronic consumption decreases it. Low 5-HT functioning is associated with a propensity toward disinhibited behavior, alcohol preference and intake, which facilitate aggression and impulsivity. Research found the presence of low serotonin activity in suicidal behavior, aggression and alcoholism, leading to the conclusion that serotonergic mechanisms underlie all these problems [6, 12, 31, 32].

Physical Illnesses, Negative Life Events, Demographic and Situational Variables

The comorbidity of a terminal, painful or debilitating physical illness with substance abuse and/or depression significantly increases the suicidal risk. A number of studies have shown an increased risk of suicide in patients with cancer, immunodeficiency syndrome (AIDS), head injuries, severe neurological illnesses, physical inabilities, insomnia, etc [4, 22].

For people with alcohol or drug abuse, old age, living alone, divorce or recent loss of someone close, financial problems or job loss, depression associated with social isolation, presence of stressful life events, easy access to highly lethal means of suicide (e. g. fire arms or drugs) are risk factors which can lead to suicidal behavior [12, 22, 24, 25]. Many studies indicate that most suicide victims with a history of alcohol misuse are men. This finding does not reflect any particular vulnerability of men to the suicide-promoting effects of alcohol, but it can be explained through the higher prevalence of alcohol misuse among men compared with women in the general population [25, 33]. In fact, female alcohol abusers are more at risk of suicidal behavior compared with men [33, 34], probably because they are more exposed to social stigmatization.

Especially in adolescence, some problems from the past such as loss of a parent during childhood, sexual abuse, a history of neglect, violence or alcohol/substance abuse manifested by one of the parents, are likely to lead to alcohol/substance abuse as a (maladaptive) coping response; associated with depression, rigid thinking or emotional vulnerability, they may significantly increase the suicidal risk [35].

The availability of highly lethal means of suicide (such as fire arms or potentially harmful medication) may not influence the rate of suicide attempts in the general population, but it certainly influences the rate of survival from suicide. When the access to highly lethal methods of suicide is difficult, people are likely to use less lethal methods, improving their chances of survival. Due to the well-known emotional and cognitive effects of consumption, people with alcohol or drug abuse are more likely to use highly lethal methods of suicide if available, increasing the proportion of completed suicide/suicide attempts, compared with the general population [36].

Alcohol or drug abuse is considered both a major predispositioning and a precipitating risk factor for suicidal behavior. Chronic alcohol/drug abuse increases the suicidal risk through its effects of inducing negative affect and hopelessness, lowered self-esteem, and negative life events (divorce, work problems, social isolation). According to some authors, acute alcohol/drug abuse is more significant in relation to suicide than chronic abuse [24]. Alcohol or substance abuse may precipitate suicidal behavior through its depressogenic effects (if low doses of alcohol may ameliorate negative states, higher doses produce depressant effects, often leading to spontaneous suicidal ideation), impaired problem solving abilities and constricted thinking, increased aggression/impulsivity, or alcohol myopia (narrowing attention to the immediate crisis or affective state) [12, 25].

In the assessment of suicidal risk the protective factors should not be ignored. Protective factors include: effective treatment for associated mental disorders (including alcoholism or substance abuse), good health, easy access to medical and counseling services, the capacity to ask for help when necessary, problem solving abilities, good coping skills, strong connections with the family members and feelings of responsibility toward them, community appreciation and support, moral, cultural and religious beliefs against suicide, fear of death [37].

SYNTHESIS: *Guidelines for the evaluation of suicidal risk for the patient with alcohol and/or drug abuse [adaptation after 22, 7]*

- Screen for alcohol or drug abuse (use clinical interviews, questionnaires, laboratory tests); evaluate the history and severity of consumption, abstinence attempts and relapses
- Screen for associated mental disorders or other psychiatric conditions (e.g. major depression, borderline personality disorder, schizophrenia, manic depression, impulsive and antisocial behavior, anxiety disorders)
- Perform a mental status examination, with emphasis on mood, affect and judgment
- Investigate the existence of actual or past suicidal ideation, plan or intent, previous suicide attempts, family history of suicide attempts, access to lethal means
- Identify symptoms associated with suicide (hopelessness, anhedonia, psychomotor agitation or extreme passivity, insomnia, impaired concentration, anxiety)
- Investigate the severity of depression
- Assess the impulsivity and aggression
- Review other risk factors associated with suicide (associated physical illnesses, negative life events, job loss and financial problems, bereavement, loneliness and lack of social support, low self-esteem, feelings of guilt, presence of family violence and disruption)
- Assess protective factors
- Interview family or significant others
- Synthesize and formulate a prevention/intervention plan

Management of the Suicidal Risk in Individuals with Alcohol and/or Drug Abuse

First Actions in Primary Care

The assessment of suicidal risk, which is practically recommended to be performed for every individual with alcoholism and/or drug abuse, is a first necessary step in the development of a coherent plan to manage the risk. During the assessment phase, family doctors, psychiatrists, social workers or other professionals in contact with people with alcohol/drug abuse play the leading role. Various assessment techniques are utilized: from medical exams and laboratory tests, to detailed inquires, interviews and questionnaires.

Depending on the assessed level of suicidal risk, the necessary level of care is established for every person. If the suicidal risk is appreciated as low - for example, when the person has a satisfactory degree of impulse/abuse control, rational thinking and good social support, then he/she can be treated as outpatient.

For the people with suicidal ideation, one of the useful and frequently employed methods in outpatient care is a "no-harm contract". In the particular case of people with alcohol/drug abuse and suicidal ideation, this contract could be adapted, adding a "non-abuse" section. The method is appropriate only for the patients who are able to understand the terms of the contract and who have control over their actions. The contract has the form of a set of clearly formulated statements, written and signed, or verbally agreed by the person at risk in the presence of the clinician or therapist, and its main role is to solidify the therapeutic alliance. The negotiation of the contract can promote discussion on patient's worries, problems or other relevant issues. In the contract, the patient agrees not to use alcohol or drugs, not to harm him/herself over a specific period of time, and to contact the physician if the situation becomes difficult to control without help. The contract is made for a short period (24 or 48 hours), and it is renewed once the stipulated period ends. It is accompanied by follow-up visits and/or telephonic contacts. The recommendation is to involve the patient's family in the negotiation and implementation of the contract; they could play an important role to monitor and sustain the patient [22, 38].

Constant evaluation over time by a specialist and social support are key elements in outpatient care. The available support systems should be identified in the patient's environment: family members, relatives, friends, colleagues, counselors, whose help the specialist should request.

It should be mentioned that, in general, patients with alcohol/drug abuse are able to contract for safety only after they have been detoxified. In most cases, before specifically addressing suicidal ideation, they should be referred to specialized centers for alcohol/drug abuse. If the specialist appreciates that certain personality factors, tensions or disturbed relations within the patient's family or his/her social environment could perpetuate suicidal ideation, the patient should also be referred for individual or family therapy.

If the suicidal risk is appreciated as moderate – for example, when the person has a persistent feeling of hopelessness associated with moderate alcohol abuse, he/she should be referred to psychiatric care. In this situation, the physician should take the time and carefully explain to the patient the reason for the referral, assure him/her that the pharmacological and psychological therapies are effective and these are the best option in his/her case, respond to the patient's anxieties about stigma and psychotropic medication, emphasize that their professional relationship continues and that referral does not mean abandonment [7].

For the people with high suicidal risk - for example, people who have chronic dependence, depression and a suicidal plan, or people with a history of suicide attempts, recurrent alcohol dependence and recent social stressors, hospitalization is mandatory. Among the indications for immediate hospitalization are: chronic alcohol abuse with severe depression, recurrent thoughts of suicide, high level of intent to die in the immediate future, psychomotor agitation and a low capacity of impulse control, existence of a plan to use a violent and immediate lethal method [7, 22]. In this case, the family should be informed about the decision. Because the admission in hospital does not automatically reduce the suicidal risk, the patients with acute suicidal risk should be kept under constant observation to ensure their safety. If the patient at risk or his family refuses hospitalization, the physician is confronted with the difficult situation to consider the involuntary admission in the hospital. In most U. S. States, a patient who refuses hospitalization could be voluntarily committed if he/she: presents an imminent danger to self and others, and an inability to care for him/herself [22, 39].

According to the World Health Organization resources for general physicians [7], every patient with alcohol and/or drug abuse should be evaluated for suicidal risk and carefully monitored. It is true that in absence of definite criteria, in many cases physicians should take into account their clinical intuition when they decide for outpatient care or hospitalization. Being the result of a complicated array of factors, suicidal behavior is still difficult to predict with a satisfactory accuracy [11].

Psychosocial Interventions

Various psychosocial interventions proved to be efficient in treating alcohol/drug abuse, depression, suicidal ideation, or other psychiatric conditions associated with suicidal risk. These include: cognitive behavioral and rational emotive interventions (e. g. cognitive restructuring, problem-solving and coping skills training, disputation of irrational thoughts), dialectical behavior interventions (e. g. emotion regulation, self-soothing, distraction tactics), psycho-educational interventions (e.g. collaborative goal-setting), motivational interviewing techniques, group and family therapy, counseling and support.

A particular emphasis in psychotherapy when working with substance abuse individuals who already have a suicidal intent or a suicidal plan should be put on the therapeutic alliance. In many cases, these patients have a poor motivation to collaborate in therapy, they are non-compliant with the treatment plan, and often show anti-therapeutic behavior (i. e. arrive late or miss the sessions, deny the problems, present low distress tolerance). In these circumstances, therapists have to show flexibility in organizing the sessions, and they have to collaborate with the patient and his/her family to anticipate and address the potential barriers to compliance [40]. The collaborative alliance with the patient's family always has a significant contribution to therapeutic success.

The core psychotherapeutic tasks for the patients with alcohol/drug abuse and suicidal risk could be summarized as follows: treat the alcohol/drug abuse; screen and address the associated psychiatric conditions which constitute risk factors for suicide (i. e. depression or personality disorders); address suicidal ideation or suicidal plan, carefully monitoring the risk; address cognitive and emotional conditions such as catastrophic or dichotomic thinking, aggression, impulsivity and lack of behavioral control, low self-esteem, feelings of guilt, hopelessness and helplessness; teach adequate problem solving strategies and coping skills; work with the patient to enhance psychosocial support and create an actively supportive environment, communicate realistic hope and progressively encourage the patient's independence and self-efficacy, explore the protective factors and emphasize the patient's strengths, communicate care and ensure support.

Pharmacological Treatment

Several systematic and well-controlled studies demonstrate that selective serotonergic antidepressants (SSRI) are efficient for treating depressive symptoms in alcoholics with comorbide major depression as well as for reducing alcohol abuse [41-44]. At the same time, SSRI present the advantage of a reduced toxicity in overdose (compared for example with the tricyclic antidepressants); this quality recommends them as a safer method of treatment for suicidal depressed alcoholics [17]. The cyclic antidepressants have proven to be efficient for treating the depressive symptoms in alcohol abusers with comorbide depression, but their effects on alcohol consumption is less clear [17, 45-47]. Electroconvulsive treatment, benzodiazepines and neuroleptics have been generally indicated as having positive effects in the treatment of suicidal patients, but their effects have not been tested on the subgroup of suicidal patients with comorbide alcohol and/or drug abuse.

A review of clinical studies available in literature has led Cornelius and his colleagues [17] to the critical observation that there is only little specific evidence regarding the effective medication for people with associated suicidal behavior, depression and alcohol/drug abuse, despite the high frequency of this comorbidity. In many practical cases, the therapeutical approaches for these patients address each pathological condition in an independent manner, ignoring any possible factor interactions. Future research has to bring further clarifications on this aspect, exploring new/alternative treatment options.

TERTIARY PREVENTION

Tertiary prevention includes measures addressed to the individuals with alcohol/drug abuse and a history of suicide attempt(s). This category of people needs special attention, given the fact that, according to empirical data, previous suicide attempt(s) is one of the best predictors of suicidal risk in individuals with alcohol/drug abuse [4, 15, 22]. Tertiary prevention aims both to limit the damage produced by the performed suicide attempt(s) and to prevent future suicidal behavior. It includes crisis interventions, a set of specific measures taken immediately after the suicide attempt, as well as assessment, rehabilitation and follow-up measures.

Because those who have attempted suicide may have serious somatic pathologies (like broken bones, brain damage, organ injuries), depression and other mental problems, clinicians and mental health professionals collaborate for their rehabilitation. Another important aspect is that, when suicide occurs, family members and friends may feel shame, shock, anger, guilt or depression, and due to the social stigma that still surrounds suicide and substance abuse, they often prefer to keep silence about their problems and refuse specialized assistance. Empirical studies have shown that a history of suicide attempt(s) in the family significantly increases the suicidal risk to other members [23]. Thus, it is recommended that the family members of a suicidal patient always be carefully evaluated for suicidal risk; they should also benefit from all the available support of the community.

Conclusion

Suicide is still the eleventh cause of death in the U. S. [10] and its strong association with alcohol and/or drug abuse is widely recognized [1-3, 6]. Prevention of suicidal behavior is a complex activity, involving population-based approaches and more specific actions targeting higher risk groups and individuals.

In this chapter, the preventive strategies have been structured in three sections: primary prevention, secondary prevention and tertiary prevention. Primary prevention includes actions addressed to the whole population, such as the control of alcohol/drug consumption, the efficient treatment of mental disorders, restricted access to guns, or a wide range of actions destined to improve the quality of life. Secondary prevention implies the assessment of risk and protective factors in substance-dependent individuals and the management of suicidal risk. Tertiary prevention refers to protective measures necessary for the people who have already had a suicide attempt. An integrated approach with actions at all these three levels probably is the best option.

According to the white paper of the U. S. Department of Health and Human Services – Substance Abuse and Mental Health Services Administration (SAMHSA) [4], a reliable prevention approach involves the following steps: identification of the problem, identification of risk and protective factors, development, implementation and evaluation of interventions and dissemination of evidence-based practices. A literature review on the prevention of suicidal behavior in alcohol and/or drug abuse has led to the conclusion that much progress has been made on the conceptualization and identification of the risk and protective factors, even if "further research is needed to transform suicide prediction into science" [48]. Instead, there is a remarkable lack of controlled studies regarding evidence-based practices.

References

[1] Kendall RE: Alcohol and suicide. *Substance and Alcohol Actions/Misuse* 1983; 4: 121-127.

[2] Preuss UW, Schuckit MA, Smith TL, Danko GP, Bucholz KK, Hesselbrock, MN, Hesselbrock V, Kramer, JR: Predictors and correlates of suicide attempts over 5 years in 1,237 alcohol-dependent men and women. *Am J Psychiatry* 2003; 160: 56-63.

[3] Murphy GE, Wetzel, RD: The lifetime risk of suicide in alcoholism. *Arch Gen Psychiatry* 1990; 47:383–92.

[4] Center for Substance Abuse Treatment. *Substance Abuse and Suicide Prevention: Evidence and Implications—A White Paper*. DHHS Pub. No. SMA-08-4352. Rockville, MD: Substance Abuse and Mental Health Services Administration, 2008.

[5] Pope KS, Vasquez MJT: *Responding to suicidal risk, in Ethics in Psychotherapy and Counseling: A Practical Guide.* Edited by Pope KS, Vasquez MJT. San Francisco, CA. Jossey-Bass, an imprint of John Wiley Publishers, 2007; 258-279.

[6] Sher L: Alcohol consumption and suicide. QJM: *An International Journal of Medicine* 2006; 99(1): 57-61.
[7] World Health Organization (WHO), Department of Mental Health: *Preventing Suicide. A resource for general physicians*. Geneva, 2000.
[8] World Health Organization (WHO), Department of Mental Health and Substance Dependence: Multisite intervention study on suicidal behaviours – SUPRE-MISS: *Protocol of SUPRE-MISS*. Geneva, 2002.
[9] World Health Organization (WHO), Department of Mental Health and Substance Dependence: *Prevention and promotion in mental health*. Geneva, 2002.
[10] National Institute of Mental Health, Suicide Prevention. http://www.nimh.nih.gov/health/topics/suicide-prevention/index.shtml, retrived at 10.06.2009.
[11] Sher L: Preventing suicide. *QJM: An International Journal of Medicine* 2004; 97: 677-680.
[12] Mann JJ, Waternaux C, Haas GL, Malone, K: Toward a clinical model of suicidal behavior in psychiatric patients. *Am J Psychiatry* 1999; 156: 181-189.
[13] Sher L. Depression and alcoholism. *QJM: An International Journal of Medicine;* 97: 237–240.
[14] Conner KR, Duberstein PR: Predisposing and precipitating factors for suicide among alcoholics: empirical review and conceptual integration. *Alcohol Clin Exp Res* 2004; 28(Suppl.): 6–17.
[15] Moscicki EK: Epidemiology of completed and attempted suicide: Toward a framework for prevention. *Clinical Neuroscience Research* 2001; 1: 310-323.
[16] Cornelius JR, Thase ME, Salloum IM, Cornelius MD, Black A, Mann JJ: Cocaine use associated with increased suicidal behavior in depressed alcoholics. *Addictive Behaviors* 1998; 23(1): 119-121.
[17] Cornelius JR, Clark DB, Salloum IM, Bukstein OG, Kelly TM: Management of suicidal behavior in alcoholism. *Clinical Neuroscience Research* 2001; 1: 381-386.
[18] Davidson KM, Ritson EB: The relationship between alcohol dependence and depression. *Alcohol and Alcoholism* 1993; 28(2): 147-155.
[19] Gilman SE, Abraham HD: A longitudinal study of the order of onset of alcohol dependence and major depression. *Drug and Alcohol Dependence* 2001; 63(3): 277-286.
[20] Nurnberger JI, Faroud T, Flury L, Meyer ET, Wiegand R: Is there a genetic relationship between alcoholism and depression? *Alcohol Research and Health* 2002; 26(3): 233-240.
[21] Pietraszek MH, Urano T, Sumioshi K, Serizawa K, Takahashi S, Takada Y, Takada A: Alcohol-induced depression: involvement of serotonin. *Alcohol and Alcoholism 1991;* 26: 155–159.
[22] Gliatto MF, Rai AK: Evaluation and Treatment of Patients with Suicidal Ideation. *American Family Physician* 1999; 67(6): 1500-1511.
[23] Roy A: Relation of family history of suicide to suicide attempts in alcoholics. *Am J Psychiatry* 2000; 157:2050-2051.
[24] Borges G, Walters EE, Kessler RC: Associations of Substance Use, Abuse, and Dependence with Subsequent Suicidal Behavior. *Am J Epidemiol* 2000; 151(8): 781-789.

[25] Brady J: The association between alcohol misuse and suicidal behaviour. *Alcohol & Alcoholism* 2006; 41(5): 473–478.

[26] Gorenstein EE, Newman JP: Disinhibitory psychopathology: a new perspective and a model for research. *Psychol Rev* 1980; 87:301–315.

[27] Murdoch D, Pihl R, Ross D: Alcohol and crimes of violence: present issues. *Int J Addict* 1990; 25: 1065-1081.

[28] Roizen J: Epidemiological issues in alcohol-related violence. *Recent Dev Alcohol* 1997;13: 7-40.

[29] Koller G, Preuss UW, Bottlender M, Wenzel K, Soyka M: Impulsivity and aggression as predictors of suicide attempts in alcoholics. *European Archives of Psychiatry and Clinical Neuroscience* 2002; 252(4): 155-160.

[30] Sher L, Oquendo MA, Galfalvy HC, Grunebaum MF, Burke AK, Zalsman G, Mann JJ: The relationship of aggression to suicidal behavior in depressed patients with a history of alcoholism. *Addict Behav* 2005; 30:1144–1153.

[31] Pihl RO, Lemarquand D: Serotonin and aggression and the alcohol-aggression relationship 1998; 33(1): 55-65.

[32] Fulwiler C, Eckstine J, Kalsy S: Impulsive-Aggressive Traits, Serotonin Function, and Alcohol-Enhanced Aggression. The Journal of Clinical Pharmacology 2005; 45: 94-100.

[33] Pirkola SP, Isometsa ET, Heikkinen ME, Lonnqvist JK: Suicides of alcohol misusers and non-misusers in a nationwide population. Alcohol and Alcoholism 2000; 35: 70–75.

[34] Ramstedt, M: Alcohol and suicide in 14 European countries. Addiction 2001; 96 (Suppl.1): 59–75.

[35] Adams DM, Overholser JC: Suicidal behavior and history of substance abuse. American Journal of Drug and Alcohol Abuse 1992; 18(3): 343 – 354.

[36] Roy A: Suicide, in Kaplan and Sadock's synopsis of psychiatry: behavioural sciences/clinical psychiatry. Edited by Kaplan HI, Sadock BJ. Baltimore, Williams & Wilkins, 1998: 321-342.

[37] Sher L: Risk and protective factors for suicide in patients with alcoholism. Scientific World Journal 2006; 6: 1405-1411.

[38] Stanford EJ, Goetz RR, Bloom JD: The no-harm contract in the emergency assessment of suicidal risk. *J Clin Psychiatry* 1994; 55: 344-348.

[39] Simon RI: *Psychiatry and law for clinicians.* Washington, D.C.: American Psychiatric Press, 1992.

[40] Meichenbaum D: 35 Years of working with suicidal patients: Lessons learned. *Canadian Psychologist* 2005; 46: 64-72.

[41] Cornelius JR, Salloum IM, Cornelius MD, Perel JM, Thase ME, Ehler JG, Mann JJ: Fluoxetine trial in suicidal depressed alcoholics. *Psychopharmacol Bull* 1993; 29: 195-199.

[42] Roy A: Placebo-controlled study of sertraline in depressed recently abstinent alcoholics. *Biol Psychiatry* 1998; 44: 633-637.

[43] Kranzler HR, Burleson JA, Korner P, Del Boca FK, Bohn MJ, Brown J, Liebowitz N: Placebo-controlled trial of fluoxetine as an adjunct to relapse prevention in alcoholics. *Am J Psychiatry* 1995; 152: 391-397.

[44] Cornelius JR, Bukstein OG, Birmaher B, Salloum IM, Lynch K, Pollock NK, Gershon S, Cark D: Fluoxetine in adolescents with major depression and an alcohol use disorder: an open-label trial. *Addict Beh* 2001; 26: 735-739.

[45] McGrath PJ, Nunez EV, Stewart JW, Goldman D, Agosti V, Ocepek-Welikson K, Ouitkin FM: Imipramine treatment of alcoholics with major depression: a placebo-controlled clinical trial. *Arch Gen Psychiatry* 1996; 53: 232-240.

[46] Powell BJ, Campbell JL, Landon JF, Liskow BI, Thomas HM, Nickel EJ, Dale TM, Penick EC, Samuelson SD, Lacoursiere RB: A double-blind placebo-controlled study of nortriptyline and bromocriptine in male alcoholics subtyped by comorbid psychiatric disorders. *Alcohol Clin Exp Res* 1995; 19: 462-468.

[47] Mason BJ, Kocsis JH, Ritvo CE, Cutler RB: A double-blind, placebo-controlled trial of desipramine for primary alcohol dependence stratified on the presence or absence of major depression. *J Am Med Assoc* 1996; 275: 761-767.

[48] Hughes, DH: Can the clinician predict suicide? *Emergency Psychiatry* 1995; 46(5): 449-451.

In: Suicidal Behavior in Alcohol and Drug Abuse... ISBN: 978-1-60876-919-3
Editors: L. Sher, A. Vilens, pp. 343-363

Chapter 20

SUICIDAL BEHAVIOR AMONG USERS OF ALCOHOL AND ILLICIT DRUGS

Jennifer R. Havens and April M. Young
University of Kentucky College of Medicine, Kentucky, USA

ABSTRACT

Psychiatric disorders, which include substance use disorders, are known antecedents of suicidal behavior. The prevalence of suicidal ideation among those using alcohol ranges from 15 to 50%, which is similar to the prevalence rate among other substance users. For suicide attempts, prevalence estimates are upwards of 50% among adults using alcohol or other substances and 20% in substance-using adolescent populations. Injection drug use in particular appears to impart the greatest risk for both fatal and non-fatal suicidal acts. Data consistently demonstrate an association between alcohol and other drug use and both fatal and non-fatal suicidal behavior, including ideation, attempts and completed suicide.

1. INTRODUCTION

This chapter will focus on the epidemiological data demonstrating an association between suicidal behavior and use of alcohol and/or illicit drugs. Epidemiology is defined by Gordis as "the study of how disease is distributed in populations and of the factors that influence or determine its distribution" (p. 3)[1], and therefore we will examine the prevalence and incidence of suicidal behavior and how substance use may influence such behaviors. In keeping with the definitions of suicide posited by O'Carroll and colleagues (1996)[2], non-fatal suicidal behavior includes suicide attempts, in which an unsuccessful attempt was made to end one's life, and suicidal ideation, in which there are thoughts of suicide [2]. The term suicide is used to describe death via a self-inflicted injury [2]. It should also be noted that suicidal behaviors, both non-fatal and fatal are thought to occur on a continuum, from ideation to plans to attempts and finally completed suicide, which is why it is important to study non-fatal suicidal acts, as they may indicate an increased risk for eventual suicide [3].

Table 1. DSM-IV Diagnostic Criteria for Substance Abuse and Dependence

Abuse

A. A maladaptive pattern of substance use leading to clinically significant impairment or distress, as manifested by one (or more) of the following, occurring within a 12-month period:
   1. Recurrent substance use resulting in a failure to fulfill major role obligations at work, school, or home (e.g., repeated absences or poor work performance related to substance use; substance-related absences, suspensions, or expulsions from school; neglect of children or household)
   2. recurrent substance use in situations in which it is physically hazardous (e.g., driving an automobile or operating a machine when impaired by substance use)
   3. Recurrent substance-related legal problems (e.g., arrests for substance-related disorderly conduct)
   4. Continued substance use despite having persistent or recurring social or interpersonal problems caused or exacerbated by the effects of the substance (e.g., arguments with spouse about consequences of intoxication, physical fights)

B. The symptoms have never met the criteria for Substance Dependence for this class of substance

Dependence

A. A maladaptive pattern of substance use, leading to clinically significant impairment or distress, as manifested by three (or more) of the following, occurring at any time in the same 12-mont period:
   1. Tolerance, as defined by either of the following:
      a. A need for markedly increased amounts of the substance to achieve intoxication or desired effects
      b. Markedly diminished effect with continued use of the same amount of the substance
   2. Withdrawal, as manifested by either of the following:
      a. The characteristic withdrawal syndrome for the substance
      b. The same (or a closely related) substance is taken to relieve or avoid withdrawal symptoms
   3. The substance is often taken in large amounts over a longer period than was intended
   4. There is a persistent desire or unsuccessful efforts to cut down or control substance use
   5. A great deal of time is spent in activities necessary to obtain the substance (e.g., visiting multiple doctors or driving long distances), use the substance (e.g., chain smoking), or recover from its effects
   6. Important social, occupational, or recreational activities are given up or reduced because of substance use
   7. The substance use is continued despite knowledge of having persistent or recurrent physical or psychological problem that is likely to have been caused or exacerbated by the substance (e.g., current cocaine use despite recognition of cocaine-induced depression, or continued drinking despite recognition that an ulcer was made worse by alcohol consumption)

Source: American Psychiatric Association, 2000.

As there are varying levels of suicidal behavior, there are also varying levels of substance use that indicate increasing psychopathology. Table 1 lists the diagnostic criteria for both substance abuse and dependence set forth by the Diagnostic and Statistical Manual, Fourth Edition (DSM-IV)[4]. It should also be noted that for specific drugs, and alcohol in particular, the diagnostic criteria may also include a measure of tolerance or withdrawal [4].

If diagnostic criteria for either abuse or dependence is met, it will often be described in the literature as a substance use disorder (SUD). When abuse or dependence criteria are not met, individuals may be classified as "users". Since diagnostic criteria are standardized, results can be compared across various study populations. For the current chapter, if standardized diagnostic criteria were utilized to determine the presence or absence of a SUD, it is specified as such so that comparisons can be made. And while drugs are often implicated in suicides as the method of fatal injury, the focus of this chapter is alcohol and illicit drug use as a risk factor for suicidal behavior rather than a method for completed suicides. Therefore data for drug poisonings are not presented.

Due to the statistical analyses and method of data capture generally used in the suicide literature, several points should be made prior to describing the research on the link between suicidal behavior and substance use. First, study designs vary greatly across the published literature, and cross-sectional studies are most common because they require a one-time data collection. Therefore, one can only describe the distribution of the disease under study at that point in time. This is termed prevalence or point prevalence [1]. However, there are inherent biases to cross-sectional studies, the most prominent being the inability to determine, with any authority, the temporal sequence of events leading up to the suicidal act. Many of the studies discussed in this chapter employed a cross-sectional design in which the disease or condition we are studying is lifetime suicide ideation or attempts and the factor we are examining for its association with suicidal behavior is a SUD. Since it is oftentimes difficult to determine whether a SUD preceded the suicidal act, it cannot be said that the presence of a SUD caused the suicidal behavior. Therefore, when analyzing cross-sectional studies with adequate sample size, the use of multiple regression is indicated. With multiple regression, potential confounders can be accounted for in the model and it can be said that the SUD is associated with the suicidal behavior, independent of the presence of other factors in the model. For the purposes of this chapter, when multiple regression was utilized it will be stated that substance use and suicidal behaviors are "independently associated." To make a causal link between a SUD and suicidal acts, a longitudinal study design is warranted. When prospectively following those at risk for suicidal behavior, measures are taken at baseline so that it is known that the suspected risk factor preceded any suicidal behavior. When we observe a suicidal act during the follow-up period, it is a new, or "incident" case. Therefore, incidence is merely the number of new cases of the suicidal behavior we are studying divided by the number of those at risk for suicidal behavior [1]. Since it is not practical to follow a cohort indefinitely to observe whether they eventually engage in suicidal behaviors, the incidence of suicidal behavior is usually far less than the prevalence. When a longitudinal study design is utilized, the terms "risk factor" or "predictor" are appropriate ways to describe the relationship between independent (i.e., SUD) and dependent (i.e., suicidal behavior) variables. This is always the case for fatal suicides; however, most often there was no "baseline" in which data on potential risk factors was captured, and therefore we rely on study designs that are unique to suicide, such as the psychological autopsy study. Finally, it should also be noted that differences in study populations may account for varying prevalence estimates. Therefore, the chapter is organized so that prevalence estimates are reported for similar populations and are therefore comparable.

2. Prevalence of Fatal and Non-Fatal Suicidal Behavior among Substance Users

Suicide is a major public health concern worldwide [5], and studies have been conducted in numerous countries to explore the antecedents of both non-fatal and fatal suicide. As noted by Wilcox (2004) in her review of the literature on suicide and substance use, "Suicidal behavior commonly occurs in the context of a convergence of multiple predisposing factors and current environmental factors that influence its development" (p. 27) [6]. Therefore, although the goal of this chapter is to describe the association between alcohol and other substance use and both fatal and non-fatal suicidal behavior, we would be remiss not to mention other potential risk factors that may be modifying the risk that substance use infers, such as comorbid psychiatric disorders.

Thoughts of suicide, or suicidal ideation (SI) is the most prevalent of the suicidal behaviors [7]. Since completed suicide is a rare event, SI, along with suicide attempts (SA) encompass much of the literature on the epidemiology of suicidal behaviors regarding alcohol and other substance use. The following section presents data specific to the prevalence and incidence of ideation and attempts as they are associated with alcohol and other substance use across a multitude of populations.

2.1. Alcohol and other Substance Users

Kessler and colleagues (1999) estimated the prevalence of suicidal ideation (SI) in the general population to be 13.5% [7]. However, among studies of those with substance use, abuse, or dependence, the prevalence is far greater. The highest prevalence of SI (63% among females and 47% among males) was observed among substance users in St. Louis [8], while several other studies reported the lifetime prevalence of SI to be anywhere from 20% among those with any diagnosed substance use disorder (SUD) [9] to 39.8% among African American cocaine users [10]. At 42%, past month suicidal ideation was higher than many lifetime estimates in a study of treated substance users in Norway [11]. In studies where alcohol is delineated from other substances, the prevalence of ideation ranges from 15.5% among females in treatment for an alcohol use disorder (AUD) [12] to 50.8% among alcohol dependent individuals enrolled in a genetics study [13].

Lifetime prevalence of suicide attempts (SA) is anywhere from < 1% to 4.6% in general population samples in the United States [7;14]. However, in these same large scale studies, the prevalence estimates were almost six times greater for those meeting the diagnostic criteria for a SUD or AUD and nine times greater among those with any substance use [15]. The prevalence of SA in other drug using populations ranges from 19% to 47% [16-19]. Amongst those primarily using alcohol, the prevalence of suicide attempts is upwards of 50.9% [15] and incidence in one study over a five year period was 4.5% [20].

In a study by Wines and colleagues (2004), in the two years following substance detoxification, the incidence of SA was 6.9% [19]. The lowest prevalence among either treated or community-based substance users was found to be 10% among non-injecting cocaine users in Australia [21]. While in other studies of cocaine users, the lifetime prevalence of SA was closer to 40% [21;22] , which is higher than that reported among methamphetamine users (28.7%) [23]. Substance treatment appears to be potentially protective against suicidal behavior. In two studies by Ilgen and colleagues (2007), longer time in treatment was protective against suicide attempts during the follow-up period [17;24]. However, a history of suicide attempts may also be a hindrance to those seeking substance abuse treatment. Using data from the Drug Abuse Treatment Outcome Survey (DATOS), Agosti and Levin (2006) examined treatment outcomes among those with and without a previous history of SA. While the overall success of treatment did not differ between the groups, those with a history of SA were at risk for additional ideation and attempts at follow-up in addition to major depressive disorder (MDD) and cocaine use [25]. In substances other than alcohol, the association between suicide attempts and opiate use has perhaps been studied most extensively and the prevalence estimates are fairly stable across study populations. Studies have found that between 31% and 48% of treated or community-based opiate users report a lifetime history of SA [26-32]. In a cohort of treated heroin users in Australia, the cumulative incidence of SA was more than 10% over a three-year period. However, the prevalence of both current SI and SA did significantly decrease following substance abuse treatment [31].

In a meta-analysis of the literature examining excess mortality, amongst the 20 cohort studies that assessed substance misuse, the risk of completed suicide was 10 times that of what was expected for non-substance users [33]. While a significant decline in suicide mortality was observed over time in a cohort of registered addicts in the United Kingdom, male drug users still had a mortality rate four times that which was expected and women had a rate almost five times that of what was to be expected [34]. Finally, in a cohort of heroin users followed for more than 20 years in Albuquerque, Goldstein and Herrera (1995) found the cumulative incidence of completed suicide was 3% [35].

Method of drug administration has also been found to be associated with suicidal behavior [36], and completed suicide in particular [37;38]. For example, injection drug users (IDUs) generally show an increased prevalence of ideation, attempts and completed suicide compared to general population estimates and even other substance users [36;39-41]. Similar to escalations in suicidal behavior from ideation, plans, attempts and finally completed suicide [2], escalations often occur in drug taking as well, from ingesting or smoking to snorting and finally, injecting [42;43]. Therefore, it follows that IDUs may be at greater risk for completed suicides given their drug use has likely progressed to abuse or dependence which is associated with greater levels of psychiatric distress [44]. Dinwiddie and colleagues determined the prevalence of SA to be 23.9% among IDUs, whereas non-drug users and even cannabis users in the same population had lifetime SA prevalence of 3.9% and 6.1%, respectively; several fold lower than the IDUs. In another study of IDUs across five U.S. cities, the past 6-month prevalence of suicide ideation and attempts was 35.8% and 7%, respectively.

In an analysis of a death registry in Scotland, the suicide rate among injection drug users was exceedingly high at 35.3% [45]. In their seminal review on the increased risk of death due to mental disorders (including substance use disorders), Harris and Barraclough (1998) found significantly greater risk for suicide deaths among opioid abusers and users of mixed drugs. Moreover, the risk of suicide death for injection drug users (IDUs) was 14 times that of the expected mortality in this group [37]. Expanding on Harris and Barraclough's review, Wilcox, Conner and Caine (2004) also found the standardized mortality ratio (SMR) for opioid users, injection drug users, as well as mixed drug users to be significantly greater than expected [38]. In a 1994 report by Rossow, the annual mortality among a cohort of treated drug users was 2.3%, 15% of which were classified as suicides [46]. In a meta-analysis of the literature examining mortality, amongst the 20 cohort studies that assessed substance use, the risk of suicide was 10 times that of what was expected for non-drug users [33]. Finally, a significant decline in the mortality rate was observed in a cohort of registered addicts in the United Kingdom; however, male drug users still had a mortality rate four times that of expected and female drug users had a rate almost five times that of what was to be expected [34].

2.2. Adolescents

Perhaps more studied than adult populations, adolescents and young adults have been the focus of a multitude of research examining the association between SUD and both non-fatal and fatal suicidal behavior. In his seminal review of suicidal behavior among adolescents, Brent (1995) found the risk for suicide attempts to be anywhere from 1.7 to 15.8 times greater among adolescents meeting criteria for substance abuse or dependence versus no substance use and 1.2 to 22.4 times greater for those with an alcohol use disorder compared to those without [47]. And in two studies examining incident suicides, alcohol and drug abuse were both found to be risk factors for suicide death [47].

Similar to adult populations, suicidal ideation is more prevalent among adolescents than other suicidal behaviors. Among treated adolescent substance users in a study by Ramchand and colleagues (2008), the authors determined the lifetime prevalence of SI to be 30% [48]. The prevalence of suicide attempts in substance using adolescents ranges from 6.1% among alcohol users to 20% among substance dependent adolescents in residential treatment [49]. A more accurate picture of the prevalence among a representative sample of high-school adolescents in the U.S. was provided by Lewinsohn (1994), who estimated the prevalence of lifetime suicide attempts to be 9.3% among substance users [50]. In a New Zealand birth cohort, amongst those with a previous history of an attempt, 65.5% had a diagnosed SUD [51]. Finally, when examined over a 20-year period, Oyefeso and colleagues (1999) found that 11.4% of adolescent drug abusers completed suicide [52].

3. Substance Use, Abuse and Dependence Associated with Suicide

Even among samples where the study population did not consist exclusively of alcohol or drug users, data consistently demonstrate an association between alcohol and other drug use and both fatal and non-fatal suicidal behavior, including ideation, attempts and completed suicide (Table 2).

Table 2. Significant Associations between Alcohol and Other Substance Use and Fatal and Non-Fatal Suicidal Behavior

Study	Population	Substance	Suicidal Behavior	Measure of Association (95% CI)
Kessler et al., 1999 [7]	Random Sample	Any SUD[a] AUD[c]	SA SA	AOR[b]: 5.8 (3.5, 9.7) AOR: 6.5 (3.6, 11.5)
Cheung et al., 2006 [53]	Random Sample	Substance Abuse	SI	AOR: 3.34 (1.57, 7.12)
Pagura et al., 2008 [56]	Random Sample	Any SUD	Multiple SA	AOR: 2.24 (1.48, 3.40)
Bolton et al, 2008 [62]	Random Sample with MDD	Any SUD	SA	AOR: 1.72 (1.02, 2.70)
Kuo et al., 2001 [57]	Random Sample	Any SUD	SA	RR[d]: 3.02 (1.14, 7.99)
Borges et al., 2000 [15]	Random Sample	Alcohol Dependence	SA	AOR: 5.90 (3.40, 10.2)
		Sedative Dependence		AOR: 3.40 (1.30, 9.00)
		Stimulant Dependence		AOR: 4.00 (2.20, 7.30)
		Marijuana Dependence		AOR: 2.70 (1.30, 5.50)
		Inhalant Dependence		AOR: 6.80 [2.40, 18.8)
Nock et al., 2008 [5]	Cross-National Sample	Any SUD	SA	AOR: 4.20 (3.50, 5.10) (high income countries) AOR: 4.60 (3.50, 6.30) (low income)
Thanh et al., 2006 [54]	Vietnamese Community Sample	Alcohol Use Sedative Use Analgesic Use	SI	AOR: 1.60 (1.10, 2.20) AOR: 2.70 (1.70, 4.30) AOR: 2.60 (1.60, 4.10)
Dube et al., 2001 [150]	Adult HMO Members	Substance Use	SA	AOR: 1.70 (1.30, 2.00)
LeMaster et al., 2004 [61]	American Indians	Any SUD	SA	AOR: 2.10 (1.38, 3.18)
Kaslow et al., 2000 [151]	African American Women	Substance Abuse	SA	AOR: 2.19 (1.02, 4.71)

Table 2. Continued

Study	Population	Substance	Suicidal Behavior	Measure of Association (95% CI)
Comtois et al., 2008 [152]	Post-partum Women	Any SUD	SA	AOR: 6.20 (2.80, 13.9)
Stallones et al., 2007 [153]	Low Income Women	Substance Abuse	SI	AOR: 2.16 (1.47, 3.19)
Havens et al., 2005 [154]	Substance Users	Poly-Drug Dependence	SA	AOR: 2.63 (1.25, 6.88)
Cottler et al., 2005 [8]	Substance Users	AUD	SI	AOR: 1.60 (1.09, 2.34) (males) AOR: 2.77 (1.56, 4.92) (females)
Landheim et al., 2006 [16]	Substance Users	SUD < age 18	SA	AOR: 2.70 (1.40, 4.90)
Glasner-Edwards et al., 2008 [23]	Methamphetamine Dependent	IDU[e]	SA	AOR: 2.25 (1.28, 3.94)
Darke et al., 2007 [31]	Heroin Users	Poly-Drug Use	SA	AOR: 1.39 (1.13, 1.72)
Dinwiddie et al., 1992 [36]	Drug Users and Controls	IDU	SA	OR: 8.27 (3.30, 20.7)
Agosti et al., 2006 [25]	Previous Attempts	Frequent Cocaine Use	SA	AOR: 1.40 (1.00, 1.90)
Vajda et al., 2000 [64]	Previous Attempts	Alcohol Abuse Drug Abuse	Re-Attempt	AOR: 3.56 (1.02, 12.4) AOR: 4.22 (1.29, 13.8)
Tidemalm et al., 2005 [72]	Mental Disorders	Any SUD	Completed	RR: 1.63 (1.04, 2.57)
Claassen et al., 2007 [65]	Major Depressive Disorder (MDD)	Alcohol Abuse Drug Abuse	SA	AOR: 2.1 (CI not reported) AOR: 1.8 (CI not reported)
Gunnell et al., in press [70]	Former Psychiatric Inpatients	Substance Misuse	SA	AHR[f]: 2.64 (2.37, 2.95)
Yen et al., 2003 [63]	Personality Disorders	Any SUD AUD	SA	AHR: 2.11 (1.43, 3.12) AHR: 1.74 (1.13, 2.68)
Zivin et al., 2007 [149]	Depressed Veterans	Substance Abuse	Completed	AHR: 1.74, 1.55, 1.96
Carrico et al., 2007 [55]	HIV-Positive	Marijuana Use	SI	AOR: 1.34 (1.03, 1.74)

Cheng et al., 2000 [140]	Taiwanese Decedents	Any SUD	Completed	AOR: 3.20 (1.00, 10.4)
Kung et al., 2005 [74]	Decedents	Alcohol Use Marijuana Use	Completed	AOR: 1.52 (1.35. 1.72) AOR: 1.60 (1.36, 1.88)
Hallfors et al., 2004 [98]	Adolescents	Marijuana Use IDU[d]	SI	AOR: 8.74 (4.29, 17.8) AOR: 19.5 (10.8, 35.4)
Hacker et al., 2006 [107]	Adolescents	Alcohol Problem Drug Use	SA	AOR: 4.70 (2.40, 9.10) AOR: 3.20 (1.80, 5.70)
Wilcox et al., 2004 [155]	Urban Youth	Marijuana Use	SA	RR: 1.80 (1.00, 3.30)
Freedenthal et al., 2007 [102]	Incarcerated Youth	Inhalant Abuse/Dependence	SA	AOR: 5.13 (2.73, 9.65)
Christofferson et al., 2003 [67]	Adolescents/Young Adults	Substance Abuse	SA	AOR: 3.00 (1.70, 5.20)
Fergusson et al., 2000 [59]	Birth Cohort – Adolescents	Any SUD	SI SA	AHR: 2.08 (1.52, 2.73) AHR: 1.84 (1.06, 3.19)
Rohde et al., 2001 [99]	Homeless Adolescents	IDU	SI	AOR: 1.94 (1.34, 2.81)
Juon et al., 1997 [116]	Urban Youth	Cocaine Use	SA	AOR: 5.11 (1.39, 18.8) (females)
Wunderlich et al., 1998 [156]	Random Sample German Adolescents	Any SUD	SA	AOR: 2.20 (1.30, 3.60)
Ialongo et al., 2002 [111]	Urban Youth	Any SUD	SA	AOR: 2.60 (1.30, 5.20)
Brener et al., 1999 [101]	University Students	Marijuana Use Cocaine/Illegal Drug Use Any Drug or Alcohol Use	SI	AOR: 2.40 (1.71, 3.36) AOR: 2.70 (1.49, 4.89) AOR: 2.10 (1.50, 2.95)

[a] Substance Use Disorder.

[b] Adjusted Odds Ratio.

[c] Alcohol Use Disorder.

[d] Relative Risk.

[e] Injection Drug Use.

[f] Adjusted Hazard Ratio.

3.1. Alcohol and other Substance Users

There have been a multitude of studies which have found alcohol and other substance use disorders to be associated with suicide attempts [5;7;56-63]. Utilizing data from the National Comorbidity Study (NCS) and NCS-Replication (NCS-R), Kessler and colleagues (1999) and Pagura and colleagues (2008) reported that the presence of a SUD was significantly associated with SA [7;56]. While in the Epidemiologic Catchment Area (ECA) survey, among a subsample of participants who were prospectively followed, SUDs were predictive of suicide attempts [57]. In an extensive study of the prevalence and correlates of suicidal behavior cross-nationally, Nock and colleagues (2008) found that in all socioeconomic strata, low, middle, and high income countries, those diagnosed with SUD were significantly more likely to have a lifetime history of SA compared to those with no substance use disorders [5]. In another representative sample of individuals, diagnosis of any substance use disorder was independently associated with suicide attempts [58]. Similar findings were observed among veterans [60], American Indians [61], and those with diagnosed major depressive disorder [62]. In longitudinal studies, one a birth cohort in New Zealand [59] and the other consisting of those with personality disorders [63], substance use disorders were found to be risk factors for subsequent suicide attempts. Two additional cohort studies found substance abuse to be a predictor of SA among those with previous attempts [64] and among individuals with major depressive disorder [65]. To examine the association involved with suicide attempts among alcohol-dependent individuals, one study divided 377 alcohol-dependent patients in an inpatient clinic into those who attempted suicide at some time in the past month and those who had not. The study also found that greater daily alcohol consumption was significantly higher among female and male attempters than in their non-attempting counterparts [66]. Finally, several cross-sectional studies have found substance abuse to be significantly associated with suicide attempts [7;60;67;68].

Among a representative sample of Chinese living in Hong Kong, Cheung (2006) found that a substance abuse diagnosis was significantly associated with suicidal ideation [53], and in Vietnam, use of specific drugs – sedatives, analgesics, and alcohol – were all associated with increased odds of SI [54]. And among a cohort of HIV-positive individuals, regular marijuana use was found to be associated with an increased prevalence of suicidal ideation [55].

Any illicit substance use was associated with suicide attempts in a study by Dube and colleagues (2001). Similarly, when suicide attempts were studied over time, substance use was predictive of subsequent attempts in studies by both Henriques (2004) and Gunnell (2008)[69;70]. When examining use of specific drugs or drug classes, in the NCS, Borges determined that use of alcohol, analgesics, sedatives, tranquilizers, marijuana, cocaine, inhalants, hallucinogens and heroin were all associated with suicide attempts, as was substance dependence for *all* drug classes examined [15]. Beautrais (2006) found that marijuana abuse or dependence was associated with SA among those in New Zealand [58], and in the U.S., the odds of a suicide attempt was significantly greater amongst those using cocaine in the ECA study [14].

In a longitudinal cohort of Finnish individuals with previous suicide attempts, diagnosis of a SUD was predictive of completed suicide [71]. Similarly, among those with serious mental disorders prospectively followed for suicide outcomes in Sweden, substance abuse/dependence was a risk factor for completed suicide [72]. Data from the 1993 National Mortality Followback Survey, a study conducted by the Centers for Disease Control and Prevention [73] in which death certificates were reviewed from 49 states and District of Columbia with special emphasis on suicides, indicated that marijuana use was predictive of completed suicides in both African American and white individuals [74]. Several case-control studies conducted among suicide decedents also found that SUD was significantly associated with completed suicide [75-78]. Finally, in a comprehensive review of the suicide literature, Fleishmann (2005) found that substance use disorders were second only to depressive disorders in terms of the number of completed suicides in which psychopathology was present (42.1% for depressive disorders versus 40.8% for SUDs)[123].

Alcohol dependence in particular is a well-established risk factor for completed suicide [79-86]. In a meta-analysis of thirty-two retrospective and prospective studies, Harris and Barraclough (1997) estimated the SMR for suicide to be almost six times greater for individuals with a DSM-III-R diagnosis of alcohol dependence and abuse versus those without [84]. More recently, Wilcox, Conner, and Caine (2004) updated and expanded the review by Harris and Barraclough and concluded the overall SMR for alcohol use disorders to be several fold greater at 979 (95% CI 898-1065) [85]. In a large, Danish prospective cohort study with a 26-year follow-up period, over 27% of all suicide completers had a registered AUD. In fact, individuals with an AUD were at nearly an 8 times higher risk of committing suicide compared to individuals without an AUD [87]. In addition to cohort studies, psychological autopsy studies have also been employed to determine risk factors for suicide. Psychological autopsies involve a combination of interviews of individuals who were closest to the victim and examinations of clinical and criminal records, case-notes, and reports. An extensive review of psychological autopsy studies of suicide by Cavanagh, Carson, Sharpe, and Lawrie (2003) demonstrated that alcohol and drug use disorders were strongly associated with suicide [86]. Further, in a review of epidemiological and clinical research in the areas of alcohol dependence and suicidal behavior, Pirkola and colleagues (2004) concluded that among unselected suicide populations, alcohol abuse or dependence was retrospectively found among 15-56% of patients who committed suicide [88].

Alcohol consumption in regards to its intensity and frequency has also been explored as a risk factor for suicidal behavior. Several studies have examined alcohol drinking as a risk factor for suicide [89-93], several of which are population-based studies [89-91;93-95]. Much of this research has found a significantly increased risk of suicide among heavy drinkers compared to nondrinkers [89-91;93]. Consistent with previous studies, a recent population-based prospective cohort study in Japanese men found that the risk of suicide among heavy drinkers (i.e., consuming $\geq$ 45.6g of alcohol per day) was two-fold higher than that of non-drinkers [96].

When compared to studies exploring the implications of heavy drinking on suicide risk, studies regarding light drinking as a risk factor for suicide show slightly more inconsistent results. Some population-based studies have reported a significantly reduced risk of suicide among light drinkers [89;91]. Yet, others have failed to show an association between light drinking and suicide risk [90;93-95]. A recent population-based prospective cohort study in Japanese men which extensively controlled for potential confounding variables found a significant association between daily amount of alcohol consumption and risk of suicide, but found that the risks of suicide among light drinkers and moderate drinkers (consuming $\leq$ 22.7g and 22.8 - 45.5g of alcohol per day, respectively) were not significantly lower than the risk among nondrinkers [96]. Likewise, a prospective cohort study of 45,000 male health professionals in the United States failed to find a significant association between overall quantity of alcohol consumed or drinking frequency and suicide death in individuals without alcohol dependence [97].

3.2. Adolescents

There are a host of studies that have found substance use to be a risk factor for suicidal behavior in adolescents. In the National Longitudinal Study of Adolescent Health (Add Health Study), injection drug use was the most robust predictor of suicidal ideation among the participants [98], with similar findings reported among homeless adolescents who were injecting [99]. The presence of any SUD has also been shown to be significantly associated with SI among adolescents [100]. For specific drugs or drug classes, suicidal ideation has been shown to be correlated with use of marijuana [6;101], alcohol [101], cocaine [101], and inhalants [6;102].

Among those reporting illicit drug use in the Add Health Study, the odds of having a lifetime history of suicide attempt was significantly greater than those with no substance use. [103-105]. Similar to Add Health, several other studies have reported any SUD [106-112] or alcohol use [46;105;107;109;112;113] to be significantly associated with non-fatal attempts. And in a longitudinal study where risk factors for suicide were assessed at age 18, it was found that the risk for SA at age 21 was significantly greater among those with a diagnosed substance use disorder [114]. Injection drug use is also significantly associated with SA among male adolescents, according to Woods and colleagues (1997)[106]. With regard to specific drugs or drug classes, SA has been demonstrated to be independently associated with use of: marijuana [46;103;113;115], cocaine [113;116], cigarettes [113], and inhalants [46;113].

4. Substance Use, Comorbid Psychiatric Disorders and Suicidal Behavior

Data have consistently demonstrated that negative affect (e.g., depressive disorders) are a robust predictor of fatal and non-fatal suicidal behavior [84;117-119]. And there is also a strong link between negative affect and both alcohol [120;121] and other SUD [44;122]. In fact, the most common risk factor identified for both fatal and non-fatal suicidal behavior is depression [123;124]; however, other psychiatric distress such as anxiety disorders [7;125], personality disorders [7;63] and other mood disorders such as bipolar or schizophrenia have also been found to be associated with suicide [7;126].

The specific role of alcohol dependence, consumption, and acute use in suicidal behavior is complex, acting on the outcome through multiple, interrelated channels. While alcohol dependence is independently associated with suicide, the potency of its ability to elicit suicidal behavior is strongly moderated by additional risk factors. In fact, the comorbidity of psychiatric disorders among alcohol-dependent patients has been reported to be relatively more important than alcohol dependence alone in determining suicidal risk [127]. Large epidemiological studies have shown that comorbid psychiatric disorders are common in patients with AUD [44;128]. The most common comorbid mental disorders include AUDs, affective disorders, and personality disorders [88]. According to a review by Pirkola and colleagues (2004), up to one-half of alcohol-dependent people who attempt suicide have comorbid psychiatric disorders [88]. In a study of alcohol dependent patients, a greater portion of attempters than non-attempters met the DSM-IV criteria for another psychiatric disorder [66]. Alcohol dependent suicide attempters were found to have multiple psychiatric diagnoses (e.g. depression, antisocial personality disorder, and substance abuse) and more severe psychiatric symptoms than non-attempters [70;129]. Individuals with alcohol dependence who attempt suicide were also more likely to have other substance abuse disorders, panic attacks, antisocial symptoms and social problems associated with alcohol abuse [130]. Male alcohol-dependent patients, in particular, who had attempted suicide were significantly more likely to have a panic disorder or a phobic disorder than were those who had not attempted suicide [130]. In a nationwide study of repeated suicide attempts and mortality among all first-time hospitalized suicide attempters in Finland from 1996-2003, having any diagnosis of a mental disorder or alcohol-related disorder before baseline was associated with a higher risk of recurrent suicide attempts and higher risk of repeated suicide attempts during follow-up [71].

While severity of alcoholism may act as a predisposing factor to suicidal behavior, major depressive episodes act as a precipitating factor [131]. Major depressive episodes increase risk for attempted and completed suicide [37;131-133] and alcoholism and depression are frequently comorbid [128;134-136]. Depression is a risk factor for suicide attempts among patients with alcohol or other substance dependence [137;138]. According to case-control psychological autopsy studies, the comorbidity of alcohol dependence and major depression confers a higher suicide risk than does either of the disorders independently [139;140]. Among a sample of hospitalized depressed patients with alcoholism, 40% had attempted suicide in the prior week and 70% had attempted suicide at some point in their lives [141] . And in an urban psychiatric facility, depressed individuals with alcoholism had significantly higher suicidality than patients with either alcohol dependence or depression, suggesting a synergistic relationship between the two conditions [142]. Studies have shown that among suicide completers with alcoholism or other substance dependence, 45-70% were experiencing major depression at the time of death [143] [140;144] [145]. In a large American epidemiological study, lifetime treatment for depression was independently associated with suicidal ideation among male and female current drinkers [146]. Sher and colleagues (2005) found that depressed individuals with a history of alcoholism had higher suicide ideation scores than counterparts who had no history of alcoholism [147].

A study by Havens and colleagues (2006) comparing suicidal ideation among IDUs and non-IDUs in Baltimorefound that once depressive symptoms were entered into the multivariate model, IDU was no longer significantly associated with SI, indicating that depression was likely moderating the relationship between IDU and suicidal ideation [41]. However, that was not the case in other populations of substance users, where given depression [148], depressive symptoms [8;41], ASPD [8], and anxiety, substance disorders were still independently associated with suicidal ideation. When studying suicide attempts, findings indicate that substance use, abuse, or dependence are associated with suicidal behavior even given the presence of major depressive disorder [16;25], depressive symptoms (but not MDD)[19;23], agoraphobia [16], bipolar disorder [26], PTSD [26], and conduct disorder [27].

Finally, in the following studies, substance use, abuse or dependence was found to be associated with suicidal behavior, even after taking into account comorbid psychiatric diagnoses, which speaks to the robustness of substance disorders as a risk factor for suicide. In the two population-based studies in the U.S., NCS and ECA, both found that mood disorders were significantly associated with SA in addition to substance abuse and dependence [14;56]. Other researchers found that even in the presence of major depressive disorder [58;60;61], antisocial personality disorder [60], and post-traumatic stress disorder [61], substance use was still independently associated with suicide attempts. In a psychological autopsy study in Taiwan, SUD was significantly associated with completed suicide as was comorbid MDD and panic disorder [140]. Finally, among depressed participants in particular, SUD has been found to be independently associated with completed suicide among both a cohort of veterans [149] and in a sample of depressed decedents less than 40 years of age [78].

6. Conclusion

In conclusion, there is evidence of a strong link between alcohol and other substance use and engagement in both fatal and non-fatal suicidal behaviors, especially for both adult and adolescent IDUs. However, it was also demonstrated that SUD is likely just one of many factors associated with increased risk for suicide and that, other psychiatric disorders, namely depressive disorders, may in fact play a larger role than SUD in determining risk. The evidence does suggest that in the presence of a SUD and other risk factors such as comorbid depression, screening for suicidal behaviors is indeed warranted.

References

[1] Gordis L. *Epidemiology*. Philadelphia: W.B. Saunders Company, 1996.

[2] O'Carroll PW, Berman AL, Maris RW, Moscicki EK, Tanney BL, Silverman MM. Beyond the Tower of Babel: a nomenclature for suicidology. Suicide Life Threat Behav 1996;26:237-252.

[3] Crosby AE, Cheltenham MP, Sacks JJ. Incidence of suicidal ideation and behavior in the United States, 1994. *Suicide Life Threat Behav* 1999;29:131-140.

[4] American Psychiatric Association. *Diagnostic and Statistical Manual of Mental Disorders, Fourth Edition*. 4th ed. Washington, DC: American Psychiatric Association, 1994.

[5] Nock MK, Borges G, Bromet EJ et al. Cross-national prevalence and risk factors for suicidal ideation, plans and attempts. *Br J Psychiatry* 2008;192:98-105.

[6] Wilcox HC. Epidemiological evidence on the link between drug use and suicidal behaviors among adolescents. *Can Child Adolesc Psychiatr Rev* 2004;13:27-30.

[7] Kessler RC, Borges G, Walters EE. Prevalence of and risk factors for lifetime suicide attempts in the National Comorbidity Survey. *Arch Gen Psychiatry* 1999;56:617-626.

[8] Cottler LB, Campbell W, Krishna VA, Cunningham-Williams RM, Abdallah AB. Predictors of high rates of suicidal ideation among drug users. *J Nerv Ment Dis* 2005;193:431-437.

[9] Tiet QQ, Finney JW, Moos RH. Recent sexual abuse, physical abuse, and suicide attempts among male veterans seeking psychiatric treatment. *Psychiatr Serv* 2006;57:107-113.

[10] Klein H, Elifson KW, Sterk CE. Predictors of suicidal ideation among "at risk" cocaine-using African American women. *Suicide Life Threat Behav* 2006;36:336-348.

[11] Rossow I, Lauritzen G. Shattered childhood: a key issue in suicidal behavior among drug addicts? *Addiction* 2001;96:227-240.

[12] Conner KR, Li Y, Meldrum S, Duberstein PR, Conwell Y. The role of drinking in suicidal ideation: analyses of Project MATCH data. *J Stud Alcohol* 2003;64:402-408.

[13] Conner KR, Hesselbrock VM, Meldrum SC et al. Transitions to, and correlates of, suicidal ideation, plans, and unplanned and planned suicide attempts among 3,729 men and women with alcohol dependence. *J Stud Alcohol Drugs* 2007;68:654-662.

[14] Petronis KR, Samuels JF, Moscicki EK, Anthony JC. An epidemiologic investigation of potential risk factors for suicide attempts. *Soc Psychiatry Psychiatr Epidemiol* 1990;25:193-199.

[15] Borges G, Walters EE, Kessler RC. Associations of substance use, abuse, and dependence with subsequent suicidal behavior. *Am J Epidemiol* 2000;151:781-789.

[16] Landheim AS, Bakken K, Vaglum P. What characterizes substance abusers who commit suicide attempts? Factors related to Axis I disorders and patterns of substance use disorders. A study of treatment-seeking substance abusers in Norway. *Eur Addict Res* 2006;12:102-108.

[17] Ilgen MA, Jain A, Lucas E, Moos RH. Substance use-disorder treatment and a decline in attempted suicide during and after treatment. *J Stud Alcohol Drugs* 2007;68:503-509.

[18] O'Boyle M, Brandon EA. Suicide attempts, substance abuse, and personality. *J Subst Abuse Treat* 1998;15:353-356.

[19] Wines JD, Jr., Saitz R, Horton NJ, Lloyd-Travaglini C, Samet JH. Suicidal behavior, drug use and depressive symptoms after detoxification: a 2-year prospective study. *Drug Alcohol Depend* 2004;76 Suppl:S21-9.:S21-S29.

[20] Preuss UW, Schuckit MA, Smith TL et al. Comparison of 3190 alcohol-dependent individuals with and without suicide attempts. *Alcohol Clin Exp Res* 2002;26:471-477.

[21] Darke S, Kaye S. Attempted suicide among injecting and noninjecting cocaine users in Sydney, Australia. *J Urban Health* 2004;81:505-515.

[22] Roy A. Characteristics of cocaine-dependent patients who attempt suicide. *Am J Psychiatry* 2001;158:1215-1219.

[23] Glasner-Edwards S, Mooney LJ, Marinelli-Casey P, Hillhouse M, Ang A, Rawson R. Risk factors for suicide attempts in methamphetamine-dependent patients. *Am J Addict* 2008;17:24-27.

[24] Ilgen MA, Harris AH, Moos RH, Tiet QQ. Predictors of a suicide attempt one year after entry into substance use disorder treatment. *Alcohol Clin Exp Res* 2007;31:635-642.

[25] Agosti V, Levin FR. One-year follow-up study of suicide attempters treated for drug dependence. *Am J Addict* 2006;15:293-296.

[26] Maloney E, Degenhardt L, Darke S, Mattick RP, Nelson E. Suicidal behaviour and associated risk factors among opioid-dependent individuals: a case-control study. *Addiction* 2007;102:1933-1941.
[27] Darke S, Ross J, Lynskey M. The relationship of conduct disorder to attempted suicide and drug use history among methadone maintenance patients. *Drug Alcohol Rev* 2003;22:21-25.
[28] Tremeau F, Darreye A, Staner L et al. Suicidality in opioid-dependent subjects. *Am J Addict* 2008;17:187-194.
[29] Conner KR, Britton PC, Sworts LM, Joiner TE, Jr. Suicide attempts among individuals with opiate dependence: the critical role of belonging. *Addict Behav* 2007;32:1395-1404.
[30] Bradvik L, Frank A, Hulenvik P, Medvedeo A, Berglund M. Heroin addicts reporting previous heroin overdoses also report suicide attempts. *Suicide Life Threat Behav* 2007;37:475-481.
[31] Darke S, Ross J, Williamson A, Mills KL, Havard A, Teesson M. Patterns and correlates of attempted suicide by heroin users over a 3-year period: findings from the Australian treatment outcome study. *Drug Alcohol Depend* 2007;87:146-152.
[32] Ross J, Teesson M, Darke S et al. The characteristics of heroin users entering treatment: findings from the Australian treatment outcome study (ATOS). *Drug Alcohol Rev* 2005;24:411-418.
[33] Neeleman J. A continuum of premature death. Meta-analysis of competing mortality in the psychosocially vulnerable. *Int J Epidemiol* 2001;30:154-162.
[34] Oyefeso A, Ghodse H, Clancy C, Corkery JM. Suicide among drug addicts in the UK. *Br J Psychiatry* 1999;175:277-82.:277-282.
[35] Goldstein A, Herrera J. Heroin addicts and methadone treatment in Albuquerque: a 22-year follow-up. *Drug Alcohol Depend* 1995;40:139-150.
[36] Dinwiddie SH, Reich T, Cloninger CR. Psychiatric comorbidity and suicidality among intravenous drug users. *J Clin Psychiatry* 1992;53:364-369.
[37] Harris EC, Barraclough B. Excess mortality of mental disorder. *Br J Psychiatry* 1998;173:11-53.:11-53.
[38] Wilcox HC, Conner KR, Caine ED. Association of alcohol and drug use disorders and completed suicide: an empirical review of cohort studies. *Drug Alcohol Depend* 2004;76 Suppl:S11-9.:S11-S19.
[39] Harris EC, Barraclough B. Excess mortality of mental disorder. *Br J Psychiatry* 1998;173:11-53.:11-53.
[40] Havens JR, Strathdee SA, Fuller CM et al. Correlates of attempted suicide among young injection drug users in a multi-site cohort. *Drug Alcohol Depend* 2004;75:261-269.
[41] Havens JR, Sherman SG, Sapun M, Strathdee SA. Prevalence and correlates of suicidal ideation among young injection vs. noninjection drug users. *Subst Use Misuse* 2006;41:245-254.
[42] Des Jarlais DC, Casriel C, Friedman SR, Rosenblum A. AIDS and the transition to illicit drug injection--results of a randomized trial prevention program. *Br J Addict* 1992;87:493-498.

[43] van Ameijden EJ, van den Hoek JA, Hartgers C, Coutinho RA. Risk factors for the transition from noninjection to injection drug use and accompanying AIDS risk behavior in a cohort of drug users. *Am J Epidemiol* 1994;139:1153-1163.
[44] Regier DA, Farmer ME, Rae DS et al. Comorbidity of mental disorders with alcohol and other drug abuse. Results from the Epidemiologic Catchment Area (ECA) Study. *JAMA* 1990;264:2511-2518.
[45] Frischer M, Bloor M, Goldberg D, Clark J, Green S, McKeganey N. Mortality among injecting drug users: a critical reappraisal. *J Epidemiol Community Health* 1993;47:59-63.
[46] Rossow I, Groholt B, Wichstrom L. Intoxicants and suicidal behaviour among adolescents: changes in levels and associations from 1992 to 2002. *Addiction* 2005;100:79-88.
[47] Brent DA. Risk factors for adolescent suicide and suicidal behavior: mental and substance abuse disorders, family environmental factors, and life stress. *Suicide Life Threat Behav* 1995;25 Suppl:52-63.:52-63.
[48] Ramchand R, Griffin BA, Harris KM, McCaffrey DF, Morral AR. A prospective investigation of suicide ideation, attempts, and use of mental health service among adolescents in substance abuse treatment. *Psychol Addict Behav* 2008;22:524-532.
[49] Cavaiola AA, Lavender N. Suicidal behavior in chemically dependent adolescents. *Adolescence* 1999;34:735-744.
[50] Lewinsohn PM, Rohde P, Seeley JR. Psychosocial risk factors for future adolescent suicide attempts. *J Consult Clin Psychol* 1994;62:297-305.
[51] Fergusson DM, Lynskey MT. Suicide attempts and suicidal ideation in a birth cohort of 16-year-old New Zealanders. *J Am Acad Child Adolesc Psychiatry* 1995;34:1308-1317.
[52] Oyefeso A, Ghodse H, Clancy C, Corkery J, Goldfinch R. Drug abuse-related mortality: a study of teenage addicts over a 20-year period. *Soc Psychiatry Psychiatr Epidemiol* 1999;34:437-441.
[53] Cheung YB, Law CK, Chan B, Liu KY, Yip PS. Suicidal ideation and suicidal attempts in a population-based study of Chinese people: risk attributable to hopelessness, depression, and social factors. *J Affect Disord* 2006;90:193-199.
[54] Tran Thi TH, Tran TN, Jiang GX, Leenaars A, Wasserman D. Life time suicidal thoughts in an urban community in Hanoi, Vietnam. *BMC Public Health* 2006;6:76.:76.
[55] Carrico AW, Johnson MO, Morin SF et al. Correlates of suicidal ideation among HIV-positive persons. *AIDS* 2007;21:1199-1203.
[56] Pagura J, Cox BJ, Sareen J, Enns MW. Factors associated with multiple versus single episode suicide attempts in the 1990-1992 and 2001-2003 United States national comorbidity surveys. *J Nerv Ment Dis* 2008;196:806-813.
[57] Kuo WH, Gallo JJ, Tien AY. Incidence of suicide ideation and attempts in adults: the 13-year follow-up of a community sample in Baltimore, Maryland. *Psychol Med* 2001;31:1181-1191.
[58] Beautrais AL, Wells JE, McGee MA, Oakley Browne MA. Suicidal behaviour in Te Rau Hinengaro: the New Zealand Mental Health Survey. *Aust N Z J Psychiatry* 2006;40:896-904.
[59] Fergusson DM, Woodward LJ, Horwood LJ. Risk factors and life processes associated with the onset of suicidal behaviour during adolescence and early adulthood. *Psychol Med* 2000;30:23-39.

[60] Price RK, Risk NK, Haden AH, Lewis CE, Spitznagel EL. Post-traumatic stress disorder, drug dependence, and suicidality among male Vietnam veterans with a history of heavy drug use. *Drug Alcohol Depend* 2004;76 Suppl:S31-43.:S31-S43.

[61] LeMaster PL, Beals J, Novins DK, Manson SM. The prevalence of suicidal behaviors among Northern Plains American Indians. *Suicide Life Threat Behav* 2004;34:242-254.

[62] Bolton JM, Belik SL, Enns MW, Cox BJ, Sareen J. Exploring the correlates of suicide attempts among individuals with major depressive disorder: findings from the national epidemiologic survey on alcohol and related conditions. *J Clin Psychiatry* 2008;69:1139-1149.

[63] Yen S, Shea MT, Pagano M et al. Axis I and axis II disorders as predictors of prospective suicide attempts: findings from the collaborative longitudinal personality disorders study. *J Abnorm Psychol* 2003;112:375-381.

[64] Vajda J, Steinbeck K. Factors associated with repeat suicide attempts among adolescents. *Aust N Z J Psychiatry* 2000;34:437-445.

[65] Claassen CA, Trivedi MH, Rush AJ et al. Clinical differences among depressed patients with and without a history of suicide attempts: findings from the STAR*D trial. *J Affect Disord* 2007;97:77-84.

[66] Pektas O, Mirsal H, Kalyoncu A, Unsalan N, Beyadzyurek M. Alcohol-dependent patients attempting and not attempting suicide: a comparison. *Acta Neuropsychiatrica* 2004;16:204-211.

[67] Christoffersen MN, Poulsen HD, Nielsen A. Attempted suicide among young people: risk factors in a prospective register based study of Danish children born in 1966. *Acta Psychiatr Scand* 2003;108:350-358.

[68] Benda BB. Gender differences in predictors of suicidal thoughts and attempts among homeless veterans that abuse substances. *Suicide Life Threat Behav* 2005;35:106-116.

[69] Henriques GR, Brown GK, Berk MS, Beck AT. Marked increases in psychopathology found in a 30-year cohort comparison of suicide attempters. *Psychol Med* 2004;34:833-841.

[70] Gunnell D, Hawton K, Ho D et al. Hospital admissions for self harm after discharge from psychiatric inpatient car*e: cohort study.* BMJ 2008;337:a2278. doi: 10.1136/bmj.a2278.:a2278.

[71] Suominen K, Isometsa E, Haukka J, Lonnqvist J. Substance use and male gender as risk factors for deaths and suicide--a 5-year follow-up study after deliberate self-harm. *Soc Psychiatry Psychiatr Epidemiol* 2004;39:720-724.

[72] Tidemalm D, Elofsson S, Stefansson CG, Waern M, Runeson B. Predictors of suicide in a community-based cohort of individuals with severe mental disorder. *Soc Psychiatry Psychiatr Epidemiol* 2005;40:595-600.

[73] Centers for Disease Control and Prevention. National Mortality Followback Survey. *National Vital Statistics System* [serial online] 2009; Accessed July 14, 2009.

[74] Kung HC, Pearson JL, Wei R. Substance use, firearm availability, depressive symptoms, and mental health service utilization among white and African American suicide decedents aged 15 to 64 years. *Ann Epidemiol* 2005;15:614-621.

[75] Stenager K, Qin P. Individual and parental psychiatric history and risk for suicide among adolescents and young adults in Denmark: a population-based study. *Soc Psychiatry Psychiatr Epidemiol* 2008;43:920-926.

[76] Schneider B, Kolves K, Blettner M, Wetterling T, Schnabel A, Varnik A. Substance use disorders as risk factors for suicide in an Eastern and a Central European city (Tallinn and Frankfurt/Main). *Psychiatry Res* 2009;165:263-272.

[77] Qin P, Nordentoft M. Suicide risk in relation to psychiatric hospitalization: evidence based on longitudinal registers. *Arch Gen Psychiatry* 2005;62:427-432.

[78] Dumais A, Lesage AD, Alda M et al. Risk factors for suicide completion in major depression: a case-control study of impulsive and aggressive behaviors in men. *Am J Psychiatry* 2005;162:2116-2124.

[79] Kendall RE. Alcohol and suicide. *Subst Alcohol Actions Misuse* 1983;4:121-127.

[80] Murphy GE, Wetzel RD. The lifetime risk of suicide in alcoholism. *Arch Gen Psychiatry* 1990;47:383-392.

[81] Bernal M, Haro JM, Bernert S et al. Risk factors for suicidality in Europe: results from the ESEMED study. *J Affect Disord* 2007;101:27-34.

[82] Roy A, Linnoila M. Alcoholism and suicide. *Suicide Life Threat Behav* 1986;16:244-273.

[83] Hirschfeld RM, Russell JM. Assessment and treatment of suicidal patients. *N Engl J Med* 1997;337:910-915.

[84] Harris EC, Barraclough B. Suicide as an outcome for mental disorders. A meta-analysis. *Br J Psychiatry* 1997;170:205-28.:205-228.

[85] Wilcox HC, Conner KR, Caine ED. Association of alcohol and drug use disorders and completed suicide: an empirical review of cohort studies. *Drug Alcohol Depend* 2004;76 Suppl:S11-9.:S11-S19.

[86] Cavanagh JT, Carson AJ, Sharpe M, Lawrie SM. Psychological autopsy studies of suicide: a systematic review. *Psychol Med* 2003;33:395-405.

[87] Flensborg-Madsen T, Knop J, Mortensen EL, Becker U, Sher L, Gronbaek M. Alcohol use disorders increase the risk of completed suicide--irrespective of other psychiatric disorders. A longitudinal cohort study. *Psychiatry Res* 2009;167:123-130.

[88] Pirkola SP, Suominen K, Isometsa ET. Suicide in alcohol-dependent individuals: epidemiology and management. *CNS Drugs* 2004;18:423-436.

[89] Akechi T, Iwasaki M, Uchitomi Y, Tsugane S. Alcohol consumption and suicide among middle-aged men in Japan. *Br J Psychiatry* 2006;188:231-6.:231-236.

[90] Klatsky AL, Armstrong MA. Alcohol use, other traits, and risk of unnatural death: a prospective study. *Alcohol Clin Exp Res* 1993;17:1156-1162.

[91] Ross RK, Bernstein L, Trent L, Henderson BE, Paganini-Hill A. A prospective study of risk factors for traumatic deaths in a retirement community. *Prev Med* 1990;19:323-334.

[92] Sorock GS, Chen LH, Gonzalgo SR, Baker SP. Alcohol-drinking history and fatal injury in older adults. *Alcohol* 2006;40:193-199.

[93] Andreasson S, Romelsjo A, Allebeck P. Alcohol, social factors and mortality among young men. *Br J Addict* 1991;86:877-887.

[94] Paffenbarger RS, Jr., King SH, Wing AL. Chronic disease in former college students. IX. Characteristics in youth that predispose to suicide and accidental death in later life. *Am J Public Health Nations Health* 1969;59:900-908.

[95] Turvey CL, Conwell Y, Jones MP et al. Risk factors for late-life suicide: a prospective, community-based study. *Am J Geriatr Psychiatry* 2002;10:398-406.

[96] Nakaya N, Kikuchi N, Shimazu T et al. Alcohol consumption and suicide mortality among Japanese men: the Ohsaki Study. *Alcohol* 2007;41:503-510.

[97] Mukamal KJ, Kawachi I, Miller M, Rimm EB. Drinking frequency and quantity and risk of suicide among men. *Soc Psychiatry Psychiatr Epidemiol* 2007;42:153-160.

[98] Hallfors DD, Waller MW, Ford CA, Halpern CT, Brodish PH, Iritani B. Adolescent depression and suicide risk: association with sex and drug behavior. *Am J Prev Med* 2004;27:224-231.

[99] Rohde P, Noell J, Ochs L, Seeley JR. Depression, suicidal ideation and STD-related risk in homeless older adolescents. *J Adolesc* 2001;24:447-460.

[100] Fergusson DM, Woodward LJ, Horwood LJ. Risk factors and life processes associated with the onset of suicidal behaviour during adolescence and early adulthood. *Psychol Med* 2000;30:23-39.

[101] Brener ND, Hassan SS, Barrios LC. Suicidal ideation among college students in the United States. *J Consult Clin Psychol* 1999;67:1004-1008.

[102] Freedenthal S, Vaughn MG, Jenson JM, Howard MO. Inhalant use and suicidality among incarcerated youth. *Drug Alcohol Depend* 2007;90:81-88.

[103] Borowsky IW, Ireland M, Resnick MD. Adolescent suicide attempts: risks and protectors. *Pediatrics* 2001;107:485-493.

[104] Pena JB, Wyman PA, Brown CH et al. Immigration generation status and its association with suicide attempts, substance use, and depressive symptoms among latino adolescents in the USA. *Prev Sci* 2008;9:299-310.

[105] Silenzio VM, Pena JB, Duberstein PR, Cerel J, Knox KL. Sexual orientation and risk factors for suicidal ideation and suicide attempts among adolescents and young adults. *Am J Public Health* 2007;97:2017-2019.

[106] Woods ER, Lin YG, Middleman A, Beckford P, Chase L, DuRant RH. The associations of suicide attempts in adolescents. *Pediatrics* 1997;99:791-796.

[107] Hacker KA, Suglia SF, Fried LE, Rappaport N, Cabral H. Developmental differences in risk factors for suicide attempts between ninth and eleventh graders. *Suicide Life Threat Behav* 2006;36:154-166.

[108] Cho H, Hallfors DD, Iritani BJ. Early initiation of substance use and subsequent risk factors related to suicide among urban high school students. *Addict Behav* 2007;32:1628-1639.

[109] Wu P, Hoven CW, Liu X, Cohen P, Fuller CJ, Shaffer D. Substance use, suicidal ideation and attempts in children and adolescents. *Suicide Life Threat Behav* 2004;34:408-420.

[110] Anteghini M, Fonseca H, Ireland M, Blum RW. Health risk behaviors and associated risk and protective factors among Brazilian adolescents in Santos, Brazil. *J Adolesc Health* 2001;28:295-302.

[111] Ialongo N, McCreary BK, Pearson JL et al. Suicidal behavior among urban, African American young adults. *Suicide Life Threat Behav* 2002;32:256-271.

[112] Vega WA, Gil A, Warheit G, Apospori E, Zimmerman R. The relationship of drug use to suicide ideation and attempts among African American, Hispanic, and white non-Hispanic male adolescents. *Suicide Life Threat Behav* 1993;23:110-119.

[113] Dunn MS, Goodrow B, Givens C, Austin S. Substance use behavior and suicide indicators among rural middle school students. *J Sch Health* 2008;78:26-31.

[114] Giaconia RM, Reinherz HZ, Paradis AD, Hauf AM, Stashwick CK. Major depression and drug disorders in adolescence: general and specific impairments in early adulthood. *J Am Acad Child Adolesc Psychiatry* 2001;40:1426-1433.

[115] Portzky G, De Wilde EJ, van HK. Deliberate self-harm in young people: differences in prevalence and risk factors between the Netherlands and Belgium. *Eur Child Adolesc Psychiatry* 2008;17:179-186.

[116] Juon HS, Ensminger ME. Childhood, adolescent, and young adult predictors of suicidal behaviors: a prospective study of African Americans. *J Child Psychol Psychiatry* 1997;38:553-563.

[117] Yen S, Shea MT, Sanislow CA et al. Personality traits as prospective predictors of suicide attempts. *Acta Psychiatr Scand* 2009.

[118] Maser JD, Akiskal HS, Schettler P et al. Can temperament identify affectively ill patients who engage in lethal or near-lethal suicidal behavior? A 14-year prospective study. *Suicide Life Threat Behav* 2002;32:10-32.

[119] Dougherty DM, Mathias CW, Marsh DM, Moeller FG, Swann AC. Suicidal behaviors and drug abuse: impulsivity and its assessment. *Drug Alcohol Depend* 2004;76 Suppl:S93-S105.:S93-S105.

[120] Kessler RC, Crum RM, Warner LA, Nelson CB, Schulenberg J, Anthony JC. Lifetime co-occurrence of DSM-III-R alcohol abuse and dependence with other psychiatric disorders in the National Comorbidity Survey. *Arch Gen Psychiatry* 1997;54:313-321.

[121] Grant BF, Harford TC. Comorbidity between DSM-IV alcohol use disorders and major depression: results of a national survey. *Drug Alcohol Depend* 1995;39:197-206.

[122] Bucholz KK. Nosology and epidemiology of addictive disorders and their comorbidity. *Psychiatr Clin North Am* 1999;22:221-240.

[123] Fleischmann A, Bertolote JM, Belfer M, Beautrais A. Completed suicide and psychiatric diagnoses in young people: a critical examination of the evidence. *Am J Orthopsychiatry* 2005;75:676-683.

[124] Arsenault-Lapierre G, Kim C, Turecki G. Psychiatric diagnoses in 3275 suicides: a meta-analysis. *BMC Psychiatry* 2004;4:37.:37.

[125] Hawgood J, De LD. Anxiety disorders and suicidal behaviour: an update. *Curr Opin Psychiatry* 2008;21:51-64.

[126] Baldassano CF. Illness course, comorbidity, gender, and suicidality in patients with bipolar disorder. *J Clin Psychiatry* 2006;67 Suppl 11:8-11.:8-11.

[127] Driessen M, Veltrup C, Weber J, John U, Wetterling T, Dilling H. Psychiatric co-morbidity, suicidal behaviour and suicidal ideation in alcoholics seeking treatment. *Addiction* 1998;93:889-894.

[128] Kessler RC, Crum RM, Warner LA, Nelson CB, Schulenberg J, Anthony JC. Lifetime co-occurrence of DSM-III-R alcohol abuse and dependence with other psychiatric disorders in the National Comorbidity Survey. *Arch Gen Psychiatry* 1997;54:313-321.

[129] Hesselbrock M, Hesselbrock V, Syzmanski K, Weidenman M. Suicide attempts and alcoholism. *J Stud Alcohol* 1988;49:436-442.

[130] Roy A, Lamparski D, DeJong J, Moore V, Linnoila M. Characteristics of alcoholics who attempt suicide. *Am J Psychiatry* 1990;147:761-765.

[131] Wilcox HC, Conner KR, Caine ED. Association of alcohol and drug use disorders and completed suicide: an empirical review of cohort studies. *Drug Alcohol Depend* 2004;76 Suppl:S11-9.:S11-S19.

[132] Cheng AT, Chen TH, Chen CC, Jenkins R. Psychosocial and psychiatric risk factors for suicide. Case-control psychological autopsy study. *Br J Psychiatry* 2000;177:360-5.:360-365.

[133] Harwitz D, Ravizza L. Suicide and depression. *Emerg Med Clin North Am* 2000;18:263-71, ix.

[134] Sher L. Depression and alcoholism. *QJM* 2004;97:237-240.

[135] Sher L. Alcoholism and seasonal affective disorder. *Compr Psychiatry* 2004;45:51-56.

[136] Kessler RC, Nelson CB, McGonagle KA, Liu J, Swartz M, Blazer DG. Comorbidity of DSM-III-R major depressive disorder in the general population: results from the US National Comorbidity Survey. *Br J Psychiatry Suppl* 1996;17-30.

[137] Celentano DD, Bond KC, Lyles CM et al. Preventive intervention to reduce sexually transmitted infections: a field trial in the Royal Thai Army. *Arch Intern Med* 2000;160:535-540.

[138] Aharonovich E, Liu X, Nunes E, Hasin DS. Suicide attempts in substance abusers: effects of major depression in relation to substance use disorders. *Am J Psychiatry* 2002;159:1600-1602.

[139] Suominen K, Henriksson M, Suokas J, Isometsa E, Ostamo A, Lonnqvist J. Mental disorders and comorbidity in attempted suicide. *Acta Psychiatr Scand* 1996;94:234-240.

[140] Cheng AT, Chen TH, Chen CC, Jenkins R. Psychosocial and psychiatric risk factors for suicide. Case-control psychological autopsy study. *Br J Psychiatry* 2000;177:360-5.:360-365.

[141] Cornelius JR, Salloum IM, Day NL, Thase ME, Mann JJ. Patterns of suicidality and alcohol use in alcoholics with major depression. *Alcohol Clin Exp Res* 1996;20:1451-1455.

[142] Cornelius JR, Salloum IM, Mezzich J et al. Disproportionate suicidality in patients with comorbid major depression and alcoholism. *Am J Psychiatry* 1995;152:358-364.

[143] Murphy GE. *Suicide in Alcoholism.* New York: Oxford University Press, 1992.

[144] Conner KR, Duberstein PR, Conwell Y. Age-related patterns of factors associated with completed suicide in men with alcohol dependence. *Am J Addict* 1999;8:312-318.

[145] Heikkinen ME, Aro HM, Henriksson MM et al. Differences in recent life events between alcoholic and depressive nonalcoholic suicides. *Alcohol Clin Exp Res* 1994;18:1143-1149.

[146] Grant BF, Hasin DS. Suicidal ideation among the United States drinking population: results from the National Longitudinal Alcohol Epidemiologic Survey. *J Stud Alcohol* 1999;60:422-429.

[147] Sher L, Oquendo MA, Galfalvy HC et al. The relationship of aggression to suicidal behavior in depressed patients with a history of alcoholism. *Addict Behav* 2005;30:1144-1153.

[148] Thompson R, Kane V, Cook JM, Greenstein R, Walker P, Woody G. Suicidal ideation in veterans receiving treatment for opiate dependence. *J Psychoactive Drugs* 2006;38:149-156.

[149] Zivin K, Kim HM, McCarthy JF et al. Suicide mortality among individuals receiving treatment for depression in the Veterans Affairs health system: associations with patient and treatment setting characteristics. *Am J Public Health* 2007;97:2193-2198.

[150] Dube SR, Anda RF, Felitti VJ, Chapman DP, Williamson DF, Giles WH. Childhood abuse, household dysfunction, and the risk of attempted suicide throughout the life

span: findings from the Adverse Childhood Experiences Study. *JAMA* 2001;286:3089-3096.

[151] Kaslow N, Thompson M, Meadows L et al. Risk factors for suicide attempts among African American women. *Depress Anxiety* 2000;12:13-20.

[152] Comtois KA, Schiff MA, Grossman DC. Psychiatric risk factors associated with postpartum suicide attempt in Washington State, 1992-2001. *Am J Obstet Gynecol* 2008;199:120-125.

[153] Stallones L, Leff M, Canetto SS, Garrett CJ, Mendelson B. Suicidal ideation among low-income women on family assistance programs. *Women Health* 2007;45:65-83.

[154] Havens JR, Ompad DC, Latkin CA et al. Suicidal ideation among African-American non-injection drug users. *Ethn Dis* 2005;15:110-115.

[155] Wilcox HC, Anthony JC. The development of suicide ideation and attempts: an epidemiologic study of first graders followed into young adulthood. Drug Alcohol Depend 2004;76 *Suppl*:S53-67.:S53-S67.

[156] Wunderlich U, Bronisch T, Wittchen HU. Comorbidity patterns in adolescents and young adults with suicide attempts. *Eur Arch Psychiatry Clin Neurosci* 1998;248:87-95.

In: Suicidal Behavior in Alcohol and Drug Abuse...
Editors: L. Sher, A. Vilens, pp. 365-391
ISBN: 978-1-60876-919-3

Chapter 21

BAD TOGETHER: ALCOHOL DEPENDENCE, IMPULSIVITY AND SUICIDE

Jessica W. M. Wong[1] and Ulrich Preuss[2]
[1]AWO Psychiatry Center, Halle, Germany
[2]Martin-Luther-University, Halle, Germany

ABSTRACT

Alcohol dependence, impulsivity and suicide are interrelated in a complex network. In this chapter, we first defined alcohol dependence and impulsivity, then we discussed the possible ways these two relate to each other. Suicide and suicidal behavior in alcohol dependent patients and in impulsive patients are discussed. The social, neurobiological and genetic backgrounds involved are presented. The role of neurotransmitters in alcohol dependence and impulsivity, including the relatively new roles cannabis and corticotrophin-releasing hormones may play, are discussed. Whether alcohol dependence leads to impulsivity or vice versa remains unclear, but they are obviously bad risk factors for the other and also a major risk factor for suicide and suicidal behaviour in alcohol dependent individuals. Lastly, a brief discussion on the therapeutic options available for suicidal behaviour and impulsivity in the context of alcohol dependence is presented.

INTRODUCTION: ALCOHOL DEPENDENCE AND SUICIDAL BEHAVIOR: EPIDEMIOLOGICAL AND CLINICAL RELATIONS

Research in clinical and epidemiological samples indicate that almost 40% of treatment-seeking inpatients with an alcohol use disorder report ever having attempted suicide, a rate that is up to six- to tenfold higher than the rate of suicide attempts in the general population [1; 2]. Approximately 5% of those with alcohol use disorders take their own lives [3; 4], 20% to 35% of completed suicides are carried out by individuals with alcohol dependence [5]. Moreover, the rate of suicide attempts in these groups of subjects is suggested to be even approximately 5 to 10 times higher [1, 6]. In 32.2% of completed suicides the victims were intoxicated [7]. Alcohol ingestion to inebriation can intensify the mood which triggers off suicidal behavior, foster aggression and reduce the inhibition threshold for suicidal behavior [8]. Thus, suicidal behavior in alcohol-dependent individuals is frequent and of clinical relevance. Suicidal behavior is related to a high rate of psychiatric comorbidity and risky behaviors such as impulsivity. The aim of this manuscript is to review available evidence for the relationship between alcohol use disorders, suicidal behavior and impulsivity.

DEFINITION OF ALCOHOL USE DISORDERS

Alcohol dependence (alcoholism) is a major health and social issue. Alcohol dependence is characterized by serious functional problems in multiple domains. In addition, alcohol-dependent individuals have a shortened lifespan of 12-20 years due to various factors, among them, suicidal behavior [9]. The National Institute on Alcohol Abuse and Alcohol dependence highlights four major symptoms: craving, loss of control, physical dependence and tolerance. Formal diagnostic criteria for clinical and research needs are based on checklists requiring the individual to have symptoms in at least three of seven [Diagnostic and Statistical Manual of Mental Disorders (DSM-IV); American Psychiatric Association 1994] or three of six [International Classification of Diseases (ICD10); World Health Organization 1993] categories within the last 12-month period. According to DSM-IV Criteria, alcohol abuse is a maladaptive pattern of use leading to clinically significant impairment or distress, as manifested by one or more of four criteria, occurring within a 12-month period: recurrent use resulting in a failure to fulfil major role obligations at work, school or home, recurrent use in situations in which it is physically hazardous, recurrent use-related legal problems and continued use despite having persistent or recurrent social or interpersonal problems caused or exacerbated by the effects of alcohol use.

Alcohol use disorders are complex genetically influenced conditions where both genetic and environmental factors explain up to 50% of the risk [10; 11]. The understanding of these factors that contribute to alcohol use, problems, and alcohol use disorders (AUDs) is expanding rapidly. To facilitate the search for genetic and environmental factors influencing the onset and course of alcohol use disorders, researchers have identified genetically influenced intermediate characteristics (endophenotypes) which explain about half of the variance for AUD risk [12]. At the same time, both cross-sectional and longitudinal studies are revealing an expanding number of behavioral, sociocultural and additional environmental characteristics that also affect drinking patterns and problems.

This is especially relevant to questions relating to how these intermediate phenotypes influence the onset and maintenance of alcohol use disorders. Beside alcohol-metabolizing enzymes, level of response to alcohol and mood an anxiety symptoms, in particular acting out or externalizing behaviors (including impulsivity) may influence drinking patterns [11,) and suicidal behavior in alcohol-dependent individuals [1].

DEFNITION OF IMPULSIVE BEHAVIOR

Impulsivity, as defined by the American Psychiatric Association (1994), is action without adequate forethought, and is a pervasive aspect of normal and abnormal human behavior. Impulsivity has also been defined as the inability to stop a behavior that has negative consequences, preference for immediate over delayed gratification, tendency to engage in risky behaviors, heightened novelty-seeking, behaving without forethought or consideration of outcomes, being impatient when asked to wait, having a short attention span, and difficulty persisting at a particular activity [13; 14; 15]. The most distinct factor of impulsivity has been identified by Lorr and Wunderlich (1985)[16], who concluded that the two components of impulsivity are not resisting urges and responding immediately to a stimulus.

Traditionally, there are three main classes of instruments to measure impulsivity: self-report measures, laboratory behavior measures and event-related potentials. Self-report measures, like the Barratt Impulsiveness Scale (BIS-11), are designed to measure motor impulsiveness, attentional impulsiveness and non-planning impulsiveness [17]. Laboratory behavior measures are divided into punishment/extinction paradigms, reward-directed paradigms and rapid-decision paradigms [18]. Studies with laboratory animals indicate that different operational measures of impulsivity are mediated by different neural mechanisms [13]. These measures were based on different operational definitions of impulsivity and have been validated independently with populations characterized by impulsive tendencies (i.e. children and adults with Attention Deficit Hyperactivity Disorder (ADHD) and juveniles diagnosed with Antisocial Personality Disorder [19; 20; 21]. The "Stop task" [19] is designed to measure a subject's ability to inhibit a pre-potent motor response, with stop reaction time (SRT) as the measure of impulsivity. The Go/no-go task [20] involves reward/punishment conflict and the ability to inhibit a punished response. Impulsivity on the Go/no-go task is indicated by errors of commission (false alarms). The Go/no-go paradigm puts a greater load on cognitive inhibition, involving response selection, while the Stop task requires the retraction of a response already initiated by the go signal, or motor inhibition [22]. The Delay Discounting task [23, 24] measures the value of immediate or certain reinforcers vs. delayed or uncertain reinforcers. Impulsive individuals are thought to value delayed or uncertain reinforcers less than immediate or certain reinforcers [21]. Finally, a time reproduction task was used to assess subjective time perception.

Lastly, impulsiveness has been shown to be related to information processing through proposed differences in attention [25], arousal [26, 27, 28] and/or maintaining a cognitive tempo or selected rate of information processing [29, 30, 31]. Measures of impulsiveness, selected verbal skills including reading, continuous motor performance and judging time intervals, define a second order factor or temporal information processing according to Stanford and Barratt (1996)[32]. A positive waveform (P300) recorded in response to target stimuli during the performance of a wide range of "oddball" tasks has been related to impulsivity and impulse control disorders [33, 34].

Evenden [13, 35] suggested that impulsivity actually comprises multiple processes that are behaviorally and neurochemically dissociable. Impulsivity can be expressed as a stable pattern across a variety of situations (trait-dependent) or may be shown transiently (state-dependent) in acute biological or environmental influences [36]. Trait-dependent theories emphasize the importance of an interaction between negative life events or psychiatric states with underlying traits of impulsivity [37], whereas state-dependent theories emphasize impulsivity as a product of the individual's diminished capacity or deconstructed state [38, 39].

The concept of rapid response, also termed response inhibition or non-planning impulsivity, encompasses several aspects of present-focused behavior, including quick decision-making, inability to withhold action, and action without regard to consequences [13; 40;41]. Some researchers have suggested that this second subtype of impulsivity is more strongly associated with psychopathology [42] and argued that each dimension of impulsivity reflects a different aspect of substance abuse (e.g., 40). The reward delay subtype of impulsivity may serve as an underlying vulnerability that may trigger substance abuse onset, whereas the rapid response subtype may contribute to the maintenance of substance abuse among individuals who already use. Another possibility is that reward delay impulsivity is triggered during an individual's active decision to use or abstain from substances, whereas rapid response impulsivity may be activated during more automatic substance use patterns such as cue-reactive behaviors.

Then there is the interesting concept of alcohol myopia [43] which states that alcohol intoxication restricts information processing, causing an individual to extract meaning solely from the most salient cues in their environment. If cues provoking an impulsive choice are more salient than cues inhibiting that choice, alcohol increases impulsivity. In contrast, if either or both of the impelling and inhibiting cues are weak, alcohol myopia does not influence responding. This differs from reflection impulsivity, that is, making decisions before enough information has been gathered and evaluated [44]

Impulsive aggression disorder has been defined as recurrent incidents of physical or verbal aggression that are out of proportion to the circumstances, occur at least twice a week for more than 1 month and lead to marked distress or impairment [45].

How Are Impulsive Behaviors and Alcohol Dependence Related?

Impulsive and aggressive behavioral patterns are hallmark clinical features of Type B [46] and Type II [47] alcoholic subtypes. Empirical studies of alcohol-induced impulsivity have generally been limited to motor impulsivity [48; 49], even though cognitive impulsivity may better represent the behavioral processes associated with intoxication (e.g. drinking and driving, unprotected sex, aggression, etc.) and long-term drug use (e.g. choice of immediate, short-term effects of intoxication over delayed, long-term effects of abstinence).

Quirk and McCormick (1998)[50] further reported that the more extreme the reported levels of depressive symptoms, aggressive/hostile cognitions, impulsiveness and maladaptive coping styles were, the higher the likelihood of abusing more than one substance. Preuss et al (2001)[51] investigated 135 alcohol-dependent patients and showed that the low-impulsivity group was slightly older and showed a later age at alcohol dependence onset than the highly impulsive group.

In extension to the concepts of impulsivity, Sugden et al (2006)[52] defined five primary symptom domains of aggressive behavior: impulsivity (rapid, thoughtless aggressive acts), affective instability (affectively charged attacks with seemingly little provocation), anxiety/hyperarousal (overwhelming anxiety and frustration leading to aggressive outbursts), cognitive disorganization (poorly organized and confused aggressive acts), and predatory/planned aggression (goal-directed preying on others). An underlying externalizing personality trait having characteristics like impulsivity, aggression, and mood swings might contribute to the etiology of all 3: alcohol dependence, externalizing personality disorders, and suicidal behavior [53; 54; 55; 56].

Are alcohol-dependent subjects and drug addicts more impulsive or is increased impulsivity caused by chronic alcohol or drug abuse? Drug-seeking behavior may result from two distinct, but inter-related, phenomena that involve impulsivity [57]: enhancement of the potency of the impulse (increased salience of the rewarding and/or reinforcing qualities of the desired drug/stimulus) and diminished ability to actively inhibit the impulse at the cognitive level. Impulsivity has been associated with early experimentation with substances of abuse and a high susceptibility to developing substance use disorders later in life [58]. Conversely, impulsive behavior may emerge as a consequence of using substances, either in the short term (e.g. acute intoxication) or after chronic use [59]. Finally, high levels of impulsivity have been reported to influence negatively both the course and the treatment outcome of substance use disorders [60]. In a review from Perry and Carroll (2008)[61] impulsivity is implicated in three phases of drug abuse. First, increased levels of impulsivity lead to acquisition of drug abuse and subsequent escalation or loss of control of drug intake. Second, drugs of abuse may increase impulsivity, an additional contributor to escalation/loss of control of consumption. Third, there is a relationship between impulsivity and other drug abuse vulnerability factors, such as sex, hormonal status, reactivity to nondrug rewards, and early environmental experiences that may impact drug intake during all phases of addiction. The chicken-or-egg question remains, however, unclear.

The causes of impulsivity and related aggressive behaviors like impulsive aggression are highly complex and multifaceted (Hollander 1995)[62]. Besides genetic influences estimated to range from 28% to 47%, there are non-shared environmental influences greater by 50% for Indirect Assault and greater by 70% for Verbal Assault [63]. Barratt et al found three differences between the groups with primarily impulsive aggression versus premeditated aggression that support a basic biological/behavioral distinction and impulsive aggressive inmates had a significant decrease in aggressive behavior [64]. All these findings support the hypothesis that an underlying externalizing trait might influence aggression, impulsivity, and alcohol dependence and facilitate suicidal behavior, for which a potential genetic locus has been detected on chromosome 2 [54].

Two of the ICD-10 criteria for alcohol and substance abuse disorders are loss of control over the substance-taking behavior and persistent substance consumption despite clear evidence of harmful consequences. Adolescence, when alcohol and substance use typically begins, is marked by both increases in the salience of reward and novelty [65, 66] and significant structural and functional development in prefrontal cortex [67]. Imaging data are consistent with enhanced reward sensitivity in adolescents [68, 69], and the rewarding properties of different drugs are likely to be especially relevant for adolescents. Everitt et al (2008)[70] hypothesized drug addiction to be the endpoint of a series of transitions from initial voluntary drug use through the loss of control over this behavior, such that it becomes habitual and ultimately compulsive. This switch represents a transition at the neural level from prefron-tal cortical to striatal control over drug-seeking and drug-taking behaviors as well as a progression from ventral to more dorsal domains of the striatum, mediated by its serially interconnecting dopaminergic circuitry. These neural transitions depend upon the neuroplasticity induced by chronic self-administration of drugs in both cortical and striatal structures, including long-lasting changes that are the consequence of toxic drug effects.

"Craving" has a central role in the continuation of alcohol and drug abuse, as well as relapse frequency. An expert committee gathered by the United Nations International Drug Control Programme and the World Health Organization defined craving as 'the desire to experience the effect(s) of a previously experienced psychoactive substance'. Craving can occur even after long-term abstinence and is typically provoked by stress, conditioned alcohol-associated stimuli and internal stimuli such as changes in mood state [71]. It is believed that residual alterations in several neurotransmitter systems that cause functional deficits in reward-related pathways and sensitization to environmental stimuli that predict drug effects are responsible for alcohol craving. Alcohol, like other drug of abuse, sensitizes neural pathways important in signalling incentive motivation and thereby drug-paired stimuli become conditioned incentives that activate a central motivational state [72; 73]. Alternatively, it is suggested that drug-paired stimuli elicit conditioned-withdrawal effects, which mimic the autonomic components of withdrawal, and thereby may also induce alcohol craving [74]. These two different mechanisms are best captured by the terms reward and relief craving [75, 76, 77]. Early stages of excessive alcohol use are characterized by impulsive drinking, that is, drinking to intoxication in binge-like episodes, common among adolescents and young adults in industrialized countries [75, 76]. This behavior is positively reinforced by pleasurable alcohol effects, and interspersed by periods of sobriety. During this stage, environmental stimuli become associated with pleasurable alcohol effects, setting the scene for 'reward craving' 77]. By contrast, following a prolonged history of dependence, low mood, elevated anxiety and increased sensitivity to stress become dominant. At this stage, alcohol use becomes primarily negatively reinforced, that is, motivated by the ability of the drug to eliminate what can collectively be labelled 'a negative emotional state', setting the scene for craving motivated by relief produced through renewed drug intake, or 'relief craving'. Among alcohol dependent patients, it is possible to distinguish between reward and relief cravers (ongoing Project PREDICT; Mann K. et al.), as it is suggested that reward craving might result from dopaminergic/opioidergic dysregulation, whereas relief craving might result from either GABAergic/glutamatergic dysregulation or dysfunction in the CRF signalling pathway [78; 79].

Conditioned drug-augmented impulsivity may have influenced relapse such that the drug abuser continues to exhibit impulsive behavior in the presence of drug- and impulsivity-related stimuli that previously signalled drug-induced impulsivity [61]. Conditioned impulsivity may lead an individual to relapse because they are not able to inhibit drug-taking behavior after exposure to drug-related cues. Elevated impulsivity is reported as a predictor of poor decision-making [80].

In summary, impulsivity has a strong role and predictive value in the development and course of alcohol dependence. Impulsivity and alcohol dependence are associated with more comorbid psychiatric diseases and more consequences, which will be elaborated on in the following paragraphs.

IS THERE AN INTERRELATIONSHIP BETWEEN ALCOHOL USE DISORDERS, IMPULSIVITY AND SUICIDALITY?

The term "suicidality" refers to the occurrence of suicidal thoughts (or suicidal ideation) or suicidal behavior [81]. Suicidal behavior may include acts of self-harm with a fatal (suicide) or a nonfatal (attempted suicide) outcome. For an extensive review of suicidality, we respectfully refer to the articles from O'Carroll et al (1996)[82] and Morton M. Silverman (2006)[83]. The National Co-Morbidity Survey [84] reported that 13.5% of the sample had at least one occurrence of persistent suicidal ideation, 3.9% reported having made a plan to commit suicide, and 4.6% reported having made at least one suicide attempt. These rates are exacerbated among people with a comorbid psychiatric disorder, including alcohol dependence. The lifetime risk for suicide completion among alcohol-dependent individuals has been reported to be almost 10%, a figure that is 5–10 times higher than that seen in the general population [2, 84, 85, 86; 87]. There are also reports of higher rates of suicide attempts among individuals with alcohol use disorders [88], and data support the conclusion of a greater than 20-fold increased risk for subsequent completed suicide among those with prior attempts [88, 89, 90, 91, 92, 93, 94]. Prior attempts are powerful predictors of suicide completion [95, 96, 97], with between 10% and 15% of attempters dying by suicide within the next 10 years [98]. In a 5-year follow-up study on 1,237 alcohol dependent subjects, 4.5% of these men and women attempted suicide [6]. More than half of the alcohol-dependent individuals who attempted suicide during the follow-up had prior attempts, compared with only 14% of the subjects with no prior suicidal behavior. An individual with a prior attempt had a 15.2% risk for a new attempt during the follow-up, compared with a 2.6% risk for the subjects without a prior attempt. Two commonly applied models to explain the occurrence of suicidal behavior include the stress–diathesis model [37] and the process model [99]. According to a stress-diathesis model [37], individuals suffering from depression and hopelessness are more likely to commit suicidal acts, if they also have high aggressive and impulsive traits. Suicidal behavior might then be even more facilitated by alcohol and drug intoxication, which often occurs before or during suicide attempts and completed suicides [1, 8, 100].

Impulsivity is hypothesized to be a predisposing factor that places individuals with alcohol use disorders at increased risk for suicidal behaviors [100]. Alcohol-dependent individuals with a history of suicidal behavior score higher on measures of impulsive traits than those without prior suicidal behavior [55]. Similarly, many suicide attempts are impulsive, as defined by a limited amount of planning prior to the attempt, and these impulsive attempts may be particularly common in those with alcohol use disorders [101]. 50% of individuals with alcohol dependence and a suicide attempt reported that they had spent less than 1 week thinking about the attempt [102], 24% to 40% of individuals with a suicide attempt spent less than 5 min planning the attempt [26, 103]. In general, individuals with an impulsive suicide attempt tend to report lower levels of depression, hopelessness, and less expectation of lethality than those who make more planned attempts [26, 102, 103, 104, 105, 106]. Suicidal patients showed more "neuroticism", which reflects emotional instability as well as impulsivity, and increased the risk for suicidal behavior [107].

Concerning impulsive aggression in violent vs. non-violent suicidal methods, there was no significant difference between the methods employed [108]. Violent suicidal methods were more frequently used by alcohol-dependent men, and the increased propensity to violence may possibly be explained by the gender-specific potential for aggression. Alcohol-dependent patients who attempted suicide were more often and more severely depressed, reported more anxiety, had a more severe course of disease (more alcohol-related problems, consumed more alcohol per day, had higher rates of other drug use and dependence) and reported more psychopathic behavior compared to those without suicide attempts [1, 55, 109, 110, 111, 112].

Regarding comorbid psychiatric diseases, Robins (1981)[113], reporting on 148 cases of suicide, found that 48% also had an affective disorder, whereas 25% were affected with alcohol dependence. Alcohol-dependent invididuals suffer from depression at a higher rate than non-alcoholics [114]. Hesselbrock et al. (1988)[109], in a study of inpatients who were being treated for alcohol dependence, found that 63% of the men with comorbid depression reported a history of suicide attempts compared with 70% of the alcohol-dependent women with a lifetime history of depression. Longitudinal studies suggest depression and anxiety disorders are more the result of, rather than the cause of, alcohol problems [115, 116, 117, 118]. More recently, Glowinski et al. (2001)[119] found that the odds of making a suicide attempt were increased 2.8 times in the presence of alcohol dependence, 8.8 times when a person has major depression, and 4-fold when a diagnosis of conduct disorder can be made. Major depressive episodes and stressful life events particularly, partner-relationship disruptions, may precipitate suicidal behavior in individuals with alcohol use disorders [114]. Alcohol misuse and psychosocial adversity can combine to increase stress on the person, and, thereby, potentially, increase the risk for suicidal behavior. Patients with co-occurring major depression (MDD) and borderline personality disorder are more likely to have a history of suicide attempts than those with MDD alone or MDD with other personality disorders [120,121]. Alcohol-dependent subjects also suffer disproportionately from anxiety disorders [122]. Impulsivity was found to correlate significantly with measures of state anxiety (+0.33), trait anxiety (+0.48), anger (+0.43) and confusion (+0.33) [123].

Preuss et al (2002)[1] analysed alcohol dependent subjects who attempted suicide and found them to be significantly younger and less educated, had a significantly higher proportion of females and probands, were less often married and more often divorced or separated, and less likely to be employed fulltime, compared to those who didn't attempt suicide. They also had an earlier onset of alcohol dependence and reported a higher maximum number of drinks in 24 hr (a drink being the alcohol content in 12 ounces of beer, 4 ounces of wine, or 1 to 1.5 ounces of 80-proof beverage). Those with suicide attempt histories also reported a higher number of alcohol dependence criteria overall, except for the items: drinking larger amounts over a longer period than intended, more alcohol-related physical disorders, more alcohol-related violence, and being more likely to have received any alcohol dependence treatment or AA. Furthermore, they were more likely to be dependent on illicit substances and more often reported a history of independent and substance-induced psychiatric disorders such as depression, mania, panic disorder, and social phobia. Surprisingly no or little relationship is found with suicide age at onset and number of suicide attempts in history [124].

The magnitude of personality disorders (PDs) correspond to rates of axis II disorders previously reported from other inpatient samples of psychoactive substance abusers [124, 125, 126], the rates reported from inpatient alcohol-dependent subjects ranges between 25 and 91% [125, 127] and is higher than the rate reported from an U.S. epidemiological sample

(39.5%, [128]). In comparison, rates of PDs in subjects with a history of suicide attempts or suicide completers were noted to range from 55 to 70% [129, 130]. Impulsivity in bipolar disorder patients has been associated with more complications like suicide [131] and substance abuse [17]. Patients with borderline personality disorder (BPD) use more substances and are more impulsive than those who do not meet criteria for borderline personality disorder [132]. Conversely, BPD patients with a history of suicide attempts had more impulsive actions, antisocial personality disorder (ASPD) comorbidity, and depression than those without a history of suicide attempts [133]. BPD and ASPD alcoholic individuals both reported more aggressive traits, more depression, and more suicidal behavior, including suicide attempts using violent methods [124]. In this sample, almost 50% of alcohol-dependent BPD subjects really wanted to die during their most serious attempt, were drunk during the attempt, indicating a significant role of alcohol use to facilitate suicidal behavior, and needed medical aid after their attempt. The combination of highly aggressive traits, depression, serious intent to die, and intoxication by alcohol and drugs puts this group of comorbid alcohol-dependent subjects at high risk to take their lives. While subjects with cluster A and C PDs, like schizotypal, avoidant, dependent, and depressive PD, had higher rates of depression, none had more aggression. Only dependent and depressive subjects had a higher rate of suicidal attempts and were more often intoxicated during the most serious suicide attempt. Thus, taking the univariate analysis, subjects with cluster B disorders are at highest risk, followed by cluster C and cluster A individuals at lowest risk. Alcohol-dependent individuals with a history of suicide attempts had significantly more schizoid PD characteristics from cluster A; more narcissistic, borderline, and antisocial characteristics from cluster B; and more avoidant, dependent, negativistic, and depressive PD characteristics from cluster C, when compared with subjects without such a history [124]. The diagnosis of histrionic and paranoid PDs was significant negative predictors of suicide attempts, making them protective factors. In the univariate analysis, paranoid PD subjects had high aggressive and histrionic PD traits, individuals had also more intensive impulsive behavior and a high rate of depression. These characteristics, however, did not result in a higher but lower rate of suicide attempts for both in the multivariate analysis. Furthermore, in both diagnostic groups, drinking or drug use during their most serious attempt was not significantly more. Considering that both PD diagnoses still reported a significant amount of risk factors, the combination of PD characteristics (e.g., suspiciousness in paranoid PD and extraversion in histrionic PD) with impulsive and aggressive traits may even be protective against suicidal behavior.

To summarize, impulsive patients who are alcohol-dependent have a higher risk of suicide, more comorbid psychiatric diseases like depression, anxiety, personality disorders and multisubstance dependence.

Neurobiology of Impulsivity and Suicidal Behavior in Alcohol Dependence

Of course, impulsive and suicidal behaviors as well as alcohol dependence have a neurobiological basis. A recent meta-analysis, confirming previous findings, indicates that there is a replicable interaction between childhood trauma and a functional polymorphism of the monoamine oxidase A (MAOA) gene, such that the genotype coding for low levels of this enzyme, which metabolizes dopamine, serotonin, and norepinephrine, is associated with more antisocial behavior, including impulsive aggression during adulthood [134, 135], and those who were sexually abused as well [136]. In work that combines brain imaging with molecular genetics, this same MAOA gene polymorphism predicted diminished reactivity of regulatory prefrontal cortex mechanisms involved in cognitive control and pronounced differences in limbic circuitry for emotion regulation, suggesting that genetic influences on these brain mechanisms are involved with impulsive aggression [137]. This research further provides evidence for an interaction of genetic factors (MAOA polymorphism) and environment (trauma).

Past research has further shown that cortical and limbic inputs to the ventral striatum (VS, arising in the prefrontal, anterior cingulate, hippocampal and amygdalar cortices) modulate Nc. accumbens function and its subsequent outputs to motor relay circuits [138, 139, 140, 141, 142, 143, 144]. Prolonged periods of forced brain exposure to BACs commonly occurring in human alcohol dependence (>150–250 mg/dL) will trigger long-term neuroadaptations leading to markedly increased voluntary alcohol intake and other consequences relevant for clinical alcohol dependence, collectively labelled 'the post-dependent state' [79] The post-dependent state reflect the sum of neuroadaptations induced as an individual becomes dependent on alcohol, and these remain for extended periods of time thereafter. These neuroadaptations can be maintained by continued brain alcohol exposure but they can remain even in its absence. Based on genetic susceptibility and other factors, the extent and duration of post-dependent neuroadaptations show considerable individual variability. In some individual, the neuroadapted, post-dependent state is hypothesized to remain indefinitely ('once an alcoholic, always an alcoholic'), while in others it remits. These neuroadaptations can be "within-systems" or "between-systems" [145].

Three categories of environmental stimuli are known to trigger relapse in alcohol-dependent individuals [146, 147]: small, 'priming' alcohol doses; conditioned cues associated with prior availability of alcohol; and stress. By altering neurochemistry throughout these neuroanatomical regions, alcohol and drugs of abuse may alter learning, lead to de-sensitization of memory and behavioral inhibition, producing abnormal susceptibility for alcohol- and drug-associated stimuli to control behavior. These common drugs of abuse are all acutely rewarding because of their actions on a final common pathway: the midbrain dopaminergic reward system, which is centred on the nucleus accumbens (NAc) in the ventral striatum [148, 149]. Through reciprocal cortical and subcortical connections, the NAc and, more broadly, the ventral striatum (VS), contribute to the motivational salience of stimuli and abet appetitive or reward-dependent behaviors [150]. Activity of the VS increases in response to both the anticipation and receipt of rewarding stimuli, including primary (e.g., food) and secondary (e.g., money) reinforcers [151]. Moreover, in addiction, craving and compulsive drug seeking, as well as sensitivity to drug cues, are associated with exaggerated VS activity and may result in behavioral disinhibition towards drug intake [152].

If drug users have less sensitivity to punishments and/or greater sensitivity to rewards [153, 154, 155], they may have difficulty changing their behavior in the face of drug-related rewards or problems and may be vulnerable to risk-taking. Deficits in impulse control and decision making observed in drug addicts result in part from hypo-function within the orbitofrontal cortex (OFC) [156, 157, 158]. Lesions to the prefrontal cortex (PFC) produce a profile of distractibility, forgetfulness, impulsivity, poor planning, and locomotor hyperactivity [159]. Consistent with Damasio's (1994)[160] somatic marker hypothesis, impaired decision-making among substance-dependent individuals has been linked to inadequate somatic signals within the ventromedial prefrontal cortex (VMPFC), which may lead to hypersensitivity to rewards without regard to future consequences and which might underlie the conversion from casual substance use to dependence [153], subsequent impulsive behaviors and suicidal behaviors. Hanson et al (2008)[161] found poorer reward-related decision-making was associated with generally heavier drug use in the past 30 days and the past year, as well as higher weekly alcohol use, more occasions of intranasal MDMA use, and meeting lifetime substance use disorder criteria for more classes of drugs. They also reported that higher impulsivity was significantly associated with more extensive drug use, as well as abuse or dependence of more types of substances, heavier weekly alcohol use, and higher self-reported depression levels. Other predictors of poor decision-making include chronic alcohol abuse, shorter duration of abstinence [162], low IQ [163], male gender [164], and elevated impulsivity [80].

The Role of Neurotransmitters

Several lines of evidence reported a relationship between low serotonergic neurotransmission and suicidal behavior. However, other underlying traits may also be associated with low serotonergic transmission. For instance, elevated impulsivity may be a reflection of low-5-HT activity in the frontal lobe [165]. Coccaro et al. (1993)[166] even hypothesized further that alcohol dependence may represent a hyposerotonergic state, and since alcohol is a potent releaser of 5-HT, some alcohol-dependent subjects may be self-medicating. Alcohol dependents with high impulsive traits showed a significant association with 5-HT2A 1438 A alleles which remained significant after excluding alcohol dependents with antisocial (APD) or borderline (BPD) personality disorders from the analysis [167]. Sher L (2006)[168] found that individuals with comorbid depression and alcohol dependence have greater serotonergic impairment which may be associated with higher risk of completed suicide. Furthermore, dopaminergic dysfunction, brain damage, neurobehavioral deficits, aggression/impulsivity and alcohol dependence severity all may affect risk for suicide among individuals with alcohol dependence. The mechanisms by which the complex 5-HT system (with at least fourteen different receptor subtypes each belonging to one of seven receptor families 5-HT1–7) modulates impulsivity are incompletely understood [169]. To shed some light on the different mechanisms involved in the 5-HT system, Talpos et al (2006)[170] compared the behavioral effects of three partially selective serotonergic (5-HT) ligands, ketanserin (5-HT2A,C receptor antagonist), SER-082 (5-HT2C,B receptor antagonist) and SB-270146-A (5-HT6 receptor antagonist) using two tests of impulsivity, i.e. five-choice serial reaction time task (5CSRTT) and delayed reward task to measure behavioral inhibition versus choice preference for a delayed reward. Dissociation was seen between the effects of ketanserin, which decreased impulsivity in the 5CSRTT, but had no effect on the delayed reward task, and SER-082, which had no effect on the 5CSRTT, but decreased impulsive responding in the delayed reward task. SB-270146-A had no effect in either paradigm. Similarly, Higgins et al. (2003)[171] found that systemic SB-242082 (a selective 5-HT2C receptor inverse agonist; 172] *increased* premature responding in the 5CSRTT, although

Koskinen et al. (2000)[173] did not see an effect with SER-082 or mCPP (5-HT2C receptor agonist) on premature responding in the same task. The effect seen by Higgins et al. in the 5CSRTT (increased impulsive responding) is opposite to that from Talpos et al (2006)[170] in the delayed reward task (decreased impulsive responding) after 5-HT2c receptor blockade, thus enhancing the degree of potential dissociation between tasks of impulsivity and 5-HT receptors.

Lowered 5-HT signalling impairs impulsive action [174, 175, 176]. Enhanced 5-HT transmission has been found to reduce premature responding in the 5CSRTT [177] and performance in a delayed reinforcement procedure has recently been reported to correlate with increased 5-HT efflux in the medial prefrontal cortex [178]. 5-HT depletions only impair impulsive action but do not delay aversion [175, 179]. These observations might indicate differential 5-HT involvement in impulsive action versus delay aversion. The trait-dependent component of impulsivity, reflected in personality measures such as the Barratt Impulsiveness Scale, may be related to relatively stable biological measures of impulsivity such as level of serotonergic function [180]. The state-dependent component, reflected by increased commission errors in a challenging version of the Continuous Performance Test (the IMT-DMT), may be related to noradrenergic function [181].

Dopamine, noradrenaline and glutamate neurotransmissions have also been implicated in impulsivity. The cannabinoid system and particularly cannabinoid CB1 receptors have been implicated in higher cognitive functions including attention, behavioral flexibility, and time estimation and working memory, based on emerging preclinical evidence [182]. In healthy volunteers, marijuana and delta9-tetrahydrocannabinol, the principle active ingredient of marijuana, have been demonstrated to increase the occurrence of risk-taking behavior in the laboratory [183] and induce impulsive action in a stop signal task, but not delay aversion [184, 185], which suggests a role for the cannabinoid system in impulsivity. Healthy subjects with low-dosed marijuana showed that THC increased impulsive responding on the Stop task and decreased patterns of impulsive responding on the time reproduction task [184]. THC did not significantly affect either the Go/no-go or Delay discounting tasks. Extinction training weakens the association between responding on the drug-paired lever and delivery of cocaine, and reduces relapse to drug seeking [186]. These beneficial effects of extinction training were suggested to arise, in part, through increased expression of GluR1 alpha-amino-3-hydroxy-5-methyl-4-isoxazolepropio-nic acid (AMPA) receptor subunits within the nucleus accumbens (NAc) [187, 188]. Chronic drug use weakens frontocortical glutamatergic input to the NAc, partly due to the internalization of AMPA receptors leading to long-term depression of cortico-striatal synapses [189] but also due to hypofunction in frontal regions [156]. This extinction-induced upregulation of the AMPA receptor GluR1 subunits may therefore strengthen excitatory cortical control of the NAc and contribute to a reduction in impulsive responding as well as a reduction in propensity to relapse. Norepinephrine enhances "signals" through postsynaptic alpha2A adrenoceptors in PFC, while dopamine decreases "noise" through modest levels of D1 receptor stimulation Brennan et al (2008)[159]. They also showed that alpha2A-Adrenoceptor stimulation strengthens the functional connectivity of PFC networks, while blockade of alpha2 receptors in the monkey PFC recreates the symptoms of ADHD, resulting in impaired working memory, increased impulsivity, and locomotor hyperactivity.

In a recent study [79], the role of “between-systems” neuroadaptations, represented by recruitment of an over-active corticotropin-releasing factor (CRF) system which mediates stress sensitivity and negative emotions in later stages of alcohol dependence, was investigated. Hypothalamic CRF neurons mediate endocrine stress responses through activation of pituitary CRF1 receptors, whereas behavioral stress responses are largely mediated by extrahypothalamic CRF1 receptors primarily in the amygdale and bed nucleus of stria terminalis, BNST [190]. Elevated anxiety is a hallmark of alcohol withdrawal, and is CRF mediated, because it is blocked by the corticotrophin-releasing factor (CRF) antagonism in the central nucleus of the amygdala, CeA [191, 192], while CRF levels or release are increased both in CeA [193] and BNST [194] during this phase. Long term upregulation of CRF1 receptors is observed in the amygdala following a history of dependence, and CRF antagonists selectively block emotionality, excessive alcohol drinking and stress-induced reinstatement of alcohol-seeking in post-dependent animals [79]. Innate upregulation of CRF1 receptor expression mimics the post-dependent phenotype, both with regard to emotional responses and ethanol self-administration. These data predict that blocking hyperactive signalling at CRF1 receptors in individuals with a history of dependence or innate susceptibility will inhibit heavy drinking and reduce the risk of relapse. As CRF1 antagonism selectively blocks stress- but not alcohol-cue associated relapse, a combination of the opioid receptor antagonist naltrexone and a CRF1 antagonist might act synergistically to prevent relapse.

In summary, many neurotransmitters have now been found to be implicated in the pathogenesis of alcohol dependence. Other than the known roles played by serotonin, noradrenalin, dopamine and glutamate, there is evidence for the involvement of cannabinoids and even corticotrophin-releasing factor. Further understanding of these roles may lead to new options in treatment and prognosis of alcohol dependence.

GENETICS

The understanding of genetics in alcohol dependence is still in its infant stage. All three, impulsivity, alcohol dependence and suicidal behaviors are genetically influenced. The purpose of studies on the genetic influences is, to disentangle effects of genetic variants on each trait or disorder alone or in combination or its influence on underlying traits which affects all traits or disorders. Several studies found evidence for an association between 5-HTTLPR-S-allele and suicide attempts in alcohol-dependent subjects, i.e. where the number of alleles showed a significant interaction with a suicide attempt history, but not with a history of depression [195, 167]. These findings correlate with some previous studies, which reported an association between the 5-HTTLPR-S-allele and completed suicides [196], and violent suicide attempts in subjects with major depression [197].

Hesselbrock et al (2004)[54] undertook a study in an attempt to identify potential chromosomal regions that may contain genes related to two different aspects of suicidal behavior—suicide attempts and suicidal behavior. For "ever tried suicide," evidence of linkage was found on chromosome 2 at 127 cM near the marker D2S1790, very close to a previously reported linkage finding for the COGA sample with the phenotype of "COGA-defined" alcohol dependence. The maximum lod score for the alcohol dependence phenotype was identified at 120.6cM near markers D2S1790 and D2S438 [198]. For the quantitative suicidality index, two separate regions of interest were found, one on chromosome 1 and one on chromosome 3. The second peak found for suicidality found in the current analyses was on chromosome 1 at 253 cM near marker D1S1602. However, the resulting lod score was considerably reduced when only independent pairs of affected siblings were examined.

A completely different approach was pursued when a gene encoding the transcription factor FosB/ΔFosB, which is induced by all common drugs and regulates downstream gene expression as part of the intracellular dopamine signalling cascade, was investigated. It was found to be associated with both novelty seeking and addiction susceptibility in animals [199]. Addictive drugs cause such long-lasting changes in behavior and brain function that alteration in gene transcription was suggested. The transcription factor DFosB has been identified as a promising candidate capable of mediating some of the behavioral changes associated with addiction [200]. Overexpression of DFosB in the orbital frontal cortex (OFC) was found to prevent the ability of an acute cocaine challenge to increase omissions and impulsive responses [201]. These raise the intriguing possibility that, although withdrawal from drug can precipitate cognitive impairments, some drug-induced changes may be adaptive, potentially invoked to protect cortical function in the face of repeated drug stimulation [152]. Winstanley et al (2008)[202] showed that the most pronounced cognitive changes occurred during initial engagement in drug seeking, during withdrawal, and when drug intake was increased.

PHARMACOTHERAPY

Few studies have dealt with the pharmacotherapy of suicidality in alcohol and substance use disorders. Hitherto, only one control study in 51 patients showed an increased rate of current suicide attemps (39%), prior suicide attempts (61%) and treatment of alcohol and substance use disorders with either Fluoxetin or Placebo [203]. Pharmacotherapy succeeded in reducing the depressive symptoms, the suicidality and alcohol consumption, and the results remained stable even after 1 year. Other studies failed to show consistent and positive effects of selective serotonin reuptake inhibitors (SSRI, which includes Fluoxetin) [204, 205, 206, 207]. Studies on suicidality with effective treatment like Lithium are either not available for alcohol-dependent individuals or are critically reviewed for interactions in alcohol relapses. Indirect effects of treatment of comorbid depression or anxiety in alcohol-dependent subjects can still be deducted from the reduced frequency of suicide attempts [208, 209, 210, 211, 212].

PSYCHOTHERAPY

Depression, prior suicide attempts and impulsive/aggressive behavior probably increase the likelihood of another suicide attempt in alcohol and substance use disorder. These can be treated with psychotherapeutic interventions, since treatment of the underlying disorder will reduce the likelihood of further repeat suicide attempts with a possible lethal outcome. Unfortunately, specific psychotherapeutic approaches designed for this high-risk group of patients are unavailable [213]. Empirical data on this group of patients are scant.

Past experience showed that cognitive behavior therapy [214] and their modifications, dialectic behavior therapy (DBT), used for treatment of Borderline Personality Disorder and their suicidality and substance abuse, [215, 216], can also reduce the frequency of suicide behavior in alcohol-dependent patients. Other psychotherapeutic approaches like problem solving strategies [217, 218, 219, 220], crisis intervention with and without intensive after-treatment [221, 222, 223] could show no consistent effects on the frequency of suidical behavior [206). A british group reported reduced suicidal ideation in patients who intoxicated themselves in suicidal intent [224, 225]. Still, the therapy was only effective on patients who showed less depressive symptoms and had no past history of self-harm.

In summary, to date there is no empirical or conceptional basis for the specific psychotherapeutic treatment of alcohol and substance use disorder patients with a history of suicidal behavior. In view of the severe consequences as well as the comorbidity with depression, personality disorders and problematic behaviors like impulse control disorder or aggression, it is necessary to devise specific therapeutic concepts for this group of alcohol-dependent patients.

REFERENCES

[1] Preuss UW, Schuckit MA, Smith TL, Danko GP, Buckman K, Bierut L, Bucholz KK, Hesselbrock MN, Hesselbrock VM, Reich T:Comparison of 3190 Alcohol-Dependent Individuals With and Without Suicide Attempts. *Alcoholism: Clinical and Experimental Research* 2002; Vol. 26, No. 4: 471–477.

[2] Inskip HM, Harris EC, Barraclough B: Lifetime risk of suicide for affective disorder, alcoholism and schizophrenia. *Br J Psychiatry* 1998; 172: 35–37.

[3] Rossow I, Amundsen A: Alcohol abuse and suicide: a 40-year prospective study of Norwegian conscripts. *Addiction* 1995; 90:685–691.

[4] Allebeck P, Allgulander C: Suicide among young men: psychiatric illness, deviant behavior and substance abuse. *Acta Psychiatr Scand* 1990; 81:565–570.

[5] Pirkola SP, Isometsa ET, Heikkinen ME, Lönnqvist JK: Suicides of alcohol misusers and non-misusers in a nationwide population. *Alcohol Alcohol* 2000; 35:70–75.

[6] Preuss UW, Schuckit MA, Smith TL, Danko GP, Bucholz K, Hesselbrock MN, Hesselbrock VM, Kramer JR: Predictors and Correlates of Suicide Attempts Over 5 Years in 1,237 *Alcohol-Dependent Men and WomenAm J Psychiatry* 2003; 160: 56–63.

[7] Carlini-Cotrim B, da Matta-Chasin AA: Blood alcohol content and death from fatal injury: a study in the metropolitan area of Sao Paulo, Brazil. *J Psychoactive Drugs* 2000; 32: 269-275.

[8] Hufford MR: Alcohol and suicidal behavior. *Clin Psychol Rev* 2001; 21(5):797–811.

[9] Poldrugo F, Chick JD, Moore N, Walburg JA: Mortality studies in the long-term evaluation of treatment of alcoholics. *Alcohol Alcohol* 1993; Suppl2, 151-155.

[10] Prescott CA, Kendler KS.: Age at first drink and risk for alcoholism: a noncausal association. *Alcohol Clin Exp Res.* 1999; 23:101-107.

[11] Schuckit MA, Smith TL, Danko GP, Reich T, Bucholz KK, Bierut LJ.: Similarities in the clinical characteristics related to alcohol dependence in two populations. *Am J Addict* 2002; 11:1-9.

[12] Duranceaux NC, Schuckit MA, Eng MY, Robinson SK, Carr LG, Wall TL.: Associations of variations in alcohol dehydrogenase genes with the level of response to alcohol in non-Asians. *Alcohol Clin Exp Res.* 2006; 30:1470-1478.

[13] Evenden JL: Varieties of impulsivity. Psychopharmacology 1999a; 146, 348–361.

[14] Mitchell SH.: Measuring impulsivity and modeling its association with cigarette smoking. Behav Cogn Neurosci Rev. 2004;3:261-75.

[15] Olmstead MC, Hellemans KG, Paine TA: Alcohol-induced impulsivity in rats: an effect of cue salience? *Psychopharmacology* (Berl). 2006;184(2):221-228.

[16] Lorr M, Wunderlich RA: A measure of impulsiveness and its relation to extroversion. *Education and Psychological Measurement,* 1985; 45: 251-257.

[17] Patton JH, Stanford MS, Barratt ES: Factor structure of the Barratt Impulsiveness Scale. *J Clin Psychol* 1995; 51:768–774.

[18] Dougherty DM, Mathias CW et al.: Laboratory measures of impulsivity. Aggression: Psychiatric Assessment and Treatment. *Medical Psychiatric Series* No.22. E.F. Coccaro. New York, Marcel Dekker Publishers 2003; 247-265.

[19] Logan GD, Sachar RJ, Tannock R: Impulsivity and inhibitory control. *Psychol Sci* 1997; 8: 60–64.

[20] Newman JP, Widom CS, Nathan S: Passive avoidance in syndromes of disinhibition: Psychopatho-logy and extraversion. *J Personality Soc Psychol* 1985; 48: 1316–1327.

[21] Crean JP, de Wit H, Richards JB: Reward discounting as a measure of impulsive behavior in a psychiatric outpatient population. *Exp Clin Psychopharmacol* 2000; 2: 155–162.

[22] Rubia K, Russell T, Overmeyer S, Brammer MJ, Bullmore ET, Sharma T et al: Mapping motor inhibition: conjunctive brain activations across different versions of go/no-go and stop tasks. *Neuroimage* 2001; 13: 250–261.

[23] Richards JB, Sabol KE, de Wit H: Effects of methamphetamine on the adjusting amount procedure, a model of impulsive behavior in rats. *Psychopharmacology (Berl)* 1999a; 146: 432–439.

[24] Richards JB, Zhuang L, Mitchell SH, de Wit H: Delay or probability discounting in a model of impulsive behavior: effect of alcohol. *J Exp Anal Behav* 1999b; 71: 121–143.

[25] Dickman SJ: Impulsivity and information processing. The Impulsive Client: Theory, Research and Treatment. *The American Psychological Association.* M.B. Shure. Washington D.C. 1993.

[26] Revelle W, Humphreys MS et al.: The interactive effect of personality, time of day and caffeine: A test of the arousal model. *J Experimental Psychol. General* 1980; 109: 1-31.

[27] Eysenck HJ, Eysenck M: *Personality and Individual Differences.* New York, Plenum Press 1985.

[28] Revelle W, Anderson KJ et al: Empirical tests and theoretical extensions of arousal based theories of personality. *Personality Dimensions and Arousal.* H.J. Eysenck. London, Pleneum Press 1987; 17-36.

[29] Barratt ES: The biological basis of impulsiveness: The significance of timing and rhythm disorders. *Personality and Individual Differences* 1983; 4: 387-391.

[30] Barratt ES: Impulsiveness and anxiety: Information processing and electroencephalographic topography. *J Res Personality* 1987; 21: 453-463.

[31] Barratt ES, Patton JH: Impulsivity: *Cognitive, behavioral and psychophysiological correlates.* Hillsdale, NJ, Erlbaum 1983.

[32] Stanford MS, Barratt ES: Verbal skills, finger tapping and cognitive tempo define a second-order factor of temporal information processing. *Brain Cognition* 1996; 31: 35-45.

[33] Harmon-Jones E, Barratt ES et al: Impulsiveness, aggression, reading and the P300 of the event-related potential. *Personality and the Individual Differences* 1997; 22: 439-445.

[34] Sunohara GA, Malone MA et al: Effect of methyphenidate on attention in children with attention deficit hyperactivity disorder (ADHD): ERP evidence. *Neuropsychopharmacology* 1999; 21: 218-228.

[35] Evenden JL: Impulsivity: a discussion of clinical and experimental findings. *J Psychopharmacol* 1999b; *13*: 180–192.

[36] Dougherty DM, Mathias CW: Suicidal behaviors and drug abuse: impulsivity and its assessment. *Drug Alcohol Depend* 2004; S76: 93-105.

[37] Mann JJ, Waternaux C, Haas GL, Malone KM. Toward a clinical model of suicidal behavior in psychiatric patients. *Am J Psychiatry* 1999;156: 181–189.

[38] Baechler J: A strategic theory: *Suicide Life Threat. Behavior* 1980; 10: 70-99.

[39] Baumeister RF: Suicide as escape from self. *Psychol Rev* 1990; 97: 90-113.

[40] Lane SD, Cherek DR, Rhoades HM, Pietras CJ, Tcheremissine OV: Relationships among laboratory and psychometric measures of impulsivity: implications in substance abuse and dependence. *Addict. Disord. Their Treatment* 2003; 2, 33–40.

[41] Moeller FG, Barratt ES, Dougherty DM, Schmitz JM, Schwann AC: Psychiatric aspects of impulsivity. *Am. J. Psychiat.* 2001a; 158, 1783–1793.

[42] Swann AC, Bjork JM, Moeller FG, Dougherty DM: Two models of impulsivity: relationship to personality traits and psychopathology. *Biol. Psychiat.* 2002; 51, 988–994.

[43] Steele CM, Josephs RA.: Alcohol myopia. Its prized and dangerous effects. *Am Psychol.* 1990;45: 921-933.

[44] Clark L et al.: Reflection impulsivity in current and former substance users. *Biol. Psychiatry* 2006; 60, 515–522.

[45] Siever LJ, Buchsbaum MS, New AS, et al: d,l-fenfluramine response in impulsive personality disorder assessed with [18F]fluorodeoxyglucose positron emission tomography. *Neuropsychopharmacology* 1999; 20*:*413–423.

[46] Babor TF, Hofmann M, Del Boca FK, Hesselbrock VM, Meyer RE, Dolinsky ZS, Rounsaville BJ: Types of alcoholics. I: Evidence for an empirically derived typology based on indicators of vulnerability and severity. *Arch. Gen. Psychiat.* 1992; 49, 599–608.

[47] Cloninger CR: Neurogenetic adaptive mechanisms in alcoholism. *Science* 1987; 236: 410–416.

[48] Finn PR, Justus A, Mazas C, Steinmetz JE: Working memory, executive processes and the effects of alcohol on Go/No-Go learning: testing a model of behavioral regulation and impulsivity. *Psychopharmacology* 1999; 146, 465–472.

[49] de Wit H, Crean J, Richards JB: Effects of d-amphetamine and ethanol on a measure of behavioral inhibition in humans. *Behavioral Neuroscienc*e 2000; 114, 830–837.

[50] Quirk SW, McCormick RA: Personality subtypes, coping styles, symptom correlates, and substances of choice among a cohort of substance abusers. *Assessment* 5, 1998; 157-169.

[51] Preuss UW, Koller G, Bondy B, Bahlmann M, Soyka M: Impulsive Traits and 5-HT2A Receptor Promoter Polymorphism in Alcohol Dependents: Possible Association but No Influence of Personality Disorders. *Neuropsychobiology* 2001; 43:186–191.

[52] Sugden SG, Kile SJ, Hendren RL: Neurodevelopmental Pathways to Aggression: A Model to Understand and Target Treatment in Youth. *J Neuropsychiatry Clin Neurosci* 2006; 18: 302–317.

[53] Bahlmann M, Preuss UW, Soyka M: Chronological relationship between antisocial personality disorder and alcohol dependence. *Eur Addict Res* 2002; 8:195–200.

[54] Hesselbrock V, Dick D, Hesselbrock M, Foroud T, Schuckit M, Edenberg H, Bucholz K, Kramer J, Reich T, Goate A, Bierut L, Rice JP, Nurnberger JI Jr.: The Search for Genetic Risk Factors Associated With Suicidal Behavior. *Alcoholism: Clinical and Experimental Research* 2004; 28: 70S-76S.

[55] Koller G, Preuss UW, Bottlender M, Wenzel K, Soyka M: Impulsivity and aggression as predictors of suicide attempts in alcoholics.*Eur Arch Psychiatry Clin Neurosci* 2002; 252:155–160.

[56] Simon OR, Swann AC, Powell KE, Potter LB, Kresnow MJ, O'Carroll PW: Characteristics of impulsive suicide attempts and attempters. *Suicide Life Threat Behav* 2001; 32 (suppl 1): 3249–3259.

[57] Jentsch JD, Taylor JR: Impulsivity resulting from frontostriatal dysfunction in drug abuse: implications for the control of behavior by reward-related stimuli. *Psychopharmacology* 1999; 146: 373–390.

[58] Tarter RE, Kirisci L, Mezzich A, Cornelius JR, Pajer K, Vanyukov M et al.: Neurobehavioral disinhibition in childhood predicts early age at onset of substance use disorder. *American Journal of Psychiatry,* 2003; 160: 1078–1085.

[59] de Wit H, Enggasser JL, Richards JB: Acute administration of d-amphetamine decreases impulsivity in healthy volunteers. *Neuropsychopharmacology,* 2002; 27: 813–825.

[60] Moeller FG, Dougherty DM, Barratt ES, Schmitz JM, Swann AC, Grabowski J: The impact of impulsivity on cocaine use and retention in treatment. *Journal of Substance Abuse Treatment,* 2001; 21: 193–198.

[61] Perry JL, Carroll ME: The role of impulsive behavior in drug abuse. *Psychopharmacology* 2008; 9: 1-26.

[62] Hollander E, Stein DJ: *Impulsivity and Aggression.* John Wiley and Sons Ltd. 1995:1.

[63] Coccaro EF, Bergeman CS, Kavoussi RJ, Seroczynski AD: Heritability of Aggression and Irritability: A Twin Study of the Buss-Durkee Aggression Scales in Adult Male Subjects. *Biol Psychiatry* 1997; 41: 273-284.

[64] Barratt ES, Stanford MS, Felthous AR, Kent TA: The effects of phenytoin on impulsive and premeditated aggression: a controlled study. *J Clin Psychopharmacol* 1997; 17: 341–349.

[65] Spear LP: The adolescent brain and age-related behavioral manifestations. *Neurosci. Biobehav. Rev.* 2000; 24: 417–463.

[66] Steinberg L: Risk taking in adolescence: new perspectives from brain and behavioral science. *Curr. Dir. Psychol. Sci.* 2007; 16: 55–59.

[67] Casey BJ, Tottenham N, Liston C, Durston S: Imaging the developing brain: What have we learned about cognitive development? *Trends Cogn. Sci.* 2005; 9:104–10.

[68] Ernst M, Nelson EE, Jazbec S, McClure EB, Monk CS, et al.: Amygdala and nucleus accumbens in responses to receipt and omission of gains in adults and adolescents. *Neuroimage* 2005; 25:1279–1291.

[69] Galvan A, Hare TA, Voss H, Glover G, Casey BJ: Risk-taking and the adolescent brain: Who is at risk*? Dev. Sci.* 2007; 10: F8–14.

[70] Everitt BJ, Belin D, Economidou D, Pelloux Y, Dalley JW, Robbins TW: Neural mechanisms underlying the vulnerability to develop compulsive drug-seeking habits and addiction.*Philos Trans R Soc Lond B Biol Sci.* 2008; 363::3125-3135.

[71] Vengeliene V, Bilbao A, Molander A, Spanagel R: Neuropharmacology of alcohol addiction. *British Journal of Pharmacology* 2008; 154, 299–315.

[72] Tiffany ST, Conklin CA: A cognitive processing model of alcohol craving and compulsive alcohol use. *Addiction* 2000; 95: S145–S153.

[73] Addolorato G, Leggio L, Abenavoli L, Gasbarrini G (2005). On behalf of the Alcoholism Treatment Study Group neurobiochemical and clinical aspects of craving in alcohol addiction: a review. *Addict Behav* 30: 1209–1224.

[74] Littleton J: Can craving be modeled in animals? The relapse prevention perspective. *Addiction* 2000; 95 (Suppl 2): 83–90.

[75] McCarty CA et al.: Continuity of binge and harmful drinking from late adolescence to early adulthood. *Pediatrics* 2004; 114: 714–719.

[76] Dawson, DA et al.: Another look at heavy episodic drinking and alcohol use disorders among college and noncollege youth. *J. Stud. Alcohol* 2004; 65: 477–488.

[77] Heinz A, Lo¨ber S, Georgi A, Wrase J, Hermann D, Rey ER et al.: Reward craving and withdrawal relief craving: assessment of different motivational pathways to alcohol intake. *Alcohol Alcohol* 2003; 38: 35–39.

[78] Verheul R, van den Brink W, Geerlings P: A three-pathway psychobiological model of craving for alcohol. *Alcohol Alcohol* 1999; 34: 197–222.

[79] Heilig M, Koob GF: A key role for corticotropin-releasing factor in alcohol dependence. *Trends Neurosci* 2007; 30: 399–406.

[80] Verdejo-Garcia A, Rivas-Perez C, Vilar-Lopez R, Perez-Garcia M: Strategic self-regulation decision-making and emotion processing in polysubstance abusers in their first year of abstinence. *Drug Alcohol Depend* 2007; 86: 139–146.

[81] Van Heeringen K: The Neurobiology of Suicide and Suicidality. *Can J Psychiatry* 2003; 48: 292-300.

[82] O'Carroll PW, Berman AL, Maris RW, Moscicki EK, Tanney BL, Silverman MM: Beyond the Tower of Babel: A nomenclature for Suicidology. *Suicide and Life-Threatening Behavior* 1996; 36: 237-252.

[83] Silverman MM: The Language of Suicidology. *Suicide and Life-Threatening Behavior* 2006; 36: 519-532.

[84] Kessler RC, Borges G, Walters E: Prevalence of and risk factors for lifetime suicide attempts in the National Comorbidity Survey. *Arch Gen Psychiatry* 1999; 56: 617–626.

[85] Murphy GE, Armstrong JW, Hermele SL, Fischer JR, Clendenin WW: Suicide and alcoholism. Interpersonal loss confirmed as a predictor. *Arch Gen Psychiatry* 1979; 36: 65–69.

[86] Murphy GE, Wetzel RD, Robins E, McEvoy L: Multiple risk factors predict suicide in alcoholism. *Arch Gen Psychiatry* 1992; 49: 459–463.

[87] Murphy GE, Wetzel RD: The lifetime risk of suicide in alcoholism.*Arch Gen Psychiatry* 1990; 47: 383–392.

[88] Rossow I, Romelsjo A, Leifman H: Alcohol abuse and suicidal behavior in young and middle aged men: differentiating between attempted and completed suicide. *Addiction* 1999; 94: 1199–1207.

[89] Dhossche D.M., Meloukheia A.M., Chakravorty S.: The association of suicide attempts and comorbid depression and substance abuse in psychiatric consultation patients. *Gen Hosp Psychiatry* 2000; 22: 281–288.

[90] Hawton K, Fagg J: Suicide, and other causes of death, following attempted suicide. *Br J Psychiatry* 1988; 152: 359–366.

[91] Isometsa ET, Lonnqvist JK: Suicide attempts preceding completed suicide. *Br J Psychiatry* 1998; 173: 531–535.

[92] Ostamo A, Lonnqvist J, Heinonen S: Epidemiology of parasuicides in Finland. *Psychiatria Fennica* 1991; 22:181–189.

[93] Rosenberg ML, Davidson LE, Smith JC, Berman AL, Buzbee H, Gantner G, Gay GA, Moore-Lewis B, Mills DH, Murray D: Operational criteria for the determination of suicide. *J Forensic Sci* 1988; 33:1445–1456.

[94] Schmidtke A: Perspective: suicide in Europe. Suicide Life Threat Behav 1997; 27:127–134.

[95] Johnsson-Fridell EJ, Öjehagen A, Träskman-Bendz L: A 5-year follow-up study of suicide attempts. *Acta Psychiatr Scand* 1996; 93: 151–157.

[96] Foster T, Gillespie K, McClelland R, Patterson C: Risk factors for suicide independent of DSM-III-R axis I disorder: case-control psychological autopsy study in Northern Ireland. *Br J Psychiatry* 1999; 175: 175–179.

[97] Suokas J, Suominen K, Isometsa E, Ostamo A, Lonnqvist J: Longterm risk factors for suicide mortality after attempted suicide-findings of a 14-year follow-up study. *Acta Psychiatr Scand* 2001; 104: 117–121.

[98] Nordström P, Samuelsson M, Åsberg M: Survival analysis of suicide risk after attempted suicide. *Acta Psychiatr Scand* 1995; 91:336–340.

[99] Van Heeringen C.: Understanding suicidal behavior: the suicidal process approach to research, treatment and prevention. *Chichester* (UK): Wiley; 2001.

[100] Conner KR, Duberstein PR: Predisposing and precipitating factors for suicide among alcoholics: empirical review and conceptual integration. *Alcohol Clin Exp Res* 2004; 28 (suppl 1): 6S–17S.

[101] Suominen, K, Isometsa E, Henriksson M, Ostamo A, Lonnqvist J: Hopelessness, impulsiveness and intent among suicide attempters with major depression, alcohol dependence, or both. *Acta Psychiatr. Scand.* 1997; 96: 142–149.

[102] Conner KR, Hesselbrock VM, Schuckit MA, Hirsch JK, Knox KL, Meldrum S, Bucholz KK, Kramer J, Kuperman S, Preuss U, Soyka M: Precontemplated and impulsive suicide attempts among individuals with alcohol dependence. *J. Stud. Alcohol* 2006; 67: 95–101.

[103] Williams C, Davidson J, Montgomery I: Impulsive suicidal behavior. *J. Clin. Psychol.* 1980;36: 90–94.

[104] Baca-García E, Diaz-Sastre C, Basurte E, Prieto R, Ceverino A, Saiz-Ruiz J, de Leon J: A prospective study of the paradoxical relationship between impulsivity and lethality of suicide attempts. *J. Clin. Psychiatry* 2001; 62: 560–564.

[105] Baca-Garcia E, Diaz-Sastre C, García Resa E, Blasco H, Braquehais Conesa D, Oquendo MA, Saiz-Ruiz J, de Leon J: Suicide attempts and impulsivity. *Eur. Arch. Psychiatry Clin. Neurosci.* 2005; 255: 152–156.
[106] Wyder M, De Leo D: Behind impulsive suicide attempts: indications from a community study. *J. Affect. Disord.* 2007; 104: 167–173.
[107] Roy A: Characteristics of drug addicts who attempt suicide. *Psychiatry Res* 2003; 121: 99-103.
[108] Preuss UW, Koller G, Bottlender M, Schultz G, Barnow S, Zimmerman J, Soyka M: Suicide Attempts in Alcohol Dependents: Clinical Characteristics and Differentiation of the Applied Methods. *Fortschr Neurol Psychiat* 2006a; 74: 77-84.
[109] Hesselbrock M, Hesselbrock V, Syzmanski K, Weidenman M: Suicide attempts and alcoholism. *J Stud Alcohol* 1988; 49:436–442.
[110] Roy AA, Lamparski DD, DeJong JJ, Moore VV, Linnoila MM: Characteristics of alcoholics who attempt suicide. *Am. J. Psychiatry* 1990; 147: 761–765.
[111] Roy A.: Childhood trauma and attempted suicide in alcoholics. *J. Nerv. Ment. Dis.* 2001;189: 120–21.
[112] Whitters AC, Cadoret RJ, Widmer RB: Factors associated with suicide attempts in alcohol abusers. *J. Affect. Disord.* 1985; 9: 19–23.
[113] Robins E: The Final Months—A Study of the Lives of 134 Persons Who Committed Suicide. Oxford University Press, New York 1981.
[114] Merikangas KR, Gelernter CS: Comorbidity for alcoholism and depression. *Psychiatr Clin North Am* 1990; 13:613–632.
[115] Vaillant GE: Natural history of male alcoholism. V. Is alcoholism the cart or the horse to sociopathy? *Br. J. Addict.* 1983; 78: 317.
[116] Vaillant GE: A long-term follow-up of male alcohol abuse. *Arch Gen Psychiatry* 1996; 53: 243.
[117] Fillmore KM, Mildanik L: Chronicity of drinking problems among men: a longitudinal study. *J Stud Alcohol* 1984; 45: 228.
[118] Fillmore KM: Prevalence, incidence and chronicity of drinking patterns and problems among men as a function of age: a longitudinal and cohort analysis. *Br J Addict* 1987; 82: 77.
[119] Glowinski AL, Bucholz KK, Nelson EC, Fu Q, Madden PAF, Reich W, Heath AC: Suicide attempts in an adolescent female twin sample. *J Am Acad Child Adolesc Psychiatry* 2001; 40:1300–1307.
[120] Corbitt EM, Malone KM, Haas GL, Mann JJ: Suicidal behavior in patients with major depression and comorbid personality disorders. *J Affect Disord* 1996; 39: 61–72.
[121] Kelly TM, Soloff PH, Lynch KG, Haas GL, Mann JJ: Recent life events, social adjustment, and suicide attempts in patients with major depression and borderline personality disorder. *J Personal Disord* 2000; 14:316–326.
[122] Weiss KJ, Rosenberg DJ: Prevalence of anxiety disorder among alcoholics. *J Clin Psychiatr* 1985; 46: 3–5.
[123] Apter A, van Praag HM, Plutschik R, Sevy S, Korn M, Brown S: Interrelation-ships among anxiety, aggression, impulsivity and mood: A serotonergically linked cluster? *Psychiatry Res.,* 1990; 148: 191-9.

[124] Preuss UW, Koller G, Barnow S, Eikmeier M, Soyka M: Suicidal Behavior in Alcohol-Dependent Subjects: The Role of Personality Disorders. *Alcohol Clin Exp Res* 2006; ,30: 866–877.
[125] Driessen M, Veltrup C, Weber J, John U, Wetterling T, Dilling H: Psychiatric co-morbidity, suicidal behavior and suicidal ideation in alcoholics seeking treatment. *Addiction* 1998; 93:889–894.
[126] Skodol AE, Oldham JM, Gallaher PE: Axis II comorbidity of substance use disorders among patients referred for treatment of personality disorders. *Am J Psychiatry* 1999; 156:733–738.
[127] DeJong CA, van den Brink W, Harteveld FM, van der Wielen EG: Personality disorders in alcoholics and drug addicts. *Comp Psychiatry* 1993; 34:87–94.
[128] Grant BF, Stinson FS, Dawson DA, Chou SP, Ruan WJ, Pickering RP: Co-occurrence of 12-month alcohol and drug use disorders and personality disorders in the United States: results from the national epidemiologic survey on alcohol and related conditions. *Arch Gen Psychiatry* 2004; 61:361–368.
[129] Chioqueta AP, Stiles TC: Assessing suicide risk in cluster C personality disorders. *Crisis* 2004; 25:128–133.
[130] Hawton K, Houston K, Haw C, Townsend E, Harriss L: Comorbidity of axis I and Axis II disorders in patients who attempt suicide. *Am J Psychiatry* 2003; 160:1494–1500.
[131] Corruble E, Damy C, Guelfi JD: Impulsivity: a relevant dimension in depression regarding suicide attempts? *J Affect Disord* 1999; 53:211–215.
[132] Kruedelbach N, McCormick RA, Schulz SC, Grueneich R: Impulsivity, coping styles, and triggers for craving in substance abusers with borderline personality disorder. *J Personal Disord* 1993; 7:214–222.
[133] Soloff PH, Lis JA, Kelly T, Cornelius J, Ulrich R: Risk factors for suicidal behavior in borderline personality disorder. *Am J Psychiatry* 1994; 151:1316–1323.
[134] Caspi A, McClay J, Moffitt TE, Mill J, Martin J, Craig IW, Taylor A, Poulton R: Role of genotype in the cycle of violence in maltreated children. *Science* 2002; 297:851-854.
[135] Kim-Cohen J, Caspi A, Taylor A, Williams B, Newcombe R, et al.: MAOA, maltreatment, and gene-environment interaction predicting children's mental health: new evidence and a meta-analysis. *Mol. Psychiatry* 2006; 11:903–913.
[136] Ducci F, Enoch MA, Hodgkinson C, Xu K, Catena M, et al.: Interaction between a functional MAOA locus and childhood sexual abuse predicts alcoholism and antisocial personality disorder in adult women. *Mol. Psychiatry2008;* 13: 334-347.
[137] Meyer-Lindenberg A, Buckholtz JW, Kolachana B, Hariri AR, Pezawas L, et al.: Neural mechanisms of genetic risk for impulsivity and violence in humans. *Proc. Natl. Acad.Sci.USA* 2006; 103:6269–74.
[138] Cador M, Robbins TW, Everitt BJ: Involvement of the amygdala in stimulus-reward associations: interaction with the ventral striatum. *Neuroscience* 1989; 30:77–86.
[139] Robbins TW, Cador M, Taylor JR, Everitt BJ: Limbic-striatal interactions in reward-related processes. *Neurosci Biobehav Rev* 1989; 13:155–162.
[140] Burns LH, Everitt BJ, Robbins TW: Differential effects of excitotoxic lesions of the basolateral amygdala, ventral subiculum and medial prefrontal cortex on responding with conditioned reinforce-ment and locomotor activity potentiated by intra-accumbens infusions of *d*-amphetamine. *Behav Brain Res* 1993; 55:167–183.

[141] Burns LH, Everitt BJ, Kelley AE, Robbins TW: Glutamatedopamine interactions in the ventral striatum: role in locomotor activity and responding with conditioned reinforcement. *Psychopharmacology* 1994; 115:516–528.

[142] O'Donnell P, Grace AA: Synaptic interaction among excitatory afferents to nucleus accumbens neurons: hippocampal gating of prefrontal cortical input. *J Neurosci* 1995; 15:3622–3639.

[143] Moore H, Grace AA: Interactions between amygdala and prefrontal cortical afferents to the nucleus accumbens and their modulation by dopamine receptor activation. *Soc Neurosci* 1996; Abstr 22:1088.

[144] Weissenborn R, Robbins TW, Everitt BJ: Effects of medial prefrontal or anterior cingulate cortex lesions on responding for cocaine under fixed-ratio and second-order schedules of reinforcement in rats. *Psychopharmacology* 1997; 134:242–257.

[145] Koob GF and Le Moal M: Plasticity of reward neurocircuitry and the 'dark side' of drug addiction. *Nat. Neurosci.* 2005; 8: 1442–1444.

[146] Brownell KD et al.: Understanding and preventing relapse. *Am. Psychol.* 1986; 41: 765–782.

[147] Shaham Y et al.: The reinstatement model of drug relapses: history, methodology and major findings. *Psychopharmacology* (Berl.) 2003; 168: 3–20.

[148] Kosten TR, George TP, Kleber HD: The neurobiology of substance dependence: implications for treatment. In *Clinical Textbook of Addictive Disorders,* ed. RJ Frances, SI Miller, AH Mack, 2005; pp. 3–15. New York: Guilford.

[149] Nestler EJ: Is there a common molecular pathway for addiction? *Nat. Neurosci.* 2005; 8:1445–49.

[150] Berridge KC, Robinson TE: Parsing reward. *Trends Neurosci,* 2003; 26:507.

[151] O'Doherty JP: Reward representations and reward-related learning in the human brain: insights from neuroimaging. *Curr Opin Neurobiol,* 2004: 14:769.

[152] Kalivas PW, Volkow ND: The neural basis of addiction: a pathology of motivation and choice. *Am J Psychiatry,* 2005; 162: 1403-1413.

[153] Bechara A, Damasio H: Decision-making and addiction (part I): impaired activation of somatic states in substance dependent individuals when pondering decisions with negative future consequences. *Neuropsychologia,* 2002; 40: 1675–1689.

[154] Bechara A, Dolan S, Hindes A: Decision-making and addiction (part II): myopia for the future of hypersensitivity to reward? *Neuropsychologia,* 2002; 40: 1690–1705.

[155] Petry NM, BickelWK, Arnett M: Shortened time horizons and insensitivity to future consequences in heroin addicts. *Addiction,* 1998; 93: 729–738.

[156] Volkow ND, Fowler JS: Addiction, a disease of compulsion and drive: involvement of the orbito-frontal cortex. *Cereb Cortex,* 2000; 10: 318-325.

[157] Rogers RD, Robbins TW: Investigating the neurocognitive deficits associated with chronic drug misuse. *Curr Opin Neurobiol.,* 2001; 11: 250-257.

[158] Schoenbaum G, Roesch MR, Stalnaker TA: Orbitofrontal cortex, decision-making and drug addiction. *Trends Neurosci.,* 2006; 29: 116-124.

[159] Brennan AR, Arnsten AF: Neuronal mechanisms underlying attention deficit hyperactivity disorder: the influence of arousal on prefrontal cortical function. *Ann N Y Acad Sci.* 2008; 1129: 236-245.

[160] Damasio AR: Descartes' Error: Emotion, Reason, and the Human Brain. Grosset/Putnam, New York 1994.

[161] Hanson KL, Luciana M, Sullwold K: Reward-related decision-making deficits and elevated impulsivity among MDMA and other drug users. *Drug and Alcohol Dependence,* 2008; 96: 99–110.

[162] Bechara A, Dolan S, Denburg N, Hindes A, Anderson SW, Nathan PE: Decision-making deficits, linked to a dysfunctional ventromedial prefrontal cortex, revealed in alcohol and stimulant abusers. *Neuropsychologia,* 2001; 39: 376–389.

[163] Mazas CA, Finn PR, Steinmetz JE: Decision-making biases, antisocial personality, and early onset alcoholism. *Alcohol. Clin. Exp. Res.,* 2000; 24: 1036–1040.

[164] Stout JC, Rock SL, Campbell MC, Busemeyer JR, Finn PR: Psychological processes underlying risky decisions in drug abusers. *Psychol Addict Behav* 2005;19(2): 148-157.

[165] Hoyenga KB, Hoyenga KT*: Psychobiology: The Neuron and Behavior.* Brooks-Cole, California. 1988.

[166] Coccaro EF, Kavoussi RJ, Stehle S: *Serotonin and impulsive aggression: Relationship to alcoholism. In: The Science and Psychiatry of Violence.* Butterworth-Heinemann, Oxford (eds C. Thompson and PJ Cowen) 1993; 62-75.

[167] Preuss UW, Koller G, Soyka M, Bondy B: Association between Suicide Attempts and 5-HTTLPR-S-Allele in Alcohol-Dependent and Control Subjects: Further Evidence from a German Alcohol-Dependent Inpatient Sample. Biol Psychiatry 2001; 50: 636–639.

[168] Sher L: Alcohol and suicide: neurobiological and clinical aspects. Scientific World Journal 2006 Jun 21; 6:700-706.

[169] Barnes NM, Sharp T: A review of central 5-HT receptors and their function. Neuropharmacology 1999; 38: 1083–1152.

[170] Talpos JC, Wilkinson LS, Robbins TW: A comparison of multiple 5-HT receptors in two tasks measuring impulsivity. *J Psychopharmacology* 2006; 20: 47-58.

[171] Higgins GA, Enderlin M, Haman M, Fletcher PJ: The 5-HT(2A) receptor antagonist M100,907 attenuates motor and 'impulsive-type' behaviors produced by NMDA receptor antagonism. *Psychopharmacology* (Berl) 2003; *170:* 309–319.

[172] De Deurwaerdere P, Navailles S, Berg KA, Clarke WP, Spampinato U: Constitutive activity of the serotonin2C receptor inhibits in vivo dopamine release in the rat striatum and nucleus accumbens. *J Neurosci* 2004; 24: 3235–3241.

[173] Koskinen T, Ruotsalainen S, Puumala T, Lappalainen R, Koivisto E, Mannisto PT, Sirvio J: Activation of 5-HT2A receptors impairs response control of rats in a five-choice serial reaction time task. *Neuropharmacology* 2000; 39: 471–481.

[174] Masaki D et al.: Relationship between limbic and cortical 5-HT neurotransmission and acquisition and reversal learning in a go/no-go task in rats. *Psychopharmacology (Berl.)* 2006; 189: 249–258.

[175] Winstanley CA et al.: Fractionating impulsivity: contrasting effects of central 5-HT depletion on different measures of impulsive behavior. *Neuropsychopharmacology* 2004a; 29, 1331–1343.

[176] Winstanley CA et al.: 5-HT2A and 5-HT2C receptor antagonists have opposing effects on a measure of impulsivity: interactions with global 5-HT depletion. *Psychopharmacology (Berl.)* 2004; 176, 376–385.

[177] Homberg JR et al.: Serotonin transporter deficiency in rats improves inhibitory control but not behavioral flexibility. *Eur. J. Neurosci.* 2007; 26: 2066–2073.

[178] Winstanley CA et al.: Double dissociation between serotonergic and dopaminergic modulation of medial prefrontal and orbitofrontal cortex during a test of impulsive choice. *Cereb. Cortex* 2006; 16: 106–114.
[179] Crean J et al.: Effect of tryptophan depletion on impulsive behavior in men with or without a family history of alcoholism. *Behav. Brain Res.* 2002; 136: 349–357.
[180] Manuck SB, Flory JD, McCaffery JM, Matthews KA, Mann JJ, Muldoon MF: Aggression, impulsivity, and central nervous system serotonergic responsivity in a nonpatient sample. *Neuropsychopharmacology* 1998; 19:287–299.
[181] Swann AC, Koslow SH, Katz MM, Maas JW, Javaid J, Secunda SK, Robins E: Lithium carbonate treatment of mania: cerebrospinal fluid and urinary monoamine metabolites and treatment outcome. *Arch Gen Psychiatry* 1987; 44:345–354.
[182] Egerton A et al.: Cannabinoids and prefrontal cortical function: insights from preclinical studies. *Neurosci. Biobehav. Rev.* 2006; 30: 680–695.
[183] Lane SD et al.: Acute marijuana effects on human risk taking. *Neuropsychopharmacology* 2005; 30: 800–809.
[184] McDonald J, Schleifer L, Richards JB, de Wit H: Effects of THC on behavioral measures of impulsivity in humans *Neuropsychopharmacology* 2003; 28: 1356–1365.
[185] Ramaekers JG et al.: High-potency marijuana impairs executive function and inhibitory motor control. *Neuropsychopharmacology* 2006; 31: 2296–2303.
[186] Bouton ME, Schwartzberg D: Sources of relapse after extinction in pavlovian and instrumental learning. *Clin Psychiatry Rev.,* 1991; 11: 123-140.
[187] Sutton MA, Schmidt EF, Choi K-H, Schad CA, Whisler K, Simmons D, Karanian DA, Monteggia L, Neve RL, Self DW: Extinction-induced upregulation in AMPA receptors reduces cocaine-seeking behavior. *Nature,* 2003; 421: 70-75.
[188] Self DW, Choi KH: Extinction-induced neuroplasticity attenuates stress-induced cocaine seeking: a state-dependent learning hypothesis. *Stress,* 2004; 7: 145-155.
[189] Thomas MJ, Beurrier C, Bonci A, Malenka RC: Long-term depression in the nucleus accumbens: a neural correlate of behavioral sensitization to cocaine. *Nat Neurosci.,* 2001; 4: 1217-1223.
[190] Dautzenberg FM and Hauger RL: The CRF peptide family and their receptors: yet more partners discovered. *Trends Pharmacol. Sci.* 2002; 23: 71–77.
[191] Baldwin HA et al.: CRF antagonist reverses the 'anxiogenic' response to ethanol withdrawal in the rat. *Psychopharmacology (Berl.)* 1991; 103: 227–232.
[192] Rassnick S et al.: Microinjection of a corticotropin-releasing factor antagonist into the central nucleus of the amygdala reverses anxiogenic-like effects of ethanol withdrawal. *Brain Res.* 1993; 605: 25–32.
[193] Merlo Pich E et al.: Increase of extracellular corticotropinreleasing factor-like immunoreactivity levels in the amygdala of awake rats during restraint stress and ethanol withdrawal as measured by microdialysis. *J. Neurosci.* 1995; 15: 5439–5447.
[194] Olive MF et al.: Elevated extracellular CRF levels in the bed nucleus of the stria terminalis during ethanol withdrawal and reduction by subsequent ethanol intake. *Pharmacol. Biochem. Behav.* 2002; 72: 213–220.
[195] Gorwood P, Batel P, Ade´s J, Hamon M, Boni C: Serotonin transporter gene polymorphisms, alcoholism and suicidal behavior. *Biol Psychiatry* 2000; 48:259–264.

[196] Bondy B, Erfurth A, de Jonge S, Kru¨ger M, Mayer H: Possible association of the short allele of the serotonin transporter promoter gene polymorphism (5-HTTLPR) with violent suicide. *Mol Psychiatry* 2000; 5:193–195.

[197] Bellivier F, Szo¨ke A, Henry C, Lacoste J, Bottos C, Nosten-Bertrand M et al: Possible association between serotonin transporter gene polymorphism and violent suicidal behavior in mood disorders. *Biol Psychiatry* 2000; 48:319–323.

[198] Foroud T, Edenberg H, Goate A, Rice J, Flury L, Koller D, Bierut L, Conneally PM, Nurnberger JI, Bucholz KK, Li T-K, Hesselbrock V, Crowe R, Schuckit M, Porjesz B, Begleiter H, Reich T: Alcoholism susceptibility loci: confirmation studies in a replicate sample and further mapping. *Alcohol Clin Exp Res* 2000; 24:933–945.

[199] Hiroi N, Agatsuma S: Genetic susceptibility to substance dependence. *Mol. Psychiatry* 2005; 10: 336–44.

[200] Nestler EJ: Molecular mechanisms of drug addiction. *Neuropharmacology,* 2004; 47(Suppl 1): 24-32.

[201] Winstanley CA, LaPlant Q, Theobald DEH, Green TA, Bachtell RK, Perrotti LI, DiLeone RJ, Russo SJ, Garth WJ, Self DW et al.: DeltaFosB induction in orbitofrontal cortex mediates tolerance to cocaine-induced cognitive dysfunction. *J Neurosci.,* 2007; 27: 10497-10507.

[202] Winstanley CA , Bachtell RK, Theobald DEH, Laali S, Green TA, Kumar A, Chakravarty S, Self DW and Nestler EJ: Increased Impulsivity during Withdrawal from Cocaine Self-Administration: Role for DFosB in the Orbitofrontal Cortex. C Cortex, 6.6. 2008.

[203] Cornelius JR, Salloum IM, Lynch K, Clark DB, Mann JJ: Treating the substance-abusing suicidal patient. *Ann N Y Acad Sci* 2001; 932: 78-90.

[204] Hirsch SR, Walsh C, Draer R: Parasuicide: a review of treatment interventions. *J Affect Disorders* 1982; 4: 299-311.

[205] Montgomery SA, Roy D, Motgomery DB: The prevention of recurrent suicidal acts. *Br J Clin Pharmacol* 1983; 15: 183-188.

[206] Hawton K, Arensman E, Townsend E, Bremner S, Feldman E, Goldney R et al: Deliberate self harm: systematic review of efficacy of psychosocial and pharmacological reatments in preventing repetition. *BMJ* 1998; 317: 441-447.

[207] Grandin LD, Yan LJ, Gray SM, Jamison KR, Sachs GS: Suicide prevention: increasing educatin and awareness. *J Clin Psychiatry* 2001; 62 Suppl 25: 12-16.

[208] Cornelius JR, Salloum IM, Ehler JG, Jarrett PJ, Cornelius MD, Perel JM et al: Fluoxetine in depressed alcoholics. A double-blind, placebo-controlled trial. *Arch Gen Psychiatry* 1997; 54: 700-705.

[209] Cornelius JR, Salloum IM, Haskett RF, Daley DC, Cornelius MD, Thase ME, Perel JM: Fluoxetine versus placebo in depressed alcoholics: a 1-year follow-up study. *Addict Behav* 2000; 25: 307-310.

[210] Johnson BA, Ait-Daoud N, Ma JZ, Wang Y: Ondansetron reduces mood disturbance among biologically predisposed, alcohol.-dependent individuals. *Alcohol Clin Exp Res* 2003; 27: 1773-1779.

[211] Liappas J, Paparrigopoulos T, Tzavellas E, Christodoulou G: Alcohol detoxification and social anxiety symptoms : a preliminary study of the impact of mirtazapine administration. *J Affect Disrod* 2003; 76: 279-284.

[212] Le Fauve CE, Litten RZ, Randall CL, Moak DH, Salloum IM, Green AI: Pharmacological treatment of alcohol abuse/dependence with psychiatric comorbidity. *Alcohol Clin Exp Res* 2004; 28: 302-312.

[213] Goldberg JF, Singer TM, Garno JL: Suicidality and substance abuse in affective disorders. *J Clin Psychiatry* 2001; 62 Suppl 25: 35-43.

[214] Lieberman R, Eckman T: Behavior therapy versus insight-oriented therapy for repeated suicide attempters. *Arch Gen Psychiatry* 1981; 38; 1126-1130.

[215] Linehan MM: Combining pharmacotherapy with psychotherapy for substance abusers with borderline personality disorders: strategies for enhancing compliance. *NIDA Res Monogr* 1995; 50: 129-142.

[216] Linehan MM, Schmidt H 3rd, Dimeff LA, Craft JC, Kanter J, Comtois K.A.: Dialectical behavior therapy for patients with borderine personality disorder and drug dependence. *Am J Addict* 1999; 8: 279-292.

[217] Gibbons JS, Butler J, Urwin P, Gibbons JL: Evaluation of a social work service for self-poisioning patients. *Br J Psychiatry* 1978; 133: 111-118.

[218] Hawton K, McKeown S, Day A, Martin P, O'Connor M, Yule J: Evaluation of out-patient counselling compared with general practitioner care following overdoses. *Psychol Med* 1987; 17: 751-761.

[219] Salkovskis PM, Atha C, Storer D: Cognitive-behavioral problem solving in the treatment of patients who repeatedly attempt suicide: a controlled trial. *Br J Psychiatry* 1990; 157: 871-876.

[220] McLeavey BC, Daly RJ, Ludgate JW, Murray CM: Interpersonal problem-solving skills training in the treatment of self-poisoning patients. *Suicide Life Threatening Behav* 1994; 24: 382-394.

[221] Hawton K, Bancroft J, Catalan J, Kingston B, Stedeford A, Welch N: Domiciliary and out-patient treatment of self-poisoning patients by medical and non-medical staff. *Psychol Med* 1981; 11: 169-177.

[222] Allard R, Marschall M, Plante MC: Intensive follow-up does not decrease the risk of repeat suicide attempts. *Suicide Life Threatening Behav* 1992; 22: 303-314.

[223] Van Heeringen CV, Jannes S, Buylaert H, Hendrick H, de Bacquer D, van Remoortel J: The management of non-compliance with referral to out-patient after-care among attempted suicide patients: a controlled intervention study. *Psychol Med* 1995; 25: 963-970.

[224] Guthrie E, Kapur N, Mackway-Jones K, Chew-Graham C, Moorey J et al: Randomised controlled trial of brief psychological intervention after deliberate self poisoning. *BMJ* 2001; 323: 135-138.

[225] Guthrie E, Kapur N, Mackway-Jones K, Chew-Graham C, Moorey J, Mendel E et al: Predictors of outcome following brief psychodynamic-interpersonal therapy for deliberate self-poisoning. *Aust N Z J Psychiatry* 2003; 37: 532-536.

In: Suicidal Behavior in Alcohol and Drug Abuse...
Editors: L. Sher, A. Vilens, pp. 393-406

ISBN: 978-1-60876-919-3

Chapter 22

SUICIDAL BEHAVIOR IN ALCOHOL USE DISORDERS: NEUROBIOLOGICAL ASPECTS

Leo Sher
Columbia University and New York State Psychiatric Institute,
New York, New York, USA

ABSTRACT

Humans have consumed alcohol for thousands of years. Alcohol and other drugs have a long history of remedial, recreational, and ceremonial functions. Nowadays, most adults in the Western countries drink alcohol. Because of its availability nearly every adult in the Western countries has tried alcohol at least once, and a sizable minority have serious problems from drinking. The conditions that lead to excessive alcohol consumption in some individuals and not in others are complex because they involve interactions among genetic, psychosocial, environmental, and neurobiological factors. The actions of alcohol that cause intoxication, initiate and maintain excessive drinking behavior, and promote relapse during abstinence occur primarily in the brain. The specific mental processes thought to underlie the development of alcoholism involve normal brain functions such as learning, attention, emotion, and cognition. Alcohol use is a major contributing factor for head injuries, motor vehicle accidents, violence, and assaults. The large population of individuals with alcohol abuse and dependence, the relative frequency of suicides and suicide-related behaviors in this population, and the devastating effects of attempted and completed suicides on individuals, families, and society make this an important area for research. Multiple lines of evidence suggest that lower serotonin activity is tied to increased aggression/impulsivity which in turn is presumed to enhance the probability of suicidal behavior. Dopaminergic dysfunction may play a role in the pathophysiology of suicidal behavior in alcoholism. Alcohol can damage the brain in many ways. The brain is vulnerable to the toxic effects of alcohol itself and can be affected by alcohol-related damage to other organs, including the liver, pancreas, and heart. Brain damage and neurobehavioral deficits are associated with suicidal behavior. It is possible that cognitive abnormalities contribute to increased suicidality in individuals with alcohol use disorders. Low selenium status is associated with depressed mood, anxiety, and cognitive decline. These symptoms are commonly observed in persons with alcohol use disorders. Selenium deficiency may play a role in the pathophysiology of depression and suicidal behavior in individuals who abuse alcohol. Understanding the integration of the interactions among multiple biological systems in the regulation of ethanol-seeking behavior and the development of ethanol dependence is an important challenge for future research. It is to be hoped that studies of the neurobiology of suicidal behavior in alcohol use disorders will improve treatment and prevention of suicidal behavior in individuals with alcohol abuse and dependence.

Introduction

Humans have consumed alcohol for thousands of years. Alcohol and other drugs have a long history of remedial, recreational, and ceremonial functions. The first recorded reference to alcohol as an addicting substance was made more than 2000 years ago by Seneca, a Roman philosopher who classified excessive drinking as a form of insanity. Nowadays, most adults in the Western countries drink alcohol. The consumption of alcoholic beverages has risen steadily since World War II, and drinking now begins at an earlier age. The steady increase in alcohol production and consumption is related to the broader growth of commodity production in industrialized societies in which alcoholic beverages are consumed in tandem with other new forms of commodities and foods. In the business world misleading and confusing information is often used to win consumers without considering the effects of the product on the health of the user. Alcohol advertising is countered by warnings from the health professions, but the individual is expected to sort out the contradictory information and make a rational decision. Seeking the causes of alcohol abuse within the person diverts attention from the invisible economic, political, and social parameters that promote the lucrative industry of alcohol production and consumption.

Societies have three basic ways of dealing with alcohol misuse. The first is to prohibit alcohol production and distribution. Over the past centuries many societies such as the United States, China, Islamic countries and some European countries tried to limit or ban the use of alcohol. Foolproof in theory, prohibition is not effective against organized global marketing. The second is to urge consumers to abstain from or limit alcohol consumption. The third way is prevention. Prevention is focuses on countering the daily cultivation of appeals and associations that render the use of alcohol compelling and resistant to change.

Alcohol is widely consumed at social gatherings, featured in television, billboard and magazine advertisements, and readily available in most households. Because of its availability nearly every adult in the Western countries has tried alcohol at least once, and a sizable minority have serious problems from drinking. The conditions that lead to excessive alcohol consumption in some individuals and not in others are complex because they involve interactions among genetic, psychosocial, environmental, and neurobiological factors.

In the eyes of the public, the word addict stirs up a negative image: a person of low moral character who willfully chooses to engage in questionable behavior. The social stigma attached to addicts reflects the great gap that exists between scientific knowledge and public perception of addiction. Just as mental illness was viewed as a social problem instead of a medical issue until the last several decades, alcohol addiction continues to be seen as a character flaw instead of as the biological problem that it is. Alcoholism is a disease that anyone who has the susceptible internal chemistry can get, be he saint or sinner, tower of strength or shriveling weakling.

Alcohol use is a major contributing factor for head injuries, motor vehicle accidents, violence, and assaults. In the U.S., it has been estimated that alcohol is involved in 45 percent of violent crimes, 45 percent of episodes of marital violence, 20 percent of nonfatal industrial accidents, and 15 percent of nonfatal traffic accidents. The cost of alcohol-related mortality and morbidity in the United States is estimated at $136 billion per year [1]. Beyond money, there is also the pain and suffering of the all individuals besides the alcoholic affected. Culturally supported behaviors that undermine health, such as the misuse of alcohol, claim many more lives than can be accounted for through lack of access to good medical care or unsuspected environmental hazards.

The link between alcohol misuse and violence probably has a biological basis. For example, both alcohol abuse and violent behavior are associated with abnormal serotonin function and low blood sugar [2,3]. Serotonin plays an important role in the regulation of glucose metabolism. Serotonin and its precursors cause the release of insulin and this, in turn, controls blood sugar. A study by Virkkunen et al. [2] found that the alcoholic, impulsive offenders with intermittent explosive disorder had significantly lower mean blood glucose levels when given glucose than did the healthy controls. There was no difference when the offenders just took the placebo of aspartame. In another study by this group, a relationship was found between hypoglycemia and low serotonin levels [3]. They found that when they measured both blood sugar and serotonin levels, they were able to predict which of their studied individuals were repeat, alcohol-abusing, violent offenders and impulsive fire-setters in 84% of cases. It is important to note that the role of alcohol abuse in criminal behavior may be overestimated. Possibly, offenders with alcohol use disorders have a higher chance to get caught compared to non-alcoholic offenders. People with criminal records are not necessarily representative of all people who have committed crimes. A police officer may be more likely to record an offense if it is committed by a drunk person. A study by Petersilia et al. [4] published in the late 1970s demonstrated that there was a distinction in arrest rates between intensive offenders who were continuously engaged in crime and committed to criminal lifestyles and who were careful to avoid arrest compared with those who committed crimes irregularly with less care and planning. This study reported that an average intense offender committed ten times as many crimes as the intermittent offender, but was five times less likely to be arrested for any one crime. Once arrested, the intensive offender was also less likely to be convicted and incarcerated. Impulsive individuals with alcoholism may be less careful to avoid arrest than non-alcoholic offenders.

The actions of alcohol that cause intoxication, initiate and maintain excessive drinking behavior, and promote relapse during abstinence occur primarily in the brain. The specific mental processes thought to underlie the development of alcoholism involve normal brain functions such as learning, attention, emotion, and cognition. To understand the factors that compel some individuals to drink excessively, alcohol research has focused on the identification of brain mechanisms that support the reinforcing actions of alcohol and the progression of changes in neural function induced by chronic ethanol consumption that lead to the development of dependence and suicidal behavior.

Alcohol and Suicide

Alcohol misuse is an important risk factor for suicidal behavior [5-10]. The large population of individuals with alcohol abuse and dependence, the relative frequency of suicides and suicide-related behaviors in this population, and the devastating effects of attempted and completed suicides on individuals, families, and society make this an important area for research. Some reports have found that lifetime mortality due to suicide in alcohol dependence is as high as 18% [7]. Murphy and Wetzel [8] reviewed the epidemiological literature and found that the lifetime risk of suicide among individuals with alcohol dependence treated in outpatient and inpatient settings was 2.2% and 3.4%, respectively. Nonetheless, individuals with alcohol dependence have a 60–120 times greater suicide risk than the non-psychiatrically ill population.

High rates of suicide attempts among individuals with alcohol use disorders have also been reported [9,10]. For example, in an urban community in the US, 24% of subjects with alcohol dependence attempted suicide, as compared with 5% with other psychiatric diagnoses [9]. Forty per cent of a sample of depressed subjects with alcohol dependence who were hospitalized had attempted suicide in the prior week and 70% had attempted suicide at some point in their lives [10]. Depressed subjects with a history of alcohol dependence have higher current suicide ideation scale scores compared with depressed subjects without a history of alcohol dependence [6]. These data indicate that a lifetime diagnosis of alcohol dependence is a major risk factor for attempted or completed suicide.

A model of suicidal behavior among subjects with alcoholism has recently been proposed [11]. Predisposing factors that are presumed to increase (moderate) risk for suicide among individuals with alcoholism are aggression/impulsivity and alcoholism severity, which represent predominantly externalizing constructs, and negative affect and hopelessness, which represent predominantly internalizing constructs. Major depressive episodes and stressful life events—particularly interpersonal difficulties — are conceptualized as precipitating factors. This model is consistent with the stress-diathesis model of suicidal behavior.

Serotonin

Multiple lines of evidence suggest that lower serotonin activity is tied to increased aggression/impulsivity which in turn is presumed to enhance the probability of suicidal behavior [12,13]. Low CSF 5-hydroxyindolacetic acid 5-HIAA has been reported in suicide attempters with major depression, schizophrenia and personality disorders as compared with people who do not attempt suicide but have the same psychiatric diagnosis [12-15]. The levels of 5-HIAA in CSF taken from abstinent individuals with a history of alcohol dependence of both sexes were shown to be lower than in controls [16]. Moreover, impulsive offenders with alcohol dependence had lower CSF 5-HIAA levels than non-impulsive offenders with alcohol dependence [2]. High-lethality depressed suicide attempters with comorbid alcoholism have lower CSF 5-HIAA levels compared with low-lethality depressed suicide attempters with comorbid alcoholism [17]. In subjects with comorbid depression and alcoholism greater serotonergic impairment may be associated with higher risk of completed suicide.

Dopamine

Research evidence suggests that pathological aggression may be related to genetically determined abnormalities in the dopaminergic system [18]. Suicidal behavior may be regarded as self-directed pathological aggression. Several lines of evidence suggest that the dopamine system is involved in the pathophysiology of suicidal behavior. Lower levels of CSF homovanillic acid (HVA) have been found in depressed patients with a history of either violent or non-violent suicide attempts than in controls [19]. In our recent study, we compared CSF HVA levels in depressed suicide attempters without comorbid Axis II disorders, depressed non-attempters without comorbid Axis II disorders, and normal controls [20]. Depressed suicide attempters had lower CSF HVA levels compared to depressed non-attempters and to controls. There was no difference in CSF HVA levels between depressed non-attempters and controls. Several studies that did not involve CSF HVA measures also suggested that the dopaminergic system may be involved in the neurobiology of suicidal behavior. For example, Pitchot et al. [21] studied the growth hormone (GH) response to apomorphine, a selective dopaminergic agonist, in depressed patients with and without history of suicide attempts and found that patients with a history of suicidal behavior exhibited a significantly lower GH response to apomorphine than patients who never attempted suicide. More recent reports from the same group confirmed their earlier finding. It has also been observed that dopamine abnormalities are associated with impulsivity, emotional dysregulation, and alcohol use disorders [22]. For example, a recent neuroimaging study suggests that alcoholism is associated with blunted dopamine transmission in the ventral striatum [23]. Alcoholism is also associated with high aggression, impulsivity, and suicidal behavior [24]. Therefore, it is reasonable to suggest that genetically determined dopaminergic dysfunction may play an important role in the pathophysiology of suicidal behavior in alcoholism.

Brain Damage

Alcohol can damage the brain in many ways [25,26]. The brain is vulnerable to the toxic effects of alcohol itself and can be affected by alcohol-related damage to other organs, including the liver, pancreas, and heart. The risk of alcohol– induced brain damage and related neurobehavioral deficits varies from person to person and is influenced by factors such as age, gender, drinking history, and nutrition. In the US, up to two million individuals with alcoholism have permanent and debilitating conditions that require lifetime custodial care. Examples of such conditions include alcohol–induced persisting amnesic disorder (also called Wernicke–Korsakoff syndrome) and dementia, which seriously affects many mental functions in addition to memory (e.g., language, reasoning, and problem–solving abilities). Brain damage and neurobehavioral deficits are associated with suicidal behavior [27,28].

THE ROLE OF COGNITIVE IMPAIRMENT

Alcohol and Cognitive Dysfunction

Etiological models for alcohol use disorders have traditionally proposed trait and cognitive explanations for initiation, maintenance, and dependence [29]. Within this framework, temperament and personality models have often focused on trait disinhibition [30], including behavioral undercontrol [31], impulsivity and sensation seeking [32], suggesting that deficits in interrupting ongoing behavior may be central to hazardous drinking. Numerous studies have shown that heavy drinkers and subjects suffering from alcohol dependence have reduced performance on neurocognitive tests such as Wisconsin Card Sorting Test, the Stroop Test, Trails A and B test/Trail Making, Tower of Hanoi/London, and the Go No-Go Test compared with controls [33-62]. These effects have been shown to persist after detoxification [36,38,44-47,55,56,58,59,63], and may be based on hereditary predispositions [64,65]. The effects appear to be correlated with years of alcohol use [35,47], although some studies have not found such an effect [43]. Subjects suffering from alcohol dependence have been found to perform like subjects with frontal brain lesions in some investigations [34,39]. It is not clear whether the results are general for substance abuse populations since two investigations have found similar effects when comparing subjects dependent on alcohol with subjects dependent on other substances [33,34]. However, one study has found worse executive functioning among alcohol dependent subjects [40]. A number of investigations have found worse performance among subjects suffering from alcohol dependence, former alcoholics and heavy social drinkers compared with controls on the standard Stroop Test [34,40,41,46,49,58] and the Stroop tests containing alcohol related words [43,51-53,56]. Two studies have found that this difference may be specific for the alcohol related version of the Stroop Test, while alcohol-dependent subjects had normal scores on the standard Stroop Test [28,29]. Another study has found that Stroop performance may predict results of detoxification treatment [67]. A recent study found differences in tests scores on the Go No-Go Test between detoxified polysubstance users with alcohol dependence and control subjects [46]. Another study found that subjects with alcohol dependence differ electrophysiologically from control individuals using the Go No-Go Test [36]. In summary, neuropsychological studies of alcohol use disorders overall suggest that individuals with alcohol abuse and dependence are cognitively impaired.

Suicide and Cognitive Impairment

Data suggest that neuropsychological dysfunction may play a role in determining risk for suicidal acts. Suicide attempters have been characterized as "cognitively rigid" on the basis of self-ratings and performance on mental flexibility tasks [68-70]. From case studies [71], Rourke et al. [72] suggested that a specific nonverbal learning disability may predispose individuals to suicidal behavior. Bartfai et al. [73], using standard neuropsychological measures, found poorer performance on measures of fluency (verbal as well as nonverbal) and reasoning in a small sample of recent suicide attempters compared to chronic pain patients and nonpatients. Subjects with a history of high-lethality suicide attempts exhibited deficits in executive functioning that were independent of deficits associated with depression alone [27].

Alcohol use disorders are associated with both cognitive impairment and suicidal behavior. It is possible that cognitive abnormalities contribute to increased suicidality in individuals with alcohol use disorders. Future studies of the role of cognitive abnormalities in the pathophysiology of suicidal behavior are merited.

Possible Role of Selenium Deficiency

Selenium and Alcohol

Selenium is an essential trace element for humans and animals [74-78]. The four natural oxidation states of selenium are elemental selenium (0), selenide (-2), selenite (+4), and selenate (+6). Inorganic selenate and selenite predominate in water whereas organic selenium compounds (selenomethionine, selenocysteine) are the major selenium species in cereal and in vegetables. For the general population, the primary pathway of exposure to selenium is food, followed by water and air. Both selenite and selenate possess substantial bioavailability. Selenium is an essential component of glutathione peroxidase, which is an important enzyme for processes that protect lipids in polyunsaturated membranes from oxidative degradation.

The selenium content in human blood varies between different areas of the world due to the soil content of selenium with consequent variations in dietary intake. Blood selenium level appears to be an index of long-term selenium status and does not change from day-to-day. There is a consensus in the literature concerning the lower concentration of plasma selenium in patients with alcoholism, even in the absence of severe liver pathology as well as in some cases of modest alcohol consumption [79-85]. Serum, erythrocyte, and whole blood levels of selenium are also decreased in patients with alcoholism [16-23,83-90]. For example, Korpela et al. [86] measured serum selenium values in patients with alcoholism having various degrees of liver damage. As a percentage of healthy control level, the average serum selenium level of alcoholics with histologically normal liver was 60%, with fatty liver was 63%, with alcoholic hepatitis was 52%, and with cirrhosis was 46%. Decrease in selenium levels in patients with alcoholism may be related to insufficient dietary intake, reduced intestinal absorption, changes in plasma proteins (much of the circulating selenium is bound to glutathione peroxidase and other proteins), and increased requirements [81-83,85,91].

Selenium, Mood, and Behavior

Selenium is thought to play an important role in brain function, because its metabolism in the brain is vastly different than in other organs [92-94]. Specifically, during times of deficiency, the brain retains selenium at the expense of tissues, such as muscle, kidney and liver. Indeed, selenium is an important modulator of mood. Effects of dietary selenium on mood in healthy men were assessed by the Profile of Mood States-Bipolar Form [95]. Eleven healthy men were confined in a metabolic research unit for 120 days. The diet of conventional foods provided 80 μg/day of selenium for the first 21 days, then either 13 or 356 μg/day for the remaining 99 days. There were no significant changes in any of the mood scales due to dietary selenium. However, in the low-selenium group, the changes in the agreeable-hostile and the elated-depressed subscales were correlated with initial erythrocyte selenium concentration; that is, the lower thev initial selenium status, the more the mood scores decreased. Finley and Penland [96] investigated effects of dietary selenium on healthy men who were fed either a low or a high selenium diet for 15 weeks. Subjects on the low selenium diet had significantly decreased clearheaded/confused and elated/depressed subscores, those on the high selenium diet significantly improved in the clearheaded/confused, confident/unsure, and composed/anxious subscores.

The possibility that a subclinical deficiency of the trace element selenium might exist in a sample of the British population was examined by Benton and Cook [97]. A selenium supplement was given for 5 weeks. Using a double-blind cross-over design, 50 subjects received either a placebo or 100 μg of selenium on a daily basis. On three occasions they filled in the Profile of Moods States. Selenium intake was associated with a general elevation of mood and in particular, a decrease in anxiety. The change in mood when taking the active tablet was correlated with the level of selenium in the diet, which was estimated from a food frequency questionnaire. The lower the level of selenium in the diet the more reports of anxiety, depression, and tiredness, decreased following 5 weeks of selenium therapy. Thus, selenium depletion may affect mood and behavior. Selenium influences compounds with hormonal activity and neurotransmitters in the brain, and this is postulated to be the reason selenium affects mood in humans and behavior in animals [74,92,98]. In a randomized trial of HIV-infected patients, researchers found that supplementation with 200 μg/day selenium caused a 20-fold reduction of depressed–dejected mood state and a trend toward improvement in quality of life scores [99].

Selenium is required for appropriate thyroid hormone synthesis, activation, and metabolism [100]. Selenium status influences thyroid function. It has been suggested that the effects of selenium status on mood, behavior, and cognition may be partly mediated by changes induced by selenium deficiency or selenium supplementation in thyroid function.

Low selenium status is associated with depressed mood, anxiety, and cognitive decline [100-105]. These symptoms are commonly observed in persons with alcohol use disorders. Selenium deficiency may play a role in the pathophysiology of depression and suicidal behavior in individuals who abuse alcohol. Healthy nutrition and possibly mineral supplementations should be a part of the treatment plan of patients with alcohol use disorders especially when alcohol misuse is comorbid with depression. Adequate nutrition is needed for many aspects of brain functioning. In general, greater attention to nutritional factors in psychiatry is warranted.

Conclusion

Just as we cannot step in the same river twice we will never be able to see the world in the same way as we did before the discoveries in neurobiology of addictions during the past 30-40 years. More recently, increasing attention has been directed toward the understanding of neurobiological and environmental factors in susceptibility to relapse. Understanding the integration of the interactions among multiple biological systems in the regulation of ethanol-seeking behavior and the development of ethanol dependence is an important challenge for future research. It is to be hoped that studies of the neurobiology of suicidal behavior in alcohol use disorders will improve treatment and prevention of suicidal behavior in individuals with alcohol abuse and dependence.

REFERENCES

[1] Burke TR. The economic impact of alcohol abuse and alcoholism. *Public Health Rep.* 1988;103(6):564-8.

[2] Virkkunen M, Rawlings R, Tokola R, Poland RE, Guidotti A, Nemeroff C, Bissette G, Kalogeras K, Karonen SL, Linnoila M. CSF biochemistries, glucose metabolism, and diurnal activity rhythms in alcoholic, violent offenders, fire setters, and healthy volunteers. *Arch Gen Psychiatry.* 1994 Jan;51(1):20-7.

[3] Roy A, Virkkunen M, Linnoila M. Monoamines, glucose metabolism, aggression towards self and others. *Int J Neurosci* 1988;41(3-4):261-4.

[4] Petersilia, Joan, Peter W. Greenwood, and Marvin Lavin. Criminal Careers of Habitual *Felons.* Washington, D.C.: U.S. Government Printing Office, July 1978.

[5] Sher L. Risk and protective factors for suicide in patients with alcoholism. *TheScientificWorldJournal* 2006;6:1405-1411.

[6] Sher L, Oquendo MA, Conason AH, Brent DA, Grunebaum MF, Zalsman G, Burke AK, Mann JJ. Clinical features of depressed patients with or without a family history of alcoholism. *Acta Psychiatr Scand* 2005;112(4):266-71.

[7] Roy A, Linnoila M. Alcoholism and suicide. *Suicide Life Threat Behav* 1986;16(2):244-73.

[8] Murphy GE, Wetzel RD. The lifetime risk of suicide in alcoholism. *Arch Gen Psychiatry* 1990;47(4):383-92.

[9] Weissman MM, Myers JK. Clinical depression in alcoholism. *Am J Psychiatry* 1980;137(3):372-3.

[10] Cornelius JR, Salloum IM, Day NL, Thase ME, Mann JJ. Patterns of suicidality and alcohol use in alcoholics with major depression. *Alcohol Clin Exp Res* 1996;20(8):1451-5.

[11] Conner KR, Duberstein PR. Predisposing and precipitating factors for suicide among alcoholics: empirical review and conceptual integration. *Alcohol Clin Exp Res* 2004; 28(5 Suppl):6S-17S.

[12] Sher L, Mann JJ. Neurobiology of suicide. In: Soares JC, Gershon S, eds. *Textbook of medical psychiatry.* New York: Marcel Dekker, 2003: 701–711.

[13] Placidi GP, Oquendo MA, Malone KM, Huang YY, Ellis SP, Mann JJ. Aggressivity, suicide attempts, and depression: relationship to cerebrospinal fluid monoamine metabolite levels. *Biol Psychiatry* 2001;50:783–791.

[14] Roy A, De Jong J, Linnoila M. Cerebrospinal fluid monoamine metabolites and suicidal behavior in depressed patients. A 5-year follow-up study. *Arch Gen Psychiatry* 1989;46:609–612.

[15] Mann JJ. A current perspective of suicide and attempted suicide. *Ann Intern Med.* 2002;19;136(4):302-11.
[16] Ratsma JE, Van Der Stelt O, Gunning WB. Neurochemical markers of alcoholism vulnerability in humans. *Alcohol Alcohol* 2002;37:522–533.
[17] Sher L, Oquendo MA, Grunebaum MF, Burke AK, Huang Y, Mann JJ. CSF monoamine metabolites and lethality of suicide attempts in depressed patients with alcohol dependence. *Eur Neuropsychopharmacology* 2007;17(1):12-15.
[18] Chen TJ, Blum K, Mathews D, et al. Are dopaminergic genes involved in a predisposition to pathological aggression? Hypothesizing the importance of "super normal controls" in psychiatric genetic research of complex behavioral disorders. *Med Hypotheses* 2005;65:703–707.
[19] Engstrom G, Alling C, Blennow K, Regnell G, Traskman-Bendz L. Reduced cerebrospinal HVA concentrations and HVA/5-HIAA ratios in suicide attempters. Monoamine metabolites in 120 suicide attempters and 47 controls. *Eur Neuropsychopharmacol* 1999;9:399–405.
[20] Sher L, Mann JJ, Traskman-Bendz L, Huang Y, Fertuck EA, Stanley BH. Lower cerebrospinal fluid homovanillic acid levels in depressed suicide attempters. *J Affect Disord* 2006;90:83–90.
[21] Pitchot W., Hansenne M., Moreno AG, Ansseau M. Suicidal behavior and growth hormone response to apomorphine test. *Biol Psychiat* 1992;31:1213–1219.
[22] Tupala E, Tiihonen J. Dopamine and alcoholism neurobiological basis of ethanol abuse. *Prog Neuropsychopharmacol Biol Psychiat* 2004;28:1221–1247.
[23] Martinez D, Gil R, Slifstein M, et al. Alcohol dependence is associated with blunted dopamine transmission in the ventral striatum. *Biol Psychiat* 2005;58:779–786.
[24] Sher L. Alcoholism and suicidal behavior: a clinical overview. *Acta Psychiatr Scand* 2006;113:13–22.
[25] Rourke SB, Loeberg T. The neurobehavioral correlates of alcoholism. In: Nixon SJ, ed. *Neuropsychological Assessment of Neuropsychiatric Disorders,* 2d edn. New York: Oxford University Press, 1996, pp. 423–485.
[26] Oscar-Berman M, Marinkovic K. Alcoholism and the brain: an overview. *Alcohol Res Health.* 2003;27(2):125-33.
[27] Keilp JG, Sackeim HA, Brodsky BS, Oquendo MA, Malone KM, Mann JJ.
[28] Neuropsychological dysfunction in depressed suicide attempters. *Am J Psychiatry* 2001;158(5):735-41.
[29] 28. Oquendo MA, Friedman JH, Grunebaum MF, Burke A, Silver JM, Mann JJ. Suicidal behavior and mild traumatic brain injury in major depression. *J Nerv Ment Dis* 2004;192(6):430-4.
[30] Anderson KG, Schweinsburg A, Paulus MP, Brown SA, Tapert S. Examining personality and alcohol expectancies using functional magnetic resonance imaging (fMRI) with adolescents. *J Stud Alcohol* 2005;66(3):323-31.
[31] McGue M, Iacono WG, Legrand LN, Malone S, Elkins I. Origins and consequences of age at first drink. I. Associations with substance-use disorders, disinhibitory behavior and psychopathology, and P3 amplitude. *Alcohol Clin Exp Res* 2001;25(8):1156-65.
[32] Sher KJ, Walitzer KS, Wood PK, Brent EE. Characteristics of children of alcoholics: putative risk factors, substance use and abuse, and psychopathology. *J Abnorm Psychol* 1991;100(4):427-48.

[33] Grau E, Ordet G. Personality traits and alcohol consumption in a sample of non-alcoholic women. *Pers Indiv Diff* 1999;27:1057-66.
[34] Beatty WW, Katzung VM, Moreland VJ, Nixon SJ. Neuropsychological performance *of recently abstinent alcoholics and cocaine abusers.* Drug Alcohol Depend 1995;37(3):247-53.
[35] Bechara A, Dolan S, Denburg N, Hindes A, Anderson SW, Nathan PE. Decision-making deficits, linked to a dysfunctional ventromedial prefrontal cortex, revealed in alcohol and stimulant abusers. *Neuropsychologia* 2001;39(4):376-89.
[36] Brokate B, Hildebrandt H, Eling P, Fichtner H, Runge K, Timm C. Frontal lobe dysfunctions in Korsakoff's syndrome and chronic alcoholism: continuity or discontinuity? *Neuropsychology* 2003;17(3):420-8.
[37] Cohen HL, Porjesz B, Begleiter H, Wang W. Neurophysiological correlates of response production and inhibition in alcoholics. *Alcohol Clin Exp Res* 1997;21(8):1398-406.
[38] Demir B, Ucar G, Ulug B, Ulusoy S, Sevinc I, Batur S. Platelet monoamine oxidase activity in alcoholism subtypes: relationship to personality traits and executive functions. *Alcohol Alcohol* 2002;37(6):597-602.
[39] Fama R, Pfefferbaum A, Sullivan EV. Perceptual learning in detoxified alcoholic men: contributions from explicit memory, executive function, and age. *Alcohol Clin Exp Res* 2004;28(11):1657-65.
[40] George MR, Potts G, Kothman D, Martin L, Mukundan CR. Frontal deficits in alcoholism: an ERP study. *Brain Cogn* 2004;54(3):245-7.
[41] Goldstein RZ, Leskovjan AC, Hoff AL, Hitzemann R, Bashan F, Khalsa SS, Wang GJ, Fowler JS, Volkow ND. Severity of neuropsychological impairment in cocaine and alcohol addiction: association with metabolism in the prefrontal cortex. *Neuropsychologia* 2004;42(11):1447-58.
[42] Ihara H, Berrios GE, London M. Group and case study of the dysexecutive syndrome in alcoholism without amnesia. *J Neurol Neurosurg Psychiatry* 2000;68(6):731-7.
[43] Joyce EM, Robbins TW. Frontal lobe function in Korsakoff and non-Korsakoff alcoholics: planning and spatial working memory. *Neuropsychologia* 1991;29(8):709-23.
[44] Lusher J, Chandler C, Ball D. Alcohol dependence and the alcohol Stroop paradigm: evidence and issues. *Drug Alcohol Depend* 2004;75(3):225-31.
[45] Moriyama Y, Mimura M, Kato M, Yoshino A, Hara T, Kashima H, Kato A, Watanabe A. Executive dysfunction and clinical outcome in chronic alcoholics. *Alcohol Clin Exp Res* 2002;26(8):1239-44.
[46] Munro CA, Saxton J, Butters MA. The neuropsychological consequences of abstinence among older alcoholics: a cross-sectional study. *Alcohol Clin Exp Res* 2000; 24(10):1510-6.
[47] Noel X, Van der Linden M, Schmidt N, Sferrazza R, Hanak C, Le Bon O, De Mol J, Kornreich C, Pelc I, Verbanck P. Supervisory attentional system in nonamnesic alcoholic men. *Arch Gen Psychiatry* 2001;58(12):1152-8.
[48] Oscar-Berman M, Kirkley SM, Gansler DA, Couture A. Comparisons of Korsakoff and non-Korsakoff alcoholics on neuropsychological tests of prefrontal brain functioning. *Alcohol Clin Exp Res* 2004;28(4):667-75.
[49] Ratti MT, Bo P, Giardini A, Soragna D. Chronic alcoholism and the frontal lobe: which executive functions are imparied? *Acta Neurol Scand* 2002;105(4):276-81.

[50] Rothlind JC, Greenfield TM, Bruce AV, Meyerhoff DJ, Flenniken DL, Lindgren JA, Weiner MW. Heavy alcohol consumption in individuals with HIV infection: effects on neuropsychological performance. *J Int Neuropsychol Soc* 2005;11(1):70-83.

[51] Schmidt KS, Gallo JL, Ferri C, Giovannetti T, Sestito N, Libon DJ, Schmidt PS. The neuropsychological profile of alcohol-related dementia suggests cortical and subcortical pathology. *Dement Geriatr Cogn Disord* 2005;20(5):286-91.

[52] Sharma D, Albery IP, Cook C. Selective attentional bias to alcohol related stimuli in problem drinkers and non-problem drinkers. *Addiction* 2001;96(2):285-95.

[53] Stetter F, Ackermann K, Bizer A, Straube ER, Mann K. Effects of disease-related cues in alcoholic inpatients: results of a controlled "Alcohol Stroop" study. *Alcohol Clin Exp Res* 1995;19(3):593-9.

[54] Stormark KM, Laberg JC, Nordby H, Hugdahl K. Alcoholics' selective attention to alcohol stimuli: automated processing? *J Stud Alcohol* 2000;61(1):18-23.

[55] Sullivan EV, Mathalon DH, Zipursky RB, Kersteen-Tucker Z, Knight RT, Pfefferbaum A. Factors of the Wisconsin Card Sorting Test as measures of frontal-lobe function in schizophrenia and in chronic alcoholism. *Psychiatry Res* 1993;46(2):175-99.

[56] Sullivan EV, Rosenbloom MJ, Pfefferbaum A. Pattern of motor and cognitive deficits in detoxified alcoholic men. *Alcohol Clin Exp Res* 2000;24(5):611-21.

[57] Sullivan EV, Fama R, Rosenbloom MJ, Pfefferbaum A. A profile of neuropsychological deficits in alcoholic women. *Neuropsychology* 2002;16(1):74-83.

[58] Tapert SF, Brown SA. Substance dependence, family history of alcohol dependence and neuropsychological functioning in adolescence. *Addiction* 2000;95(7):1043-53.

[59] Tedstone D, Coyle K. Cognitive impairments in sober alcoholics: performance on selective and divided attention tasks. *Drug Alcohol Depend* 2004;75(3):277-86.

[60] Uekermann J, Daum I, Schlebusch P, Wiebel B, Trenckmann U. Depression and cognitive functioning in alcoholism. *Addiction* 2003;98(11):1521-9.

[61] Uekermann J, Daum I, Schlebusch P, Trenckmann U. Processing of affective stimuli in alcoholism. *Cortex* 2005;41(2):189-94.

[62] van Gorp WG, Altshuler L, Theberge DC, Wilkins J, Dixon W. Cognitive impairment in euthymic bipolar patients with and without prior alcohol dependence. A preliminary study. *Arch Gen Psychiatry* 1998;55(1):41-6.

[63] Zinn S, Stein R, Swartzwelder HS. Executive functioning early in abstinence from alcohol. *Alcohol Clin Exp Res* 2004;28(9):1338-1346.

[64] Smith ME, Oscar-Berman M. Resource-limited information processing in alcoholism. *J Stud Alcohol* 1992;53(5):514-8.

[65] Corral M, Holguin SR, Cadaveira F. Neuropsychological characteristics of young children from high-density alcoholism families: a three-year follow-up. *J Stud Alcohol* 2003;64(2):195-9.

[66] Nigg JT, Glass JM, Wong MM, Poon E, Jester JM, Fitzgerald HE, Puttler LI, Adams KM, Zucker RA. Neuropsychological executive functioning in children at elevated risk for alcoholism: findings in early adolescence. *J Abnorm Psychol* 2004;113(2):302-14.

[67] Cox WM, Yeates GN, Regan CM. Effects of alcohol cues on cognitive processing in heavy and light drinkers. *Drug Alcohol Depend* 1999;55(1-2):85-9.

[68] Cox WM, Hogan LM, Kristian MR, Race JH. Alcohol attentional bias as a predictor of alcohol abusers' treatment outcome. *Drug Alcohol Depend* 2002;68(3):237-43.

[69] Levenson M, Neuringer C: Problem-solving behavior in suicidal adolescents. *J Consult Clin Psychol* 1971;37:433–6.
[70] Neuringer C: Rigid thinking in suicidal individuals. *J Consult Psychol* 1964;28:54–8.
[71] Patsiokas AT, Clum GA, Luscomb RL: Cognitive characteristics of suicide attempters. *J Consult Clin Psychol* 1979;47:478–84.
[72] Bigler E: On the neuropsychology of suicide. *J Learn Disabil* 1989; 22:181–5.
[73] Rourke BP, Young GC, Leenaars AA: A childhood learning disability that predisposes those afflicted to adolescent and adult depression and suicide risk. *J Learn Disabil* 1989; 22:169–75.
[74] Bartfai A, Winborg I, Nordstrom P, Asberg M: Suicidal behavior and cognitive flexibility: design and verbal fluency after attempted suicide. *Suicide Life Threat Behav* 1990;20:254–65.
[75] Sher L. Role of selenium depletion in the etiopathogenesis of depression in patients with alcoholism. *Med Hypoth* 2002;59:330-3.
[76] Rayman MP. The importance of selenium to human health. *Lancet* 2000;356:233-41.
[77] Barceloux DG. Selenium. *J Toxicol Clin Toxicol.* 1999;37(2):145-72.
[78] Flohe L, Andreesen JR, Brigelius-Flohe R, Maiorino M, Ursini F. Selenium, the element of the moon, in life on earth. *Life* 2000;49: 411-20.
[79] Alertsen AR, Aukrust A, Skaug OE. Selenium concentrations in blood and serum from patients with mental diseases. *Acta Psychiatr Scand* 1986;74:217-9.
[80] Lecomte E, Herbert B, Pirollet P, Chancerelle Y, Arnaud J, Musse N, Paille F, Siest G, Artur Y. Effect of alcohol consumption on blood antioxydant nutrients and oxidative stress indicators. *Am J Clin Nutr* 1994;60:255-61.
[81] Ward RJ, Julta J, Peters TJ. Antioxidant status in alcoholic liver disease. *Adv Biosci* 1989;76:343-51.
[82] Tanner AR, Bantock I, Hinks L, Lloyd B, Turner NR, Wright R. Depressed selenium and vitamin E levels in a alcoholic population. *Dig Dis Sci* 1986;31:1307-12.
[83] Johansson U, Johnsson F, Joelsson B, Berglund M, Akesson B. Selenium status in patients with liver cirrhosis and alcoholism. *Br J Nutr* 1986;55:227-33.
[84] Girre C, Hispard E, Therond P, Guedj S, Bourdon R, Dally S. Effect of abstinence from alcohol on the depression of glutathione peroxidase activity and selenium and vitamins E levels in chronic alcoholic patients. *Alcohol Clin Exp Res* 1990;14:909-12.
[85] Dworkin BM, Rosenthal WS, Gordon GG, Jankowski RH. Diminished blood selenium levels in alcoholics. *Alcohol Clin Exp Res* 1984;8:535-8.
[86] Ringstad J, Knutsen SF, Nilssen OR, Thomassen Y. A comparative study of serum selenium and vitamin E levels in a population of male risk drinkers and abstainers. *Biol Trace Elem Res* 1993;36:65-71.
[87] Korpela H, Kumpulainen J, Luoma PV, Arranto AJ, Sotaniemi EA. Decreased serum selenium in alcoholics as related to liver structure and function. *Am J Clin Nutr* 1985;42:147-51.
[88] Watson RR, Mohs ME, Eskelson C, Sampliner RE, Hartmann B. Identification of alcohol abuse and alcoholism with biological parameters. *Alcohol Clin Exp Res* 1986;10:364-85.
[89] Välimäki MJ, Harju KJ, Ylikahri RH. Decreased serum selenium in alcoholics - a consequence of liver dysfunction. *Clin Chim Acta* 1983;130:291-6.

[90] Corrigan FM, Besson JAO, Ward NI. Red cell caesium, lithium and selenium in abstinent alcoholics. *Alcohol Alcoholism* 1991;26:309-14.

[91] Bjorneboe GE, Johnsen J, Bjorneboe A, Bache-Wiig JE, Morland J, Drevon CA. Diminished serum concentration of vitamin E in alcoholics. *Ann Nutr Metab* 1988;32:56-61.

[92] Lieber CS. Alcohol and the liver. In: Arias IM, Frenkel MS, Wilson JHP, eds. Liver Annual-VI. Amsterdam: *Excerpta Medica,* 1987: 163-240.

[93] Dutta SK, Miller PA, Greenberg LB, Levander OA. Selenium and acute alcoholism. *Am J Nutr* 1983;38:21-9.

[94] Whanger PD. Selenium and the brain: A review. *Nutr Neurosci* 2001;4:81-97.

[95] Bodnar LM, Wisner KL. Nutrition and depression: implications for improving mental health among childbearing-aged women. *Biol Psychiatry* 2005;58(9):679-85.

[96] Hawkes WC, Hornbostel L. Effects of dietary selenium on mood in healthy men living in a metabolic research unit. *Biol Psychiatry* 1996;39:121-8.

[97] Finley JW, Penland JG. Adequacy or deprivation of dietary selenium in healthy men: clinical and psychological findings. *J Trace Elem Exp Med* 1998;11:11-27.

[98] Benton D, Cook R. Selenium supplementation improves mood in a double-blind crossover trial. *Biol Psychiatry* 1991;29:1-92-1098.

[99] Brtkova A, Brtko J. Selenium: metabolism and endocrines (minireview). *Endocrine Regulations* 1996;30:117-28.

[100] Shor-Posner G, Lecusay R, Miguez MJ, Moreno-Black G, Zhang G, Rodriguez N, Burbano X, Baum M, Wilkie F. Psychological burden in the era of HAART: impact of selenium therapy. *Int J Psychiatry Med* 2003;33(1):55-69.

[101] Sher L. Role of thyroid hormones in the effects of selenium on mood, behavior, and cognitive function. *Med Hypoth* 2001;57:480-3.

[102] Sher L. Depression and suicidal behavior in alcohol abusing adolescents: possible role of selenium deficiency. *Minerva Pediatr.* 2008;60(2):201-9.

[103] Hong LL, Tian DP, Su M, Shen XN, Gao Y. Effect of selenium deficiency on the F344 inbred line offspring rats' neuro-behavior, ability of learning and memory. *Wei Sheng Yan Jiu* 2006;35(1):54-8.

[104] Rayman M, Thompson A, Warren-Perry M, Galassini R, Catterick J, Hall E, Lawrence D, Bliss J. Impact of selenium on mood and quality of life: a randomized, controlled trial. *Biol Psychiatry* 200615;59(2):147-54.

[105] Benton D. Selenium intake, mood and other aspects of psychological functioning. *Nutr Neurosci.* 2002;5(6):363-74.

[106] Chen J, Berry MJ. Selenium and selenoproteins in the brain and brain diseases. *J Neurochem.* 2003;86(1):1-12.

In: Suicidal Behavior in Alcohol and Drug Abuse...
Editors: L. Sher, A. Vilens, pp. 407-422
ISBN: 978-1-60876-919-3

Chapter 23

SOCIO-POLITICAL DILEMMAS: ALCOHOL/SUBSTANCE ABUSE AND SUICIDE

Said Shahtahmasebi
The Good Life Research Centre Trust, Rangiora, New Zealand

ABSTRACT

Research has long focused on the relationship between depression and suicide, the literature also links alcohol and drugs as causes of depression thus inferring a causal relationship to suicide. However, there is some doubt as to the true nature of the relationship between depression and suicide. Therefore, a weak depression-suicide link would undermine the alcohol/drug abuse-suicide scenario (and other suicide scenarios which are based on depression and mental illness). As discussed elsewhere the whole approach to suicide research will need to be evaluated to benefit current health and social policies and future policy development. Indeed, there is anecdotal evidence highlighting the relationship between an understanding of the dynamics of human behaviour and the current policy of insisting on manipulating the perceived link between mental health and suicide to reduce the suicide rate. The role alcohol plays in the process of suicide, it is argued, may be related to the means and method of suicide and not the cause of suicide. To place emphasis on the alcohol-suicide link would be repeating the depression-suicide link leading to a large volume of research but very little understanding of suicide as a process of decision making. Furthermore, it diverts attention from other relationships e.g. between alcohol/drugs with the economy, culture, society and social perceptions and expectations. In other words, despite the harmful effects of drugs, drinking alcohol and substance taking (e.g. party pills) are socially acceptable. This chapter provides a discussion of the relevant issues surrounding human behaviour and argues that, at least in part, the dynamics of the decision making process are motivated by social, educational, and economic policies.

Introduction

The relationship between alcohol and suicide is not a clear one. Suicide has been associated with mental ill-health and depression (e.g. see [1-5]). Regardless of its short-term inhibition properties and its association with a state of happiness, alcohol is a depressant [6]. It is, therefore, reasonable to assume and pursue a line of enquiry into the contribution of alcohol to the suicide rates. However, as in the depression-suicide scenario, the alcohol-suicide studies have, on average relied on those admitted to hospital accident and emergency wards (emergency rooms) or specialised clinics for overdose or the treatment of addiction. For the most part we are not sure of the population from which some patients may be reported to have attempted or committed suicide. It is important to have identified and have an estimate of this population in order to calculate the proportion of committed or attempted suicides where alcohol would have been involved. Nevertheless, some authors have claimed that the alcohol-suicide causal relationship is well documented (e.g. see [7]), whilst others (e.g. see [8]) reported a lack of evidence to support this link.

On the other hand, drinking alcohol is so well embedded in our culture that, not only does it feature in most aspects of our lives but it has its own culture: *the drinking culture*. Our entire lives appear to have been designed around alcohol: we celebrate with a drink or two; we attempt to cope with depression and stress with a drink or two; social life without alcohol is unthinkable to such an extent that the social culture and traditions have changed accordingly. For example, the shifting of emphasis and word association is fairly evident in phrases such as 'merry Christmas' and 'happy hour'! The former is associated with an increased consumption of alcohol through a special occasion whilst the latter due to reduced costs (most pubs and bars sell half-price alcoholic beverages during a daily period they call 'happy hour'). A drinking culture is encouraged within all sections of society including the medical establishment who have helped the alcohol industry by proclaiming the protective effects of alcohol against heart disease, e.g. drinking moderate amounts of red wine. On the other hand, there is ample evidence to support the adverse consequences of alcohol on health outcomes (e.g. see [9]). The literature lacks a critical approach. Alcohol/drug abuse are decision outcomes governed by the dynamics of human behaviour. The relevant issues of dynamics such as the feed-back effect are discussed elsewhere [10-13]. Due to the nature of addiction, the dynamics of decision making in the population of substance abusers may be different to the general population and that of the suicide completers. For example, while pain, trauma and distress might be presumed sufficient reasons for suicidal behaviour in some sections of the population, the dynamics of addiction might be operating in a different direction e.g. the need to satisfy "cravings" will heighten the instinct for survival rather than non-survival despite possible suicidal thoughts. By the same token some of the proposed evidence for the alcohol-suicide link has been based on studies of suicide attempters where alcohol had been involved [14, 15]. But, we know for example, that suicide attempters and suicide completers are not from the same population [16-18]. We also know that alcohol features prominently as part of the method of suicide (e.g. in an overdose).

The question that arises is whether appropriate questions have been asked by concentrating solely on alcohol as a cause of suicide. More specifically, it is proposed in this chapter that a more appropriate line of enquiry may be in the context of human behaviour in relation to drinking patterns and suicide.

SUICIDE

Suicide is a major public health concern globally. In some countries it ranks between the first and third leading cause of death [19, 20]. The suicide literature provides a historical, cultural, religious and philosophical background to suicide e.g. see [21, 22]. For example, Ventegodt and Merrick [22] suggest that in some cultures suicide was viewed as a legitimate way out albeit to restore honour, as a rectification for mistakes or unforgivable acts, or a as solution for difficult circumstances e.g. to avoid committing other unforgivable acts. All the major religions forbid suicide; in most western societies, suicide and suicidal thoughts and contemplation is viewed negatively and correlated with mental illness. However, Ventegodt and Merrick [22] rightly argue that life and death are real outcomes that provide real choices to think about and are relevant to good living and very sound considerations. Indeed, making a choice is a process and processes are by nature dynamic involving other social and economic and environmental processes. Although all the major religions warn against suicide nevertheless these are presented as stern warnings with severe eternal consequences. But at the end of the day the choice is left to the individual "whoever commit suicide..." or "he who commits suicide..." will be punished in hell by the same method used for suicide. Therefore, as argued elsewhere [23, 24], suicide is the outcome of a decision making process. Making a decision is often governed by individual characteristics, social, economic and environmental processes [25].

In New Zealand, like other countries, there has been a long established view of the direction of causality from mental illness, specifically depression to suicide. This has been achieved by the hasty reporting of so called research and in particular the media's slant and uncritical reporting. In announcing a $6.4 million campaign to reduce the impact of depression, the New Zealand Government claimed "We know that up to 90% of suicides are *caused* by depression and that each year 500 New Zealanders are dying by suicide." The Government further claimed "The World Health Organisation has predicted that by the year 2020, depression will be second only to cardiovascular disease, in contributing to the global burden of disease. We must tackle this problem head on and the National Depression Initiative will go a long way to achieving this objective." [http://www.beehive.govt.nz/View Document.aspx?DocumentID=27352]. This announcement is a reflection of the ineffectiveness of health and social policies in reducing cardiovascular disease. However, a more conservative estimate of depression in the population suggests up to one in four women and one in ten men can expect to experience depression at some time in their lives [http://www.everybody.co.nz/page-75c9ff3f-7aa4-4b07-b63d-eaf5d92b88bb.aspx]. Applying these estimates to the New Zealand 2001 population estimates for males and females aged 15-85+ in 2001 yields over one hundred and forty-five thousands males and over three hundred and eighty-eight thousands females may be suffering from depression. If depression is such a strong causal factor then should we not expect a much larger suicide mortality than the 500 quoted by the government? It is not surprising that when suicide occurs the public mindset automatically blames depression/mental illness as the cause. The wisdom of the uncritical acceptance of this causal relationship was also challenged in earlier papers [23, 24]. Within the suicide literature, despite the large volume of work, criticisms have been aired that our knowledge of suicide is based on scant scientific evidence [26-28]. The study design and the quality of data have been cited as being responsible for the ambiguities in the evidence. One of the consequences of accepting this relationship to explain suicide is to concentrate on building a case that would associate the suicide case with mental illness. Given the public mindset it would be only too easy to suggest a link to mental illness after the event. For example, in suicide research Bronisch and Wittchen [29] suggest no direct association between depression and suicide, Beautrais [30-32] claims that depression and mental illness are the cause of suicide, Khan et al [33] claim that antidepressants do not reduce suicide and may increase the risk of suicide while Hall et al [34] claim that antidepressants reduce suicide rates. The latter study [34] compared the first point in the time series with the last point which happened to be lower than the first point and did not make much of the upward trend of suicide rates in between. Suicide data, in particular those based on psychological autopsy type investigations such as Beautrais [30-32], are often plagued with a high degree of bias, as well as the confounding and compounding of random effects such as error-in-variables with the structural error. Given the current public mindset, helped by the medical model and the media, that depression causes suicide, the collection of data on suicide cases after the event from friends and relatives will be highly biased towards mental ill-health as in the Canterbury Suicide Project [30-32]. These studies have failed to address the methodological issues related to design, data collection and analysis, thus, resulting in misleading conclusions. Furthermore, the NZ Medical Journal claims depression is a common, serious and significant illness and links it to suicide and recommends medication [http://www.nzma.org.nz/journal/117-1206/1200/]. It is not surprising to hear that young people have been prescribed antidepressants including preschool children. But more alarming is the prescribing of antidepressants to children under a year old [http://www.nzherald.co.nz/section/1/story.cfm?c_id=1&objectid=10462684].

Viewed as an illness of the mind, suicide research has, over and above depression, followed many directions such as a link with fatty acids [35, 36], eating disorders and anorexia nervosa, [37, 38], persons with intellectual disability [39, 40], cannabis and alcohol misuse [39, 41-43] , allergy symptoms [44] and clinical settings [42, 45], also see [23] for more categories. Pharmacological treatment of mental illness, depression and suicidal behaviour on its own may be controversial [46] others suggest holistic medicine as a more effective treatment [47-50].

There is, however, some evidence to support the view that self-harm or parasuicide has a different distribution to that of suicide [16-18]. There is no doubt that there will be an overlap between the two populations perhaps due to a suicide attempt going fatally wrong, or, conversely a failed first attempt. Clearly, the hospitalisation rates may not be taken as an indicator of suicide rates and the two populations are different.

Alcohol and Suicide

The literature suggests a link between alcohol and suicide and suicide attempts [7, 14, 42, 43, 51-55]. Studies of suicide or parasuicides which are searching for a link with alcohol consumption often conclude that consumption prior to the suicide attempt is a major risk factor [14, 51, 52]. They go on to recommend that prevention, treatment and future research should take serious note of this relationship. However, unless the authorities are aware of an impending suicide so that drinking prior to suicide may be identified, it will be an impossible task to monitor all drinking at all times. On the other hand, knowledge of an impending suicide dictates appropriate intervention rather than wait for the pre-suicide drinking to take place.

It has been claimed that the social studies of suicide have missed alcohol as a risk factor [53, 54]. It appears that the supporting evidence often comes from admissions to hospital, psychiatric or alcohol treatment units for attempted suicide [7, 14, 15, 51, 56]. For example, Rossow and Amundsen [56] suggest a strong link between alcohol abuse and suicide in Norwegian conscripts. Suicide in the army has been discussed elsewhere [57, 58] which suggests drug (including alcohol) abuse may be a first attempt to deal with life issues. Furthermore, alcohol is a depressant agent and thus it is linked to suicide: alcohol dependence leads to less self-esteem and hence depression and suicide [59]. Unfortunately, similar to the studies of the depression-suicide link, studies of the alcohol-suicide relationship have in the main been focussed on admissions to hospital or treatment units for either suicide attempts or the treatment of alcoholism. The pitfalls of suicide research were briefly mentioned in the introduction and have been discussed elsewhere [10, 13, 23, 24, 57, 58, 60]. Indeed, there are examples of authors not escaping such pitfalls when pursuing a psychological autopsy and interviewing relatives of suicide cases to conclude statistical significance of alcohol abuse in suicide (e.g. see [55]). One of the methodological issues associated with data obtained from a third party about a suicide case is its objectivity, accuracy, and validity. Information obtained in this way cannot be corroborated because the case is no longer alive (e.g. see [10]).

There is, however, variation in the literature on how the alcohol-suicide relationship is emphasised. The literature may, in general, be divided into alcohol consumption and parasuicide, alcohol addiction and completed suicide, and alcohol overdosing. For example, Flensborg-Madsen and colleagues[61] claimed that alcohol abuse disorder increases the risk of completed suicide. Others link alcohol with self-harm and suicide attempts (e.g. see [14, 15, 51]), and alcohol overdosing in addicts (e.g. see [56, 62]).

Suokas and Lonnqvist [15] reported that a high proportion of suicide attempters admitted to emergency rooms had high blood alcohol levels. They also reported that alcohol consumption shortly before and at the time of parasuicide was common, 3.3.% of the alcohol users went on to commit suicide after 5.5 years, and that compared with those who had not consumed alcohol, the suicide risk of drinkers was assessed as less severe and they were less often referred to a psychiatrist. Clearly, either the health care professionals had not recognised the important role of alcohol consumption in suicide, or those who had consumed alcohol prior to parasuicide had not intended to commit suicide. If the latter is true then the relationship between alcohol and suicide should have been questioned and re-assessed.

Others have attempted to provide evidence of an association between alcohol consumption and suicide by drawing conclusions from the effect of intoxication (e.g. see [63]). Intoxication and alcohol overdosing is, in its own right, an outcome and may be viewed a type of self-harm. Intoxication is a consequence of alcohol overdose and it is frequently a choice that is made by individuals for whatever reason.

Bronisch and Wittchen [29] found no statistical association between depression and suicide but they suggested that the link with suicide is through the combined effect of anxiety and depression. An important issue that arises is that suicide, depression and anxiety are all outcomes which may be subject to influence by other factors. For example, the literature suggests a relationship between anxiety and alcohol [64-66]. It is suggested that alcohol may be used as a coping agent for anxiety and other disorders such as phobias (e.g. [64, 65])

possibly leading to alcohol dependence. On the other hand, Flensborg-Madsen and colleagues [61] claimed that psychiatric disorders (e.g. anxiety) are neither sufficient nor necessary causes in the association between alcohol disorder and an increased risk of completed suicide. Thus, the three way relationship between depression, anxiety and suicide becomes more complicated. Whether or not there is a direct effect on suicide, it appears that the reasons for alcohol consumption may vary from group to group. For example, alcoholics and addicts may co-administer and overdose alcohol with other drugs for a maximum "effect", while within the suicide attempters population, alcohol consumption may well be a motivator (e.g. see [52, 67-69]) to carry out a decision made previously to commit suicide. It is therefore, unwise to infer cause and effect.

Drug abuse and multiple drugs co-administered with alcohol have also been linked to suicide and suicidal behaviour [69, 70] in particular within the addict population. Furthermore, the consumption of alcohol and drug abuse have been linked, in other words, heavy drinkers are more likely to experiment with drugs [11, 70, 71]. It is not surprising that within the addict population co-administering of alcohol has been reported and thus linked to suicide through overdosing (e.g. see [62]). However, Hayward et al. [8] suggested no significant association between alcohol and suicide. It is plausible that overdosing is an artefact of drug abuse rather than an intention to commit suicide. Although the literature does not appear to confidently clarify the causal relationship between alcohol and suicide, nevertheless, the issues that have arisen are, in themselves, important results.

The resulting issues and questions relate to the dynamics of alcohol consumption [68, 72]. In other words, does the literature provide sufficient evidence to assume a direct and independent alcohol-effect on suicide behaviour in general (e.g. self-harm, suicide attempt, completed suicide)?

To understand and develop theories on the alcohol-suicide relationship we must try to understand the dynamics of human behaviour; more specifically, we must explore the alcohol-suicide relationship in the context of the social culture of alcohol.

THE CULTURE OF DRINKING ALCOHOL

Alcohol is associated with both positive and negative life outcomes [73]: drink and be merry (in bad times), or drink and celebrate the good times. Throughout history, for its property of reducing inhibitions, alcohol has been portrayed as beneficial (e.g. see [74]). Alcohol has been used both as a social enhancer and a remedy for maladies as well as the positive psychological benefits of light to moderate alcohol use including reducing stress and increasing happiness [75]. It is not surprising that in the public psyche "good health", "one for the road", "a night cap", "cheers", "to good fortunes" and "to happiness" are some of the wishful phrases synonymous with an alcohol drinking culture which tend to mask the consequences of drinking alcohol on health and social behaviour.

Alcohol has been associated with morbidity including cancer and heart disease, and mortality [9, 76, 77]. The literature links smoking with drinking. Both smoking and drinking are strongly associated with young people's experimenting with and future use of illicit drugs [78-80]. In addition to smoking, individual characteristics, parental drinking patterns and socio-economic variables have also been used to predict drinking patterns e.g. see [81-83].

For example, drinking has been associated with demographic, economic, social and environmental factors; smoking and other drug use, TV advertising; emotional and psychological (parental and peer pressure influence) factors [71, 84-93]. Smoking behaviour, in turn, has been associated with the psycho-social effect of wishing to belong to a peer social group [94], self-esteem and parental smoking behaviour [95], the psychological process of risk assessment and risk taking [96-98]. Others suggest smoking/drinking behaviour is likely to be influenced through the family environment, which affects psychological well-being, adjustment and problem behaviour, perceived academic performance and school conduct [99, 100]. Furthermore, the prevalence of smoking is associated with the subjective effect of smoking e.g. feelings of higher self-esteem and being in control [95, 101], and a perceived 'benefit' effect as utilised in the risk models [96, 97].

However, current knowledge is based on evidence from cross-sectional studies using survey designs. Drinking, like smoking, is the outcome of a decision process. An earlier paper [11], using longitudinal data, reported that drinking patterns in the teenage population were influenced by the dynamics of individual and social behaviour. For example, heavy drinking appeared to be associated with age, parental involvement, drugs experimentation, being a male; and a lack of concern about own health.

It is of interest, but not surprising, to note the parental effect on drinking patterns. As mentioned above, the family environment provides not only the main but also the early exposure to the culture of drinking alcohol. Dawson et al. ([89]) reported a positive association between the age that a person had their first drink with future heavy drinking habits.

The home environment often promotes first exposure to alcohol. Outside of the family lifestyle, tobacco and alcohol, despite their negative economic, social and health consequences, are also well established economic avenues for generating revenue by governments (e.g. see [102-104]). The individual's '*freedom*' of choice has been a popular political justification of keeping this avenue open to the treasury. However, since the 1970s most governments have caved in under pressure from scientists, health professionals and anti-smoking groups, and cigarette packets began to carry a health warning. Over subsequent decades, this health warning has developed into anti-smoking legislation to include, in some countries, a total ban on tobacco advertising, a ban on dispensing tobacco products (vending machines), and a ban on smoking in enclosed public places such as offices, cafes, restaurants and pubs. Alcoholic drinks appear to have followed a reverse pattern: not only are there no health warnings visible on alcoholic drink bottles but that drinking is encouraged within the media, in particular the entertainment medium [86]. In most western societies, alcoholic beverages may be consumed anywhere and anytime. Furthermore, the 'happy hour' when alcohol may be purchased at half price, is a regular feature in most clubs and pubs. Governments, health ministries and health promotion schemes appear to recommend guidelines for *safe* alcohol consumption. Commonly, most anti-drinking campaigns are often associated with drink-driving prevention schemes. In New Zealand, the message of the anti-drinking campaign condones drinking which explicitly declares "it is not the drinking, it is how we're drinking". Additional encouragement appears to come from an unlikely source; the medical profession's proclamation, widely reported through the popular media, that alcohol is a preventive agent against heart disease.

Alcohol and Suicide Revisited

It is believed that alcohol helps diminish or reduce inhibitions enabling individuals to behave out of character [72]. "Inhibitions" are themselves behaviour outcomes governed by an individuals' characteristics and social ideals/perceptions and expectations. However, alcohol has long been used as a motivator or "Dutch courage" in a variety of social settings leading to various outcomes such as aggression, rape, and suicide [52, 67-69].

It may be argued that there are two main issues with this scenario. First, the consequences of drinking, over and above morbidity, mortality and issues related to addiction, are the possible changes in conduct and behaviour that are not normally associated with an individual. Second, when people intend to perform an out of character or out of ordinary task, be it violence against themselves or another person, cope with stress or stand up to their boss, or perform on stage they may intentionally drink alcohol prior to performing the task. The literature acknowledges the latter as "Dutch courage" [67, 72, 105-109]. For example, alcohol has been used to motivate courage to perform tasks perceived by individuals as difficult e.g. getting into a fight [70], or even going through a planned suicide attempt. In other words, it is less likely that without the motivator (alcohol) the individuals would have started a fight or made a suicide attempt.

As mentioned above, alcohol has been promoted as having medicinal properties (e.g. see [74]). Alcohol may also be looked upon as a first step treatment against emotional and psychological downturn. Alcohol has been used in self-medication [64], and as a mediator [65]. On the other hand, the consumption of alcohol may lead to various emotional and mental health problems e.g. consumption of alcohol may lead to alcohol dependence, cause phobia and tension [66, 109]. A question that arises is which comes first; alcohol dependence or the life event e.g. does phobia lead to heavy alcohol consumption or drinking increase tension and phobia [72, 109]? Once again, the cause and effect is not as clear-cut, i.e. whether alcohol dependence is the result of anxiety and other disorders, or alcohol dependence is the cause of mental and behaviour disorders. The relationship between alcohol and mental health must be re-evaluated.

Due to the social culture of drinking discussed above, including the mixed and conflicting messages from the "experts", politicians, and health and socio-economic policies, alcohol and life events may have been highly intertwined to confuse cause and effect. For example, consumption of alcohol to cope with life events such as stress and phobia [72, 109] may lead to higher levels of stress and alcohol dependence. Similarly, Finch and Munro [68] argue that a negative social attitude of irresponsible drinking has had more of an impact on the intoxicated victims than intoxicated defendants. On the other hand gender may well be a confounder effect as the majority of alcohol related rape victims are women. In other words, it appears that socially the onus is on women to be more careful as opposed to the crime that has been committed. While, in legal defence, alcohol has been blamed as the cause of irresponsible and criminal behaviour, the reverse should also be argued strongly: alcohol is being used as a motivator. In other words, those who commit anti-social or criminal acts whilst under the influence of drugs/alcohol chose to drink alcohol and/or used drugs to be empowered. We chose to drink inspite the consequences of dinking alcohol. When exploring the relationship between alcohol and alcoholism with other life events then the dynamic interaction between the consequences of drinking and 'choice' must be included in the study.

The addiction-suicide relationship appears vague. A medical model of suicide assumes that the consequences of heavy drinking and addiction are the individual's loss of control, depression and mental illness which lead to suicide or suicidal behaviour. On the other hand, it is plausible that the craving that is caused by addiction sensitises and motivates the desire to satisfy the craving first and foremost. In other words, the process of decision making is, despite the consequences of addiction, influenced by temporal dependencies, i.e. the duration spent in a state of addiction influences the probability of survival. It is argued that such a feedback effect will lead to the maintenance of addiction. For example, in the context of smoking it is reported that a cessation will often be accompanied by feelings of unease and anxiety [101, 110]. The feedback effect of unease and anxiety is more smoking rather than suicide or suicidal behaviour.

However, those who drink alcohol, smoke or use/abuse other substances/drugs form a population similar to those with depression/mental illness, the military or students, and like in any other population an expected proportion will commit suicide. And like any other population the expected proportion of suicide should not be based on estimates of those visiting psychiatric and mental health units. To investigate the path to suicide, we must explore the process of decision making (see [10, 57, 58, 60]).

The literature on suicide makes the connection with alcohol by suggesting that alcohol was involved [8, 15, 52]. In an earlier paper [23], it was reported that addiction was the reason for 13% of the sample of completed suicide cases to have had a psychiatric record. In a subsequent paper [24], it was reported that out of all the suicide cases completed over the period September-December 204, only one had alcohol dependency for which the case had sought treatment. But two cases were reported to have had blood alcohol levels of 1.5 times and 2.5 times that of the legal driving limit. Similarly, Hayward and colleagues [8] reported no association between alcohol consumption and suicide.

On the other hand, it may be perceived that alcohol is associated with suicide through overdosing. An overdose of prescribed medication with alcohol is one of the more frequently used methods of committing suicide [62]. However, death as a result of co-administering alcohol with other depressant drugs such as heroin in the population of addicts will have a different dynamic than that of the suicide population. The former is preventable [111]. On the other hand, although alcohol is a depressant [6], the causal relationship between alcohol and depression is vague i.e. whether depressive spells are the consequences of alcohol consumption or vice versa i.e. to alleviate symptoms of depression with a few drinks. Similarly, the longer the duration of drug dependency the higher the dependency and the higher the likelihood of an increased dose (either in frequency or quantity) to alleviate the dependency symptoms e.g. depression [62]. Although, Darke and colleagues [62] referred to this phenomena as overdosing by opium addicts and linked it to the duration of opium/drug dependency, higher dependency and higher levels of alcohol consumption. By the same token it is likely that drug users were heavy drinkers at the onset of drug use and before addiction.

Therefore, involvement of alcohol in a suicide or suicide attempt may not necessarily be the cause but the motivator or as a means to commit the act of suicide, or, the result of overdosing behaviour.

Equally likely, as discussed above, alcohol is perceived as a personal and social treatment of an individual's adverse life events and misfortunes. Therefore, self-medication with alcohol may be an unconscious decision to resolve one's problems and prevent suicidal behaviour. The reverse may also be true, i.e. that the short-term calming effect of alcohol may make it easier to act on impulse and choose death rather than life. The longer-term consequences of such an approach in dealing with life's problems are alcoholism and alcohol related morbidity and death. It is likely that suicide may have been considered early at the onset of heavy drinking. It is unlikely that alcoholism can be claimed as the cause of suicide.

CONCLUSION

The substantive issues raised in this chapter are addressed formally elsewhere [12]. In the context of this chapter, the issue is the clarification of the substantive issues before attempting to interpret observed behaviour. As mentioned above, we need to consider the feedback effect in our attempts to explore the relationship between drinking habits with life events or outcomes. For example, overdosing may well be due to the level of drug dependence. Higher levels of dependence, in turn, may be governed by the length of time as a drug user. In other words, the longer a drug user, the higher the level of drug dependence and the higher the dosage. As reported earlier [11], teenage heavy-drinking is associated with drug experimentation. It is not uncommon to co-administer drugs with alcohol and, therefore, overdosing may be an artefact of the culture of heavy drinking and drug use. Overdosing that leads to hospitalisation or are fatal may not be viewed as intentional suicide or suicide attempts. In Darke's study [62] there were no reported intentions of self-harm or suicide.

It is clear that, to reduce drug dependence and death rates in the population, an understanding of the dynamics of a decision to use drugs must be sought. Otherwise, like in all other health, social, and economic areas, policy making becomes only a patching job. In other words, new policies are ofen in response to symptoms that are the result of the feedback effect from earlier policies aimed at addressing an issue e.g. alcohol-health issues. It is argued [25] that such an approach will exacerbate the dynamics of human behaviour which will make researchers and policy makers and the public the problem rather than part of any solution.

Although there is ample evidence to support the ill-effects of alcohol at a social and individual level, drinking is a choice and is the outcome of a decision process. Governments across the world (including the British Government e.g. see [105]) blame alcohol for all manner of criminal behaviour and ill-health but social and economic policies do not reflect this concern. The opposite may be true that they promote alcohol consumption. Therefore, should we be blaming alcohol for our social ills or the society that produces the drinkers?

REFERENCES

[1] Asukai N. Suicide and mental disorders. *Psychiatry & Clinical Neurosciences.* 1995;49(Suppl 1):S91-97.

[2] Besseghini VH. Depression and suicide in children and adolescents. *Annals of the New York Academy of Sciences.* 1997;816:94-98.

[3] Conwell Y, Duberstein PR, Caine ED. Risk factors for suicide in later life. *Biol Psychiatry.* Aug 1 2002;52(3):193-204.

[4] Lonnqvist JK, Henriksson MM, Isometsa ET, et al. Mental disorders and suicide prevention. *Psychiatry & Clinical Neurosciences.* 1995;49(Suppl 1):S111-116.

[5] Maris RW. Suicide prevention in adults (age 30-65). *Suicide & Life-Threatening Behavior.* 1995;25(1):171-179.
[6] Pettinati H. Antidepressant treatment of co-occurring depression and alcohol dependence. *Biological Psychiatry.* 2004;56(10):785-792.
[7] Caces F, Harford T. Time series analysis of alcohol consumption and suicide mortality in the United States, 1934-1987. *Journal of studies on alcohol.* 1998;59(4).
[8] Hayward L, Zubrick SR, Silburn S. Blood alcohol levels in suicide cases. *British Medical Journal.* 1992;46(3):256-260.
[9] Duffy JC, ed. *Alcohol and illness: the epidemiological view point.* Edinburgh: Edinburgh University Press; 1992. Health and Society.
[10] Shahtahmasebi S. Suicide Research and Adolescent Suicide Trends in New Zealand. *TheScientificWorldJournal.* 2008;8:287-302.
[11] Shahtahmasebi S, Berridge D. Teenage drinking patterns: A longitudinal analysis. *Int J Adolesc Med & Health.* 2009;21(3):forthcoming.
[12] Shahtahmasebi S, Berridge D. Conceptualising behaviour: a practical guide to data analysis. New York: Nova Sci; 2009.
[13] Shahtahmasebi S, Shahtahmasebi R. Society, Change and Suicide. *Journal of Alternative Medicine Research.* 2009;2010:2 (1):forthcoming.
[14] Hawton K, Fagg J, McKeown SP. Alcoholism, alcohol and attempted suicide. *Alcohol and Alcoholism.* 1989;24(1):3-9.
[15] Suokas J, Lonnqvist J. Suicide attempts in which alcohol is involved: a special group in general hospital emergency rooms. *Acta Psychiatrica Scandinavica.* 1995;91(1):36-40.
[16] Favazza A. The coming of age of self-mutilation. *J Nerv Ment Diseases.* 1998;186:250-268.
[17] Pattisson E, Kahan J. The deliberate self-harm syndrome. *Am J Psychiatry.* 1983;107:867-872.
[18] Simeon D, Stein J, Holander E. Depersonalization disorder and self-injurious behaviour. *J Clin. Psychiatry.* 1998;56((suppl 4)):36-39.
[19] Mann JJ. Forword. In: Merrick J, Zalsman G, eds. *Suicidal behaviour in adolescence: an international perspective* Tel Aviv: Freund Publishing House LTD; 2005:1-2.
[20] Merrick J, Zalsman G. Suicide from an international perspective. *TheScientificWorldJournal.* 2005;5:888-890.
[21] Maharajh HD, Abdool PS. Cultural aspects of suicide. *TheScientificWorldJOURNAL.* 2005;5:736-746.
[22] Ventegodt S, Merrick J. Philosophy of life and suicide: to be or not to be is still the question. In: J M, G Z, eds. *Suicidal behaviour in adolescence: an international perspective.* Tel Aviv: Freund Publishing House LTD; 2005:9-17.
[23] Shahtahmasebi S. Suicides by Mentally Ill People. *TheScientificWorldJournal.* 2003;3:684-693.
[24] Shahtahmasebi S. Suicides in New Zealand. *TheScientificWorldJournal.* 2005;5:527-534.
[25] Shahtahmasebi S. The Good life: A holistic approach to the health of the population. *ScientificWorldJournal.* 2006;6:2117-2132.
[26] Cutcliffe JR. Research endeavours into suicide: a need to shift the emphasis. *Br J Nurs.* Jan 23-Feb 12 2003;12(2):92-99.

[27] De Leo D. Why are we not getting any closer to preventing suicide? *Br J Psychiatry.* Nov 2002;181:372-374.
[28] Institute of Medicine. *Reducing Suicide: A National Imperative.* Washington DC 2002.
[29] Bronisch T, Wittchen H. Suicidal ideation and suicide attempts: comorbidity with depression, anxiety disorders, and substance abuse disorder. *European archives of psychiatry and clinical neuroscience.* 1994;244(2):93-98.
[30] Beautrais AL. *Serious suicide attempts in young people: a case control study* [PhD]. Christchurch: Dept. of Psycholigical Medicine, Christchurch School of Medicine; 1996.
[31] Beautrais AL. Suicides and serious suicide attempts: two populations or one? *Psychol Med.* 2001;31:837-845.
[32] Beautrais AL, Joyce PR, Mulder RT. The Canterbury suicide project: Aims, overview and progress. *Community Mental Health in New Zealand.* 1994;8(2):32-39.
[33] Khan A, Warner HA, Brown WA. Symptom Reduction and Suicide Risk in Patients Treated With Placebo in Antidepressant Clinical Trials: An Analysis of the Food and Drug Administration Database. *Arch Gen Psychiatry.* 2000;57:311-317.
[34] Hall WD, Mant A, Mitchell PB, Rendle VA, Hickie IB, McManus P. Association between antidepressant prescribing and suicide in Australia, 1991-2000: trend analysis. *BMJ.* 2003;326.
[35] Ainiyet J, Rybakowski J. [Low concentration level of total serum cholesterol as a risk factor for suicidal and aggressive behavior]. *Psychiatria Polska.* 1996;30(3):499-509.
[36] Brunner J, Parhofer KG, Schwandt P, Bronisch T. Cholesterol, essential fatty acids, and suicide. *Pharmacopsychiatry.* Jan 2002;35(1):1-5.
[37] Dancyger IF, Fornari VM. A review of eating disorders and suicide risk in adolescence. *TheScientificWorldJOURNAL.* 2005;5: 803-811.
[38] Meltzer HY, Cola PA. The pharmacoeconomics of clozapine: a review. *Journal of Clinical Psychiatry.* 1994;55(Suppl B):161-165.
[39] Maharajh HD, Konings M. Cannabis and suicidal behaviour among adolescents: a pilot study from Trinidad. *TheScientificWorldJOURNAL.* 2005;5:576-585.
[40] Merrick J, Merrick E, Morad M, Kendel I. Adolescents with intellectual disability and suicidal behaviour *TheScientificWorldJournal.* 2005; 5:724-728.
[41] Sher L. Risk and protective Factors for suicide in patients with alcholism. *TheScientificWorldJOURNAL.* 2006;6:1405-1411.
[42] Sher L. Alcohol and suicide: neurobiological and clinical aspects *TheScientificWorldJOURNAL.* 2006;6:700-706.
[43] Sher L. Relation between rates of geriatric suicide and consumption of alcohol beverages in European countries. *TheScientificWorldJOURNAL.* 2006;6:383-387.
[44] Postolache TT, Lapidus M, Sander ER, Langenberg PH, Robert G, al. e. Changes in allergy symptoms and depression scores are positively correlated in patients with recurrent mood disorders exposed to seasonal peaks in aeroallergens *TheScientificWorldJOURNAL.* 2007;7:1968-1977.
[45] Pompili M, Girardi P, Lester D, Tatarelli R. Suicide soon after generalizd tonic-clonic seizure. A possible Peri-Ictal Phenomenon? *TheScientificWorldJOURNAL.* 2006;6:356-360.
[46] Farley RL. Pharmacological treatment of major depressive disorder in adolescents. *TheScientificWorldJOURNAL.* 2005;5:420-426.

[47] Ventegodt S, Andersen N, Neikrug S, Kandel I, Merrick J. Clinical holistic medicine: holistc treatment of mental disorders. *TheScientificWorldJOURNAL.* 2005;5:427-445.
[48] Ventegodt S, Clausen B, Merrick J. Clinical Holistic Medicine: The Case Story of Anna. III. Rehabilitation of Philosophy of Life During Holistic Existential Therapy for Childhood Sexual Abuse. *TheScientificWorldJOURNAL.* 2006;6:2080-2091.
[49] Ventegodt S, Kandel I, Neikrug S, Merrick J. Clinical holistic medicine: the existential crisis- life crisis, stress, and burnout. *TheScientificWorldJOURNAL.* 2005;5:300-312.
[50] Ventegodt S, Merrick J. Suicide from a holistic point of view. *TheScientificWorld JOURNAL.* 2005;5:958-766.
[51] Borges G, Rosovsky H. Suicide attempts and alcohol consumption in an emergency room sample. *Journal of studies on alcohol.* 1996;57(5):543-548.
[52] Bennett S, Coggan C, Hooper R, Lovell C, Adams P. Presentations by youth to Auckland emergency departments following a suicide attempt. *Int J Ment Health Nurs.* Sep 2002;11(3):144-153.
[53] Skog OJ. Alcohol and suicide-Durkheim revisited. *Acta Sociologica.* 1991;34(3):193.
[54] Norstrom T. Impact of Alcohol, Divorce, and Unemployment on Suicide: A Multilevel Analysis. *Social Forces.* 1995;74:293.
[55] Kõlves K, Värnik A, Tooding L, Wasserman D. The role of alcohol in suicide: a case-control psychological autopsy study. *Psychological Medicine.* 2006;36(07):923-930.
[56] Rossow I, Amundsen A. Alcohol abuse and suicide: a 40-year prospective study of Norwegian conscripts. *Addiction.* 1995;90(5):685-691.
[57] Shahtahmasebi S. War, massive personal and social change and suicide. In: Sher L, ed. *War and suicide.* New York: Nova Sci; 2009.
[58] Shahtahmasebi S. A top-down society, the military and suicide. In: Sher L, ed. *Suicide in the military.* Vol forthcoming. New York: Nova Sci 2009.
[59] Kendall R. Alcohol and suicide. *Substance and alcohol actions/misuse.* 1983;4(2-3):121.
[60] Shahtahmasebi S. Can suicide be quantified and categorised? In: Sher L, ed. *Internet and Suicide.* Vol in press. New York: Nova Sci; 2008.
[61] Flensborg-Madsen T, Knop J, Mortensen EL, Becker U, Sher L, Gronbaek M. Alcohol use disorders increase the risk of completed suicide - Irrespective of other psychiatric disorders. A longitudinal cohort study. *Psychiatry Research.* May 2009;167(1-2):123-130.
[62] Darke S, Ross J, Hall W. Overdose among heroin users in Sydney, Australia: I. Prevalence and correlates of non-fatal overdose. *Addiction.* 1996;91(3):405-411.
[63] Rossow I, Ystgaard M, Hawton K, et al. Cross-national comparisons of the association between alcohol consumption and deliberate self-harm in adolescents. *Suicide and Life-Threatening Behavior.* Dec 2007;37(6):605-615.
[64] Bolton JM, Robinson J, Sareen J. Self-medication of mood disorders with alcohol and drugs in the National Epidemiologic Survey on Alcohol and Related Conditions. *Journal of Affective Disorders.* Jun 2009;115(3):367-375.
[65] Goldsmith AA, Tran GQ, Smith JP, Howe SR. Alcohol expectancies and drinking motives in college drinkers: Mediating effects on the relationship between generalized anxiety and heavy drinking in negative-affect situations. *Addictive Behaviors.* 2009;34(6/7):505-513.

[66] Stevens S, Rist F, Gerlach AL. Influence of alcohol on the processing of emotional facial expressions in individuals with social phobia. *British Journal of Clinical Psychology.* Jun 2009;48:125-140.

[67] Evans C. Alcohol, violence and aggression. *Alcohol and Alcoholism.* 1980;15(3):104-117.

[68] Finch E, Munro V. The demon drink and the demonized woman: Socio-sexual stereotypes and responsibility attribution in rape trials involving intoxicants. *Social & Legal Studies.* 2007;16(4):591.

[69] Wilcox H, Conner K, Caine E. Association of alcohol and drug use disorders and completed suicide: an empirical review of cohort studies. *Drug and alcohol dependence.* 2004;76:11-19.

[70] Dawson D. Alcohol, Drugs, Fighting and Suicide Attempt/Ideation. *Addiction Research & Theory.* 1997;5(6):451 - 472.

[71] Grucza RA, Bierut LJ. Cigarette smoking and the risk for alcohol use disorders among adolescent drinkers. *Alcohol Clin Exp Res.* Dec 2006;30(12):2046-2054.

[72] Stockwell T, Bolderston H. Alcohol and phobias. *Addiction.* 1987;82(9):971-979.

[73] Murphy JG, McDevitt-Murphy ME, Barnett NP. Drink and be merry? Gender, life satisfaction, and alcohol consumption among college students. *Psychology of Addictive Behaviors.* 2005;19(2):184.

[74] Lowe G. Alcohol: a ppositive enhancer of pleasurable expectancies? *Addiction Controversies.* 1992:53.

[75] Baum-Baicker C. The psychological benefits of moderate alcohol consumption: a review of the literature. *Drug and alcohol dependence.* 1985;15(4):305.

[76] Marcus P, Newman B, Millikan R, Moorman P, Baird D, Qaqish B. The associations of adolescent cigarette smoking, alcoholic beverage consumption, environmental tobacco smoke, and ionizing radiation with subsequent breast cancer risk (United States). *Cancer Causes and Control.* 2000;11(3):271-278.

[77] Naranjo CA, Bremner KE. Behavioural correlates of alcohol intoxication. *Addiction.* 1993;88(1):25-35.

[78] Kosterman R. The dynamics of alcohol and marijuana initiation: patterns and predictors of first use in adolescence. *American Journal of Public Health.* Vol 90: Am Public Health Assoc; 2000:360-366.

[79] Rashad I, Kaestner R. Teenage sex, drugs and alcohol use: problems identifying the cause of risky behaviors. *J Health Econ.* 2004;23(3):493-503.

[80] Weinberg N, Rahdert E, Colliver J, Glantz M. Adolescent substance abuse: a review of the past 10 years. *J Am Acad Child Adolesc Psychiatry.* 1998;37(3):252-261.

[81] Peterson P, Hawkins J, Abbott R, Catalano R. Disentangling the Effects of Parental Drinking, Family Management, and Parental Alcohol Norms on Current Drinking by Black and White Adolescents. *J Res Adolesc.* 1994;4(2):203-227.

[82] White HR, McMorris BJ, Catalano RF, Fleming CB, Haggerty KP, Abbott RD. Increases in alcohol and marijuana use during the transition out of high school into emerging adulthood: The effects of leaving home, going to college, and high school protective factors. *J Stud Alcohol.* Nov 2006;67(6):810-822.

[83] Wilks J, Callan V, Austin D. Parent, Peer and Personal Determinants of Adolescent Drinking. *Addiction.* 1989;84(6):619-630.

[84] Agrawal A, Grant JD, Waldron M, et al. Risk for initiation of substance use as a function of age of onset of cigarette, alcohol and cannabis use: findings in a Midwestern female twin cohort. *Prev Med.* Aug 2006;43(2):125-128.

[85] Amonini C, Donovan RJ. The relationship between youth's moral and legal perceptions of alcohol, tobacco and marijuana and use of these substances. *Health Educ Res.* Apr 2006;21(2):276-286.

[86] Atkin C. Effects of televised alcohol messages on teenage drinking patterns. *J Adolesc Health Care.* 1990;11(1):10-24.

[87] Bates M, Labouvie E. Adolescent risk factors and the prediction of persistent alcohol and drug use into adulthood. *Alcohol Clin Exp Res.* 1997;21(5):944-950.

[88] Chuang YC, Ennett ST, Bauman KE, Foshee VA. Neighborhood influences on adolescent cigarette and alcohol use: mediating effects through parent and peer behaviors. *J Health Soc Behav.* Jun 2005;46(2):187-204.

[89] Dawson DA, Grant BF, Li TK. Impact of age at first drink on stress-reactive drinking. *Alcohol Clin Exp Res.* Jan 2007;31(1):69-77.

[90] de Visser RO, Rissel CE, Smith AM, Richters J. Sociodemographic correlates of selected health risk behaviors in a representative sample of Australian young people. *Int J Behav Med.* 2006;13(2):153-162.

[91] Engels RC, Scholte RH, van Lieshout CF, de Kemp R, Overbeek G. Peer group reputation and smoking and alcohol consumption in early adolescence. *Addict Behav.* Mar 2006;31(3):440-449.

[92] Loury S, Kulbok P. Correlates of alcohol and tobacco use among Mexican immigrants in rural North Carolina. *Fam Community Health.* Jul-Sep 2007;30(3):247-256.

[93] Orlando M, Tucker JS, Ellickson PL, Klein DJ. Concurrent use of alcohol and cigarettes from adolescence to young adulthood: an examination of developmental trajectories and outcomes. *Subst Use Misuse.* 2005;40(8):1051-1069.

[94] Sussman SC, Dent W. Group self-identification and adolescent cigarette smoking: a 1-year prospective study. *J Abnorm Psychol.* 1994;103(3):576-580.

[95] Murphy NT, Price CJ. The influence of self-esteem, parental smoking and living in tobacco production region on adolescent smoking behaviour. *J Sch Health.* 1988;58(10):401-405.

[96] Parsons JT, Siegel AW, Cousins JH. Late adolescent risk-taking: effect of perceived benefits and perceived risks on behavioural intentions and behavioural change. *J Adolesc.* 1997;20:381-392.

[97] Moore S, Gullone E. Predicting adolescent risk behaviour using a personalized cost-benefit analysis. *J Youth Adolesc.* 1996;25(3):343-359.

[98] Smith AMA, Rosenthal DA. Adolescents' perceptions of their risk environment. *J Adolesc.* 1995;18:229-245.

[99] Shek DT. Family environment and adolescent psychological well-being, school adjustment, and problem behaviour: a pioneer study in a Chinese context. *J Genet Psychol.* 1997;158(1):113-128.

[100] Upadhyaya HP, Deas D, Brady KT, Kruesi M. Cigarette smoking and psychiatric comorbidity in children and adolescents. *J Am Acad Child Adolesc Psychiatry.* Nov 2002;41(11):1294-1305.

[101] McNeill AD, Jarvis M, West R. Subjective effects of cigarette smoking in adolescents. *Psychopharmacology-(Berl).* 1987;92(1):115-117.

[102] Shahtahmasebi S. Teenage smoking: researching behaviour. *Int J of Psychology Research.* 2007;2(1/2).

[103] Shahtahmasebi S. Teenage smoking: what are the main issues? In: Lapointe MM, ed. *Adolescent Smoking and Health Research.* New York: Nova Sci; 2007:91-102.

[104] Shahtahmasebi S. Teenage smoking: longitudinal vs. cross-sectional modeling. In: Grenell RS, ed. *Adolescent Behaviour Research Studies.* New York: Nova Sci; 2007:77-107.

[105] Deehan A. Alcohol and crime. Crime reduction research series paper. 1999;3.

[106] Evans C. Alcohol and violence: Problems relating to methodology, statistics and causation. *Alcohol and Aggression.* 1986:138-160.

[107] Freed P, Rudolph S. Protecting Partial-Hospitalization Patients from Suicide. *Perspectives in Psychiatric Care.* 1998;34(2).

[108] Roche A. Drinking behavior: A multifaceted and multiphasic phenomenon. *Learning about drinking.* 2001:1-33.

[109] Stockwell T. Stress and alcohol. *Stress Medicine.* 1985;1(3).

[110] McNeill AD. The development of dependence on smoking in children. *Psychopharmacology-(Berl).* 1991;92(1):115-117.

[111] Zador D, Sunjic S, Darke S. Heroin-related deaths in New South Wales, 1992: toxicological findings and circumstances. *Medical Journal of Australia.* 1996;164(4):204-206.

Part VI. Substance Use Disorders and Suicide in Adolescents and the Elderly

In: Suicidal Behavior in Alcohol and Drug Abuse...
Editors: L. Sher, A. Vilens, pp. 425-441
ISBN: 978-1-60876-919-3

Chapter 24

SUBSTANCE ABUSE AND SUICIDE RISK AMONG ADOLESCENTS

Maurizio Pompili[1,2], Eleonora Piacentini[1], Marco Innamorati[3], Letizia Capezzali[1], Mariantonietta Milelli[1], Roberto Tatarelli[1] and David Lester[4]

[1]Sant'Andrea Hospital, Rome, Italy, Sapienza University of Rome, Rome, Italy
[2]Harvard Medical School, Boston, Massachusetts, USA
[3]Università Europea di Roma, Rome, Italy
[4]The Richard Stockton College of New Jersey, Pomona, New Jersey, USA

ABSTRACT

The World Health Organization has declared that suicide is the third leading cause after car accidents and cancer among those aged 15-24. Suicide in youths has become a public health problem that remains unresolved. Several risk factors have been proposed by researchers, and substance abuse is one of the best known of these. Experimental analysis and psychological autopsy studies have demonstrated that alcohol and other illicit drugs are associated with suicidal behaviour. We are going to examine the relationship between suicidal and substance abuse behaviours, focusing on epidemiology, comorbidity and prevention programs.

Then we will analyze specific characteristics concerning the association between alcohol, cocaine, heroin and cannabis abuse and suicidal behaviours in adolescents.

Individuals with substance abuse disorder who attempt or complete suicide can be characterized as having mood disorders, stressful life events, interpersonal problems, poor social support, lonely lives, and hopelessness.

Results emerging from the literature confirm a strong relationship between suicide and substance abuse so that preventive programs may be based on risk factors associated with both suicide and substance abuse disorder. Management programs should combine different therapeutic strategies such as psychotherapy and pharmacological treatment.

Introduction

Adolescence is a challenging period of cognitive, biological, physiological and psychological transition, often described as occurring between 10 and 19 years of age [1]. The psychological and social transitions of adolescence lead to the needs for independence, autonomy, identity formation and acceptance by peers. All of these contribute to the risk-taking behaviors of adolescence, of which substance use is the most damaging [2, 3]. The term 'misuse' encompasses a wide spectrum of problematic or harmful use, consistent with the conceptualisation of substance use and misuse, as broadly defined by the DSM-IV [4]. Moreover, Borst et al. [5] postulated that, with the advent of puberty, social-cognitive changes lead more often to internal rather than external attributions of unhappiness. This shift in attributional style leads to more self-blame in response to interpersonal stressors and, in some adolescents, results in suicidal behavior.

Adolescent suicide is a pressing international health problem. The World Health Organization declared suicide to be the third leading cause of death among those aged 15-24, after car accidents and cancer. Adolescent suicide not only represents a tragic loss of a young life, but it is an intensely painful experience for victims' loved ones (and also for the mental health professionals who work with the suicides).

Suicide and Substance Use among Adolescents: Epidemiologic Aspects

Researchers lack sufficient data to provide an accurate picture about adolescent suicide rates. Data for the 1990s indicate that the highest rates of suicide among men aged 15-24 are found in Russia, Lithuania, New Zealand, Latvia and Finland, while for women the highest rates are found in Cuba, Singapore, New Zealand, Mauritius, Kazakhstan, Kyrgyzstan [6]. Some researchers have reported that this suicide rate has increased by 245% between 1956 and 1994 [7]. The increase in the rate of suicide from the 1970s through the early 1990s has been attributed to rising rates of depression, the increased availability of firearms, and an increase in substance abuse among adolescents [8].

As with adult males, adolescent males complete suicide at rates approximately five times higher than rates for adolescent females [9]. One reason for the lower rates of suicide in females than in males is that the preferred method for suicide in females is overdoses, which can be treated more effectively in Western countries than are attempts by other means such as firearms or hanging. In addition, as discussed below, completed suicide is often associated with conduct difficulties/aggressive behavior and substance abuse, all of which are more common in males than in females [10].

With regard to suicide attempts, data obtained from the 2003 Youth Risk Behavior Surveillance (YRBS) survey in the United States, from more than 15,000 high school students in 32 states and 18 local municipalities, indicate that, within a twelve-month period, 16.9% of adolescents seriously considered attempting suicide, 16.5% developed a suicide plan, 8.5% attempted suicide (females, 11.5%; males, 5.4%), and 2.9% attempted suicide in a manner requiring emergency medical treatment [11].

A strong relationship has been found between substance use disorders and completed suicide in adolescents. Substance use is one of the behaviors that place adolescents at greatest risk for suicidal behavior [12]. Over a century ago, Durkheim noted the association between substance abuse and suicide attempts. He tested the possible association between suicide rates and rates of alcoholism and alcohol consumption levels [13]. In order to identify with the teenage culture, become autonomous and differentiate from their parents, some adolescents choose to use drugs, cigarettes, alcohol and cannabis, as well as other illicit drugs such as opiates and stimulants. Mind-altering substances tend to disinhibit impulsivity and facilitate the expression of suicidal impulses that might otherwise have been contained. In addition, substance abuse can result in social isolation and increase the risk of depressive moods by distancing adolescents from their families or by diminishing their opportunities because of school failure, lost jobs or legal problems. Furthermore, chemical dependence may place the adolescent in close contact with drug dealers and users who have easy access to handguns. The combination of substance abuse and the availability of handguns may place adolescents in high-risk situations.

School-based surveys provide prevalence estimates of substance use, but do not capture street and homeless youth and other high risk adolescents not found in the school environment. Some authors [14] report that, after remaining fairly stable across the 1980's, there was a substantial increase in rates of tobacco use (any use of cigarettes) among American adolescents in the early 1990's. Alcohol use (defined as any drinking) also remains pervasive in adolescence. Marijuana is the most widely used illicit drug among adolescents. Albeit less dramatic than the increase in marijuana use, the rise in cocaine and hallucinogen use since the early 1990's is also notable. The MTF study (Monitoring The Future, an ongoing study of the behaviors, attitudes, and values of American students and young adults funded by the National Institute on Drug Abuse) also highlights an important increase in MDMA use in the past few years such that ecstasy use has now become more prevalent among American teenagers than cocaine use. In contrast, the use of inhalants, LSD, crystal methamphetamine, and Rohypnol has decreased since the peak in the mid 1990's. In general, males report slightly higher rates of illicit drug use (primarily marijuana use) than females, a trend that is also seen for smokeless tobacco, steroid use and heavy drinking. Marijuana is the most frequently used substance in this age group followed by hallucinogens.

Substance Use, Substance Abuse and Substance Use Disorders among Adolescent Suicide Attempters

Suicide attempters exhibit high rates of substance use. Spirito et al. [15] studied substance use among adolescent suicide attempters and found that about 50% of 12-18 year-old adolescents (N=106) who presented at an emergency department after a suicide attempt had drank alcohol in the previous 3 months. One-third reported having been drunk in the past 3 months, and one fifth reached the clinical cut-off for alcohol problems on the Adolescent Drinking Inventory [16].

As for substance abusers, Cavaiola and Lavender [17] reported that 20%of a sample of 250 adolescents in a residential treatment program for chemical dependency had made a suicide attempt in the two years before admission. A total of 101 attempts were made by these

50 adolescents. Deykin and Buka [18] reported high lifetime rates of suicide attempts among 300 adolescent substance abusers aged 15-19 years in residential treatment. Twenty-eight percent of boys and 60% of girls reported at least one previous suicide attempt.

Suicide rates are slightly lower among adolescents who seek outpatient treatment for substance abuse compared with those in residential treatment, but they are still elevated relative to suicide rates in general population. Berman and Schwartz [19] assessed 298 adolescent outpatients, aged 13 to 19, who were substance abusers and found that 30% reported a previous suicide attempt.

High rates of alcohol and other substance use disorders have also been reported among suicidal adolescents admitted to general hospitals. Vajda and Steinbeck [20] conducted a retrospective record review of 112 adolescents, aged 13 to 20 years, who presented after a suicide attempt at an emergency department. They found that 35% met the criteria for an alcohol use disorder, and 27% met criteria for an illicit drug use disorder at the time of the attempt. Moreover, the study found that a diagnosis of alcohol abuse increased the risk of a repeat suicide attempt three-fold, while a diagnosis of illicit drug abuse increased the risk of a repeat suicide attempt four-fold within the following 12 months. In contrast, Spirito et al. [15] found lower rates of substance abuse than those reported by Vajda and Steinbeck [20]. Spirito et al. reported that 12% of adolescent suicide attempters who presented at an emergency department, aged 12 to 18 years, met the criteria for an alcohol use disorder (6% alcohol abuse and 6% alcohol dependence) and 18% met the criteria for cannabis use disorder (8.4% cannabis abuse and 9.6% cannabis dependence). This difference could be explained by two factors. First the diagnostic method used by Spirito et al. to make diagnoses (the National Institute of Mental Health Diagnostic Interview Schedule for Children [21]) may yield a more conservative diagnostic picture relative to the nonstructured clinical interviews used in the Vajda and Steinbeck study. Second, the sample studied by Spirito et al. was younger (mean age 15 years) than that in the Vajda and Steinbeck study (male mean age 18 years; female mean age 17 years).

In summary, a substance abuse or substance use disorder increases the risk of attempted suicide dramatically.

Suicide, Substance Abuse and other Psychiatric Disorders: Comorbidity Matters

Co-occurring substance use and other psychiatric problems is a particularly prominent characteristic of those seeking help for either substance abuse or mental health services [22-26]. Using a clinical population of adolescents from substance abuse treatment settings, Diamond and colleagues [27] reported that 72% of adolescent marijuana users had two or more psychiatric syndromes when entering treatment. While attention-deficit hyperactivity disorder (ADHD) and conduct disorder (CD) were common among adolescent clients, depression and anxiety disorders were also relatively common in adolescents with conduct and substance use disorders [28, 29]. In a case-control study of adolescents with alcohol dependence, compared with community-dwelling adolescents without alcohol dependence, Clark et al. [30] found that the most common form of psychopathology observed in alcohol-dependent adolescents included CD, ADHD, major depressive disorder and post traumatic stress disorder (PTSD).

Comorbidity increases the risk of suicidal behavior, particularly mood disorders with substance use disorders (SUD) [31-33] and disruptive behavior disorders with SUD [34]. Harrington et al. [35] found that depression in childhood was a strong predictor of a suicide attempt in early adult life. The risk is increased when depression is associated with drug abuse and external disturbances, cognitive distortions, hopelessness and low self-esteem, a passive coping style, social maladjustment, interpersonal problems, and familial and environmental stresses (conflict and loss, mental health problems in one or both parents, and suicidal events in the family or in the social network) [36]. Gould et al. [37] investigated suicidal ideation and attempts in an epidemiologic study and concluded that substance use disorders may mediate the relationship between disruptive behavior disorders and suicidal behavior in adolescents. However, there is little detailed information on the connection between disruptive behavior disorders, substance use, and suicidal behavior because there is little in-depth research of psychiatric disorders and suicidal behavior among adolescents with substance use disorders.

Kelly et al. [38] screened 1303 adolescents, of whom 969 (74%) completed the assessment. 515 (53%) were diagnosed with an Alcohol Use Disorder (AUD) and/or one or more other Substance Use Disorder (SUD), as defined by the DSM-IV [4]. Adolescents were classified into those who denied prior attempted suicide and those who had at least one lifetime suicide attempt. Kelly et al. found that major depression and bipolar disorder placed both sexes at highest risk for making a suicide attempt. ADHD was also associated with increased risk for males attempted suicide while conduct disorder was significantly associated with attempted suicide among females. The present authors were interested in the effect of individual substance use disorders on the risk for attempted suicide in this study. Only the male sample had high enough rates of individual substance use disorders to allow for the investigation. For the female sample, we collapsed all SUD other than cannabis use disorder into one category. There were no significant differences in rates of AUD among suicide attempters and non-attempters. We did not find that cannabis use disorders increased the risk for attempted suicide for either sex. Males with hallucinogen use disorders, inhalant use disorders and sedative-hypnotic use disorders had a higher risk for attempting suicide, while females with substance disorders other than cannabis use disorder had a higher risk for attempting suicide. The study indicated that adolescents with SUD were most likely to attempt suicide when they also had a mood disorder. This increased suicide risk begins at age 11 for females and around age 12½ for males.

THE RELATIONSHIP BETWEEN SUICIDE AND SUBSTANCE ABUSE: EXPLANATIONS

Given the association between substance abuse and suicidality, the next question is why are these two behaviors associated?

Substance abuse is a well-known risk factor in suicide attempters, but some authors raise the question of whether it is a proximal or a distal risk factor? Hufford [39] suggested that the acute effects of intoxication may represent a proximal risk factor for suicidal behavior. There is evidence that excessive alcohol use heightens psychological distress, increases aggressiveness (toward the self and others), enhances suicide-specific alcohol expectancies (e.g., "alcohol will give me the courage to make a suicide attempt"), and inhibits the generation and implementation of adaptive coping strategies. Among individuals who contemplate suicide, this concurrent increase in psychological distress, aggressiveness, and cognitive distortion may be sufficient to propel suicidal thoughts into action. Support for this theory comes from research that suggests that adolescents who make fatal and nonfatal suicide attempts exhibit elevated rates of alcohol use and intoxication at the time of the attempt [40-43].

However, substance use may also function as a more distal risk factor for suicidal behavior [39]. The research reviewed above indicates that substance use increases the statistical risk of future suicidal behavior. The results of the review conducted by Hufford [39] suggest that substance use disorder may be associated with increased stress and co-occurring psychopathology, which in turn increase the risk of suicidal behavior. Under heightened stress, severe depressive symptoms and/or conduct disturbance, caused in part by a history of substance use, adolescents may be more likely to attempt suicide as a means to cope with perceived insurmountable problems and intense emotional arousal.

Some research finds that substance use among adolescents is positively related to heightened levels of stress across many areas of life. For example, substance use has been associated with poor academic performance, legal/disciplinary problems, and interpersonal conflict among adolescents [33, 44, 45]. In turn, the same stressors have also been directly associated with suicidal behavior among adolescents [44, 46, 47]. Substance use has also been hypothesized to exacerbate psychological symptoms such as depression and disruptive behavior among adolescents [48].

Following Buksteinet al. [49], three main hypotheses can be postulated to explain the escalation process in substance use and suicide:

(a) Substance abuse → breakdown in personal relationships → increased suicide risk;
(b) Substance abuse → change in mood → suicidal ideation or depression → suicide attempt;
(c) Substance abuse → intoxicating effects → impaired judgement → increased suicide risk.

Goldston [50] suggested that some adolescents who attempt suicide may be motivated by a desire to escape from unbearable stressors and difficulties or aversive self-awareness such as the realization of inadequacies and unmet expectations. Some substance abusers also use substances to "escape" or dampen distress, to provide tension reduction, to distract from life difficulties, and to "self-medicate" [39, 51].

To the extent that relief is achieved, both types of behaviors will have a greater chance of being maintained. Consistent with this, there are several factors (e.g., impulsivity and depression) that have been posited to increase the likelihood of both suicidal and substance abusing behaviors. Hence, there may be similarities in the precipitants and factors increasing the risks and maintenance of suicidal and substance abusing behaviors.

Finally, there are physiological explanations. For example, altered serotonergic functioning has been found among suicides and individuals who make suicide attempts [52, 53]. Alterations in serotonergic functioning also have been found to be associated with the abuse of some substances [54]. Volkow [55] has suggested that physiological changes secondary to substance abuse may worsen mood, increasing the likelihood of suicidal behaviors in vulnerable populations.

The Risk of Suicide in the Different Kinds of Drug Abuse

Heroin

Research on suicide in heroin-dependent patients has received attention in recent years, but there is little research on the adolescent patient. However the major general population risk factors for suicide also apply to heroin users, and they include variables such as sex, psychopathology, family dysfunction and social isolation. Darke and Ross [56] noted that heroin users have even greater exposure to these factors than suicidal individuals and often manifest additional risk factors, such as poly-drug use.

Roy et al. [57] studied the characteristics of opiate-dependent patients (in whom heroin was the illicit drug of first choice) who had attempted suicide. One hundred of the 246 patients had attempted suicide, and significantly more of the opiate-dependent patients who had attempted suicide had a family history of both completed and attempted suicide. Opiate-dependent patients who had attempted suicide reported significantly more childhood emotional abuse, physical abuse, sexual abuse, and emotional and physical neglect. Moreover, opiate-dependent patients who had attempted suicide were found to be significantly more introverted, hostile and neurotic. Finally, significantly more of the patients who had attempted suicide were female and unemployed. Thus, the results of the study suggest that suicidal behavior may be multi-determined, with psychosocial, family, personality and psychiatric risk factors.

Kalyoncu et al. [58] examined the socio-demographic and clinical characteristics of a sample of young adult heroin-dependent patients (aged 18-24 years). The female suicide attempters were significantly younger at the onset of heroin use than those who had not attempted suicide. The male suicide attempters were also younger at the onset of heroin use, but this difference was not statistically significant. The starting age of heroin use, therefore, may be a risk factor for suicide attempts. The suicide attempters had experienced greater family psychopathology and dysfunction than the non-attempters and had significantly higher scores on the Childhood Trauma Questionnaire. These findings suggest that previous traumatic experiences are strongly associated with suicide attempts in young adult heroin-dependent patients. The heroin-dependent patients who had attempted suicide also differed with respect to the presence of other current psychiatric disorders (depressive, anxiety and antisocial personality disorders) that met DSM-IV criteria. In particular, the male suicide attempters more often met the criteria for antisocial personality disorder.

Cocaine

Cocaine dependence is a major public health problem, and patients with cocaine dependence have a greater risk of suicidal behavior. For example, Marzuk et al. [59] found that 29% of completed suicides in New York City aged 21–30 tested positive for cocaine. Roy [60] studied the characteristics of cocaine-dependent patients who attempt suicide. Thirty-nine percent of the cocaine-dependent patients had attempted suicide at some time in their lives. The cocaine-dependent patients who had attempted suicide more often had a family history of suicidal behavior, and they reported significantly more childhood trauma. They also had higher personality scores for introversion, neuroticism and hostility; and they had significantly more comorbidity with use of other substances, as well as psychiatric and physical disorders.

Garlow [61] studied 416 cases of suicide in those aged 14-25 and found differences by race, sex, and age among the suicides who had used cocaine and alcohol before committing suicide. Almost all (94.6%) of the suicides in whom cocaine was detected were male, 51.4% of the cocaine-positive victims were African American men, and 43.2% were white men. Substance use by teenage victims differed dramatically across ethnic lines. The vast majority (86.7%) of African American teenagers did not use either substance before committing suicide, whereas 50.0% of the white teenage suicides had used one or both substances, with 41.7% of the white teenagers having used alcohol. Overall, alcohol use was much more common among white suicides of all age groups. The same authors [62] later studied 1296 adolescent suicides and found a similar result. The use of cocaine and alcohol prior to suicide differed for African American and white teenage suicides, with rates of intoxicant use significantly higher in whites than in blacks. Whereas black teens had the highest rate of completed suicide, white teenagers had higher rates of cocaine and alcohol use preceding suicide. These results have important implications for surveillance of at-risk youths and for prevention programs. Substance abuse appears to play a role in almost half of white teenage suicides, and so drug and alcohol use in this group could be a warning sign of emerging suicidality whereas, in black teens, the presence of substance abuse might not identify at-risk teenagers.

Cannabis

Cannabis is one of more frequently used drugs by adolescents. Ramsay and Partridge [63] report a prevalence of cannabis use of 40% and 47% among British adolescents 16-19 years old and young adults 20-24 years old, respectively. A report on young people's attitudes and opinion about drugs in the European Union [64] pointed out that 28.9% of their sample of over 7000 European youths 15-24 years old had tried cannabis at least once in their life, while 11.3% had used it in the month before the survey.

A case-control study published by Beautrais et al. [65] examined the relationship between cannabis abuse-dependence and the risk of medically serious suicide attempts. Beautrais et al. compared 302 individuals who had made suicide attempts with 1028 randomly selected control subjects. The results showed that individuals who had made serious suicide attempts had significantly higher rates of cannabis abuse/dependence than comparison subjects. The authors suggested that this result could result from socio-demographic disadvantages and disadvantageous childhood family circumstances. Before adjustment for socio-demographic and family factors, the odds ratio for cannabis abuse/dependence and serious suicide attempt risk was 10.3, while after adjustment for these factors the odds ratio was only 3.2. Another hypothesis was that this association could be largely explained by the co-morbidity of cannabis abuse/dependence with other mental disorders (notably, mood disorder, other substance use disorder and antisocial personality disorder). After controlling for confounding factors and comorbid psychiatric disorder, the odds ratio between cannabis abuse/dependence and making a serious suicide attempt was 2.0 and only marginally statistically significant.

Fergusson et al. [66] studied the association between the frequency of cannabis use and psychosocial outcomes in adolescence/young adulthood. The sample included 1265 children who were studied at birth, 4 months, 1 year and at annual intervals up to age 16 years and again at age 18 years and 21 years. The results showed that cannabis use, and particularly regular cannabis use, was associated with a dramatic increase in risk of other forms of illicit drug use, even when confounding variables were taken into account. In particular, regular cannabis abuse was associated with increases in delinquency, depression and suicidal behavior. The adverse effects of cannabis on adjustment seemed to be most pronounced for younger users and declined with increasing age. These findings reinforce public health concerns about minimizing the use of cannabis among school-aged populations.

Rey et al. [67] investigated the mental health of 1490 Australian adolescents aged 13-17 who used cannabis. One-quarter of this sample reported having used cannabis, and males were twice as likely as females to have used cannabis before the age of 13. Rey et al. found an association between depression (one of the most important risk factors for suicide) and cannabis use. The results also showed that cannabis use increased the incidence of disruptive behaviors such as conduct problems, tobacco smoking, excessive drinking and the use of illicit drugs.

Chabrol, Chauchard and Girabet [68] evaluated the relative contributions of cannabis use, depression symptoms and anxiety symptoms in the prediction of suicidal behaviors in a sample of 248 high-school students from Toulouse, France. Those who had used cannabis at least once in the last 6 months had significantly higher rates of suicidal behaviors, depression symptoms and anxiety symptoms compared to non-users. Moreover, cannabis use appeared to be an independent predictor of suicidal behaviors after controlling for symptoms of depression and anxiety, suggesting that cannabis use contributes to suicidal behaviors independently from depression and anxiety symptoms.

Innamorati, Pompili, Tatarelli, Girardi, Ferrari, Tamburello and Lester [69] studied 246 university students in Italy, with a mean age of 21.9 years, who completed the Zung scales for anxiety and depression, a Suicide Score Scale and an *ad hoc* questionnaire assessing risky behaviors. The results showed that 48% of the students reported having used cannabis at least once during the prior year. Heavy cannabis users seemed to be more prone to engage in risky behavior than non-users or casual users. Heavy users were also more likely to report higher use of tobacco and illicit drugs. Thus, the current regular use of cannabis is associated with an externalizing "syndrome" of current and past risky behavior. This syndrome of risky behavior is directly and indirectly associated with potential threats to the psychological and physical well-being of the individual. Concurrent use of cannabis and other illicit drugs is associated with a stronger risk. Regarding the association with suicide risk, the authors suggested that the effect of cannabis use was weak, but poly-drug users had the highest suicide risk. The effect of illicit drug use was evident even when the presence of other risky behaviors, depression and anxiety were controlled for. The results indicated that the lifetime use of any illicit drug other than cannabis may be a predictor of higher suicide risk in depressed students. The results suggest the need for community programs oriented toward preventing substance use among young adults and adolescents, such as educating the youth about the linkage between drug use and depressive disorders and other psychiatric problems.

Suicidal Behavior and Alcohol Abuse

Epidemiology

The Centers for Disease Control and Prevention have reported that since the 1950s, the rate of suicide in children and adolescents has increased by more than 300 percent [70]. Epidemiologic studies in the United States indicate that the rate of suicide among adolescent has increased in the last twenty years. According to recent data from the Youth Risk Behavior Surveillance in the United States, 16.9% of high school students had considered attempting suicide and about 8.4% had attempted suicide in 2005 [71].

Suicide, in Europe and Anglo-Saxon Countries, is statistically the second leading cause of death among adolescents after car accidents. According to WHO, 40% of youths who do not succeed in dying in their first attempt repeat the attempt. Furthermore, 20% of youths aged 14-19 have thought about the own death.

Empirical reviews of cohort studies [72] and psychological autopsy studies [73] have demonstrated that alcohol and drug use disorders are associated with suicide. The Centers for Disease Control and Prevention [74] estimated that 30% of high school students have had their first alcoholic drink by age 13, and that 29.7% admit to having drunk five or more alcoholic drinks in a row within the last two weeks. Alcoholism, both acute and chronic, is highly associated with suicidal tendencies [75].

Empirical studies have demonstrated that alcohol abuse, along with the consumption of drugs, is one of the three principal causes of death among the youth (along with car accidents and homicide). Depressed individuals who consume drugs or alcohol have a higher probability of attempting suicide compared to depressed individuals who do not.

Glowinski et al. [76] estimated that, in cases of alcohol dependence, the probability of making a suicide attempt increases by a factor of 2.8. Miles [77] demonstrated that the risk of suicide in alcoholics is 15% or higher as compared to a risk of only 1% to 1.3% in the general population.

Relieving the symptoms of depression by drinking alcohol or using drugs can raise the risk of suicide by altering the impulsiveness of the subject.

Risk Factors

Adolescent suicide does not have any single cause but rather springs from a multitude of factors. It is a multidimensional phenomenon, and to understand, prevent, and intervene on this kind of behavior it is necessary to take in consideration all of the factors (biological, genetic, physiological, social, cultural and environmental) that have importance in the genesis of such a behavior. The presence of a psychiatric disorder creates the greatest risk of suicide, especially the major mood disorders (major depression and bipolar disorders), alcohol abuse and schizophrenia. Among depressed individuals, the risk of suicide is higher if the patient does not follow the therapy correctly or if they show a resistance to taking prescribed medications.

Among the causes of suicide, alcoholism is second only to mood disorders. Among alcoholics, the risk of suicide at some point in their lifetime is estimated to be 10%-15%. Barraclough et al. [78] found, in a sample of 100 cases of suicide, that 85% had experienced depression and/or alcoholism, and it is common to find comorbidity between mood disorders and alcohol abuse in people who have attempted suicide [79, 80]. While suicide usually comes in the first phases of the major mood disorders, in alcoholics suicide comes in the final phases, often in conjunction with breaks in interpersonal relations, social marginalisation and poverty or from somatic complications of the sickness.

PREVENTION

The high incidence of completed and attempted suicide among adolescents makes prevention difficult. The CDC's National Center for Injury Prevention and Control has published a program with guidelines for intervention strategies for communities that are interested in developing prevention programs for adolescents [81]. The strategies for suicide prevention for adolescents concentrate on two general themes: strategies to identify subjects at risk so as to direct them to healthcare centers and strategies to increase their social support network and their management of stress.The CDC guide contains the following suggestions:

- Make sure that programs for suicide prevention are strongly linked with the professional mental health resources of the community.
- A good prevention program adopts a broad approach. Prevention programs must be designed so that they can deal with complex and multidimensional factors.
- Avoid reliance on one prevention strategy.
- Incorporate promising, but underused, strategies into current programs where possible.
- Expand suicide prevention efforts for young adults.
- Employ screening programs and evaluation of the prevention programs.

In the clinical context, patients avoid bringing up their suicidal thoughts and plans, but they are more willing to discuss these if the clinician asks specific questions about the intention to commit suicide [82]. Educating general practitioners [83] and nurses [84] about suicide, depression and substance abuse can have a major impact on how patients at risk are evaluated and managed. The same approach can be useful in non-clinical contexts, and education programs for teachers, school staff and family members can improve the recognition of suicidal tendencies.

In summary, one of the most effective strategies for suicide prevention is to teach people how to recognize and respond to the signals of suicidal tendencies since this increases the likelihood of at-risk youths seeking help. Identifying psychiatric disorders in adolescents and reducing the risk factors for suicide are especially important. In particular, the identification and treatment of drug and alcohol misuse and abuse is critical in reducing the suicidal behavior of adolescents.

Common risk-factors for suicide in adolescents include:

- Previous suicide attempts
- Feelings of desperation
- Impulsive or aggressive tendencies
- Ease of access to lethal instruments such as firearms
- A history sexual or mental abuse
- Difficult relationships between parents and children
- Stress, particularly sudden losses of interpersonal relationships and legal or discipline problems
- Lack of involvement in scholastic life or in work
- Suicide in the family
- Psychosis in the parents

Conclusion: A Note on Intervention

Many interventions exist that are oriented toward the adolescents at risk of suicide. Interventions for suicidal adolescents have to consider adolescents in context. The problem of alcohol and substance abuse can be treated with the help of psychotherapy with the aim of helping clients to find a motivation for stopping drinking, identifying the circumstances that motive them to drink, and identifying the factors that play a significant role for the genesis of this conduct. Psychotherapy helps the individual learn new methods for facing stressful situations and develop better social relationships. For adolescent clients, it is important also to involve the whole family for the family plays a fundamental role both in the cause of the problem and in the recovery of the patient.

References

[1] Crockett LJ, Petersen AC: Adolescent development: health risks and opportunities for health promotion, in *Promoting the health of adolescents: new directions for the twenty-first century.* Edited by Millstein SG, Petersen EO, Nightingale EO. New York, Oxford University Press, 1993, pp 13-38.

[2] Franzkowiak P: Risk-taking and adolescent development: the functions of smoking and alcohol consumption in adolescence and its consequences for prevention. *Health Promot* 1987; 2:51-61.

[3] Fergusson DM, Horwood LJ: Transitions to cigarette smoking during adolescence. *Addict Behav* 1995; 20:627-642.

[4] American Psychiatric Association: *Diagnostic and statistical manual of mental disorders*, 4th ed. Washington, DC, American Psychiatric Association, 1994.

[5] Borst SR, Noam GG, Bartok JA: Adolescent suicidality: a clinical-developmental approach. *J Am Acad Child Adolesc Psychiatry* 1991; 30:796-803.
[6] Lester D: Adolescent suicide from an international perspective. *Am Behav Sci* 2003; 46:1157-1170.
[7] Peters KD, Kochanek KD, Murphy SL: Deaths: final data for 1996. *National Statistics Report* 1998; 47:9.
[8] Commission on Adolescent Suicide Prevention: *Youth suicide, in Treating and preventing adolescent mental health problems: what we know and what we don't know.* Edited by Evans DL, Foa EB, Gur RE, et al. New York, Oxford University Press, 2005, pp 434–443.
[9] Kochanek KD, Murphy SL, Anderson RN, et al: *Deaths: final data for 2002 National Vital Statistics Reports.* DHHS Publication No. (PHS) 2005–1120, 53(5), Hyattsville, National Center of Health Statistics, 2004.
[10] Brent DA, Baugher M, Bridge J, et al: Age- and sex-related risk factors for adolescent suicide. *J Am Acad Child Adolesc Psychiatry* 1999; 38:1497-1505.
[11] Grunbaum JA, Kann L, Kinchen S, et al: Youth risk behavior surveillance - United States, 2003 MMWR Morb Mortal Wkly Rep 2004; 53:1-96.
[12] Brent DA: Risk factors for adolescent suicide and suicidal behavior: mental and substance abuse disorders, family environmental factors, and life stress. Suicide Life *Threat Behav* 1995; 25 Suppl:52-63.
[13] Durkheim E: *Suicide,* New York, Free Press, 1951.
[14] Young SE, Corley RP, Stallings MC, et al: Substance use, abuse and dependence in adolescence: prevalence, symptom profiles and correlates. *Drug Alcohol Depend* 2002; 68:309-322.
[15] Spirito A, Mehlenbeck R, Barnett N, et al: The relation of mood and behavior to alcohol use in adolescent suicide attempters. *J Child Adolesc Subst Abuse* 2003; 12:35-53.
[16] Harrell A, Wirtz PW: Adolescent Drinking Index: professional manual, Odessa, *Psychological Assessment Resources, 1*989.
[17] Cavaiola AA, Lavender N: Suicidal behavior in chemically dependent adolescents. *Adolescence* 1999; 34:735-744.
[18] Deykin EY, Buka SL: Suicidal ideation and attempts among chemically dependent adolescents. *Am J Public Health* 1994; 84:634-639.
[19] Berman AL, Schwartz RH: Suicide attempts among adolescent drug users. *Am J Dis Child* 1990; 144:310-314.
[20] Vajda J, Steinbeck K: Factors associated with repeat suicide attempts among adolescents. *Aust N Z J Psychiatry* 2000; 34:437-445.
[21] Costello EJ, Edelbrock CS, Dulcan MK, et al: *Diagnostic Interview Schedule for Children,* Pittsburgh, Western Psychiatric Institute and Clinic, School of Medicine, University of Pittsburgh, 1987.
[22] Brooner RK, King VL, Kidorf M, et al: Psychiatric and substance use comorbidity among treatment-seeking opioid abusers. *Arch Gen Psychiatry* 1997; 54:71-80.
[23] Bukstein OG, Glancy LJ, Kaminer Y: Patterns of affective comorbidity in a clinical population of dually diagnosed adolescent substance abusers. *J Am Acad Child Adolesc Psychiatry* 1992; 31:1041-1045.

[24] Mueser KT, Yarnold PR, Levinson DF, et al: Prevalence of substance abuse in schizophrenia: demographic and clinical correlates. *Schizophr Bull* 1990; 16:31-56.

[25] Hien D, Zimberg S, Weisman S, et al: Dual diagnosis subtypes in urban substance abuse and mental health clinics. *Psychiatr Serv* 1997; 48:1058-1063.

[26] Ross HE, Glaser FB, Germanson T: The prevalence of psychiatric disorders in patients with alcohol and other drug problems. *Arch Gen Psychiatry* 1988; 45:1023-1031.

[27] Diamond G, Panichelli-Mindel SM, Shera D, et al: Psychiatric syndromes in adolescents seeking outpatient treatment for marijuana with abuse and dependency in outpatient treatment. J*ournal of Child and Adolescent Substance Abuse* 2006; 15:37–54.

[28] Crowley TJ, Riggs PD: Adolescent substance use disorder with conduct disorder and comorbid conditions, in Adolescent drug abuse: clinical assessment and therapeutic interventions. Edited by Rahdert ER, Czechowicz D. Rockville, *National Institute on Drug Abuse,* 1995, pp 49-111.

[29] Grilo CM, Becker DF, Fehon DC, et al: Conduct disorder, substance use disorders, and coexisting conduct and substance use disorders in adolescent inpatients. *Am J Psychiatry* 1996; 153:914-920.

[30] Clark DB, Pollock N, Bukstein OG, et al: Gender and comorbid psychopathology in adolescents with alcohol dependence. *J Am Acad Child Adolesc Psychiatry* 1997; 36:1195-1203.

[31] Brent DA, Johnson B, Bartle S, et al: Personality disorder, tendency to impulsive violence, and suicidal behavior in adolescents. *J Am Acad Child Adolesc Psychiatry* 1993; 32:69-75.

[32] Brent DA, Kolko DJ, Wartella ME, et al: Adolescent psychiatric inpatients' risk of suicide attempt at 6-month follow-up. *J Am Acad Child Adolesc Psychiatry* 1993; 32:95-105.

[33] Lewinsohn PM, Gotlib IH, Seeley JR: Adolescent psychopathology: IV. Specificity of psychosocial risk factors for depression and substance abuse in older adolescents. *J Am Acad Child Adolesc Psychiatry* 1995; 34:1221-1229.

[34] Marttunen MJ, Aro HM, Henriksson MM, et al: Antisocial behaviour in adolescent suicide. *Acta Psychiatr Scand* 1994; 89:167-173.

[35] Harrington R, Bredenkamp D, Groothues C, et al: Adult outcomes of childhood and adolescent depression. III. Links with suicidal behaviours. *J Child Psychol Psychiatry* 1994; 35:1309-1319.

[36] Bolognini M, Plancherel B, Laget J, et al: Adolescent's suicide attempts: populations at risk, vulnerability, and substance use. *Subst Use Misuse* 2003; 38:1651-1669.

[37] Gould MS, King R, Greenwald S, et al: Psychopathology associated with suicidal ideation and attempts among children and adolescents. *J Am Acad Child Adolesc Psychiatry* 1998; 37:915-923.

[38] Kelly TM, Cornelius JR, Clark DB: Psychiatric disorders and attempted suicide among adolescents with substance use disorders. *Drug Alcohol Depend* 2004; 73:87-97.

[39] Hufford MR: Alcohol and suicidal behavior. Clin Psychol Rev 2001; 21:797-811.

[40] Marttunen MJ, Aro HM, Henriksson MM, et al: Mental disorders in adolescent suicide. DSM-III-R axes I and II diagnoses in suicides among 13- to 19-year-olds in Finland. *Arch Gen Psychiatry* 1991; 48:834-839.

[41] Runeson B: Psychoactive substance use disorder in youth suicide. *Alcohol Alcohol* 1990; 25:561-568.

[42] Hawton K, Fagg J: Deliberate self-poisoning and self-injury in adolescents. A study of characteristics and trends in Oxford, 1976-89. *Br J Psychiatry* 1992; 161:816-823.

[43] Kotila L, Lonnqvist J: Adolescent suicide attempts: sex differences predicting suicide. *Acta Psychiatr Scand* 1988; 77:264-270.

[44] Brent DA, Perper JA, Moritz G, et al: Stressful life events, psychopathology, and adolescent suicide: a case control study. *Suicide Life Threat Behav* 1993; 23:179-187.

[45] Needle R, McCubbin H, Lorence J, et al: Reliability and validity of adolescent self-reported drug use in a family-based study: a methodological report. *Int J Addict* 1983; 18:901-912.

[46] Adams DM, Overholser JC, Spirito A: Stressful life events associated with adolescent suicide attempts. *Can J Psychiatry* 1994; 39:43-48.

[47] Lewinsohn PM, Rohde P, Seeley JR: Psychosocial characteristics of adolescents with a history of suicide attempt. *J Am Acad Child Adolesc Psychiatry* 1993; 32:60-68.

[48] Greenbaum PE, Foster-Johnson L, Petrila A: Co-occurring addictive and mental disorders among adolescents: prevalence research and future directions. *Am J Orthopsychiatry* 1996; 66:52-60.

[49] Bukstein OG, Brent DA, Perper JA, et al: Risk factors for completed suicide among adolescents with a lifetime history of substance abuse: a case-control study. *Acta Psychiatr Scand* 1993; 88:403-408.

[50] Goldston DB: Conceptual issues in understanding the relationship between suicidal behavior and substance use during adolescence. *Drug Alcohol Depend* 2004; 76 Suppl:S79-91.

[51] Khantzian EJ: The self-medication hypothesis of substance use disorders: a reconsideration and recent applications. *Harv Rev Psychiatry* 1997; 4:231-244.

[52] Mann JJ, Brent DA, Arango V: The neurobiology and genetics of suicide and attempted suicide: a focus on the serotonergic system. *Neuropsychopharmacology* 2001; 24:467-477.

[53] Mann JJ, Oquendo M, Underwood MD, et al: The neurobiology of suicide risk: a review for the clinician. *J Clin Psychiatry 1999*; 60 Suppl 2:7-11; discussion 18-20, 113-116.

[54] Morgan MJ: Ecstasy (MDMA): a review of its possible persistent psychological effects. *Psychopharmacology* (Berl) 2000; 152:230-248.

[55] Volkow ND: Drug abuse and mental illness: progress in understanding comorbidity. *Am J Psychiatry* 2001; 158:1181-1183.

[56] Darke S, Ross J: Suicide among heroin users: rates, risk factors and methods. *Addiction* 2002; 97:1383-1394.

[57] Roy A: Characteristics of opiate dependent patients who attempt suicide. *J Clin Psychiatry* 2002; 63:403-407.

[58] Kalyoncu A, Mırsal H, Pektaş Ö, et al: Heroin-dependent patients attempting and not attempting suicide: a comparison. *Acta Neuropsychiatrica* 2007; 19:297-303.

[59] Marzuk PM, Tardiff K, Leon AC, et al: Prevalence of cocaine use among residents of New York City who committed suicide during a one-year period. *Am J Psychiatry* 1992; 149:371-375.

[60] Roy A: Characteristics of cocaine-dependent patients who attempt suicide. *Am J Psychiatry* 2001; 158:1215-1219.
[61] Garlow SJ: Age, gender, and ethnicity differences in patterns of cocaine and ethanol use preceding suicide. *Am J Psychiatry* 2002; 159:615-619.
[62] Garlow SJ, Purselle DC, Heninger M: Cocaine and alcohol use preceding suicide in African American and White adolescents. *J Psychiatr Res* 2007; 41:530-536.
[63] Ramsay M, Partridge S: *Drug misuse declared in 1998: results from the British Crime Survey,* London, Home Office, 1999.
[64] European Opinion Research Group: *Attitudes and opinions of young people in the European Union on drugs:* Eurobarometer 57.2, Special Eurobarometer 172, Brussels, European Commission, Public Opinion Analysis sector, 2002.
[65] Beautrais AL, Joyce PR, Mulder RT: *Cannabis abuse and serious suicide attempts. Addiction* 1999; 94:1155-1164.
[66] Fergusson DM, Horwood LJ, Swain-Campbell N: Cannabis use and psychosocial adjustment in adolescence and young adulthood. *Addiction* 2002; 97:1123-1135.
[67] Rey JM, Sawyer MG, Raphael B, et al: Mental health of teenagers who use cannabis. Results of an Australian survey. *Br J Psychiatry* 2002; 180:216-221.
[68] Chabrol H, Chauchard E, Girabet J: Cannabis use and suicidal behaviours in high-school students. *Addict Behav* 2008; 33:152-155.
[69] Innamorati M, Pompili M, Ferrari V, et al: Cannabis use and the risk behavior syndrome in Italian university students: are they related to suicide risk? *Psychol Rep* 2008; 102:577-594.
[70] Scherff AR, Eckert TL, Miller DN: Youth suicide prevention: a survey of public school superintendents' acceptability of school-based programs. *Suicide Life Threat Behav* 2005; 35:154-169.
[71] Eaton DK, Kann L, Kinchen S, et al: Youth Risk Behaviors Surveillance- United States 2005. *MMWR Surveill Summ* 2006; 55:1-33.
[72] Harris EC, Barraclough B: Suicide as an outcome for mental disorders. A meta-analysis. *Br J Psychiatry* 1997; 170:205-228.
[73] Cavanagh JT, Carson AJ, Sharpe M, et al: Psychological autopsy studies of suicide: a systematic review. *Psychol Med* 2003; 33:395-405.
[74] Grunbaum JA, Kann L, Kinchen SA, et al: Youth risk behavior surveillance--United States, 2001. *MMWR Surveill Summ* 2002; 51:1-62.
[75] Berglund M, Ojehagen A: The influence of alcohol drinking and alcohol use disorders on psychiatric disorders and suicidal behavior. *Alcohol Clin Exp Res* 1998; 22:333S-345S.
[76] Glowinski AL, Bucholz KK, Nelson EC, et al: Suicide attempts in an adolescent female twin sample. *J Am Acad Child Adolesc Psychiatry* 2001; 40:1300-1307.
[77] Miles CP: Conditions predisposing to suicide: a review. *J Nerv Ment Dis* 1977; 164:231-246.
[78] Barraclough B, Bunch J, Nelson B, et al: A hundred cases of suicide: clinical aspects. *Br J Psychiatry* 1974; 125:355-373.
[79] Beautrais AL, Joyce PR, Mulder RT, et al: Prevalence and comorbidity of mental disorders in persons making serious suicide attempts: a case-control study. *Am J Psychiatry* 1996; 153:1009-1014.

[80] Conwell Y, Duberstein PR, Cox C, et al: Relationships of age and axis I diagnoses in victims of completed suicide: a psychological autopsy study. *Am J Psychiatry* 1996; 153:1001-1008.

[81] O'Carroll PW, Potter LB, Mercy JA: Programs for the prevention of suicide among adolescents and young adults. *MMWR Recomm Rep* 1994; 43:1-7.

[82] Pompili M, Innamorati M, Del Casale A, et al: La prevenzione del suicidio e il ruolo strategico dei medici di base. Prevenzione e Stili di Vita. *Rivista della Società Italiana di Medicina Generale* 2009; 1:35-41.

[83] Rutz W, von Knorring L, Walinder J: Frequency of suicide on Gotland after systematic postgraduate education of general practitioners. *Acta Psychiatr Scand* 1989; 80:151-154.

[84] Pompili M, Girardi P, Ruberto A, et al: Emergency staff reactions to suicidal and self-harming patients. *Eur J Emerg Med* 2005; 12:169-178.

In: Suicidal Behavior in Alcohol and Drug Abuse... ISBN: 978-1-60876-919-3
Editors: L. Sher, A. Vilens, pp. 443-452

Chapter 25

ALCOHOLISM AND SUICIDAL BEHAVIOR IN THE ELDERLY

Margda Waern
Institution for Neuroscience and Physiology,
Sahlgrenska Academy at the University of Gothenburg, Gothenburg, Sweden

ABSTRACT

Suicide rates are particularly high among elderly in most western countries. Studies from a number of different western settings demonstrate increased risk of suicide in elderly persons with alcohol use disorders. The association is not consistent worldwide, and this might in part be attributed to differences in alcohol consumption patterns. Controlled studies are needed to clarify the role of alcohol in non-lethal suicidal behaviours in late life. Given the aging of populations worldwide, and changing trends in alcohol consumption, some regions may need to expand prevention efforts in order to target elderly with problematic alcohol consumption, especially those with comorbid depression.

INTRODUCTION

Populations are aging worldwide. Suicide rates are particularly high among elderly in most western countries [1] [2, 3]. Yet there are surprisingly few studies that focus specifically on the relationship between alcohol use disorders and suicide in late life. Suicide prevention programs seldom emphasize the detection and treatment of alcoholism in this age group. Further, assessments of alcohol use are not always the routine in the clinical management of the depressed elderly. The fictitious case of Mr. B. that follows demonstrates a number of features frequently associated with suicide in elderly persons with alcoholism.

Mr. B. was an eighty-year-old widower who consulted his GP because he felt fatigued and had lost weight during the last month. He reported sleep problems, describing how he spent many night hours ruminating about a conflict regarding his only son. The son lived in another part of the country, and was seldom in touch. The elderly patient acknowledged that he had been feeling low during the past couple of months. He denied current suicidal ideation upon the doctor's direct questioning. He related that he had taken an overdose of sleeping pills many years ago, in connection with marital problems. Mr. B. left his doctor's office with a prescription for an antidepressant. Three weeks after the consultation, the neighbours heard a gunshot. Mr. B had taken his life. The medical examiner's investigation revealed an enlarged liver and the forensic lab work-up showed a high blood alcohol concentration. Analysis of psychotropic drugs and their metabolites in blood and urine suggested that Mr. B. had taken 1) the antidepressant as prescribed and 2) a minor tranquilizer in an amount beyond the usual therapeutic dosage. Review of case notes showed that the latter drug had been prescribed by a second physician at consultation that took place a week before the suicide, when Mr. B. sought help for diffuse symptoms of anxiety. Neither of the physicians whom Mr. B. consulted shortly before his suicide had posed questions concerning his use of alcohol.

At the time of his death, Mr. B. fulfilled criteria for both major depression and alcohol use disorder, which is a common pattern of comorbidity in elders who commit suicide [4]. Mr. B. had treatment for his affective disorder only. Why might there be a tendency for physicians to overlook alcohol overconsumption in their elderly patients? First, there may be a misconception that elderly people do not drink. Second, stereotypes regarding old age might lead to permissive attitudes ("a little alcohol will brighten things up"). Third, doctors may feel uncomfortable posing questions about alcohol consumption to their elderly patients. Fourth, diagnostic criteria regarding alcohol dependence and abuse may not be particularly suitable for elderly [4]; problematic alcohol use may thus go undetected. Fifth, lack of experience in the management of late-life alcohol overconsumption might render the doctor less inclined to identify such problems. Finally, recent attention regarding the advantageous health effects of mild to moderate alcohol consumption on cardiac and cerebrovascular health and cognition may affect attitudes in both health professionals and in the general public [5]. A number of different health outcomes seem to follow the "U-shaped" curve with regard to alcohol consumption, also in elders aged 70 and above [6]. However, it remains unclear whether the association between alcohol consumption and suicide mortality follows such a pattern. The authors of a large prospective cohort study on Japanese men (aged 40-79 years) reported a positive linear association, with no evidence of decreased suicide risk in light drinkers [7].

Alcohol Use Disorders and Suicide in the Elderly

Most of what is known about alcohol use disorders in completed suicide late in life is gleaned from retrospective studies based on interviews with close informants of suicide decedents. Rates of alcoholism vary widely in these "psychological autopsy" studies. Figures as low as 3% [8]; [9] and as high as 44% [10] have been reported. A number of methodological problems make direct comparisons among studies difficult. Interpretation is hampered by lack of comparison groups; base rates of alcohol use disorders in the underlying population are unknown. Inclusion age and sex distributions vary among studies, as do the diagnostics employed. Also, cause of death classification and routines regarding forensic examination may differ. Some persons with problematic substance use may be missed in studies that exclude uncertain causes of death, as substance users are more common among uncertain suicides. Cultural background may influence attitudes towards both suicide and alcohol-related behaviors, and informants in some settings might feel less comfortable discussing the elderly decedent's alcohol habits.

Support for proxy interviews in suicide research was supplied by Conner and colleagues [11], who demonstrated substantial agreement between alcohol dependence diagnoses generated from close informant reports and those determined by a clinician. Results were not as good regarding a diagnosis of alcohol abuse, however. During the past decade, the literature on suicide in late life has been enriched by several controlled studies. Rates of alcohol use disorders were extremely low in both cases and controls in the studies set in Britain [12] and in Hong Kong [9]. Somewhat higher proportions were reported from Canada [13], but proportions did not differ between cases and controls in that study (8% of the suicides had alcohol dependence as compared with 5% of the control group). Three case-controlled studies showed increased risk [14], [15]; [16]. One of these studies [16] presented risk data in men and women separately. A history of alcohol dependence or abuse was observed in 35% of the elderly men who died by suicide and in 18% of the women. This disorder was uncommon among persons in the population comparison group (2% of the men and 1% of the women). A significant association between alcohol use disorder and suicide remained in both sexes after adjustment for a number of potential confounders including depression. An 8-fold risk increase was noted for men and a 13-fold risk increase was observed in women. These findings are in line with those reported in a review of mixed age cohort studies [3], highlighting the importance for clinicians to consider suicide risk also among women with alcohol use disorders.

There is one cohort study suggesting that the association between alcohol dependence and suicide is amplified with increased age [17], but it is unclear whether this applies also in very late life. One psychological autopsy report focusing on the "older" elderly (75+) observed a history of substance use disorder in 16%, which could be compared with 43% in the younger elderly [18]. It was not possible to generate risk data for the "old" elderly group as none of the population controls aged 75 and above in that study had an alcohol use disorder. Persons with alcoholism are less likely to reach "old" old age, and those who do might be less inclined to participate in a research study than their peers without the disorder.

Detailed information regarding comorbidity in elderly suicide cases with alcoholism is lacking in most studies. One [16] demonstrated that proportions with various affective disorders were similar to those observed among suicide decedents with no history of alcohol use disorder (recurrent major depression 30%, single episode major depression 9% and bipolar disorder 9%). Minor depression, in accordance with DSM-IV research criteria, was present in 17%. Over a fifth of the elderly suicide cases with alcohol use disorder in that study also fulfilled criteria for an anxiety disorder. Proportions with a prescription for an antidepressant at the time of the suicide were similar in persons with (53%) and without (61%) alcohol use disorders. It is notable that only one of the suicide decedents had specific treatment for alcoholism during the year prior to the suicide. His G.P. had prescribed disulfuram. None of the elderly suicide decedents had contact with a specialist substance-use service.

Examining alcohol consumption rather than diagnostics, Grabbe and colleagues [19] analysed data from the National Mortality Followback Survey, and observed that suicide was overrepresented among elderly persons with both moderate and heavy drinking compared to those who did not drink. Another study [20] could not show associations between suicide and 1) frequency and 2) quantity of alcohol consumption in the elderly. An association between binge drinking and a history of attempted suicide in persons aged 60 and above was demonstrated in a study set in Australia [21]. A "drinking habit" distinguished elderly suicide attempters (28%) from community controls (9%) in a recent Taiwan-based study [22]. When interpreting results of population studies that utilize alcohol consumption measures, it is important to keep in mind that persons with serious health problems and former alcoholics are overrepresented among the teetotallers. Mortality is high in elders who abstain, and persons who discontinue alcohol use in late life are more likely to die than those who continue to drink [6].

Alcohol Use Disorders and Attempted Suicide

Elderly persons are far less likely to engage in non-fatal suicidal behavior in comparison with younger persons [1]. However, when elders do self-harm, the behavior is often more serious, with higher level of suicide intent and increased risk of completed suicide [23].

A recent review on attempted suicide in later life [24] showed a wide variation in rates of substance misuse (2%-36%). Half of all the reviewed studies on self-harm in older people lacked diagnostic data regarding substance misuse, demonstrating that this is an under researched topic. The overall pattern observed in the studies that did report substance use disorders seems to mirror that for completed suicide in this age group. Low rates were reported from Asian settings, and intermediate rates from Australasia. High rates were observed in Nordic and US settings. One Taiwanese study not included in the review reported an intermediate proportion with alcohol abuse (20%) in Chinese suicide attempters admitted to a geropsychiatric unit [25]. Controlled studies are needed, as the base rate of alcohol use disorders in the underlying population will affect results. Culturally determined patterns of alcohol consumption may play an important role. On a population level, suicide rates appear to be higher in countries with "drink to get drunk" consumption patterns [26]. The Southern European alcohol use pattern appears to be less conducive to suicidal behavior. In line with this theory, a low rate of alcoholism (3%) was noted in a recent French study on suicide attempters aged 60 and above [27].

There are several clinical studies that compare substance use disorders in older and younger suicide attempters. Twelve percent of the elderly (65+) patients who were referred to an Australian poison unit had alcohol dependence/ abuse, and this proportion did not differ from that observed in patients under age 65 [28]. An age difference was noted in a Finnish study, however [29]; 28% of elderly (60+) suicide attempters had a substance use disorder, compared to 57% among those under the age of 60. One study that focused on sex differences in late life suicide attempts (65+) found that the association between suicide intent and attempt lethality was greater in men than in women, but the impact of lifetime substance use disorders did not differ by sex [30]. Swedish researchers examined rates of alcohol use disorders in elderly suicide completers and attempters residing in the same catchment area.

Proportions with alcohol use disorders were strikingly similar in the two groups [31], providing further evidence for the observation that determinants of attempted and completed suicide tend to overlap in the elderly [32].

Acute Alcohol Intoxication and Suicidal Behavior

Conwell and colleagues reported positive post-mortem screening for blood alcohol in 15% of a cohort of U.S. suicides aged 64-73 years and in 6% of those aged 74 and above [33]. A higher proportion (29%) was observed in a Swedish suicide cohort aged 65 and above [16]. As expected, the proportion with a positive screening was greater among those with a history of alcohol use disorder (64%) than those without (18%).

Regarding attempted suicide, over half (55%) of the elderly suicide attempters who took part in a Finnish study reported having used alcohol prior to the attempt [29]. While high, this proportion was significantly less than noted for attempters aged under 60 years (78%). Acute alcohol use has been shown to increase suicide attempt lethality in mixed age attempters [34], but data is lacking to date regarding elderly.

A Model of Suicidal Behavior in Alcoholism

Conner and Duberstein [35] introduced a model of suicidal behavior in individuals with alcoholism. Aggression/impulsivity, severity of alcoholism, negative affect and hopelessness were seen as factors of importance. Precipitating factors included major depression and stressful life events, and in this connection interpersonal problems were seen to play a central role. The model makes clinical sense, but it is yet to be tested on a large cohort of elderly suicide decedents and attempters. A factor that might be expected to play a less prominent role in late-life suicides might be impulsive-aggressive traits. There is some evidence that the importance of these traits decreases with increasing age [36]. A violent suicide method might be construed as a marker of aggression aimed at one self, and two separate studies suggest that older persons with alcohol use disorder might actually be less apt to use violent suicide methods than their peers without this disorder [37]; [16].

While one might argue that persons with a familial propensity might commit suicide before reaching old age, results from an exploratory study on suicide in first-degree relatives of elderly suicide victims suggested familial aggregation of suicides [38]. Previous episodes of suicidal behavior were more common among elderly suicide decedents who lost first-degree relatives by suicide than in those without family member suicides. This points to a "suicidal diathesis," that is, a vulnerability to react with suicidality in times of stress [39]. In 6 of the 85 elderly suicide cases, proxy informants reported that a suicide had occurred in an offspring prior to the suicide of the elderly decedent. All six of the elderly suicide victims who lost offspring by suicide had substance use disorders and all but one of the offspring who committed suicide were alcoholics. While results of this northern European study cannot be directly extrapolated to other settings, findings parallel reports of parental alcohol dependence and offspring suicidal behavior in younger cohorts in varied geographical settings [40] [41] [42].

IMPLICATIONS FROM A PUBLIC HEALTH PERSPECTIVE

An association between alcohol use disorders and suicide has been observed in some geographical settings, but not in others. Discrepant results may reflect cultural diversity with regard to alcohol availability, patterns of consumption, differing base rates of alcohol use disorders in the underlying population and regional variation with regard to the epidemiology of both fatal and non-fatal self-harm. The impact of changing demographics, in combination with increasing alcohol consumption in Baby Boomers [4] and in females [43] remains to be seen. Larger studies are needed to ascertain the role of alcohol use disorders and suicidal behavior in the elderly in different world regions.

From a public health perspective, primary prevention of alcohol use disorders across the life cycle could in time impact on elderly suicide rates. In this connection, reduction in alcohol availability might provide an important strategy [44].

The availability of suicide methods is another important focus for suicide prevention strategies. Relatively high rates of suicide by medication overdose among elderly alcoholic suicides signal a need for clinicians to be restrictive in prescribing sedatives and hypnotics to this patient group. These drugs were associated with increased risk of suicide even after adjustment for confounding by indication [45], and persons with a background in alcohol use disorder might be more prone to have a prescription for such drugs. Impaired judgement and increased disinhibition brought on by acute alcohol intoxication can elicit impulsive suicidal acts in vulnerable individuals, making decreased access to both drugs and firearms an important prevention priority.

IMPLICATIONS FOR CARE PROVIDERS

Recent research points to the important role to be played by depression care managers in the treatment of late life depression in primary care [46]. Given the observation regarding the co-occurence of major depression and alcoholism in elderly suicides, persons who monitor elders with depression should be on the lookout for signs of alcohol overconsumption. Screening questionnaires could be useful in this context. The CAGE questionnaire has been shown to have relatively good psychometric properties in older patients [47]. The authors of a recent literature review regarding screening for alcohol misuse [48] concluded that while the CAGE was more appropriate for detecting dependence, the AUDIT [49] was more useful for the detection of risky drinking in elderly primary care patients.

Short treatments could be initiated for risk consumers. While it is unclear at this point whether such interventions could actually reduce suicide risk in elders who over consume alcohol, it is interesting to note that short treatments appear to be more successful in decreasing alcohol consumption in men than in women [50]. The reverse (i.e., lack of effect in males) has been reported for suicide prevention strategies that specifically target depression [51].

As pointed out above, depression is common in elderly suicide decedents with alcohol use disorders. It has been suggested that adults with comorbid major depressive disorder and alcohol use disorder have earlier onset, more comorbidity and more severe course of illness than their counterparts without alcohol use disorder [52]. While elderly-specific data are lacking in this regard, clinical experience speaks for a need for individualized treatments for elderly with major depression and comorbid alcohol use disorder. Management in this age group may be further complicated by the existence of physical illness and functional disability, which can compound suicide risk. Comorbid cases may require specialist psychogeriatric services, working in close conjunction with providers of alcohol services and, in the case of the medically ill/functionally impaired, with G.P.s/somatic specialists and home care assistants. The latter are an important group from a suicide prevention perspective because they can serve as "gatekeepers", sensing changes in mood and suicidality that might otherwise go undetected. Contact between health care providers and the family is also essential. Family members may be aware of the elderly person's death wishes/suicidal ideation [53], and it is imperative that this information reaches the clinician so that management can be intensified.

The need for repeat assessments of suicide risk in elderly persons with comorbid depression and alcohol use disorders cannot be overemphasized. Clinical experience shows us that the level of suicidality can change rapidly in persons with this diagnostic pattern. Some elders with early onset alcoholism and recurrent depression may have extremely long "suicidal careers", but survival to old age should not be misconstrued as a sign of low risk in the future. Monitoring of suicidality is particularly important during the month following hospital discharge. A clinical tool that might prove useful in the management of elderly with comorbid depression and alcohol use disorder is the Reasons for living--Older Adults Scale [54].

CONCLUSION

Results from psychological autopsy studies from a number of western settings suggest a rather strong association between alcohol use disorder and suicide in late life. The association is not consistent worldwide, and this might in part be attributed to differences in alcohol consumption patterns, base rates of alcohol use disorders and rates of both lethal and non-lethal self-harm. National suicide prevention strategies need to be tailored to meet the risks of underlying populations. Given the aging of populations worldwide, and changing trends in alcohol consumption, some regions may need to expand prevention efforts in order to target elderly alcoholics, especially those with comorbid depression.

REFERENCES

[1] Conwell Y, Duberstein PR, Caine ED: Risk factors for suicide in later life. *Biol Psychiatry* 2002; 52(3): 193-204.

[2] Harris EC, Barraclough B: Suicide as an outcome for mental disorders. A meta-analysis. *Br J Psychiatry* 1997; 170: 205-228.

[3] Wilcox HC, Conner KR, Caine ED: Association of alcohol and drug use disorders and completed suicide: an empirical review of cohort studies. *Drug Alcohol Depend* 2004; 76 Suppl: S11-19.

[4] Blow FC, Brockmann LM, Barry KL: Role of alcohol in late-life suicide. *Alcohol Clin Exp Res* 2004; 28(5 Suppl): 48S-56S.

[5] Ogborne AC, Smart RG: Public opinion on the health benefits of moderate drinking: results from a Canadian National Population Health Survey. *Addiction* 2001; 96(4): 641-649.

[6] Turvey CL, Schultz SK, Klein DM: Alcohol use and health outcomes in the oldest old. *Substance Abuse Treatment Prevention and Policy* 2006; 1:8.

[7] Nakaya N, Kikuchi N, Shimazu T, Ohmori K, Kakizaki M, Sone T, Awata S, Kuriyama S, Tsuji I: Alcohol consumption and suicide mortality among Japanese men: the Ohsaki Study. *Alcohol* 2007; 41(7): 503-510.

[8] Barraclough BM: Suicide in the elderly. *British Journal of Psychiatry* 1971; 120 (suppl 6): 87-97.

[9] Chiu HF, Yip PS, Chi I, Chan S, Tsoh J, Kwan CW, LI SF, Conwell Y, Caine E: Elderly suicide in Hong Kong--a case-controlled psychological autopsy study. *Acta Psychiatr Scand* 2004; 109(4): 299-305.

[10] Conwell Y, Olsen K, Caine ED, Flannery C: Suicide in later life: psychological autopsy findings. *Int Psychogeriatr* 1991; 3(1): 59-66.

[11] Conner KR, Duberstein PR, Conwell Y: The validity of proxy-based data in suicide research: a study of patients 50 years of age and older who attempted suicide. I. Psychiatric diagnoses. *Acta Psychiatr Scand* 2001; 104(3): 204-209.

[12] Harwood D, Hawton K, Hope T, Jacoby R: Psychiatric disorder and personality factors associated with suicide in older people: a descriptive and case-control study. *Int J Geriatr Psychiatry* 2001; 16(2): 155-165.

[13] Preville M, Hebert R, Boyer R, Bravo G, Seguin M: Physical health and mental disorder in elderly suicide: a case-control study. *Aging Ment Health* 2005; 9(6): 576-584.

[14] Conwell Y, Lyness JM, Duberstein P, Cox C, Seidlitz L, DiGiorgio A, Caine ED: Completed suicide among older patients in primary care practices: a controlled study. *J Am Geriatr Soc* 2000; 48(1): 23-29.

[15] Beautrais AL: A case control study of suicide and attempted suicide in older adults. *Suicide Life Threat Behav* 2002; 32(1): 1-9.

[16] Waern M: Alcohol dependence and misuse in elderly suicides: *Alcohol and Alcoholism* 2003; 38(3): 249-254.

[17] Conner KR, Beautrais AL, Conwell Y: Moderators of the relationship between alcohol dependence and suicide and medically serious suicide attempts: analyses of Canterbury Suicide Project data. *Alcohol Clin Exp Res* 2003; 27(7): 1156-1161.

[18] Waern M, Rubenowitz E, Wilhelmson K: Predictors of suicide in the old elderly. *Gerontology* 2003; 49(5): 328-334.

[19] Grabbe L, Demi A, Camann MA, Potter LV: The health status of elderly persons in the last year of life: a comparison of deaths by suicide, injury, and natural causes. *Am J Public Health* 1997; 87(3): 434-437.

[20] Turvey CL, Conwell Y, Jones MP, Phillips C, Simonsick E, Pearson JL, Wallace R: Risk factors for late-life suicide: a prospective, community-based study. *Am J Geriatr Psychiatry* 2002; 10(4): 398-406.

[21] Pfaff JJ, Almeida OP, Witte TK, Waesche MC, Joiner TE, Jr: Relationship between quantity and frequency of alcohol use and indices of suicidal behavior in an elderly Australian sample. *Suicide Life Threat Behav* 2007; 37(6): 616-626.
[22] Liu IC, Chiu CH: Case-control study of suicide attempts in the elderly. *Int Psychogeriatr* 2009; 19: 1-7.
[23] Hawton K, Harriss L: Deliberate self-harm in people aged 60 years and over: characteristics and outcome of a 20-year cohort. *Int J Geriatr Psychiatry* 2006; 21(6): 572-581.
[24] Chan J, Draper B, Banerjee S: Deliberate self-harm in older adults: a review of the literature from 1995 to 2004. *Int J Geriatr Psychiatry* 2007; 22(8): 720-732.
[25] Yang CH, Tsai SJ, Chang JW, Hwang JP: Characteristics of Chinese suicide attempters admitted to a geropsychiatric unit. *Int J Geriatr Psychiatry* 2001; 16(11): 1033-1036.
[26] Ramstedt M: Alcohol and suicide in 14 European countries. *Addiction* 2001; 96 Suppl 1: S59-75.
[27] Lebret S, Perret-Vaille E, Mulliez A, Gerbaud L, Jalenques I: Elderly suicide attempters: characteristics and outcome. *Int J Geriatr Psychiatry* 2006; 21(11): 1052-1059.
[28] Ticehurst S, Carter GL, Clover KA, Whyte IM, Raymond J, Fryer J: Elderly patients with deliberate self-poisoning treated in an Australian general hospital. *Int Psychogeriatr* 2002; 14(1): 97-105.
[29] Suominen K, Isometsa E, Lonnqvist J: Elderly suicide attempters with depression are often diagnosed only after the attempt. *Int J Geriatr Psychiatry* 2004; 19(1): 35-40.
[30] Dombrovski AY, Szanto K, Duberstein P, Conner KR, Houck PR, Conwell Y: Sex differences in correlates of suicide attempt lethality in late life. *Am J Geriatr Psychiatry* 2008; 16(11): 905-913.
[31] Waern M, Wiktorsson S: Alcohol use and suicide in older persons. *International Psychogeriatrics* 2005; 17 S2: 28-29.
[32] Pearson JL, Conwell Y: Suicide in late life: challenges and opportunities for research. Introduction. *Int Psychogeriatr* 1995; 7(2): 131-136.
[33] Conwell Y, Rotenberg M, Caine ED: Completed suicide at age 50 and over. *J Am Geriatr Soc* 1990; 38(6): 640-644.
[34] Sher L, Oquendo MA, Richardson-Vejlgaard R, Makhija NM, Posner K, Mann JJ, Stanley BH: Effect of acute alcohol use on the lethality of suicide attempts in patients with mood disorders. *J Psychiatr Res* 2009; 43(10): 901-905.
[35] Conner KR, Duberstein PR: Predisposing and precipitating factors for suicide among alcoholics: empirical review and conceptual integration. *Alcohol Clin Exp Res* 2004; 28(5 Suppl): 6S-17S.
[36] McGirr A, Renaud J, Bureau A, Seguin M, Lesage A, Turecki G: Impulsive-aggressive behaviours and completed suicide across the life cycle: a predisposition for younger age of suicide. *Psychol Med* 2008; 38(3): 407-417.
[37] Conwell Y, Duberstein PR, Cox C, Herrmann J, Forbes N, Caine ED: Age differences in behaviors leading to completed suicide. *Am J Geriatr Psychiatry* 1998; 6(2): 122-126.
[38] Waern M: Suicides among family members of elderly suicide victims: an exploratory study. *Suicide Life Threat Behav* 2005; 35(3): 356-364.

[39] Mann JJ, Waternaux C, Haas GL, Malone KM: Toward a clinical model of suicidal behavior in psychiatric patients. *Am J Psychiatry* 1999; 156(2): 181-189.

[40] Brent DA, Bridge J, Johnson BA, Connolly J: Suicidal behavior runs in families. A controlled family study of adolescent suicide victims. *Arch Gen Psychiatry* 1996; 53(12): 1145-1152.

[41] Runeson B: Psychoactive substance use disorder in youth suicide. *Alcohol Alcohol* 1990; 25(5): 561-568.

[42] Statham DJ, Heath AC, Madden PA, Bucholz KK, Bierut L, Dinwiddie SH, Slutske WS, Dunne MP, Martin NG: Suicidal behaviour: an epidemiological and genetic study. *Psychol Med* 1998; 28(4): 839-855.

[43] Haw C, Hawton K, Casey D, Bale E, Shepherd A: Alcohol dependence, excessive drinking and deliberate self-harm: trends and patterns in Oxford, 1989-2002. *Soc Psychiatry Psychiatr Epidemiol* 2005; 40(12): 964-971.

[44] Brady J: The association between alcohol misuse and suicidal behaviour. *Alcohol and Alcoholism* 2006; 41(5): 473-478.

[45] Carlsten A, Waern M: Are sedatives and hypnotics associated with increased suicide risk of suicide in the elderly? *BMC Geriatr* 2009; 9: 20.

[46] Schulberg HC, Bruce ML, Lee PW, Williams JW, Jr., Dietrich AJ: Preventing suicide in primary care patients: the primary care physician's role. *Gen Hosp Psychiatry* 2004; 26(5): 337-345.

[47] Ewing JA: Detecting alcoholism. The CAGE questionnaire. *Jama* 1984; 252(14): 1905-1907.

[48] Berks J, McCormick R: Screening for alcohol misuse in elderly primary care patients: a systematic literature review. *Int Psychogeriatr* 2008; 20(6): 1090-1103.

[49] Saunders JB, Aasland OG, Babor TF, de la Fuente JR, Grant M: Development of the Alcohol Use Disorders Identification Test (AUDIT): WHO Collaborative Project on Early Detection of Persons with Harmful Alcohol Consumption--II. *Addiction* 1993; 88(6): 791-804.

[50] Kaner EF, Dickinson HO, Beyer F, Pienaar E, Schlesinger C, Campbell F, Saunders JB, Burnand B, Heather N: The effectiveness of brief alcohol interventions in primary care settings: A systematic review. *Drug Alcohol Rev* 2009; 28(3): 301-323.

[51] Rutz W: Preventing suicide and premature death by education and treatment. *J Affect Disord* 2001; 62(1-2): 123-129.

[52] Sher L, Stanley BH, Harkavy-Friedman JM, Carballo JJ, Arendt M, Brent DA, Sperling D, Lizardi D, Mann JJ, Oquendo MA: Depressed patients with co-occurring alcohol use disorders: a unique patient population. *J Clin Psychiatry* 2008; 69(6): 907-915.

[53] Waern M, Beskow J, Runeson B, Skoog I: Suicidal feelings in the last year of life in elderly people who commit suicide. *Lancet* 1999; 354(9182): 917-918.

[54] Edelstein BA, Heisel MJ, McKee DR, Martin RR, Koven LP, Duberstein PR, Britton PC: Development and Psychometric Evaluation of the Reasons for Living--Older Adults Scale: A Suicide Risk Assessment Inventory. *Gerontologist* 2009 Jul 21.

Part VII. Suicidal Behavior in Individuals with Comorbid Substance Use Disorders and Other Psychiatric Disorders

In: Suicidal Behavior in Alcohol and Drug Abuse... ISBN: 978-1-60876-919-3
Editors: L. Sher, A. Vilens, pp. 455-475

Chapter 26

COMORBID BIPOLAR AND SUBSTANCE USE DISORDERS: IMPACT ON SUICIDAL BEHAVIOR

Brit Haver and Ketil J. Oedegaard
University of Bergen, Bergen, Norway

ABSTRACT

Bipolar disorders (BPD) are common, with a lifelong risk of episodes of mood swings, deteriorating interepisode functioning, lower quality of life, as well as increased mortality. Comorbidity between BPD and substance use disorders (SUD) is more frequent than for any other psychiatric disorder. Substance abuse may precede, precipitate or follow the first episode of mood disorder, leading to poorer treatment compliance, an overall worse outcome, and an even higher suicide risk. We hypothesize that a common underpinning may explain the frequent association between BPD and substance abuse, namely impulsivity and irritable, hyperthymic or cyclothymic temperaments. Substance abuse causes impaired cognitive functioning in the frontal-cortical areas, including the inhibition of impulsive responses, thereby setting up a negative spiraling effect during the course of time. Abstinence may on the other hand set up neurogenesis in the damaged areas of the brain, thereby regaining executive cognitive functions necessary for compliance with treatment. We believe that a significant part of the poor prognosis related to BPD – and specifically mortality related to suicide – can be explained by undetected SUD which accompany the disorder. Early detection and prevention of SUD among bipolar patients, systematic use of recommended treatment regimes, and long-term follow-up may help these patients obtain a significantly better prognosis and quality of life. Integrated treatment of the BPD and substance abuse may prevent new mood swings, improve patient compliance and reduce suicidal acts. Specific programs for this subgroup of bipolar patients need to be implemented in general psychiatry and mood clinics.

INTRODUCTION

A survey among 500 psychiatrists in the UK and the US about treatment challenges for bipolar patients showed that patients comorbid with substance abuse were rated as having the highest level of unmet treatment needs, followed by patients with rapid cycling [1].

Most psychiatrists have met this specific group of patients: males or females with a bipolar disorder who have frequent inpatient stays related to substance abuse. These patients are not easily forgotten because they may be involved in strange activities, stirring up emotions in their environments. Often they are brought to the hospital by the police because of noisy or peculiar behavior in public places during an episode of elated mood. Shortly afterwards, they may however develop a full-blown picture of major depression, ruminating over the sad consequences of their recent behavior.

Bipolar disorders generally are a major health problem, resulting in reduced capacity for work and social relations, as well as higher mortality and lower quality of life [2]. The subgroup of patients comorbid with substance abuse have an even more serious outcome [3], especially when it comes to suicide attempts and suicide. These patients are heavy consumers of health services, and represent major challenges for the psychiatrists. In addition, it is a clinical impression that they may suffer even more than any other subgroup of psychiatric patients. They often start with the very best prospects, ending up with little success in most aspects of life. Also, they may represent heavy burdens for their families, if there is any family or friends left in the long run. Many of these patients end their lives by suicide. Ernest Hemingway's life and death illustrates this tragic outcome of comorbid alcohol dependence and bipolar disorder [4]. As therapists responsible for the treatment of this group of patients we might wonder: could we help prevent this fatal course of the disorder?

Bipolar patients with substance abuse impose high quality clinical skills to be delivered by the specialist services. At the same time, many unanswered questions exist as to which treatment regimes work best. In this chapter we will focus on both the epidemiology and the clinical aspects of comorbid bipolar and substance use disorders. Since alcohol is the drug of choice for most people – with and without bipolar disorders (BPD) - the majority of our clinical experience and research evidence focuses on the relationship between alcohol and BPD. The relationship between cannabis, other drugs and BPD will be mentioned when of special relevance. We will discuss various theories and try to understand the frequent coexistence of these disorders – and their differential impact on suicidal behavior. Also, we will provide evidence of sex differences related to this area of clinical research.

EPIDEMIOLOGY OF BIPOLAR DISORDERS

The reported lifetime prevalence rates for bipolar I (BP I) (Major depression and mania) disorder are fairly stable about 1 %, but may vary between studies (0.8-3.3 %) [5-10]. Only minor sex differences are disclosed. The prevalence rates increase to 10.9 % for bipolar II disorders (BP II) (Major depression and hypomania), and when using a wider definition of bipolar disorders, including minor depression, hypomanic symptoms and subthreshold disorders - without specifying the time period of symptom expression [11, 12]. The concept of bipolar spectrum disorder has been validated in a French clinical study, estimating that bipolar II disorders constitute 39 % of major depressive episodes [13]. Also, recurrent unipolar major depression (UP) may turn into bipolar disorder, adding to the prevalence rates reported above [14]. As mentioned, bipolar I disorder is evenly distributed among women and men, while depressive disorders are consistently overrepresented among women. The bipolar disorders starting in childhood and adolescence are other areas of importance, since these subgroups often are unrecognized and untreated, carry high risks of developing alcohol and drug abuse, as well as suicide [15-18]. The prevalence rates of physical or sexual abuse and PTSD are high among this group of youngsters with a bipolar disorder, and the chances of teenage pregnancy, trouble with the police, and an impaired course of the bipolar disorder including suicide attempts and substance abuse are high [17, 19, 20].

Epidemiology of Substance Abuse

The prevalence rates of substance abuse and dependence may vary widely between countries, and sex differences are pervasive, showing consistently higher frequencies among males. For example, in the National Comorbidity Survey from the US, the lifetime prevalence of alcohol abuse was 9.4 and of alcohol dependence 14.1, whilst the lifetime prevalence rates of drug abuse and dependence were 4.4 % and 7.5 % respectively. In a Norwegian epidemiological study the rates for alcohol abuse and dependence were fairly similar to those reported from the US. On the other hand, the rates for drug abuse and dependence were markedly lower: only 1.9 and 1.5 respectively [10]. Concerning sex differences, any substance use disorder was three times more common among men compared to women in Norway. Similarly, sex differences were substantial for all kinds of drugs in the US [8].

Epidemiology of Comorbid Bipolar and Substance Use Disorders

The rates of comorbid substance use and bipolar disorders are substantially higher than expected by chance. Although comorbidity between substance abuse and psychiatric disorders is a general phenomenon, the rates for bipolar disorders are higher than for any other Axis I disorder. This has been extensively documented in epidemiological studies from the US [7, 21, 22] as well as in Europe [23]. For example, in the Epidemiologic Catchment Area Study (ECA), subjects with mania were 6 times more likely to have a substance use disorder than the general population [22]. In the National Epidemiologic Survey on Alcohol and Related Conditions (NESARC) study, bipolar I subjects had an OR 3.5 for any alcohol use disorder and an OR of 4.8 for any drug use disorder [6]. Previous studies have shown an even higher comorbidity between mania and drug dependence, namely an OR about 8.4 [21]. In clinical populations of bipolar I disorder, substance use disorders are present in at least 40 % of the patients [24]. In a study of bipolar I and II patients, Bauer et al. found that 72 % of bipolar patients had a lifetime – and about 34 % a current - substance use disorder [25]. Mania has been closely related to both alcohol and cannabis use [26].

Generally, the substance use comorbidity between bipolar II and bipolar spectrum disorders has been less extensively studied based on general population data. In clinical populations, however, alcohol abuse has been specifically related to bipolar II disorder [23]. Recently, a study of the lifetime comorbidity of bipolar disorder with other *DSM-IV*/CIDI disorders in the United States (National Comorbidity Survey–Replication) found significantly increased OR for comorbid substance abuse in both bipolar I (OR: 8.8) and bipolar II (OR: 3.9) [9]. Interestingly, this study also found an increased OR for substance abuse in patients with bipolar spectrum disorders (OR: 3.2).This bipolar spectrum group was also studied in the Zürich study [12], where it was found that the group of patients that are encompassed by a broader BP-II definition accounts for most of the comorbidity of alcohol use disorders (AUD) with major depressive disorders. The broadest concept of BP-II explained two thirds of all cases of comorbidity of AUD with major depressive episodes [27].

Comorbidity of BPD with ADHD, anxiety disorders, eating disorders, and personality disorders is also pervasive [28-36]. These comorbidities may add to treatment challenges associated with BPD and SUD.

Theories about the Relationship between BPD and Substance Abuse

When substance abuse is coupled with a bipolar disorder, this is in current psychiatric diagnostic classification systems expressed as a dual diagnosis, implicitly saying that the co-morbid disorders are separate entities, rather than related psychopathological syndromes. While concomitant disorders may branch from a common substrate, comorbidity usually implies that substance abuse and other mental disorders spring from relatively distinct processes. Nonetheless, it has been hypothesized that the common interaction between them, is indeed the result of a combined pathophysiological underpinning [37].

One theory about the relationship between bipolar disorders and substance abuse that could reflect such a shared pathophysiological underpinning, focuses on impulsivity, which is found to be a trait among both BP I and II subjects, even present between episodes of mania or hypomania [37]. However, the presence of substance abuse increases this interepisode impulsivity [38]. Impulsivity generally refers to premature, unduly risky, poorly conceived tasks. Dysfunctional impulsivity includes deficits in attention, lack of reflection and/or insensitivity to consequences, which is a common part of the addictive process in substance abusers [39]. In a review on the relationship between impulsivity and drug use, it is hypothesized that different aspects of impulsivity may play a differential impact on drug use: trait impulsivity may be more important for drug use during adolescence, while state impulsivity may be more important among adults [40]. Also, acute and chronic drug use may increase impulsive behavior, setting up a negative spiral, causing neurotoxic effects in the frontal-cortical areas of the brain. This results in impairment of executive functioning, which include abstract thinking, motivation, planning, attention to tasks and inhibition of impulsive responses [39]. Thereby, impulsiveness – which may be an initial driving force during the start of alcohol abuse – is reinforced by the drug itself. Also, the general impairment of executive functioning caused by alcohol may enhance the chances that impulsivity "wins" in a situation where reflection and thoughts about the consequences would have stopped the actions earlier in the drinking career. Thus, impulsivity was related to seriousness of suicide attempts in a study of bipolar patients, while substance abuse did not have an effect after impulsivity was taken into account [41]. Abstinence, on the other hand, causes burst of neurogenesis and brain regrowth, which makes it possible to regain executive functioning [39].

The Role of Temperament

The issue of comorbidity in bipolar disorder is wide-ranging, encompassing numerous conditions, among others anxiety disorders, impulse control disorders, eating disorders, substance abuse, and personality disorders. Increased proneness to substance abuse is evidenced across the entire bipolar spectrum [42], and even a family history of bipolar-II spectrum disorders has been related to alcohol abuse among socially phobic patients [43]. Several studies have observed the role of affective temperaments in substance related issues, suggesting they represent a constitutional predisposition to risk-taking, amplifying the problem of substance abuse. Accordingly, healthy individuals, evaluated along Akiskal and Mallya's s interview TEMPS-I [44-46] and a questionnaire on substance-use were found to be at risk of substance use if they had a hyperthymic or irritable temperament. Others found a clear association between hyperthymia and alcohol use [47] and cyclothymia and alcohol abuse [48]. Cyclothymic temperament was also found to distinguish a sample of methadone-maintained addicts from a control group of non-abusers independently of dual diagnosis status [42] .

It is likely that the affective dysregulation of bipolar disorder extends beyond elation and depression to include irritability, impulsivity, substance abuse and suicidal behaviour, leading to an unstable, unpredictable and stormy life [49, 50].This is particularly true for bipolar patients with cyclothymic temperaments because of their extreme mood instability [51]. Recently a large French study identified cyclothymic temperament as a significant risk factor for suicidal behavior [52]. Previously, cyclothymic temperament has been found to be a prospective predictor of bipolarity and suicidality in children and adolescents with major depressive disorder [53]. We suggest that the cyclothymic temperamental character might represent a mediating or underlying trait in the intricate pattern of substance abuse and suicidal behavior that so many bipolar patients demonstrate during their life span. Also, affective temperaments are related to earlier age of onset of both major depressive disorder and bipolar disorder [54].

The self-medication hypothesis, especially between alcohol and bipolar disorder - although popular among the patients – is however not much supported by empirical evidence [55-57].

The Temporal Sequence between BPD and Substance Abuse

Few longitudinal studies exist on the temporal sequence of substance abuse and bipolar disorders in a lifetime perspective. We would need epidemiological studies from early adolescence, as well as studies of different clinical populations of BPD over a long time, in order to better understand the intricate interaction between these disorders. A review published in 2005 reported a strong association between bipolar disorder and substance abuse, the direction of causality was however uncertain [27]. Important findings have later come from the longitudinal epidemiological study in Zurich [58]. A key finding of their study was that bipolar disorder tends to manifest first in the comorbid sequence, i.e., in the majority of cases the onset of bipolar disorder occurred before age 20, whereas at this age alcohol use disorder was a minor problem but grew quickly in the third decade of life. In the prospective period from age 20/21 to 40/41 changes from bipolar-II to alcohol use disorder were several times more frequent than the reverse. In a Danish epidemiological study based on register data, the results were however the opposite: The risk of developing a psychiatric disorder in individuals who were already registered with alcohol use disorder (AUD) was larger than the risk of developing AUD in individuals already registered with another psychiatric disorder [59].

At the time of first clinical contact, about a third of the patients with BP I have developed substance abuse, and a trend towards increasing frequency was described over two years' observation period [60]. In a clinical study of the time sequence between BP I over 4.7 years, cannabis and alcohol use preceded or coincided with mania/ hypomania, and alcohol use preceded or coincided with depression [61]. An attempt to classify the BPI/ substance abuse sequence into Alcohol First, Bipolar First and BPD only showed that the affective symptomatic recurrence curves were fairly similar over five years among the groups [62]. However, the group of patients who developed alcohol abuse following first hospitalization had a less favorable outcome, and the symptomatic recurrences of alcohol use disorders were common among both comorbid groups of patients.

On the other hand, in many clinical settings and research studies, a comprehensive evaluation of the use of drugs and alcohol among first time diagnosed BP patients is not performed. Thus, the basis for preventive and treatment strategies is not established, and the impact of substance use and abuse can not be correctly evaluated over the course of time. Also, different substances have been associated with different clinical patterns and the course of BPD. For example, alcohol is more commonly associated with depressive episodes of bipolar disorder, while cannabis is almost exclusively associated with mania [60, 63]. Some important negative consequences of substance abuse generally on the outcome of BPD have nevertheless been well documented: a lack of compliance with the treatment regime, more frequent hospitalizations and increased mortality and suicide rates. Also, a slow recovery from the mood episodes has been reported [55, 57].

Bipolar Disorder and Suicide

Although varying suicide rates among bipolar patients are reported in the literature, these patients are highly overrepresented among those who complete suicide. About 15-20 % of the patients (variation between 5-60 %) end their life by suicide, and the risk is highest during the first illness period [55]. Certain seasonality has been observed, since suicide peaks during springtime, while bipolar depression peaks during wintertime. It has been assumed that activation caused by extensive light during late springtime may bring depressed subjects to commit suicide. Suicide generally runs in certain families, irrespective of psychiatric disorder, indicating genetic and shared environmental influences. A family history of both suicide and bipolar disorder would indicate an even higher risk of suicide. Also, a study among bipolar patients found that alcoholism and suicide attempts clustered in certain families [64].

In addition to substance abuse, clinical predictors of suicide among bipolar patients include a history of suicide attempts, mixed states and rapid cycling, as well as serious depression and psychosis [55].

IMPACT OF SUBSTANCE ABUSE ON SUICIDAL BEHAVIOR

Alcohol plays a major role in suicide attempts and completed suicides, and alcohol increases the risk of completed suicide, irrespective of other psychiatric disorder [65]. In an Estonian case control study of completed suicides, altogether 61 % had either alcohol abuse or dependence based on psychological autopsy [66]. Similar results are found in several studies from other Western countries. Irrespective of the general population's level of alcohol consumption, subjects with alcohol abuse or dependence are highly overrepresented among suicide completers [67]. In itself, chronic alcohol ingestion often precipitates depression, which partly could explain this overrepresentation. In addition, alcohol ingestion or acute intoxication often occurs as part of the suicidal action in subjects who have no previous alcohol problem. Thus, alcohol is found in the blood of suicide completers in a majority of cases, as well as in subjects performing serious suicide attempts. At a certain blood level, alcohol impairs judgment, increases impulsivity and aggression, and also reduces the impact of thoughts that usually inhibit the action of suicide. For example, thoughts about children and family may seem less relevant or even disappear during alcohol intoxication. Another action of alcohol is to reduce anxiety: maybe the fear of death is taken away, as well as the fear of being seriously harmed as a consequence of the suicidal act. On the other hand, alcohol restrictions or reduction in alcohol consumption at a general population level, do not necessarily reduce suicide mortality [68].

In a longitudinal study of 955 affectively ill patients over 14 years, it was found that temperament attributes such as impulsiveness and assertiveness were the best prospective predictors of completed suicide beyond the first 12 months after coming to treatment [69]. Suicides before 12 months were on the other hand predicted by clinical characteristics such as mixed affective syndromes with psychotic symptoms, rapid cycling, emotional turmoil plus depression. Substance abuse was however a significant predictor for short time and long-term suicide completion, as well as serious suicide attempts.

IMPACT OF SUBSTANCE ABUSE ON SUICIDAL BEHAVIOR RELATED TO BP

The overall risk for suicide attempts among bipolar I and bipolar II patients are higher than for any other Axis I psychiatric disorder, and the lifetime prevalence of suicidal ideation or attempts are about 80 % [70]. However, the incidence of suicide attempts differs remarkably during different phases of the BP disorder, being highest in the depressive and mixed phases of the disorder [71]. The connection between substance abuse and BPD and suicide may be attributed to increased impulsivity or impaired sleep, as well as destabilization of the illness itself [55]. Low levels of the serotonin metabolite 5-HIAA have been found in cerebrospinal fluid of violent suicide cases and in families with depression and alcoholism, as well as among subjects who have recovered from alcoholism. Thus, a genetic factor may play an important role, making certain subjects vulnerable to both suicide and alcohol abuse. This biological vulnerability may add to the effects on judgment exerted by the drug itself during intoxication [55]. Another factor is that subjects with mood disorders and substance abuse may receive less optimal health care contacts following suicide attempts [72].

The suicide mortality among psychiatric patients is generally high, especially for patients with affective disorders and substance abuse [73]. That specific study revealed sharp peaks of suicide mortality the first weeks after admission and discharge, making these time periods of special relevance for intervention. Among 15386 Swedish bipolar patients, the suicide rates were 15 for males and 22.4 for females, compared to the general population [74]. Similar results were found in a large Danish study (n=54103) covering all patients admitted for the first time to a psychiatric hospital during 1973-93 with an affective disorder [75]. Both studies report the highest suicide rate during the first year after the initial diagnosis, and younger age as a risk factor. Improved treatment strategies, better follow-up practices, and the involvement of family members after discharge was suggested to reduce suicide related to hospital stays.

However, the relative impact of alcohol abuse or dependence on the reported suicide mortality among patients with affective disorders cannot be evaluated from these large studies, since the initial assessment of substance use or substance use disorders generally is lacking from the register data and the clinical studies. Since we know that alcohol use disorders – and alcohol by itself – are closely related to suicidal acts, this limits the interpretation of the above referenced studies.

On the other hand, psychiatric disorders were found to be of little relevance in suicides among alcohol dependent patients – with or without comorbid psychiatric disorders [65]. This means that the impact of psychiatric disorders generally is lower when alcohol dependence is the primary disorder.

Sex Differences in BPD, Substance Abuse and Suicidal Behavior

There is a general sex difference between men and women when it comes to use and abuse of alcohol and illegal drugs: men drink more and do more drugs on a worldwide basis. Although there has been a reduction in the gap concerning alcohol and drug use between the sexes during the last decades, this still holds true. However, when it comes to alcohol use among female and male bipolar patients, there is a tendency that women with BP disorders use and abuse alcohol much the same way as their male counterparts. The usual sex difference is here more evened out. Thus, in a clinical study of lifetime risk for alcoholism among bipolar patients, it was found that bipolar men had a 2.77 higher risk while women had a 7.35 higher risk, compared to the general population. Nevertheless, a lifetime history of alcoholism was still more frequent among males with a bipolar disorder, compared to females [76]. Also, these bipolar men had a family history of alcoholism, while the women had a history of polysubstance abuse. This is an important observation for understanding the relationship between substance abuse and BPD generally, and specifically when it comes to the impact on suicidal behavior between the sexes.

Another important sex difference is related to suicidal behavior, where women generally are overrepresented among those who attempt suicide, while men are substantially overrepresented among those who commit suicide, although culturally based differences exist in a global perspective [67, 77, 78]. The female/ male sex ratio is usually about 1/ 3 for completed suicides but may vary up to 1/10 [79]. This may be related to the suicide methods applied: women generally use less lethal methods, since a majority intoxicate themselves, are discovered or seek help by themselves, while men more often use violent methods like shooting, jumping, hanging, carbon monoxide intoxication (let the car engine run in a closed garage), intentionally involve themselves in lethal traffic accidents or drowning at sea. Using these methods, few chances of survival exist. However, among completed suicides, hanging is the most prevalent suicide method in Europe for both women and men [80].

Among affectively ill patients – including unipolar depression – men still are overrepresented when it comes to completed suicides, and females are overrepresented concerning both harmless gestures, self mutilations with minimal intent to die, and serious suicide attempts. However, men were only 1.7 times as likely to commit suicide as females, while females were only 1.7 times as likely to engage in serious suicide attempts [69]. Among bipolar patients, however, women and men are as likely to commit suicide [55]. Thus, among affectively ill subjects, it seems that the sex differences are evened out compared to the total population of those who commit suicidal acts. Also, bipolar II disorders maybe significantly more prevalent among women compared to men, and even the response to lithium may show some sex differences [12, 81].

The Special Group of Bipolar Patients with PTSD, Childhood Sex Abuse and Severe Comorbid Alcohol Use Disorder

Prior research suggests that there may be gender differences in the longitudinal course of bipolar disorder (BD), women being more likely to have rapid cycling [82], mixed mania [83] and a history of severe childhood sexual and physical abuse [84, 85] and PTSD [29, 86]. Furthernore, most individuals with bipolar I disorder (BD I) have a lifetime substance use disorder (SUD)[9], and although more men than women with BD have a SUD, the risk of developing an alcohol use disorder is greater for women with BD compared to men with BD, relative to the general population [76]. Hence, both SUD and PTSD are associated with greater BD severity, more depressive symptoms, shorter euthymic periods, greater functional impairment, poorer quality of life, and more suicide attempts [87, 88]. The last study, which is recently published from the McLean Hospital, prospectively followed 89 bipolar patients with co-occurring substance use disorders for eight months. They were able to demonstrate that the effect of gender on mood outcomes was attenuated after accounting for lifetime sexual/physical abuse and PTSD diagnosis. This raises the question whether early trauma is connected with exaggerated cycles of mood shifts, increasing the probability of developing enduring changes in the brain physiology associated with substance abuse, a rapid cycling/dysphoric mood instability, and increased suicidality.

In sum, the existing literature indicates there is a particular group of bipolar women manifesting with mixed episodes, rapid cycling, PTSD, co-occurring substance abuse and suicidal behavior, with a less favorable prognosis. These women need special attention and interventions in order to improve their otherwise poor outcomes. However, a high frequency of physical or sexual abuse in childhood was found also among male veterans with bipolar disorder, which was associated with PTSD, substance abuse and higher likelihood of at least one suicide attempt during the follow-up period [89].

TREATMENT ASPECTS: BIPOLAR DISORDERS COMORBID WITH SUBSTANCE ABUSE

There are numerous guidelines for the pharmacological treatment of bipolar disorder, mostly presenting similar recommendations. Although the high prevalence of comorbid alcohol and substance abuse is everywhere recognized, no specific guidelines exist for this group of patients. Recommendations must therefore be based upon general advice for the treatment of bipolar disorder, taking into consideration additional information particularly relevant for patients with alcohol and substance abuse disorders. The Canadian Network for Mood and Anxiety Treatments (CANMAT) recently published updated guidelines in conjunction with the International Society for Bipolar Disorders (ISBD) [90].

The recommendations for the management of acute mania include lithium, valproate, and several atypical antipsychotics as first-line treatments. For the management of bipolar depression only, lithium, lamotrigine, and quietapine are acceptable as monotherapy. Also, olanzapine plus a selective serotonin reuptake inhibitor (SSRI), and lithium or valproate plus SSRI/ bupropion are recommended. First-line options for maintenance treatment of bipolar disorder include either lithium, lamotrigine or valproate, and olanzapine. However new data support the use of quetiapine monotherapy for the prevention of manic and depressive events, and aripiprazole monotherapy for the prevention of manic events.

In addition to pharmacotherapy, psychosocial interventions are recommended in the treatment of bipolar disorders. Both group psychoeducation, cognitive behaviour therapy (CBT), and interpersonal and social rhythm therapy (IPSRT) have confirmed a number of important benefits, such as decreased relapse rates, mood fluctuations, need for medications, and hospitalizations, as well as increased functioning and medication adherence [91]. Therefore, providing psychoeducation is an essential part of managing patients with BPD.

There is an apparent contradiction that emerges when selecting a suitable pharmacotherapy for bipolar patients with both substance abuse and suicidal behavior. First, according to clinical experience, and supported by clinical research, lithium has proven to be an effective strategy for prevention of suicide among bipolar patients, and should therefore be a first line consideration in the treatment of bipolar patients with a personal history of serious suicide attempts or a family history of completed suicides [55, 92-94]. However, lithium is the drug of choice first and foremost when it comes to prevention of mood swings among subjects with a classical BP I disorder. Typical lithium responders have euphoric manic episodes and a high degree of inter-episodic recovery [55]. They may represent a specific subgroup of bipolar patients with a certain neurobiological basis. Since laboratory tests are not yet available, the prediction of lithium response still rests upon a clinical judgment [95].

On the other hand, bipolar patients with comorbid alcohol and substance abuse often have a clinical presentation that includes mixed episodes, rapid cycling and high levels of inter-episodic symptomatology, all indicators of a lithium non-responder. For these patients, other treatment strategies must be applied. Often valproate is considered the first line treatment for patients with predominantly mixed episodes [91]. Valproate is easier to take, represents less risk of intoxication and may have less subjectively experienced side effects. On the other hand, polycystic ovaries and possible teratogenic side effects limit the use of this drug among young women.

Another major obstacle when using lithium is the non-compliance seen among substance abusers. The risk of intoxication is higher, since substance abusers may forget that they have taken their daily dose, and take an extra dose. Alternatively, they do not take the drug during periods of substance abuse, thereby increasing the risk of recurrence of depression or mania by a combined effect: the substance abuse itself and the sudden change of lithium level in the serum. So, if you prescribe lithium to anyone who has an established alcohol problem, the follow-up procedure must be even more frequent than usual. You may even add an anticraving drug – such as naltrexone or acamprosate - or disulfiram (Antabus) - to prevent substance abuse. The conclusion is that lithium can be used only among patients who live a reasonably stable life – and who can abstain from alcohol and drugs during periods of high risk for relapse – to either new episodes of mood disorder or substance abuse – or both. Thus, patients in their early phases of bipolar disorder – without an established substance abuse or dependence - may benefit from lithium in terms of prevention of mood cycles, substance abuse and suicide.

On the other hand, the risk of intentional lithium intoxication as a suicidal gesture or completed suicide exists, and should be considered. Hence, it appears that combining the optimal treatments for suicide protection and substance abuse is impossible in many cases, since a typical bipolar patient with substance abuse may be a lithium non-responder or non-compliant drug taker.

Pharmacotherapy of co-occurring bipolar disorder and substance abuse disorders was reviewed in 2006 [96]. The authors identified three randomized double blind placebo controlled trials demonstrating that valproate decreased alcohol use [97], that carbamazepine decreased the use of cocaine [98], and that lithium reduced the number of positive urine screens for polysubstance use in adolescents [99]. Furthermore, quetiapin reduced the craving for cocaine and amphetamine in an open randomized controlled study [100]. In addition, some data from open–label trials suggest that lamotrigine reduces cocaine craving [101, 102], and aripiprazole can decrease alcohol and cocaine use [103].

Integrated Pharmacological and Psychosocial Treatment for BPD and SUD

In spite of the common comorbidity and poor prognosis of substance abuse in bipolar patients, little research has focused on integrated pharmacological and psychosocial treatments. One specific group intervention program for patients with bipolar disorders and substance abuse was developed by a group at Harvard University. It has been thoroughly described and also tested in a randomized controlled trial[104-106]. The program called Integrated Group Treatment (IGT) consists of 20 weekly group sessions lasting one hour, each of which is dedicated to a specific topic. An important aspect of this program is to integrate the two disorders into a single disorder called "bipolar substance abuse", thereby enhancing the patients' understanding of how abstinence from alcohol and drugs helps one's bipolar disorder, as well as how taking a mood stabilizer helps one's substance abuse. A randomized controlled trial of IGT was found to reduce substance use significantly in this population. This suggests that integrated group therapy could fill a treatment gap for this population, which traditionally has poor outcomes [106].

However, to the authors' knowledge, no studies have specifically addressed treatments affecting the high suicide rates among bipolar patients with comorbid SUD. In the last decade effective pharmacotherapy has been combined with more and more effective psychosocial interventions. The main targets of these interventions have been to prevent medication non-compliance, lifestyle modifications, early detection of relapse, and modification of family and interpersonal conflicts [107, 108]. These interventions, while reducing relapse and recurrences, may indirectly reduce the risk of suicide. In a study of intensive psychotherapy targeted at reducing suicidality in bipolar patients, it was found that patients receiving pharmacotherapy (lithium, valproate, carbamazepine) and psychosocial interventions over a two year period experienced a threefold reduction in suicide attempts during the acute treatment phase, and a 18-fold reduction during maintenance. No significant difference between the group receiving psychotherapy specific to bipolar disorder and the group receiving non-specific clinical management was found [109].

The interaction between pharmacotherapy and psychosocial interventions in bipolar patients with substance abuse and suicidal behavior is complex, and further studies are needed to present interventions reducing the chance of suicide in these patients who carry the highest risk of self-inflicted death.

FURTHER TREATMENT RECOMMENDATIONS

A recent study showed that bipolar depressed patients - with and without alcohol use disorders (AUD) - received inadequate antidepressant treatment, with even higher frequency of inadequate treatment among patients with AUD (75 %) than those without (67%) [110]. This might contribute to the high frequency of attempted and completed suicides in this population. On the other hand, antidepressant medication may worsen cycling and provoke mania in patients with a BPD [111]. Thus, the general attitude in psychiatry as well as guidelines recommend that patients with BPD should receive a mood stabilizer when antidepressants are given [90]. Also, the antidepressant should be stopped when the depression is in remission.

STRATEGIES FOR REDUCING ALCOHOL INGESTION

The most effective strategy for the detection of a possible alcohol problem is a comprehensive alcohol and drug history. Such a history is often missing in clinical practice at start of treatment. Also, structured interviews like SCID or MINI SCID help the clinician delineate BPD and SUD, and PRISM (Psychiatric Research Interview for Substance and Mental disorders) is available for research purposes [112]. In addition, the use of questionnaires such as AUDIT [113], biomarkers for detection of recent or chronic alcohol abuse may be helpful [114]. The same instruments may be used in the follow-up of patients with incipient or established alcohol problems and BPD. The use of a diary on alcohol and drug use between sessions, Quantity – Frequency interviews or Quick Screens [115], discussing high risk situations for relapses into drinking, as well as using motivational and cognitive techniques addressing substance use may be effective [116]. To the authors' knowledge, we lack intervention studies showing the effectiveness of such techniques among patients with BPD.

Suggestions for Future Research

It is a paradox that substance abusers so often are excluded from clinical studies of BPD, since they more often than not represent a majority of those coming to treatment. Thereby we do not know very much about the interaction between substance abuse and BPD, especially when it comes to different treatment regimes. We would therefore recommend the following studies to be prioritized:

- Longitudinal cohort studies of adolescents focusing on drug and alcohol use, and the debut of BPD;
- Follow-up studies of clinical populations with BPD, focusing on the intricate relationship between alcohol and drug use – between and during affective episodes;
- Longitudinal clinical studies, focusing on the impact of alcohol and drug use on suicide prevalence among BP patients;
- Randomized clinical studies on treatment regimes for patients with both BPD and SUD;
- Genetic studies of subgroups of BPD – with and without SUD;
- Intervention studies affecting alcohol and drug use among patients with BPD.

Conclusion

Alcohol and substance abuse frequently accompanies bipolar disorders, leading to a higher suicide rate as well as a poorer prognosis. Early identification of incipient alcohol problems as well as preventive and specific treatment strategies during follow-up may improve the outcome for many bipolar patients. Among the patients with a well established alcohol dependence or abuse, fewer treatment strategies are available, and a higher suicide rate is expected. Specific clinical programs should be established for bipolar patients comorbid with substance abuse, and increased research activities should deal with this subgroup of bipolar patients.

[1] Chengappa KR, Williams P: Barriers to the effective management of bipolar disorder: a survey of psychiatrists based in the UK and USA. *Bipolar Disord*, 2005; 7 Suppl 1:38-42.

[2] Fajutrao L, Locklear J, Priaulx J, Heyes A: A systematic review of the evidence of the burden of bipolar disorder in Europe. *Clin Pract Epidemol Ment Health*, 2009; 5:3.

[3] Cardoso BM, Kauer Sant'Anna M, Dias VV, Andreazza AC, Cereser KM, Kapczinski F: The impact of co-morbid alcohol use disorder in bipolar patients. *Alcohol*, 2008; 42(6):451-7.

[4] Martin CD: Ernest Hemingway: a psychological autopsy of a suicide. *Psychiatry*, 2006; 69(4):351-61.

[5] Narrow WE, Rae DS, Robins LN, Regier DA: Revised prevalence estimates of mental disorders in the United States: using a clinical significance criterion to reconcile 2 surveys' estimates. *Arch Gen Psychiatry*, 2002; 59(2):115-23.

[6] Grant BF, Stinson FS, Hasin DS, Dawson DA, Chou SP, Ruan WJ, Huang B: Prevalence, correlates, and comorbidity of bipolar I disorder and axis I and II disorders: results from the National Epidemiologic Survey on Alcohol and Related Conditions. *J Clin Psychiatry*, 2005; 66(10):1205-15.

[7] Regier DA, Farmer ME, Rae DS, Locke BZ, Keith SJ, Judd LL, Goodwin FK: Comorbidity of mental disorders with alcohol and other drug abuse. Results from the Epidemiologic Catchment Area (ECA) Study. *JAMA*, 1990; 264(19):2511-8.

[8] Kessler RC, McGonagle KA, Zhao S, Nelson CB, Hughes M, Eshleman S, Wittchen HU, Kendler KS: Lifetime and 12-month prevalence of DSM-III-R psychiatric disorders in the United States. Results from the National Comorbidity Survey. *Arch Gen Psychiatry*, 1994; 51(1):8-19.

[9] Merikangas KR, Akiskal HS, Angst J, Greenberg PE, Hirschfeld RM, Petukhova M, Kessler RC: Lifetime and 12-month prevalence of bipolar spectrum disorder in the National Comorbidity Survey replication. *Arch Gen Psychiatry*, 2007; 64(5):543-52.

[10] Kringlen E, Torgersen S, Cramer V: A Norwegian psychiatric epidemiological study. *Am J Psychiatry*, 2001; 158(7):1091-8.

[11] Akiskal HS, Bourgeois ML, Angst J, Post R, Moller H, Hirschfeld R: Re-evaluating the prevalence of and diagnostic composition within the broad clinical spectrum of bipolar disorders. *J Affect Disord*, 2000; 59 Suppl 1:S5-S30.

[12] Angst J, Gamma A, Benazzi F, Ajdacic V, Eich D, Rossler W: Toward a re-definition of subthreshold bipolarity: epidemiology and proposed criteria for bipolar-II, minor bipolar disorders and hypomania. *J Affect Disord*, 2003; 73(1-2):133-46.

[13] Akiskal HS, Akiskal KK, Lancrenon S, Hantouche EG, Fraud JP, Gury C, Allilaire JF: Validating the bipolar spectrum in the French National EPIDEP Study: overview of the phenomenology and relative prevalence of its clinical prototypes. *J Affect Disord*, 2006; 96(3):197-205.

[14] Goodwin GM, Anderson I, Arango C, Bowden CL, Henry C, Mitchell PB, Nolen WA, Vieta E, Wittchen HU: ECNP consensus meeting. Bipolar depression. Nice, March 2007. *Eur Neuropsychopharmacol*, 2008; 18(7):535-49.

[15] Faedda GL, Baldessarini RJ, Suppes T, Tondo L, Becker I, Lipschitz DS: Pediatric-onset bipolar disorder: a neglected clinical and public health problem. *Harv Rev Psychiatry*, 1995; 3(4):171-95.

[16] Goldstein BI, Levitt AJ: Prevalence and correlates of bipolar I disorder among adults with primary youth-onset anxiety disorders. *J Affect Disord*, 2007; 103(1-3):187-95.

[17] Goldstein BI, Strober MA, Birmaher B, Axelson DA, Esposito-Smythers C, Goldstein TR, Leonard H, Hunt J, Gill MK, Iyengar S, Grimm C, Yang M, Ryan

ND, Keller MB: Substance use disorders among adolescents with bipolar spectrum disorders. *Bipolar Disord*, 2008; 10(4):469-78.
[18] Wilens TE, Biederman J, Adamson JJ, Henin A, Sgambati S, Gignac M, Sawtelle R, Santry A, Monuteaux MC: Further evidence of an association between adolescent bipolar disorder with smoking and substance use disorders: a controlled study. *Drug Alcohol Depend*, 2008; 95(3):188-98.
[19] Romero S, Birmaher B, Axelson D, Goldstein T, Goldstein BI, Gill MK, Iosif AM, Strober MA, Hunt J, Esposito-Smythers C, Ryan ND, Leonard H, Keller M: Prevalence and correlates of physical and sexual abuse in children and adolescents with bipolar disorder. *J Affect Disord*, 2009; 112(1-3):144-50.
[20] Carballo JJ, Harkavy-Friedman J, Burke AK, Sher L, Baca-Garcia E, Sullivan GM, Grunebaum MF, Parsey RV, Mann JJ, Oquendo MA: Family history of suicidal behavior and early traumatic experiences: additive effect on suicidality and course of bipolar illness? *J Affect Disord*, 2008; 109(1-2):57-63.
[21] Kessler RC, Crum RM, Warner LA, Nelson CB, Schulenberg J, Anthony JC: Lifetime co-occurrence of DSM-III-R alcohol abuse and dependence with other psychiatric disorders in the National Comorbidity Survey. *Arch Gen Psychiatry*, 1997; 54(4):313-21.
[22] Helzer JE, Pryzbeck TR: The co-occurrence of alcoholism with other psychiatric disorders in the general population and its impact on treatment. *J Stud Alcohol*, 1988; 49(3):219-24.
[23] Merikangas KR, Herrell R, Swendsen J, Rossler W, Ajdacic-Gross V, Angst J: Specificity of bipolar spectrum conditions in the comorbidity of mood and substance use disorders: results from the Zurich cohort study. *Arch Gen Psychiatry*, 2008; 65(1):47-52.
[24] Cerullo MA, Strakowski SM: The prevalence and significance of substance use disorders in bipolar type I and II disorder. *Subst Abuse Treat Prev Policy*, 2007; 2:29.
[25] Bauer Mark S AL, Evans DR, Beresford T, Williford WO and Hauger R: Prevalence and distinct correlates of anxiety, substance and combined comorbidity in a multi-site public sector sample with bipolar disorder. *Jorunal of Affective Disorders*, 2005; 85:301-315.
[26] Henquet C, Krabbendam L, de Graaf R, ten Have M, van Os J: Cannabis use and expression of mania in the general population. *J Affect Disord*, 2006; 95(1-3):103-10.
[27] Krishnan KR: Psychiatric and medical comorbidities of bipolar disorder. *Psychosom Med*, 2005; 67(1):1-8.
[28] Kessler RC, Adler L, Barkley R, Biederman J, Conners CK, Demler O, Faraone SV, Greenhill LL, Howes MJ, Secnik K, Spencer T, Ustun TB, Walters EE, Zaslavsky AM: The prevalence and correlates of adult ADHD in the United States: results from the National Comorbidity Survey Replication. *Am J Psychiatry*, 2006; 163(4):716-23.
[29] Kolodziej ME, Griffin ML, Najavits LM, Otto MW, Greenfield SF, Weiss RD: Anxiety disorders among patients with co-occurring bipolar and substance use disorders. *Drug Alcohol Depend*, 2005; 80(2):251-7.
[30] Simon NM: Generalized anxiety disorder and psychiatric comorbidities such as depression, bipolar disorder, and substance abuse. *J Clin Psychiatry*, 2009; 70 Suppl 2:10-4.
[31] Luckenbaugh DA, Findling RL, Leverich GS, Pizzarello SM, Post RM: Earliest symptoms discriminating juvenile-onset bipolar illness from ADHD. *Bipolar Disord*, 2009; 11(4):441-51.

[32] Zepf FD: Attention deficit-hyperactivity disorder and early-onset bipolar disorder: two facets of one entity? *Dialogues Clin Neurosci*, 2009; 11(1):63-72.
[33] Biederman J, Petty CR, Byrne D, Wong P, Wozniak J, Faraone SV: Risk for switch from unipolar to bipolar disorder in youth with ADHD: A long term prospective controlled study. *J Affect Disord*, 2009.
[34] Tijssen MJ, van Os J, Wittchen HU, Lieb R, Beesdo K, Mengelers R, Krabbendam L, Wichers M: Evidence that bipolar disorder is the poor outcome fraction of a common developmental phenotype: an 8-year cohort study in young people. *Psychol Med*, 2009:1-11.
[35] Zanarini MC, Barison LK, Frankenburg FR, Reich DB, Hudson JI: Family history study of the familial coaggregation of borderline personality disorder with axis I and nonborderline dramatic cluster axis II disorders. *J Pers Disord*, 2009; 23(4):357-69.
[36] Maremmani I, Perugi G, Pacini M, Akiskal HS: Toward a unitary perspective on the bipolar spectrum and substance abuse: opiate addiction as a paradigm. *J Affect Disord*, 2006; 93(1-3):1-12.
[37] Najt P, Perez J, Sanches M, Peluso MA, Glahn D, Soares JC: Impulsivity and bipolar disorder. *Eur Neuropsychopharmacol*, 2007; 17(5):313-20.
[38] Swann AC, Dougherty DM, Pazzaglia PJ, Pham M, Moeller FG: Impulsivity: a link between bipolar disorder and substance abuse. *Bipolar Disord*, 2004; 6(3):204-12.
[39] Crews FT, Boettiger CA: Impulsivity, frontal lobes and risk for addiction. *Pharmacol Biochem Behav*, 2009; 93(3):237-47.
[40] de Wit H: Impulsivity as a determinant and consequence of drug use: a review of underlying processes. *Addict Biol*, 2009; 14(1):22-31.
[41] Swann AC, Dougherty DM, Pazzaglia PJ, Pham M, Steinberg JL, Moeller FG: Increased impulsivity associated with severity of suicide attempt history in patients with bipolar disorder. *Am J Psychiatry*, 2005; 162(9):1680-7.
[42] Maremmani I, M P, S L: Dual diagnosis heroin addicts. The clinical and therapeutic aspects. *Heroin Addiction Related Clinical Problems*, 2003; 5:7-98.
[43] Perugi G, Frare F, Madaro D, Maremmani I, Akiskal HS: Alcohol abuse in social phobic patients: is there a bipolar connection? *J Affect Disord*, 2002; 68(1):33-9.
[44] Akiskal HS, Mallya G: Criteria for the "soft" bipolar spectrum: treatment implications. *Psychopharmacol Bull*, 1987; 23(1):68-73.
[45] Akiskal HS, Placidi GF, Maremmani I, Signoretta S, Liguori A, Gervasi R, Mallya G, Puzantian VR: TEMPS-I: delineating the most discriminant traits of the cyclothymic, depressive, hyperthymic and irritable temperaments in a nonpatient population. *J Affect Disord*, 1998; 51(1):7-19.
[46] Placidi GF, Signoretta S, Liguori A, Gervasi R, Maremmani I, Akiskal HS: The semi-structured affective temperament interview (TEMPS-I). Reliability and psychometric properties in 1010 14-26-year old students. *J Affect Disord*, 1998; 47(1-3):1-10.
[47] Signoretta S, Maremmani I, Liguori A, Perugi G, Akiskal HS: Affective temperament traits measured by TEMPS-I and emotional-behavioral problems in clinically-well children, adolescents, and young adults. *J Affect Disord*, 2005; 85(1-2):169-80.
[48] Perugi G, Toni C, Travierso MC, Akiskal HS: The role of cyclothymia in atypical depression: toward a data-based reconceptualization of the borderline-bipolar II connection. *J Affect Disord*, 2003; 73(1-2):87-98.
[49] Akiskal HS, Maser JD, Zeller PJ, Endicott J, Coryell W, Keller M, Warshaw M, Clayton P, Goodwin F: Switching from 'unipolar' to bipolar II. An 11-year

prospective study of clinical and temperamental predictors in 559 patients. *Arch Gen Psychiatry*, 1995; 52(2):114-23.

[50] Perugi G, Akiskal HS, Ramacciotti S, Nassini S, Toni C, Milanfranchi A, Musetti L: Depressive comorbidity of panic, social phobic, and obsessive-compulsive disorders re-examined: is there a bipolar II connection? *J Psychiatr Res*, 1999; 33(1):53-61.

[51] Akiskal HS, Djenderedjian AM, Rosenthal RH, Khani MK: Cyclothymic disorder: validating criteria for inclusion in the bipolar affective group. *Am J Psychiatry*, 1977; 134(11):1227-33.

[52] Azorin JM, Kaladjian A, Adida M, Hantouche E, Hameg A, Lancrenon S, Akiskal HS: Risk factors associated with lifetime suicide attempts in bipolar I patients: findings from a French National Cohort. *Compr Psychiatry*, 2009; 50(2):115-20.

[53] Kochman FJ, Hantouche EG, Ferrari P, Lancrenon S, Bayart D, Akiskal HS: Cyclothymic temperament as a prospective predictor of bipolarity and suicidality in children and adolescents with major depressive disorder. *J Affect Disord*, 2005; 85(1-2):181-9.

[54] Oedegaard KJ, Syrstad VE, Morken G, Akiskal HS, Fasmer OB: A study of age at onset and affective temperaments in a Norwegian sample of patients with mood disorders. *J Affect Disord*, 2009.

[55] Goodwin FK, Jamison KR: *Manic-Depressive Ilness. Bipolar Disorders and Recurrent Depression. Second Edition*: Oxford University Press. 247-269. 2007.

[56] Khantzian EJ: The self-medication hypothesis of substance use disorders: a reconsideration and recent applications. *Harv Rev Psychiatry*, 1997; 4(5):231-44.

[57] Weiss RD: Treating patients with bipolar disorder and substance dependence: lessons learned. *J Subst Abuse Treat*, 2004; 27(4):307-12.

[58] Angst J, Gamma A, Endrass J, Rossler W, Ajdacic-Gross V, Eich D, Herrell R, Merikangas KR: Is the association of alcohol use disorders with major depressive disorder a consequence of undiagnosed bipolar-II disorder? *Eur Arch Psychiatry Clin Neurosci*, 2006; 256(7):452-7.

[59] Flensborg-Madsen T, Mortensen EL, Knop J, Becker U, Sher L, Gronbaek M: Comorbidity and temporal ordering of alcohol use disorders and other psychiatric disorders: results from a Danish register-based study. *Compr Psychiatry*, 2009; 50(4):307-14.

[60] Baethge C, Baldessarini RJ, Khalsa HM, Hennen J, Salvatore P, Tohen M: Substance abuse in first-episode bipolar I disorder: indications for early intervention. *Am J Psychiatry*, 2005; 162(5):1008-10.

[61] Baethge C, Hennen J, Khalsa HM, Salvatore P, Tohen M, Baldessarini RJ: Sequencing of substance use and affective morbidity in 166 first-episode bipolar I disorder patients. *Bipolar Disord*, 2008; 10(6):738-41.

[62] Strakowski SM, DelBello MP, Fleck DE, Adler CM, Anthenelli RM, Keck PE, Jr., Arnold LM, Amicone J: Effects of co-occurring alcohol abuse on the course of bipolar disorder following a first hospitalization for mania. *Arch Gen Psychiatry*, 2005; 62(8):851-8.

[63] Jaffee WB, Griffin ML, Gallop R, Meade CS, Graff F, Bender RE, Weiss RD: Depression precipitated by alcohol use in patients with co-occurring bipolar and substance use disorders. *J Clin Psychiatry*, 2009; 70(2):171-6.

[64] Potash JB, Kane HS, Chiu YF, Simpson SG, MacKinnon DF, McInnis MG, McMahon FJ, DePaulo JR, Jr.: Attempted suicide and alcoholism in bipolar disorder: clinical and familial relationships. *Am J Psychiatry*, 2000; 157(12):2048-50.

[65] Flensborg-Madsen T, Knop J, Mortensen EL, Becker U, Sher L, Gronbaek M: Alcohol use disorders increase the risk of completed suicide--irrespective of other

psychiatric disorders. A longitudinal cohort study. *Psychiatry Res*, 2009; 167(1-2):123-30.
[66] Kolves K, Varnik A, Tooding LM, Wasserman D: The role of alcohol in suicide: a case-control psychological autopsy study. *Psychol Med*, 2006; 36(7):923-30.
[67] Wasserman D, Wasserman C, eds. *Oxford Textbook of Suicidology and Suicide Prevention. A global perspective*. 2009, Oxford University Press.
[68] Varnik A, Kolves K, Vali M, Tooding LM, Wasserman D: Do alcohol restrictions reduce suicide mortality? *Addiction*, 2007; 102(2):251-6.
[69] Maser JD, Akiskal HS, Schettler P, Scheftner W, Mueller T, Endicott J, Solomon D, Clayton P: Can temperament identify affectively ill patients who engage in lethal or near-lethal suicidal behavior? A 14-year prospective study. *Suicide Life Threat Behav*, 2002; 32(1):10-32.
[70] Valtonen H, Suominen K, Mantere O, Leppamaki S, Arvilommi P, Isometsa ET: Suicidal ideation and attempts in bipolar I and II disorders. *J Clin Psychiatry*, 2005; 66(11):1456-62.
[71] Valtonen HM, Suominen K, Haukka J, Mantere O, Leppamaki S, Arvilommi P, Isometsa ET: Differences in incidence of suicide attempts during phases of bipolar I and II disorders. *Bipolar Disord*, 2008; 10(5):588-96.
[72] Suominen KH, Isometsa ET, Lonnqvist JK: Comorbid substance use reduces the health care contacts of suicide attempters with schizophrenia spectrum or mood disorders. *Schizophr Bull*, 2002; 28(4):637-47.
[73] Qin P, Nordentoft M: Suicide risk in relation to psychiatric hospitalization: evidence based on longitudinal registers. *Arch Gen Psychiatry*, 2005; 62(4):427-32.
[74] Osby U, Brandt L, Correia N, Ekbom A, Sparen P: Excess mortality in bipolar and unipolar disorder in Sweden. *Arch Gen Psychiatry*, 2001; 58(9):844-50.
[75] Hoyer EH, Mortensen PB, Olesen AV: Mortality and causes of death in a total national sample of patients with affective disorders admitted for the first time between 1973 and 1993. *Br J Psychiatry*, 2000; 176:76-82.
[76] Frye MA, Altshuler LL, McElroy SL, Suppes T, Keck PE, Denicoff K, Nolen WA, Kupka R, Leverich GS, Pollio C, Grunze H, Walden J, Post RM: Gender differences in prevalence, risk, and clinical correlates of alcoholism comorbidity in bipolar disorder. *Am J Psychiatry*, 2003; 160(5):883-9.
[77] Canetto SS: Women and suicidal behavior: a cultural analysis. *Am J Orthopsychiatry*, 2008; 78(2):259-66.
[78] Bertolote J, Fleischman A: *A global perspective on the magnitude of suicide mortality.*, in *Oxford Textbook of Suicidology and Suicide Prevention. A global perspective.* , D. Wasserman and C. Wasserman, Editors. 2009, Oxford University Press.
[79] Isometsa ET, Lonnqvist JK: Suicide attempts preceding completed suicide. *Br J Psychiatry*, 1998; 173:531-5.
[80] Varnik A, Kolves K, van der Feltz-Cornelis CM, Marusic A, Oskarsson H, Palmer A, Reisch T, Scheerder G, Arensman E, Aromaa E, Giupponi G, Gusmao R, Maxwell M, Pull C, Szekely A, Sola VP, Hegerl U: Suicide methods in Europe: a gender-specific analysis of countries participating in the "European Alliance Against Depression". *J Epidemiol Community Health*, 2008; 62(6):545-51.
[81] Viguera AC, Baldessarini RJ, Tondo L: Response to lithium maintenance treatment in bipolar disorders: comparison of women and men. *Bipolar Disord*, 2001; 3(5):245-52.
[82] Coryell W, Endicott J, Keller M: Rapidly cycling affective disorder. Demographics, diagnosis, family history, and course. *Arch Gen Psychiatry*, 1992; 49(2):126-31.

[83] Akiskal HS, Hantouche EG, Bourgeois ML, Azorin JM, Sechter D, Allilaire JF, Lancrenon S, Fraud JP, Chatenet-Duchene L: Gender, temperament, and the clinical picture in dysphoric mixed mania: findings from a French national study (EPIMAN). *J Affect Disord*, 1998; 50(2-3):175-86.

[84] Briere J, Elliott DM: Prevalence and psychological sequelae of self-reported childhood physical and sexual abuse in a general population sample of men and women. *Child Abuse Negl*, 2003; 27(10):1205-22.

[85] Elliott DM, Mok DS, Briere J: Adult sexual assault: prevalence, symptomatology, and sex differences in the general population. *J Trauma Stress*, 2004; 17(3):203-11.

[86] Baldassano CF, Marangell LB, Gyulai L, Nassir Ghaemi S, Joffe H, Kim DR, Sagduyu K, Truman CJ, Wisniewski SR, Sachs GS, Cohen LS: Gender differences in bipolar disorder: retrospective data from the first 500 STEP-BD participants. *Bipolar Disord*, 2005; 7(5):465-70.

[87] Goldberg JF, Garno JL: Development of posttraumatic stress disorder in adult bipolar patients with histories of severe childhood abuse. *J Psychiatr Res*, 2005; 39(6):595-601.

[88] Meade CS, McDonald LJ, Graff FS, Fitzmaurice GM, Griffin ML, Weiss RD: A prospective study examining the effects of gender and sexual/physical abuse on mood outcomes in patients with co-occurring bipolar I and substance use disorders. *Bipolar Disord*, 2009; 11(4):425-33.

[89] Brown GR, McBride L, Bauer MS, Williford WO: Impact of childhood abuse on the course of bipolar disorder: a replication study in U.S. veterans. *J Affect Disord*, 2005; 89(1-3):57-67.

[90] Yatham LN, Kennedy SH, Schaffer A, Parikh SV, Beaulieu S, O'Donovan C, MacQueen G, McIntyre RS, Sharma V, Ravindran A, Young LT, Young AH, Alda M, Milev R, Vieta E, Calabrese JR, Berk M, Ha K, Kapczinski F: Canadian Network for Mood and Anxiety Treatments (CANMAT) and International Society for Bipolar Disorders (ISBD) collaborative update of CANMAT guidelines for the management of patients with bipolar disorder: update 2009. *Bipolar Disord*, 2009; 11(3):225-55.

[91] Yatham LN, Kennedy SH, O'Donovan C, Parikh S, MacQueen G, McIntyre R, Sharma V, Silverstone P, Alda M, Baruch P, Beaulieu S, Daigneault A, Milev R, Young LT, Ravindran A, Schaffer A, Connolly M, Gorman CP: Canadian Network for Mood and Anxiety Treatments (CANMAT) guidelines for the management of patients with bipolar disorder: consensus and controversies. *Bipolar Disord*, 2005; 7 Suppl 3:5-69.

[92] Cipriani A, Pretty H, Hawton K, Geddes JR: Lithium in the prevention of suicidal behavior and all-cause mortality in patients with mood disorders: a systematic review of randomized trials. *Am J Psychiatry*, 2005; 162(10):1805-19.

[93] Baldessarini RJ, Tondo L, Hennen J, Viguera AC: Is lithium still worth using? An update of selected recent research. *Harv Rev Psychiatry*, 2002; 10(2):59-75.

[94] Ahrens B, Grof P, Moller HJ, Muller-Oerlinghausen B, Wolf T: Extended survival of patients on long-term lithium treatment. *Can J Psychiatry*, 1995; 40(5):241-6.

[95] Ikeda A, Kato T: Biological predictors of lithium response in bipolar disorder. *Psychiatry Clin Neurosci*, 2003; 57(3):243-50.

[96] Vornik LA, Brown ES: Management of comorbid bipolar disorder and substance abuse. *J Clin Psychiatry*, 2006; 67 Suppl 7:24-30.

[97] Salloum IM, Cornelius JR, Daley DC, Kirisci L, Himmelhoch JM, Thase ME: Efficacy of valproate maintenance in patients with bipolar disorder and alcoholism: a double-blind placebo-controlled study. *Arch Gen Psychiatry*, 2005; 62(1):37-45.

[98] Brady KT, Sonne SC, Malcolm RJ, Randall CL, Dansky BS, Simpson K, Roberts JS, Brondino M: Carbamazepine in the treatment of cocaine dependence: subtyping by affective disorder. *Exp Clin Psychopharmacol*, 2002; 10(3):276-85.

[99] Geller B, Cooper TB, Sun K, Zimerman B, Frazier J, Williams M, Heath J: Double-blind and placebo-controlled study of lithium for adolescent bipolar disorders with secondary substance dependency. *J Am Acad Child Adolesc Psychiatry*, 1998; 37(2):171-8.

[100] Brown ES, Nejtek VA, Perantie DC, Rajan Thomas N, Rush AJ: Cocaine and amphetamine use in patients with psychiatric illness: a randomized trial of typical antipsychotic continuation or discontinuation. *J Clin Psychopharmacol*, 2003; 23(4):384-8.

[101] Brown ES, Nejtek VA, Perantie DC, Orsulak PJ, Bobadilla L: Lamotrigine in patients with bipolar disorder and cocaine dependence. *J Clin Psychiatry*, 2003; 64(2):197-201.

[102] Brown ES, Perantie DC, Dhanani N, Beard L, Orsulak P, Rush AJ: Lamotrigine for bipolar disorder and comorbid cocaine dependence: a replication and extension study. *J Affect Disord*, 2006; 93(1-3):219-22.

[103] Brown ES, Jeffress J, Liggin JD, Garza M, Beard L: Switching outpatients with bipolar or schizoaffective disorders and substance abuse from their current antipsychotic to aripiprazole. *J Clin Psychiatry*, 2005; 66(6):756-60.

[104] Weiss RD, Najavits LM, Greenfield SF: A relapse prevention group for patients with bipolar and substance use disorders. *J Subst Abuse Treat*, 1999; 16(1):47-54.

[105] Weiss RD, Kolodziej M, Griffin ML, Najavits LM, Jacobson LM, Greenfield SF: Substance use and perceived symptom improvement among patients with bipolar disorder and substance dependence. *J Affect Disord*, 2004; 79(1-3):279-83.

[106] Weiss RD, Griffin ML, Kolodziej ME, Greenfield SF, Najavits LM, Daley DC, Doreau HR, Hennen JA: A randomized trial of integrated group therapy versus group drug counseling for patients with bipolar disorder and substance dependence. *Am J Psychiatry*, 2007; 164(1):100-7.

[107] Colom F, Vieta E, Reinares M, Martinez-Aran A, Torrent C, Goikolea JM, Gasto C: Psychoeducation efficacy in bipolar disorders: beyond compliance enhancement. *J Clin Psychiatry*, 2003; 64(9):1101-5.

[108] Lam DH, Burbeck R, Wright K, Pilling S: Psychological therapies in bipolar disorder: the effect of illness history on relapse prevention - a systematic review. *Bipolar Disord*, 2009; 11(5):474-82.

[109] Rucci P, Frank E, Kostelnik B, Fagiolini A, Mallinger AG, Swartz HA, Thase ME, Siegel L, Wilson D, Kupfer DJ: Suicide attempts in patients with bipolar I disorder during acute and maintenance phases of intensive treatment with pharmacotherapy and adjunctive psychotherapy. *Am J Psychiatry*, 2002; 159(7):1160-4.

[110] Baca-Garcia E, Sher L, Perez-Rodriguez MM, Burke AK, Sullivan GM, Grunebaum MF, Stanley BH, Mann JJ, Oquendo MA: Treatment of depressed bipolar patients with alcohol use disorders: plenty of room for improvement. *J Affect Disord*, 2009; 115(1-2):262-8.

[111] Ghaemi SN, Hsu DJ, Soldani F, Goodwin FK: Antidepressants in bipolar disorder: the case for caution. *Bipolar Disord*, 2003; 5(6):421-33.

[112] Caton CL, Samet S, Hasin DS: When acute-stage psychosis and substance use co-occur: differentiating substance-induced and primary psychotic disorders. *J Psychiatr Pract*, 2000; 6(5):256-66.

[113] Saunders JB, Aasland OG, Babor TF, de la Fuente JR, Grant M: Development of the Alcohol Use Disorders Identification Test (AUDIT): WHO Collaborative Project on

Early Detection of Persons with Harmful Alcohol Consumption--II. *Addiction*, 1993; 88(6):791-804.

[114] Hock B, Schwarz M, Domke I, Grunert VP, Wuertemberger M, Schiemann U, Horster S, Limmer C, Stecker G, Soyka M: Validity of carbohydrate-deficient transferrin (%CDT), gamma-glutamyltransferase (gamma-GT) and mean corpuscular erythrocyte volume (MCV) as biomarkers for chronic alcohol abuse: a study in patients with alcohol dependence and liver disorders of non-alcoholic and alcoholic origin. *Addiction*, 2005; 100(10):1477-86.

[115] Roy M, Dum M, Sobell LC, Sobell MB, Simco ER, Manor H, Palmerio R: Comparison of the quick drinking screen and the alcohol timeline followback with outpatient alcohol abusers. *Subst Use Misuse*, 2008; 43(14):2116-23.

[116] McIntosh MC, Leigh G, Baldwin NJ, Marmulak J: Reducing alcohol consumption. Comparing three brief methods in family practice. *Can Fam Physician*, 1997; 43:1959-62, 1965-7.

In: Suicidal Behavior in Alcohol and Drug Abuse...
Editors: L. Sher, A. Vilens, pp. 477-495
ISBN: 978-1-60876-919-3

Chapter 27

COMORBIDITY OF BIPOLAR DISORDER WITH ALCOHOL AND DRUG ABUSE, LEADING TO SUICIDAL BEHAVIOR

***Amanda Galvão-de Almeida*[1,2], *Fabiana Nery-Fernandes*[1], *Ilza Rosa Batista*[2], *Camila Guindalini*[2], *Esdras Cabus Moreira*[1] *and Ângela Miranda-Scippa*[1]**

[1]Universidade Federal da Bahia, Bahia, Brazil
[2]Universidade Federal de São Paulo, São Paulo, Brazil

ABSTRACT

Background

Bipolar disorder is a frequent and chronic affective illness associated with significant global dysfunction and suicidal behavior. Bipolar patients frequently have other Axis I psychiatric disorders such as substance abuse or dependence affecting up to 60% of these individuals. Substance use disorders can independently lead to risk-taking behaviors and suicidality. Therefore, we gathered data about bipolar disorder and substance use disorders as single and as combined factors leading to suicidal behavior. We also discussed some neurobiological findings related to this comorbidity.

Methods

We reviewed the Medline database in search for studies published in English, Spanish or Portuguese until June 1st 2009, containing the following keywords: "bipolar disorder", "suicidal behavior", "suicide", "substance use disorders", "alcohol", "drugs", "cocaine", "*cannabis*", "marijuana", "opiate", "amphetamine", "comorbidity".

Results

Comorbididy with substance use disorders, especially alcohol abuse and dependence, impose higher rates of suicidal behavior on bipolar patients. The presence of the comorbidity seems to be significantly more associated with suicidality than either bipolar or alcohol/drug use disorder. Some factors seem to mediate the frequency and severity of suicidal behavior in bipolar patients with substance use disorders: early onset of bipolar disorder, drug abuse after the onset of affective illness, aggressive and/or hostile behavior, impulsivity, and frequency of mixed depression.

Conclusion

Assessment of suicidal thoughts and past history of suicide attempts is especially important in patients with comorbid bipolar and substance use disorders in order to adequately treat these individuals and reduce the frequency and consequences of suicidal behavior.

Introduction

Bipolar disorder (BD) is the psychiatric disorder that carries the highest lifetime risk of death by suicide [1-3]. Alcohol and drug use disorders are important factors associated with suicidal behavior in both the general population and in such clinical samples as the ones comprised of BD subjects [4, 5]. At least half of BD patients have a lifetime history of substance use disorders (SUDs). This comorbidity leads to clinical and functional impairment, poor treatment adherence, and additional risk of suicide [6].

In this chapter, we will discuss some important issues related to the comorbidity of BD and alcohol/drugs use disorders, and to suicidality as the main outcome. We didactically divided the chapter into sections and subsections and discussed the relations between BD and suicidal behavior, BD and SUDs, and BD, SUDs and suicidality. We also briefly added some neurobiological data of the matter discussed in each section. It is important to emphasize that this chapter does not intend to approach any of the therapeutical aspects of the comorbidity between BD and SUDs.

1. Bipolar Disorder and Suicidal Behavior

Bipolar disorder is a chronic and cyclic affective disease. It is one of the most common severe mental illnesses and may be broken down into type I, characterized by the occurrence of manic and usually recurrent depressive episodes; and type II, characterized by recurrent depression and hypomania [7]. Besides those, episodes of BD can combine depressive and manic symptoms, known as mixed episodes. Mixed episodes are defined in the Diagnostic and Statistical Manual of Mental Disorders - fourth edition (DSM-IV) as manic episodes with syndromal depression or depressive episodes with syndromal mania [8].

Findings of recent studies generally indicate that an overall lifetime prevalence of BD-I is approximately 1%. The array of rates is not wide, even from different countries, with most ranging from 1% to 1.5%. However, studies including the bipolar *spectrum*, a more broadly defined condition that also includes BD-II and cyclothymia, produce much higher lifetime prevalence rates from 3% to 8.3% [9].

Bipolar disorder can be extraordinarily costly financially, clinically and socially [10]. In 2000, according to the World Health Organization, BD ranked ninth among the main causes of global dysfunction in individuals between 15 and 45 years of age and, in 2020, it is estimated that it will reach the fourth position [11]. The course of BD is episodic and highly variable, with potential for high level severity and recurrence intensity, and disproportionately high depressive morbidity [12]. Additionally, BD is associated with a substantial burden of illness-related morbidity and mortality, and has proven fatal in a high proportion of patients, in that it complicates risk-taking behavior, comorbid stress-sensitive medical illnesses, and especially suicide [13].

Numerous studies have documented a strong association between BD and both suicide attempts and completion [14]. This affective disorder is not only among the top 10 illnesses in terms of disease burden worldwide, but may be the psychiatric condition associated with the highest lifetime risk of suicide completions and attempts [1, 15]. Individuals with BD have lifetime suicide attempt rates of 20% to 56%, almost 15 times higher than the rates found in the general population in the U.S. [2], and twice higher than those of individuals with unipolar depression. Of these, almost one third ultimately die from suicide [9, 16]. Table 1 shows the risk of death by suicide among psychiatric disorders, according to some authors [2, 3].

It has been demonstrated that suicidal behavior in major mood disorder patients occur mostly during major depressive episode (70%–89%), especially the mixed or agitated ones, and less frequently in mixed mania (11%–20%), but practically never during euphoric mania and euthymia [17, 18]. An American study evaluating the Epidemiologic Catchment Area (ECA) database, with more than 18,000 patients, reported a prevalence of 29.2% of one or more suicide attempts throughout life in patients with BD, as well as of 15.9% in patients with unipolar depression and of 4.2% in patients having other Axis I psychiatric pathologies, according to DSM-III criteria. In accordance with the same study, BD patients have a relative risk of attempting suicide 6.2 times higher than patients with other psychiatric disorders [19]. The National Comorbidity Survey also found that the odds ratio for lifetime history of suicide attempts in BD was almost 30 times higher when compared with any other disorder [20].

Moreover, suicide attempts by patients with BD have an increased lethal potential. Data from a study comparing the risk of completed suicide suggested that BD cases have a higher proportion of high lethal risk of suicidal attempt than unipolar depression patients [21]. Among bipolar patients, rates of suicide attempts are only 5 times the rates of completed suicides, whereas in the general population rates of suicide attempts are 10 to 20 times the rates of completed suicides [22].

Table 1. Risk of death by suicide among psychiatric disorders

Psychiatric Disorder	Relative Risk	Suicide Rate (%/Year)	Lifetime Risk (%)
Bipolar Disorder	28	0.39	23.4
Severe Major Depressive Disorder	21	0.29	17.4
Multiple Drug Abuse	20	0.28	16.8
Moderate Major Depressive Disorder	9	0.13	7.8
Schizophrenia	9	0.12	7.2
Personality Disorders	7	0.10	6.0
General Population	1.0	0.014	0.8

Adapted from Harris; Barraclough, 1997; Tondo, Isacson, Baldessarini, 2003.

Table 2. Risk factors and clinical characteristics associated with suicidal behavior in bipolar patients [16, 23-32]

Demographic factors	Clinical factors	Cognitive-Behavioral Characteristics and Personal/Family History
Male gender #	Greater number of depressive episodes*	Presence of aggressiveness throughout life*
Single marital status	Greater number of psychiatric hospitalizations*	Impulsivity
	Early onset age*	Presence of hopelessness
	History of suicidal attempts*	Lack of confidence
	History of suicidal ideation*	Few motives to live
	Absence of psychosis	Family history of suicide and attempted suicide
	Predominance of depressive symptoms	History of physical abuse
	Severity of the episodes	History of sexual abuse
	Mixed states	
	Rapid cycling	
	Comorbidity with Axis I psychiatric disorders	
	Comorbidity with borderline, narcisist and antisocial personality disorders	
	Drug/alcohol abuse	
	Mania induced by antidepressants	
	Anxiety	
	Shorter duration of BD	
	Early age at hospitalization	
	Depression severity at first episode	

* Factors more often cited in the literature; # Controversial findings.

Several factors and clinical characteristics have been associated with suicide attempts in BD patients. However, the data regarding this association is sometimes conflicting. Table 2 summarizes the risk factors associated with suicidal behavior in BD patients according to some authors [16, 23-32].

The rates of accidental and other forms of injury or violent death among BD patients are high in some samples, and bear an uncertain relationship to suicidality [33]. In a British cohort of 235 BD patients, deaths from other causes were not excessive considering the age groups studied, but alcohol abuse and deterioration from premorbid level of functioning up to a year after the disease onset were associated with increased risk of suicide [34].

In Khalsa et al.'s study (2008), suicidality was associated with initial mixed-state, higher proportion of follow-up weeks in mixed-states or depression, and prior suicide attempts. In the same study, accidents were associated selectively with initial mania or psychosis, later mania or hypomania, and alcohol abuse [33].

Data on risk factors for suicide attempts and completed suicide among patients with BD are limited and controversial. Several cohort studies have examined risk factors for lifetime suicide attempts, but none of those had a sufficient sample size to examine prospective suicide attempts or suicide death. A systematic review found that most previous studies of risk factors for suicide death included too few events to accurately identify clinical or demographic risk factors [31]. Nevertheless, there is a recent cohort study that evaluated more than 32,000 health plan users with BD. This study indicated that suicide attempts were significantly more frequent among women, whereas suicide death was significantly more frequent among men. It also indicated that suicide attempt was strongly related to younger age, but probability of suicide death was relatively similar across age categories. Suicide attempt was more likely to occur among those with recorded diagnoses of substance abuse, although suicide death did not significantly differ by substance abuse diagnosis. Diagnoses of anxiety disorders were associated with significantly higher probability of both suicide attempts and suicide death. This data suggested that risk factors for suicide attempts and suicide death in individuals with BD are generally similar to those in the general population and in the clinical samples with unipolar depression subjects [35].

1.1. Neurobiology of Suicidal Behavior in Bipolar Disorder Individuals

Most of the studies evaluated mainly the clinical risk factors leading to suicide attempts [27, 31]. The knowledge about the neurobiology of complete suicide is still limited. Considering that suicide is a potentially preventable cause of death, understanding the neural correlates of suicidal behavior may be helpful with reducing suicide rates in BD and other psychiatric disorders.

According to Oquendo et al. (1997), the suicidal behavior is complex and results from the association of two components: biological vulnerability and psychosocial stressors. In this model, the biological vulnerability refers to a person's propensity to manifest suicidal behavior and may be considered trait-related. In contrast, psychosocial stressors, or triggers, are precipitants that determine the timing for suicidal acts, but also contribute to the probability of them. In this case, triggers may be considered state-related [36].

Since both neurobiological and psychological factors combine to play an important role in suicidality, research findings now converge on the view that two general categories of risk for suicide can be identified: (*a*) dysregulated impulse control; and (*b*) propensity to intense psychological pain (e.g., social isolation, hopelessness), often in the context of mental disorders, especially mood disorders. Each of these categories of risk is underlain, at least to some degree, by specific genetic and neurobiological factors, which are in general not well characterized although there is emerging consensus that most, if not all, reside in or affect the serotonergic system [37].

In fact, many studies have also found an association between suicide and serotonin hypofunction in BD patients [38, 39]. The finding of serotonin hypofunction, pointing to genetic contributions to suicide, led to a search for candidate genes whose products control serotonin biosynthesis, degradation, or reuptake. Studies have sought to link higher prevalence of polymorphisms in serotonin-related genes to suicidal behavior [40, 41]. However, some studies failed to find an association between these polymorphisms and suicidality [42]. Studies have also identified alterations in *locus coeruleus* norepinephrine transmission in relation to suicide in BD [9] although this neurotransmission is less often and intensely studied.

Another important point is the hyperactivity of the hypothalamic-pituitary-adrenal (HPA) axis that has been hypothesized as a biochemical marker of suicide, since it is an important modulator of the relationship between acute stress exposure and physiological activation. Increased activity of the HPA axis has been observed in unipolar and bipolar patients with suicidal behavior [43]. Besides that, neuroimaging studies describe higher rate and intensity of white matter hyperintensities associated with suicide attempts in bipolar patients in comparison with individuals who were not ill, after controlling for age [44, 45, De Oliveira et al., 2009 *submitted*]. Neurocognitive deficits associated with abnormalities of prefrontal cortex were found to be more profound in the suicide attempters than in the non-attempters, in a group of bipolar depressed patients, regardless of depression severity [46].

Although the precise causes of suicide in BD remain unclear and researchers have not yet found any particular combination of risk factors to be sensitive enough to predict suicide, long-term use of lithium is one treatment consistently associated with much lower rates of suicide and lifetime suicide attempts in bipolar patients. A meta-analysis of 22 studies showed that the computed risk of completed suicide was 8.85 times lower with long-term lithium treatment than without it [47]. Nevertheless, rates of completed suicides among BD patients treated with lithium still remain 10 times higher than those in the general population [48] and we are unaware of the biological basis of the anti-suicide properties of lithium.

1.2. Bipolar Disorder and Alcohol/Drug Comorbidity

First of all, it is important to briefly discuss the concept of comorbidity. The term comorbidity was first used in 1970 by Feinstein to refer to any co-existent additional disease in a patient with a particular indexed illness [49]. In the late 80's, the term was applied in Psychiatry, after the publishing of DSM-III-R, which accepted the co-occurrence of multiple diagnostic categories in the same individual based on population epidemiological studies [50]. The association of diagnostic categories is frequently described based on the chronology of the manifestation of the disorders. The former diagnosis or disorder is known as "primary" and the latter, as the "secondary". Such nomenclature is confusing because it implicitly establishes a cause-effect relation between the disorders, which is not true for all cases [51].

To some authors, even nowadays, comorbidity simply refers to the occurrence of two syndromes in the same patient. Defined literally, every pair of syndromes in which the diagnosis of one does not categorically exclude the diagnosis of the other is potentially comorbid [52]. However, others question whether the presence of various diagnoses in the same individual, a rule in the psychiatric practice, wouldn't be an artifact of an inappropriate diagnostic system.

In this context, McHugh and Slavney propose four perspectives on a mental disorder: as a disease (similar to a categorical diagnosis), as a dimension (personality disorders, for example), as a behavior (one of the models used for substance dependence) and as an event of life (psychological or mental alteration as a result of traumatic experience) [53]. In light of this proposal, a comorbidity can occur between distinct categories (specific mental illnesses), or between a specific category and a dimensional aspect of the subject's behavior, which does not fulfill the criteria for a mental disorder. Finally, the diagnosing processes should combine descriptive, categorical and dimensional approaches. For a broader definition of comorbidity, transversal and longitudinal evaluations, in which nuclear, atypical and subclinical symptoms must be considered, are important [49].

According to the several studies described below, bipolar disorder and SUDs are relevant comorbid conditions. In fact, BD may be is the Axis I disorder associated with the highest risk for co-existing alcohol and drug use disorder [54]. Data from the ECA study show that substance abuse occurred in over 60% of type I BD patients. Some authors suggest that such comorbidity may have increased in recent decades [6, 55].

Substance abuse syndromes are elevated in bipolar patients even at the time of their first hospitalization. These elevated rates were consistently replicated in many different countries, treatment settings, and clinical and research populations. Correspondingly, rates of BD are elevated five to eight times in patients with SUDs [55].

The National Epidemiologic Survey on Alcohol and Related Conditions (NESARC) examined the prevalence and co-occurrence of DSM-IV substance, mood, and anxiety disorders in a representative sample of 43,093 respondents in the U.S. In subjects with bipolar I disorder, there was a 58% lifetime prevalence of co-occurring alcohol use disorders and a 38% lifetime prevalence of any drug use disorder [56].

Other studies have shown that estimates of lifetime substance abuse comorbidity in BD range from 6% to 69% for alcohol abuse, with rates of at least 30% in most studies; and from 14% to 60% for drug abuse. Males with BD have higher rates of substance abuse than do females (59.7% vs. 37.8% for alcohol; 54.5% vs. 33.8% for other drugs), specifically higher rates of comorbid alcohol abuse/dependence and *cannabis* abuse/dependence than BD women. Some authors failed to find gender differences in rates of cocaine and opiate use among BD patients [57, 58].

When compared to unipolar depression, BD seems to be more strongly associated with panic disorder (21% vs. 10%), obsessive-compulsive disorder (21% vs. 12.2%), borderline personality disorder (41% vs. 31.6%) and substance dependence (56.1% vs. 27.2%). These differences can be even more pronounced in samples of BD inpatients [59-61].

Substance use disorders can precede or ensue the onset of BD and may occur in any phase of the disorder. Additionally, when compared to individuals with BD and no alcohol or drug use, individuals with BD who use alcohol and/ or illicit substances have: *1* - higher rates of hospitalization, *2* - lower rates of remission during hospitalization, *3* - more mixed episodes, rapid mood cycling, persistent mood symptoms with treatment, and residual symptoms during recovery, *4* - poor or non- response to lithium, 5- poor treatment adherence, 6- higher rates of comorbid anxiety disorders, 7- more impaired functional status, and 8- higher risk of suicide [4, 6, 62]. Most of the outcomes listed above were associated to suicidal behavior in BD subjects (See Table 2).

Bipolar disorder is the DSM-IV Axis I diagnosis more associated with alcoholism, with a lifetime prevalence of 50%-60%, while these rates in schizophrenia are 30%-40%, and 30% in unipolar depression [63]. Besides the fact that alcohol is the preferred drug of abuse in BD patients, up to 60% of the subjects who present with alcohol problems may have undiagnosed BD. Non-recognition of the co-occurrence of alcohol abuse or dependence (AAD) and BD increases the impact of its numerous negative consequences: greater risk of medication noncompliance, slower recovery from mood episodes, more frequent hospitalizations, suicides, and accidents [54, 64]. Moreover, after becoming dependents on alcohol, BD patients seem to be unlikely to return to premorbid functioning even after a long period of abstinence [65].

Additionally, the reports of association between BD and AAD are mainly during dysphoric or mixed mania episodes, and in rapid cycling course and treatment-resistant variants of BD. When gender analysis were performed, female BD patients with pathological alcohol use presented with significantly higher levels of depressive symptoms than non-AAD BD females or BD males with or without comorbid AAD. It has been suggested that alcohol use among BD females enhances their vulnerability to depressive symptomatology when compared to either female non-alcoholic or male BD patients [66].

In one study, Frye and colleagues (2003) show that the risk of alcohol dependence in patients with BD seem to be higher among women than among men, when compared to the risk in the general population [67]. Escamilla et al. (2002) also showed that gender was strongly associated with SUDs (primarily alcohol dependence) among BD patients in Central America (Costa Rica) [68].

The results of a recent Brazilian study showed that AAD was associated with male gender, lower education, earlier age of BD onset, psychosis during the first episode, more depressive symptoms, and worse psychosocial functioning. In addition, the presence of AAD was associated with high rates of suicide attempts [54].

When it comes to *cannabis*, some authors suggest that it is the most commonly illicit drug abused by individuals with BD, mirroring the relative rates of drugs of abuse in the general population. Studies investigating especially younger BD patients showed that rates of *cannabis* use disorders either equal or exceed those of alcohol abuse or dependence [69].

Studies published suggest that *cannabis* abuse in particular was associated with poor treatment adherence, increased duration or severity of mania, and negative outcomes in BD. Moreover, *cannabis* abuse complicated the treatment of co-occurring alcohol use disorders in patients with BD [70]

A recent study revealed that, by quarters, *cannabis* use selectively and strongly preceded and coincided with mania / hypomania. Alcohol use preceded or coincided with depression; whereas substance use was unassociated with mood states in preceding quarters [6]. Moreover, a BD-patient group with *cannabis* use problems was associated with a longer time in affective episodes and with rapid cycling. Although these individuals remitted immediately after hospitalization, BD/*cannabis* patients had rapid rates of recurrence [70].

Specifically about cocaine, studies show evidence of more social, vocational, and legal problems when psychiatric disorders, including BD, co-occur with cocaine dependence than with alcohol dependence. The diagnosis of BD is related with the index of cocaine dependence severity and is also associated with more days of use in the period of the heaviest cocaine use. Thus, individuals with BD should be carefully assessed in the case of cocaine misuse [71].

Herrero et al. (2008) examined the psychiatric status of young cocaine users recruited in non-clinical settings and found that nearly 42.5% of the subjects presented psychiatric comorbidity. The most common Axis I diagnoses were mood disorders (26.6%) and anxiety disorders (13%) [72].

The use of drugs has been associated with a more severe course and outcome in both schizophrenia and BD. Use of stimulant drugs (e.g. cocaine and methamphetamine) has been linked with criminality, violence and homelessness in severe mental disorders. High levels of *cannabis* use have been associated with increased psychopathology in both schizophrenia and BD [70, 73].

The understanding of the underlying causes of the high rate of comorbidity between BD and SUDs remain limited. Previous studies have suggested that vulnerability to the development of SUD during the course of BP may be related to the presence of specific neurological impairments. In this way, structural and functional abnormalities in portions of the prefrontal cortex, as well as the medial temporal and subcortical regions implicated in motivational and emotional processing, have been suggested in adolescents with BD and have also been associated with the development of SUDs [74].

Considering the clinical aspects of the bipolar disorder and SUDs comorbidity, we can say that one disorder influences the course, outcome, or treatment response of a second coexisting disorder. Determining whether both disorders develop in the same patient at different times or concurrently may help to clarify the mechanism of comorbidity [52]. However, many times it is not possible to determine the sequential occurrence of the phenomena.

Strakowski and DelBello (2000) discussed four potential hypotheses for why substance use and BD co-occur: (a) substance abuse occurs as a symptom of BD; (b) substance abuse is an attempt by BD patients to self-medicate symptoms; (c) substance abuse causes BD; and (d) substance use and BD share a common risk factor. Since none of these hypotheses has unequivocal support to explain all cases of BD and SUDs co-occurrence, it is probable that all four mechanisms play some role in the excess of substance abuse observed in bipolar patients [55].

Examining the hypothesis that substance dependence may have its roots in self-medication, Maremmani and colleagues (2006) have observed that BD patients with SUDs often continue to use substances even after the substance has proven lacking to continue providing symptom relief. Therefore, these authors suggest that hypomania is the driving force behind the addiction in individuals with bipolar spectrum disorders, leading to both sensation seeking behavior and a failure to appreciate its consequences [75].

The authors of the chapter also agree that, in the case of BD/SUDs comorbidity, symptoms of BD play a crucial role in the incidence and maintenance of substance use problems. Also, abuse of a drug may trigger the development of the mood disorders in a vulnerable individual. However, further analyses of this complex matter are beyond the scope of this chapter.

2. Impact of Comorbid Bipolar Disorder and Alcohol/Drug Use Disorders on Suicidal Behavior

Complications of substance abuse in BD include more suicide attempts, and increased risk for completed suicide. There are reports to the extent that rates of suicide rise up to 3 times in this comorbid population and that suicide attempts tend to be recurrent in BD patients with SUDs [52, 54, 71, 76]. Moreover, a retrospective chart review study associated the comorbid sample BD/SUDs with significantly higher suicidality than either BD or SUDs [77].

Some other specific comorbidities are also associated with the increase of suicidal behavior in BD patients: borderline personality disorder and panic disorder [78-82].

In fact, alcohol abuse or dependence represents an independent risk to suicidal behavior [83]. Around 7%-18% of alcohol dependents die by suicide [5, 84] and individuals with alcohol dependence have a 60–120 times higher suicide risk than the non-psychiatrically-ill population [5]. It has been observed that, in the general population, the greater likelihood of future suicide attempt occurs in individuals with problematic alcohol use, prior suicide attempt, younger age, unmarried status, dependence on other substances, and the presence of another substance-induced psychiatric disorder [85].

Although most of the studies focused on the chronic use of alcohol, acute alcohol use is also associated with suicide. Suicide completers have high rates (33%-69%) of positive blood alcohol and intoxicated individuals are more likely to attempt suicide using more lethal methods (e.g. firearm, hanging). Acute use of alcohol or intoxication increases the risk of suicide in 90 times and may be especially decisive in suicides among persons with no previous psychiatric history [5].

A history of other SUDs, such as cocaine, amphetamines, opiates and *cannabis*, has also been linked to suicidality in BD samples [52], and in the general population [20]. In a recent study, although rates of SUDs and suicide attempts were similar in BD-I and -II individuals, SUDs emerged as BD-I-specific correlates of suicide attempt. The great majority of the subjects with BD-I with illicit drug (93%), alcohol (89%), or combined substance (97%) use disorders had made attempts. However, these findings only partially explained the risk, since slightly over half of the BD-I suicide attempters had a illicit drug (52%) or alcohol (56%) use problem, and BD-I subjects in this study without SUDs also had high rates of suicide attempt (67%) [86].

Data from the National Violent Death Reporting System (NVDRS) which included 6865 suicide incidents from 13 states in the U.S. were analyzed by Karch and colleagues (2006). This study identified race/ethnicity and the sample is described as being comprised of 5797 (84.4%) non-Hispanic whites, 501 (7.3%) non-Hispanic blacks, 257 (3.7%) Hispanics, and 310 (4.5%) persons from other racial/ethnic groups [87].

At the time of the suicide event, non-Hispanic blacks had lower blood alcohol levels than other groups. Non-Hispanic whites had lower cocaine levels, but higher levels of opiates. There were no differences between the levels of amphetamines or marijuana by race/ethnicity. Hispanics were less likely to have been diagnosed with a mental illness or given accordant treatment, although family reports of depression were comparable to non-Hispanic whites and other racial/ethnic groups. Non-Hispanic whites were more likely to be diagnosed with depression or BD and non-Hispanic blacks with schizophrenia. Comorbid substance abuse and mental health problems were more likely among non-Hispanic whites and non-Hispanic blacks, while Hispanics were more likely to have a substance abuse problem without history of comorbid mental health problems. The authors suggest that suicide prevention efforts must address not only substance abuse and mental health problems in general, but the unique personal, family, and social characteristics of different racial/ethnic groups [87].

2.1. Risk Factors of Suicidal Behavior Considering SUD and BD Comorbidity

Some features seem to mediate the frequency and severity of suicidal behavior in BD patients with SUDs. For example, higher rates of suicide attempts have been reported in BD patients whose drug abuse began after the onset of affective illness [88].

Some BD-I-specific factors appear to be involved in the effects of SUDs on suicide attempt risk. The combination of SUDs and BD-I symptoms may foster aggression, impulsivity, and hostility, which in turn increase the chances of acting on suicidal thoughts. However, a difficult question related to understanding the precise role of aggression, hostility, and impulsivity in suicide attempts among BD patients is that 'trait' and 'state' attributes are not always easily separable, as many individuals may spend the majority of their lives at least partially symptomatic [86].

Impulsivity results from dysregulation of the initiation of action, an integral part of BD. It can be operationalized as a predisposition to action without reflection or without regard for consequences, and has interacting state- and trait-like characteristics [89].

Potential consequences of the increased impulsivity in BD individuals include substance abuse, suicidal behavior, and other serious behavioral problems. Trait impulsivity, as measured by the Barratt Impulsiveness Scale (BIS-11), is also increased in BD, even when patients are euthymic. Additionally, elevated BIS-11 scores were associated with early onset, more frequent episodes of illness, and a history of suicide attempts, the relationships of which persisted even when age, gender, and education were taken into account [89].

Since higher measures of impulsivity are associated with manic episodes rather than to euthymic periods in BD patients, a mixed episode, especially a mixed depression, may represent the higher-risk phase of BD patients. This combination is potentially dangerous in terms of risk for violence, substance abuse, or suicide [8]. The tendency of understanding mood disorders phases in terms more of a *continuum* than a rigid classification helps to clarify the definition of mixed episodes in BD. Manic symptoms during depressive episodes may be better understood as a dimensional construct. In fact, Swann and colleagues (2007) found that even modest manic symptoms during BD depressive episodes were associated with greater impulsivity, and with histories of alcohol abuse and suicide attempts [8]. Impulsivity, as a trait, was also associated with violent suicide attempts in another study evaluating borderline personality disorder and alcoholism in a sample of BD patients [32].

Many researches agree with the observation that BD-I patients with an earlier age of onset are a correlate of suicide attempt in those with alcohol use disorders [86]. However, it seems that the effect of earlier onset of BD illness on the association between alcohol use disorder and suicidality is not mainly due to longer duration of illness. In fact, early BD-I onset also could include stunted progress in social, academic, or employment spheres, which, speculatively, in the context of the increased impulsivity and risk-taking behaviors and/or abnormal mood might combine to influence an adolescent toward injudicious use of alcohol [86].

Box 1 summarizes the factors associated with suicidal behavior in BD patients with comorbid SUDs [8, 32, 86, 89]

Box 1. Factors associated with suicidal behavior in bipolar individuals with substance use disorders

Alcohol abuse or dependence
Early onset of bipolar disorder
Drug abuse after the onset of affective illness
Aggressive behavior
Hostility
Impulsivity
Mixed depression

2.2. Neurobiology of Suicidal Behavior in Comorbidity between Bipolar Disorder and Alcohol/Drug Individuals

There are scarce data concerning the neurobiology of suicidal behavior in BD patients with comorbid SUDs. However, some clinical observations suggest that neurobiological matters demand further investigation in this setting, and at least one report suggests that early onset of BD-I and alcoholism may even share a common genetic etiology [90].

Genetic factors could account for the association: BD, alcoholism, and attempted suicide cluster in some families identified through a BD-I proband. The increased suicide risk could also arise from additional neurobiological factor(s) that have associations with both SUDs and BD. For example, abnormal serotonin function has been linked to suicide risk, lifetime severity of aggression, and BD [86].

Chronic alcohol consumption has also been linked to abnormal serotonin function. Post-mortem studies of brain tissue from patients with alcohol dependence revealed reduced serotonin transporter binding in the hippocampus. Similarly, binding was reduced in the 5-HT1A receptors of alcohol-consumers, compared to those of subjects who did not use alcohol [5, 86]. An association was found between frequency of the short (S) allele of the serotonin transporter (5-HTTLPR) and alcohol dependence. This association was stronger among individuals with alcohol dependence complicated by a comorbid psychiatric condition [86].

3. Conclusion

Alcohol and other drug use disorders appear to be particularly salient factors for increasing suicidality in bipolar patients, along with aggressive/impulsive traits. Patients with BD and SUDs have poorer quality of life and more instability of the illness, the combination of which results in higher suicide rates and more frequent suicidal attempts, as well as some physical consequences of this self-destructive act. Therefore, assessment of suicidal thoughts and past history of suicide attempts is especially critical in the comorbid BD/SUDs group in order to adequately treat these individuals and to reduce the frequency and consequences of suicidal behavior.

Additionally, considering the proposal and possible validity of a bipolar *spectrum*, understanding the comorbidity phenomena with SUDs and how it impacts on suicidality may be even more challenging. Future studies, besides evaluating the consistency of the bipolar *spectrum* construct, should try to establish a parallel between the bipolar categories and SUDs as a relevant comorbidity, and between these comorbidities and suicidal behavior, as a severe and preventable outcome.

Moreover, it is fundamental to have a broader comprehension of the comorbidity concept, and to clarify the complex relationship among psychiatric disorders co-occurring in the same individual, providing theoretical models for new practical interventions and research questions.

Among the questions unanswered is the role of drugs in BD adolescents in terms of neurodevelopment, and whether this association is related to suicidal behavior in adulthood.

Finally, future studies focusing on neurobiological aspects may play a fundamental role in distinguishing categories of the bipolar *spectrum*, their relation to the SUDs comorbidity, including chronology of this association, and to suicidal behavior.

REFERENCES

[1] Azorin JM, Kaladjian A, Adida M, Hantouche E, Hameg A, Lancrenon S, Akiskal HS: Risk factors associated with lifetime suicide attempts in bipolar I patients: findings from a French National Cohort. *Compr Psychiatry* 2009; 50(2):115-20.

[2] Harris EC, Barraclough B: Suicide as an outcome for mental disorders: a meta-analysis. *Br J Psychiatry* 1997; 170:205–28.

[3] Tondo L, Isacsson G, Baldessarini R: Suicidal behaviour in bipolar disorder: risk and prevention. *CNS Drugs* 2003; 17(7):491-511.

[4] World Health Organization: Neuroscience of psychoactive substance use and dependence. Geneva, Switzerland, *WHO Library Cataloguing-in-Publication Data,* 2004.

[5] Sher L: Alcohol consumption and suicide. *QJM* 2006; 99(1):57-61.

[6] Baethge C, Hennen J, Khalsa HM, Salvatore P, Tohen M, Baldessarini RJ: Sequencing of substance use and affective morbidity in 166 first-episode bipolar I disorder patients. *Bipolar Disord* 2008; 10(6):738-41.

[7] American Psychiatric Association. *Diagnostic and Statistical Manual of Mental Disorders*. Fourth Edition, Text Revision. Washington, DC, APA Press, 2000.

[8] Swann AC, Gerard Moeller F, Steinberg JL, Schneider L, Barratt ES, Dougherty DM: Manic symptoms and impulsivity during bipolar depressive episodes. *Bipolar Disord* 2007; 9(3):206-12.

[9] Goodwin F, Jamison K: *Manic-Depressive Illness.* New York, NY, Oxford University Press, 2007, pp 89-269.

[10] Peele PB, Xu Y, Kupfer DJ: Insurance expenditures on bipolar disorder: clinical and parity implications. *Am J Psychiatry* 2003; 160:1286-1290.

[11] World Health Organization: The World Health Report, 2001: *Mental Health – new understanding, new hope.* 2001. www.who.int

[12] Tohen M, Angst J: Epidemiology of bipolar disorder. In: Tsuang MT, Tohen M, eds. *Psychiatric Epidemiology.* New York, NY, Wiley-Liss, 2002, pp 427-444.

[13] Angst F, Stassen H, Clayton P, Angst J: Mortality of patients with mood disorders: follow-up over 34-38 years. *J Affect Disord* 2002; 68:167-181.

[14] Carballo JJ, Harkavy-Friedman J, Burke AK, Sher L, Baca-Garcia E, Sullivan GM, Grunebaum MF, Parsey RV, Mann JJ, Oquendo MA: Family history of suicidal behavior and early traumatic experiences: additive effect on suicidality and course of bipolar illness? *J Affect Disord* 2008; 109(1-2):57-63.

[15] Oquendo MA, Chaudhury SR, Mann JJ: Pharmacotherapy of suicidal behavior in bipolar disorder. *Arch Suicide Res* 2005; 9: 237–250.

[16] Valtonen H, Suominen K, Mantere O, Leppämäki S, Arvilommi P, Isometsä E: Suicidal ideation and attempts in bipolar I and II disorders. *J Clin Psychiatry* 2005; 66:1456-1462.

[17] Balázs J, Benazzi F, Rihmer Z, Rihmer A, Akiskal KK, Akiskal HS: The close link between suicide attempts and mixed (bipolar) depression: implications for suicide prevention. *J Affect Disord* 2006; 91(2-3):133-8.

[18] Rihmer Z: Suicide risk in mood disorders. *Curr Opin Psychiatry* 2007; 20:17-22.

[19] Chen YW, Dilsavier SC: Lifetime rates of suicide attempts among subjects with bipolar and unipolar disorders relative to subjects with other Axis 1 disorders. *Biol Psychiatry* 1996; 39:896-899.

[20] Kessler RC, Borges G, Walters EE: Prevalence of and risk factors for lifetime suicide attempts in National Comorbidity Survey. *Arch Gen Psychiatry* 1999; 56:617- 626.

[21] Raja M, Azzoni A: Suicide attempts: differences between unipolar and bipolar patients and among groups with different lethality risk. *J Affect Disord* 2004; 82(3):437-42.

[22] Baldessarini RJ, Tondo L, Hennen J: Lithium tratment and suicide risk in major affective disorders:update and new findings. *J Clin Psychiatry* 2003; 64(suppl 5):440-452.

[23] Oquendo MA, Waternaux C, Brodsky B, Parsons B, Haas GL, Malone KM, Mann JJ: Suicidal behavior in bipolar mood disorder: clinical characteristics of attempters and nonattempters. *J Affect Disord* 2000; 59(2):107-17.

[24] Oquendo M, Currier D, Mann J: Prospective studies of suicidal behavior in major depressive and bipolar disorders: what is the evidence for predictive risk factors? *Acta Psychiatr Scand* 2006; 114:151-8.

[25] Slama F, Bellivier F, Henry C, Rousseva A, Etain B, Rouillon F, Leboyer M: Bipolar patients with suicidal behavior: toward the identification of a clinical subgroup. *J Clin Psychiatry* 2004; 65(8):1035-9.

[26] Valtonen H, Suominen K, Mantere O, Leppämäki S, Arvilommi P, Isometsä E: Prospective study of risk factors for attempted suicide among patients with bipolar disorder. *Bipolar Disord* 2006; 8:576-85.

[27] Marangell LB, Bauer MS, Dennehy EB, Wisniewski SR, Allen MH, Miklowitz DJ, Oquendo MA, Frank E, Perlis RH, Martinez JM, Fagiolini A, Otto MW, Chessick CA, Zboyan HA, Miyahara S, Sachs G, Thase ME: Prospective preditors of suicide and

suicide attemps in 1556 patients with bipolar disorders followed for up to 2 years. *Bipolar Disord* 2006; 8:566-75.

[28] Leverich GS, Altshuler LL, Frye MA, Suppes T, Keck PE Jr, McElroy SL, Denicoff KD, Obrocea G, Nolen WA, Kupka R, Walden J, Grunze H, Perez S, Luckenbaugh DA, Post RM: Factors associated with suicide attempts in 648 patients with bipolar disorder in the Stanley Foundation Bipolar Network. *J Clin Psychiatry* 2003; 64:506-15.

[29] Grunebaum MF, Ramsay SR, Galfalvy HC, Ellis SP, Burke AK, Sher L, Printz DJ, Kahn DA, Mann JJ, Oquendo MA: Correlates of suicide attempt history in bipolar disorder: a stress-diathesis perspective. *Bipolar Disord* 2006; 8:551-7.

[30] Tsai S, Lee J, Chen C: Characteristics and psychosocial problems of patients with bipolar disorder at high risk for suicide attempt. *J Affect Disord* 1999; 52:145-52.

[31] Hawton K, Sutton L, Haw C, Sinclair J, Harris L: Suicide and attempted suicide in bipolar disorder: a systematic review of risk factors. *J Clin Psychiatry* 2005; 66:693-704.

[32] Neves FS, Malloy-Diniz LF, Corrêa H: Suicidal behavior in bipolar disorder: what is the influence of psychiatric comorbidities? *J Clin Psychiatry* 2009; 70(1):13-8.

[33] Khalsa HM, Salvatore P, Hennen J, Baethge C, Tohen M, Baldessarini RJ: Suicidal events and accidents in 216 first-episode bipolar I disorder patients: predictive factors. *J Affect Disord* 2008; 106(1-2):179-84.

[34] Dutta R, Boydell J, Kennedy N, VAN Os J, Fearon P, Murray RM: Suicide and other causes of mortality in bipolar disorder: a longitudinal study. *Psychol Med* 2007; 37(6):839-47.

[35] Simon G, Hunkeler E, Fireman B, Lee J, Savarino J: Risk of suicide attempt and suicide death in oatients treated for bipolar disorder. *Bipolar Disord* 2007; 9:526-530.

[36] Oquendo M, Malone K, Mann J: Suicide: Risk factors and prevention in refractory major depression. *Depress Anxiety* 1997; 5(4):202-11.

[37] Joiner TE Jr, Brown JS, Wingate LR: The psychology and neurobiology of suicidal behavior. *Annu Rev Psychol* 2005; 56:287-314.

[38] Oquendo MA, Placidi GP, Malone KM, Campbell C, Keilp J, Brodsky B, Kegeles LS, Cooper TB, Parsey RV, van Heertum RL, Mann JJ: Positron emission tomography of regional brain metabolic responses to a serotonergic challenge and lethality of suicide attempts in major depression. *Arch Gen Psychiatry* 2003; 60(1):14-22.

[39] Turecki G, Sequeira A, Gingras Y, Séguin M, Lesage A, Tousignant M, Chawky N, Vanier C, Lipp O, Benkelfat C, Rouleau GA: Suicide and serotonin: study of variation at seven serotonin receptor genes in suicide completers. *Am J Med Genet B Neuropsychiatr Genet* 2003; 118B(1):36-40.

[40] Kim S, Choi K, Baykiz A, Gershenfeld H: Suicide candidate genes associated with bipolar disorder and schizophrenia: An exploratory gene expression profiling analysis of post-mortem prefrontal cortex. *BMC Genomics* 2007; 8:413-422.

[41] De Luca V, Strauss J, Kennedy J: Power based association analysis (PBAT) of serotonergic and noradrenergic polymorphisms in bipolar patients with suicidal behavior. *Prog Neuropsychopharmacol Biol Psychiatry* 2008; 32:197-203.

[42] Mann JJ, Currier D, Murphy L, Huang YY, Galfalvy H, Brent D, Greenhill L, Oquendo M: No association between a TPH2 promoter polymorphism and mood disorders or monoamine turnover. *J Affect Disord* 2008; 106(1-2):117-21.

[43] Nemeroff CB, Owens MJ, Bissette G, Andorn AC, Stanley M: Reduced corticotropin releasing factor binding sites in the frontal cortex of suicide victims. *Arch Gen Psychiatry* 1988; 45(6):577-9.

[44] Zanetti MV, Cordeiro Q, Busatto G: Late onset bipolar disorder associated with White matter hyperintensities: a phathophysiological hypothesis. *Prog Neuropsychopharmacol Biol Psychiatry* 2007; 31:551-558.

[45] Pompili M, Innamorati M, Mann JJ, Oquendo MA, Lester D, Del Casale A, Serafini G, Rigucci S, Romano A, Tamburello A, Manfredi G, De Pisa E, Ehrlich S, Giupponi G, Amore M, Tatarelli R, Girardi P: Periventricular White matter hyperintensities as predictors of suicide attempts in bipolar disorders and unipolar depression. *Prog Neuropsychopharmacol Biol Psychiatry* 2008; 32:1501-1507.

[46] Keilp J, SackeimH, Brodsky B Oquendo M,Malone K, Mann J: Neuropsychological dysfunction in depressed suicide attempters. *Am J Psychiatry* 2001; 158:735-741.

[47] Tondo L, Hennen J, Baldassarini R: Reduced suicide risk with long-term lithium treatment in major affective ilness: a meta-analysis. *Acta Psychiatr Scand 2001*; 104:163-172.

[48] Baldessarini R, Tondo L, Hennen J: Reduced suicide risk during long-term treatment with lithium. *Ann N Y Acad Sci 2001;* 932:24-43.

[49] Maser JD, Cassano GB, Michelini S: Treatment Implications of Comorbid Mental Disorders. In: Treatment Strategies for Patients with Psychiatric Comorbidity. Em Scott W, Sanderson W, editors. *Treatment strategies for patients with psychiatric comorbidity.* New York, NY, Wiley, 1997, p 3-22.

[50] Krueger RF, Markon KE: Reinterpreting comorbidity: a model-based approach to understanding and classifying psychopathology. *Annu Rev Clin Psychol* 2006; 2:111-33.

[51] Nunes EV, Rounsaville BJ: Comorbidity of substance use with depression and other mental disorders: from Diagnostic and Statistical Manual of Mental Disorders, fourth edition (DSM-IV) to DSM-V. Addiction 2006; 101(suppl 1):89-96.

[52] Krishnan KR: Psychiatric and medical comorbidities of bipolar disorder. *Psychosom Med* 2005; 67(1):1-8.

[53] McHugh PR, Slavney PR: *The Perspectives of Psychiatry.* Baltimore (MA), The Johns Hopkins University Press, 1998, pp 14-15.

[54] Cardoso BM, Kauer Sant'Anna M, Dias VV, Andreazza AC, Ceresér KM, Kapczinski F: The impact of co-morbid alcohol use disorder in bipolar patients. *Alcohol* 2008; 42(6):451-7.

[55] Strakowski SM, DelBello MP: The co-occurrence of bipolar and substance use disorders. *Clin Psychol Rev* 2000; 20(2):191-206.

[56] Cerullo MA, Strakowski SM: The prevalence and significance of substance use disorders in bipolar type I and II disorder. *Subst Abuse Treat Prev Policy* 2007; 2:29.

[57] Cassidy F, Ahearn EP, Carroll BJ: Substance abuse in bipolar disorder. *Bipolar Disor*d 2001; 3:181– 8.

[58] Kawa I, Carter JD, Joyce PR, Doughty CJ, Frampton CM, Wells JE, Walsh AE, Olds RJ: Gender differences in bipolar disorder: age of onset, course, comorbidity, and symptom presentation. *Bipolar Disord* 2005; 7(2):119-25.

[59] Kessler RC: Comorbidity of unipolar and bipolar depression with other psychiatric disorders in a general population survey, in *Comorbidity in Affective Disorders.* Edited by Tohen M. New York, NY, Marcel Dekker, 1999, pp 1-25.

[60] McElroy SL: Diagnosing and treating comorbid (complicated) bipolar disorder. *J Clin Psychiatry* 2004; 65 Suppl 15:35-44.

[61] Schiavone P, Dorz S, Conforti D, Scarso C, Borgherini G: Comorbidity of DSM-IV Personality Disorders in unipolar and bipolar affective disorders: a comparative study. *Psychol Rep* 2004; 95(1):121-8.

[62] Strakowski SM, DelBello MP, Fleck DE, Arndt S: The impact of substance abuse on the course of bipolar disorder. *Biol Psychiatry* 2000; 48:477–485.

[63] Kessler RC, Rubinow DR, Holmes C, Abelson JM, Zhao S: The epidemiology of DSM-III-R bipolar I disorder in a general population survey. *Psychol Med* 1997; 27(5):1079-89.

[64] Aagaard J, Vestergaard P: Predictors of outcome in prophylactic lithium treatment: a 2-year prospective study. *J Affect Disord* 1990; 18(4):259-66.

[65] Weiss RD, Ostacher MJ, Otto MW, Calabrese JR, Fossey M, Wisniewski SR, Bowden CL, Nierenberg AA, Pollack MH, Salloum IM, Simon NM, Thase ME, Sachs GS; for STEP-BD Investigators: Does recovery from substance use disorder matter in patients with bipolar disorder? *J Clin Psychiatry* 2005; 66(6):730-5.

[66] Salloum IM, Cornelius JR, Mezzich JE, Kirisci L, Daley DC, Spotts CR, Zuckoff A: Characterizing female bipolar alcoholic patients presenting for initial evaluation. *Addict Behav* 2001; 26(3):341-8.

[67] Frye MA, Altshuler LL, McElroy SL, Suppes T, Keck PE, Denicoff K, Nolen WA, Kupka R, Leverich GS, Pollio C, Grunze H, Walden J, Post RM: Gender differences in prevalence, risk, and clinical correlates of alcoholism comorbidity in bipolar disorder. *Am J Psychiatry* 2003; 160(5):883-9.

[68] Escamilla MA, Batki S, Reus VI, Spesny M, Molina J, Service S, Vinogradov S, Neylan T, Mathews C, Meza L, Gallegos A, Montero AP, Cruz ML, Neuhaus J, Roche E, Smith L, Leon P, Freimer NB: Comorbidity of bipolar disorder and substance abuse in Costa Rica: pedigree- and population-based studies. *J Affect Disord* 2002; 71(1-3):71-83.

[69] Leweke FM, Koethe D: Cannabis and psychiatric disorders: it is not only addiction. *Addiction Biology* 2008; 13:264–275.

[70] Strakowski SM, DelBello MP, Fleck DE, Adler CM, Anthenelli RM, Keck PE, Jr, Arnold LM, Amicone J: Effects of co-occurring cannabis use disorders on the course of bipolar disorder after a first hospitalization for mania. *Arch Gen Psychiatry* 2007; 64:57–64.

[71] Ford J, Gelernter J, DeVoe J, Zhang W, Weiss R, Brady K, Farrer L, Kranzler H: Association of psychiatric and substance use disorder comorbidity with cocaine dependence severity and treatment utilization in cocaine-dependent individuals. *Drug and Alcohol Dependence* 2009; 99:193–203.

[72] Herrero MJ, Domingo-Salvany A, Torrens M, Brugal MT; ITINERE Investigators: Psychiatric comorbidity in young cocaine users: induced versus independent disorders. *Addiction* 2008; 103(2):284-93.

[73] Ringen PA, Lagerberg TV, Birkenaes AB, Engn J, Faerden A, Jónsdottir H, Nesvåg R, Friis S, Opjordsmoen S, Larsen F, Melle I, Andreassen OA: Differences in prevalence

and patterns of substance use in schizophrenia and bipolar disorder. *Psychol Med* 2008; 38(9):1241–1249.

[74] Jarvis K, DelBello MP, Mills N, Elman I, Strakowski SM, Adler CM: Neuroanatomic comparison of bipolar adolescents with and without cannabis use disorders. *J Child Adolesc Psychopharmacol* 2008; 18(6):557-63.

[75] 75- Maremmani I, Perugi G, Pacini M, Akiskal HS: Toward a unitary perspective on the bipolar spectrum and substance abuse: opiate addiction as a paradigm. *J Affect Disord* 2006; 93(1-3):1-12.

[76] Comtois KA, Russo JE, Roy-Byrne P, Ries RK: Clinicians' assessments of bipolar disorder and substance abuse as predictors of suicidal behavior in acutely hospitalized psychiatric inpatients. *Biol Psychiatry* 2004; 56(10):757-63.

[77] Verduin ML, Carter RE, Brady KT, Myrick H, Timmerman MA: Health service use among persons with comorbid bipolar and substance use disorders. *Psychiatr Serv* 2005; 56(4):475-80.

[78] Simon NM, Otto MW, Wisniewski SR, Fossey M, Sagduyu K, Frank E, Sachs GS, Nierenberg AA, Thase ME, Pollack MH: Anxiety disorder comorbidity in bipolar disorder patients: data from the first 500 participants in the Systematic Treatment Enhancement Program for Bipolar Disorder (STEP-BD). *Am J Psychiatry* 2004; 161(12):2222-9.

[79] Garno JL, Goldberg JF, Ramirez PM, Ritzler BA: Bipolar disorder with comorbid cluster B personality disorder features: impact on suicidality. *J Clin Psychiatry* 2005; 66(3):339-45.

[80] Goldberg JF: Bipolar disorder with comorbid substance abuse: diagnosis, prognosis, and treatment. *J Psychiatr Pract* 2001; 7(2):109-22.

[81] Goldstein TR, Birmaher B, Axelson D, Ryan ND, Strober MA, Gill MK, Valeri S, Chiappetta L, Leonard H, Hunt J, Bridge JA, Brent DA, Keller M: History of suicide attempts in pediatric bipolar disorder: factors associated with increased risk. *Bipolar Disord* 2005; 7(6):525-35.

[82] Keller MB: Prevalence and impact of comorbid anxiety and bipolar disorder. *J Clin Psychiatry* 2006; 67 Suppl 1:5-7.

[83] Swann AC, Dougherty DM, Pazzaglia PJ, Pham M, Steinberg JL, Moeller FG: Increased impulsivity associated with severity of suicide attempt history in patients with bipolar disorder. *Am J Psychiatry* 2005; 162(9):1680-7.

[84] Inskip HM, Harris EC, Barraclough B: Lifetime risk of suicide for affective disorder, alcoholism and schizophrenia. *Br J Psychiatry* 1998; 172:35-7.

[85] Ilgen MA, Harris AH, Moos RH, Tiet QQ: Predictors of a suicide attempt one year after entry into substance use disorder treatment. *Alcohol Clin Exp Res* 2007; 31(4):635-42.

[86] Sublette ME, Carballo JJ, Moreno C, Galfalvy HC, Brent DA, Birmaher B, John Mann J, Oquendo MA: Substance use disorders and suicide attempts in bipolar subtypes. *J Psychiatr Res* 2009; 43(3):230-8.

[87] Karch DL, Barker L, Strine TW: Race/ethnicity, substance abuse, and mental illness among suicide victims in 13 US states: 2004 data from the National Violent Death Reporting System. *Inj Prev* 2006; 12 Suppl 2:ii22-ii27.

[88] Baethge C, Baldessarini RJ, Khalsa HM, Hennen J, Salvatore P, Tohen M: Substance abuse in first-episode bipolar I disorder: indications for early intervention. *Am J Psychiatry* 2005; 162(5):1008-10.

[89] Swann AC, Lijffijt M, Lane SD, Steinberg JL, Moeller FG: Increased trait-like impulsivity and course of illness in bipolar disorder. *Bipolar Disord* 2009; 11(3):280-8.
[90] Lin PI, McInnis MG, Potash JB, Willour V, MacKinnon DF, DePaulo JR, Zandi PP: Clinical correlates and familial aggregation of age at onset in bipolar disorder. *Am J Psychiatry* 2006; 163(2):240-6.

In: Suicidal Behavior in Alcohol and Drug Abuse... ISBN: 978-1-60876-919-3
Editors: L. Sher, A. Vilens, pp. 497-511

Chapter 28

COMORBID FEATURES OF SUICIDAL BEHAVIOR, DEPRESSION AND ALCOHOL ABUSE

Debora Ganz and Leo Sher
Columbia University and New York State Psychiatric Institute,
New York, New York, USA

ABSTRACT

Internationally, alcohol use disorders and depression are both highly associated with suicidality. Such association is not surprising since many of the causes of alcoholism and depression overlap and both contribute to suicidal tendencies. Suicidal risk is even higher in individuals suffering from comorbid depression and alcohol abuse than it is in individuals presenting with depression or alcohol abuse alone. This connection between alcohol use, depression and suicidality appears to vary across gender, age, race and socio-economic background.

There are many clinical features, as well as biological and social contributors, that are commonly present in individuals suffering from comorbid alcoholism, depression and suicidal tendencies. Most of these clinical features are enhanced by the comorbidity of alcohol abuse, depression and suicidality. Alcohol abuse, depression and suicidal behavior have been found to have biochemical and genetic correlates. Alcohol abuse, depression and suicidality are also commonly comorbid with other psychiatric disorders, childhood abuse, aggression, substance use, life stressors, and low self esteem. This article also discusses the social stigma associated with alcoholism, depression and suicidality, and how that may serve to enhance these disorders. Many directional models are presented (1) based on past research and (2) as suggestions for future research. There is a lot that can be done by clinicians, legal and educational professionals and society at large that may help to prevent and treat such problems.

INTRODUCTION AND EPIDEMIOLOGY

Suicidal behavior is a major medical and social problem. Every year, approximately one million people die from suicide worldwide. A survey done in the U.S. in 2004 found the 12-month prevalence of DSM-IV alcohol use disorders to be 12.4% in males and 4.9% in females [1]. Alcohol use disorders are associated with suicides, with an 8% lifetime risk for suicide in individuals with alcohol dependence [2,3]. International studies have found up to a 6 times increased risk for suicide in alcohol abuse and dependence when compared to the general population (DSM-III-R) [4,5]. Across age and gender, autopsy studies have shown that between 15% and 61% of all suicides previously suffered from alcohol use disorders [6].

Depression has also been implicated in suicidal behaviors ranging from suicidal thoughts to completed suicides [7,8]. Such association (between alcohol, depression and suicide) is not surprising since many of the causes of alcoholism and depression overlap and both contribute to suicidal tendencies [2-8]. In regards to alcohol use, there are consistent positive correlations between alcohol use and suicidal ideation and behaviors, and a few longitudinal studies have found further evidence that drinking that begins earlier in life is related to increases in suicidal ideation and suicide attempts over time [7,9,10]. In fact, heavier alcohol use among teens was associated with a 3- to 4-fold increase in the probability of a lifetime suicide attempt [11,12]. It is even true that depression and suicidal ideation are intrinsically connected due to the fact that one of the definitions of depression is "suicidal thoughts or intentions" [13]. Regarding depression and suicidality, depression is the most prominent predictor of suicidal ideation, telling someone about plans to commit suicide, and attempting suicide [8]. Such suicidal risk may rise if the depression is accompanied by alcohol abuse [14]. Individuals with comorbid depression and alcohol use more frequently reported a history of suicide and higher ideation scores than did individuals with alcohol use or depression alone [15].

Approximately 40% of people with an AOD (alcohol and other drug) use disorder developed their first symptom between the ages of 15 and 19 [14,15], and individuals who start using alcohol earlier in life are left with a greater vulnerability to the effects of alcohol [16]. It is therefore important to stop alcohol use in these young populations. However, the association of alcohol dependence and suicide has been shown to be higher with increased age (between 20 and 50 years; even when controlling for comorbid mood disorders and gender) [17].

There are many clinical features, as well as biological and social contributors, that are commonly present in individuals suffering from comorbid alcoholism, depression and suicidal tendencies. Most of these clinical features and associations, such as personality disorders, are enhanced by the comorbidity of alcohol abuse, depression and suicidality.

CAUSATION OR CORRELATION?

According to some models, it appears possible that it is AOD intoxication that is neurobiologically responsible for depressive symptoms [15,17]. It is estimated that about 60% of all depressive episodes in alcoholics might be substance-induced [19]. Primarily however, it appears that depression may be a risk factor for AOD use, with depressive symptoms predating AOD use up to 80% of the time [20,21]. When considering suicidal ideation, the connection between alcohol use and suicidality appears to vary across gender with suicidality leading to increased alcohol-related problems for females, while alcohol-related problems are predictive of suicidality among males [7]. It is also theorized that while alcohol use in general may have a more distal interaction with suicidality, binge drinking is implicated as a more proximal precipitating factor of suicide attempts [8,22].

In consideration of clinical factors, it is also possible that a third factor (ie: aggression or child abuse) contributes to the initiation and/or maintenance of all three factors independent of each other. It is therefore important that the sequence of clinical features is taken into careful consideration when diagnosing such comorbidities. In accordance with Hovens model [18], clinicians should not preemptively diagnose individuals who show signs of severe depression immediately after having stopped heavy doses of AOD consumption with a mood disorder. Only individuals who were severely depressed before consuming alcohol and those whose symptoms persist for more than six weeks after can accurately be diagnosed with comorbid depression [23].

On the other hand, it may be true that alcohol abuse causes depression, in which case initial prevention of acohol consumtion is essential. The biological reason that alcohol may be responsible for causing depression is because alcohol can cause an individual to take part in risk taking behaviors [24]. Or it is possible that depression may lead an individual to imbibe alcohol. The initial intoxication can then directly or indirectly lower resistance to suicidal impulses, causing either intoxicated suicide attempts due to increased aggression or decreased inhibition, eventual deterioration of judgment, increased feelings of depression and/or eventual undermining of social support [7,8,25]. The comorbidity of suicidal inclinations may also present as an individuals' extreme attempt to be rid of external pressures when alcohol consumption either fails to do so or enhances initial depressive feelings [18]. It is also possible that the initial alcohol consumption will increase stress and thereby trigger the depressive symptoms that are then predictive of suicidality [7,8,18].

Either way, suicide, depression, and alcohol abuse can certainly be enhanced by one another. These disparate directional models, which consider many different combinations of suicidality, alcohol use and depression, certainly expose a need for more research in comorbid diagnoses. These models should also serve to encourage clinicians to consider gender and underlying and/or comorbid factors when clients present with suicidal features in order to better evaluate where to best implement treatment initiatives.

BIOLOGICAL FACTORS

Alcohol abuse, depression and suicidal behavior have been found to have biochemical and genetic correlates [27-46]. Twin and adoption studies suggest that 50% to 60% of risk to develop alcohol dependence is due to heritable factors, and linkage and association studies have identified chromosomal regions and individual genes that most likely contribute to the development of this condition [28,29]. In a study of the two syndromes in female twins, Kendler et al. [30] showed a genetic correlation of 0.4–0. A genetic basis was suggested on chromosome 1 that may predispose some individuals to alcoholism and others to depression (which may be alcohol induced). Due to the high genetic relationships, loci on other chromosomes, notably chromosomes 2, 7 and 4, may also be of interest [31]. Such genetic factors are likely to increase in strength as the individual ages [32]. Furthermore, it is hypothesized that people with a family history of alcoholism are more sensitive to the stimulating effects and less sensitive to the sedative effects of alcohol [33-35].

Regarding suicidality, liability to suicidal behavior might be familialy transmitted as a trait independent of axis I or II diagnoses [36]. Association between serotonin dysfunction and suicide, as well as suicide-related behaviors such as violence, aggression, anger, anxiety and impulsivity have been demonstrated in a considerable number of studies. Thus, genes related to serotonergic pathways became a focus of attention of genetic researchers studying mood and suicidal behavior. The insertion/deletion polymorphism in the promoter region of the serotonin transporter promoter (5-HTTLPR) may be involved in suicidal behavior, especially when anger traits are present [37].

A recent study found an anterior medial prefrontal cortical area where patients with comorbid major depression and alcohol use disorders had more severe hypofrontality compared to MDD (Major Depressive Disorder) only patients [38]. This group difference disappeared after fenfluramine administration. The fact that the observed group difference disappeared after the fenfluramine challenge suggests that serotonergic mechanisms play a role in the observed differences between the groups. Many behaviors and emotional mechanisms that participate in inducing alcohol abuse are known to be critically dependent on the prefrontal cortical areas [39,40]. This means that prefrontal cortex abnormalities could be present in individuals with alcohol use disorders before they start drinking. Although it is possible that some individuals begin drinking before age 13 and their behavioral problems are related to alcohol use, this is not very likely because a recent study suggests that only 8.6% of patients with comorbid major depression and alcohol use disorders began drinking/using drugs before age 13 [41].

Abnormalities in the dopamine and hypothalamic-pituitary-adrenal (HPA) systems may also be involved in depression, alcohol abuse, and suicidality [42]. Cerebrospinal fluid (CSF) homovanillic acid (HVA) levels were lower in depressed subjects with a history of alcoholism than in depressed subjects without a history of alcoholism, even after adjustment for sex, aggression and depression scores, cigarette smoking, antisocial and borderline personality disorders, psychomotor retardation, and delusions [43]. An earlier study reported that depressed subjects with alcoholism had significantly lower concentrations of HVA than never depressed subjects with alcoholism [42]. Low CSF HVA may have more to do with psychopathology related to alcoholism than mood disorder biology. Recent data on HPA system activation suggest that environmental stress and paternal history of alcoholism can interact to produce an exaggerated endocrine stress response, which is normalized by alcohol [45]. Multiple research reports suggest that HPA abnormalities are also involved in the neurobiology of depression and suicidal behavior [46].

Other Psychiatric Disorders

Researchers indicate that almost 75% of people with alcohol use disorders suffer from some other psychiatric disorder. While this includes the diagnosis of major depression, other mood disorders, personality disorders and bipolar disorder are also often comorbid diagnoses [47-50].

Alcohol-misuse has been found to be commonly comorbid with major depression, suicide attempts, PTSD, generalized anxiety, social phobia and agoraphobia (particularly as it relates to childhood abuse) [51]. One study with a population of Swiss army conscripts found that psychiatric illness and depression scores were higher among suicide victims than controls [52]. Another commonly comorbid diagnosis to suicidality is that of oppositional behavior disorders, particularly in adolescents, which may result in part from alcohol or other substance misuse [18,42,53]. These studies all noted the need for consideration of other psychiatric illnesses and personality factors as indicators of increased suicide risk. Many disorders are inherently bound to suicide risk factors and such suicidality can be increased by depression, alcohol use or both in comorbidity.

Childhood Abuse

One common precursor to comorbid alcoholism and depression is childhood abuse [51,54,55]. Consequences of childhood abuse can be internalizing disorders such as depression and suicidal ideation, and externalizing behaviors such as alcohol use and suicide attempts [55,15].

Regardless of the connecting factors, it is clear that depression and alcohol abuse often result from early childhood abuse. In an article by Makhija & Sher [55], alcohol abuse is described as a consequence of the depression and feelings of worthlessness that resulted from childhood abuse. Alcoholism acts as a type of coping mechanism for such individuals in that alcoholism can provide an escape from the emotional and psychological feelings associated with these environments by creating an effect of stress reduction and/or enhancing the feelings of disassociation that may have been used to deal with the horror of abuse in the first place.

Even without the additions of AOD use or depression, childhood abuse significantly increases suicide risk [7,41,56-58]. Adult women with a history of abuse are a particularly relevant cohort with regards to this topic, as they are more likely to report depression, substance abuse and suicidality than are women without such a history [58]. This loss of self-esteem due to abuse contributes to depression and suicidal impulses [15]. Alcohol misuse is frequently the facilitator of suicide attempts and completions among abused populations [25]. In fact, it was discovered that, if such individuals continue to abuse alcohol, one out of every twenty active alcoholics with comorbid major depression will die by suicide within two years of hospitalization [59].

Self Medication Model

There are many different reasons given for the causation of both depression and alcohol abuse as well as the correlation of comorbid depression and alcohol abuse. There exists a self-medication model of alcoholism that would regard alcohol abuse as an attempt by depressed persons to dismiss their feelings of depression [18]. Drinking may serve to medicate suicidality in the same way that it is purported to medicate depressive symptoms, suggesting that alcohol abuse may follow suicidal ideation within the self-medication framework. This is true based on alcohols neurobiological ability to reduce high levels of stress, anxiety and other distressing emotions through its anxiolytic effects [7]. Research suggests that depression and AOD use may lead to a suicide attempt as a means of coping with perceived insurmountable problems and/or alcohol related emotional arousal [59].

Developmental and Situational Contributors

Aggression

Individuals with both alcoholism and depression who attempt or complete suicide often present with significantly high levels of aggression and impulsivity [15,42,51,52,60-62]. The comorbidity of depression and alcoholism was reported to have higher lifetime aggression and impulsivity as well as higher suicidal ideation scores [15]. Compared to MDD only patients, MDD/AUD patients reported more behavioral problems and significantly higher aggression scores during their childhood [40]. However, even in individuals without alcohol use disorders, violent behavior in the final year of life was a significant predictor of completed suicides, particularly among females [60].

Alcohol use may increase the aggressiveness of an attempter, serve to enhance suicide-specific alcohol expectancies (ie: alcohol will give me the courage to complete my suicide), or create a disinhibiting affect allowing for the breakthrough of self-destructive impulses into actual behavior [15]. This aggression may be a distal contributor to suicidality as it may serve to increase delinquency and/or promote interpersonal disruptions that may in turn increase suicide risk. Alcohol may also, or alternatively, serve as a direct causative factor by increasing aggressiveness and therefore propelling suicidal ideation into action [42], even when the initial alcohol consumption was associated with destructive self-medication (ie: for depression, stress reduction etc).

However, studies show that completed suicides by males with alcohol dependence or abuse over the ages of 50 and 65 years were more likely to use non-violent suicide methods, have proof of alcohol post-mortem and were less likely to have severe physical illnesses, separation, and unemployment at the time of suicide [61,62].

Substance Use

AOD use and AUD's appear frequently and interchangeably throughout many articles (including this one). This is likely because of the high comorbidity between the two, and possibly due to the self-medication model as a cause for AOD use in response to both depression and suicidal ideation [18]. In general, individuals who are sensation seekers or involved in risk taking behaviors such as drug use are more likely to drink and also more likely to exhibit suicidal ideation [7]. (Such sensation seeking is likely to be more prevalent among adolescent and young adult populations.)

Stress

Studies have shown that the brain changes associated with stressful experiences are also associated with more sensitivity to the effects of the stress as well as to drugs of abuse [63]. Whether or not this is due to new stressors, it is not surprising that stress may result in depression and suicidality and that these factors (AOD use, depression and suicidality) alone as well as in comorbidity may serve to enhance stress as well as stress relieving activities (ie: smoking and drinking). Stressors may include the loss of a parent or loved one, the break up of a romantic relationship, abuse or neglect, chronic illness, natural disasters, and other trauma [2,64-68]. Homelessness, unemployment, and low socio-economic status may more generally contribute to stress in the home and therefore indirectly contribute to feelings of depression, suicidal ideation and AOD use [69-71]. While some stressful risk factors may be present in alcoholism, depression or suicidality individually, many of these risks are often augmented when these features present themselves in comorbity [3,7,11,67,70].

While alcoholism and depression are often associated with suicide attempts, most psychiatric patients never attempt suicide, leading to the conclusion that there are additional risk factors and/or stressors that drive individuals to commit suicide. Studies indicate that it is life stressors that may contribute to or be increased by suicide attempts and suicidal ideation. High life stress can reduce adaptive coping efforts [72], which can lead into further depression and suicidality. Families or communities with high levels of stress (i.e. financial, psychological) may have less developed coping mechanisms, which can likely lead to alcohol use as a self-medication or suicide as an unhealthy resolution: possibly encouraged by alcohol-induced myopia (see self-medication model above) [7]. Stressful life events and depressive episodes are thought to precipitate aggression, alcoholism and negative affect [48,73]. In particular, partner-relationship disruptions are most strongly associated with attempted and completed suicides in persons with alcoholism and in females with depression [42,74,75]. Furthermore, prolonged depression, alcohol abuse or both in comorbidity can lead to a decrease in social support and further suicidal tendencies [7].

Stigmatization and Low Self-esteem

The self-medication model may often be a result of the taboos associated with being an alcoholic and therefore seeking treatment for alcoholism, the taboos associated with seeking treatment for depression, and/or the ambiguity within the definition of depression. In a novel article regarding the stigma of alcohol misuse, Aviram [76] elucidates the pressures that cause individuals to consume alcohol as well as the stigmas associated with seeking treatment for alcoholism and being labeled as 'an alcoholic.' Depression and/or suicidal ideation may be the initial response to feelings of low self-esteem and/or external pressures, with alcoholism developing later as a method of self-medication in place of seeking treatment for depression.

Alternatively, an individual may attempt to cope with his or her depression, which is seen as a mere phase or sense of weakness, by resorting to alcohol use. Suicidality may be considered as a solution to seemingly insurmountable and unsalvageable emotional problems that one is faced with, often independently; especially when alcohol fails to assuage them [59]. Individuals may also be (or feel that they are) facing these issues on their own due to the fact that their alcoholism, depression, aggression, etc. have diminished their social support. Once alcohol use has been initiated, depressed individuals may fail to acknowledge the consequences of further alcohol use, especially if use results in initial alleviation of depressive or anxiety symptoms. This alcohol use may then lead such individuals into suicidality due to a lack of inhibition or new sense of brazenness [15,77].

It is also possible that it is not the social stigma associated with having depression, but rather the ambiguity associated with defining depression that pushes self-medication; rather than treatment seeking. With depression occurring earlier in life nowadays then in the past [1] and an estimated 17.1 million adults reporting experiencing one major depressive episode in the past year [78], there should be many individuals being treated for depression. However, one to two thirds of those who are depressed never seek treatment for their depression [78,79]. This may be true because people may assume that feeling depressed is normal after increased levels of stress or simply be uneducated as to the definition of clinical depression as a mental illness.

Suggestions for Prevention

Screening

When an individual presents with alcoholic features, depressive features and/or other psychiatric symptoms are often comorbid [80,81]. There is a deficiency present in professional psychological venues that pertain to the screening of such populations. A full psychiatric screening should be encouraged within both psychiatric emergency rooms as well as other clinical settings [15,18]. Factors that should be assessed, which have been found to be common risk-factors for alcohol induced suicide, include depression and other mood disorders, recent heavy drinking, threat of suicide, lack of social support, being unemployed, living alone, older age, male gender, interpersonal life events, substance dependence, high nicotine intake, and low education [6]. Considering the comorbidity of such disorders, detailed screenings can help to better address all of the contributing factors and ultimately better resolve these illnesses and prevent suicide.

Individual Treatment

It has been suggested that within treatment of comorbid alcoholism and depression, clinicians should first focus on abstinence and then treat the depression. Studies have shown that individuals depressed after one week of abstinence have superior outcomes with antidepressant treatment than those without a period of abstinence [15]. However, treatment of depression should not be withheld in recovering alcoholics because of the concern that the symptoms may represent prolonged intoxication or withdrawal effects, because it has also been found that treatment of recovering alcoholics may actually reduce the risk of relapse in comorbid conditions [66].

Persons presenting with alcohol abuse and suicidal ideations and/or behaviors should be taught to identify the life stressors or circumstances that precipitated or are contributing to their distress [82]. An integral part of the therapy should be identifying and targeting suicidal cognitions. They should be asked to review their binge drinking behavior, including positive and negative expectancies, experiences, and consequences.

Multiple studies, including a recent meta-analysis, suggest that cognitive-behavioral therapy (CBT) can reduce suicidal behavior [83,84]. This highly significant result was in spite of the considerable variability in the populations being treated, the treatments implemented, and the outcomes used. This heterogeneity is a cause for optimism in CBT's promising ability to reduce suicidal behavior in a variety of circumstances: CBT does prove effective when compared with minimal treatment or "treatment as usual," and importantly, CBT was still effective when studies using control groups involving active psychological treatments were included in the analysis. This suggests that CBT may have a specific effect, but it does not mean that other treatments cannot be used to counter suicidal thoughts and behaviors. Indeed, a key question concerns what aspects of therapies are common and effective in helping those who are suicidal and which are specific. Treatment is effective when directly focused on reducing some aspect of suicidal behavior but not when focused on other symptoms (such as depression or distress) with a view to reducing suicidal behavior as a secondary effect. Thus, to be effective, specific CBT suicide prevention treatment programs need to be designed, tailored, and implemented to focus on suicidal behavior. It is also important to note that CBT can also reduce alcohol and substance abuse [85].

Community and Environmental Factors

Environmental causes must be considered and responded to as well. It is essential that parental abuse and negligence be recognized early and that such children are removed from their homes as a means of prevention. When problems do present themselves, culturally and developmentally appropriate approaches are needed to address these issues.

Education and open discussion of the problems associated with drinking and depression should also be encouraged [86]. An individual who is unaware of the reality and features of alcohol abuse and/or clinical depression may feel that their depressed state is normal or something to be ashamed of and therefore self-medicate rather than seek professional treatment [76,86]. Suicide preventions should target specific groups at highest risk for suicide based on age, gender, location, etc.

Legal suggestions that should be applied to prevent alcohol misuse include alcohol taxes, warning labels, zero-tolerance laws, and other laws regarding serving alcohol and acting under the influence of alcohol [87]. Law officials must also consider that it may not be merely the laws themselves that need to be enhanced, but rather the implementation of these laws, specifically in communities where alcohol misuse is prevalent. These factors can and have already contributed to decreased accessibility of alcohol and education regarding the negative affects of alcohol consumption [87], but more measures are still needed to increase these awareness's.

As is the case with many current psychological illnesses, the stigmatization that surrounds being labeled as having a mental illness is a very real threat to seeking treatment [87]. Some models may fail to recognize low self-esteem as a risk factor for AOD abuse [73], but that does not mean that stigma is not involved. Recognition and literature regarding stigmatization of mental illnesses is becoming more widespread, yet there is still much to be done before the stigma regarding illnesses such as alcoholism and depression are significantly diminished. This is needed before we can expect individuals to feel comfortable addressing these issues and seeking treatment - a necessary first step in the implementation of treatment for alcohol abuse, depression and suicidality.

Future Research Suggestions

More studies are still needed regarding the complicated associations between comorbid diagnoses; specifically regarding suicide, depression and AOD use disorders. Furthermore, the genetic influences of alcohol-related disorders on the suicide risk of relatives has yet to be assessed [6]. Specific risk constellations and possibly even diagnostic scales and clear clinician requirements or suggestions for patient intake would also be helpful in recognizing and preventing risk factors for alcoholism, depression, and suicidality individually as well as collectively.

References

[1] Grant BF, Hasin DS, Chou SP, et al.: Nicotine Dependence and Psychiatric Disorders in the United States. Results for the National and Epedimiologic Survey on Alcohol and Related Conditions. *Archives of General Psychiatry* 2004;61:1107-15.

[2] Bertolote MJ, Fleischmann A: *World Psychiatry* 2002;1:181-5.

[3] Inskip HM, Harris C, Barraclough B: Lifetime risk of suicide for affective disorder, alcoholism and skitzophrenia. The British Journal of Psychiatry 1998;172:35-37.

[4] Harris EC, Baraclough B: Excess Mortality of Mental Disorder. *The British Journal of Psychiatry* 1998;173:11-53.

[5] Wilcox HC, Conner KR, Caine ED: Association of alcohol and drug use disorders and completed suicide: an empirical review of cohort studies. *Drug and Alcohol Dependence* 2004;76 suppl:S11-19.

[6] Schneider B: *Substance use disorders and risk for completed suicide. Review.* Frankfurt, Germany: in press.

[7] Light J, Grubea J, Maddena P, Goverb J: Adolescent alcohol use and suicidal ideation. A nonrecursive model. *Addictive Behaviors* 2003;28:705-24.

[8] Windle M: Suicidal Behaviors and Alcohol Use Among Adolescents: A Developmental Psychopathology Perspective. Alcoholism: *Clinical and Experimental Research* 2004; 5S.

[9] Reifman A, Windle M: Adolescent suicidal behaviors as a function of depression, hopelessness, alcohol use, and social support: a longitudinal investigation. *Am J Community Psychol* 1995;23:329–54.

[10] Vega WA, Gil A, Warheit G, Apospori E, Zimmerman R: The relationship of drug use to suicide ideation and attempts among African American, Hispanic, and white non-Hispanic male adolescents. *Suicide and Life-Threatening Behavior* 1993;23:110–19.

[11] Borowsky IW, Ireland M, Resnick MD: Adolescent suicide attempts: risks and protectors. *Pediatrics* 2001;107:485–93.

[12] Windle M, Miller-Tutzauer C, Domenico D: Alcohol use, suicidal behavior, and risky activities among adolescents. *J Res Adolesc* 1992;2:317–30.

[13] American Psychiatric Association. *Diagnostic and Statistical Manual on Mental Disorders, fourth edition (DSM-IV).* Washington, DC: American Psychiatric Press, 1995.

[14] Shaffer D, Craft L: Methods of adolescent suicide prevention. *Journal of Clinical Psychiatry* 1999;60(2):70-74.

[15] Sher L, Oquendo MA, Galfalvy HC, Grunebaum MF, Burke AK, Zalsman G, Mann JJ: The relationship of aggression to suicidal behavior in depressed patients with a history of alcoholism. *Addict Behav* 2005;30:1144-1153.

[16] Grant BF, Stinson FS, Harford TC: Age at onset of alcohol use and DSM-IV alcohol abuse and dependence: a 12-year follow-up. *J Subst Abuse* 2001;13:493–504.

[17] Conner KR, Beautrais AL, Conwell Y: Moderators of the relationship between alcohol dependence and suicide and medically serious suicide attempts: analyses of Canterbury Suicide Project data. Alcoholism: *Clinical and Experimental Research* 2003;27:1156-61.

[18] Hovens JG, Cantwell DP, Kiriakos R: Psychiatric comorbidity in hospitalized adolescent substance misusers. *Journal of the American Academy of Child & Adolescent Psychiatry* 1994;33(4):476–83.

[19] Schuckit MA, Tipp JE, Bergman M et al.: Comparison of induced and independent major depressive disorders in 2,945 alcoholics. *American Journal of Psychiatry* 1997;154:948-57.

[20] Burke JD, Burke KC, Rae DS: Increased rates of drug abuse and dependence after onset of mood or anxiety disorders in adolescence. *Hospital and Community Psychiatry* 1994;45(5):451–55.

[21] Rohde P, Lewinsohn PM, Seeley JR: Comorbidity of unipolar depression: II. Comorbidity with other mental disorders in adolescents and adults. *Journal of Abnormal Psychology* 1991;100(2):214–22.

[22] Pirkola SP, Isometsa ET, Heikkinen M, et al.: Employment status influences the weekly patterns of suicide among alcohol misusers. Alcoholism: *Clinical and Experimental Research* 1997;21:1704-6.

[23] Mack AH, Frances RJ: Treatment of Alcohol Use Disorders in Adolescents. *Journal of Psychiatric Practice* 2003;9(3):195-208.

[24] Monti PM, Robert M, Nixon K, Sher KJ, Swartzwelder HS, Tapert SF, White A, Crews FT: Adolescence: Booze, Brains, and Behavior. *Alcoholism: Clinical & Experimental Research* 2005;29(2):207-20.

[25] Crombie IK, Pounder DJ. Who takes alcohol prior to suicide? *J Clin Forensic Med* 1998;5:65-8.

[26] Renaud J, Berlim MT, McGirr A, Tousignant M, Tureki G: Current psychiatric morbidity, aggression/impulsivity, and personality dimensions in child and adolescent suicide: A case-control study. *J Affect Disord* 2008;105(1-3):221-8.

[27] Sher L, Mann JJ. Neurobiology of suicide. In: Soares J.C., Gershon S. (editors). *Textbook of Medical Psychiatry.* New York: Marcel Dekker, 2003, pp. 701-711.

[28] Enoch MA, Goldman D: The genetics of alcoholism and alcohol abuse. *Curr Psychiatry Rep.* 2001;3(2):144-51.

[29] Heath AC, Whitfield JB, Madden PA, Bucholz KK, Dinwiddie SH, Slutske WS, Bierut LJ, Statham DB, Martin NG: Towards a molecular epidemiology of alcohol dependence: analysing the interplay of genetic and environmental risk factors. *Br J Psychiatry Suppl.* 2001;40:s33-40.

[30] Kendler KS, Heath AC, Neale MC, Kessler RC, Eaves LJ: Alcoholism and major depression in women: a twin study of the causes of comorbidity. *Arch Gen Psychiatry* 1993;50:690–8.

[31] Nurnberger JI Jr, Foroud T, Flury L, Su J, Meyer ET, Hu K, Crowe R, Edenberg H, Goate A, Bierut L, Reich T, Schuckit M, Reich W: Evidence for a locus on chromosome 1 that influences vulnerability to alcoholism and affective disorder. *American Journal of Psychiatry* 2001;158(5):718-24.

[32] Kutlenios RM: Genetics and alcoholism: Implications for advanced practice psychiatric/mental health nursing. *Archives of Psychiatric Nursing* 1988;12(3):154-61.

[33] Newlin DB, Thompson, JB: Alcohol Challenge with sons of alcoholics: *A critical Review and AnalysisPsychological Bulletin* 1990;108:383-402.

[34] Pollock VE: Meta-analysis of subjective sensitivity to alcohol in sons of alcoholics. *American Journal of Psychiatry* 1992;149:1534-8.

[35] Schuckit MA, Smith TL, Kalmijn J, et al.: Response to alcohol in daughters of alcoholics: A pilot study and a comparison with sons of alcoholics. *Alcohol and Alcoholism* 2000;35:242-8.

[36] Brent DA, Bridge J, Johnson BA, Connolly J: Suicidal behavior runs in families. A controlled family study of adolescent suicide victims. *Arch Gen Psychiatry* 1996;53(12):1145-52.

[37] Zalsman G, Anderson GM, Peskin M, Frisch A, King RA, Vekslerchik M, Sommerfeld E, Michaelovsky E, Sher L, Weizman A, Apter A: Relationships between serotonin transporter promoter polymorphism, platelet serotonin transporter binding and clinical phenotype in suicidal and non-suicidal adolescent inpatients. *Journal of Neural Transmission,* 2005, Vol. 112, No. 2, pp. 309-315.

[38] Sher L, Milak MS, Parsey RV, Carballo JJ, Cooper TB, Malone KM, Oquendo MA, Mann JJ: Positron emission tomography study of regional brain metabolic responses to a serotonergic challenge in major depressive disorder with and without comorbid lifetime alcohol dependence. *European Neuropsychopharmacology* 2007;17(9)608-15.
[39] Adinoff, B: "Neurobiologic processes in drug reward and addiction." *Harv. Rev. Psychiatry* 2004;12(6)305-20.
[40] Lyvers M: Loss of control in alcoholism and drug addiction: a neuroscientific interpretation. *Exp Clin Psychopharmacol* 2000;8(2):225-49.
[41] Sher L, Stanley BH, Harkavy-Friedman J, Carballo JJ, Arendt M, Brent D, Sperling D, Lizardi D, Mann JJ, Oquendo MA: Depressed patients with co-occurring alcohol use disorders: a unique patient population. *J Clin Psychiatry* 2008;69(6):907-15.
[42] Fromme K, D'Amico EJ. Neurobiological bases of alcohol's psychological effects. In: Leonard KE, Blane HT (Ed). *Psychological Theories of Drinking and Alcoholism.* Guilford, New York, 1999, pp. 422-455.
[43] Sher L, Oquendo MA, Li S, Huang Y, Grunebaum MF, Burke AK, Malone KM, Mann JJ: Lower CSF homovanillic acid levels in depressed patients with a history of alcoholism. *Neuropsychopharmacology* 2003;28(9):1712-19.
[44] Roy A, DeJong J, Lamparski D, George T, Linnoila M: "Depression among alcoholics. Relationship to clinical and cerebrospinal fluid variables" *Arch.Gen.Psychiatry,* 1991;48(5):428-32.
[45] Zimmermann U, Spring K, Kunz-Ebrecht SR, Uhr M, Wittchen HU, Holsboer F: Effect of ethanol on hypothalamic-pituitary-adrenal system response to psychosocial stress in sons of alcohol-dependent fathers. *Neuropsychopharmacology* 2004;29(6):1156-65.
[46] Sher L: Combined dexamethasone suppression-corticotropin-releasing hormone stimulation test in studies of depression, alcoholism, and suicidal behavior. *The Scientific World Journal* 2006;6:1398-1404.
[47] Compton WM, Cottler LB, Jacobs JL, Ben-Abdullah A, Spitznagel EL: The Role of Psychiatric Disorders in Predicting Drug Dependence Treatment Outcomes. *Am J Psychiatry* 2003;160:890–895.
[48] Schneider B, Georgi K, Weber B, et al.: Risk factors for suicide in substance-related disorders. *Psychiatrische Praxis* 2006;33:81-87.
[49] Duffy J, Kreitman N: Risk factors for suicide and undetermined death among in-patient alcoholics in Scotland. *Addiction* 1993;88:757-66.
[50] Cheng ATA, Mann AH, Chan KA: Personality disorder and suicide. A case-control study. *British Journal of Psychiatry* 1997;170:441-6.
[51] Buydens-Branchey L, Branchey M, Noumair D: Age of alcoholism onset, relationship to psychopathology. *Arch Gen Psychiatry* 1989;46:225-30.
[52] Angsta J, Claytonb PJ: Personality, smoking and suicide: a prospective study. *Journal of Affective Disorders* 1998;51(1):55-62.
[53] Cavaiola A, Schiff M: Self-esteem in abused chemically dependent children. *Child Abuse Negl* 1989;13:327–34.
[54] Paolucci EO, Genuis ML, Violato C: A meta-analysis of the published research on the effects of child sexual abuse. *J Psychol* 2001;135:17–36.
[55] Makhija N, Sher L: Childhood abuse, adult alcohol use disorders and suicidal behaviour QJM: *An International Journal of Medicine* 2007;100(5):305-9.

[56] Hasin DS, Grant BF: Major depression in 6050 former drinkers. Association with past alcohol dependence. *Arch Gen Psychiatry September* 2002;59:794-800.

[57] Briere J, Runtz M: Suicidal thoughts and behaviours in formal sexual abuse victims. *Can J Behavioural Science* 1986;18:413-23.

[58] Borges G, Rosovsky H: Suicide attempts and alcohol consumption in an emergerncy room sample. *J Studies Alc* 1996; 7:543-8.

[59] Hufford MR: Alcohol and suicidal behavior. *Clin Psychol Rev* 2001;21:797– 811.

[60] Conner KR, Cox C, Duberstein PR, Tian L, Nisbet PA, Conwell Y: Violence, Alcohol, and Completed Suicide: A Case-Control Study. *Am J Psychiatry* 2001;158:1701-5.

[61] Conner KR, Duberstein PR, Conwell Y: Age-related patterns of factors associated with completed suicide in men with alcohol dependence. *The American Journal of Addictions* 1999;8:312-18.

[62] Waern M: Alcohol dependence and misuse in elderly suicides. *Alcohol and Alcoholism* 2003;38:249-54.

[63] Romeo RD, McEwen BS: Stress and the adolescent brain. Annals of the New York *Academy of Sciences* 2006;1094:202-14.

[64] Wells VE, Deykin EY, Klerman GL: Risk factors for depression in adolescence. *Psychiatric Development* 1985;3(1):83-108.

[65] Monroe SM, Rohde P, Seeley JR, et al.: Life events and depression in adolescence: relationship loss as a prospective risk factor for first onset of major depressive disorder. *Journal of Abnormal Psychology* 1999;108(4):606-14.

[66] Brown J, Cohen P, Johnson JG, et al.: Childhood abuse and neglect: specificity of effects on adolescent and young adult depression and suicidality. *Journal of the American Academy of Child and Adolescent Psychiatry* 1999;38(12):1490-6.

[67] Krug EG, Kresnow M, Peddicord JP, et al.: Suicide after natural disasters. *New England Journal of Medicine* 1998; 338(6): 373-8.

[68] Kovacs M: Psychiatric disorders in youths with IDDM: rates and risk factors. *Diabetes Care,* 1997;20(1):36-44.

[69] Deas D, Thomas S: Comorbid Psychiatric Factors Contributing to Adolescent Alcohol and Other Drug Use. *Alcohol Research & Health* 2002;26(2):116-21.

[70] Agerbo E, Nordentoft M, Mortensen PB: Familial, psychiatric, and socioeconomic risk factors for suicide in young people: nested case-control study. *BMJ* 2002;325:7355.

[71] Heikkinen ME, Aro HM, Henriksson MM, et al.: Differences in recent life events between alcoholic and depressive nonalcoholic suicides. *Alcoholism: Clinical and Experimental Research* 1994;18:1143-9.

[72] Wilson KG' Stelzer J, Bergman JN, Kral MJ, Inayatullah M, Elliott CA: Problem solving, stress, and coping in adolescent suicide attempts. *Suicide & life-threatening behavior* 1995;25(2):241-52.

[73] Conner KR, Beautrais AL, Conwell Y: Risk factors for suicide and medically serious suicide attempts among alcoholics: analyses of Canterbury Suicide Project data. *Journal of Studies on Alcohol* 2003;64:551-4.

[74] Rich CL, Warstadt GM, Nemiroff RA, Fowler RC, Young D: Suicide, stressors, and the life cycle. *Am J Psychiatry* 1991;148:960.

[75] Heikkinen ME, Isometsä ET, Aro HM, Sarna SJ, Lönnqvist JK: Age-related variation in recent life events preceding suicide. *J Nerv Ment Dis* 1995;183:325-31.

[76] Aviram, RB: The Stigma of Alcohol Misuse, in Adolescence and Alcohol An international perspective. Edited by Kandel I, Merrick J, Sher L. London and Tel Aviv: *Freud Publishing House Ltd.*, 2006, pp 175-179.

[77] Rao U, Ryan ND, Dahl RE, Birmaher B, Roa R, Williamson DE, Perel JM: Factors associated with the development of substance use disorder in depressed adolescents. *J Am Acad Child Adolesc Psychiatry* 1999;38:1109–17.

[78] Substance Abuse and Mental Health Services Administration (SAMHSA). Depression among Adults. *The National Survey on Drug Use and Health Report,* November, 2005. Retrieved July 31, 2009, from http://www.oas.samhsa.gov.

[79] National Institute on Alcohol Abuse and Alcoholism (NIAAA). *Depression.* NIH pub. No. 99-3561. Bethesda, MD: 1999.

[80] Rohde P, Lewinsohn PM, Seeley JR: Psychiatric comorbidity with problematic alcohol use in high school students. *J Am Acad Child Adolesc Psychiatry* 1996;35(1):101-109.

[81] Carballo JJ, Oquendo MA, Garcio-Moreno M, Poza B, Giner L, Baca E, Zalsman G, Roche A, Sher L: *Alcohol related disorders, adolescents and the emergency room* Edited by Kandel I, Merrick J, Sher L. London and Tel Aviv: Freud Publishing House Ltd., 2006, pp 145-155.

[82] Jeglic EL: *Targeted intervention for suicidal college students who binge drink.* Retrieved Nov. 12, 2008, from http://suicidecenter.org/studies/4.html.

[83] Tarrier N, Taylor K, Gooding P: Cognitive-behavioral interventions to reduce suicide behavior: a systematic review and meta-analysis. *Behav Modif.* 2008;32(1):77-108.

[84] Barbe RP, Bridge J, Birmaher B, Kolko D, Brent DA: Suicidality and its relationship to treatment outcome in depressed adolescents. *Suicide Life Threat Behav* 2004;34(1):44-55.

[85] Liddle HA, Dakof GA, Turner RM, Henderson CE, Greenbaum PE: Treating adolescent drug abuse: a randomized trial comparing multidimensional family therapy and cognitive behavior therapy. *Addiction* 2008;103(10):1660-70.

[86] Ganz D, Sher L: Suicidal behavior in adolescents with comorbid depression and alcohol abuse. *Minerva Pediatrica* 2009;61(3):333-47.

[87] Preventing Alcohol Abuse and Related Problems, in *NIAAA Research Monograph* No. 34. Alcohol Alert (NIH Publication No. 34 PH 370). Bethesda, MD, 1996. Retrieved May 11, 2008, from http://pubs.niaaa.nih.gov/publications/aa34.htm. 2007;42(2):106-117.

INDEX

B

C

D

E

F

G

H

I

N

O

P

Q

R

S

T

U

V

W

Y